THE CALUMET REGION

INDIANA'S LAST FRONTIER

INDIANA HISTORICAL COLLECTIONS
VOLUME XXXIX

The

CALUMET
REGION

INDIANA'S LAST FRONTIER

By

Powell A. Moore

INDIANA HISTORICAL BUREAU
1959

To

RUTH, ANN, AND HUGH

PREFACE

THIS IS A HISTORY of the Calumet Region of Indiana from the beginning to the close of 1933, which I regard as its formative period. While the area's industries expanded and population increased in proportion after 1933, its economic, social, and cultural patterns were well established by that date.

The region's history may be divided into three periods. The first comprises the years before 1833 when the Indians, particularly the Potawatomi, occupied the area, and when it was controlled in succession by the French, English, and Americans. From the earliest times the Calumet attracted the attention of the Indians and the white men. Its sloughs and swamps teemed with the fur-bearing animals so important to both the Indians and the fur traders. Also, because of its location at the foot of Lake Michigan, the region was crossed by numerous Indian trails which in later years were used by explorers, missionaries, fur traders, and finally by the pioneers to reach the Illinois Country and other places farther west. The first and only permanent white settlement in this initial phase of the Calumet's history was a fur-trading post, established by Joseph Bailly in 1822 on the north bank of the Little Calumet River in what is now Porter County.

The second period, which extends roughly from 1833 to 1869, began with the arrival of the first settlers. Since the Calumet was the last distinct section in Indiana to be settled, it was truly the state's last frontier. The

development of the area was delayed by the great Kankakee Marsh which for many years acted as a barrier
against the movement of population from the more southern parts of the state; by the absence of harbors along
the Indiana shore of Lake Michigan; and because the
Federal government waited until 1832 to extinguish the
claims of the Potawatomi to the land. This was a slow
and plodding era which could boast of only two incorporated towns, Valparaiso and Crown Point, the county
seats of the region. Although the first railroads to reach
Chicago from the East crossed the Calumet in 1851-52,
some years passed before the iron horse had any noticeable effect on the lives of the people.

America's industrial revolution, pushing slowly but
surely into the lower Great Lakes region, ushered in the
final phase of the Calumet's history. In 1869, George H.
Hammond, pioneer in the shipping of dressed beef by
refrigeration, established a meat-packing plant on the site
of the city that now bears his name. But the real impact
of the industrial revolution upon the area was delayed
until suitable sites for basic industries were no longer
available in Chicago. Industry then expanded eastward
into Indiana along the coast of Lake Michigan, leaving
in its wake Whiting, started by the Standard Oil Company in 1889; East Chicago, incorporated in the same
year, where Inland Steel began its operations in 1901;
and finally Gary, founded in 1906 when the United States
Steel Corporation began the construction of its great mills
amid the sloughs and sand ridges along the lake front.

Firm in the belief that a regional history should be
devoted to things economic, social, and cultural, I have
placed a minimum of emphasis on political affairs. Since
in modern times a great industrial area cannot stand
alone, I have made every effort to place the Calumet

Region in its proper national setting. I have also endeavored to recapture the color and atmosphere of the
times of Joseph Bailly, Solon Robinson, and George
Earle; the rough and tumble years of early Hammond,
Whiting, East Chicago, and Gary; and of the sand hills
that Diana of the Dunes loved so well.

Several of my colleagues at Indiana University gave
cheerfully and unselfishly of their time and knowledge
to aid in the preparation of this work. Hugh W. Norman not only suggested that I do this volume but kept
me at the task until it was completed. My greatest debt
of gratitude is to Donald F. Carmony, who sacrificed
the progress of his own work to a painstaking reading
of every page of the manuscript and whose wise counsel
enabled me to avoid many of the pitfalls that lie in an
author's path. John D. Barnhart and R. Carlyle Buley
read portions of the manuscript and made many helpful
suggestions.

I am also indebted to Frances Krauskopf, of West
Virginia University, who made significant improvements
in the greater portion of the manuscript. Hubert Haw-
kins, of the Indiana Historical Bureau, was generous
with his advice and counsel. My most sincere thanks
go to Dorothy Riker and Gayle Thornbrough, also of
the Indiana Historical Bureau, whose able and meticu-
lous editing detected many weaknesses and corrected in-
numerable errors in the manuscript.

I want to thank a host of librarians in the Calumet
and Chicago areas, without whose assistance this book
could not have been written. Officials of the major
industries went beyond the call of duty to provide employment statistics and other important information
about their company's operations and history. At no
time were efforts made by these men to influence the

writing of this volume. Finally, I am grateful for the generous financial grants extended by the Graduate Research Council of Indiana University for research and the typing of the manuscript.

Whatever faults or shortcomings this book may have in any respect are the sole responsibility of the author.

POWELL A. MOORE

INDIANA UNIVERSITY CALUMET CENTER
EAST CHICAGO, INDIANA

CONTENTS

ILLUSTRATIONS

MAPS

1

THE CALUMET STORY

THE CALUMET REGION of Indiana is that part of the northwestern corner of the state drained by the Grand Calumet and Little Calumet rivers. It is on the southern shore of Lake Michigan and includes approximately the northern halves of the counties of Porter and Lake. The cities of Gary, East Chicago, Hammond, Whiting, Crown Point, and Valparaiso are in the region which is today one of the most heavily industrialized centers of the United States.

Origin of the Name "Calumet"

Originally, the Grand Calumet and the Little Calumet rivers were sluggish streams with low banks fringed by a heavy growth of reeds, and the French, who named them, were apparently influenced by those features. Calumet is the corruption of the Old French "Chalemel," and also the Low Latin "Calamellus," both meaning "reed." It has also been asserted that Calumet is the French version of the Indian words, "GE-KEL-E-MUK" in the Delaware and "KEN-NOM-KYAH" in the Potawatomi, meaning a low body of deep, still water.[1]

[1] Jacob P. Dunn, "Indiana Geographical Nomenclature," in *Indiana Magazine of History,* 8(1912):109. Calumet appears on early maps as Cal-La-Mick, Kil-La-Mick, Calumic, etc. See Sara Jones Tucker (comp.), *Indian Villages of the Illinois Country* (Illinois State Museum, *Scientific Papers,* Vol. 2, Part 1, Atlas (Springfield, 1942), plates XXXVIII, XL, XLIX.

The French called the ceremonial tobacco pipes of the Indians the Calumet because the stems were made from reeds or canes.[2] The use of the Calumet was widespread in the Upper Mississippi Valley and in the Great Lakes Region. Father Louis Hennepin, a colleague of La Salle, described the pipe as being made "of a red, black or white marble. The head is finely polished. The quill, which is commonly two and a half feet long, is made of a pretty strong reed or cane, adorned with feathers of all colors, interlaced with locks of women's hair. Every nation adorns it as they think fit, and according to the birds they have in their country."[3] The Indians designed or decorated them for each occasion. There were Calumets for war, peace, commerce and trade, and for social and political purposes. The Indians believed that some misfortune would befall them if they should violate the public faith in the Calumet. However, it was vitally important that one be able to distinguish between the war and peace pipes lest through ignorance or inattention he should become a victim of treachery.[4]

Father Jacques Marquette, while on his voyage down the Mississippi River with Louis Joliet, 1673, was impressed by the reverence of the Indians for the Calumet:

There is nothing more mysterious or respected among them. Less honor is paid to the Crowns and scepters of Kings than the savages bestow upon this. It seems to be the God of peace and of war, the

[2] Frederick W. Hodge (ed.), *Handbook of American Indians North of Mexico* (2 vols. Smithsonian Institution, Bureau of American Ethnology, *Bulletin 30* [Washington, D. C., 1907, 1910]), 1:191; Henry Gannett, "Indiana Geographical Nomenclature," in *Indiana Magazine of History,* 8 (1912):71.

[3] Isaac J. Cox (ed.), *The Journeys of Réné Robert Cavelier, Sieur de La Salle* . . . (2 vols. New York, 1922), 1:77-78.

[4] Hodge (ed.), *Handbook of American Indians,* 1:194.

Arbiter of life and of death. It has but to be carried upon one's person, and displayed, to enable one to walk safely through the midst of Enemies—who, in the hottest of the Fight, lay down their Arms when it is shown. For that reason, the Ilinois gave me one, to serve as a safeguard among all the Nations through whom I had to pass during my voyage.[5]

The Valparaiso Moraine and Lake Chicago

The principal physiographic features of the Calumet Region were produced by the invasion of the last glacier which is believed to have reached its maximum stage about 25,000 years ago.[6] This was the Lake Michigan lobe of the late Wisconsin ice sheet, and is said to have extended slightly south of Indianapolis. During the glacier's retreat northward, because of changes in temperature, moraines were deposited whenever it became stationary for any considerable length of time. The most conspicuous of these is the Valparaiso Moraine, named for the city of Valparaiso in Porter County, Indiana, which stands near its crest.

This moraine embraces Lake Michigan like an immense U. It begins near the boundary line between Illinois and Wisconsin, and extends southward through Lake, McHenry, Cook, DuPage, and Will counties in Illinois; then it turns toward the southeast and enters Indiana from the southeastern part of Will County. From there the trend is northeastward across Lake, Porter, and La Porte counties into Michigan, where its course has been traced as far as Montcalm County. The parallelism of the moraine to the lake shore is one of

5 Edna Kenton (ed.), *The Jesuit Relations and Allied Documents* . . . (New York, 1925), 352.

6 George B. Cressey, *The Indiana Sand Dunes and Shore Lines of the Lake Michigan Basin* (The Geographic Society of Chicago, *Bulletin No. 8*, 1928), 51.

its most striking features. Its elevation in Indiana is not
more than 750 feet until it reaches Valparaiso, where it
rises above 800 feet.[7]

The moraine is about 17 miles wide as it crosses Lake
County and passes into Porter County to the east. There
it gradually narrows until its width is only about 7 miles
as it enters La Porte County. The continental divide,
or watershed, corresponds very closely to the crest of
the moraine, and with two exceptions,[8] all streams which
start south of the crest line find their way to the Mississippi River by way of the Kankakee and Illinois and
eventually mingle with the waters of the Gulf of Mexico.
Until engineers began to tamper with them, those that
have their origin north of the divide ultimately reached
the Atlantic through the Great Lakes and the St. Lawrence River. In Lake County the Lake Michigan watershed extends farther southward than at any other point
in Indiana.[9]

To the north of the Valparaiso Moraine is the lake
plain which was once covered by the glacial Lake Chicago. As the edge of the ice sheet receded north of the
moraine, the water from the melting glacier and from
rains formed a lake between the glacier to the north and
the moraine to the south. The waters of this lake were
dammed up to the north and northeast by the ice of the
retreating glacier and on all sides by the moraine which
the glacier had left behind it. The lake continued to
rise until it overflowed the moraine at its lowest point,

[7] Frank Leverett, *The Pleistocene Features and Deposits of the Chicago Area* (Chicago Academy of Sciences, Geological and Natural History Survey, *Bulletin No. II,* May, 1897), 23-24.

[8] These are the branch of Deep River rising near Leroy and a branch
of Salt Creek.

[9] Willis S. Blatchley, "The Geology of Lake and Porter Counties,
Indiana," in Indiana *Geological Report,* 1897, pp. 26, 53-54.

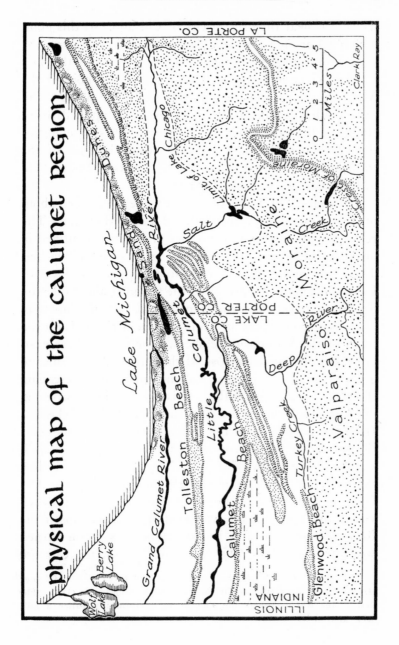

physical map of the calumet region

which was near the present city of Chicago. At this point a channel eroded through which, for a long period, the waters of the glacial lake found their way to the Des Plaines River and thence by way of the Illinois to the Mississippi. To this channel was given the name "Chicago Outlet." Lake Chicago is the name applied to all stages of the lake from the time of the first opening of the Chicago outlet until its final closing because of the overflow of the Great Lakes finding for itself a new channel through the Niagara River.[10]

The waters of Lake Chicago at one time were about 60 feet above the present level of Lake Michigan. The retreat of its waters left a series of beaches identified in order as the Glenwood, Calumet, and Tolleston beaches. The cause of the two marked lowerings of the level of Lake Chicago which produced the Calumet and Tolleston beaches is to be found in events in the life of contemporaneous glacial lakes in front of the Erie and Huron lobes of the Wisconsin ice sheet. For a time these eastern lakes discharged across Michigan into Lake Chicago greatly augmenting the volume previously escaping through the Chicago outlet. This resulted in a deepening or erosion of the outlet and the level of the lake fell from the Glenwood to the Calumet stage. At this point the retreat of the Huron and Erie lobes exposed a spillway to the Mohawk River in New York and the flow through the Chicago outlet shrank accordingly. The level of the lake was stabilized and the Calumet Beach was formed. A later advance of the glacier closed the Mohawk spillway and the overflow was again turned westward into Lake Chicago. The floor of the Chicago

10 Leverett, *The Pleistocene Features and Deposits of the Chicago Area*, 12, 65. Leverett gave it the name Lake Chicago in 1897. The flow of the water through the Chicago outlet formed a valley a mile wide in Illinois.

outlet was further deepened by this great flood and the level of the lake was lowered to the Tolleston stage. The level of the lake was stabilized at this point by the uncovering of a bedrock sill in the outlet floor which prevented further erosion and resulted in the formation of the Tolleston Beach.[11]

The Glenwood Beach was named for the village of Glenwood, Illinois, near the Indiana boundary, where it is well exposed, and is about 55 feet above the present level of Lake Michigan. The beach at Dyer, Indiana, averages about 10 feet in height and is from 500 to 700 feet in width. The Lincoln Highway was built near its crest for several miles east of Dyer. The beach extends across Lake County through Schererville, Merrillville, and Ainsworth. In Porter County it is not so easy to trace. However, south of Baillytown it is clearly marked and is well developed east to Michigan City. East of Chesterton there was a long bay, known as the Chesterton embayment, which extended to the La Porte County line, having an average width of a mile and a half. It is now the course of the Little Calumet River. Mastodons and mammoth elephants apparently wandered along this beach, for their remains have been found in Illinois in gravel pits as old as the beach itself.[12]

The Calumet Beach is named for the Little Calumet River since it lies just to the south of that stream through most of its course. In Lake County the beach is about 20 feet below the Glenwood stage, and is easily traced along Ridge Road from Munster through Highland to Glen Park in south Gary. Although the beach is about ten miles from Lake Michigan at the Illinois line, it

[11] J. Harlen Bretz, "The Stages of Lake Chicago: Their Causes and Correlations," in *American Journal of Science*, 249 (1951) :401-6.

[12] Cressey, *Indiana Sand Dunes and Shore Lines of the Lake Michigan Basin*, 56-59; Leverett, *op. cit.*, 66-71.

turns northeastward and enters Porter County about three miles from the lake. The beach has a regular course as far as Salt Creek, and is quite distinct east of Baillytown. The water apparently stood at this level longer than it did at the Glenwood stage. Dune accumulations are extensive along this beach, many dunes reaching 40 feet in height.[13]

Following the Calumet stage, the level of Lake Chicago fell about 15 feet, and at this point the Tolleston Beach was formed. It was from 20 to 25 feet above the surface of Lake Michigan. The beach was named for the village of Tolleston, which is now a part of Gary. It enters Indiana through south Hammond and extends eastward through Hessville, Tolleston, Aetna, and into Porter County just south of Ogden Dunes. Everywhere in Indiana this beach is built of sand about 25 feet deep. In Porter County it is partially covered by dunes of a later age, and even where the beach is exposed, it is difficult to recognize. The bones of mastodons and mammoths have also been found in the deposits of this beach.[14]

The present level of Lake Michigan, about 578 feet, was reached when a series of low-water stages lower than the Tolleston occurred. When the ice sheet withdrew entirely from the Huron and Erie basins, lower outlets were discovered and the western channels went dry. In one of these stages the lake plain emerged almost completely as it stands today. The location of the outlets of these low-water stages must have been well toward the north end of the Michigan basin and may have been

---

[13] Cressey, *op. cit.*, 62-64; Leverett, *op. cit.*, 72.

[14] Cressey, *op. cit.*, 65-67; C. L. Bieber, "Tolleston and Post-Tolleston Beaches and Bars in Lake County, Indiana," in Indiana Academy of Science, *Proceedings*, 1951, p. 176.

the straits of Mackinac.[15] Lake Chicago became Lake Michigan at that time.

Rivers and Streams

With the exception of the Grand and Little Calumet rivers, all streams of consequence draining the Calumet Region have their sources on or near the crest of the Valparaiso Moraine. Originally, the more important reached Lake Michigan by way of the Little Calumet River. In Porter County one branch of Salt Creek has its origin in Bull Eye Lake just south of the crest of the moraine. It pierces the divide and flows into the Little Calumet in Portage Township. Coffee Creek, also in Porter County, rises near the crest of the moraine and joins the Little Calumet at Chesterton. Deep River, in Lake County, one branch of which has its source near Leroy, south of the divide, and the other in Fancher's Lake, flows northward through Hobart and, before the digging of Burns Ditch, into the Little Calumet just east of Gary.[16]

Men and nature have conspired to make many changes in the Grand and Little Calumet rivers. These once formed a single river that followed a hairpin course. The source was in La Porte County near its western boundary. Leaving that county about one half mile north of the morainic region, it flowed westward across Porter and Lake counties into Illinois. There it followed a northwestward course to the bluffs at Blue Island. Here the river made a sharp curve to the northeast, re-entered Lake County and continued eastward where it emptied

15 Bretz, "The Stages of Lake Chicago," in *American Journal of Science,* 249:409-10.

16 Blatchley, "The Geology of Lake and Porter Counties," in Indiana *Geological Report,* 1897, pp. 41, 53-55.

into Lake Michigan at what is now Gary's Marquette Park. A new channel to Lake Michigan in Illinois was opened by the Indians more than a hundred and fifty years ago. They pushed and pulled their canoes through the marshes between Wolf Lake and Lake Calumet until a permanent channel was opened to Lake Michigan about twelve miles south of the Chicago River. This created two rivers: the southern one, the Little Calumet, which flowed westward across the Calumet Region and discharged its waters through the new channel into Lake Michigan at South Chicago; the northern one, the Grand Calumet, which flowed eastward and emptied into Lake Michigan through the old mouth at Marquette Park.[17]

The opening of the new mouth in South Chicago apparently affected the current of the Grand Calumet, and by 1872 its mouth in Indiana was found to be closed by aquatic vegetation and by drifting sand.[18] It would be difficult to determine the exact time when this occurred. A traveler in 1809 reported the mouth was about twenty yards wide and very deep.[19] Henry R. Schoolcraft, who came along the beach in 1820, wrote: "We passed the Grand Konomick [Grand Calumet], the mouth of which is choaked up with sand, and the appearance of the coun-

[17] Blatchley, *loc. cit.*, 42. At several points in Indiana these streams are only about three miles apart.

[18] "Examination and Survey of the Mouth of Grand Calumet River, Indiana," 1872, in Report of the Secretary of War, in *Senate Documents*, 42 Congress, 3 session, No. 25, p. 8.

[19] "Notes Taken on a Journey from Fort Wayne to Fort Dearborn, in June, 1809," in the Peru (Indiana) *Saturday Gazette,* August 10, 1839, reprinted in *Indiana Magazine of History,* 36(1940):48. This was apparently by William Johnston whose manuscript, "Notes on a Tour from Fort Wayne to Chicago, 1809," is in the library of the Chicago Historical Society. See Milo M. Quaife, *Chicago and the Old Northwest, 1673-1835* (Chicago, 1913), 447.

try, in the vicinity, is very barren, and uninviting."[20]
A map made by the U. S. Topographical Bureau in 1845
showed that the Grand Calumet no longer flowed into
Lake Michigan in Indiana. Instead, the river's current
had been reversed and its waters united with those of
the Little Calumet in Illinois to form the Calumet River
which emptied into Lake Michigan at South Chicago.[21]

Before the digging of Burns Ditch and before the industries began taking liberties with these streams, their
channels were so clogged with vegetation that a boat
could scarcely be pushed along. The Grand Calumet,
particularly, was more of a bayou than a river.[22] The
streams were at no time navigable except for small cargo
and pleasure craft. In 1870 the Federal government
began the development of the South Chicago Harbor
at the mouth of the Calumet River. Prior to 1895 futile
attempts were made to make the Grand Calumet navigable through Hammond to a point one half mile to the
east. Some parts of the river were dredged to a depth
of ten feet three different times, and were as often filled
by refuse from the George H. Hammond Packing Company and by sewage from Hammond and Burnham.
In 1903 U. S. Army engineers reported no navigation on
the river and the project was abandoned.[23]

[20] Henry R. Schoolcraft, *Narrative Journal of Travels from Detroit
Northwest Through the Great Chain of American Lakes to the Sources
of the Mississippi River in the Year 1820* (Albany, N. Y., 1821), 393.

[21] Photostat in the Gary Public Library of a map of the coast of
Lake Michigan from Chicago to Michigan City, surveyed in 1845 by
G. R. Moury under the direction of Capt. J. McClellan of the U. S.
Topographical Bureau.

[22] "Examination and Survey of the Mouth of Grand Calumet River,"
in Report of the Secretary of War, in *Senate Documents,* 42 Congress; 3
Session, No. 25, p. 8.

[23] "Examination of Calumet River, Illinois and Indiana," 1903, in
Report of the Secretary of War, in *House Documents,* 58 Congress, 2
session, No. 172, p. 4.

When the United States Steel Corporation built its great plants on the lake front in Gary, it was necessary to relocate the Grand Calumet. The river was moved from its ancient bed in the plant area to a new and straighter channel about a half mile to the south. For some distance through its property the steel company imprisoned the stream in a narrow bed of masonry, and then for several miles its current was held in place by solid banks of steel slag. Although the stream had its faint origin in what is now the Marquette Park lagoon in the eastern part of Gary, it really did not become a river until it reached the steel mills. In the course of its operations the steel company pumped millions of gallons of water each day out of Lake Michigan and ultimately this was emptied into the stream. To this was added other millions from the roofs and paved streets of Gary.

The nature and course of the Little Calumet were changed when Burns Ditch was completed in 1926. Because of the river's periodic floods most of the adjacent area was a great marsh and worthless except for hunting and fishing. In the early spring the river was frequently a mile wide where it crossed Broadway in Gary, and on one occasion when there was an ice jam at the Broadway bridge, it was almost two miles wide.[24] In 1908 Randall W. Burns of Chicago, who owned 1,200 acres of the marsh and for whom the canal was ultimately named, launched a movement to reclaim the land. The legal fight, in which Burns was supported by civic leaders in Gary,[25] lasted for more than fifteen years. Opposition to the project came largely from farmers, who feared an increase in taxes, and from the railroads, which ob-

24 Gary *Evening Post,* March 30, 1912.
25 Gary *Weekly Tribune,* August 7, 1908.

jected to the cost of the building and maintenance of bridges.[26] The reclaiming of the Calumet Marsh may be compared to the draining of the Pontine marshes in Italy. It was necessary to cut through the high sand barrier of the Tolleston Beach and the dunes that separated the marsh and Lake Michigan. The waters of the Little Calumet and those of Deep River, which empties into the Little Calumet, were diverted into the lake a short distance east of Ogden Dunes. The main channel of the ditch through the sand dunes is 1⅛ miles long, and the river section from the head of the ditch to Deep River is about 6½ miles in length. The Little Calumet was also dredged to the mouth of Salt Creek. The project permitted the reclamation of more than 20,000 acres in Porter County and in Gary.[27]

The natural drainage of the greater part of the Calumet Region was shifted from the St. Lawrence to the Mississippi drainage system by the construction of the Calumet Sag Canal, completed in 1922. The pattern for this move was set by the construction of the Chicago Sanitary and Ship Canal, opened in 1900, which reversed the flow of the Chicago River away from Lake Michigan and southward through the watershed to join the Des Plaines River at Lockport, Illinois. This was done to save Lake Michigan from pollution by Chicago's sewage although in 1933 it became a link in the Lakes-to-Gulf waterway. The Calumet Sag Canal diverted the flow of that portion of the Little Calumet River west of Burns Ditch and that of the Grand Calumet from Lake Michigan at South Chicago across the low divide at Blue Island to join the Chicago Sanitary and Ship

26 Gary *Post-Tribune,* September 26, 1925.

27 Arthur P. Melton, construction engineer of the Burns Ditch project, in Gary *Post-Tribune,* August 6, 1926. The landowners were assessed to pay the cost of the ditch.

Canal. Thus the natural drainage was turned to the Mississippi. The former mouths of the Chicago and Calumet rivers now are outlets from Lake Michigan.[28]

Economic Geography

The portion of the region best suited for agriculture lies between the crest of the Valparaiso Moraine and the Calumet Beach and, after the completion of Burns Ditch, in the valley of the Little Calumet. The northern slope of the moraine in Lake County is more fertile than it is in Porter County to the east. It contains several small prairies and a number of low ridges or gently undulating swells, with intervening sags. The soil on the prairies is a rich black loam, while on some of the ridges it is a whitish clay.[29] The plain between the Glenwood and Calumet beaches has poor drainage and is covered with muck and clay soils. That portion north of Griffith and Dyer was known as the Cady Marsh, and peat was cut there for many years. Later, cheap coal transported by the railroads brought an end to that industry. The western portion of the marsh was called Lake George, and the water there was from five to seven feet deep. In the early nineties the lake was drained by the great Hart Ditch which extends from the vicinity of Dyer to the northeast and joins the Little Calumet at Wicker Park, south of Hammond.[30] The soil in the Little Calu-

28 J. Harlen Bretz, *Geology of the Chicago Region, Part II—The Pleistocene* (Illinois State Geological Survey, *Bulletin No. 65,* Part 2, Urbana, Ill., 1955), 21-22.

29 Blatchley, "The Geology of Lake and Porter Counties," in Indiana *Geological Report,* 1897, p. 58.

30 Timothy H. Ball, "The Cady Marsh," in Indiana Academy of Science, *Proceedings,* 1897, p. 240. The Cady Marsh was named for Jack Cady, who operated a tavern for stagecoach travelers near the marsh. See Alfred H. Meyer, "Toponomy in Sequent Occupance Geography, Calumet Region, Indiana-Illinois," in Indiana Academy of Science, *Proceedings,* 1944, p. 150.

met Valley is a rich muck and many portions are tillable only in unusually dry weather. Rich deposits of heavy lake clay and boulder clay were discovered in the vicinity of Dyer, Hobart, Porter, and Chesterton. The clay deposits at Hobart were more than forty feet deep. For many years these formed the basis of a profitable brick and tile industry in those communities. Valuable deposits of molding sand were uncovered near McCool, in Porter County, which found a ready market in the steel mills of the region.[31]

The western portion of the lake plain where the cities of East Chicago, Whiting, Hammond, and Gary now stand was a region of sand ridges, swamps, and sloughs. These ridges, which ran parallel to the Lake Shore, were originally covered with a valuable growth of white pine and cedar trees. This timber was cut off, much of it being stolen, and used in the building of Chicago, a growth of scrub oak taking its place.[32] Originally, there were three lakes in this section: Wolf, George, and Berry. These were remnants of a once shallow bay of Lake Michigan. Berry Lake was drained to make way for the industrial development of Whiting and East Chicago, and Lake George has been filled in by neighboring industries and no longer appears on the map. Wolf Lake remains and is of interest to sportsmen. The swamps were once almost impenetrable because of a thick and tangled growth of shrubs and vines. John Tipton, while surveying the Indiana-Illinois boundary line in

[31] Blatchley, "The Geology of Lake and Porter Counties," in *loc. cit.,* 71; Fritiof M. Fryxell, *The Physiography of the Region of Chicago* (Chicago, 1927), 48.

[32] Herbert A. Kellar (ed.), *Solon Robinson, Pioneer and Agriculturist* (2 vols. *Indiana Historical Collections,* Vols. 21 and 22, Indianapolis, 1936, 1937), 2:80; Timothy H. Ball, *Encyclopedia of Genealogy and Biography of Lake County, Indiana* (Chicago, 1904), 7.

1821, thought the region could never be settled and that it would never be of any value to the state.[33]

The Dune Country

Along the shores of Lake Michigan east of Gary is one of the most remarkable regions in America, the Indiana dune country. The face of the earth here appears as if Nature, by some powerful convulsion, had torn the earth asunder and thrown it into sand hills, leaving the intervening spaces to be filled with ponds and marshes. The wide sandy beach between the water's edge and the dunes is ever changing, water and wind tearing it in one place and adding to it in another. A person may walk along the margin of the water and see that each wave throws up a minute ridge of sand, so minute, in fact, that it is scarcely visible. Perhaps the next wave carries it away, but if it be thrown high enough to remain unmolested until it has time to dry, its particles are caught up by the wind and carried farther inland. In most cases they are piled up for a time along the foot of a ridge or a dune, which is found from 50 to 100 yards back from the water. If a stiff breeze is blowing, a traveler along this beach is bombarded by the fine, sharp-edged particles of sand, many of which strike against the face and produce a stinging sensation. Nowhere else in the Great Lakes Region are the beaches more beautiful and interesting than in the Indiana dune country.

The dunes, postglacial in origin, were formed by the westerly and northwesterly winds blowing from the lake across areas of sand that were deposited along the shore. Winds, blowing from the lake over the beach, pick up

33 Nellie A. Robertson and Dorothy Riker (eds.), *The John Tipton Papers* (3 vols. *Indiana Historical Collections,* Vols. 24-26, Indianapolis, 1942), 1:271.

particles of sand and carry them inland. Where some
obstacle is encountered the velocity of the wind is decreased and the sand is dropped. So dunes may originate
about trees and clumps of grass. The cottonwood tree,
which abounds in the region, and the sand reed or dune
grass are the most successful dune-forming plants.[34]
The infant dune itself becomes an obstacle to the wind
and rapid growth takes place. Dunes have been found
to move as rapidly as ten or fifteen feet each year.[35] As
they move inland the dunes may cover up forests, fill
up ponds and lakes, and invade lowlands and fields. In
many places the drifting sands have wholly or partly
covered a tall pine or oak tree. Where but partly covered
its top projects for a few feet above the crest of the
dune. One may rest in its shade and not realize that he
is sheltered by the upper limbs of a large tree whose
trunk and main branches lie far beneath him embedded
in the sand. When a dune becomes stationary, due to
the cutting off of its sand supply by new dunes, it then
becomes covered with vegetation.

There is a constant, tormented warfare involving the
wind, sand, and vegetation. The wind hurls the sand with
great force against any obstacle in its path and one has
only to stoop down and face it to feel its power. Single
trees and entire groups of plants have the soil blown out
from under them, leaving the roots exposed high above
the surface, and in time they collapse and die. The wind
is a destroyer as well as a builder of dunes. The uproot-
ing of a tree, a forest fire burning off the vegetation, or
the burrowing of an animal in the side of a stationary
dune, may create a bare spot over which the winds

[34] Henry C. Cowles, "The Ecological Relations of the Vegetation of
the Sand Dunes of Lake Michigan," in *Botanical Gazette,* 27(1899) :107-8.
[35] Fryxell, *Physiography of the Region of Chicago,* 35.

freely play. A great storm scoops out a small bowl-shaped cavity, and, carrying the sand either south or southeastward drops it over the hillside. The cavity is cut deeper and wider by succeeding storms, and a great "blow-out" in time results. Where a few years before stood a high dune now exists a valley in which, in many instances, may be seen the dead trunks and stumps of trees that had been covered by the now departed dune.[36] Hence, the dune country is ever changing as the processes of construction and destruction continue side by side. Before the white man came to disturb them, the stable or "dead" dunes were covered by a forest of white pine, which here reached its extreme southern range. As the pine was lumbered off, it was generally replaced by scrub oak and jack pine which often follow the white pine. Some of the dunes remained bare and were changed by the wind into "live" or shifting dunes.

The dune belt ranges in width from a mile and a quarter at Miller to about three fourths of a mile at Waverly Beach, now in the Indiana Dunes State Park, and then narrows to the northeast. Mt. Tom, at Waverly Beach, almost 200 feet above the lake, is the highest of the Indiana dunes. In the same vicinity are Mt. Holden, and Mt. Green, which rise 170 and 160 feet respectively. These were called the "Three Sisters" by the pioneers, and the village of Tremont took its name from the three sand mountains.[37]   In 1835 an English

36 In 1917 the Jens Jensen Blowout near Waverly Beach was a bowl-like blowout about a half mile in width with sides or walls between fifty and sixty feet high. See George A. Brennan, *The Wonders of the Dunes* (Indianapolis, 1923), 147.

37 Cressey, *Indiana Sand Dunes and Shore Lines of the Lake Michigan Basin*, 4, 7. It is thought that Mt. Tom was named for Thomas Brady, who was captured by the English and Indians at the battle near the Petite Fort, December 5, 1780, during the Revolutionary War. Mt. Holden was named for E. J. Holden, of Chicago, the first president of the Prairie Club, and Mt. Green for a pioneer who operated a tavern

traveler coming through the dune country from Michigan City to Chicago found it as hot and dazzling as a great desert.

But not all of the dune country is sand. Here are miles of forests, fertile lowlands, flower-grown valleys, spring-fed streams, and impenetrable swamps. Between the beaches of old Lake Chicago and the dune belt is a strip of marshy meadow land, the soil of which is muck. An inferior quality of peat is found here which burns indefinitely after the marshes have been swept by a forest fire. Interesting areas of quaking bogs, which contain a wealth of flora, are found in this strip. The most unusual is the Cowles Tamarack Swamp, named for Dr. Henry Chandler Cowles, botanist and authority on the plants of the dunes. On walking over this bog, which lies just north of Mineral Springs, the vegetation quivers within a 10-foot radius. A clump of tamaracks 25 feet high were found in this bog and the water beneath it was 10 feet deep.[38]

The dune country is a wild and fascinating treasure land of plant life. Its botanical features may be considered under two heads: first, the dunes as a meeting place of trees and wild flowers from all directions; and second, as a picturesque battleground between plant life and the elements.[39] Here may be found more than 1,300 species of flowering plants and ferns.[40] Within a small

near Tremont. See below, 32, and Meyer, "Toponomy in Sequent Occupance Geography," in Indiana Academy of Science, *Proceedings,* 1944, pp. 156-57.

[38] Cressey, *op. cit.,* 68; E. Stillman Bailey, *The Sand Dunes of Indiana* (Chicago, 1917), 156; Orpheus M. Schantz, "Indiana's Unrivaled Sand-Dunes," in *The National Geographic Magazine,* 35(1919):437.

[39] Henry C. Cowles, quoted in Stephen T. Mather, *Report on the Proposed Sand Dunes National Park, Indiana* (Department of the Interior, Washington, D. C., 1917), 44.

[40] Donald C. Peattie, *Flora of the Indiana Dunes* . . . (Chicago, 1930), 7.

area one may find plants of the desert and plants of the rich woodlands, plants of the pine woods and plants of the swamps, plants of the oak woods and plants of the prairies. The prickly pear cactus of our southwestern deserts grows side by side with the bearberry of the arctic regions. The most common pine of the dunes, the jack pine, is far out of its main range, and reaches here its farthest southern growth.[41] Many other species of plants flourish in the dunes that are found nowhere for many miles outside the region. Dr Cowles found a remarkable similarity in the flora of the Danish and Indiana Dunes, in that the same genera and often the same species occur in the two regions.[42]

Because of the congenial cover afforded by the vegetation and the presence of abundant food in the swamps and marshes, more than three hundred varieties of birds have been found in the region. About half of these are seasonal residents.[43] Many, during the spring and fall migrations, finding excellent protection against the weather, loiter days and weeks longer than is normal in this climatic belt. And yet, among the live dunes and windswept open spaces near the beach of the lake where vegetation is sparse, the twitter and chirp of a bird are seldom heard. Only the wind disturbs the silence that prevails in this desert. The scamper of a lizard here and there is usually the only activity to be seen. The golden and bald eagles were common in the dune country until recent years.[44] Drusilla Carr, who came to live at

[41] Cowles, quoted in Mather, *Report on the Proposed Sand Dunes National Park*, 44.

[42] Cowles, "The Ecological Relation of the Vegetation of the Sand Dunes of Lake Michigan," in *Botanical Gazette*, 27 (1899) :386.

[43] Brennan, *The Wonders of the Dunes*, 263-312.

[44] Edwin Way Teale, *Dune Boy, The Early Years of a Naturalist* (New York, 1943), 2.

Miller Beach in 1872, saw hundreds of bald eagles in that vicinity. On one occasion, she fought one of the great birds with her sunbonnet when it attacked her baby on the beach.[45]

Wild Life and Climate

The wild life of the region was typical of that found by the pioneers in the Middle West. Deer, bears, and timber wolves roamed the dunes and sand ridges. Although the deer and bears soon disappeared when the first settlers came, the wolves lingered, and, as late as 1907, one was seen crossing Broadway Street in Gary after the paving of that thoroughfare began.[46] The Indians, and later the settlers, reaped a rich harvest by trapping the mink and muskrats which infested the numerous swamps and sloughs. Wild ducks and geese abounded in unbelievable numbers in the spring and fall, and wealthy sportsmen from Chicago maintained hunting preserves on the site of Gary until after the turn of the present century.

Lake Michigan exercises a pronounced influence on the climate. The fact that the Lake remains cool throughout the summer, gives welcome coolness to the winds from off that large body of water, with the result that the average summer temperatures are lower near the Lake than elsewhere in Indiana. In autumn and winter, the Lake does not become as cold as the land, and this

[45] "Mrs. Drusilla Carr Tells of Early Days at Miller Beach," in J. W. Lester (ed.), Papers by Various Hands (Scrapbooks in Gary Public Library), 1:232.

[46] Gary Evening Post, October 6, 1909. For other accounts of the fauna of the region, see Edwin W. Dinwiddie, "The Fauna of Lake County," in Timothy H. Ball (ed.), Lake County, Indiana, 1884 . . . (Crown Point, Ind., 1884), 151-52; Brennan, The Wonders of the Dunes, 242.

causes a delay in the cooling of the adjacent belt. The first killing frost of autumn comes twenty and even thirty days later near the Lake than in areas a few miles farther south. Autumn is generally warm and delightful. Spring arrives late and is usually cold and wet. In some years the springs are so cold as to make it seem that the region plunges abruptly from winter to summer. The Lake's coolness also delays the coming of the warmest average day of the summer until some thirty-four days after the summer solstice, in contrast with a delay of about thirty days for most of the state. The amount of snowfall east of the end of the Lake is the heaviest in Indiana. This is partly due to the fact that when the land is colder than the Lake, clouds often develop as the wind from the Lake is chilled and this condition sometimes results in snow. And yet the influence of the Lake upon precipitation is slight. The increase of snowfall attributable to the presence of the Lake, on the average, is not more than twenty inches and this represents only about two inches of rain. This is a rather insignificant part of the annual precipitation of about thirty-five inches in the region.[47]

[47] Stephen S. Visher, *Climate of Indiana* (Bloomington, Ind., 1944), 55-56, 63-64; U. S. Weather Bureau, Ogden Dunes Co-operative Station, "Local Climatological Summary for the Ten-year Period, 1949-1958," compiled by Robert Allen Ward (mimeographed report).

2

FRENCH, ENGLISH, AND INDIANS

UNTIL 1763, the Calumet Region was a part of the French Empire in America. The first white visitors to the area were probably the picturesque and adventurous *coureurs de bois* or "bush rangers," and the *voyageurs* or boatmen. Some of the former were from the best families in New France, and took to the wilderness actuated by a love for adventure and a desire to profit from the fur trade.[1] As the swamps and sloughs of the Calumet teemed with fur-bearing animals, it is hardly possible that these Frenchmen were not familiar with the area. Unfortunately, the *coureurs de bois* seldom kept records, and no written accounts have been found of their activities in the region.

Father Jacques Marquette and the *voyageurs* Pierre Porteret and Jacques Largilliers passed through the Calumet Region in 1675. Two years before, Louis Joliet and Marquette had been sent by Jean Talon, intendant of New France, to determine whether the Mississippi River emptied into the Gulf of Mexico or into the Vermillion Sea, now the Gulf of Southern California.

[1] For accounts of the *coureurs de bois,* see William Bennett Munro, *Crusaders of New France* (Yale University Press, 1921), 155-79; Grace Lee Nute, *Caesars of the Wilderness, Médard Chouart, Sieur des Groseilliers, and Pierre Esprit Radisson, 1618-1710* (New York, 1943), 39-74; Jacob P. Dunn, *Indiana, A Redemption from Slavery* (Boston and New York, 1905), 85-92. For the later period, see R. Carlyle Buley, *The Old Northwest, Pioneer Period 1815-1840* (2 Vols. Indiana Historical Society, 1950), 1:403-8.

Marquette was so impressed by the hospitality of the Illinois Indians, whom he encountered while on this journey, that he promised to return and establish a mission among them.[2] In October, 1674, he started out from the mission of St. Francis Xavier at Green Bay to fulfill this pledge. Because of the illness of Marquette, the party spent the winter at the Chicago Portage between the Chicago and Des Plaines rivers.[3]

On the three days before Easter in April, 1675, Marquette preached to more than fifteen hundred Indians at a village a few miles south of the present city of Ottawa, Illinois. Again stricken with illness, the priest expressed the desire to return immediately to the mission of St. Ignace near Michilimackinac. Thus began the long journey up the Illinois and the Des Plaines rivers and across the Chicago Portage to Lake Michigan. From the mouth of the Chicago River the *voyageurs* chose the shorter and easier route to Michilimackinac by canoe along the southern and eastern shore of the lake.[4] In view of Marquette's exhausted condition, it appears certain the party camped or paused for rest at more than one point in the Calumet Region as they passed along the southern shore of Lake Michigan. It is even probable they camped at the mouth of the Grand Calumet and that Mass was celebrated there, as so many believe.[5] Marquette died on

2 Kenton (ed.), *Jesuit Relations and Allied Documents*, 366. Marquette's journal of the expedition is also to be found in Reuben G. Thwaites (ed.), *The Jesuit Relations and Allied Documents* (73 vols. Cleveland, 1896-1901), Vol. 59. For standard accounts, see Francis Parkman, *La Salle and the Discovery of the Great West* (Frontenac ed., Boston, 1905), and Reuben Gold Thwaites, *Father Marquette* (New York, 1902).

3 Kenton (ed.), *Jesuit Relations and Allied Documents*, 367-87.

4 Thwaites (ed.), *Jesuit Relations and Allied Documents*, 59:17, 185-211.

5 In 1912 the silver lid of a small lavorium or baptismal font, used

May 18 and was buried on the banks of the river that bears his name near the present city of Ludington, Michigan. Two years later some of his Ottawa disciples disinterred the body, cleaned and dried the bones, and took them to their final resting place at St. Ignace.[6]

The history of the Calumet Region in this early period was closely intertwined with that of the St. Joseph Mission and with Fort St. Joseph, which were located near the present city of Niles, Michigan, on the St. Joseph River about sixty miles from where it empties into Lake Michigan. For more than a century Fort St. Joseph was the principal seat of civilization around the southern end of the Lake. About 1680, the Potawatomi Indians began to move southward from Wisconsin to settle around the lower end of the Lake and in the fertile St. Joseph River Valley.[7] The Jesuits established the St. Joseph Mission some time around 1689 to minister to the spiritual needs of the Potawatomi and other tribes in that area.[8]

by the priests for baptismal ceremonies was found in the dried-up bed of the old mouth of the Grand Calumet River in Gary. The relic was sent to Paris where French scholars expressed the opinion that it was made in the sixteenth century. Another piece of a lavorium was found in the same vicinity. It is possible that it was lost by priests, even by Marquette himself. The relic later came into the possession of Daniel E. Kelly, a Valparaiso, Indiana, attorney. See Brennan, *The Wonders of the Dunes,* 28; Gary *Daily Tribune,* June 25, 1914.

[6] Thwaites (ed.), *Jesuit Relations and Allied Documents,* 59:185-211; Thwaites, *Father Marquette,* 207-8, 221. It was the custom among some Indian tribes to clean and dry the bones of their dead as a mark of respect as well as to prevent wild animals from molesting the graves.

[7] Hodge (ed.), *Handbook of American Indians,* 1:290; Louise Phelps Kellogg, *The French Régime in Wisconsin and the Northwest* (State Historical Society of Wisconsin, 1925), 271. Fort St. Joseph should not be confused with the present city of St. Joseph, Michigan, which was later established at the mouth of the St. Joseph River on Lake Michigan.

[8] George Paré, "The St. Joseph Mission," in *Mississippi Valley Historical Review,* 17(1930-31):31; Kellogg, *The French Régime in Wisconsin and the Northwest,* 168, 271.

A few years later, Fort St. Joseph was erected and garrisoned by the French to command one of the canoe routes and the important portage between the St. Joseph and Kankakee rivers. The fort was also intended to act as a barrier between the Iroquois and the tribes in the country around Lake Michigan.[9] With the exception of a brief interim when the troops were withdrawn, the place was garrisoned by the French, and later by the English until its capture by the Potawatomi in 1763 during Pontiac's uprising.[10] It was not reoccupied by troops at the close of hostilities, but because of its strategic and commercial importance, British officials in Detroit and Michilimackinac watched it closely before and during the American Revolution.

Fort St. Joseph was an important center of the fur trade and in 1750 there were between forty and fifty French families residing in its vicinity.[11] Before the establishment of Fort Dearborn in 1803, many of the Indians in what are now Indiana, Illinois, and southern Wisconsin brought their pelts to St. Joseph. While the Indians apparently had no permanent homes in the Calumet Region, they did prize the area as a rich source of furs, fish, and various kinds of wild berries. The Potawatomi, in particular, regarded the region as one of their favorite hunting grounds and continued to do so

[9] George Paré and Milo M. Quaife (eds.), "The St. Joseph Baptismal Register," in *Mississippi Valley Historical Review*, 13:(1926-27):201; Kellogg, *The French Régime in Wisconsin and the Northwest*, 292, 313. Milo M. Quaife, *Lake Michigan* (Indianapolis, 1944), 54, states that the fort was built in 1681, while Daniel McCoy, "Old Fort St. Joseph," in *Michigan Pioneer and Historical Collections*, 35(1907), 546-47, insisted it was erected in 1697.

[10] See Howard H. Peckham, *Pontiac and the Indian Uprising* (Princeton University Press, 1947), 159.

[11] Paré "The St. Joseph Mission," in *Mississippi Valley Historical Review*, 17:51.

even after they moved to the area just north of the Wabash River.

The English Period, 1763-1783

The French period in the history of the Old Northwest ended in 1763 with their defeat by the English in the French and Indian War. By the terms of the Treaty of Paris, ratified in February, 1763, France ceded to England all her territory between the Appalachian Mountains and the Mississippi River, save New Orleans. The remainder of her holdings in what is now Canada also went to the English. At the same time, France gave New Orleans and that part of Louisiana west of the Mississippi to her ally, Spain. France was thus eliminated from continental North America. The lasting impression of the French on the Calumet Region was slight, and in later years there was little to remind the people that their marshes and sand dunes had once been a part of New France.

Throughout the long conflict between the English and the French, 1689-1763, the Potawatomi and the other tribes of the Great Lakes Region were loyal allies of the French. The defeat of their friends left them bewildered and uncertain as to what the future held for them. The restlessness of the tribes was increased when the English governmental officials proved to be less generous than the French in the matter of gifts and unscrupulous English traders tried to cheat and plunder them. The arrogance and reserve demonstrated by the English also aroused resentment of the proud Indians. Moreover, they were alarmed by the prospect of English settlers pushing westward across the Appalachians to deprive them of their lands. The terrible uprising, rather erroneously known as Pontiac's Conspiracy, occurred when Frenchmen whispered into the ears of Indian chiefs that, although the French king had been asleep while the English took their lands, he was now awake and was sending armies to help them drive the hated English out of Canada and the West.[12]

Most of the tribes of the Northwest went on the war-path, those in the vicinity of Detroit and Lake Michigan being led by Pontiac, a war chief of the Ottawa tribe. The Ottawa, Ojibwa (Chippewa), and the Potawatomi had long been united in a loose confederacy and, as was expected, joined in the attack on the English. In May, 1763, a reign of terror began among the western settlements as the English forts were attacked with great fury by the Indians. The garrisons at Fort St. Joseph and at Miamis (Fort Wayne) surrendered and the men were taken prisoners or massacred. A few days later, Ouiatanon, on the Wabash River, was taken. Its garrison, apparently due to the intervention of the local French inhabitants, was spared. Michilimackinac was captured on June 4. While these attacks were taking place, Pontiac was wasting the full power of his Ottawa, Ojibwa, Potawatomi alliance in a vain effort to take Detroit. Also in the east, Fort Pitt successfully resisted the Indian attack. By the end of 1764 the Indians, convinced they could not depend upon France for aid in the war, sued for peace.[13] Never again did the Potawatomi of the Calumet Region take up arms against the English.

12 Francis Parkman, *The Conspiracy of Pontiac and the Indian War after the Conquest of Canada* (Frontenac ed., 2 vols. Boston, 1905), 1:178-87; Nelson Vance Russell, *The British Régime in Michigan and the Old Northwest, 1760-1796* (Northfield, Minn., 1939), 18-19; Peckham, *Pontiac and the Indian Uprising*, 96-98, 101-6; John D. Barnhart and Donald F. Carmony, *Indiana, From Frontier to Industrial Commonwealth* (4 vols. New York, 1954), 1:44-51.

13 Peckham, *Pontiac and the Indian Uprising*, 156-61, 212, 272, 281; Parkman, *The Conspiracy of Pontiac*, 1:283, 285. Pontiac, although im-

The news of the Indian uprising convinced the English that something had to be done to quiet the fears of the Indians and to remedy some of their grievances. On October 7, the King issued the "Proclamation of 1763" which forbade further settlement of the country west of the crest of the Appalachian Mountains; the residents in that region were to "forthwith remove themselves." The great West was to be an Indian reserve, and all tres-passers were to be seized and sent out of the country. To protect the Indians from unscrupulous traders, traffic in furs was limited to those of good character who could qualify for a license. Actually, the proclamation was intended as a temporary expedient to placate the Indians and to secure time for the consideration of better methods to regulate trade.[14] The French settlers and traders at St. Joseph, Detroit, and Michilimackinac were left with-out a government and were expected to leave the country. They remained, however, and many continued to trade with the Indians without licenses.[15]

The Proclamation of 1763 was not satisfactory, and in 1774 was supplanted by the Quebec Act. This act was designed to establish a civil government for the Northwest, provide for better supervision of the Indians, and to regulate the fur trade more effectively. The French Catholics were also given religious freedom. Al-though all the Northwest was joined to the crown colony of Quebec, what are now lower Michigan and the upper part of Indiana were placed under the jurisdiction of a

portant in this conflict, was but one of several Indian chiefs and not the leader of the entire uprising.

[14] Louise Phelps Kellogg, *The British Régime in Wisconsin and the Northwest* (State Historical Society of Wisconsin, 1935), 29; Clarence W. Alvord, *The Mississippi Valley in British Politics* (2 vols. Cleveland, 1917), 1:202-10.

[15] Russell, *The British Régime in Michigan and the Old Northwest,* 61-62.

lieutenant governor, or commander, at Detroit.[16] This act was never given a fair trial as the Revolutionary War, breaking out the next year, brought turmoil and confusion to the West.

The English made every effort to enlist the aid of the Indians against the Americans in the Revolutionary War. In the Great Lakes Region, the Potawatomi, Ottawa, and Ojibwa (Chippewa) were won over with liberal presents, weapons, rum, and promises. Governor Henry Hamilton, at Detroit, promised to pay for scalps as he would for beaver skins. In 1778 the British listed 150 dozen scalping knives among their trade goods at Detroit. But not all the tribes supported the English. The French and Spanish, friendly to the American cause, had influence with many Indians including some that were pledged to the enemy.[17]

The war did not leave the Calumet Region entirely undisturbed. For a brief moment the sand dunes echoed to the sound of musket fire and war whoops as adherents of the English and the Americans were locked in combat. This was the battle, December 5, 1780, near the Petite Fort at the mouth of Fort Creek in what is now the Indiana Dunes State Park. The French built this fort, or stockade, probably between 1750 and 1755, to help them command the fur trade of the Calumet Region. It is possible that it was used by the St. Joseph traders as a collection point and storage place for furs obtained by the Potawatomi in the marshes of the area. The place was later occupied by the English but abandoned as

---

16 Russell, *op. cit.,* 72-73; Logan Esarey, *A History of Indiana* (3d ed., 2 vols. Fort Wayne, 1924), 1:51.

17 Russell, *The British Régime in Michigan and the Old Northwest,* 191; see John D. Barnhart, *Henry Hamilton and George Rogers Clark in the American Revolution* (Crawfordsville, Ind., 1951), 1-189, for an account of the principal campaigns of the Revolutionary War in Indiana.

untenable in 1779. Although American sympathizers
were said to have held it for a time, there is nothing to
indicate it was inhabited when the battle occurred.[18]

In 1780 several events affected adversely the prestige
of the Spanish and Americans among the Indians of the
northwest. In May a force of English and Indians from
Michilimackinac attacked St. Louis and ravaged the surrounding country.[19] About this time, Augustin Mottin
de la Balme, a former inspector general of cavalry in
Washington's army, appeared among the French inhabitants in the Illinois Country. Acting on the assumption
that the French at Detroit and in Canada were as friendly
toward the American cause as were those in Illinois, he
led an expedition of French Creoles from the villages
in Illinois and on the Wabash to attack Detroit. If successful there, he planned to invade Canada and arouse
the French against the English. In November of 1780
La Balme's men captured the English post of Miamis near
the present city of Fort Wayne. After plundering the
stores of the traders, they encamped a short distance
away. During the night, the party was attacked by Indians led by Little Turtle. La Balme was slain along
with about half of his men.[20] Thus ended the projected
conquest of Detroit and the invasion of Canada.

Before his departure from the Illinois Country, de la
Balme sent a detachment of sixteen men from Cahokia
with pack horses, under the command of Jean Baptiste
Hamelin, against the St. Joseph post.[21] Included in this

[18] Brennan, *The Wonders of the Dunes,* 77.

[19] Quaife, *Chicago and the Old Northwest,* 94-97.

[20] Russell, *The British Régime in Michigan and the Old Northwest,*
219-21; Esarey, *History of Indiana,* 1:92.

[21] Arent S. DePeyster to H. Watson Powell, January 8, 1781, in
Michigan Pioneer and Historical Collections, 19 (1892) :591-92. DePeyster
had succeeded Hamilton as the British commandant at Detroit.

party was Lieutenant Thomas Brady, a former superintendent of Indian affairs for the English in the Illinois
Country. Although there was no garrison at St. Joseph,
the post was an important center of the fur trade. It
was also a rendezvous of the Potawatomi and a gathering
place for their war parties sent out to harass the American settlements. Hamelin so timed his march that when
he arrived at St. Joseph the Indians were absent on their
first winter hunt. Hamelin looted the place, which was
deserted except for a few traders and an old Indian chief
and his family, loaded the pack horses with about fifty
bales of goods and furs and departed hastily, taking the
route around Lake Michigan toward the Chicago Portage.[22]

Lieutenant Dagneau de Quindre, English commander
in that region, who was absent when the post was attacked, collected a party of Potawatomi and pursued the
marauders. They overtook Hamelin near the Petite
Fort, which was about a day's journey beyond the Riviere
du Chemin, or Trail Creek, the stream at the mouth of
which Michigan City now stands. In the battle that
followed, December 5, 1780, Hamelin and three of his
men were killed, two were wounded, and seven captured.
Thomas Brady was among those taken prisoner. De
Quindre did not lose a man.[23] This affair greatly en-

[22] Ibid.; Quaife, Chicago and the Old Northwest, 99; Paré, "The
St. Joseph Mission," in Mississippi Valley Historical Review, 17:47-48;
Clarence W. Alvord, "The Conquest of St. Joseph, Michigan, by the
Spaniards in 1781," in Missouri Historical Review, 2(1908):205.

[23] De Peyster to Powell, January 8, 1781, in Michigan Pioneer and
Historical Collections, 19:591-92. De Peyster, to whom De Quindre made
his report, wrote that the battle occurred a day's journey beyond the
Riviere du Chemin, or Trail Creek. As the distance from Trail Creek
to the Petite Fort was about eleven miles, and as the going for loaded
pack horses through the sand dunes would have been difficult, it is
reasonable to believe that the battle was fought at the Petite Fort and

hanced the prestige of the English among the Indians.[24]

The reverses at Miamis (Fort Wayne) and at the Petite Fort apparently convinced the Spanish officials at St. Louis that a successful blow must be struck at the enemy before the winter was over. On January 2, 1781, Don Eugenio Pierro, the commandant at St. Louis, with a large party of Spaniards, Frenchmen, and Indians began the long march of about four hundred miles through the ice and snow to attack the St. Joseph post. It was captured a few weeks later and, as the Potawatomi were again on a hunt, Pierro suffered no casualties.[25] The post was looted, huts of the traders burned, and a large supply of corn which the English had collected there in anticipation of an attack on St. Louis that spring was destroyed. The Spanish flag flew over the place for twenty-four hours, after which Pierro and his men departed in haste for St. Louis. De Quindre, who was again absent when the post was taken, was unable to assemble a force of Indians to pursue the raiders.[26]

Some historians indicate that the St. Joseph expedition in 1781 was a part of the general plan of the Spanish

not on Trail Creek. George Brennan was positive that it occurred on Trail Creek. See Brennan, *The Wonders of the Dunes,* 52. Quaife, unable to locate the site of the Petite Fort, thought the engagement was fought near the "Calumet River." See Quaife, *Chicago and the Old Northwest,* 100n.

[24] Russell, *The British Régime in Michigan and the Old Northwest,* 212; Kellogg, *The British Régime in Wisconsin and the Northwest,* 174.

[25] Daniel McCoy, "Old Fort St. Joseph," in *Michigan Pioneer and Historical Collections,* 35(1907):549; Alvord, "The Conquest of St. Joseph, Michigan," in *Missouri Historical Review,* 2:206; Quaife, *Chicago and the Old Northwest,* 100-2.

[26] De Peyster to Powell, March 17, 1781, in *Michigan Pioneer and Historical Collections,* 19:600; Quaife, *Chicago and the Old Northwest,* 100-2. That Pierro divided the goods seized at the post between the St. Joseph Indians, who remained neutral in the affair, and those accompanying him, indicates that the sole objective of the Spanish was not plunder.

to seize important places in the West to strengthen their claim to that country at the end of the war; that they hoped to prevent the Americans from getting the great West.[27] On the other hand, more recent evidence leads to the belief that the campaign was conceived in order to maintain the prestige of the Spanish and Americans among the Indians, and also to discourage the English from further attacks on their posts on the Wabash, in the Illinois Country, and in upper Louisiana.[28]

In the years immediately following the Revolutionary War the Potawatomi remained loyal to England. Encouraged by the English, they were present at the defeat of General Arthur St. Clair, 1791; fought Anthony Wayne at Fallen Timbers, 1794; and participated in the Battle of Tippecanoe against William Henry Harrison in 1811. They took up arms against the United States for the last time in the War of 1812.

[27] Esarey and Thwaites appear to favor this conclusion. See Esarey, *History of Indiana*, 1:93 and Reuben G. Thwaites, *France in America, 1497-1763* (*The American Nation: A History,* Vol. 7, New York, 1905), 291.

[28] In an article in the *Gaceta de Madrid (Madrid Gazette)*, March 12, 1782, the Spanish claimed their governor at Havana ordered the campaign against St. Joseph. Alvord denied this and charged that Spanish diplomats inserted the article in the *Gaceta* to strengthen Spain's claim to the West. According to Alvord, the real motive of the expedition was the desire of the Cahokians to revenge the defeat of their people at the Petite Fort, and also to plunder the St. Joseph post. "The Conquest of St. Joseph, Michigan," in *Missouri Historical Review,* 2:197-210. Lawrence Kinnaird stated that the St. Joseph affair was a manifesto of Spain's Indian policy, that it was a matter of maintaining Spanish prestige among the Indians. He based his opinion upon a letter from Francesco Cruzat, Spanish commandant at St. Louis, to Governor Galvez at New Orleans, January 10, 1781. "The Spanish Expedition against Fort St. Joseph in 1781, A New Interpretation," in *Mississippi Valley Historical Review,* 19(1932-33):173-91. Kellogg accepted Kinnaird's conclusions. *The British Régime in Wisconsin and the Northwest,* 175. This author is inclined to agree with Kinnaird and Kellogg.

Indian Land Cessions

After Indiana became a state in 1816 the Federal government took steps to move the Indians west of the Mississippi River. In 1818 the Delaware surrendered all their claims to land in Indiana. At the same time, the Wea, Kickapoo, and the Miami relinquished their territory south of the Wabash River, with the exception of a few reserves. These cessions, known as the "New Purchase," amounted to more than one third of the total area of the state.

The northwestern corner of the state, including the Calumet Region, was one of the last sections given up by the Indians. In 1826 the Treaty of Mississinewa was negotiated with the Potawatomi. The tract ceded, later known as the "Ten Mile Purchase," was described as follows: "Beginning at a point on Lake Michigan, ten miles due north of the southern extreme thereof; running thence due east to the land ceded by the Indians to the United States by the Treaty of Chicago (1821); thence south with the boundary thereof, ten miles; thence west to the southern extreme of Lake Michigan; thence with the shore thereof to the place of the beginning."[29] This grant extended eastward to the St. Joseph River, and in the Calumet Region included the Miller section of what is now Gary and the dune country to the east. In later years the southern boundary of this area was known as the "Indian Boundary Line."

In the Treaty of Tippecanoe, 1832, the Potawatomi Indians gave up most of their remaining land in northwestern Indiana, retaining sections on which were located their villages, settlements, and agricultural plots.[30] The

[29] Charles C. Royce (comp.), *Indian Land Cessions in the United States* (2 vols. U. S. Bureau of American Ethnology, *Eighteenth Annual Report,* 1896-97), 1: 716.

[30] *Ibid.,* 1:740. The next year, 1833, in a great conclave at Chicago,

Federal government purchased all these reservations in 1836 with the understanding that the Indians would move in 1838, at the expense of the government, to reservations west of the Mississippi.[31] However, the exodus of the Potawatomi was gradual and some remained in the Calumet Region for a few years after that date. Others returned from time to time in later years to visit the burial grounds of their ancestors.[32]

Indian Villages and Trails

As the greater part of the Calumet Region was composed of sand dunes, swamps, and sloughs, it is doubtful that the Potawatomi ever had any of their principal towns and villages in the area. Indian towns were seldom permanent and usually changed with the seasons. The tribes followed hunting parties and readily abandoned their residences when menaced by an enemy. Notwithstanding this lack of permanency, they did have favorite locations. Summer homes were maintained on Fancher's Lake, in the vicinity of what is now Hobart, and on a creek near the present town of Dyer.[33] The Indians had

the Potawatomi ceded their remaining lands in Illinois and southern Michigan.

[31] Dwight L. Smith, "A Continuation of the Journal of an Emigrating Party of Potawatomi Indians, 1838," in *Indiana Magazine of History,* 44(1948):395.

[32] Barnhart and Carmony, *Indiana,* 1:213-16; Esarey, *History of Indiana,* 1:381-85. In 1873 Simon Pokagon, son of the famous Potawatomi chief, Leopold Pokagon, and other Indians visited the burial ground near Lake Station (East Gary). Arthur Patterson, "The Pottawatomie Trail of Lake County," in *History of Lake County,* edited by Alice M. Demmon, *et al.* (Lake County Historical Association *Publication,* Vol. 11, 1934), 51.

[33] Armanis F. Knotts, "Indian Trails, Towns and Mounds in Lake County," in *History of Lake County,* edited by John O. Bowers, *et al.* (Lake County Historical Association *Publication,* vol. 10, 1929), 94. Patterson, "The Pottawatomie Trail of Lake County," in Demmon (ed.), *History of Lake County* (1934), 51. Solon Robinson, writing in 1835,

a workshop and dancing ground near what is now East Gary. Chiqua's Town, just east of the present city of Valparaiso, was a popular gathering place for various tribes. When winter came, the Potawatomi usually retired to homes on the "islands" in the great marshes of the Kankakee River.[34] Not only was this one of the finest hunting and trapping areas in the West but here they were protected against the icy winds from off Lake Michigan.

Solon Robinson, who settled near what is now Crown Point in the fall of 1834, said the only Indians he saw were a few around Cedar Lake, a few miles to the south. Robinson and his brother Milo operated the first store in Lake County, and at the start their best customers were the Potawatomi who traded furs and cranberries at their place of business. Cranberries and huckleberries grew abundantly in the marshes and sand of the region, and the Indians traveled great distances to pick them for the market.[35] It is probable that Robinson's dusky customers were merely seasonal residents of the area.

The Calumet Region, located at the foot of Lake Michigan, was traversed through the years by the Indians on their various missions. Some of their trails were worn smooth by years of constant use. Others were not so

said the Indians in Lake County had no fixed residence, some families occupying as many as a dozen sites in a year. Kellar (ed.), *Solon Robinson,* 1:63.

[34] Alfred H. Meyer, "The Kankakee 'Marsh' of Northern Indiana and Illinois," in Michigan Academy of Science, Arts, and Letters, *Papers,* 21(1935):367. These "islands" were actually groves of trees whose surface rose ten to twenty feet above the level of the marsh. See Blatchley, "The Geology of Lake and Porter Counties," in Indiana *Geological Report,* 1897, pp. 57-58.

[35] Kellar (ed.), *Solon Robinson,* 1:61; Darus P. Blake, "Early Days in Lake and Porter Counties," in Bowers (ed.), *History of Lake County* (1929), 82-83.

plainly marked. In places they were lost in the expanse of the prairie, or disappeared in marshes and lowlands. The general outlines of the larger trails were fairly well fixed. There might be two or three paths in some places, but these would converge and run together. In places the track might be entirely obliterated, but would later appear again. In later years, engineers quickly discovered the Indians always followed the easiest, the best, and the shortest way from point to point. If many of the trails are no longer visible today, it is because the builders of the railroads and highways found they were the most practical routes through the dunes and swamps of the region.

The most famous of the trails was the "Old Sauk Trail," so named because at the time Michigan, northern Indiana, and northern Illinois were being settled, the Sauk or Sac were using it the most. For many years the Sauk received an annuity in goods from the English and later from the United States. To collect these payments they traveled each year, men, women, children, ponies, and dogs, from their home in western Illinois to Malden, in Canada, and later to Detroit. The Sauk followed the great transcontinental trail which had been used by the Indians for centuries. That portion of the trail from near Rock Island, Illinois, to Detroit became known as the Sauk Trail. It entered the Calumet Region at Dyer and followed for a distance the Glenwood beach of old Lake Chicago through Schererville and Merrillville. From there the trail continued through the present city of Valparaiso and thence in a northeasterly direction through what are now Westville, La Porte, and New Carlisle.[36] The Lincoln Highway follows this route

36 Knotts, "Indian Trails, Towns, and Mounds in Lake County," in Bowers (ed.), *History of Lake County* (1929), 90-91; Brennan, *The Wonders of the Dunes*, 79.

rather closely to a point east of Valparaiso. A northern tributary to the Sauk Trail, the Dakota-Wisconsin branch, followed the Lake Michigan beach eastward from Chicago and through the sand dunes past Joseph Bailly's trading post, thence through the present Porter and Chesterton to join the main trail.[37]

The Cedar Lake Trail ran from the Chicago-to-Vincennes Trail, crossing the Kankakee River at a ford about a mile east of what is now Momence, Illinois. From there it turned to the northeast past the northern end of Red Cedar Lake to the present Crown Point and Merrillville. At Merrillville it crossed the Sauk Trail and went on to the Deep River crossing at what was later Liverpool, where it joined the Calumet Beach Trail.[38] The Potawatomi Trail followed the Cedar Lake Trail from the crossing of the Kankakee and turned to the northeast between the Kankakee Marsh and the edge of the Valparaiso Moraine. It then divided, one branch joining the Sauk Trail about a mile east of Valparaiso. Chiqua's Town, a dancing ground and rendezvous of the Indians, was located at this junction. The other branch went on to the Deep River crossing at Liverpool and thence past Joseph Bailly's trading post to what is now Michigan City. Here it divided, one branch going north to St. Joseph, and the other east to Detroit.[39]

The Calumet Beach Trail came out of Illinois along the ridge south of the Little Calumet River, now Ridge

[37] Sister Mary Borromeo Brown, *The History of the Sisters of Providence of Saint Mary-of-the-Woods, Vol. I* (New York, 1949), 126; Brennan, *The Wonders of the Dunes*, 76, 101. Many writers consider this northern tributary as the main trail.

[38] Knotts, "Indian Trails, Towns and Mounds in Lake County," in Bowers (ed.), *History of Lake County* (1929), 91.

[39] *Ibid.*, 92; Brennan, *The Wonders of the Dunes*, 101; Hubert M. Skinner, *History of Valparaiso from the Earliest Times to the Present* (Valparaiso, Ind., 1876), 4-5.

Road, to about one half mile east of what is now Broadway Street in Gary. From there it left the present highway and went along the ridge next to the marsh to East Gary, then on past Joseph Bailly's trading post to Michigan City. The Tolleston Beach or Dunes Trail came from the west through what is now south Hammond, followed the ridge north of the Little Calumet Marsh and on to Michigan City.[40] The Calumet River Trail crossed the present Illinois state line along the route later followed by the Michigan Central Railroad west of Hammond. At Hammond, it followed the Grand Calumet River closer than did the railroad to the old mouth of the river in what is now Gary's Marquette Park, where it joined the Lake Shore Trail. The Lake Shore Trail followed the Lake Michigan beach, or, in time of bad weather, the first valley just south of the beach. Until recent years, it could be easily traced through the sand dunes. East of Fort Creek, near Mt. Tom, one branch joined the Dunes Trail to Michigan City. The other followed the lake beach to that place.[41]

There were other trails, but apparently those described here were the principal ones. Along these trails marched the war parties of the Indians. Other Indians followed one trail or another in their never ending search for furs to trade for the white man's goods. These trails simplified the task of the land-hungry pioneers when they came to deprive the Indians of their hunting grounds. If one were looking for some lasting influence of the Indians upon the Calumet Region, he would find it in the trails they left for the white man to use.

[40] Knotts, "Indian Trails, Towns and Mounds in Lake County," in Bowers (ed.), *History of Lake County* (1929), 92.

[41] *Ibid.*, 92-93; Brennan, *The Wonders of the Dunes*, 77; Patterson, "The Pottawatomie Trail of Lake County," in Demmon (ed.), *History of Lake County* (1934), 50.

3

THE LOG CABIN ERA, 1816-1852

THE ORIGINAL BOUNDARIES of the present states of
Ohio, Indiana, and Illinois were fixed, subject to certain
specified revisions, in the Ordinance of 1787. According
to this document, the northern boundary of these states
was to be a line drawn east and west through the southern
extremity of Lake Michigan. Had this boundary remained unchanged, the Miller section of Gary, the dune
country, Michigan City, South Bend, and Toledo, Ohio,
would now be in Michigan. Also, to the west of the
southern extremity of the lake, that part of Gary where
the great steel mills are located, East Chicago, Whiting,
a strip of Hammond, Chicago, and much of northern
Illinois would now be a part of Wisconsin. Again, had
the Ordinance line been retained as a boundary, Indiana
and Illinois would not now have a foot of frontage on
Lake Michigan.[1]

Ohio, when preparing for statehood, ignored the
Ordinance of 1787 in the matter of her northern boundary. Determined to have possession of the mouth of
the Maumee River, where Toledo now stands, her con-
stitutional convention of 1802 extended the northern
boundary to the northerly cape of Maumee Bay, thereby

[1] Mrs. Frank J. Sheehan, *The Northern Boundary of Indiana* (Indiana Historical Society Publications, Vol. 8, No. 6, Indianapolis, 1928),
291-92; Charles Kettleborough (ed.), *Constitution Making in Indiana,
Volume I, 1780-1851* (*Indiana Historical Collections*, Vol. I, Indianapolis,
1916), 33.

acquiring some 468 square miles of territory originally assigned to what is now Michigan. Michigan leaders later bitterly protested Ohio's encroachment on their territory. The controversy reached its climax in 1835 in what was called the "Toledo War," at which time the Ohio militia and that of the Michigan Territory were dispatched to the disputed area. In 1836 Congress awarded the "Toledo strip" to Ohio, and in compensation gave Michigan the region northwest of Lake Michigan known as the Upper Peninsula.[2]

In 1815 Jonathan Jennings, delegate to Congress from the Indiana Territory, drafted a bill to enable Indiana to become a state, and in its early consideration by Congress proposed that the northern boundary be fixed on a line twenty-five miles north of the southern extremity of Lake Michigan. This arrangement would have extended Indiana's area to a point just south of St. Joseph, Michigan. The ambitious Jennings apparently decided he had asked for too much of Michigan's territory, and the bill was amended to locate the boundary on a line ten miles north of the southern tip of the lake. This gave Indiana a frontage of forty-one miles on Lake Michigan.[3] Michigan had no territorial delegate in Congress at that time, and there was no opposition to the change. It is said that the "only man interested was the delegate from Indiana and he was the chairman of the committee that arranged the boundaries."[4] Indiana little

2 See Buley, *The Old Northwest,* 1:63-65, 67; 2:190-203, for accurate maps depicting these boundary disputes and for an excellent account of the "Toledo War."

3 *Ibid.,* 1:66-67; Kettleborough, *Constitution Making in Indiana, 1780-1851,* 72-74; George Pence and Nellie C. Armstrong, *Indiana Boundaries, Territory, State and County (Indiana Historical Collections,* Vol. 19, Indianapolis, 1933), 11-12; Sheehan, *The Northern Boundary of Indiana,* 294-96.

4 Claude S. Larzelere, "The Boundaries of Michigan," in *Michigan Pioneer and Historical Collections,* 30(1906):6.

knew how valuable this ten-mile strip, which totaled some 1,100 square miles, would become in the future, and at the time, the change in the boundary aroused no comment, favorable or unfavorable.

Upon becoming a state in 1818, Illinois followed the example set by Ohio and Indiana and obtained a northern boundary more than sixty-one miles north of the southern extremity of Lake Michigan.[5] In the framing of her constitution in 1835 Michigan adhered to the line as set by the Ordinance of 1787 for her southern boundary. Congressmen from Ohio, Indiana, and Illinois apparently united their strength to defeat this provision. Instead, the act enabling Michigan to become a state in 1836 described the new state as bounded on the south by Ohio and Indiana.

Joseph Bailly on the Little Calumet

The first permanent settlement in the Calumet Region, was founded in 1822 by Joseph Bailly, a fur trader. Bailly established his home and trading post on the north bank of the Little Calumet River in Porter County, near the present towns of Porter and Chesterton. With Bailly came his wife, Marie Le Fevre Bailly, their children, Esther, Rose, Eleanor, and Robert, and also Therese de la Vigne, a daughter of Mrs. Bailly by a former marriage. Another daughter, Hortense, was born later.[6]

Joseph Bailly, or Joseph Aubert de Gaspe Bailly de Messein, was born in 1774 at Quebec of a prominent French family. At an early age, he went west and engaged in the fur trade in the vicinity of Michilimackinac.[7]

---

[5] Buley, *The Old Northwest*, 1:81.

[6] Frances R. Howe, *The Story of a French Homestead in the Old Northwest* (Columbus, Ohio, 1907), 42. Frances Howe was a granddaughter of Joseph and Marie Bailly.

[7] *Ibid.*, 24-25.

At this time he was described as well educated, noisy, no matter what part of the island might contain him. He was exceptionally good-natured, and fond of entertaining his friends.[8] By the turn of the nineteenth century Bailly was conducting trading operations on the Grand, Muskegon, Kalamazoo, and St. Joseph rivers in Lower Michigan. In this area he was associated with the traders William Burnett, John Kinzie, and the famous Potawatomi chief, Alexander Robinson. By 1805 Bailly had extended his fur-trading activites to the Kankakee River in the Indiana Territory.[9]

In the years after the War of 1812 John Jacob Astor's American Fur Company virtually controlled the fur trade of the Great Lakes Region. The records of the company at Michilimackinac for 1821-22 show that Bailly and John Kinzie were trading at their own risk and account in Lower Michigan. Such evidence indicates that Bailly and Kinzie were independent traders and not agents of the Astor company.[10] About this time Bailly's license as a fur trader, issued by the Federal government, assigned him to the Calumet Region. As the northern boundary of Indiana had not been officially surveyed, he thought he was still in Michigan when he settled on the Little Calumet River.[11] His operations extended out from the

8 Elizabeth Thérèse Baird, "Reminiscences of Early Days on Mackinac Island," in *Wisconsin Historical Collections,* 14(1898):43.

9 Joseph Bailly to Toussaint Pothier, November 18, 1800, and Joseph Bailly to Louis Bourie, May 28, 1805. Bailly Papers, in possession of Mrs. John O. Bowers, Gary. Pothier was a merchant and fur trader at Mackinac Island; Bourie, a resident of Fort Wayne, obtained a license at this time for Bailly from the Indian Agency at Fort Wayne to trade in the Kankakee Valley.

10 Ida Amanda Johnson, *The Michigan Fur Trade* (Lansing, 1919), 125.

11 Howe, *The Story of a French Homestead,* 40-41. Joseph Bailly was apparently a British citizen until after the War of 1812. As Congress passed a law in 1816 that licenses to trade with the Indians were to be

Calumet post through southern Michigan, the Kankakee
Valley, and into the Wabash country. Bailly obtained
trade goods from Detroit and Michilimackinac and in
turn sold his furs at those places.[12]

As was common among Frenchmen in the Great Lakes
Region in the early years, Joseph Bailly married Indian
women. His first wife was the daughter of an Indian
chief and to this union six children, Alexis, Joseph, Michel, Philip, Francis, and Sophia were born. The sons,
with the exception of Francis, who chose to be a medicine man or herb doctor among the Indians, were educated at Montreal.[13] Alexis, the oldest son, had a notable
career. He entered the service of the Northwest Fur
Company, a British trading firm, and after the War of
1812 was employed by Astor's American Fur Company.
For a time he was stationed at Prairie du Chien in what
is now Wisconsin and was later the company's agent
at Mendota in what was to be the Minnesota Territory.
At Mendota, Alexis married a daughter of Jean Baptiste Faribault, one of the most prominent figures in the

issued only to American citizens unless by express direction of the
President, Bailly must have found it necessary to become an American
citizen. His son Alexis was naturalized a few years later so that he
could participate in the fur trade. See William Folwell, *A History of
Minnesota* (4 vols. St. Paul, 1921-30), 1:133.

[12] By the time Bailly established his fur-trading post on the Little
Calumet River, St. Joseph, Michigan, was a regular port of call for
cargo-carrying boats on Lake Michigan. The American Fur Company
also sent brigades to collect pelts from the traders at various points
along the lake's shore. See Quaife, *Lake Michigan,* 113-16, 174-75, 178,
180, 183. It is possible that Bailly transported his furs in his own boats
up Lake Michigan to St. Joseph, whence they were shipped in regular
carriers to Michilimackinac and Detroit, or he may have used pack horses
to transport his pelts to St. Joseph. The harbor at Michigan City was
not developed until the 1830's.

[13] Information about the education and careers of the children may
be obtained from typewritten notes of John O. Bowers in possession of
Mrs. John O. Bowers, Gary, Indiana. See also Baird, "Reminiscences of

Indian trade in those years.[14] In 1851 he was in charge of the commissary which provided food for the Sioux Indians during the negotiations which led to the sale of their lands in Iowa and in the Minnesota Territory to the Federal government. Alexis was elected to Minnesota's first General Assembly in 1858 and was also appointed a colonel in the state's militia.[15] In 1835 he served as one of the administrators of his father's estate on the Little Calumet River.

Joseph Bailly and his first wife separated by mutual consent but the date of their parting is not clear. Marie Le Fevre, his second wife, was born in 1783 in the French settlement known as the Rivière des Raisin on the site of the present city of Monroe, Michigan. Marie's father was a French merchant and her mother was an Ottawa Indian. At an early age she had married an Ottawa medicine man named de la Vigne. Two daughters, Agatha and Therese, were born to this union. In time Marie availed herself of the Ottawa tribal privilege and purchased her freedom from her husband. In 1810 she met Joseph Bailly at Michilimackinac where they agreed to be husband and wife. Available records do not show when they were legally married, but evidence indicates the ceremony took place some years later.[16] Marie was

Early Days on Mackinac Island," in *Wisconsin Historical Collections,* 14:43-44.

14 Baird, in *loc. cit.* 14:43; Folwell, *History of Minnesota,* 1:437.

15 Folwell, *History of Minnesota,* 1:279.

16 In a notarized statement made at Drummond's Island, May 2, 1817, where they were living at the time, Bailly assigned to "Marie Le Fevre" all his household goods to satisfy a debt of 150 pounds which he owed her for services rendered as a "Maid-servant in his home and for clothing and money advanced by her to him." Since Marie is named in this document as "Marie Le Fevre," they apparently were not formally married at that time. It is possible this settlement was made just prior to their legal marriage. (A typewritten copy of this document is in the possession of Mrs. John O. Bowers, Gary, Indiana.) John O.

described as being a "good woman, and possessed the gift so much prized among her own people—that of a good storyteller. Her stories quite surpassed the '*Arabian Nights*' in interest; one could have listened to her all day and never tired."[17] She continued to speak her Indian tongue after her marriage to Bailly and could understand French only when it was spoken slowly.

In 1819 Agatha de la Vigne, one of Marie's daughters, was married to Edward Biddle, a member of the prominent Philadelphia family of that name, who was engaged in business at Mackinac Island. Joseph Bailly was reported to have been "more noisy than ever over this marriage. Proud of his stepdaughter, such a marriage and connection was more than he could bear quietly."[18]

From 1822 to 1833 Joseph Bailly and his family apparently were the only settlers in the Calumet Region. And yet their home and trading post were not typical of pioneer American settlements. Here was reproduced the social, economic, and religious atmosphere of old Michilimackinac and other French outposts in the Old Northwest. Located on a principal Indian trail and near others, the trading post became a favorite rendezvous for Indians and trappers. The inn, which Bailly operated only a short distance from his residence, was popular with travelers who passed over the old post road between

Bowers, in his typewritten notes about the Bailly family, stated that Mr. Wright, a grandson of Sophia Bailly Graveraet, the latter a daughter of Joseph Bailly's first marriage, told him in 1922 that the Catholic Church refused to grant Joseph Bailly a divorce from his first wife. However, this would not have prevented Joseph and Marie from being married in a civil ceremony. Elizabeth Thérèse Baird, who knew them at Mackinac Island, said that "in the course of time," they were married. "Reminiscences of Early Days on Mackinac Island," in *Wisconsin Historical Collections*, 14:43.

17 *Ibid.*, 14:44.
18 *Ibid.*, 14:44-47.

Detroit and Chicago. Charles Hoffman, while on his tour of the West in 1833, was impressed with the comfort and hospitality of the Bailly establishment. He described the settlement as consisting of "six or eight log-cabins of a most primitive construction, all of them gray with age, and so grouped on the bank of the river as to present a picturesque appearance."[19]

Ottawa Indians came from what is now Michigan to trade at the Bailly post, and the place was also a favorite haunt of the Potawatomi. Mrs. Bailly, no doubt in part because of her Ottawa background, was highly respected by the Indians and was addressed as "Aunt" by their children.[20] The Ottawa and Potawatomi, who often camped for months at a time in the vicinity of the post, frequently left their personal property in the care of the Baillys when they went on their prolonged hunts.[21]

The Baillys being devout Catholics, the homestead was a regular stopping place for priests en route to and from Chicago and Detroit. There being no chapel at the settlement in the early period, religious services were held in the residence. On these occasions confessions were heard in the parlor and Mass was celebrated in the dining room. If there were Indians in the vicinity at those particular times, they were encouraged by the Baillys to attend the services. Bailly, himself, translated orally the old Royaumont French Bible history one winter for the Indians, and later made a translation of the entire New Testament into Potawatomi.[22]

19 Charles F. Hoffman, *A Winter in the West* (2 vols. New York, 1835), 1:230.

20 Brown, *The History of the Sisters of Providence of Saint Mary-of-the-Woods,* 127.

21 Howe, *The Story of a French Homestead,* 63.

22 Brown, *op. cit.,* 127, 128, 129-30; John O. Bowers, *The Old Bailly Homestead* (Gary, 1922), 7. The chapel at the homestead was built some years after Marie Bailly's death in 1866. Its bell, from the old Saint

Photograph by Russell V. Hamm for Chicago Daily News

THE BAILLY HOMESTEAD

SOLON ROBINSON

Courtesy Wisconsin State Historical Society

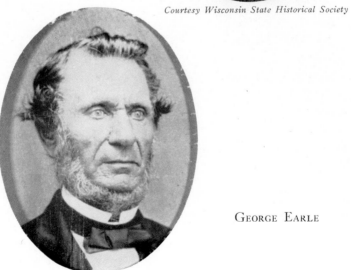

GEORGE EARLE

Courtesy Walter Pickart, Gary

Bailly, a well-educated and intelligent man, gave his children all the educational advantages that were available at that time. The library at the homestead consisted of about three hundred volumes in French and English, most of them classics. Rose and Esther attended school at Mackinac Island for a brief time before the family moved to the Calumet Region. During the 1820's, the children attended the Carey Mission School near the present Niles, Michigan, conducted by Isaac McCoy, a Baptist missionary to the Indians.[23]

Bailly's only son by his second marriage died in 1827 at the age of ten. The Bailly sisters mingled with the Beaubiens, the Kinzies, the Ogdens, and other prominent families in the social life of early Chicago. Esther, the eldest, married John H. Whistler, grandson of Captain John Whistler, the builder of Fort Dearborn, and a cousin of James Abbott McNeill Whistler, the famous artist. Rose became the wife of Francis Howe, a Chicago civil engineer. Hortense, the youngest, married Joel H. Wicker, a merchant at nearby Deep River, Indiana.[24] Apparently, Therese, their half-sister, who lived at the homestead, never married.

Eleanor Cecilia Kinzie Bailly, born at Mackinac Island in 1815, had the most distinguished career of any of Joseph Bailly's daughters. Because of her the Bailly family was associated with Saint Mary-of-the-Woods, near Terre Haute, Indiana, for many years. A group of the Sisters of Providence came from France to establish

Mary's Academy (Saint Mary-of-the-Woods), was a present from the Sisters of Providence. See Howe, *The Story of a French Homestead*, 163.

[23] Bowers, *The Old Bailly Homestead*, 10; Baird, "Reminiscences of Early Days on Mackinac Island," in *Wisconsin Historical Collections*, 14:43; Howe, *The Story of a French Homestead*, 47-51. Miss Howe states that Rose and Esther Bailly also attended the Mission School while it was at Fort Wayne, prior to its removal to Michigan Territory.

[24] Bowers, *The Old Bailly Homestead*, 10.

this famous school in 1840. Eleanor entered the novitiate at St. Mary's in November, 1841. Her arrival was reported to have been "a red letter day for the little band of Sisters battling so bravely with pioneer difficulties. A native American, educated, refined, familiar with the French and English languages—little wonder they considered her a God-send."[25] Eleanor, who chose the name of Sister Mary Cecilia, later taught English and music at St. Mary's.

In 1844, after several years of controversy with the Bishop of Vincennes, the Sisters of Providence considered seriously the removal of the school from his diocese. Sister Mary Cecilia offered land at the Bailly homestead and the Sisters were inclined to accept this generous offer. But within a short time it was discovered that the homestead was in the diocese of Vincennes and not in the Chicago diocese, as had been thought. The Sisters also decided the location on the Little Calumet River was too remote and isolated for a girls' school.[26]

Sister Mary Cecilia became Superior General at St. Mary's in 1856, and was head of the school until 1868. In 1860 her niece, Rose Howe, was the first student to graduate from Saint Mary-of-the-Woods Academy. Another niece, Frances Howe, attended the school in 1868 but left before the end of the year to go abroad with her mother.[27] In 1869 Mrs. Francis Howe, Mother Mary Cecilia's sister, suggested that the Sisters of Providence establish a school at Calumet, now Chesterton,

[25] Sister Anita Cotter, "Mother Mary Cecilia Bailly," in *In God's Acre, Biographical Sketches, Series I* (Sisters of Providence, Saint Mary-of-the-Woods, 1940), 9-10.

[26] Brown, *The History of the Sisters of Providence of Saint Mary-of-the-Woods,* 1:398-99.

[27] Sister Mary Borromeo Brown to the Author, October 7, 1953; Cotter, *In God's Acre,* 4.

and invited the Sisters who might come there to reside at the Bailly homestead. The school was started with Mother Mary Cecilia, assisted by a faculty of three sisters and two secular teachers, in charge. A short time later Mother Mary Cecilia recommended moving the school to the Bailly place, Mrs. Howe having offered about one hundred acres of improved land for such a purpose. The project was abandoned when the Superior of St. Mary's declined the offer and the Bishop of Fort Wayne found he could not provide a chaplain. The school at Chesterton was closed in 1872.[28]

On leaving Chesterton, Mother Mary Cecilia filled an assignment at St. Augustine's in Fort Wayne for eight years. Then, at her own request, she was sent to St. Ann's Orphan Asylum at Terre Haute, where she died in 1898. The biographer of Mother Mary Cecilia at St. Mary's paid tribute to her: "Here we see the little Indian of the northern lakes becoming one of the Torch-Bearers of Christian education in southern Indiana and a notable factor in the expansion of St. Mary-of-the-Woods."[29]

The departure of most of the Indians and the coming of the settlers marked the end of the fur-trading era. Joseph Bailly turned to other projects and became interested in the location of a harbor and city at the old mouth of the Grand Calumet River in what is now Gary's Marquette Park. In connection with this matter, and also to control more of the Little Calumet, he added a large tract of land on both sides of the river to the original homestead. The arrival of the first settlers in 1833 led Bailly to lay out a town on the north bank of the Little Calumet which he called the "Town of Bailly." Streets

[28] Cotter, *In God's Acre*, 33-34. The name Calumet was changed to Chesterton in 1869.

[29] *Ibid.*, 35-36. Mother Mary Cecilia was buried at St. Mary's.

were named for members of his family. One, he called
Le Fevre, in honor of his wife, and others were named
Esther, Rose, Eleanor, and Hortense for his daughters.
Since the site was near the principal trails and routes
leading to Chicago and also on the Little Calumet, Bailly
believed it would be a profitable project. However, newcomers sought the land suitable for farms to the south
rather than the marshes and dunes to the north, which
were unfit for cultivation, and the place proved to be a
poor site for an urban center. Few lots were sold and
the dreams of a town ended with Bailly's death in 1835.[30]

Joseph Bailly's widow remained at the homestead
after his death with other members of the family, except
for a sojourn at Mackinac Island with Agatha and her
husband, Edward Biddle. She died at the homestead
in 1866. Her daughter Rose, who married Francis
Howe, and her children, Rose and Frances, occupied
the place after the death of Francis Howe in 1856. In
the meantime, much of the timber on the homestead was
sold for the construction of the first railroads in the
region.[31] Frances Howe lived there from time to time
until her death in 1918. The following year the homestead was sold to the School Sisters of Notre Dame,

30 Howe, *The Story of a French Homestead*, 90; Bowers, *The Old
Bailly Homestead*, 7, 9. Bailly owned shares in the "Michigan," one of
the finest steamboats on the Great Lakes at that time. This ship was built
and operated by Oliver Newberry, Detroit merchant and ship owner.
Newberry was widely known as the "Admiral of the Lakes." See Marie
Bailly and Alexis Bailly to Oliver Newberry, August 20, 1836, in Bailly
Papers, and Quaife, *Lake Michigan,* 147-57. The plat of the "Town of
Bailly" is in La Porte County Deed Records, A:241. Bailly located the
family cemetery on a ridge a short distance from the residence when
his son Robert died. Today most of the graves are poorly marked and
positive identification of those buried there is difficult. Evidence indicates that the graves of Joseph and Marie Bailly, Robert, Rose Bailly
Howe, Francis Howe, Hortense, and Therese are there.
31 Howe, *The Story of a French Homestead,* 138-39, 154.

Milwaukee, Wisconsin, who wished to use it as a retreat for ill Sisters. The Sisters called the place Villa St. Joseph, and a number of them lived there during the warm months of each year until 1932, when it was abandoned because of a shortage of personnel.[32] A few years later the homestead passed into private hands.

Early Roads, Travelers, and Taverns

The Calumet Region was one of the last portions of Indiana to be settled. The Black Swamp in northwestern Ohio blocked the most direct route from the East into northern Indiana. Although the opening of the Erie Canal in 1825 provided roundabout transportation for settlers in the Lake Michigan region, the lack of harbors and the presence of sand dunes along the southern shore of the lake in Indiana caused immigrants to follow the line of least resistance into Michigan, northern Illinois, and southern Wisconsin. The great Kankakee Marsh to the south handicapped the movement of people from that direction.[33] This marsh was from three to five miles wide, and the depth of its water was from one to four feet deep for eight or nine months of each year.[34] Few people ever saw the Kankakee River except in times of

[32] Sister Mary Antonice, School Sisters of Notre Dame, Milwaukee, Wisconsin, to the author, November 19, 1958. The homestead, which had dwindled to a little more than 44 acres, was purchased by the Sisters of Notre Dame for $8,050. See Porter County Deed Records, 180:536.

[33] Frederick Jackson Turner, *The United States, 1830-1850, The Nation and Its Sections* (New York, 1935), 269-70. Although Congress began appropriating funds for the development of the Michigan City harbor in 1836, it was some years before it was a satisfactory port. See Charles Roll, *Indiana, One Hundred and Fifty Years of American Development* (5 vols. Chicago, 1931), 2:45.

[34] Meyer, "The Kankakee 'Marsh' of Northern Indiana and Illinois," in Michigan Academy of Science, Arts, and Letters, *Papers*, 21(1935):366.

severe droughts or in the winter when the marsh was
frozen over. The region's first historian wrote that "so
far as any ordinary access to it from this county [Lake]
is concerned it is like a fabulous river, or one the existence of which we take on trust."[35] As a result, immigrants from the more southern parts of Indiana and
Ohio chose the easier routes along the Michigan Road
or up the Wabash River into the tier of counties east
of Porter and Lake.[36] The late removal of the Indians
also delayed the area's settlement for a time.

The beach along the southern shore of Lake Michigan
provided one of the first routes for settlers and travelers.
The going was easy when the sand was wet and packed,
and particularly so in the winter when it was frozen. A
traveler in December, 1833, said "the beach twenty
yards from the surf was nearly as hard as stone, and
the finest Macadamized road in the world could not
compare with the one over which we now galloped."
But all was not perfect in the winter, for the same traveler reported that "after passing around the end of the
lake and taking a northwardly direction, the way in
which the icy blast would come down the bleak shore of
the lake 'was a caution.' . . . The rough ice piled up
on the coast prevented us from watering our beasts; and
we did not draw a rein till the rushing current of the
Calaminc [Calumet], which debouches into Lake Michigan some ten miles from Chicago, stayed our course."[37]

In the summer and early fall, when the sand was
generally loose and dry, travel was slow and difficult.
Passengers were often compelled to walk while the tired
horses struggled to pull the heavy vehicles through the

[35] Timothy H. Ball, *Lake County, Indiana, from 1834 to 1872* (Chicago, 1873), 17.

[36] Esarey, *History of Indiana*, 1:276-77.

[37] Hoffman, *A Winter in the West*, 1:232, 235-36.

deep sand. A good team reportedly took six days to make the trip from Michigan City to Chicago, a distance at that time of about fifty miles.[38] Streams flowing into the lake slowed down the travelers. The crossing of the Calumet River in what is now South Chicago, was particularly difficult and hazardous. The river was too deep to be fordable, and many of the vehicles took an uncertain and dangerous course through the shallow water of the lake to a sand bar a few hundred feet from the shore, and thence on it past the mouth of the river to the other side. Since other travelers at this same time reported a ferry at this point, it is possible that only the more daring, or the thrifty, took the sand-bar crossing.[39]

Many travelers and settlers came by way of the Great Lakes to Detroit, whence they chose the less hazardous route overland to Niles, La Porte, and Michigan City. From there they followed the Lake Michigan beach to Chicago. Later a branch of the road reached the beach by way of the Bailly trading post.[40] This became known as the Chicago-Detroit Road, and in winter when ice prevented navigation on the upper reaches of the Great Lakes, traffic on this route was particularly heavy. Lieut. James Strode Swearingen led his troops over this route in 1803 to establish Fort Dearborn,[41] and in 1816 other

[38] Milo M. Quaife, *Chicago Highways, Old and New, from Indian Trail to Motor Road* (Chicago, 1923), 45.

[39] *Ibid.*, 45; Hoffman, *A Winter in the West*, 1:236. James H. Luther recalled that he drove teams between La Porte and Chicago until the fall of 1836 and knew of no other route but the one along the beach. He used other routes after that date. See James H. Luther, "History of Northern Lake County," in Timothy H. Ball (ed.), *Lake County, Indiana, 1884* . . . (Crown Point, Ind., 1884), 114-15.

[40] Charles J. Latrobe, *The Rambler in North America, MDCCCXXXII-MDCCCXXXIII* (2 vols. London, 1835), 2:185.

[41] See the "Journal of James Strode Swearingen," in Quaife, *Chicago and the Old Northwest*, 376.

soldiers came along the beach to rebuild the fort which had been destroyed by the Indians during the massacre there in 1812. In the early years mail and dispatches were brought this way by soldiers to the military and civilian population of Fort Dearborn. The United States was granted by treaty with the Indians in 1821 the right to use the road and in 1825 it became a post road.

The first important stage on the road between Detroit and Chicago was established in 1833. Begun as a weekly stage from Niles to Chicago, it developed rapidly with the increase of immigration and travel in the succeeding years until 1835 when one stage ran each day between the two centers. The various stage interests on the Detroit-Chicago Road combined to form the Western Stage Company and in the summer of 1839 its stages left Chicago daily for the East. The stage route later formed a connecting link with the railhead of the Michigan Central Railroad as it pushed westward from Detroit toward Chicago.[42]

As travel increased, inns made of logs were established at various points along the beach. The Bennett Tavern was built at the old mouth of the Grand Calumet River in 1833, and the next year Hannah Berry opened an inn farther west on the beach.[43] Berry Lake was probably named for this family. Most of these taverns were crude affairs and little attention was given to the comfort of the guests. An English visitor reported the sleeping accommodations at one of these inns were "inferior to the bed of an East Lothian Pig."[44] Another was served

[42] Bessie L. Pierce, A History of Chicago. Volume I . . . (New York, 1937), 96, 100-1.

[43] Solon Robinson, "A Lecture on the Early History of Lake Co.," in Kellar (ed.), Solon Robinson, 2:51-52.

[44] Patrick Shirreff, A Tour Through North America (New York, 1837), 257-58.

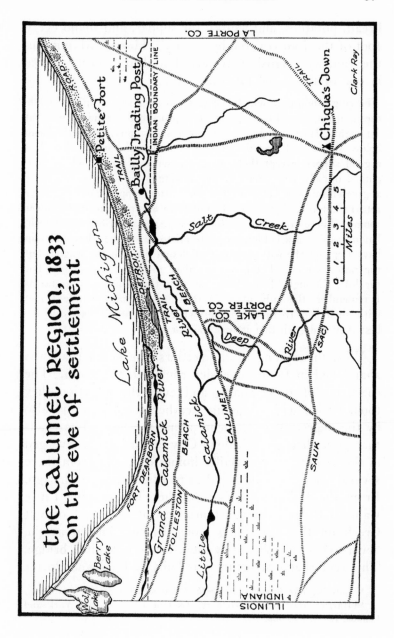

the Calumet Region, 1833
on the eve of settlement

bread, potatoes, and whisky for supper, and found every foot of the floor covered by guests.[45] Harriet Martineau, the famous English traveler, described her experience in one of the beach taverns:

The single house at which we were to stop for the night, while the mail-wagon, with its passengers, proceeded, promised well, at 1st sight. It was a log house on a sand bank, perfectly clean below stairs, and prettily dressed with green boughs. We had a good supper, except there was an absence of milk, and we concluded ourselves fortunate in our resting place. Never was there a greater mistake. We walked out, after supper, and when we returned, found that we could not have any portion of the lower rooms. There was a loft, which I will not describe, into which, having ascended a ladder, we were all to be stowed. I would fain have slept on the soft sand out of doors, beneath the wagon, but the rain came on. There was no place to put our heads into but the loft. Enough. I will only say that this house was, as far as I remember, the only place in the United States where I met with such bad treatment. Everywhere else people gave me the best they had—whether it was good or bad.[46]

With the coming of the settlers, the beach road was abandoned in favor of easier routes to the south. The character of these roads, and even the direction they took, varied with changing weather conditions and also by the degree of settlements along the way. The roads that came through Michigan City or La Porte converged in the vicinity of the Bailly homestead, and from there several branches could be taken to Illinois and to Chicago. From the Bailly place one of these crossed the Little Calumet River a short distance west of the mouth of Salt Creek on the Terrifying Long Bridge, known as the "ever-to-be-remembered-by-those-who-crossed-it" bridge. This remarkable structure was built by Lake and Porter

45 Latrobe, *The Rambler in North America*, 2:194.

46 Harriet Martineau, *Society in America* (2 vols. New York and London, 1837), 1:257-58.

counties in 1836. It was about a thousand feet long and was made of poles throughout. Poles were used to build the cribs or piers, for the stringers, and small poles and split timbers were used for the floor. One hardy pioneer was more frightened while crossing this bridge than he was in getting around the mouth of the Calumet River on the sand bar in South Chicago.[47] Most travelers were so wary of this structure that they chose to walk, rather than ride over it on horseback or in a vehicle. With this experience behind them, they followed the road south and west of the Little Calumet through Liverpool, Munster, Thornton, and Blue Island to Chicago. Another branch followed what is now the Dunes Highway by way of Aetna, and from there it ran through Tolleston to Hegewisch, where there was a ferry across the Little Calumet. A more difficult route ran through what is now Hammond to South Chicago, which necessitated the crossing of both Little and Grand Calumet rivers. As early as 1833, some settlers began to use the Old Sauk Trail into the Calumet Region as well as to points in Illinois.[48]

The taverns on these roads were more attractive and hospitable than those on the beach. Some were operated by families who provided a friendly atmosphere, good food, and comfortable lodgings for the weary travelers. The better known of these were the Old Maid's Tavern at Willow Creek, the Gibson Inn in what is now Gary, the Brass Tavern in Munster, and the Hohman Inn in

[47] Luther, "History of Northern Lake County," in Ball (ed.), *Lake County, Indiana, 1884*, 117; Quaife, *Chicago Highways, Old and New*, 46.

[48] Darius P. Blake, "Early Days in Lake and Porter Counties," in Bowers (ed.), *History of Lake County* (1929), 82, 87; "Reminiscences of Mrs. Henrietta Gibson," in John W. Lester (ed.), Papers by Various Hands (scrapbooks in the Gary Public Library), 1:241; Luther, "History of Northern Lake County," in Ball (ed.), *Lake County, Indiana, 1884*, 117-18; Ball, *Lake County, Indiana 1834-1872*, 20.

the present city of Hammond.[49] The Gibson Inn, the
first permanent white settlement on the site of Gary, was
erected by Thomas Gibson and his wife, Anna Maria,
in 1837 or 1838. It was a two-story hewn-log building
with a large sitting room and a dining room on the first
floor. There were two large bedrooms on the second
floor, and the beds were separated by curtains to assure
a degree of privacy for the guests. There was a lean-to
at the rear of the building where men could congregate.
Mrs. Gibson, known as "Mother Gibson," continued to
operate the inn for some years after her husband's death
in 1850. A son of the Gibsons ran a tavern on the same
road to Chicago at Hegewisch, Illinois.[50]

Settlement of Porter County

The purchase of the land from the Indians by the
Federal government brought the first settlers and claim
seekers into the region. Government surveyors completed
the survey of the land in the greater part of the area in
the summer of 1834. At that time a party of surveyors
camped for a week in a grove on the site of the present
city of Crown Point and found no settlers or cabins in
that vicinity. With the exception of an occasional en-
campment of Indians whose ponies grazed on the empty
prairies, there was nothing to interfere with the preparations being made for the coming of the white man.[51]

49 Blake, "Early Days in Lake and Porter Counties," in Bowers (ed.),
History of Lake County (1929), 85-86. The Brass Tavern was operated
by Allen H. Brass. See Wilhelmine S. Kaske, "Early Days in Munster,"
in Demmon (ed.), *History of Lake County* (1934), 87.

50 "Reminiscences of Mrs. Henrietta Gibson," in Lester (ed.), Papers
by Various Hands, 1:240-41. The Gibson Inn was located at what is
now the junction of 14th Avenue and Madison Street near the Froebel
School. Anna Maria Gibson sold the inn during the packing-house boom
of the 1890's.

51 Ball, *Lake County, Indiana, 1834-1872*, 21.

Although settlers arrived in the eastern portion of the region in 1833, the public lands in Porter County were not offered for sale by the Federal government until 1835 and those in Lake County could not be purchased until 1839. The Calumet Region was in the last land district to be laid out in Indiana. In the beginning the Federal land office was located at La Porte but was removed in the summer of 1839 to Winamac. Its location at Winamac worked a hardship on those who had to go on foot to make their purchases.[52]

The Porter County part of the region received the first settlers. Early in 1833 the Morgan brothers, Jesse, Isaac, and William, natives of Virginia, established land claims in the area. Two years before, Jesse had brought his family to La Porte County, and in 1832 he and his brothers were prominent in the organization of that county. On leaving La Porte County, Jesse chose a farm a few miles from the Bailly homestead and became an intimate friend of Joseph Bailly.[53] For many years he operated a tavern called the "Stage House" on the Chicago-Detroit Road which ran through his claim. Isaac and William Morgan settled on what was later known as Morgan's Prairie.[54] In 1834 Thomas A. E. Campbell,

[52] See land survey map in Esarey, *History of Indiana*, 1:344. Heinrich Eggers, one of the pioneers of Whiting, walked from Chicago to Winamac in 1851 to purchase land. See below, 183.

[53] Mary Morgan and Olga Mae Schiemann, "Coffee Creek Post Office," in *Indiana History Bulletin* 30(1953):49. Jesse Morgan was the "lister of taxable property," and Isaac Morgan was a member of the county board of commissioners of La Porte County in 1832. See Jasper Packard, *History of La Porte County, Indiana* (La Porte, Ind., 1876), 37-39. Frances Howe, who had a poor opinion of her grandfather's neighbors, thought Jesse Morgan was the best of the settlers. See Howe, *The Story of a French Homestead*, 65.

[54] Weston A. Goodspeed and Charles Blanchard (eds.), *Counties of Porter and Lake Indiana* (Chicago, 1882), 17; Cannon, Loring, and Robb (eds.), *History of the Lake and Calumet Region*, 1:84, 87.

of Montgomery County, New York, visited the site of
the present city of Valparaiso and located a farm in that
vicinity. Campbell is generally regarded as the founder
of Valparaiso.[55] A large number of the early settlers in
this part of the region came from New York and Ohio,
as well as from other parts of Indiana.[56]

The earliest post office in the Calumet Region was
called Coffee Creek, now Chesterton, and was established
in January, 1835. Jesse Morgan was the first postmaster.
This post office, named for a small stream in its vicinity,
had a varied history. It was discontinued in September,
1837, re-established in April, 1840, with Jesse Morgan
as postmaster, and again discontinued in August, 1842.
It was re-established in December, 1846, with Jesse Morgan again as postmaster. Its name was changed from
Coffee Creek to Calumet in December, 1849.[57] The village of Calumet, taking its name from the post office, was
laid out in 1852 on the Lake Shore and Michigan Southern Railroad. Among its first citizens were Vincent
Thomas, Enos Thomas, William Thomas, Jesse Morgan,
and William Coleman.[58] In 1869 the community was
incorporated as a town and its name changed to Chesterton. This was done because the name "Calumet," which
was associated with two rivers and the region as a whole,
caused much confusion.[59] In January, 1870, the Post

55 Hubert M. Skinner, Complete History of Porter County, prepared
for Valparaiso Messenger, 1878 (Typewritten MS in Indiana State
Library).

56 Goodspeed and Blanchard (eds.), Counties of Porter and Lake, 17.

57 Albert W. Highsmith, Office of the Postmaster General, Washington, D. C., to the Author, October 12, 1953; Index of Indiana Post Offices,
Indiana Division, Indiana State Library. The Chesterton Westchester
Tribune, April 16, 1896, carried a statement that the Coffee Creek post
office was established in 1833. It is probable that Jesse Morgan collected
and distributed mail unofficially in his home at that early date.

58 Valparaiso Porter County Vidette and Republican, December 24,
1868.

59 Ibid., September 9, 1869.

Office Department, to avoid complications, designated the local office as Chesterton.[60] The town incorporation was abandoned in 1878 when the taxes proved insufficient for the maintenance of a town organization. Industrial development, accompanied by an increase in population, brought about the second incorporation of the community in 1899.[61]

Waverly, the second town to be laid out in the region, was founded in 1834 on a site about two miles northwest of the present Chesterton and not far from the Bailly homestead. Here John W. Foster began what he hoped would be a prosperous lumber town. Valuable improvements were made only to be destroyed in 1839 by a forest fire. Waverly Beach, named for the Waverly Road which passed the town site on its way to the lake shore, is the only reminder today of Foster's dream of a town in those early years.[62]

Until 1836 the area comprising the counties of Porter and Lake was under the political and judicial jurisdiction of La Porte County. In January of that year, Porter County was organized by the General Assembly, and the boundaries of Lake County were defined in the same bill.[63] Lake County was to be separated from Porter when its population justified the step. Porter County was named for Admiral David Dixon Porter, a hero of the War of 1812, and the father of Admiral David Porter of Civil War fame.[64]

[60] Highsmith to the Author, October 12, 1953.

[61] Louis Menke, in *Indiana History Bulletin,* 30(1953):169.

[62] John O. Bowers, *Dream Cities of the Calumet* (Gary, 1929), 24; Goodspeed and Blanchard (eds.), *Counties of Porter and Lake,* 18, 162. See Deed Records, A:157, in La Porte County recorder's office for plat of the town of Waverly.

[63] Pence and Armstrong, *Indiana Boundaries,* 550, 676; Kellar (ed.), *Solon Robinson,* 2:57-58.

[64] Skinner, *History of Valparaiso,* 9. Porter County is the only county

The Portersville Land Company, organized by Benjamin McCarty, platted the town of Portersville in July, 1836, near the crest of what is now called the Valparaiso Moraine.[65] McCarty had helped locate the county seat towns of South Bend and La Porte, and apparently found such efforts to be profitable.[66] His company offered Portersville to the county commissioners as a site for the county seat. Three other sites were considered by the commissioners appointed by the General Assembly of the state to locate the county seat: one of these was at Prattville, another at Flint Lake, and the third about a mile and a half northwest of Portersville.[67] Since the McCarty property was in approximately the geographical center of the county, and as the land company offered to donate a site for the courthouse, ninety-six lots in the town, and $1,200 in cash to the county, the decision was in favor of Portersville.[68]

The name of the county seat was changed from Portersville to Valparaiso in 1837. Hubert M. Skinner, one of the first historians of the town, explained the reason for the change: "It happened that a party of old sailors from the South Pacific stopped one night [during the winter of 1836-37] at Hall's old tavern, and passed the evening telling stories of the old Chilean seaport of that

of that name in the United States. Thomas A. E. Campbell designed the county seal, which represents the battleship "Essex" commanded by Admiral Porter in the War of 1812. See Skinner, Complete History of Porter County.

65 See Deed Records, A:13-14, in Porter County recorder's office for a plat of the town of Portersville.

66 *History of St. Joseph County, Indiana* (Chas. C. Chapman & Co., Chicago, 1880), 662; Packard, *History of La Porte County*, 197; Ball, *Lake County, Indiana, 1834-1872*, 320.

67 Ernest V. Shockley, "County Seats and County Seat Wars in Indiana," in *Indiana Magazine of History*, 10(1914):31.

68 Cannon, Loring, and Robb (eds.) *History of the Lake and Calumet Region*, 1:699.

name. It was at old Valparaiso that the hero for whom our county was named, fought his famous battle on board the *'Essex,'* and at the suggestion of the party of marines the young county seat was appropriately named for the Spanish-American seaport."[69] The new name was approved by the Indiana General Assembly.[70]

James Snow reportedly erected the first frame building in Porter County on the Old Sauk Trail in Union Township west of Valparaiso, and here he opened the first store in the township. In 1837 it was purchased by Oliver Shepard, who added a tavern to the establishment. Shepard, an enterprising New England Yankee, put up a sign calling it the "Hoosier's Nest."[71] This was no doubt inspired by the famous poem of the same name by John Finley, which was published by the Indianapolis *Indiana Journal* on January 1, 1833.[72] The sign on Shepard's store and inn attracted the attention of travelers and in time the inn became famous.

The Beginnings of Lake County

The settlement of the Lake County portion of the region began in the summer of 1833 with the arrival of William Ross from Decatur County, Indiana. Ross built a cabin in the vicinity of Deep River near the present town of Hobart, planted a crop of corn, and spent the following winter there with his family. He was killed

[69] Skinner, *History of Valparaiso,* 12.

[70] See *Laws of Indiana,* 1836-37 (local), p. 382; Pence and Armstrong, *Indiana Boundaries,* 676.

[71] Goodspeed and Blanchard (eds.), *Counties of Porter and Lake,* 197-98.

[72] The poem was not published in the Indianapolis *Indiana Journal,* but separately as a "carrier's address"; it was republished each New Year's Day for several years. See Jacob Piatt Dunn, *The Word Hoosier* (*Indiana Historical Society Publications,* Vol. 4, No. 2, Indianapolis, 1907), 2, 4.

by a falling tree in 1836.[73] In September, 1834, Richard
Fancher, Charles Wilson, Robert Wilkinson, and two
nephews of Wilkinson, came from Attica on the Wabash
River to explore the country and establish claims. Fancher chose land on the little lake just south of what is
now Crown Point which has since borne his name. They
stayed about three weeks and then returned to the Wabash for the winter.[74] On October 30, 1834, Solon
Robinson and his family established their home on the
site of Crown Point. They were preceded by a few
days by Thomas Childers. Henry Wells and Luman
Fowler arrived next and in the spring their families came.
During the winter of 1834-35, William Clark, William
Holton, and Warner Holton, old friends of Robinson's
from southern Indiana, settled in the vicinity of the
Robinson claim. These men and their families almost
perished while crossing the Kankakee Marsh. Fortunately Robinson had anticipated their coming and erected sign posts to guide them across the prairies. Other
settlers came in such numbers during the next few months
that the tax collector from La Porte paid them a visit
in the fall of 1835.[75]

Robinson is regarded by many as the founder of Crown
Point. He was also known as the "Squatter King" of
Lake County. He was born in Tolland, Connecticut, in
1803. Robinson had little formal education, which is
rather surprising in view of his literary achievements in
later years. He came to Cincinnati in 1828 and there
he married Mariah Evans of Philadelphia, a woman
of strong character and refinement, who was well edu-

[73] Robinson, "A Lecture Upon the Early History of Lake Co.," in
Kellar (ed.), *Solon Robinson,* 2:53. Because of their temporary nature,
the taverns along the beach were not regarded as settlements.

[74] Ball, *Lake County, Indiana, 1834-1872,* 21-22.

[75] Kellar (ed.), *Solon Robinson,* 2:53, 54-56, 58.

cated for the time and proved to be a worthy helpmate for her husband in the early years of his career. The Robinsons moved to Jennings County, Indiana, where he laid out the town of "Solon," which proved to be a failure because he was unable to attract buyers for the lots. Discouraged by this setback and believing his health was affected by the climate along the Ohio River, Robinson decided to seek his fortune in northwestern Indiana. Accordingly, in the early fall of 1834 the family traveled in a wagon drawn by oxen to Door Prairie, in La Porte County. Discovering this area was well settled and hearing that good land was available just a few miles to the west, he brought his family over the Old Sauk Trail into the Calumet Region.[76]

Robinson apparently influenced many people from various parts of the country to settle in Lake County. In his voluminous correspondence with the editors of newspapers and farm publications he extolled the virtues of the region, and informed prospective settlers as to the expense involved and the equipment they would need to farm there.[77] Most of his correspondence was with the Albany (New York) *Cultivator*, and it is of interest that more than 23 per cent of the people living in Lake County in 1850 were born in New York and Pennsylvania. Only Indiana provided more settlers for Lake County in this early period than did the Empire State.[78]

[76] See *ibid.*, 1:3-41. There were two children in the family when they came to Lake County: Solon Oscar, born in 1831, and Josephine Salinda, born in 1833. Three others were born at Crown Point: Charles Tracy in 1836, Leila Gertrude in 1838, and Allen Downing in 1842. *Ibid.*, 1:33. For an account of Robinson's career prior to his move to Lake County, and a description of his new surroundings, see his communication to the Madison *Republican and Banner*, January 15, 1835, in *ibid.*, 1:51-57.

[77] See Robinson's advice to Western Emigrants, November 1 and November 25, 1842, in *ibid.*, 1:331-33, 340-43.

[78] Indiana provided 28.74 per cent and New York 16.04 per cent

The first post office in the county was at what is now Crown Point but then called Lake Court House, usually written Lake C. H. From here Robinson dated his writings and the name thus became familiar to thousands of farmers throughout the country.[79] As mentioned above, Robinson erected sign posts to guide the pioneers across the bewildering prairies to his settlement.

The first winters, which were unusually severe, brought hardships and privations to the settlers. Although the prairies were reasonably devoid of trees, the first plowing of the tough sod was so difficult that the areas of tillable land were limited. The farmers were able to raise enough foodstuffs in the summer of 1835 for their own use, but new settlers came in such large numbers in the following fall and winter that food became scarce and many cattle starved to death.[80] Many found it necessary to travel with wagons, drawn by horses or oxen, to La Porte or Michigan City for food, and there were some who obtained supplies from the Wabash Country, almost one hundred miles away.[81] The scarcity of gristmills presented problems for those fortunate enough to have a supply of corn or wheat. Frequent trips to the mills were necessary because flour and corn meal had a tendency to become moldy within a short time. The mills that were run by water power ceased operations in extremely cold weather when the streams were frozen over. Consequently, congestion was so great at the mills that it was not unusual for a pioneer to wait two or three

of the total population of Lake County in 1850. Elfrieda Lang, "The Inhabitants of Center Township, Lake County, Indiana, According to the Federal Census of 1850," in *Indiana Magazine of History,* 44(1948): 281-82.

[79] Kellar (ed.), *Solon Robinson,* 1:18; 2:59.

[80] *Ibid.,* 2:58-59.

[81] *Ibid.,* 2:59; Ball, *Lake County, Indiana, 1834-1872,* 36.

days for his grain to be ground.[82] More than one man died from cold and exposure while bringing food across the bleak prairies to his family.[83]

When Robinson first came to the region he named it "Oakland County," as descriptive of most of the timber in it. The vicinity of his cabin was called "Robinson's Prairie."[84] A new mail route from Michigan City to Peoria, which passed through Robinson's Prairie, led to the establishment of the first post office in the county, known as Lake Court House, March, 1836, with Robinson as postmaster. He brought the mail from Michigan City the first year at his own expense. Although the name Crown Point was adopted locally in 1840, the post office designation was not changed until 1845.[85] Robinson and his brother Milo also opened the first store in the county in 1836 at Lake Court House. Their best customers at first were the Potawatomi who still lingered in the region. The brothers accepted furs and cranberries from the Indians in exchange for their goods, "while those calling themselves far superior to the poor Indians in all the moral attributes, gave us promises to pay, some of which are promises to this day."[86] Robinson, an advocate of temperance, not only refused to sell liquor to the Indians but tried to discourage its use by them.

Although these settlers had selected excellent land, built homes, erected fences, and made other improve-

[82] Blake, "Early Days in Lake and Porter Counties," in Bowers (ed.), *History of Lake County* (1929), 81.

[83] Robinson to the Editors of *The Cultivator*, November 25, 1842, in Kellar (ed.), *Solon Robinson*, 1:340-43.

[84] Robinson to the Editors of the Madison *Republican and Banner*, December 16, 1834, in *ibid.*, 1:51.

[85] Robinson, "A Lecture on the Early History of Lake Co.," in *ibid.*, 2:59. Robinson, a Whig, was removed from office by President John Tyler in 1843. See *ibid.*, 1:18.

[86] *Ibid.*, 2:60-61.

ments, they were still only squatters and would have no legal title to their farms until the Federal government offered the land in Lake County for sale. Public lands were sold at auction by the government, the minimum price being $1.25 an acre, an arrangement which tempted speculators to outbid the pioneers for their improved farms. Land sales were not announced in the county until 1839 but, on July 4, 1836, the settlers met at the house of Solon Robinson and formed the Squatters' Union, the purpose of which was to protect their holdings. William Clark was elected president and Robinson secretary of the organization. A constitution was drawn up, to which 476 signatures were in time attached, and a course of action agreed upon.[87] When the land sales were finally held at La Porte in March, 1839, the squatters of Lake County were present, armed with rifles and knives, and the pressure was such that speculators refrained from bidding against them.[88]

George Earle and the County Seat Controversy

The history of the region is not confined to the settlers who worked to establish homes for themselves in the wilderness. Others played an important role in the development of the area. Some were men of vision while others were speculators interested only in quick profits. In 1835 Nathaniel Davis purchased a "float" or land warrant from a Potawatomi named Ben-Ack.[89] This

[87] This constitution is published in Kellar (ed.), *Solon Robinson,* 1:68-76; and in Ball, *Lake County, Indiana, 1834-1872,* 39-48.

[88] Kellar (ed.), *Solon Robinson,* 1:11-12. Such actions were not unusual in the West in that period. See Sandford C. Cox, *Recollections of the Early Settlement of the Wabash Valley* (Lafayette, Ind., 1860), 18.

[89] The patent issued by the Federal government to Ben-Ack was recorded in Lake County Deed Records, A:3. Nathaniel Davis' purchase from Ben-Ack was recorded in *ibid.,* C:19-20. In the Treaty of Tippecanoe, 1832, "floats" or floating reserves were issued to certain Indians,

warrant gave him possession of 640 acres of land on both sides of Deep River near its junction with the Little Calumet. Later in the same year, Davis bought 320 acres in the same vicinity from Kau-Bee, also a Potawatomi.[90] Nathaniel Davis sold this property in July, 1836, to John C. Davis and Henry Frederickson of Philadelphia.[91] The new proprietors, together with John Chapman of Elkhart County, Indiana, proceeded to plat a town on both sides of Deep River, which they called Liverpool.[92] Because of its location on one branch of the Chicago-Detroit Road and because the Little Calumet was considered navigable at that point, the promoters predicted a bright future for Liverpool. This being an era of wild speculation, the proceeds from a three-day sale of lots in July, 1836, was reported to have been about $18,000.00.[93]

George Earle, of Falmouth, England, was among those who purchased land at Liverpool. The role played by Earle, a cultured and intelligent man, in the development of this part of the region was equal, if not superior, to that played by Solon Robinson. An architect and also an artist of considerable ability, Earle came to Philadelphia in 1835 to erect some buildings. While there he became acquainted with John C. Davis. The latter, with the Liverpool project in mind, aroused Earle's interest in the Calumet Region.[94] In 1836 the Englishman

entitling them to sections or quarter sections of land of their own choosing. See John O. Bowers, *Dream Cities of the Calumet*, 11.

[90] La Porte County Deed Records, B:49.

[91] This was the first deed recorded in Lake County. Ben-Ack's patent from the United States government was the first instrument recorded.

[92] The plat of Liverpool was filed with the Porter County recorder, May 17, 1837. See Deed Records, A:236-37.

[93] Robinson, "A Lecture on the Early History of Lake Co.," in Kellar (ed.), *Solon Robinson*, 2:60.

[94] William Earle, "The Earle Family in Lake County," in Lester

brought his family to Liverpool. When the sale of lots
fell below the expectations of the promoters, Earle purchased the site and much of the other land in that vicinity.[95]

The statute providing for the organization of Lake
County was passed by the General Assembly in January,
1837, and went into effect on February 15 of the same
year.[96] However, the location of the permanent county
seat was delayed for several years. As the choice of a
county capital would greatly increase the value of land
in that vicinity, landowners vied with each other for the
rich prize. The competition in Lake County was between Solon Robinson, George Earle, and Benjamin
McCarty. Robinson did not settle on almost the exact
geographical center of the county by accident. Before
leaving La Porte County in 1834 he obtained a plat of
the prospective county from the surveyors and got their
advice on the quality of the land.[97] Robinson also had
the site of the county seat in mind when he named the
post office on his property "Lake Court House." Benjamin McCarty was an old hand at locating county seats
as indicated earlier by his success in St. Joseph, La Porte,
and Porter counties. In 1839 he laid out the town of
West Point on the northeast side of Cedar Lake on land

(ed.), Papers by Various Hands, 1:260. William Earle was a grandson
of George Earle.

95 Blake, "Early Days in Lake and Porter Counties," in Bowers (ed.),
History of Lake County (1929), 86-87; Bowers, Dream Cities of the
Calumet, 13.

96 Pence and Armstrong, Indiana Boundaries, 550. The first county
elections were held in March, 1837.

97 Since Robinson said he first visited Lake County "in the company
of one other person," it is possible that his companion was one of the
surveyors. See Robinson to the editors of the Madison Republican and
Banner, December 16, 1834, in Kellar (ed.), Solon Robinson, 1:53; Ball,
Lake County, Indiana, 1834-1872, 22.

formerly belonging to Dr. Calvin Lilley.[98] The site of the county seat was probably uppermost in the thoughts of George Earle when he purchased Liverpool.

In March, 1837, Solon Robinson was elected clerk of Lake County, a position he held until 1843. The Robinson brothers erected a log building in which to hold court, its first session taking place in October of 1837. In February, 1838, the General Assembly of Indiana passed an act locating the county government temporarily in the Robinson's log structure at Lake Court House. This act also created a new set of commissioners to locate the permanent county seat, as one member of the original board had died and another refused to serve. After considering Lake Court House, Liverpool and West Point, the commissioners in May, 1839, decided in favor of Liverpool. Because this site was on the northern fringe of settlement, the citizens in the central and southern portions of the county were greatly dissatisfied with the arrangement. The county officers were urged not to move their offices to Liverpool, and the General Assembly was petitioned to make a relocation. Also, according to a state law, the officials could not be compelled to move to a new county seat until suitable buildings were erected. Although George Earle hurriedly began the building of a courthouse at Liverpool, the county officials never moved there. Once more the General Assembly took action. A third set of commissioners came into the county and in June, 1840, agreed upon the site of Lake Court House.[99]

[98] Robinson, "A Lecture on the Early History of Lake Co.," in Kellar (ed.), *Solon Robinson*, 2:70; Ball, *Lake County, Indiana, 1834-1872*, 85. For McCarty's activities in St. Joseph and La Porte counties see *History of St. Joseph County* (1880), 662, and Packard, *History of La Porte County*, 197.

[99] Kellar (ed.), *Solon Robinson*, 1:16-17, 2:69, 71; Shockley, "County

The plat of the town, made in 1840, included some forty acres of Robinson's land and twenty acres belonging to Judge William Clark. Robinson and Clark donated the space for the streets, the site for the courthouse, acreage for a school and public square, and half of their lots, plus additional acreage. Since the name Lake Court House was considered too awkward, Robinson, Earle, and Judge Clark were chosen to select a new name for the town. They immediately agreed upon Crown Point. According to one of the county's first historians, this name was selected in contrast to West Point, which had sought the county seat, and also as an illusion to Robinson's title of "Squatter King" of Lake County.[1] No evidence has been found to indicate it was named for Crown Point, New York.

The loss of the county seat ruined the hopes of George Earle for a town at Liverpool. In 1845 he took the Liverpool post office up Deep River to the site of Hobart. Here he built a flour mill and a sawmill, and in 1849 laid out the town of Hobart, named for his brother, Frederick Hobart Earle, of Falmouth, England. Earle retained his holdings at Liverpool and, firm in the belief that some day a large city would rise in Indiana at the southern end of Lake Michigan, advised his heirs against selling the property. Liverpool gradually deteriorated until it became a ghost town. It was revived as a part of East Gary in 1908.[2]

Seats and County Seat Wars," in *Indiana Magazine of History*, 10:34; Pence and Armstrong, *Indiana Boundaries*, 550.

[1] Robinson, "A Lecture on the Early History of Lake Co.," in Kellar (ed.), *Solon Robinson*, 2:71; Ball, *Lake County, Indiana, 1834-1872*, 86. Crown Point was incorporated as a town in 1868.

[2] Earle, "The Earle Family in Lake County," in Lester (ed.), Papers by Various Hands, 1:261, 264.

The Dream Cities

While the pioneers were building their homes and farms on the prairies to the south, another form of activity was taking place along the shores of Lake Michigan. Speculators were busy planning harbors and cities which they hoped would surpass in importance Michigan City and the bustling young town of Chicago. In 1837 Jacob Bigelow, William Morse, and Joshua Hobart of Michigan City, and Leverett Bradley of Porter County laid out a town which they called City West.[3] It was located on both sides of Fort Creek where that stream flows into Lake Michigan in what is now the Indiana Dunes State Park. Bigelow erected a hotel, the "Exchange," with twenty-two rooms, the largest tavern in the region. A sawmill, blacksmith shop, and a store were opened and about twenty families, including the promoters, established homes in the new town. The promoters proposed to build a canal, to be known as the Lake Michigan and Kankakee Canal, which would intersect the Little Calumet River at the mouth of Salt Creek.[4]

The greatest day in the brief life of City West was July 1, 1837, when Daniel Webster visited the town while on a tour of the West. The senator, his wife, and

[3] Jacob Bigelow, who filed the plat at the Porter County recorder's office on July 12, 1837, was listed as the president of the Michigan City and Kankakee Railroad Company. It is possible that the promoters planned to build a railroad from City West to the Kankakee River. See Porter County Deed Records, A:262-64.

[4] John O. Bowers, "Indiana Lake Frontage and the Early Days of Its Development," in J. W. Lester (ed.), Papers by Various Hands (scrapbooks in Gary Public Library), 1:297-98. In August, 1836, the administrators of the Joseph Bailly estate offered to sell 120 acres of land near City West to Jacob Bigelow for $6,000.00 and six choice lots in City West. Apparently the offer was declined. Bailly Papers, in possession of Mrs. John O. Bowers, Gary.

daughter Julia, were making a leisurely voyage on a lake steamer from Chicago to Buffalo. Eager for a Congressional appropriation to build their harbor, the promoters invited Webster to inspect the town.[5] Although he was entertained lavishly and made a brief speech to the hopeful residents, the senator made no commitments in favor of a harbor there.[6] Webster was also invited to visit Michigan City. He was not only royally entertained there but was given a lot by the boosters of that town.[7] The partisans of City West later intimated that the decision of the Federal government to build the harbor at Michigan City was the result of Webster's influence, which was won because the entertainment he received there was more to his liking.[8] This view is hardly reasonable since the initial appropriation for the harbor at Michigan City was made the year before Webster visited the rival sites.[9]

Failure to get Federal aid for the harbor brought an end to the plans for a city at the mouth of Fort Creek. By the end of 1838 all the inhabitants had moved

5 Some writers give July 4, 1837, as the date of Webster's visit to City West. According to his biographer, he embarked from Chicago on July 1 for Michigan City. Therefore, it is logical to place him in City West on the same day. See Claude M. Fuess, *Daniel Webster* (2 vols. New York, 1930), 2:65.

6 Bowers, "Indiana Lake Frontage and the Early Days of Its Development," in Lester (ed.), Papers by Various Hands, 1:299.

7 Michigan City *News-Dispatch*, January 18, 1932. The deed to this lot stated that Webster paid $2,000.00 for it. In view of the fact that he borrowed $3,000.00 to finance his western tour, it is reasonable to believe the lot was a gift. Webster sold it in 1841. See Fuess, *Daniel Webster*, 2:62. That promoters of Michigan City gave Webster an urgent invitation to visit their town is indicated in C. H. Van Tyne (ed.), *The Letters of Daniel Webster* (New York, 1902), 210.

8 Bowers, "Indiana Lake Frontage and the Early Days of Its Development," in Lester (ed.), Papers by Various Hands, 1:299.

9 Rollo B. Oglesbee and Albert Hale, *History of Michigan City* (La Porte, Ind., 1908), 107.

away.[10] Some of the buildings were moved to other sites and those that remained were destroyed by fire a few years later. The Chesterton *Tribune* in 1908 published this fitting epitaph for City West:

The last vestige of City West, the once hopeful rival of Chicago for the mercantile supremacy of the west was wiped out early this morning when fire laid waste to the Central Hotel in Chesterton. This building was moved from City West in 1850, thereby escaping the devastation by fire that swept City West a few years later. In the thirties when ox teams mired in the marsh mud of Chicago's main street, and when small schooners anchored outside the bar to discharge their cargos by lighters, it was not unreasonable for far sighted men to look upon other and more solid spots as equally promising of municipal greatness. As far as men could see, Chicago was no cinch at the outset.[11]

Manchester was planned and platted by hopeful promoters just west of the mouth of Salt Creek in 1837.[12] As a branch of the Chicago-Detroit Road crossed the Little Calumet River on the famous Long Bridge at that point, the place was considered an excellent site for a city. It was also at what was in those years considered to be the head of navigation of the Little Calumet, that stream then having a larger volume of water than at present. As has already been indicated, a canal was planned to provide access from this river to Lake Michigan at City West. A few lots were sold, and later the remainder of the site was auctioned to satisfy a mortgage on the property.[13] The promoters of Man-

[10] Bowers, "Indiana Lake Frontage and the Early Days of Its Development," in Lester (ed.), Papers by Various Hands, 1:300.

[11] Chesterton *Tribune,* April 8, 1908.

[12] The plat of Manchester was filed May 13, 1837, by Austin Chittenden and Silas Lamson at the Porter County recorder's office. See Deed Records, A:230-31.

[13] Porter County Deed Records, A:386, and Bowers, *Dream Cities of the Calumet,* 26-28.

chester were apparently interested only in making a quick profit from gullible investors.

In 1837 Indiana City was laid out on the lake front just west of the old mouth of the Grand Calumet River in what is now Gary's Marquette Park. The place was apparently a "paper city" for no records have been found that any lots were sold or that it ever had any inhabitants.[14] Although some writers have attributed the failure of the "dream cities" to the panic of 1837, it is significant that the only cities around the southern bend of Lake Michigan to survive and prosper in this period were Chicago and Michigan City, and these were the only ones that received Federal aid for the development of their harbors.

Population and Pioneer Life

John Hack, the first of the German settlers in the Lake County portion of the region, acquired a farm on Prairie West near the site of the present village of St. John. He was for some years the leader and patriarch of the Germans in the area.[15] Most of the Germans who came to Lake County in the early years were Roman Catholics. Hack built a chapel on his land in 1843 and in 1856 the Church of St. John the Evangelist, the first Catholic church in the county, was erected. Hack also established a small distillery at St. John in 1842, where he made peach brandy and whisky for several years.[16]

[14] Bowers, *Dream Cities of the Calumet*, 15. City West, Indiana City, and Liverpool were listed on the map in J. H. Colton, *Indiana, Delineated, Geographical, Historical* (New York, 1838).

[15] Alma Gettler, "Town of Dyer," in Demmon (ed.), *History of Lake County* (1934), 80; Robinson, "A Lecture on the Early History of Lake Co.," in Kellar (ed.), *Solon Robinson*, 2:65; Ball, *Lake County, Indiana, 1834-1872,* 303-4.

[16] Gettler, "Town of Dyer," in Demmon (ed.), *History of Lake County* (1934), 84.

In 1847 Solon Robinson estimated there were about one hundred German families in Lake County.[17] The census of 1850 showed that more than 52 per cent of the population of St. John Township were German.[18] In 1849 and 1850 about forty German families settled just north of what is now Merrillville.[19]

The population of Porter County increased from 2,162 in 1840 to 5,234 in 1850, while that of Lake County was 1,468 in 1840 and 3,991 in 1850.[20] As almost all the people were farmers, most of them were living south of the Little Calumet River. The sand dunes, sand ridges, and marshes adjacent to Lake Michigan, where the industrial cities of Hammond, East Chicago, Whiting, and Gary now stand, were almost devoid of inhabitants. North Township, which in 1850 included all the area between the Little Calumet and the lake, had a population of ninety-seven persons in nineteen households, and none of its children attended school that year.[21] In 1849 Crown Point was just a village of thirty-five dwellings and three stores.[22] Valparaiso, with a population of 522,

[17] Ball, *Lake County, Indiana, 1834-1872,* 180; Robinson, "A Lecture on the Early History of Lake Co.," in Kellar (ed.), *Solon Robinson,* 2:78.

[18] U. S. Bureau of the Census, *Seventh Census* (1850), 768; Lang "The Inhabitants of Center Township, Lake County," in *Indiana Magazine of History,* 22 (1948) :283.

[19] Hiram Barton, "Merrillville," in Bowers (ed.), *History of Lake County* (1929), 73; Goodspeed and Blanchard (eds.), *Counties of Porter and Lake,* 545-46. Merrillville, south of the present Gary, was originally called Wiggins' Point for Jeremiah Wiggins who settled there in 1835. Later it was called Centerville until the post office was established there in 1848. The name was then changed to Merrillville for Dudley Merrill who lived there with his family. See William F. Howat (ed.), *A Standard History of Lake County, Indiana, and the Calumet Region* (2 vols. Chicago, 1915), 1:40-41.

[20] U. S. Bureau of the Census, *Compendium of the Sixth Census* (1840), 82; *Seventh Census* (1850), 768, 772.

[21] *Seventh Census* (1850), 768.

[22] *The Indiana Gazetteer, or Topographical Dictionary of the State of Indiana* (Indianapolis, 1849), 202.

was the only incorporated town in the region, and it did not receive its charter until 1850.

Because of poor transportation facilities, the people led isolated lives and had little connection with the outside world. Even Chicago was a landlocked city for about six months of each year when navigation was curtailed by ice on the upper reaches of Lake Michigan. The principal agricultural products were cheese, butter, hay, oats, and Irish potatoes.[23] Wheat was not grown successfully because the nature of the soil was such that its freezing caused it to heave, thereby disturbing the roots of the plants.[24] The only markets for agricultural products and the only source of supplies were at Chicago, Michigan City, and for some, La Porte. While the farmers in the eastern portion of the region had a shorter distance to travel to Michigan City, those in the west were compelled to haul their products in wagons drawn by horses and oxen to Chicago, at least forty miles away.[25] In order to avoid the crossing of the Calumet rivers, many went by the way of Blue Island, Illinois, where the water on the Blue Island Sag was often two and three feet deep. When such conditions prevailed, double teams were necessary to pull the wagons.[26] In many instances the expense involved in making the trip exceeded the amount received for the products. For example, in 1838 a farmer spent nine days in hauling thirty bushels of wheat to Chicago, for which he received $18.00.[27]

23 J. D. DeBow, *Statistical View of the United States . . . Being a Compendium of the Seventh Census. . . .* (Washington, D. C., 1854), 227.

24 Blatchley, "The Geology of Lake and Porter Counties," in *Indiana Geological Report,* 1897, p. 67; Kellar (ed.), *Solon Robinson,* 1:374.

25 Robinson, "A Lecture on the Early History of Lake Co.," in Kellar (ed.), *Solon Robinson,* 2:75.

26 Ball, *Lake County, Indiana, 1834-1872,* 96-97.

27 "Narrative of Judge David Turner as told to Z. F. Summers, in the 1850's," in Crown Point *Lake County Star,* November 10, 1905.

LAKE COUNTY COURTHOUSE, 1848-79

VALPARAISO MALE AND FEMALE COLLEGE

INTERSECTION OF HOHMAN AND
STATE STREETS, HAMMOND, 1903

EMPLOYEES OF GEORGE H. HAMMOND
PACKING COMPANY

Under these conditions, the farmers made little money, yet they had to pay a high price for tools, nails, glass, and other necessities. The log cabins of the settlers were furnished only with those articles absolutely necessary for the maintenance of their health. Many became discouraged and moved farther west to more attractive sites. Solon Robinson said in 1847 that "of the 249 persons who were assessed here [Crown Point] only ten years ago, *eighty only remain* and twenty-seven have died here —so that 142 have rolled on in that irresistable wave of Western emigration. . . ."[28]

Robinson was among those who left the region for more promising fields of endeavor. Although not a practical farmer, he came to have a wide and accurate knowledge of agriculture in the United States. Between 1841 and 1851, he visited almost every state in the Union and also many portions of Canada. Robinson was a traveling correspondent for the Albany (N. Y.) *Cultivator* from 1845 to 1849, and from the latter date until 1851, he sent reports of his journeys to the *American Agriculturalist*, and was its assistant editor. In 1851 he became editor of *The Plow*, a monthly planter's and farmer's journal, published in New York. He was appointed agricultural editor of the New York *Tribune* by Horace Greeley in 1853 and remained with that paper until his death in 1880. While in the Calumet Region, Robinson published two novels, *The Will*, and *The Last of the Buffaloes*, which were well received by the critics. In later years his *Me-won-i-toc*, a tale of frontier and Indian life, passed through several editions. He published *Facts for Farmers*, a reference work of over a

28 Robinson, "A Lecture on the Early History of Lake Co.," in Kellar (ed.), *Solon Robinson.* 2:63.

thousand pages in 1864. This volume was in such great demand as to warrant a translation into German.[29]

The end of the era of isolation and log cabins was near at hand as the second half of the century began. The problem of transportation, which had plagued the region from the very start, was about to be solved as the railroads pushed their tracks slowly but surely toward the robust young city of Chicago. Not only would the coming of the iron horse brighten the lives of the farmers but would open for development the heretofore inaccessible marshes and sand dunes in the vicinity of Lake Michigan.

[29] See Kellar (ed.), *Solon Robinson,* 1:23-25, and Ball, *Lake County, Indiana, 1834-1872,* 277-83, for these phases of Robinson's career.

4

THE IMPACT OF THE RAILROADS

BECAUSE OF THE CALUMET REGION'S location at the southern end of Lake Michigan it was logical that the railroads, seeking the shortest routes from the East to Chicago, would build their tracks across the area. As a result, the interests of the region became closely intertwined with those of Chicago, and the development of that city in turn greatly affected the heretofore worthless marshes and sand dunes along the Indiana shore of Lake Michigan.

The Building of the Railroads

The first phase of the railroad building era may be confined to the years from 1852 to 1865 when four roads crossed the region to reach Chicago. These were the Michigan Central, the Michigan Southern and Northern Indiana (later known as the Lake Shore and Michigan Southern), the Pittsburgh, Fort Wayne and Chicago, and the Cincinnati Air Line which came to be known as the "Panhandle." The first two roads were later absorbed by the New York Central, and the others became a part of the Pennsylvania system. As these were the first roads, their effect on the region and its people was more noticeable than was that of the later railroads.

Although in the twenty years before 1852 separate networks of railroads were in process of development both east and west of the Alleghenies, there was no direct rail connection between the Atlantic seaboard and Chicago. And yet it was obvious to farsighted men that Chicago could well become the great railroad center of Middle America. Consequently, the two "Michigan Roads," the Michigan Central and the Michigan Southern, engaged in a dramatic race to be the first to reach Chicago and thereby provide the vital link between the East and the Old Northwest.

By April, 1849, the Michigan Central had built its tracks from Detroit to New Buffalo, Michigan, a few miles northeast of Michigan City. In July, 1851, the Michigan Southern, which had its eastern terminus at Monroe, reached the village of White Pigeon, Michigan, several miles northeast of Elkhart, Indiana.[1] This was about as far as they could go on their Michigan charters, and the state of Indiana stood as a barrier between them and Chicago. To cross Indiana, they must either obtain a franchise from its General Assembly or make some sort of an arrangement with the railroads already established in the state. The Assembly was interested in the development of Indianapolis as a great railroad center and refused to grant charters to the Michigan roads. As a result they found it necessary to resort to the second alternative, that of co-operating with Indiana companies which held franchises to build roads in the northern part of the state.

As early as 1835 the Indiana General Assembly had granted a charter to the Buffalo and Mississippi Railroad Company to build a railroad across the northern part of the state as a link in a transcontinental route.[2] No construction was undertaken under this franchise. In

[1] Alvin F. Harlow, *The Road of the Century. The Story of the New York Central* (New York, 1947), 220, 255; Michigan Southern and Northern Indiana Rail-Road Companies, *Report*, 1853, p. 5.

[2] *Laws of Indiana*, 1834-35 (local), pp. 16-24.

1850 the Northern Indiana Railroad Company was organized under an act of 1843 to build a railroad from Michigan City to La Porte or as much farther east as they saw proper.[3] The Michigan Southern made an argeement with the latter company to use their franchise to build their road from the Michigan State line to La Porte, and then through an arrangement with the Buffalo and Mississippi, the line was extended west to Illinois. The road entered Illinois over the tracks of the Rock Island Railroad and reached Ainsworth's, at the city limits of Chicago, in February, 1852.[4]

Fortunately for the Michigan Central, the New Albany and Salem Railroad, later known as the Monon, held a franchise from the State of Indiana to build a line from New Albany to Salem and "to such other point or points" as the company might deem expedient. With such an unlimited charter, the company was able to build northward to Michigan City, and then across the state to the Illinois line.[5] The construction of the railroad between New Albany and Lafayette was financed largely by the sale of stock to the citizens of the towns and to the farmers along its route. Since there were no towns of

3 *Ibid.,* 1842-43 (local), pp. 65-66.

4 Michigan Southern and Northern Indiana Rail-Road Companies, *Reports,* 1850, 1853, 1855; E. D. Daniels, *A Twentieth Century History and Biographical Record of La Porte County, Indiana . . .* (Chicago, 1904), 68-71.

5 Frank F. Hargrave, *A Pioneer Indiana Railroad. The Origin and Development of the Monon* (Indianapolis, 1932), 26-32, 73-76. The Michigan Southern contested the right of the New Albany and Salem to build this line. A suit was filed in the U. S. District Court for the District of Michigan asking for an injunction to prevent its construction. That court dismissed the case in the belief that it did not have jurisdiction in the matter, whereupon the case was appealed to the Supreme Court. After hearing testimony at the December term of 1853, that court also declined to act. Northern Indiana Railroad Company *v.* The Michigan Central Railroad Company, in U. S. Supreme Court, *Reports,* 15:232-52.

any considerable size between Lafayette and Michigan City and as it was necessary for its tracks to cross the Kankakee marsh, the company found itself in financial difficulties. The Michigan Central came to its rescue by purchasing $500,000 worth of its stock and by agreeing to construct that part of the road from Michigan City to the Illinois line. In turn, the New Albany and Salem permitted the Michigan Central to run its trains over this route. That part of the road south of Michigan City was completed in the summer of 1854.[6]

In the meantime, the Michigan Central had opened its road from New Buffalo to Michigan City in October, 1850.[7] The following year its tracks were pushed slowly across the marshes and sand ridges of the Calumet Region to the Illinois state line. The Michigan Central lacked a franchise to enter Illinois as that state was also reluctant to grant charters to out-of-state railroads. The Illinois Central, badly in need of rails and rolling stock from the East, agreed to bring the Michigan Central into Chicago over its tracks. Although the Michigan Southern had reached the city limits of Chicago in February, 1852, the Michigan Central was the first to run a train into Chicago, this being accomplished in May, 1852, over a temporary track built by the Illinois Central

---

[6] Michigan Central Railroad, *Fifth Annual Report*, 1851, p. 50; *Eighth Annual Report*, 1854, p. 16; Hargrave, *Origin and Development of the Monon*, 42-45, 105-8, 127-29. In 1855 the Cincinnati Express began running from Chicago over the tracks of the Michigan Central to Michigan City, thence by the New Albany and Salem to Lafayette, and then by other roads to Indianapolis and Cincinnati. Harlow, *The Story of the New York Central*, 228.

[7] Michigan Central Railroad, *Fifth Annual Report*, 1851, p. 15; *Sixth Annual Report*, 1852, p. 16. In 1869 the Michigan Central obtained a legal title to the line from Michigan City to Illinois from the New Albany and Salem. Hargrave, *Origin and Development of the Monon*, 194.

to a point near Michigan Avenue and Twelfth Street.[8]

As the railroads penetrated the region, stations and shipping points were established along their routes. These in time became the nucleus of settlements by those who found employment repairing the road beds and replacing the soft iron rails which wore out with alarming frequency. Porter, on the Michigan Central near the present town of Porter, was the first railroad station in the region. When the Michigan Southern crossed the Michigan Central tracks about a mile to the east, the station was moved to the crossing and the sign, "Porter," was left over the depot door. A town was laid out on the north side of the railroads by Henry Hageman in 1872 and named for him. The railroads never recognized that designation but persisted in calling it Porter, and in time the name Hageman was discarded. Calumet, now Chesterton, was laid out in 1852 on the Michigan Southern less than a mile from where it crossed the Michigan Central.[9]

In 1852 George Earle started the town of Lake Station on the Michigan Central near the site of old Liverpool. The railroad built a handsome depot, grain elevator, large freighthouse, and other facilities for the shipping of farm products and livestock. It also erected a large woodshed, and at one time farmers were paid two dollars a cord for wood delivered there for use in the

8 Paul W. Gates, *The Illinois Central Railroad and Its Colonization Work* (*Harvard Economic Studies*, Vol. 42, 1934), 44-46, 90-92; Caroline E. MacGill, *History of Transportation in the United States before 1860* (Washington, D. C., 1917), 541-42. The Michigan Southern united with the Northern Indiana in 1855. It became the Lake Shore and Michigan Southern in 1869 as a result of an amalgamation arranged by Cornelius Vanderbilt with other roads. Harlow, *The Story of the New York Central*, 281.

9 Chesterton *Tribune*, November 25, 1892; Chesterton *Westchester Tribune*, April 16, 1896; Goodspeed and Blanchard (eds.), *Counties of Porter and Lake*, 163-64.

railroad engines. A restaurant was located at the depot and all trains were ordered to stop there long enough for the passengers to eat their meals.[10] In 1854 the Joliet and Northern Indiana Railroad was completed. This line, better known as the "Joliet Cut-Off," joined the Michigan Central at Lake Station, whence it ran westward to Joliet, Illinois. There it made a connection with the Rock Island road and the Chicago, Alton, and St. Louis line.[11] Stations and shipping facilities were established on the Joliet branch at Dyer in 1855 and at Ross in 1857. The town of Dyer was platted in 1858, and soon exceeded Lake Station in the shipping of agricultural products.[12] As other railroads were built in the region and other shipping points were established, Lake Station declined in population and prosperity. For the second time, George Earle saw the failure of his hopes to build a city near the junction of Deep River and the Little Calumet.[13]

Valparaiso and Crown Point, the county seats of the region, slumbered as "inland towns" for several years. A plank road was started from Valparaiso to Michigan City in 1850, but after the railroads reached Porter, work on it was discontinued.[14] The citizens of Valparaiso

10 Patterson, "Lake Station," in Bowers (ed.), *History of Lake County* (1929), 109; Earle, "The Earle Family in Lake County," in Lester (ed.), Papers by Various Hands, 1:262; Blake, "Reminiscences of Darius Blake," in Lester (ed.), Papers by Various Hands, 1:245.

11 The Michigan Central obtained a perpetual lease on the Joliet Cut-Off in September, 1854. See Michigan Central Railroad, *Ninth Annual Report*, 1855, p. 10.

12 Gettler, "Town of Dyer," in Demmon (ed.), *History of Lake County* (1934), 77; Ball, *Lake County, Indiana, 1834-1872*, 153-54.

13 Lake Station had a population of 250 in 1866. See *The Indiana State Gazetteer and Shippers' Guide for 1866-1867* (Lafayette, Ind., 1866), 34.

14 Goodspeed and Blanchard (eds.), *Counties of Porter and Lake*, 210-11.

went to Porter or to La Porte to send their telegrams, take the cars, and to ship and receive freight. Hacks or stages made daily trips to Porter and Calumet (Chesterton) to connect with the trains at these stations.[15] Crown Point's citizens sought similar services at Lake Station, and later at Ross and Hobart. A stage made daily trips from Crown Point to Lake Station with mail and passengers, a distance of fifteen miles.[16] The county seats were quiet and sleepy little towns before the coming of the railroads. The editor of the local paper in Crown Point reported in 1858 that he counted seven large sows in one day, each with a litter of pigs, running at large on Main Street.[17]

The Pittsburgh, Fort Wayne and Chicago, financed largely by the Pennsylvania Railroad, reached Valparaiso in 1858.[18] From there it passed through Hobart and the present cities of Gary, East Chicago, and Whiting to Chicago. While awaiting the arrival of the railroad, the Valparaiso *Republican* of August 11, 1857, predicted "this road will bring to our doors what we so greatly need—a market; and will concentrate to one spot nearly all the trade of a fertile, well-wooded and above all a healthy county." The railroad's influence on the town was felt immediately. In 1859 the Valparaiso Male and Female College, forerunner of Valparaiso University, was started by the Methodist Church.[19] The town's industrial development began in 1866 with the establish-

15 Valparaiso *Republican,* May 25, 1858.

16 Ball, *Lake County, Indiana, 1834-1872,* 97-98.

17 "Old Time News, Reminiscences of Lake County, April 27 to May 4, 1858," from the Crown Point *Register,* in Crown Point *Lake County Star,* June 14, 1901.

18 Valparaiso *Republican,* September 30, 1858.

19 George W. Stimpson, *The Story of Valparaiso University* (Chicago, 1921), 9.

ment of a woolen mill and also a paper mill.[20] Valparaiso's population more than doubled in the ten years after the arrival of the railroad.[21] The village of Wheeler was laid out in 1858 on the new railroad some miles west of Valparaiso. Thomas A. E. Campbell, who played a part in the founding of Valparaiso, was the father of Wheeler. The village boasted a population of about one hundred people in 1859.[22]

In 1865 the Cincinnati Air Line Railroad, later known as the "Panhandle," reached Crown Point on its way from Cincinnati to Chicago. The road's arrival was accompanied by the building of additional dwellings, business houses, and grain elevators. For a time every available house was filled with newcomers.[23] The presence of the railroad moved Timothy H. Ball in 1865 to establish the Crown Point Institute, an institution to provide collegiate instruction for young ladies and young men.[24] The town's population more than doubled in the decade following the advent of the railroad.[25] The prediction was made in 1883 that Crown Point would some day be a suburb of Chicago.[26]

Immediate Effects of the Railroads

The railroads, by improving transportation facilities, exercised an immediate influence upon the lives of the

[20] Valparaiso *Vidette and Republican,* December 24, 1868.

[21] According to the census reports, Valparaiso's population was 522 in 1850, 1,698 in 1860, and 2,765 in 1870.

[22] Valparaiso *Republican,* May 19, 1859.

[23] Ball, *Lake County, Indiana, 1834-1872,* 127; "Old Time News," from Crown Point *Register,* April 13, 1865, in Crown Point *Lake County Star,* March 31, 1905.

[24] Ball, *Lake County, Indiana, 1834-1872,* 127-29.

[25] The *Indiana State Gazetteer and Shippers' Guide for 1866-1867* estimated Crown Point's population at 750. It was 1,708 in 1880.

[26] Crown Point *Lake County Star,* February 16, 1883.

farmers and upon agriculture in general. The Civil War, which greatly increased the price of farm products, was also a stimulating factor. Corn, which sold for seventeen cents a bushel in 1861, brought ninety cents in 1864, and the price of pork soared to sixteen cents a pound by the end of the war. The fertile prairie soil yielded bountiful crops of corn, oats, hay, and potatoes while the close proximity of Chicago stimulated the production of poultry, eggs, and dairy products. Lake was first among the counties of the state in the production of butter, hay, and oats in 1870. In 1880, Lake led the counties of the state in the amount of cheese produced upon the farms.[27] While Porter County farmers also prospered, their total production did not equal that of Lake County.

This prosperity was reflected in the lives of the farmers. Dressed lumber, which had heretofore been scarce and expensive, was now available at reasonable prices. Consequently, the people abandoned their log cabins for frame and brick residences. Churches, schools, and business houses were likewise improved and modernized. The log cabins were rapidly relegated to the status of stables, cribs for corn, and granaries. Articles practically unknown in the pioneer period appeared on the shelves of stores. Homes were more attractive and comfortable now with their plastered walls, mirrors, and carpets. Stoves, for cooking and heating purposes, replaced the open fireplaces. Pianos, organs, and sewing machines, extremely rare in the earlier days, came into common use. The lives of the people were enriched by the availability of books, magazines, and newspapers. Horses took the place of the patient and slow-moving oxen. Improved farming implements were purchased, and on some farms

27 Ball, *Lake County, Indiana, 1834-1872*, 126; *Compendium of the Ninth Census* (1870), 730, 731; *Compendium of the Tenth Census* (1880), pt. 1: 856-57.

reapers made the task of farming less arduous and more profitable.[28]

Later Railroads

In 1874 the second phase of the railroad building era began. In that year the Baltimore, Pittsburgh and Chicago road, built and owned by the Baltimore and Ohio, passed through Miller; from there it followed the shore of Lake Michigan to Chicago.[29] In 1880 the Chicago and Grand Trunk, later known as the Grand Trunk Western, reached Chicago by way of Valparaiso. The year 1882 saw the Nickel Plate and Erie enter Chicago by way of Hammond.[30] In the same year, the Louisville, New Albany and Chicago (Monon), formerly the New Albany and Salem, pushed its tracks northward through the Kankakee Marsh to Dyer and to Hammond. In 1884 this road entered Chicago. According to one version, "Monon" is from the Potawatomi word meaning to "carry," while others insist it is from the Indian for "swiftly moving."[31] In 1895 the Wabash crossed the region, and in 1902 the Chesapeake and Ohio entered Hammond. The Pere Marquette made its western terminus at Porter and reached Chicago over the tracks of other roads in 1903. The third phase of the railroad building era, the construction of the belt lines and of the Chicago, South Shore and South Bend electric road, will be told later in this volume.

[28] Timothy H. Ball, *Northwestern Indiana from 1800 to 1900* . . . (Crown Point, 1900), 125-27.

[29] Edward Hungerford, *The Story of the Baltimore and Ohio Railroad, 1827-1927* (2 vols. New York, 1928), 2:108; Ball, *Encyclopedia of Genealogy and Biography of Lake County*, 31.

[30] Howat (ed.), *A Standard History of Lake County*, 1:268; *The Calumet Region Historical Guide* . . . , compiled by the Writers' Program of the Work Projects Administration ([East Chicago], 1939), 76-77.

[31] Hargrave, *The Origin and Development of the Monon*, 195, 196.

Public Lands and Land Sales

The swamps and marshes of the region also felt the impact of the railroads. As has been noted, the early settlers avoided the marshes and also the land that was subject to periodic floods. As a result, there were less than one hundred people living north of the Little Calumet River in Lake County as late as 1850. In that year Congress ceded what were regarded as "swamp lands" to the states in which they were located. The act provided that "the proceeds of said lands shall be applied, exclusively, so far as necessary, to the purpose of reclaiming said lands by means of levees and drains."[32] Indiana received 1,226,706 acres of the swamp lands in 1851. Of this total, 111,400 acres were located in Lake County, and 55,305 acres were in Porter County. With the exception of the Kankakee Marsh, most of this land was located in the Calumet Region. The average price received by the state of Indiana for the swamp lands before January 1, 1854, was $1.29 an acre.[33] A check of the records in the Recorder's office at Crown Point revealed that most of the swamp lands in Lake County sold for $1.25 an acre.

The General Assembly passed an act in 1852 to regulate the sale of these lands and to provide for their drainage and reclamation as specified by Congress. A commissioner of swamp lands for each county was appointed by the governor, who in turn appointed an engineer whose duty it was to make arrangements with contractors for the drainage of the land. Any funds remaining from the sale of the lands after drainage was completed were to be placed in the school fund of the

[32] Benjamin H. Hibbard, *A History of the Public Land Policies* (New York, 1924), 269-70.

[33] Auditor's Report, in Indiana *Documentary Journal,* 1851-52, pp. 379-82; *ibid.,* 1854, pp. 56-57.

state. The law was so imperfectly written that the administration of the funds was characterized by graft and fraud. This was particularly true in the Lake County portion of the Calumet Region. As a result, very little of the swamp lands were actually drained as provided by the law.[34]

The railroads greatly increased the value of the land in the areas through which they passed. Consequently, shrewd and farsighted men took advantage of the low price asked by the state for the swamp lands. George W. Clark, a civil engineer in Chicago, was one of the most important of these investors. Clark, according to his own report, was an engineer for the locating of the Baltimore and Ohio and the Illinois Central railroads, and for the Illinois and Michigan Canal.[35] Apparently, he was well acquainted with the favorable effect the railroads had exercised on the value of land in other parts of the country.

Clark purchased fifty-four tracts of land amounting to 2,979 acres from the State of Indiana in 1854, and to this was added eighty-three tracts totaling 8,552 acres, also from the state, in 1856. He acquired 1,176 acres at private sale between 1857 and 1859 for prices considerably higher than those paid for the state's lands. Clark was also a consistent bidder for land offered by the sheriff at tax sales. He found some excellent bargains at these auction sales as indicated by his purchase of a parcel of 1,096 acres for $31.93, and another of 880 acres for $42.92. A total of 6,842 acres were added to his holdings in this manner. The records show that

[34] Esarey, *History of Indiana*, 2:621-23; Ball, *Lake County, Indiana, 1834-1872*, 105-10.

[35] Clark gave this information about his career in a mortgage suit against William W. Beach and Jonathan Mabie. Lake County Deed Records, T:229.

by the end of 1860 Clark's purchases amounted to 19,549 acres.[36] This vast area included roughly the sites of the present cities of Whiting and East Chicago, a portion of Hammond, and that part of Gary north of the Little Calumet River and west of Broadway Street.

At his death in 1866 Clark left this estate to his sisters, Caroline M. Forsythe, Sarah Jane Clark, and Harriett Clark, and to his brothers, Robert Dunlop Clark and Brig. Gen. Henry Francis Clark. Clark showed his confidence in Caroline's husband, Jacob Forsythe, by giving him the power of attorney for his interests a few weeks before his death. Forsythe and Robert Dunlop Clark were the executors and trustees of the estate.[37] Forsythe was general freight agent and passenger agent of the Erie Railroad in Chicago at that time.[38] In order to administer the property personally, the Forsythes moved with their children in 1867 to a new home near the present city of Whiting.[39] They purchased the shares of the other heirs and were in full possession of the estate by the end of 1868.[40]

Aaron N. Hart's purchases of land in the region equalled or perhaps surpassed those of George W. Clark. Hart originally was associated with the publishing firm of Rice and Hart in Philadelphia. In 1854 he became interested in the possibilities of the Calumet Region. He helped form the real estate company of Hart and Biggs in Chicago and was active there until the great fire.

[36] It would not be practical to list the references to each of Clark's purchases. The author made an exhaustive study of the deed books in the Recorder's Office at Crown Point and has every reason to believe these figures to be correct.

[37] Clark's will was recorded in Lake County Deed Records, V:256-58.

[38] Whiting *Call,* October 9, 1910.

[39] Hammond *Times,* July 2, 1939.

[40] See Lake County Deed Records, 10:468, 518-22, 524, 526, for these transactions.

Hart's persistence in buying land in the area from 1856 until his death in 1883 was amazing, and the records of his multitudinous transactions in the deed books are bewildering. An accurate estimate of his total purchases is not available, but the records indicate they approximated 20,000 acres.[41]

Hart acquired about 15,000 acres in the vicinity of Dyer including much of the Old Cady Marsh. Other large tracts were obtained near Lake Station and Crown Point. In 1882 he bought 1,023 acres in what is now Hammond for $12,000.00. The records show that in 1881 and 1885 the Aetna Powder Company bought a total of 360 acres in what is now the eastern part of Gary from him and from his estate. It is of interest that 4,680 acres of swamp land obtained from the state in 1856 and 1857 were not recorded in the Recorder's Office at Crown Point until after his death.[42]

In 1861 Hart moved his family to Hartsdale Farm, consisting of about 8,000 acres, near Dyer. This farm was widely regarded as a model establishment. In time it was crossed by five railroads and Hartsdale, located at the crossing of the Joliet Cut-Off and the Pennsylvania Railroad, was the railway station of the Hart estate. Hart recorded an addition to the town of Dyer in 1859 and subsequently played an important part in its development.[43] Nicholas Scherer, who came from Prussia in 1848, laid out the town of Schererville in 1865 on land purchased

---

41 Ball, *Encyclopedia of Genealogy and Biography,* 83, 554-55. See partition deed in Deed Records, 36:333-41, for a description of Hart's holdings at the time of his death. Since he disposed of some of his property before his death, all his purchases were not listed in this record.

42 Lake County Deed Records, W:269-347; 30:212; 36:334-35.

43 Gettler, "Town of Dyer," in Demmon (ed.), *History of Lake County* (1934), 77, 80; Cannon, Loring, and Robb (eds.), *History of the Lake and Calumet Region,* 1:145.

from Hart.[44] The landowner died in 1883 when the banks of a drainage ditch upon which he was working at the time collapsed. His vast estate was left to his wife and four children who continued to develop the property, and in the early 1890's constructed the great Hart Ditch. This project, which drained what was once called Lake George, extended for about five miles from Dyer to the Little Calumet River just west of what is now Wicker Park.

Ernst W. Hohman and George M. Roberts were two other large landowners in the region. Hohman, generally regarded as the first settler on the site of the present city of Hammond, purchased 366 acres of swamp land in the period from 1851 to 1858 from the state and from private owners. Roberts bought 471 acres in the years from 1851 to 1857 from soldiers holding Federal land warrants and also from the state.[45] He donated a right-of-way across his land to the Pennsylvania Railroad, which built the station of Robertsdale, in what is now North Hammond, in recognition of the gift. This part of Hammond has since borne his name.

Early Railroad Stations and Settlements

The most important stations and settlements located on the Michigan Southern Railroad in the early days were Miller, Pine, and Whiting. Miller was reportedly named for a foreman of the railroad in charge of the erection of the station there. Although he left when the work was completed, one of his children was buried at Miller.[46] Pine was hardly more than a depot. In

44 Gettler, "Town of Dyer," in *loc. cit.*, 80-81.
45 See Lake County Deed Records, Vol. 10, for Hohman's and Roberts' purchases.
46 "Mrs. Drusilla Carr Tells of Early Days at Miller Beach," in

the early days Whiting was known as Whiting's Crossing. The settlement obtained this name from a conductor on the Michigan Southern whose train was wrecked when it collided with another at the crossing there. Following the accident, the railroad built a siding to avoid future collisions. The place was called Whiting's Crossing or Whiting's Turn Out, later shortened to Whitings. When the Standard Oil Company built its great refinery there, officials of the company changed this awkward sounding name to its present form.[47]

George Tolle, a manufacturer of surgical instruments in Chicago, laid out Tolleston in 1857 on the Michigan Central. Aaron N. Hart, who owned land in that vicinity, and Tolle recorded a plat of the town in July, 1863.[48] The importance of this place was enhanced when the Pittsburgh, Fort Wayne and Chicago road, now the Pennsylvania, crossed the Michigan Central at that point. Tolleston is now a part of Gary.

The Michigan Central had its western terminus for a time at West Point, later called Gibson Station, in what is now Hammond. Passengers left the railroad there and completed the trip into Chicago by stagecoach. Joseph Hess, a native of Alsace-Lorraine, opened a restaurant at West Point in 1851. He was also the first postmaster of the town. A few years later he moved about a mile south and started the settlement of Hessville, where he operated a general store, engaged in the cattle business, and served as postmaster for nearly forty

J. W. Lester (ed.), Papers by Various Hands (scrapbooks in Gary Public Library), 1:232.

[47] U. G. Swartz, "Some Early Days of the Whiting Refinery," in *The Stanolind Record,* July, 1923, p. 6.

[48] August Rump, "Tolleston and the Calumet Region," in Demmon (ed.), *History of Lake County* (1934), 64. The plat of Tolleston is in the Miscellaneous Records, A:446-47, in the Recorder's Office at Crown Point.

years. He also was trustee of North Township for twenty-two years.[49] Hessville was later annexed to Hammond.

Most of the people who populated these settlements were Germans. Tolleston was largely a German Lutheran community.[50] Miller was settled by Swedes as well as Germans. Tolleston, which in 1882 boasted a population of about four hundred inhabitants, was the largest of these villages for some years.[51] The only satisfactory connection these communities had with each other was by railroad. Sand was a factor in nearly every phase of their lives. It discouraged overland travel, and without the railroad they would have been isolated from the outside world. A large number of the settlers in the early years were employed as maintenance workers by the railroads. They supplemented their incomes by cultivating patches of the sandy soil and by grazing a few cows on the anemic vegetation.[52]

Products of the Dunes and Marshes

The people soon discovered that the dunes and marshes, instead of being liabilities entirely, did produce a degree of wealth. Strawberries, wintergreen berries, and huckleberries grew on the sand ridges in unbelievable quantities. The women and children scooped them up

[49] Alys Hess, "Hessville and Joseph Hess," in Bowers (ed.), *History of Lake County* (1929), 117-18. Alys Hess was a son of Joseph Hess. This West Point should not be confused with the one platted in the 1830's.

[50] Clara E. Ford, "Pioneer Days of Robertsdale, Whiting, Berry Lake," and Rump, "Tolleston and the Calumet Region," in Demmon (ed.), *History of Lake County* (1934), 224, 65.

[51] *Indiana State Gazetteer and Business Directory, 1882-1883,* compiled by R. L. Polk & Company (Indianapolis, 1882), 773.

[52] Frank Borman, "Reminiscences of Tolleston," in Demmon (ed.), *History of Lake County* (1934), 85.

with their hands. Huckleberries grew so luxuriantly they could be raked from the vines into bed sheets. Cranberries were equally abundant in the swamps and marshes. The berries were packed in barrels and shipped by rail to Chicago. The fruit crop of North Township was said to have amounted in some years to more than the whole grain crop of Centre Township, and that township was one of the best agricultural sections in Lake County. A thousand bushels of huckleberries were shipped from Tolleston in a single season, and the annual shipment of berries in the Lake County portion of the region was about 5,000 bushels.[53]

Sand provided a source of income for much of the population for many years. There was a great demand for sand by the railroads for track elevation in Chicago and other cities. Municipalities and private contractors used it for filling-in purposes. The site of the Chicago World's Fair, the Columbian Exposition of 1893, was filled in with sand from the dune country just east of Miller. The Calumet Region sand was cheap and easy to obtain. The railroads built their sidings against the dunes and loaded the cars with steam shovels. In some instances sand was chuted directly into the cars. Some of the highest and most beautiful of the sand dunes were obliterated in this manner. Sandsuckers from Chicago lurked in Lake Michigan between Miller and Michigan City and sucked sand from the shallow water into barges and scows. Since the sand companies operating inland paid for the sand obtained from private property and those using sandsuckers paid nothing, vigorous demands were made to the Federal government to halt the op-

[53] Edwin W. Dinwiddie, "The Flora of Lake County," in Ball (ed.), *Lake County, Indiana, 1884,* 159; Ball, *Lake County, Indiana, 1834-1872,* 239-40; David Turner, "Our Exports," in Ball (ed.), *Lake County, Indiana, 1884,* 159, 188.

erations of the latter. As late as 1913 a Gary editor declared that the sandsuckers were stealing the bottom of the Lake.[54]

Tolleston, Miller, and Dune Park, the latter known as Wilson today, were the most important points for the shipping of sand. In 1889 the Sante Fe Railroad was reported to have placed an order for 150,000 cars of sand to be obtained from the Miller area. In the same year Dune Park was said to be the best paying freight station on the Michigan Southern between Elkhart and Chicago. In 1898 more than three hundred cars of sand were shipped from Dune Park every twenty-four hours. The *Lake County Star* estimated that 50,000 cars would be shipped from the Tolleston region in 1897. Gravel, consisting of pebbles ranging in size between a hen's egg and a small marble, was obtained on the Lake Michigan beach. It was raked out of the shallow water by hand and carted beyond the reach of the high storm waves. This material was shipped to Chicago for use in roofing and concrete pavements.[55]

The cutting, storing, and shipping of ice from the Calumet rivers and from inland lakes was also a flourishing business. Ice was not obtained for commercial purposes from Lake Michigan as its quality was poor and the operations difficult as well as dangerous. Miller and Clark were centers of this industry and large ice houses or storage places were maintained at both stations. In 1882 approximately 5,000 cars were shipped from Clark. Chicago companies reaped a large harvest from Berry

[54] Chesterton *Tribune,* September 13, 1890; Gary *Evening Post,* December 27, 1913.

[55] Chesterton *Tribune,* May 16 and August 22, 1889, May 7, 1898; Crown Point *Lake County Star,* January 1, 1897; Blatchley, "The Geology of Lake and Porter Counties," in Indiana *Geological Report,* 1897, p. 41.

and Wolf lakes. Fancher's Lake, south of Crown Point, produced a good yield each year.[56] The railroads used much of the ice in their refrigerator cars and large amounts were shipped to Chicago for refrigeration purposes.

Miller was also the center of a profitable fishing industry which operated along the beach of Lake Michigan. The Lake teemed with whitefish and sturgeon in the early years. In 1905 Albert Sabinske, one of the pioneer fishermen at Miller Beach, was reported to have caught a sturgeon that was eight feet long and weighed two hundred pounds. Professional fishermen operated at Miller as early as 1882. The fish were caught in nets which were pulled out of the water by windlasses set up on the beach. Huge fires were built at night to aid the fishermen in their operations. Some took their catch in sailboats to the market in Chicago. Others iced their fish in tubs and barrels for shipment by railroad. Farmers came to Miller to trade flour, pork, and butter for fish.[57]

Originally, the sand ridges and dunes were covered with a luxuriant growth of white pine and cedar. Timber thieves operated in the wilderness along the lake front undisturbed by the county officials at Crown Point and Valparaiso. Young Chicago was partly built with lumber obtained in this manner.[58] And yet enough timber remained in later years to provide a source of income for many people. Hobart was at one time an important center of the timber trade in the region. The old Lake

[56] *Indiana State Gazetteer and Business Directory, 1882-1883,* 170; Clara E. Ford, "Heinrich D. Eggers," in Demmon (ed.), *History of Lake County* (1934), 223; Ball, *Lake County, Indiana, 1834-1872,* 349-51.

[57] Chesterton *Tribune,* August 3, 1905; "Drusilla Carr Tells of Early Days at Miller Beach," in Lester (ed.), Papers by Various Hands, 1:228, 230, 231.

[58] Robinson, "A Lecture on the Early History of Lake Co.," in Kellar (ed.), *Solon Robinson,* 2:80.

Street plank road in Chicago was built of lumber from the Hobart mills, and the first cedar block road in Chicago was made of block sawed at Hobart.[59] There was a pier at Waverly Beach after the Civil War which was used by boats hauling timber and firewood to Chicago.[60] Jacob Forsythe established a sawmill at Cassella, where Indiana Harbor now stands, to cut lumber and firewood from trees on the George W. Clark estate. Forsythe purchased all the "cordwood and standing timber and trees" on Clark's property and the latter estimated in his will that the yield would be at least 50,000 cords of wood. Settlers in the vicinity of Whiting cut timber at points as close as possible to Lake Michigan. The logs were made into rafts and were pulled by men and teams through the shallow water of the Lake to the mouth of the Calumet River in South Chicago. Tugs completed the tow from that point to the market in Chicago.[61]

The marshes adjacent to the Calumet rivers abounded in mink and muskrats and in the spring and fall they were the favorite haunt of geese and wild ducks. Professional trappers, farmers, and villagers trapped and hunted in this wilderness. An estimated 30,000 muskrats were taken each year and for a hunter to bag from fifty to one hundred ducks in a single day was a common occurrence. Ducks were sold in Chicago for from ninety cents to one dollar and fifteen cents a dozen.[62]

[59] William Earle, "The Early History of Northern Lake County," in Demmon (ed.), *History of Lake County* (1934), 54.

[60] Isaac Crisman, "Autobiography of Isaac Crisman," in J. W. Lester (ed.), Papers by Various Hands (scrapbooks in Gary Public Library), 1:227. Crisman, one of the pioneers of Portage Township, frequently saw boats being loaded with timber.

[61] See Clark's will in Lake County Deed Records, V:257, and Ford, "Pioneer Days of Robertsdale, Whiting, and Berry Lake," in Demmon (ed.), *History of Lake County* (1934), 225.

[62] J. W. Lester, "Pioneer Stories of the Calumet," in *Indiana Magazine of History*, 18(1922) :173, 174.

The Tolleston Club of Chicago

The story of the Tolleston Club of Chicago, extending over more than half a century, could be written into a novel of real romance and tragedy. This club, incorporated in 1873, was composed of wealthy businessmen and leaders of finance and industry. It secured control of about five thousand acres of marsh land along the Little Calumet River between Black Oak and Liverpool.[63] J. Ogden Armour, Marshall Field, Potter Palmer, J. J. Knickerbocker, and John W. (Bet-a-Million) Gates, president of the Illinois Steel Company, were associated with the club.[64] C. D. Peacock, W. H. McCormick, Dr. Nicholas Senn, and Albert G. Spaulding, founder of the famous sporting goods firm, were listed as members in 1902.[65] About an hour's travel by rail brought the sportsmen to one of the finest hunting and fishing grounds in the Middle West.

A spacious club house was erected in the vicinity of what is now Twenty-fifth Avenue and Clark Road in Gary. The entire first floor consisted of a large club room, dining room, and kitchen. At one end of the club room was a huge fireplace and at the other end, a handsome mahogany sideboard. The silverware and furnishings of the club buffet were valued at $50,000.00. There were forty beds in the sleeping quarters on the second floor. A large barn for horses, dog kennels, pigeon cotes, and an icehouse were built on the grounds. There were also living quarters for the large staff of servants and

---

63 The Lake County Deed Records show that the Club purchased 1,174 acres of land during the years from 1873 to 1898. The other acreage was leased. See Gary *Post-Tribune*, January 3, 1928.

64 Chesterton *Tribune,* January 27, 1897; Gary *Post-Tribune,* January 3, 1928.

65 *The Tolleston Club of Chicago* (published by the Tolleston Club, 1902). Pamphlet in Gary Public Library.

guides who administered to the needs of the members and their guests. A canal was constructed from the Little Calumet to a boathouse near the club.[66]

Grand old times were had at the club during the best years of its life. Members and their guests were transported to and from the Tolleston railroad station in stately victorias and surreys drawn by blooded horses and driven by liveried servants. The more active engaged in hunting and fishing. Game was so abundant that it was not unusual for a hunter to bag a hundred ducks in a single day. The record for ducks killed by one of the members was 189 between sunrise and 10:00 A. M. Others came in the club to enjoy the excellent food and to relax in the peace and quiet of the wilderness. It was whispered in the servants' quarters that some came for a "little rest," and they got it—just as little as possible. Cards were the principal attraction for many and it was rumored there were occasions when at least $50,000.00 changed hands in a single poker game.[67]

The club fenced most of its property and hired game wardens, or guards, to prevent outsiders from poaching on its preserve. Farmers and others in the vicinity resented the restrictions imposed by what they regarded as a "foreign" hunting club. Many of the natives in the region supplemented their incomes in the winter and early spring by hunting wild fowl and trapping mink and muskrats in the marshes. The club's edicts were intolerable to them. A feud, characterized by violence and bloodshed, raged between the club and the local people for over twenty-five years, during which time poachers and game wardens were wounded and even killed.

[66] Goodspeed and Blanchard (eds.), *Counties of Porter and Lake,* 542.
[67] Gary *Weekly Tribune,* May 5, 1908; Gary *Post-Tribune,* January 3, 1928.

The poachers slipped into the marshlands at night, set traps, and returned to their homes in the morning with mink and muskrats. The more daring openly defied the guards of the club by hunting and trapping in broad daylight. In retaliation, the guards smashed boats and confiscated guns, traps, and fishing tackle belonging to the local residents. The guards could distinguish between the noise made by the muzzle-loading guns of the poachers and the more modern weapons used by the club's members. This enabled them to locate or ambush the unwary trespassers. A pitched battle involving more than twenty men was fought on the ice in the marsh in 1897. When this affair was over, four of the participants were wounded, one fatally.[68]

The worst tragedy occurred in 1894 when a poacher, Albert Looker, killed James Conroy and William Cleary, game wardens employed by the club, when they assaulted him in a Tolleston saloon.[69] Looker, hailed as a hero by the local populace, was acquitted in a Hammond court on the grounds that he had acted in self-defense. According to reports, Looker later killed one of Conroy's brothers in Texas, who had followed him there to avenge his brother's death.[70] The following poem by Silas E. Green, one-time postmaster at Jerusalem, reflects the sentiment of the local citizens in regard to this episode:[71]

[68] Crown Point *Lake County Star,* 1895 (date of issue obliterated); Whiting *Sun,* March 20, 1897; Chesterton *Westchester Tribune,* January 23, 1897.

[69] Otto C. Bormann, member of a pioneer Tolleston family, witnessed the shooting from under a pool table. See Gary *Evening Post,* July 20, 1911; Chesterton *Tribune,* April 6, 1894.

[70] Cannon, Loring, and Robb (eds.), *History of the Lake and Calumet Region,* 1:177-81.

[71] The shooting occurred in James Hargin's saloon and not in Harrigan's Hotel. This poem is in pamphlet form in the Gary Public Library.

THE TOLLESTON TRAGEDY

Come, all you young heroes, wherever you be,
I'll sing you a song if you'll listen to me,
How one Albert Looker in Bradford did dwell,
Killed two burly watchmen in Harrigan's Hotel.

Twenty-first of March at the close of the day,
Those two jolly men for recreation did stray.
And it seemed when they entered that
    place on that night,
Those two burly watchmen were prepared
    for a fight.

With nuckles of brass and pistols to boot,
All ready to beat, all ready to shoot;
But they ran on a snag and before very long,
The coroner was sent for, the sheriff along.

The young man they tackled without any cause,
In strict violation of all of our laws,
Till he, being tired of this kind of play
Pulled out a gun and began firing away.

Soon one of the watchmen cried out, "I am hit."
And dropped to the floor like a man in a fit.
The other got a lead pill in his head,
And in less than a minute both watchmen were dead.

The trial is over and Looker is free;
The people are glad and, of course, so is he.
Lake County is rid of terrible pests,
Their spirits gone hunting, their bodies at rest.

All glory to Looker, let every one sing
The praise of a man that would do such a thing.
The Calumet marshes will miss their soft tread,
For the terrors of Calumet Township are dead.

The local newspapers supported the poachers against
the club. In 1897 the editor of the Whiting *Sun* said:
"the legislature should pass a law this winter, wiping
out those shooting clubs and not allow the fencing up
of land for game purposes. Already too many murders
have been committed at Tolleston." In 1891 the Hobart
Gazette denounced the club for what it called the brutal
treatment of trespassers.[72] Since members of the club were
reluctant to discuss the troubles with newspaper men, the
reporters went to the poachers, who were always willing
to talk, for their stories. The spokesmen for the club
stoutly insisted they never ordered, or even sanctioned,
violent tactics on the part of their employees. They also
thought many of the crimes committed in the marsh were
unjustly blamed on their game wardens.

In the end it was the growth of Gary, which adversely
affected hunting and fishing in the region, that spelled
the end of the Tolleston Club. The Indiana General Assembly also dealt it a blow when it legalized hunting on
private property that was not under cultivation. In 1911
the Lake County Country Club, now the Gary Country
Club, leased the club house and adjoining acreage for a
golf course.[73] Gary real estate firms tried for many
years to buy the club's property, but as the proposed
Burns Ditch would drain the Calumet Marsh and hence
increase its value, the members of the club were in no
hurry to sell. By 1923 the last legal barriers against the
Burns Ditch project were removed, and the club began
to sell its land to realty companies and to the school city
of Gary.[74] Within a few years the Tolleston Club of
Chicago was just a memory.

72 Whiting *Sun*, January 30, 1897; Hobart *Gazette*, May 19, 1891.
73 Gary *Weekly Tribune*, May 15, 1908.
74 See Lake County Deed Records, Vols. 342, 351, 353, 381, 388.

In 1885 other Chicago sportsmen organized the Calumet Gun Club. A club house and fifteen cottages were erected on the Lake Michigan beach just east of the present harbor of the Gary Steel Works. A piano, bowling alleys, and billiard tables were installed. Trap shooting facilities and a rifle range were built on the beach where contests were frequently held with clubs from Chicago. The members and their families enjoyed sledding and tobogganing on the sand dunes and skating on the Grand Calumet River. The Baltimore and Ohio Railroad established the Calumet Heights Station for the accommodation of the club. As several miles of sand and swamps separated the club from the settlements south of the Little Calumet River, there was apparently no conflict between it and the local populace. The club's buildings were still intact when the United States Steel Corporation bought the site in 1905. A number of engineers engaged in the construction of the steel mills enjoyed the comfort of the cottages until they could obtain housing in the new town of Gary.[75]

Horse Racing and Gambling at Roby

The extreme northwest corner of Hammond bordering on Lake Michigan is known as Roby. The place was named for Edward H. Roby, who in 1873 purchased more than six hundred acres of land there from Caroline Forsythe.[76] Gambling, horse racing, and prize fighting went on at Roby toward the end of the last century. Since prize fighting was illegal at that time in Illinois and as Chicago officials were making one of their sporadic attempts to stamp out gambling, the gamblers turned

[75] Chicago *Sunday Tribune,* March 22, 1896; Gary *Daily Tribune,* July 3, 1914 and February 26, 1917.
[76] See Lake County Deed Records, Vols. 4 and 17.

their attention to Roby. Prize fighting was also forbidden in Indiana, but the state did permit exhibitions of the "manly art of self defense." Roby was an ideal site for gambling activities. It was believed that the wilderness then separating Roby from Hammond proper would discourage any interference with illegal activities. The place was close to Chicago and only a few miles from the site of the World's Fair which was expected to attract large crowds from all parts of the nation.

In 1892 a syndicate of gamblers from Cicero, Illinois, operating as the Columbian Athletic Club, established a race track, a gambling casino, an arena for boxing matches, and a hotel at Roby. The boxing arena was designed to accommodate 12,000 spectators. At first there was only one race course, the Forsythe Track, the back stretch of which was only three feet from the Illinois state line. Two additional tracks, the Lakeside and the Sheffield, were constructed in 1895 following enactment of an Indiana law permitting only fifteen days of continuous racing at any one track and requiring an interval of thirty days between meetings at the same course. By holding meetings of fifteen days at Forsythe, then at Lakeside, and next at Sheffield, the gamblers expected to conduct legal racing for several months each year. The syndicate controlled the gambling by permitting only its own bookmakers to operate at the tracks.[77]

Chicagoans and Hoosiers flocked to this sporting center in great numbers, crowds of 6,000 people being common at the prize fights. In 1893 Governor Claude Matthews, apparently aroused by the boldness of the gambling syndicate in advertising the attractions at Roby

[77] Chicago *Times,* August 1, 1892; Chicago *Tribune,* June 13, 1893, November 1, 1897; Whiting *Democrat,* September 12, 1895; *Laws of Indiana,* 1895, pp. 92-93.

in Indianapolis, forced the cancellation of its Labor Day boxing program by dispatching two companies of the state militia to the scene. But gambling was resumed after the troops departed. On Sundays an estimated 1,500 eager customers fought with one another to get to the gambling tables at the Casino. Special trains were run from Chicago and the streetcars were frequently so crowded that the trips to and from the city were made without stopping to pick up passengers along the way. The Whiting *Sun* described these visitors to Indiana: "It's the same old crowd that used to infest upper Clark Street, sullen, loud, noisy, and glum at the law which drove them into the wilderness and across the prairie to carry on their business."[78]

Whiting and Hammond merchants launched a crusade against the gambling at Roby, and several newspapers brought pressure on the county sheriff and Hammond officials to enforce the laws against such activities. Merchants complained that the gamblers were siphoning money out of Hammond. According to reports, men earning $1.08 a day at the Hammond packing house were pooling their money and sending it to Roby to bet on the races. When the sheriff and the Hammond authorities failed to take action, charges were made that practically every official in Hammond and in the county was in the pay of the gambling syndicate. Also, that every newspaper in Hammond, except a German publication, was on the payroll of the Roby interests. The Whiting *Sun* alleged that Hammond's city administration was owned by the gamblers. Hammond, the paper declared, was in the toils of the "Roby Octopus" and its people were "Robyized."[79]

[78] Chicago *Tribune* June 13, September 5, 1893; Chesterton *Tribune,* June 3, 1893, June 26, 1894; Whiting *Sun,* January 22, 1898.

[79] Chesterton *Tribune,* June 21, 1895; Whiting *Sun,* January 22, 1898.

However, forces and influences beyond the control of the gamblers restricted the horse-racing program in the area. Because the elaborate Chicago tracks were more accessible to the public, Roby found it profitable to operate only for a brief period before the Chicago tracks opened in the spring and after they closed in the fall.[80] Also, in 1895, the Indiana Supreme Court ruled that as the three tracks at Roby were owned and operated by the same people, they fell under the restriction of the law requiring an interim of thirty days between fifteen-day racing periods.[81] Consequently, in later years meetings were held only at the Lakeside Track. In 1902 a Chicago newspaper described the Roby track:[82]

Lakeside is the most original track not only around Chicago but almost any place in the United States. To say it is primitive would be mild. It manages to get along without a grandstand. It maintains the old fashioned syndicate betting ring now to be found nowhere else except in Charleston, S. C., Atlanta, Ga., and Rome, Italy. But Lakeside has a good track, a safe track, and likewise a sure one. The heavy rains yesterday merely washed the dust off the steps. It has plenty of sand and that is why it is hard to put the track out of business. Despite its shortcomings, Lakeside draws the Faithful. It does it every fall and spring. It also draws some pretty fair horses.

In 1905 the era of large-scale gambling came to an end at Roby. In that year the Indiana General Assembly forbade betting on horse races, thereby crippling the sport in the state.[83] At the same time Governor J. Frank Hanly, aroused by the vice conditions in Ham-

---

80 A survey of the sports pages of the Chicago newspapers indicated that Lakeside's most important meeting was held in November of each year.

81 State *v.* Forsythe, 147 Ind. 466-76; Chesterton *Westchester Tribune,* June 21, 1895.

82 Chicago *Tribune,* November 3, 1902.

83 *Laws of Indiana,* 1905, p. 717.

mond, dismissed the city's police commissioners and appointed a new board to enforce the laws. The new officials acted with such vigor that gamblers and other purveyors of vice were driven westward into Illinois.[84] Also, the advance of population and industry into that part of the region made Roby a less congenial place for illegal activities.[85]

[84] Chesterton *Tribune,* December 3, 1905.

[85] The Western Glucose Company established a large plant in the Roby area in 1906 for the manufacture of corn syrup and other corn products. This company was absorbed by the American Maize Products Company in 1908. Hammond *Lake County Times,* August 22, 1906.

5

EARLY INDUSTRIAL DEVELOPMENT

THE FIRST PHASE of the region's industrial development was stimulated almost entirely by the railroads. The very presence of the railroads fired the imaginations of civic leaders and promoters, and many citizens were led to believe their communities were destined to become important manufacturing centers. Several areas, tempted by the prospect of increased land values and large payrolls, embarked upon industrial projects of doubtful soundness. Towns and villages, residential in character and whose existence depended upon the patronage of farmers, competed with each other for factories. Hopeful promoters sought to create new towns and cities in the sand and marshes of the region. While a few of these efforts met with a reasonable degree of success, their story is largely one of failure and disillusionment.

A few places sought industries to exploit such natural resources as clay, sand, and timber, and some of these projects were profitable for several years. On the other hand, certain communities attracted manufacturers whose products bore no relationship to the natural wealth in their immediate vicinity. Companies, more popularly known as "bonus industries," were induced to establish plants in various places by gifts of money, buildings, free water, and the promise of low taxes. Such industries were generally fly-by-night affairs whose owners had no intention of remaining permanently in any one place. Instead, they were quick to move on to other localities if lucrative offers could be obtained. If the factory ceased operations, as many did, the problem of unemployment confronted the community. When the workers sought employment elsewhere, empty houses and unpaid bills remained to remind the merchants of their former customers.

Industry in Valparaiso

Valparaiso's industrial history began before the first railroad arrived. A blacksmith and wagon-making shop, established by the Buel brothers in 1839, was continued by Andrew Jackson Buel until his death in 1868. In 1845 a small iron foundry, the first in the Calumet Region, was established to make iron castings. In later years this foundry manufactured steam engines for the local market. Another foundry was started in 1850.[1] The Valparaiso Woolen Manufacturing Company was incorporated in 1866 for $60,000.00, a large sum for that time. This plant contained fourteen looms and employed thirty-two workers. Its blankets won the first prize at the Chicago Fair in 1868. In 1867 the Valparaiso Paper Mill, capitalized for $20,000.00 and with twenty employees, began the manufacture of straw wrapping paper.[2]

For a brief time the business recession which followed the Civil War brought gloom and discouragement to the town. In 1871 the Valparaiso Male and Female College, which had been in operation since 1859, closed its doors. The woolen mill went out of business the following year when it encountered financial difficulties. The picture was

[1] Goodspeed and Blanchard (eds.), *Counties of Porter and Lake,* 119; Valparaiso *Vidette and Republican,* December 24, 1868. Available sources fail to indicate when these foundries ceased to operate.

[2] Skinner, *History of Valparaiso,* 21; Goodspeed and Blanchard (eds.), *Counties of Porter and Lake,* 121.

further darkened when the Winchell House, the town's largest hotel, was closed. Valparaiso, for the moment at least, faced the specter of unemployment.[3]

The depression was of short duration and a brighter era soon began for the town. In 1872 or 1873 a pin factory, said to have been the only one of its kind west of New York State, was located in the plant of the defunct woolen mill.[4] Henry Baker Brown came from Ohio in the same year and established the Northern Indiana Normal School on the campus of the former Valparaiso Male and Female College. This institution, later to develop into Valparaiso University, contributed much to the economic stability of the community. Although the pin factory ceased its operations in 1876, hosiery and yarn were manufactured in the plant for several years. The town's citizens had an unhappy experience in 1892 with the Dulaney Electric Clock Company. Two brothers named Dulaney came from Canton, Ohio, with a recently invented electric clock which they proposed to manufacture and sell outright instead of leasing, as was done by the Western Union Telegraph Company. Several Valparaiso citizens invested rather heavily in their stock. A building was leased, machinery installed, and production was about to begin when the sheriff from Canton arrived to file a claim against the brothers for debts owed in Ohio. All that the local stockholders realized from their investment was experience.[5]

Valparaiso was fortunate in never having a "boom" such as plagued other towns. Several small factories were established there in the early years of the present cen-

---

[3] Skinner, Complete History of Porter County, 30.

[4] Skinner, History of Valparaiso, 23; Goodspeed and Blanchard (eds.), Counties of Porter and Lake, 121.

[5] Harry G. Cutler, History of Porter County, Indiana (2 vols. Chicago, 1912), 1:233-34.

tury, and the community was never dependent on one large industry. One of these smaller enterprises, a "bonus industry," proved to be an asset to the town, a rare occurrence in those years. In 1900 the town council donated $5,000.00 to persuade the Chicago Mica Company to locate there. This company, which manufactured electric insulators and various bakelite products, occupied the buildings of the old woolen mill. It began operations in 1901 and by 1912 there were seventy-five people on its payroll.[6] In 1904 James H. McGill, founder of the Valparaiso telephone system, established the McGill Manufacturing Company in the building formerly occupied by one of the early foundries. This plant produced electrical specialties for telephone companies. In 1908 the Urschel Laboratories began the manufacture of canning machinery. Two years later the Indiana Steel Products Company, makers of electric magnets, battery re-chargers, and a variety of electrical supplies established its plant in the town. The Fibroc Insulation Company, whose products were bakelite fuse plugs and switchboards for telephones, arrived in 1921. A paint and varnish factory was also located there during this period.[7] Valparaiso's industrial experience was much happier than that of certain other communities. That its population suffered a slight decrease from 1910 to 1920, was no doubt due to the decline of the fortunes of Valparaiso University in those years.[8]

Crown Point

The Letz Manufacturing Company was the only important industry ever established at Crown Point. In 1882 Louis Holland-Letz set up a plant there for the

[6] *Ibid.*, 1 :234-35.

[7] *Ibid.*, 1 :235 ; Valparaiso *Daily Vidette,* February 11, 1924.

[8] Valparaiso's population was 6,987 in 1910 and 6,518 in 1920.

manufacture of feed grinders for use by farmers. The Letz grinder won the gold medal first prize at the Columbian Exposition in Chicago in 1893. Three years later the company began to manufacture what was said to have been the first corn husker and shredder. In 1909 improvements were made on the Letz feed grinder which enabled it to crush the whole ear of corn instead of just the grains. This was followed in 1912 by the production of a roughage mill which permitted farmers to utilize every possible type of home-grown feed at low cost. In 1920 the productive capacity of the company was greatly increased by the erection of new buildings and the installation of new equipment. The Letz Company was one of the most prosperous of the smaller industries in the region.[9]

Civic leaders apparently made little effort to attract industries to the town. Citizens seemed more interested in Crown Point being a residential town, and as hoped by some, a rural suburb of Chicago.[10] Competition between its two railroads, the Erie and Pennsylvania, was so keen that commutation tickets for passengers to Chicago in 1884 were only fifty-four cents a trip. Crown Point was also depicted as a town where retired farmers could make their homes and be free from the hazards which generally accompanied strikes in manufacturing centers. The presence of the county government was an economic asset to the town. The condition of the roads and the distribution of population being what they were in those years, county officials and lawyers had a tendency to reside in the vicinity of the courthouse.[11] In later years

[9] Cannon, Loring, and Robb (eds.), *History of the Lake and Calumet Region*, 2:92-94.

[10] Crown Point *Lake County Star*, February 16, 1883. Crown Point's population was 1,708 in 1880 and 2,336 in 1900.

[11] Ball (ed.), *Lake County, Indiana, 1884*, 146-47; Crown Point *Lake County Star*, April 4, 1884.

the quiet enjoyed by Crown Point was affected by the coming of the automobile and by the development of the industrial cities along the shore of Lake Michigan.

George Earle and Hobart

George Earle laid out the town of Hobart in 1849, and for many years he and his family exercised an important influence on the cultural and economic life of the town. Earle operated a flour mill and a sawmill at Hobart. In connection with these activities he constructed a dam on Deep River which formed a lake, called Lake George in his honor. Earle maintained a palatial residence and conducted an extensive real estate business at Hobart. Although he spent much time in England and France, he continued to regard the town as his home until he moved to Philadelphia in 1872. An architect and artist, Earle collected or painted about three hundred pictures which he housed in an art gallery at Hobart, thus adding to the cultural life of the region.[12] In 1875 the founder of Hobart died in his native England. John Earle, the only son, inherited his father's vast estate in the Hobart-Liverpool area. Ball described George Earle as "tall in person, dignified and courteous in manners, manifesting the bearing of an American and English gentleman."[13]

Hobart's prosperity and industrial experience were based largely upon its natural resources. Rich deposits of heavy lake clay and boulder clay which were found

[12] The editor of the Valparaiso *Republican* visited the gallery on July 4, 1859, and was impressed by Earle's talent as an artist. Among his works were portraits of Emperor Napoleon III and the Empress Eugenie. These were done on paper with colored crayons. Also displayed were oil paintings done by Earle's father. Valparaiso *Republican*, July 28, 1859.

[13] Ball (ed.), *Lake County, Indiana, 1834-1872*, 286.

at Hobart formed the basis of a profitable brick and tile industry for many years.[14] Similar deposits were also found in the vicinity of Munster, Porter, and Chesterton. The clay was of the "blue-rubber" variety and was so free of impurities such as grit, lime, and other foreign substances that it could be used just as it came from the pits. The clay formation had a depth of 130 feet and was thought to be almost inexhaustible.[15]

In 1881 William B. Owen established the National Fire Proofing Company at Hobart. This plant manufactured hollow porous tile for fireproof building construction, the tile being known at first as terra-cotta lumber because it could be sawed and nailed as readily as lumber itself. The company also manufactured almost every variety of roofing, flooring, and porous building tile.[16] In 1882 four brickyards, a pottery, a foundry, and an oil stove factory were reported in operation at Hobart.[17] The population of the town, which was incorporated in 1889, increased from 600 in 1880 to 1,010 in 1890.[18] In 1909 the National Fire Proofing plant employed 125 workers and covered more than 85 acres. A large brickyard, the Kulage Brick Works, was also in operation in Hobart at that time.[19]

[14] Blatchley, "The Geology of Lake and Porter Counties," in Indiana *Geological Report,* 1897, p. 71; "Brickmaking in Porter," by Herman F. Wagner as told to Warren R. Canright, in Chesterton *Tribune,* November 25 and December 2, 1954.

[15] Hobart *Gazette* (souvenir edition), May 20, 1898.

[16] *Ibid.*

[17] *Indiana State Gazetteer and Business Directory, 1882-1883,* 329.

[18] U. S. Bureau of the Census, *Eleventh Census* (1890)*:Population,* pt. 1:123.

[19] *The Lake County Directory* . . . , 1909 (Gary, 1909), 68, 802. Munster with a population of 543 had seventy workers in its brick and tile factory. Indiana Bureau of Statistics, *Thirteenth Biennial Report,* 1909-10, p. 1153.

The "Sheffield Boom"

From time to time local historians have written of efforts to establish a city called Sheffield in the present Roby and Robertsdale sections of Hammond. According to their accounts, in 1872 a number of bankers formed a syndicate which purchased 8,000 acres of land for $1,000,000 from Caroline and Jacob Forsythe. A short time later, $3,000,000 worth of bonds were issued to build an industrial city to be called Sheffield after the English manufacturing center of the same name. The plat of the city was reportedly filed in 1874 at the Lake County Recorder's Office at Crown Point, and the promoters were said to have spent about $80,000.00 to erect a hotel and to construct numerous streets and sidewalks. The panic of 1873 made it impossible for the syndicate to continue with its plans and the area reverted to the Forsythes. Sheffield Avenue in Hammond was accepted as evidence that the "Sheffield Boom" did occur.[20]

An exhaustive study of the deed and plat books in the Lake County Recorder's Office failed to substantiate the stories of the Sheffield project. No evidence was found in the deed books that the Forsythes sold such a large parcel of land in the 1870's, nor was a plat of Sheffield recorded in the plat books. In 1881 the Forsythes did sell 8,000 acres of land for $1,000,000 to William Green of New Jersey. Green immediately transferred this acreage to the East Chicago Improvement Company, organized by the London Banking House of Melville, Evans and Company, for $3,000,000.[21] But this parcel of land lay some distance east of the alleged Sheffield

[20] Goodspeed and Blanchard (eds.), *Counties of Porter and Lake,* 540; *The Calumet Region Historical Guide,* 24; Bowers, *Dream Cities of the Calumet,* 30-31.

[21] Lake County Deed Records, Vols. 32:50-56.

project and a few years later was the site of the city of
East Chicago. Historians of Sheffield were apparently
misled by this transaction. There was a Sheffield Hotel
at the junction of what was in the early years Sheffield
and Forsythe (Indianapolis Boulevard) avenues. This
hotel, well known to citizens of the region, was destroyed
by fire in 1910.[22] Apparently this hostelry was named
for the street on which it was located and not for the
alleged city of Sheffield.

The Aetna Powder Plant

In 1881 the Miami Powder Company of Xenia, Ohio,
began the erection of the Aetna Powder Plant in the
sand dunes about one and one-quarter miles west of
Miller Station. The site was chosen not because of railway facilities and the proximity of an adequate labor
supply, as was the case with most factories, but because
of their absence. A powder plant was considered a
nuisance industry and isolation was desirable because
location near heavily populated areas often resulted in
the payment of damages when explosions occurred. In
1881 the company purchased 240 acres from Aaron N.
Hart, and by 1888 acquisitions from various sources
amounted to more than nine hundred acres.[23] At the end
of its first year of operation, the plant had twenty-six
buildings, employed forty-five men, and had the capacity
to produce 60,000 pounds of powder a day.[24] The buildings were so located as to have a sand dune or ridge
between them to assure the maximum of safety for the
workers when explosions occurred. The company created

22 Bowers, *op. cit.*, 31.

23 Lake County Deed Records, 30:212. The plant was apparently
named for Mt. Aetna, an Italian volcano.

24 Goodspeed and Blanchard (eds.), *Counties of Porter and Lake,*
541-42.

a market for its products among the region's farmers by demonstrating how stumps could be destroyed at a cost of twenty to fifty cents each.[25] Aetna's products were transported in wagons to Miller for shipment over the Baltimore and Ohio Railroad. The Wabash Railroad, built through the area in 1895, provided more convenient shipping facilities to the plant.

The powder company employed about three hundred men at its peak of operations before World War I. Some of the workers lived in Miller while others resided in Tolleston. The majority of the employees who lived at the plant site were single men. To accommodate these, the company erected dormitories and encouraged private interests to operate boarding houses. The only concern it had with the latter was to make certain that the men paid their bills. Employees with families occupied attractive cottages erected by the company. A club house, provided by the company and well supplied with newspapers, books, and magazines eased the monotony of the isolated place for the workers.[26]

Aetna, because of the hazardous nature of its operations, occupied an unusual place in the area. Miller citizens avoided the plant and its businessmen were not tempted to expand in that direction. In 1907 there was only one store at Aetna and its stock consisted chiefly of overalls and chewing tobacco. The sale of alcoholic liquors was forbidden and the company would not knowingly employ men addicted to their use. Nor would the company even allow the sale of soft drinks in the plant area. Although there were no churches at Aetna, ministers from Miller and Hobart frequently conducted serv-

[25] Crown Point *Lake County Star,* August 11, 1882.
[26] Gary *Weekly Tribune,* August 16, 1907; Gary *Post-Tribune,* May 16, 1929.

ices in the parlors of the various boarding houses. The community had a post office before it achieved the status of a town.[27]

The expansion of the bustling young town of Gary threatened the existence of the plant. To preserve its isolation as much as possible and also to prevent it being absorbed by Gary, the company had the community incorporated in 1907 as a town.[28] Gary and Miller citizens opposed the presence of this dangerous industry and tried to have it removed from their borders. While Miller merchants admitted they had profited from the trade of the Aetna employees, this was offset by the reluctance of people to buy homes in Miller because of its nearness to the powder plant.[29] The plant was a hazard to the adjoining community. In 1912 an explosion of eight hundred pounds of dynamite killed six of its employees and injured many others. The tragedy occurred a few minutes before a heavily loaded passenger train on the South Shore electric line passed the plant. Two years later, a terrific explosion of two thousand pounds of nitroglycerine rocked the very foundations of Gary.[30] Every plate glass window on Broadway, Gary's main thoroughfare, between Fourth and Fifteenth avenues, about two miles from the plant, reportedly were shattered. The affair was not without its humorous side, it being alleged that some citizens took advantage of this opportunity to replace windows cracked or broken before the explosion at the powder company's expense.[31] The little cemetery

27 Gary *Weekly Tribune,* August 16, 1907.

28 U. S. Bureau of the Census, *Thirteenth Census* (1910): *Abstract . . . with Supplement for Indiana* (Washington, D. C., 1913), 581.

29 Gary *Evening Post,* May 26, 1911.

30 Gary *Daily Tribune,* November 12, 1912; November 23, 1914.

31 Autobiography of Tom Cannon (Typewritten MS in Gary Public Library), 78.

on the dune just south of where the Dunes Highway passes over the Baltimore and Ohio tracks at Miller stands a mute evidence of the tragedies at Aetna.[32]

The great demand for explosives during World War I gave the powder plant a new lease on life. In 1915 it was remodeled for the production of gun cotton for the Allies, and by April of that year about 1,200 men were engaged in the manufacture of that important product.[33] Gary was stirred to great excitement in 1917 when fire destroyed about half of the plant. There were the inevitable rumors of sabotage and the finger of suspicion was pointed at workers of German descent. Investigation by Federal agents failed to disclose any activity on the part of the enemy. Production was halted for only thirty days. With the end of the war, it was obvious there was no longer any justification for such a dangerous industry right on Gary's doorstep, and the plant closed its doors. In May, 1919, only 73 persons remained at Aetna. Gary annexed the town in 1924.[34]

Industry at Chesterton and Porter

Along toward the close of the last century the sister communities of Chesterton and Porter had high hopes of becoming large industrial centers. Their excellent railroad connections, the rich deposits of clay in the vicinity, and the promotional genius of Arthur J. Bowser, owner and editor of the Chesterton *Tribune*, combined

[32] According to several older citizens of Miller, the remains of at least twenty workers at the powder plant, victims of an explosion, were buried in the same grave at this cemetery.

[33] Gary *Evening Post*, April 5, 1915. As late as 1953, several children were injured while playing with gun cotton at the site of the old powder plant.

[34] Gary *Daily Tribune*, August 11, 1917; Gary *Evening Post*, May 30, 1919.

to present the story of a dream that almost came true. Porter was located at the junction of the Michigan Central and the Lake Shore and Michigan Southern railroads, while Chesterton was less than a mile away on the latter railroad. In 1893 the Elgin, Joliet, and Eastern (Chicago Outer Belt Line) located its eastern terminus at Porter, and in 1903 the tracks of Pere Marquette Trunk Line reached there.

Unusually rich deposits of heavy lake and boulder clay were discovered at Porter. The first brickyards were established in that area as early as 1872, and in 1883 three yards, employing forty men, were in operation.[35] The quality of Porter brick was soon widely recognized throughout the Chicago area. In 1880 C. O. Hillstrom, who had operated an organ factory in Chicago since 1869, moved his plant to Chesterton. Hillstrom also manufactured organ and piano stools. A large number of Swedes were employed at the organ factory, Hillstrom himself being of that nationality. The peak of the company's operations was reached in 1892 when 125 men were on its payroll.[36] By 1890 Chesterton's population was 931.[37]

The purchase of the Porter brickyards in 1890 by the Chicago Hydraulic Pressed Brick Company launched a boom in the two communities that waxed and waned for some years. Arthur J. Bowser, who was engaged in the real estate business himself, attracted the attention of Chicago financial interests to the area through the medium of the Chesterton *Tribune*. In 1892 a group of Chicago promoters organized the Chicago-Porter Home

[35] Indiana Department of Statistics, *Fifth Annual Report*, 1883, p. 161.

[36] Louis A. Menke, "The Story of Chesterton," in *Chesterton Retail Merchants' Directory* (Chesterton, 1949), 39; Chesterton *Tribune*, November 25, 1892.

[37] Chesterton's population in 1880 was 488.

Investment Company at Porter, and platted a tract of land into lots and streets. The company ran excursion trains from Chicago on Sundays as a part of its program to attract buyers for its lots. Free beer and lunches were served to the visitors.[38]

Such a spirit of optimism prevailed that Bowser predicted the merger of Chesterton and Porter and their growth into a city of 50,000 population. For a moment it appeared that the boom was to have a sound foundation. Early in 1892 a paint factory was established in Chesterton. In the same year the Vienna Enameling and Stamping Company, manufacturing enameled kitchenware, was located at Porter. This factory, owned and operated by Germans, employed about fifty men. The Hydraulic Brick Company was doing a flourishing business. This plant, which employed 250 men in the winter and 400 in the summer seasons, produced 250,000 bricks a day. According to reports, more than a million dollars were invested in the industries of the area. In 1893 the local manufacturers maintained a display of brick, enameled ware, and organs at Chicago's Columbian Exposition.[39]

The panic which swept the nation in 1893 struck the sister communities a hard blow. They were deprived of a payroll of $3,000.00 a month when the Vienna Enamel and Stamping plant shut down. The brick company and organ factory curtailed operations, and by the middle of August the paint company was the only factory in the township that had not closed its doors.[40] For a brief interval a pall hung over the towns. A note of optimism

[38] Chesterton *Tribune,* November 25, 1892; Valparaiso *Messenger,* September 25, 1892.

[39] Chesterton *Tribune,* June 24 and November 25, 1892; Valparaiso *Messenger,* April 27, 1893.

[40] Chesterton *Tribune,* August 11 and 18, 1893.

was sounded in November when an announcement was made that a Chicago group, which had absorbed the Chesterton-Porter Home Investment Company, intended to erect an opera house, water works, and electric light plant at Porter. The Valparaiso *Messenger,* in making a reference to Porter, said, "The little burg is already putting on city airs and threatens to annex Chesterton."[41] More solid evidence that the situation was improving appeared when the American Brass Works, manufacturers of plumbing supplies and brass lamps, moved its plant from Massachusetts to Porter. According to reports, the brass company intended to construct twenty-six houses to accommodate the families that were to accompany the plant from the Bay State.[42] Editor Bowser demonstrated his confidence in the area's future by establishing the Porter *Tribune* in 1894 in addition to the Chesterton *Tribune* which he was already publishing.[43]

Events soon proved the picture was not as bright as it had seemed. In 1895 the Porter Land and Manufacturing Company, successor to the Chicago-Porter Home Investment Company, was forced into bankruptcy. Editor Bowser was chosen by the court to preside over its demise, and the company's property was sold at auction. The American Brass Works, from which so much had been expected, was also placed in the hands of a receiver and its property sold to satisfy the creditors. The stockholders received nothing from their investment. At this juncture the distressed editor of the Chesterton *Tribune* told his readers that "it is now or never for Porter. The boom must either boom or bust. The new owners of the Land Company and the Brass Works hold its future in their hands." A "bust" appeared to be in the offing a

41 Valparaiso *Messenger,* November 2, 1893.
42 Chesterton *Tribune,* May 4 and 11, 1894.
43 *Ibid.,* June 22, 1894.

few months later when the Vienna Enameling and Stamping Company went out of business.[44]

In the summer of 1897 things took a turn for the better at Porter when the Warren Featherbone Company of Three Oaks, Michigan, established a branch factory in the building of the defunct brass works. Featherbone, a substitute for whalebone, was used in women's corsets, petticoats, and shirt collars, and also in the dress shirts worn by the men of that era. The product was made from the quills of the wing and tail feathers of the common turkey. What remained of the feathers was made into pillows and cushions.[45] Early in 1896 the Daniel Webster Manufacturing Company, makers of rattan chairs, moved into the building formerly occupied by the enameling and stamping works.

Encouraged by this activity, the Porter Land Company, which had purchased the holdings of the Porter Land and Manufacturing Company, ran full-page advertisements in the Chesterton *Tribune* depicting Porter as a suburb of Chicago. The company also advertised the community as the finest health resort in Indiana. Artesian springs having been discovered in the vicinity of what is now Mineral Springs, the realty people extolled the medicinal and healing properties of their water. A resort, known as Carlsbad Mineral Springs, was started around the turn of the century with cabins and a restaurant for the accommodation of invalids and vacationists.[46]

The prosperity of Porter and Chesterton alternately waxed and waned in the next few years. In 1896 C. O. Hillstrom, who had founded the organ factory at Ches-

44 *Ibid.*, April 12, July 19, November 1, 1895.
45 *Ibid.*, August 28, 1897; Cutler, *History of Porter County*, 1:237.
46 Chesterton *Tribune*, August 6, 1898; September 4, 1903.

terton, died. The administrators of the estate attempted
to operate the plant with varying degrees of success and
in 1898 sold it to local interests. The following year, a
strike of piano workers in Chicago led the Russell-Lane
Piano Company to move a portion of its work to the
organ factory at Chesterton. This arrangement, however, was temporary. In June, 1896, the Daniel Webster Manufacturing Company shut down when it was
unable to meet the first payment on its building. The
brickyards closed down for several months because of
the lack of a market for bricks. Once more Editor Bowser sounded a gloomy note when he reported that many
families were moving away from the sister communities.[47]
The population of Chesterton declined from 931 in 1890
to 788 in 1900.[48]

In 1903 the Chicago Flint and Line Glass Company,
manufacturers of chinaware, tried to negotiate a typical
"bonus" agreement with Porter's citizens. In return for
a cash bonus of $10,000.00 and fifty building lots, the
company promised to convert the old enameling and
stamping factory into a glass works at a cost of $50,000.-
00 and to employ not less than 150 men. The Porter
Land Company, eager to obtain what appeared to be a
prosperous industry for the community, offered to deed
one hundred lots to those who subscribed to the $10,-
000.00 bonus fund. Unable to raise that large an
amount, the land company ultimately gave eighty-four
lots and $1,600.00 in cash to secure the location of the
glass works at Porter. The new company was a great
disappointment to the community. In 1905 it closed its

[47] Cutler, *History of Porter County,* 1:235; Chesterton *Westchester
Tribune,* June 20, 1896; Chesterton *Tribune,* November 6, 1896; August
6, 1898.

[48] U. S. Bureau of the Census, *Twelfth Census* (1900); *Population,*
pt. 1:141.

doors and moved to Valparaiso when the citizens of that city offered it a bonus of $8,000.00.[49]

In 1905 the Featherbone Company left Porter. Its property passed into the hands of the Sall Mountain Asbestos Company, manufacturers of rubber and mica roofing and other fire proofing materials. This was a prosperous industry for several years. In 1912, with 105 men on the payroll, it was regarded as the largest industry in Porter County. In 1920 the Hillstrom Organ Factory was formally dissolved. Its property was purchased by the Gary Chemical Company which proved to be a short-lived industry. Thus ended the era when Porter and Chesterton aspired to be the great industrial center of the Calumet Region.[50]

The Stockyards Boom

In 1890 the most spectacular real estate boom before the coming of steel to the region was caused by rumors that the "Big Three" of the meat-packing industry, Armour, Swift, and Morris, intended to move their plants into the swamps and sand ridges where Gary now stands. So many reasons have been given for this action by the packers that it is difficult to separate fact from fiction. According to reports, the packing house people were unhappy in their relations with the Union Stock Yards Company because of excessive charges for yard privileges, railroad switching, and the like.[51] Also, that the people of Chicago, disturbed by the rank odors from the packing houses and concerned about the pollution

[49] Cutler, *History of Porter County*, 1:236; Chesterton *Tribune*, June 29, 1905.

[50] Cutler, *History of Porter County*, 1:237; Chesterton *Tribune*, April 29, 1920. Present-day industries in Porter and Chesterton are of recent origin and do not fall within the scope of this study.

[51] Philip D. Armour, quoted in Chicago *Inter-Ocean*, June 11, 1891.

of the Chicago River, demanded the city take steps to
exercise greater control over the industry. Finally, the
packers were alarmed by the opinions of many Chicagoans that such a nuisance industry should not be allowed
to exist at all in the congested areas of the city.[52] All
of this was true, but there is much evidence to indicate
that the packers' threat to leave Chicago was caused
by considerations which were kept under cover at that
time.

The behind-the-scenes story is one of conflict between
financial giants for power and profits. For some time
the Big Three of the packing industry had been trying
to get control of the Union Stock Yards. Their ownership of the stockyards in other cities was profitable because of the collection of terminal charges, feeding charges, yardage fees, and high rentals. The Big Three's
profits began in these yards the very moment the animals
arrived from the farm for sale. Control of the yards
enabled them to undersell the smaller packers and thereby
dominate the meat industry. The Chicago Union Stock
Yards, the largest in the nation and a lucrative property
paying 30 per cent annual dividends, would be a valuable
addition to their meat empire.[53]

In 1890 matters came to a head when the Vanderbilt
family and certain English interests purchased the Chicago Union Stock Yards for a price said to have been
$19,000,000.[54] This was bad news for the big packers
in so far as it thwarted, at least for the time being, their
own ambitions to get possession of the yards. Whether
the packers' threats to move their plants to Indiana are

[52] J. J. Quillen, The Industrial City (Ph.D. thesis, Yale University,
1942, on microfilm in the Gary Public Library), 14.

[53] Harper Leech and John C. Carroll, *Armour and His Times* (New
York, 1938), 199-200.

[54] *Ibid.;* Chicago *Tribune,* June 29, 1890.

to be interpreted as defensive tactics against a threat of strangulation by the yards and by their old railroad enemies, or whether they were measures to obtain for themselves a share in the profits of the stockyards are still a matter of dispute. But whether their move was defensive or aggressive it is agreed that the Big Three proceeded to act with boldness and decision.

The first step was taken by Nelson Morris. Backed by Gustavus Swift and Philip D. Armour, Morris bought a large tract of land south of the old yards, which he called the Central Stock Yards, and announced he was soliciting shipments of cattle and hogs with promises of fair treatment and no commissions. The railroads made short work of Morris' plan by simply refusing to deliver any cars to his new yards and hauled the cars instead to the Union Stock Yards. The carriers notified Morris that he could have his cars by paying the switching charges.[55] As additional switching charges would make the Central Stock Yards unprofitable, the packers lost the first round of the contest.

Undaunted by this setback, the Big Three renewed the attack along a different line. They organized the Chicago and Calumet Stock Yards Company and announced their intention to move the livestock market to Tolleston, Indiana, where they had purchased several thousand acres of land between that village and Lake Michigan. The big packing houses would follow the animals to the new yards and predictions were made that the smaller packers would do likewise.[56] There is little agreement as to how much land the packers bought in the Calumet Region at this time as the acquisitions were not made in their names. Evidence indicates that Albert H. Veeder and Edward

[55] Leech and Carroll, *Armour and His Times,* 200.
[56] Armour, quoted in the Chicago *Inter-Ocean,* June 11, 1891.

Martyn did the buying. Veeder, an attorney for Gustavus Swift, was a prominent figure in the meat industry. The Big Three met regularly in his office to form the "Veeder Pool" by which agreements were made as to how much each company would ship to various parts of the country at certain times.[57] Competition between them was eliminated in this manner. The records in the Lake County Recorder's Office at Crown Point show that Veeder and Martyn in October and November, 1890, purchased five parcels of land for $678,000.00.[58] One parcel included the site of the Calumet Gun Club near the present harbor of the Gary Steel Works. A study of the deeds indicated about 4,000 acres were purchased by the packers at that time.

There is doubt that the Big Three ever intended to move their plants to Indiana. The Chicago *Tribune,* which did not take their threats seriously, insisted the expense involved in moving the plants and building new stockyards and houses for the workers would be too great for the packers to bear.[59] Whether the packers were bluffing or not, the Union Stock Yards' officials were sufficiently impressed by their tactics to offer to negotiate a settlement. The Big Three demanded that the stockyards company pay them $3,000,000 for their sandy acres in Indiana and also make certain rate concessions. The stockyards people denounced this as a holdup. Late in 1891 a settlement was made by which the Big Three received $4,500,000 worth of five per cent bonds of the stockyards corporation, and in turn agreed to remain in Chicago and to buy no cattle or hogs within one hundred miles of the city except at the Union Stock

57 Leech and Carroll, *Armour and His Times,* 197.
58 Lake County Deed Records, 51:285, 309, 372; 52:170, 172.
59 Chicago *Tribune,* July 11, 1890.

Yards for a period of fifteen years.[60] The packers retained much of their land in the Calumet Region which they later sold to the United States Steel Corporation as part of the sites of the steel mills and the city of Gary. Although the Big Three did not get control of the stockyards, they certainly won a share of its profits.

The news that the packers planned to move their plants started a real estate boom in the vicinity of Tolleston, locally known as the "stockyards boom." Fred D. and Henry A. Bradford, Chicago promoters, organized the Chicago-Tolleston Land and Improvement Company in 1890 for the purpose of founding a town near the proposed packing-house area. The company bought a strip of land between the Michigan Central and the Pennsylvania Railroad tracks which ran parallel on the west to Burton Avenue, now Broadway Street in Gary. Burton Avenue was named for a younger brother of the Bradfords. In 1890 and 1891 the Bradfords also platted the land between the Wabash Railroad tracks and what is now 29th Street into lots. During the regime of the Chicago-Tolleston Land and Improvement Company the "town" was known successively as Bradford, East Tolleston, and Jerusalem. The name Jerusalem was acquired when Silas E. Green, an employee of the realty company, weary of pleading for the location of a post office there, finally wrote the Post Office Department that the people would have to have a post office even if it were to be called Jerusalem. Green's plea so appealed to the sense of humor of the postal officials that he was notified in 1894 an office would be established there and that its name would be Jerusalem.[61]

[60] Leech and Carroll, *Armour and His Times,* 202-3.

[61] Silas E. Green, "Jerusalem, or East Tolleston, A Town Founded on the Site of Gary," and Ruby M. Graham, "Historical Report of the Gary Region," in Lester (ed.), Papers by Various Hands, 2:250, 252; 1:273; Index of Indiana Post Offices, in Indiana State Library.

The Bradford brothers advertised their new town in the Chicago newspapers and ran excursion trains, loaded with prospective customers for their lots, over the Pennsylvania Railroad to Tolleston. An impressive circular, containing a map, predicted a bright future for the area: "This district is destined to become the great manufacturing center in America. The removal of the stock yards to this locality, the building of railroads, ship canals, docks, electric and horse car lines, electric light system, water works, factories, and numerous other industries which go to make up a large city, give to the purchaser a real chance for an investment." The circular also claimed that 5,000 lots had been sold in the town.[62] There were only three houses in the vicinity when the boom started and its subsequent population was brought in almost in a body through the efforts of the realty company. The Bradfords made every effort to put their town on a sound foundation. A furniture factory and a paint and varnish plant were erected to provide employment for its citizens. The educational needs of the community were satisfied by the building of a school.[63]

Other promoters planned the town of Ivanhoe between Tolleston and Hammond. The place was depicted as being far enough away from the proposed stockyards district to avoid the unpleasant odors associated with the meat industry in those years and yet near enough for its citizens to find employment there. This new town was laid out just west of what is now Clark Road; some lots were sold, and work was started on a factory building. The latter was never completed and for years its

[62] Chicago-Tolleston Land and Improvement Company, Circular and Map (pamphlet in Gary Public Library).

[63] Chicago *Sunday Tribune,* January 17, 1897; Green, "Jerusalem, or East Tolleston," in Lester (ed.), Papers by Various Hands, 2:252.

foundation was all that remained of the dream city of Ivanhoe.[64]

The Bradford real estate boom collapsed when it was apparent that the packers were going to remain in Chicago. A short time later the panic of 1893 destroyed what vitality was left in the community. The furniture factory closed its doors and the paint and varnish plant was destroyed by fire. Charges were made that its owners burned the building to collect the insurance, but the insurance was never paid. Many persons who had purchased their lots on contract, lost their investment because of inability to complete the payments. Others lost their property by refusing to pay the taxes, which were in some instances as low as seven cents a lot. A few, with rare foresight and faith in the region's future, were richly rewarded for retaining their holdings when the steel mills were built a few years later. One individual was reported to have traded an old bicycle for a lot on present Broadway between Ninth and Tenth avenues which he sold later for $10,000.00. In 1897 Jerusalem's sad state was revealed when the first death in the town's history occurred and the citizens discovered it was without a physician, an undertaker, or a graveyard. After much consultation, arrangements were made to inter the deceased in the Tolleston cemetery about two miles away.[65]

The Jerusalem community might have died had it not attracted the attention and interest of Louis A. Bryan, a Chicago lawyer. In 1896 Bryan and his brother, Pulaski J. Bryan, organized the Chicago-Tolleston Land and

[64] *The Calumet* (published by the Gary Commercial Club), August 1, 1913, p. 16.

[65] Green, "Jerusalem, or East Tolleston," in Lester (ed.), Papers by Various Hands, 2:252; *The Calumet,* August 1, 1913; Chicago *Sunday Tribune,* January 17, 1897.

Investment Company and purchased what was left of
the holdings of the Bradford brothers. The following
year, the Calumet Land Company, headed by Louis A.
Bryan, absorbed the Chicago-Tolleston Land and Investment Company. Bryan laid out and partially improved
about twenty miles of streets from the Wabash tracks
south to the Little Calumet River, including what is now
Broadway Street.[66] The name of the town was changed
from Jerusalem to Calumet.

Bryan obtained the location of a large piano stool factory at what is now 22d Avenue and Jefferson Street.
This industry provided some degree of stability to the
community for several years. The Bryans also conducted
a profitable sand business at Tolleston and cultivated
about 250 acres of land just north of the Little Calumet
River.[67] Louis Bryan established the Calumet *Advance*
in 1896, the first newspaper published on the site of
Gary. This busy and versatile man was postmaster of
Calumet from 1897 to 1906, and also served as a justice
of the peace.

Bryan built a substantial home in a grove at what is
now 23d Avenue and Jefferson Street and called it Island
Park. He reportedly carved this estate of about twenty
acres with his own hands out of a jungle of sand and
swale.[68] Bryan was the first to petition for the incorporation of Gary in 1906, directed its first election, and
became the town's first treasurer.[69] He brought the first
automobile to Gary. At one time Bryan drove his car

[66] Lake County Deed Records, 79:390; 80:261; Howat (ed.), *A
Standard History of Lake County*, 2:476.

[67] Chicago *Sunday Tribune*, January 17, 1897; Howat (ed.), *A
Standard History of Lake County*, 2:476.

[68] Gary *Post-Tribune*, May 17, 1926.

[69] C. Oliver Holmes, "How We Incorporated the Town of Gary,"
in Cannon, Loring, and Robb (ed.), *History of the Lake and Calumet
Region*, 1:766.

over the rails of the Santa Fé Railroad from Los Angeles to Chicago in eight days. The automobile was fitted with special wheels and was operated as a special car under regular dispatcher's orders. It reportedly arrived in Chicago on schedule.[70] Louis A. Bryan may well be regarded as the first citizen of Gary. He died at Island Park in 1926.

Griffith's Brief Boom

In the early nineties Griffith had an unpleasant experience as a boom town. It had excellent railroad connections as the Erie, the Grand Trunk, the Elgin, Joliet and Eastern, and the Joliet Cut-Off all crossed at that point. In 1890 the community's only inhabitants were the railroad station agent and his family who lived a lonely life amid sand and thickets there. The town was laid out the next year by Jay Dwiggins and Company of Chicago. According to reports, this realty company sold lots to people in various parts of the country for what were regarded as fabulous prices at that time.[71]

Griffith made a promising beginning and for the moment its future appeared bright. By 1892 four factory buildings were in process of construction. Residences, stores, and a school were built to accommodate the new citizens. The panic of 1893 ruined the boom and despair was reported to have settled down on the inhabitants. Many persons left for other parts and for a time the town was practically deserted. Only the few who had employment with the railroads remained. In later years Griffith was given a new lease on life. In 1910 the town, with a population of 523, had a small foundry, a glove factory, and two saloons.[72]

[70] Gary *Post-Tribune,* May 17, 1926.
[71] Valparaiso *Messenger,* April 27, 1893.
[72] Ball, *Encyclopedia of Genealogy and Biography,* 40; Howat (ed.),

Such were the beginnings of industry in the Calumet Region. It is remarkable that this northwestern corner of Indiana, right at Chicago's doorstep, was still largely a wilderness of swamp and sand as late as the turn of the twentieth century. Nature, it seems, had reserved it for the greater developments that were soon to come. By 1900 the American frontier was gone, and the nation's center of population had shifted into the Middle West. As a result, the Great Lakes area was about to receive the full impact of America's industrial revolution. A brighter era for the Calumet Region was just around the corner.

A Standard History of Lake County, 1:131; Valparaiso *Messenger,* April 27, 1893; Indiana Bureau of Statistics, *Thirteenth Biennial Report,* 1909-10, p. 1151. Griffith was incorporated as a town in 1904.

6

HAMMOND, DRESSED BEEF, AND GERMANS

THE EARLY HISTORY of Hammond, oldest of the larger cities of the region, is closely intertwined with the movement of German immigrants into the Middle West and with the beginning of the modern meat-packing industry in the United States. Although German settlers arrived on the scene some years before the packing house was established, that plant attracted others to the community in large numbers. Hammond was largely a city of Germans for many years and their influence on its cultural and economic life is evident to the present time.[1]

The First Settlers

In 1850 the area where Hammond now stands was covered with sand ridges and swamps. Its settlement began when the Michigan Central Railroad, built across the region the following year, made it easily accessible from Chicago. As most of the area was swamp land and could be purchased from the State of Indiana at the minimum price of $1.25 an acre, and as the railroads were expected to increase the value of land, here was an excel-

---

[1] Among the German families that have been prominent in Hammond's history are the following: Hohman, Sohl, Ahlendorf, Goodman, Drecker, Drackert, Meyn, Rimbach, Lohse, Schrieber, Muenich, Humpfer, Mott, Weis, Schloer, Eder, Knoerzer, Kleihege, Roth, Huehn, Heckman, Wilhelm, Wendisch, Prohl, and Schroeter.

lent opportunity for profitable investments in real estate. Cheap land was the attraction that brought thrifty Germans from Chicago to what was then a wilderness.

Ernst W. Hohman and his wife, Caroline Sibley Hohman, were the first to settle on the site of Hammond. Hohman, born in Königsberg, East Prussia, and a tailor by trade, was one of the many Germans who left their native land around the middle of the last century. He came to the United States by way of London, where he met and married Caroline Sibley, who was born in Wales. Their courtship, according to reports, was conducted in French as Ernst could not speak English and Caroline was not familiar with German. The couple sailed for America a few days after their marriage and arrived at New York in August, 1849. They went from there to Chicago, where Hohman opened a tailor shop.

Because of a cholera epidemic in Chicago, the Hohmans resided for a time early in 1850 with friends at Merrillville. Ernst retained his tailor shop in Chicago for a short time and traveled to and from his work on horseback. He became acquainted with the opportunities available in the Calumet Region while making these trips. In 1851 Hohman sold the tailor shop and purchased thirty-nine acres of land on the north bank of the Grand Calumet River for $262.50. Here he built the Hohman Inn, a comfortable log house with six rooms, which was soon a favorite stopping place for travelers. To this was added a clapboard section containing two bedrooms and a living room. A bridge, which came to be known as Hohman's Bridge, was built across the Grand Calumet south of the inn, and Hohman also aided in the construction of a corduroy road in the direction of Crown Point. In July 1859, Stephen A. Douglas, at that time an attorney for the Michigan Central Railroad, and his wife were guests at the inn. Douglas, pleased with the hospitality of the Hohmans, presented a fine brooch to Caroline as a token of appreciation.

Hohman speculated in land and within a few years was in comfortable circumstances. Some of his purchases were swamp lands, which he obtained from the State of Indiana for $1.25 an acre. He also acquired other holdings in private transactions for prices as high as $5.00 an acre. By 1858 his accumulations amounted to more than four hundred acres. There are so many records of land bought and sold by Hohman in later years that it would be difficult to arrive at a correct estimate of his holdings at any one time. After his death in 1873, his wife administered the estate with ability and played an important part in the development of Hammond. She built its first business section, the Hohman Opera House Block. Although an Episcopalian, she donated the site of St. Joseph's Catholic Church. In 1900 the bells of St. Joseph's were tolled as her funeral procession passed the church.[2]

William Sohl, also born in Germany, settled in the area at an early date. Like Ernst Hohman, Sohl paused in England on his way to America, and also as did Hohman, found a bride in the Sibley family. He married Louisa Isabella Sibley, a sister of Caroline Hohman, in London. In 1851 the couple came to America. Sohl purchased a large tract of land in what is now the center of Hammond, and built his residence near the Hohman Inn.

2 Diary of Caroline Hohman, April 26, 1850; July, 1859, p. 5 (Typed copy in possession of Warren A. Reeder, Hammond, Indiana); Howat (ed.), *A Standard History of Lake County,* 1:287-88; 2:512-13; Hammond *Times* (centennial edition), June 17, 1951, p. 2A; Lake County Deed Records, E:579. Ernst and Caroline Hohman had six children: Ottelia, Charles, Louis, Agnes, Emma, and Lena. The American Steel Foundries Plant now occupies the site of the Hohman Inn.

He also opened a grocery store. August and Theodore
Ahlendorf and Jacob Drecker were among the early
neighbors of the Hohmans and the Sohls.[3] In 1854 Jacob
Rimbach came to Gibson Station to work on the Michigan Central Railroad, and remained to make a fortune
by speculating in Hammond real estate.[4]

The area remained a wilderness of swamp and sand
for some years after its settlement began. There was
a dense growth of wild rice and marsh grass adjacent to
the Grand Calumet River, while an almost impenetrable
tangle of scrub oak covered the sand ridges. The residents earned their living by farming the sandy soil,
by trapping muskrats in the winter, and by acting as
guides for Chicago hunters and fishermen. They went
to Gibson Station on the Michigan Central, about two
miles away, to get their mail, send telegrams, and take
the trains to Chicago. Another settlement, Hessville,
clustered around a store and post office a mile south
of Gibson Station. In 1863 a small schoolhouse was
erected in the vicinity of the Hohman Inn. The German
character of the community was indicated by the personnel of this school. Of the twelve children in attendance
during its first session, the Hohmans sent three, the
Goodmans three, the Sohls two, the Drackerts two; the
teacher was Amanda Koontz. Only twelve families lived
in the area when construction of the slaughterhouse was
started in 1869.[5]

3 Diary of Caroline Hohman, May, 1852, p. 3; Myrtelle Huehn,
"Brief Review on the History of Hammond," in Demmon (ed.), *History
of Lake County* (1934), 57; Howat (ed.), *A Standard History of Lake
County,* 1:288-89.

4 Ball, *Encyclopedia of Genealogy and Biography,* 273.

5 Howat (ed.), *A Standard History of Lake County,* 1:289; Hammond
Times, June 17, 1951, pp. 2A, 4C; Huehn, "Brief Review on the History
of Hammond," in Demmon (ed.), *History of Lake County* (1934), 56-57.

George H. Hammond and Marcus M. Towle

The building of Hammond was a part of the most significant development in the history of the meat-packing industry, the successful shipping of dressed beef over the railroads to distant markets. Until this occurred, the great eastern markets depended upon locally grown beef and upon cattle shipped hundreds of miles over the railroads from the West. The shipping of live cattle was not profitable for the packers nor was it economical for the consumers. Both had to pay for the hauling of about 45 per cent useless and dead weight. A western steer weighing a thousand pounds would produce about 550 pounds of edible beef at the slaughterhouse near the eastern market. At that time few profitable by-products had been developed and the 450 pounds were not only useless but a costly nuisance to be disposed of. Moreover, cattle lost weight and were frequently injured while en route to the market. This great waste was the concern of every packer, and out of it came the refrigerator car and the modern trade in dressed beef.[6] The refrigerator car became inevitable after natural ice began to be used around 1857 to keep meat during the warm months of the year. About the same time artificial refrigeration was being introduced in meat-packing plants and breweries. The refrigerator car, like nearly every other basic invention of modern industry, was the work of a large number of pioneers who built upon each other's failures and partial successes.

While George H. Hammond was not the first to ship beef by refrigeration, he was undoubtedly the first to build and operate a satisfactory refrigerator car for the transportation of beef. Hammond, for whom the city of Hammond was named, was born in 1838 at Fitchburg,

[6] Leech and Carroll, *Armour and His Times,* 125.

Massachusetts. It seems he had scarcely any boyhood as he left school at ten years of age. He obtained employment making pocketbooks and soon obtained control of the firm, employing eight girls and doing a profitable business. In 1864 Hammond went to Detroit where he operated a furniture and mattress factory for more than two years. When this business was destroyed by fire, he opened a meat market. By 1868 the business had expanded until it included a large wholesale department and a slaughterhouse.[7]

In Detroit, Hammond became acquainted with Marcus M. Towle, who later founded and developed the city of Hammond, and also played an important part in the starting of East Chicago. Towle was born in 1841 at Danville, New Hampshire, and learned the butchering business in Brighton, Massachusetts. He came to Detroit in 1865. From there he shipped dressed beef in ordinary railroad cars to Boston with the carcasses covered with ice. This method was not satisfactory as the meat was discolored because of its contact with the ice.[8] While discoloration of the beef did not affect its nutritious value, consumer prejudice could not be overcome. This mode of shipment was also expensive as enormous amounts of ice were necessary to preserve the beef. Also, as the railroads frequently neglected to re-ice the cars, the beef often spoiled while en route to the market.[9] Despite these features, Towle apparently impressed upon Hammond the possibilities of shipments by refrigeration.

Hammond approached William Davis, owner of a Detroit fish market who was shipping fish, peaches, and

[7] Rudolf A. Clemen, *George H. Hammond, 1838-1886, Pioneer in Refrigerator Transportation* (New York, 1946), 11.

[8] Ball, *Encyclopedia of Genealogy and Biography,* 307; Howat (ed.), *A Standard History of Lake County,* 1 :292; 2 :504.

[9] Leech and Carroll, *Armour and His Times,* 127, 129.

strawberries to the eastern markets, and asked him to design a car to carry beef. Davis did so, using the same principle of refrigeration he had found satisfactory for the transportation of fish and fruit. The car was built, and in April, 1869, carried its first shipment of beef to Boston. The Boston *Daily Advertiser* took notice of the historic event and gave its readers a description of the car: "A refrigerator car . . . arrived in this city yesterday morning [Wednesday] laden with 16,000 pounds of beef placed on board at Detroit on Wednesday of last week. This car was in charge of Mr. George H. Hammond on its passage. The ice is placed in narrow chambers at each side of the car, opening only at the top from the outside, and does not, therefore, come in contact with the meat or the air in the car which is kept cold and dry. The meat was in better condition than that received directly from our home markets."[10]

The State Line Slaughter-House

Encouraged by this success, Hammond and Caleb Ives, a Detroit banker, obtained the exclusive use of the Davis car from the latter's heirs. A partnership was formed with Hammond and Ives each taking a one-third interest, and Marcus M. Towle and George W. Plumer each taking a one-sixth interest. The original capital was reported to have been only $6,000.00. As the livestock market was centered in Chicago, the partners decided to locate their plant in its vicinity. The choice of the site on the Grand Calumet River was determined largely by the need for ice in large amounts. Ice could be obtained from the river and near-by lakes for less than it would

10 Boston *Daily Advertiser*, April 22, 1869, quoted in Clemen, *George H. Hammond*, 14.

cost to ship the cattle from the Chicago stockyards.[11] Although Hammond preferred a site farther west in Illinois, Towle persuaded his colleagues to locate the slaughterhouse across the river from the Hohman Inn. Early in September, 1869, they purchased fifteen acres from Ernst and Caroline Hohman for $750.00; an additional twenty-three acres were acquired from the Hohmans in 1873 for $2,287.00. Purchases from other owners brought the size of the original plant area to forty-two acres.[12] The site was bounded by the Illinois-Indiana line on the west, the Grand Calumet on the north, the Michigan Central on the south, and the eastern boundary was what is now Hohman Avenue.[13]

Construction of the plant was started immediately after the acquisition of the site. An icehouse and a boarding-house were also erected. The men engaged in the construction work were crowded into the small houses of the few resident farmers and at the Hohman Inn. The building material was unloaded at the plant site from the Michigan Central although its official destination was Gibson Station, about two miles away. For some years the packing house was called the State Line Slaughter-House. By the late fall of 1869 it was a going concern with regular shipments of beef being made to the eastern markets.[14]

There was much opposition to the shipment and use of dressed beef in the early years of the industry. The railroads refused to build refrigerator cars for use by the

[11] Cannon, Loring and Robb (eds.), *History of the Lake and Calumet Region,* 1:727-29; Clemen, *George H. Hammond,* 15.

[12] See Lake County Deed Records, 12:195; 17:411; 18:412, for these purchases.

[13] By 1900 the packing-house area had expanded across the state line into Illinois.

[14] Howat (ed.), *A Standard History of Lake County,* 1:291; Clemen, *George H. Hammond,* 16.

packers and in some instances charged them excessive rates to transport their products. The carriers, having a large amount of capital tied up in livestock cars, loading docks, and feeding stations, were reluctant to invest money in refrigerator cars. As a result, the packers were compelled to build and operate their own cars. In 1885 the George H. Hammond Company owned at least eight hundred cars, three hundred of which were refrigerator cars.[15]

The consuming public in the eastern states had the idea that refrigerated beef from the West was inferior to the local product. People would apologize to guests for serving western dressed beef, and explain that the local butcher was all out of city-dressed beef. The local butchers, whose profits from the handling of the whole slaughtering process were larger than from the sale of predressed beef, helped fan this prejudice for years. They also hinted that western beef was unhealthy. The Wholesale Butchers' Union of New York charged in 1883 that western dressed beef was poisoned with ammonia. In time people came to realize that beef should be chilled and kept awhile before it was eaten, and by the time the meat was transported for four or five days from the Chicago area to the East, it was ripe for eating. Western dressed beef was also from one to two cents a pound cheaper than locally dressed beef at the peak of this era of prejudice. The public could not long resist this economy.[16]

The State Line Slaughter-House prospered despite the early opposition to its product. The firm began opera-

[15] Louis F. Swift, *The Yankee of the Yards. The Biography of Gustavus F. Swift* (New York, 1927), 187-88; Clemen, *George H. Hammond*, 16, 18.

[16] Rudolf A. Clemen, *The American Livestock and Meat Industry* (New York, 1923), 242.

tions with little capital and only eighteen employees, and yet it shipped three or more cars of beef each day to Boston during the first months of its existence. Thomas Hammond joined his brother in 1872 and managed the department that made sausage casings and tripe out of the entrails and stomach linings of cattle. It was he, according to reports, who first demonstrated that tripe could be marketed on a commercial scale. When George W. Plumer died in 1874, the firm was reorganized as George H. Hammond and Company, with George H. Hammond as president and Marcus M. Towle as vice-president. At that time its capital was increased to $2,500,000.[17]

The Hammond Company was also among the pioneers in the exportation of dressed beef to foreign countries. In April, 1879, a shipment of meat from the Indiana plant arrived in Liverpool in good condition.[18] Hammond also operated a meat establishment in Detroit and a large slaughterhouse in Omaha, Nebraska. In 1890, four years after George H. Hammond's death, the company passed into the hands of English interests, and its name was changed to G. H. Hammond and Company.[19] It was recapitalized for $6,400,000 and the size of the plant in Hammond increased. In 1891 the plant, according to reports, employed 1,000 workers and had an annual slaughtering capacity of 300,000 cattle, 25,000

[17] Ball, *Encyclopedia of Genealogy and Biography,* 31, 307; Howat (ed.), *A Standard History of Lake County,* 2:554-55; Clemen, *George H. Hammond,* 16.

[18] Clemen, *George H. Hammond,* 19.

[19] Alexander Harvey of New York City negotiated the purchase of George H. Hammond and Company on April 24, 1890, for "ten dollars and other valuable considerations." Harvey, who was apparently the representative of the English interests, "sold" the property to G. H. Hammond and Company on the same day. See Lake County Deed Records, 47:456-61, for more details of this transaction.

sheep, and 10,000 hogs. It also manufactured butterine, now called oleomargarine. The *Hammond City Directory* in 1891 boasted that the local slaughterhouse was "the greatest single dressed beef plant in the world."[20] In stockyard language, at that time, the "Big Four" usually meant Armour, Swift, Morris, and Hammond.[21]

George H. Hammond died in 1886 at the age of forty-eight, reputedly of hard work. According to his own statements, he spent over two hundred nights a year on Pullman cars, and in the last years of his life found it impossible to get a good night's rest in an ordinary bed. Hammond was devoted to Detroit, where he lived with his family and owned considerable real estate. He founded the Museum of Art in Detroit and also built a church near his residence. He was never interested in the development of the Indiana city which bore his name, nor did he ever demonstrate any concern about the welfare of its people. His biographer thought that part of the capital he always put into the expansion of his plants could have been better spent improving the social conditions and the standard of health of his employees.[22]

The Founding of Hammond

The State Line Slaughter-House, located in a wilderness, was for years virtually isolated from the world outside. The roads which led through the deep sand and swamps to Chicago and Crown Point could be traversed successfully only by horsemen and light vehicles, and were generally impassable in wet weather. There was, of course, the Grand Calumet River, but it was navigable

---

[20] Frank E. Geros, *Hammond City Directory, 1891-1892* (Hammond, 1891), 20.

[21] Leech and Carroll, *Armour and His Times*, 109.

[22] Clemen, *George H. Hammond*, 20.

only for small boats.[23] Lake Michigan was only four
or five miles away, but as far as any contact between it
and the slaughterhouse community was concerned, the
distance separating the two might as well have been a
hundred miles. According to Timothy H. Ball: "Hammond seemed far away from any Christian civilization
in 1870. For a footman on a cloudy day to have undertaken to cross, then, from the slaughter house to the
little station called Whiting on the Michigan Southern
road, would have been very risky. The distance in a
straight line is about five miles; but the swampy underbrush then was well called impenetrable. This writer
tried crossing there once, years after 1870. He failed,
and he has been in many a wild."[24] For some years, the
Michigan Central Railroad provided the only satisfactory
connection with the East and with the Chicago area only
a few miles to the west.

Nor was the village an attractive place for the workers
in the slaughterhouse to live. Modern packing-house
methods were unknown at that time and great piles of
bones accumulated at the plant. Rough sheds were built
along the railroad tracks, filled with skulls and horns,
and throwing off a stench which was nauseating to persons
not accustomed to it. When the wind was from the
wrong direction, those in its path found the odors almost
unbearable. Some of the employees maintained homes in
Chicago and resided at the company's boardinghouses,
visiting their families whenever it was possible. For a
time George H. Hammond insisted on his employees
working seven days a week; time off had to be taken at
their own expense.[25] These conditions, and the demand

[23] "Examination and Survey of the Mouth of Grand Calumet River,
Indiana," 1872, in *Senate Documents*, 42 Congress, 3 session, No. 25,
pp. 7-9.

[24] Ball, *Encyclopedia of Genealogy and Biography*, 32.

[25] Ball (ed.), *Lake County, Indiana, 1884*, 464.

for butchers in Chicago, made it difficult for the company to attract and retain skilled workers.

Despite such handicaps, many people made their permanent homes there and the population of the community grew steadily. The first effort to establish a town was made by William Swinburn, a Chicago speculator. In May, 1870, he filed the plat of the "Town of Hohman" at the county recorder's office at Crown Point. The proposed town lay south of the Michigan Central tracks and included what is now the business section of Hammond west of Hohman Avenue and south to the location of the present Russell Street. The east and west streets were named William, Warren, Green, and John, and those running north and south were called Calumet, First, Second, Third, and Fourth. The eastern boundary of the town was what Swinburn called Calumet Avenue and the western limit was the Indiana-Illinois line.[26] This proved to be another "dream city" as no evidence has been found that it was developed beyond the platting stage.

Marcus M. Towle was the founder of Hammond. From the very beginning, he sank his roots deep into the community and took an active interest in its development. Unlike George H. Hammond, who preferred Detroit as his place of residence, Towle established his home near the slaughterhouse. He and his wife operated one of the company's boardinghouses until their home was built. In 1884 Timothy H. Ball thought the Towle residence, with its greenhouse and beautiful lawn, was the finest and most imposing home in the city.[27]

26 Miscellaneous Records, A:546-47, in Lake County Recorder's Office, Crown Point. "Calumet Avenue" in Swinburn's plat should not be confused with Hammond's present street by that name.

27 Howat (ed.), *A Standard History of Lake County,* 1:292; Ball (ed.), *Lake County, Indiana, 1884,* 464.

Towle and George H. Hammond differed sharply as to the permanency of the slaughterhouse as well as to the building of a town. Hammond reasoned that it might be necessary ultimately to move the plant farther west to be closer to the growing center of the cattle business. Also, in bargaining with the Michigan Central, their only railroad outlet at that time, for advantageous rates and better service, Hammond wanted to hold the threat that the firm could always pick up and build a new plant elsewhere. The construction of houses for their workers, which would logically lead to the incorporation of the community, might indicate the permanency of the plant to the railroad, thereby weakening the company's bargaining powers. Towle, on the other hand, insisted the company owed something to its employees in the way of better living conditions. He also pointed out that if adequate housing was provided for the employees and if law and order were assured by the incorporation of the community, there would be no shortage of workers in the future. George W. Plumer supported Towle in his argument with Hammond.[28] Despite Hammond's opposition, Towle went on with his plans to build a town.

Towle was the first postmaster at State Line, a position he held for sixteen years. He also established the first store there. As there was a town with the name of State Line in Illinois, difficulty was often experienced in getting mail. In 1873 Towle persuaded the postal authorities to change the name of the office in the slaughterhouse community to Hammond, in honor of George H. Hammond.[29] In 1875 Towle purchased land from Caroline Hohman and from other residents and platted the

[28] Hammond *Times,* June 17, 1951, p. 2A; Howat (ed.), *A Standard History of Lake County,* 1:293.

[29] Cannon, Loring and Robb (eds.), *History of the Lake and Calumet Region,* 1:725-27.

town of Hammond. In 1880 the Federal census, which took notice of the place for the first time, reported 699 residents in the area. By 1890 there were 5,428.[30] There was no municipal government in the community for almost fourteen years after the slaughterhouse was established. It had to depend on the county sheriff for the maintenance of law and order, and because of the distance involved and the difficulty encountered in reaching the place, that official paid little attention to its welfare. As a result, the conditions and atmosphere so typical of the frontier towns of the Old West prevailed in the vicinity of the plant. In 1882 the editor of the *Lake County Star* found it "a lively town, full of business and progressing nicely. The town needs a government. It should be incorporated. Strangers from the rural districts do not like to see men dragged out and knocked down and pounded within an inch of their lives by bullies of the corner. A free fight, and nobody to interfere on the side of law and order."[31] The community was incorporated in 1883. It became a city the following year with Towle as mayor. He headed the city's administration until 1888.[32]

Towle sold lots to the packing-house employees at reasonable prices. He also furnished the lumber and in many instances the money to build the houses. The loans were repaid with payments taken from the workers' earnings at the slaughterhouse. Towle built a dock on the north side of the Grand Calumet and opened a lumber yard, the lumber being brought on barges from South Chicago. The great demand for houses led to the estab-

[30] U. S. Bureau of the Census, *Eleventh Census* (1890): *Population*, pt. 1:123.

[31] Crown Point *Lake County Star*, September 1, 1882.

[32] Lake County Deed Records, 21:266; 22:1, 116; 25:286; Howat (ed.), *A Standard History of Lake County*, 1:293-94, 336, 338.

lishment of a sawmill, a planing mill, and a sash, door, and blind factory. In 1884 Towle severed his connection with the packing company and devoted his time to the development of the city.[33]

The German Influence

Hammond was a German community from the very beginning of its existence. As the Germans were recognized as expert butchers and sausage makers, many found employment at the packing house. Others engaged in various types of business. The Federal census of 1910, the first to analyze the city's population, showed that almost 30 per cent of its people were born in Germany or Austria or their parents were natives of those countries.[34] This proportion was undoubtedly greater in the earlier years.

The skilled butcher was the aristocrat among the workers at the packing house. He was said to have been usually a large man and the picture of health and well-being. Tales of his strength, skill, and habits are legendary. We are told he often drank beef blood from the healthiest animals. His badge of office was a leather apron with which he kept the blood off his clothes. In this apron was a scabbard for his butcher knives which he never allowed out of his sight. The event of each year was the butchers' picnic at Drackert's Grove, the most spectacular part of the program being the contest to determine the most skillful butcher at the packing house. A dead steer was hung from a scaffold for each

[33] Howat (ed.), *op. cit.*, 1:294; Ball, *Encyclopedia of Genealogy and Biography,* 307.

[34] In 1910 there were 6,172 residents who were of German and Austrian extraction. Hammond's population in that year was 20,925. See U. S. Bureau of the Census, *Thirteenth Census* (1910): *Population,* pt. 2:531.

contestant to skin, dress, and split the carcass. The honors went to the one to complete the task in the shortest time. The splitting of the carcass into halves was the crowning moment for each contestant, a feat accomplished with such a demonstration of strength and accuracy as to elicit cries of admiration from the crowd of onlookers.[35]

In 1895 the highest wage for a ten-hour day at the packing house was $4.00 for skilled workers and $1.50 for the unskilled. Boys earned 90 cents and women 80 cents for a day's work. In that year about 1,500 workers were employed at the plant.[36] Women were largely used in the manufacture and packing of butterine.[37]

Hammond's large German element was reflected in other ways during the early years. Of the three churches in the city in 1885, two were established by Germans. According to reports, the first Christian service in the community was conducted in 1871 at the residence of Jacob Rimbach by the Reverend Herman Wunderlich, founder and pastor of St. John's Lutheran Church in Tolleston. Reverend Wunderlich also ministered to the spiritual needs of the German Lutheran population of Hessville at that time. In 1882 St. Paul's Evangelical Lutheran Church was organized. Its first building, located on a lot donated by Marcus M. Towle, was dedicated the following year. The earliest Catholic services were held in the late 1870's at the home of John L. Knoerzer. In 1879 St. Joseph's Catholic Church, for

[35] Hammond *Times,* June 17, 1951, p. 14A.

[36] Indiana Department of Statistics, *Sixth Biennial Report,* 1895-96, p. 128.

[37] Valparaiso *Messenger,* October 17, 1893. The *Messenger* of November 24, 1893, reported a daily production of 40,000 pounds of butterine at the Hammond plant.

many years the largest Catholic church in the region, was organized by the German Catholics of the city. A parochial school was started in 1885 at St. Joseph's.[38]

Because of the large German population, there were no customers for English language newspapers until the second generation of Hammond's population matured.[39] German language newspapers published in Chicago and Milwaukee found many subscribers in the city. One of the most widely distributed papers in the community in 1891 was the *Deutsche Volks Zeitung,* a German weekly published in Hammond.[40] In 1906 the Citizens German National Bank was incorporated and soon had deposits of over $1,000,000.[41] In 1914 there were nine German cultural and singing societies in Hammond and in the same year the local chapter of the National German-American Alliance had 1,200 members enrolled.[42]

The outbreak of World War I in 1914 focused the attention of the region upon Hammond's German-American citizens. In the main, their attitude toward the war was one of sympathy for the homeland. The local branch of the National German-American Alliance met in Roth's Hall and, while making it clear that its members were loyal American citizens, adopted a resolution appealing to the American sense of fair play to accord the German cause unbiased consideration. The Alliance also pledged the funds of the organization to the German Red Cross.[43]

38 Howat (ed.), *A Standard History of Lake County,* 1:361-62, 363-64; Cannon, Loring and Robb (eds.), *History of the Lake and Calumet Region,* 1:491. Methodist services were held in Hammond as early as 1872, and a church was organized in 1881. Marcus M. Towle was active in the organization and gave the site for the erection of a church building. Howat (ed.), *op. cit.,* 1:362-63.

39 Hammond *Times,* June 17, 1951, p. 2C.

40 Geros, *Hammond City Directory, 1891-1892,* 23.

41 Howat (ed.), *A Standard History of Lake County,* 1:330.

42 Hammond *Lake County Times,* May 14, 1914.

43 *Ibid.,* August 14, 1914.

Hammond's *Lake County Times,* fearing a clash between the German-Americans and the citizens of Slavic origin whose countries were then at war with Germany, pled for the exercise of sanity and restraint: "There is altogether too much readiness on the part of citizens of this country who are of foreign birth to quarrel over the causes of conflict and to air their personal and private feelings as they take sides in the controversy. Let us tend to our knitting."[44]

On August 29, 1914, the Indiana State Convention of the National German-American Alliance met in Hammond. Fearing serious trouble, Mayor John D. Smalley appealed to all citizens to extend a warm welcome to the visitors. The *Lake County Times* printed the program of the convention and much of its first page in German. Several local business houses had their advertisements in the newspaper also printed in German. The principal feature of the convention was a picnic at Kendel's Grove which was attended by about five thousand people. At this gathering "Die Wacht am Rhein" and the "Star Spangled Banner" were sung. Mayor Smalley later congratulated the citizens that not a single fight over war issues was recorded by the police. Hammond, he declared, was a neutral city.[45]

Nevertheless, a large segment of Hammond's Germans took an active interest in their homeland's cause for some months. In February, 1915, a German-Irish meeting appealed to Congress to prohibit shipments of war materials to the warring powers in Europe.[46] As Germany was unable to obtain supplies from the United States and whereas the Allies were doing so, such action by our government would have weakened Germany's opponents

44 *Ibid.,* August 17, 1914.
45 *Ibid.,* August 27, September 1, 23, 1914.
46 *Ibid.,* February 3, 1915.

in the war. However, after the United States entered
the war in 1917, available evidence indicates that Hammond's German-American citizens were loyal to their
adopted country.[47]

Early Industrial Development

James N. Young, protégé and associate of Marcus
M. Towle, played an important part in the early industrial development of the city. Young came to the
region as a telegraph operator at Gibson Station. Impressed by the abundance of wild game in the vicinity,
he conceived the idea of shipping wild ducks to the eastern market in the extra space available in the Hammond
Company's refrigerator cars after they were loaded with
meat, and used the profits from this venture to attend
law school in Chicago. Towle, impressed by the young
man's initiative, persuaded him to abandon the law and
join his real estate organization. Although Young apparently never actually resided in Hammond, the city
owes much to his genius. Four brothers of Towle were
also prominent in the community. Carrol N. Towle was
associated with him in the construction business; Edward
E. Towle operated a meat market; Amos G. Towle was
a foreman at the packing house; and Porter B. Towle
operated a printing firm.[48]

In 1874, J. M. Hirsh, a German, established a small
albumin factory near the old Hohman Street bridge over
the Grand Calumet River. This in time became the
Hirsh, Stein & Company's glue and fertilizer factory.

---

[47] A study of the Hammond papers during the war indicated no
pro-German activities among the city's German-American citizens.

[48] Myrtelle Huehn, "Incidents in Early History of Hammond," in
Demmon (ed.), *History of Lake County* (1934), 59; Howat (ed.),
A Standard History of Lake County, 1:297-98; Goodspeed and Blanchard
(eds.), *Counties of Porter and Lake,* 539.

In 1915 it employed about four hundred men and was reported to produce 5 per cent of the glue used in the United States. The name of the plant was later changed to the United Chemical and Organic Products Company. In 1880 Towle and Young induced William and Frank Tuthill to build the Tuthill Spring Works for the manufacture of wagon and carriage springs. Towle and Young later acquired a half interest in this factory. In 1882 Towle and William H. Gostlin, the latter a Canadian, established the Hammond Corn Syrup Works. The Chicago Steel Company, organized in 1886, was one of Towle's unfortunate investments. This plant, which included a foundry and a nail factory, began production in 1887 but shut down about six months later. In 1890 the Lakeside Nail Company, organized by financial interests from Cleveland, Ohio, acquired Towle's interest in the Chicago Steel Company. The Lakeside plant, which manufactured nails from old steel rails, was employing 250 men and producing 1,000 kegs of nails a day in 1891. This plant, destroyed by fire in 1904, was later reorganized as the Chicago Steel Manufacturing Company. As such, it made nails, shovels, scoops, horeshoes, and steel posts. In 1909 about 250 men were employed at this plant.[49]

Towle and Young financed and built the Chicago and Calumet Terminal Railroad, the second of the belt-line roads in the region. This road, which began operations in 1888, lay inside the circuit of the Elgin, Joliet and Eastern belt line, and at that time more nearly encircled Chicago than did any road of that type. The Chicago and Calumet Terminal provided rail connections between

[49] Huehn, *op. cit.*, 59; Howat (ed.), *op. cit.*, 1:296, 298; Geros, *Hammond City Directory, 1891-1892*, 21, 22; Goodspeed and Blanchard (eds.), *Counties of Porter and Lake*, 541; *Lake County Directory*, 1909, p. 67.

Hammond's industries and the trunk-line railroads in the Chicago area. In 1889 Towle and Young sold the road to interests headed by Gen. Joseph T. Torrence, one of the founders of East Chicago.[50]

One of Marcus M. Towle's most solid contributions to the city's economic life was the organization in 1886 of the First National Bank. This was the only bank in the city for several years. Towle's other ventures included the Hammond Buggy Company, the Chicago Carriage Works, the Kingsley Foundry, two distilleries, and two flour mills. In 1903 he opened the Towle Opera House to the public. This building, located on Hohman Avenue near Sibley Street, was for some years Hammond's center of entertainment. In the years before his death in 1910, a large floral business was Towle's chief interest.[51]

The role of Thomas Hammond, brother of George H. Hammond, in the early development of the city was second only to that of Towle. In 1886 Thomas Hammond left the packing-house business to devote his time to the economic and political affairs of the city. He was a resident of the community for thirty-five years and was for a time its leading banker and one of its wealthiest men. Hammond defeated Marcus M. Towle for mayor in 1888, was re-elected in 1890, and again in 1892. He resigned as mayor in 1893 following his election to Congress where he served one term. Hammond organized the Commercial Bank of Hammond in 1892 and was its president for sixteen years. As president of the Hammond Land and Improvement Company, he was instru-

50 East Chicago *Journal,* October 15, 1889; Howat (ed.), *A Standard History of Lake County,* 1:296; 2:504.

51 Howat (ed.), *op. cit.,* 2:504; Cannon, Loring and Robb (eds.), *History of the Lake and Calumet Region,* 1:729, 797; Ball, *Encyclopedia of Genealogy and Biography,* 307.

mental in bringing the W. B. Conkey Printing Company and other industries to the city. Hammond was given the name of "Honest Tom" while in Congress, a title he bore until his death in 1909.[52]

By 1893 Hammond was in need of a more adequate source of water than its artesian wells. Gostlin Street being its northern boundary at that time, the city had no frontage on Lake Michigan. To obtain access to the Lake, civic leaders decided to annex the narrow strip of land between Whiting and the Indiana-Illinois State Line. This move was vigorously opposed by the Forsythe family and by other owners of land in that area. In 1897, after four years of litigation in the Indiana and Federal courts, the United States Supreme Court ruled in favor of Hammond.[53] This victory gave the city a frontage on Lake Michigan of about one and one half miles and also the communities of Roby and Robertsdale.

Hammond was handicapped in its development by the lack of a navigable river and a harbor on Lake Michigan. In the early years, citizens believed the solution to the problem of cheap transportation lay in the improvement of the Grand Calumet River for use by ships that plied the Great Lakes. In 1870 the Federal government began the development of the Calumet Harbor at the mouth of the Calumet River in South Chicago. As this river was formed by the junction of the Grand Calumet and Little Calumet rivers about three miles west of Hammond, the Federal government was urged to make the Grand Calumet navigable for lake boats, at least as far inland as Hammond.

52 Howat (ed.), *op. cit.,* 1:297; Thomas Hammond, Brief History of the City of Hammond (manuscript found in the cornerstone of the Hammond Central High School built in 1893, and now in the cornerstone of the Hammond Technical High School).

53 Whiting *Sun,* March 6, 1897; *Calumet Region Historical Guide,* 203-4.

In 1872 United States army engineers surveyed the Grand Calumet, but opposed the dredging of the stream because of its low banks and adjacent marshes.[54] Nevertheless, in 1888 Congress appropriated funds to improve the river to a point one-half mile east of Hammond. Subsequently, a channel sixty feet wide and ten feet deep was partially dredged. Because of the sluggish current and the dumping of refuse from the packing house and sewage from Hammond into the river, its channel filled up rapidly. Dredging was discontinued in 1895.[55]

Construction of the Indiana Harbor Ship Canal early in the present century brought a recommendation from the army engineers in 1915 that the Grand Calumet be improved to its junction with the ship canal a short distance east of Hammond. This proposal was contingent upon the donation of the land along the river for the construction of a channel two hundred feet wide.[56] Since no reference to the project was found in subsequent reports of the War Department, Congress apparently did not look with favor upon the engineers' recommendation. As late as 1928 Hammond was warned that unless the Grand Calumet was made navigable, new industries would locate along the Indiana Ship Canal in East Chicago.[57]

At the turn of the present century, Indiana's only harbor on Lake Michigan was at Michigan City. When Hammond's foothold on the Lake was assured, plans

[54] "Examination and Survey of the Mouth of Grand Calumet River, Indiana," 1872, in *Senate Documents,* 42 Congress, 3 session, No. 25, pp. 7-9.

[55] "Calumet River, Ill.," in letter from the Secretary of War, 1916, in *House Documents,* 64 Congress, 1 session, No. 470, p. 5.

[56] *Ibid.,* 1-7.

[57] Hammond *Lake County Times,* July 12, 1928.

were made to build a harbor and to convert the region
in that vicinity into an industrial area. The guiding
force behind this project was Armanis F. Knotts, a
Hammond attorney. Knotts's plan called for the dredging of a channel along the course of the tiny Wolf River
to Wolf Lake, a short distance to the south. Wolf Lake,
he insisted, could be converted into a harbor large enough
to accommodate all the shipping on the Great Lakes.
As it would be an inland harbor, claims were made that
its maintenance cost would be less than that necessary
to keep the outer harbors at the mouths of the Calumet
and Chicago rivers in a navigable condition. Knotts
also pointed out that the Chicago and Calumet harbors
must be entered from the east and, in times of storms and
rough weather on the Lake, pilots found it difficult and
often hazardous to bring their ships into these ports.
As the proposed Wolf Lake harbor would be entered
from the north, ships could reach their docks with ease
and safety. In 1896 Knotts, known at that time as "Harbor Knotts" because of his enthusiasm for the project,
headed a delegation of Hammond's citizens to Washington to seek Federal aid for the building of the harbor.[58]
Had their mission been a success, Hammond might have
shared in the expansion of the steel industry which was
soon to affect East Chicago and which also built the city
of Gary a few years later.

Despite the lack of a harbor or a navigable river,
Hammond grew in population and industrial importance.
Its population increased from 5,428 in 1890 to 12,376
in 1900.[59] The city council sought to attract "bonus"
industries with an ordinance that permitted factories

[58] Howat (ed.), *A Standard History of Lake County,* 1:238; Chesterton *Tribune,* February 21, 1896.

[59] U. S. Bureau of the Census, *Twelfth Census* (1900): *Population,*
pt. 1:139.

locating there to be tax free for five years and have water at extremely low rates.[60] In 1898 the W. B. Conkey Printing and Bookbinding Company, considered the largest of its kind in the nation, moved its plant to the city from Chicago. Although it is not clear what inducements, other than those offered by the city, were given to the printing company, it was in a sense a "bonus" industry. The Hammond Land and Improvement Company, headed by Thomas Hammond, was reported to have presented $75,000.00 in cash and 80 acres of land to the firm. According to another version, a Chicago realty company donated ten acres for the site of the plant and also sold seventy acres to the Conkey people at a nominal price. The Printing Company employed about one thousand workers when it was put into operation. In 1909 there were two thousand employees at the establishment. Also in 1898, the Simplex Railway Appliance Company located its factory on the north bank of the Grand Calumet near the Hohman Street bridge. This company was merged with the American Steel Foundries in 1905.[61] The railway appliance company made such a solid contribution to Hammond's economy that many of the citizens, even to this day, refer to the American Steel Foundries' establishment as the "Simplex" plant.

The County Seat War

In the early years the industrial development of the northern part of Lake County was concentrated largely in North Township, where the cities of Hammond, East

---

60 Chesterton *Tribune,* July 17, 1897.

61 Whiting *Sun,* February 12, 1898; Howat (ed.), *op. cit.,* 1:298-99; *Lake County Directory,* 1909, pp. 62, 67; Franklin M. Reck, *Sand in Their Shoes. The Story of American Steel Foundries* (Chicago, 1952), 19-20.

Chicago, and Whiting are located. The great increase in the population of this township created legal and political problems which vexed the people of the county for many years. Crown Point, the county seat, located in almost the exact center of the county, was, for several decades, also near the center of the county's population. In 1870 only about 13 per cent of the county's population of 12,339 lived in North Township. By 1890 North Township had 40 per cent of the county's 23,886 residents within its borders. At the close of the century Lake County's population had soared to 37,892, and of this number, 21,020, or about 58 per cent of the county's total, were inhabitants of North Township.[62]

As the population of North Township increased, the volume of legal and political business transacted by its citizens at Crown Point increased in proportion. The distance between the cities and towns of North Township and Crown Point was such that much time and money were spent by those attending court or doing business with the various county offices. Railroad connections were so poor that at least a day was consumed in making the round trip. Although the maximum distance from any point in the county to the county seat did not exceed twenty miles, travel by horseback or in carriages was so slow that the trip generally took two days. To make matters worse, the dirt roads were often impassable in wet weather and in the winter time. Also, for those who made frequent trips, or whose business necessitated a prolonged stay in Crown Point, there was the expense for meals and lodging in the hotels or boardinghouses.

As far as the citizens of North Township were concerned, the logical solution to the problem was to have

[62] *Ninth Census* (1870): *Population*, 126; *Eleventh Census* (1890): *Population*, pt. 1:123; *Twelfth Census* (1900): *Population*, pt. 1:139.

the county seat moved to Hammond, at that time the largest city in the county. In the winter of 1890 and 1891 a determined effort was made by Hammond's citizens to get a bill through the General Assembly which would lead to the removal of the county government to their city. Michigan City, whose problems in regard to La Porte, the county seat of La Porte County, were the same as those of North Township, supported Hammond in the matter. Their efforts proved futile as the inhabitants of Crown Point and southern Lake County, aided by La Porte's citizens, were able to prevent the passage of the bill.[63]

Hammond's effort to obtain the county seat focused the attention of the General Assembly on the needs of North Township and Michigan City. Since 1873 Lake and Porter counties and for a time Starke and Pulaski, had constituted the Thirty-first Judicial District of the State, the Circuit Court of which held its sessions in Crown Point and in Valparaiso. This arrangement was inconvenient for the citizens in the northern halves of Lake and Porter counties. Also, the increase of population in both counties placed a burden on the Circuit Court greater than it could bear with any degree of efficiency. In 1895 the General Assembly created a Superior Court for Lake, Porter, and La Porte counties with one judge. As the sessions of the court were to be held in towns and cities of over 4,000 population, in addition to the county seats, Hammond and Michigan City, were each provided with a court. Although in the beginning the Superior Court's jurisdiction was limited,

---

[63] Ball, *Encyclopedia of Genealogy and Biography,* 39; Howat (ed.), *A Standard History of Lake County,* 1:110. The Journals of the General Assembly reveal that there were two or three bills introduced in the 1891 session regarding relocation of county seats. They were lost before final passage and their provisions are not known.

in 1897 the General Assembly gave it equal jurisdiction with the Circuit Court.[64]

In 1903 a compromise between the northern and southern parts of Lake County in regard to the location of the county seat was reached by the erection of a courthouse in Hammond. This building housed the Superior Court, a law library, offices of the sheriff, clerk, recorder, and other county officials.[65] The county government and its services were thus brought to the industrial region near the shore of Lake Michigan, although the county seat remained at Crown Point.

In 1907 the rapid industrial development of the area adjacent to the Lake influenced the General Assembly to establish Lake County as a separate judicial district of the Superior Court, with its sessions to be held in Hammond. The city was still the largest in the region and the possession of the only Superior Court in the county further enhanced its prestige. In 1911 Hammond's light was slightly dimmed when the General Assembly added two divisions to the Superior Court, designated as Rooms 2 and 3, each with a judge. At first, Room 1 and Room 2 held their sessions in Hammond while Room 3 divided its sessions between Hammond and Crown Point. In 1909 the bustling young city of Gary demanded one of Hammond's Superior Courts. Hammond thwarted Gary's desires with stubbornness and determination. Finally, in 1917, the General Assembly transferred Room 3 to Gary. In 1927 the Assembly completely reorganized the county's superior court system. Rooms 1 and 5 were allocated to Hammond,

[64] Johannes Kopelke, "The Bench and Bar of Lake County" and Harry B. Tuthill, "The Bench and Bar of La Porte County," in Cannon, Loring and Robb (eds.), *History of the Lake and Calumet Region,* 1:402, 404, 431.

[65] Howat (ed.), *op. cit.,* 1:110.

Rooms 3 and 4 to Gary, and Room 2 held its sessions in East Chicago. Hammond remained the "county seat" of the industrial half of the county until 1929 when county offices were also established in the new Gateway Courthouse in Gary.[66]

Local and Interurban Transportation

The development of Hammond's street railway system began as early as 1892. In that year the Hammond Electric Railway Company was given a franchise to operate an electric railway over a two-mile route on Hohman Avenue, the city's main thoroughfare. The company was permitted to use animal power only if the electric cars broke down and then for only thirty days. In 1893 the franchise was sold to the Hammond, Whiting, and East Chicago Railway Company.[67] As these cities were separated from each other only by their boundary lines, the new company proceeded to connect them with a system of street railways. Hammond being the largest city in North Township, and as the county offices and the Superior Court were in time located there, the street railways were a great convenience to the area's citizens. Hammond's merchants also benefited as the people of East Chicago and Whiting found it easy to shop in their more elaborate and better-stocked stores. As a result, Hammond's business district expanded, while those of East Chicago and Whiting remained far below the standard their populations would have justified had

[66] *Laws of Indiana*, 1907, p. 170; 1911, pp. 34-36; 1917, pp. 34-35; 1927, pp. 5-9; Kopelke, "Bench and Bar of Lake County," in Cannon, Loring and Robb (eds.), *History of the Lake and Calumet Region*, 1:405-6; Gary *Weekly Tribune*, January 1, 1909; Gary *Daily Tribune*, February 9, 1917; *Calumet Region Historical Guide*, 183-84.

[67] *Calumet Region Historical Guide*, 79; Howat (ed.), *A Standard History of Lake County*, 1:281.

the transportation facilities been different. By 1895 the electric streetcars were running between the three cities. In 1904 the first interurban line from Hammond to the Indiana Harbor section of East Chicago was opened for public use. Until this street railway was built, Indiana Harbor was accessible only by way of the trunk-line railroads.[68]

While Hammond was connected with Chicago by several trunk-line railroads, the local service provided by these lines was not satisfactory. The trunk-line stations were not conveniently located for the region's population and there were few trains that catered to the commuting trade. In 1895 the local street railway company laid a track to the Indiana-Illinois line at Roby, whence passengers reached Chicago over street railways operating under Illinois franchises. This arrangement was said to have provided the first easy contact between the Calumet Region and Chicago.[69]

The region's cities were brought closer to Chicago by the construction of what is now the Chicago, South Shore and South Bend Railroad, popularly known as the "South Shore." The plan, which called for a high-speed electric line between Chicago and South Bend, Indiana, originated with Samuel Insull. In 1901 Insull incorporated the Chicago and Indiana Airline Railway Company, but financial difficulties delayed the construction of the road for several years. As the Chicago, Lake Shore and South Bend, it reached Hammond from South Bend by way of Gary and East Chicago in 1908. Because the Insull company had difficulty obtaining a right of way into Chicago, arrangements were made with the Illinois

[68] *Calumet Region Historical Guide,* 79; Howat (ed.), *op. cit.,* 1:281.
[69] *Calumet Region Historical Guide,* 79; Ball, *Encyclopedia of Genealogy and Biography,* 41.

Central for its steam engines to bring the electric trains from the State Line to Kensington. From there the passengers took the Illinois Central suburban trains for the remainder of the trip to downtown Chicago. This service was started in July, 1908. In 1911 the cars were attached to the Illinois Central trains at Pullman for what was called the "direct run" to Chicago's Randolph Street. A short time later, the Chicago, Lake Shore and South Bend obtained the right to run its trains over the Illinois Central tracks all the way to Randolph Street.[70]

Insull's electric line and the automobile brought the entire Calumet Region well within the economic and cultural orbit of Chicago. The "South Shore" not only stressed speed but its trains were scheduled at half-hour intervals between Gary and Chicago during the hours of the day when travel was the heaviest and at one hour intervals in the late evenings when travel was light. Its trains made the trip from Hammond to downtown Chicago in about thirty minutes and from Gary the running time was seldom more than forty-five minutes. Because of this excellent service, many residents of the region found it convenient to work in Chicago. In turn, numerous Chicagoans established homes in their city's Indiana suburbs. On the negative side, Chicago siphoned business from the region's cities, thereby adversely affecting the character of their retail stores, newspapers, theaters, and places of amusement. As a result, the municipalities of the Calumet Region became in a sense the satellites of the great city which lay just across the state line.

[70] Glen A. Blackburn. "Interurban Railroads of Indiana" in *Indiana Magazine of History,* 20(1924):420-21; Hammond *Lake County Times,* July 11, 1908; Gary *Evening Post,* June 10, 1911; Cannon, Loring and Robb (eds.), *History of the Lake and Calumet Region,* 1:677.

Later Industrial Development

In the late afternoon of October 23, 1901, a great fire swept through the buildings of the G. H. Hammond meat-packing plant. Despite the combined efforts of the local fire departments and a fire company from South Chicago, whose men and equipment were rushed to the scene by railroad, the frame structures burned like tinder. About four acres of buildings were destroyed and damages to the plant were estimated at $500,000.00. At the time of the disaster, the packing house had an annual slaughtering capacity of 400,000 cattle, 500,000 sheep, and 850,000 hogs. It was also producing 5,000,000 pounds of butterine each year. About 1,800 workers were employed at the plant at the time of the fire.[71] The owners of the company made no efforts to replace the destroyed buildings. Hundreds of workers lost their jobs and the city was faced with a serious economic crisis.

J. Ogden Armour purchased the holdings of the G. H. Hammond and Company throughout the country in February, 1903, thereby extinguishing the name of Hammond as one of the "Big Four" of the packing industry. Armour intended for the Hammond Company to be the nucleus of the National Packing Company which he organized in conjunction with Gustavus F. Swift and Edward Morris.[72] The plan called for the National Packing Company to quietly absorb the small packers, after which Armour, Swift, and Morris were to unite to

[71] Howat (ed.), *A Standard History of Lake County,* 1:297; Hammond *Times,* June 17, 1951, p. 3A; Chicago *Daily Tribune,* October 24, 1901. According to the *Tribune,* a jurisdictional dispute between the chief of the Hammond Fire Department and the captain of the Chicago company delayed the fighting of the fire.

[72] Everett Wilson, manager of Armour and Company's branch offices, negotiated the purchase of the Hammond property of G. H. Hammond and Company, February 6, 1903, for J. Ogden Armour. The price was "one dollar and other valuable considerations." Wilson "sold" the Ham-

form a gigantic meat trust.[73] Unfortunately for the success of their plans, President Theodore Roosevelt and the public took a dim view of such combinations, and the National Packing Company was dissolved by the Federal courts.[74] In May, 1903, Armour closed the doors of the plant in Hammond and moved what was left of it to his theater of operations in Chicago.[75]

The loss of the packing house, the largest industry in the city, appeared for the moment to be a major disaster for Hammond. To make matters worse, a prolonged strike at the Conkey printing plant occurred about the same time as the packing-house fire. Hundreds of people found themselves without employment and many families moved away. The gloom that prevailed affected the value of real estate, and property was offered for sale at ridiculously low prices. Fortunately, the period of discouragement and indecision soon came to an end. Armanis F. Knotts, mayor of the city, 1902-4, took the lead in the launching of a new industrial era. The Hammond Industrial Committee, organized by Knotts, attracted eleven factories to the city during his administration as mayor. In 1902 William H. Gostlin, Peter W. Meyn, and A. Murray Turner, all local men, formed the Gostlin, Meyn Realty Company.[76] This combination was

mond property, February 2, 1904, to the National Packing Company for the same price. See Lake County Deed Records, 106:536-39; 107:582-84.

73 According to Louis F. Swift, "J. O. Armour and Edward Morris formed the National Packing Company in 1902. It was capitalized at fifteen million dollars. Its components were a group of 'small packers,' the term which includes all but the handful of very large companies. The plan was to continue with the merger, taking in the smaller of the large packers. Then, when all these were welded into one unit, the National Packing Company would absorb the 'Big Three'—Swift, Armour, and Morris." *Yankee of the Yards,* 209.

74 Leech and Carroll, *Armour and His Times,* 205.

75 Howat (ed.), *A Standard History of Lake County,* 1:297.

76 Hammond *Lake County Times,* July 30, 1919; Gary *Post-Tribune,* October 4, 1937; Howat (ed.), *A Standard History of Lake County,* 2:500.

responsible for much of the city's industrial development during the next twenty-five years. Although many of the new plants were small, they were diversified, and never again did Hammond have to depend on a few industries for its economic stability.

In 1902 John Fitzgerald established the Hammond Distilling Company. This plant, with a production capacity of 25,000 gallons of whisky a day, was one of the largest of its kind in the nation. In 1903 Otto Knoerzer organized the Champion Potato Machinery Company to manufacture potato diggers, seed cutters, planters, and sprayers. Knoerzer, born on a farm near Hammond and a blacksmith and wagonmaker by trade, invented the first potato machine. This was said to have been strictly a local industry, founded and financed by local men. In 1904 the Straube Piano Company came to Hammond from Downer's Grove, Illinois. The Straube plant employed about two hundred men and had a capacity of 3,000 pianos a year. Frank S. Betz, manufacturer of surgical instruments and hospital supplies, built a factory on the north bank of the Grand Calumet River in 1904. This proved to be one of Hammond's most stable industries.[77]

The Standard Steel Car Company started the construction of a huge plant in the southeastern part of the city in 1906. Sidmon McHie, publisher of the *Lake County Times,* sold the land for the site; he and William H. Gostlin were largely instrumental in bringing this firm to the community. James B. ("Diamond Jim") Brady was vice-president of this company which manufactured freight and passenger cars for the railroads. This in-

[77] *Lake County Directory,* 1909, pp. 62, 67, 71; Howat (ed.), *op. cit.,* 1:303; Cannon, Loring and Robb (eds.), *History of the Lake and Calumet Region,* 1:799.

dustry, which became the city's largest, employed about 3,500 men in 1912.[78]

In 1919 a syndicate of local realtors purchased the forty-acre site of the old packing house and subdivided it for small industries. A record was established when four new industries located in this city during a single week in 1922.[79] The Roxana Refinery of the Shell Petroleum Company, construction of which was started in 1926, provided employment for hundreds of Hammond's citizens. In 1930 Lever Brothers, manufacturers of soap and of vegetable shortenings, purchased a site in the Robertsdale section for the erection of a large plant. This was the last important development in Hammond's industrial life before the great depression paralyzed the Calumet Region.

Population and Expansion

Although Hammond's population almost doubled between 1910 and 1920, Gary took its place as the largest city in the region. In 1920 Hammond's population was 36,004 while that of Gary soared from 16,803 in 1910 to 55,378 in 1920. By 1930 Gary had 100,426 residents and Hammond's population was 64,560. The German character of the latter city's population was diminished by the influx of immigrants from other European countries in the years before World War I. In 1920 Hammond's foreign-born population included 2,717 Austrians and Germans and 3,107 of Slavic origin. Ten years later there was 1,994 natives of Austria and Germany in the city while 4,812 were from the Slavic countries and Hungary. As immigrants from eastern Europe had a

[78] Hammond *Lake County Times,* August 22 and October 19, 1906; November 12, 1912; Cannon, Loring and Robb (eds.), *op. cit.,* 1:799.
[79] Hammond *Lake County Times,* February 5, 1920; May 8, 1922.

tendency to seek employment in the heavy industries, Hammond's Slavic and Hungarian population was much smaller than that of East Chicago, Gary, and Whiting. The same was true of Negroes and Mexicans. In 1930 there were only 623 Negroes in the city.[80] Hammond's Negro, Slavic, and Hungarian citizens were concentrated in the vicinity of the Standard Steel Car plant where they found employment.

Hammond expanded its area as well as its industries after the turn of the century. In 1911 the city annexed all the territory in North Township north of the Little Calumet River that was not already occupied by East Chicago and Whiting. This area included the Gibson Railroad Yards and the Hessville community. Residents of Hessville filed a remonstrance against Hammond's action in the Circuit Court. In 1913 the court ruled in favor of Hammond but in the same decision forbade the actual annexation of Hessville for five years. In 1925, alarmed by rumors that Gary intended to absorb Highland, Munster, and what is now Wicker Park, Hammond tried to annex those communities.[81] Property owners in those places united to resist the move. When Gary indicated it had no ambitions in that direction, Hammond did not pursue the matter. Highland and Munster retain their independence and Wicker Park remains under the control of the township. The Little Calumet River remains the southern boundary of Hammond.

[80] *Fourteenth Census* (1920): *Population*, pt. 2:316, 760; *Fifteenth Census* (1930): *Population*, 3:pt. 1:721, 744.

[81] Hammond *Times*, June 17, 1951, pp. 3A-4A; Hammond *Lake County Times*, November 6, 1925.

7

WHITING AND STANDARD OIL

IN 1889 THE CALUMET REGION experienced the first substantial impact of the American Industrial Revolution when the Standard Oil Company began the construction of a great refinery at Whiting. This was also the first major industrial development along the Indiana shore of Lake Michigan. The history of Whiting is closely connected with that of the oil industry in the Middle West. The city was the birthplace of the Standard Oil Company of Indiana and is known as the capital of that great oil empire. Whiting was also the scene of some of the most significant developments in the history of the oil industry. Oil was the life blood of the city from the moment the construction of the refinery began, and in later years its influence was apparent in every phase of the community's life. The Whiting Refinery is regarded today as the largest complete oil refinery in the world.

Early Settlers

The site of Whiting was one of the most uninviting portions of the region. The greater part of the area was a wilderness of sand and swamps covered with a luxuriant growth of marsh grass, wild rice, and scrub oak. Great sand ridges lay parallel to Lake Michigan and between these were deep sloughs and swamps. The section was almost entirely surrounded by water. Lake

178

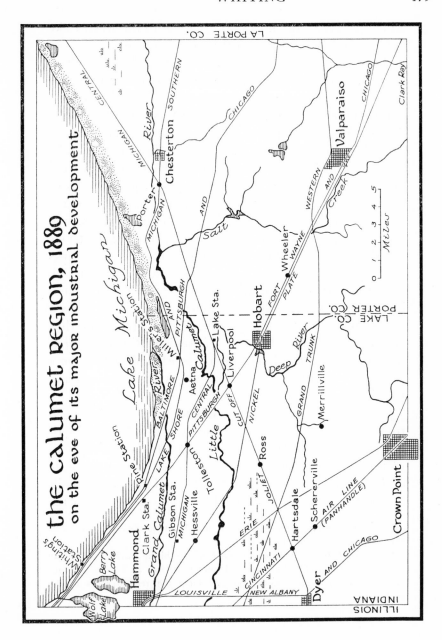

the calumet region, 1889
on the eve of its major industrial development

Michigan lay to the north, Wolf Lake to the west, Lake George and Berry Lake to the south and east.[1]

Travel by any mode of transportation was difficult in this area. The early settlers found it comparatively easy to walk or drive ox teams along the ridges but it was quite a different matter to get over to some other ridge. Travelers were compelled to take circuitous routes along the ridges to reach their destinations. Transportation by water was usually inconvenient, for although there were many waterways, they did not always extend in the directions the people wanted to travel. The railroads made no scheduled stops in this section for many years, and those who came by rail were compelled to leave the trains at Ainsworth, now South Chicago, and walk the tracks eastward for about five miles. Some settlers from Chicago found it necessary to bring their families and household goods as far south as Hegewisch where there was a bridge over the Calumet River. From that point they entered the region by way of Indian Ridge to what was then called the East Side of South Chicago where a trail was found that led to the Lake Michigan beach and thence to what is now Whiting.[2]

In 1850 the greater part of the area still belonged to the Federal government and was almost devoid of settlement. That year Congress classified practically all of this section as "swamp land" and ceded it to the State of Indiana.[3] The Michigan Southern Railroad was built across this wilderness in 1851 and entered Chicago the

<hr/>

[1] Swartz, "Some Early Days of the Whiting Refinery," in *The Stanolind Record,* July, 1923, p. 12.

[2] *Whiting City Almanac and Cook Book* (Whiting Savings and Loan Association, 1911), 10. This unusual source contains an excellent history of the Whiting area compiled largely from the reminiscences of the early settlers.

[3] See above, 93.

next year. In 1858 the Pittsburgh, Fort Wayne and Chicago Road, now the Pennsylvania, built its tracks parallel to the route of the Michigan Southern to reach Chicago. These railroads were followed in 1874 by the Baltimore, Pittsburgh and Chicago, built by the Baltimore and Ohio.

The advent of the railroads and the low prices asked by the State for the swamp lands attracted shrewd investors and speculators to the region. George M. Roberts was apparently the first to acquire land in the Whiting area, his purchases from 1851 to 1858 amounting to 471 acres. This land was bought from the Federal government, from the State of Indiana, and from Mexican War veterans for $1.25 an acre. In later years the Pennsylvania Railroad named its station in that vicinity "Robertsdale," in appreciation of land donated to it by Roberts. The latter gave his address as Robertsdale in legal transactions as early as 1872.[4] That part of Hammond adjacent to Whiting still bears his name.

George W. Clark, whose investments have already been discussed in detail, was the largest landowner in the Whiting area. Following his death in 1866, his vast estate, as already noted, passed into the hands of his sister, Caroline Forsythe, and her husband, Jacob Forsythe.[5] They moved to a home in what is now East Chicago, about three miles southeast of Whiting.[6]

The railroads brought the first settlers into the region, most of whom were Germans who found employment in the construction and maintenance of the railroad tracks. Whiting, like Hammond and Tolleston, was largely a German community in its early years. Henry Reese was one of the first to settle in the Whiting area.

4 Lake County Deed Records, 10:409, 410, 411, 413; 17:208.

5 See above, 94-95, for Clark's purchases and for the settlement of his estate.

6 Whiting *Call* (souvenir edition), October, 1910.

On the day of his departure for America from his native city of Hesse, a neighbor, who obviously had no conception of the size of the United States, urged him to ask the first person he met where Carl Steiber, another emigrant from Hesse, lived. Reese was working at Chicago Heights, Illinois, when a friend, also a Hessian, told him that Steiber was the section boss on a new railroad in near-by Indiana and was paying his men the high wages of $1.00 a day. Reese then brought his wife and baby to the area where Whiting now stands and was given a job by Steiber. There was no house to be had, so the section boss stopped the work for a couple of hours while his crew of fifteen men built a log house for the Reese family on the railroad's right of way. The nucleus of Whiting was started along the railroad tracks as other families built similar homes from timbers hewn in the adjacent woods.[7]

Heinrich D. Eggers, born in Hanover, and John F. K. Vater, a native of Saxony, were closely associated as pioneers of Whiting. The two apparently became acquainted in Chicago where Vater married Georgina Eggers, Heinrich's sister, and Amelia, Vater's sister, became the wife of Heinrich. Vater operated a general store in South Chicago.[8] The brothers-in-law were ardent hunters and thought nothing of walking several miles from their homes in South Chicago to hunt deer in what is now the Whiting area. On one occasion, according to a family story, Vater was so engrossed in eating his lunch that he missed a deer which Eggers had driven in his direction. Exasperated by Vater's carelessness and

[7] Henry Reese in *Whiting City Almanac and Cook Book,* 10, and in Whiting *Times* (historical edition), August 4, 1939; Whiting *Call* (souvenir edition), October, 1910.

[8] Henry S. Davidson, "A Pioneer Account Book," in Bowers (ed.), *History of Lake County* (1929), 128, 132. This record book was kept by John F. K. Vater at his first store in Chicago.

poor marksmanship, Eggers refused to speak to his crest-
fallen friend during the long walk back to South
Chicago.[9]

While Eggers reportedly moved to the Whiting site
in 1848 the deed for his first two purchases of land,
totaling 306 acres, were not recorded until July, 1851.
This land, for which Eggers paid the minimum price of
$1.25 an acre, was originally given to two veterans of
the Mexican War by the Federal government and they,
in turn, deposited the warrants for sale at the Federal
Land Office in Winamac, Indiana. Eggers walked from
Chicago to Winamac to make these purchases, a round
trip of about 175 miles. In 1874 Eggers added eighty
acres to his original holdings. Frederick Eggers, a
brother, bought 321 acres in 1851, and a tract of eighty
acres in 1869, all in the Whiting area. In 1868 John
F. K. Vater moved his residence to the region, having
become the owner and part owner of about 170 acres of
swamp and sand.[10]

Vater and Heinrich Eggers pioneered the shipping of
ice from the inland lakes of the Whiting area to Chicago.
They formed a partnership with Frederick Zuttermeister
and erected a large icehouse on Berry Lake. The part-
ners also shipped sand and gravel by railroad to the
Chicago market. In 1890, when it was evident that Berry
Lake would ultimately be drained by the Standard Oil
Company and by a drainage project in East Chicago,
Eggers sold his interest in the ice business to Zutter-
meister.[11]

---

[9] *Ibid.,* 130-31; Ernst Vater in the Whiting *Times,* August 4, 1939.

[10] Ford, "Heinrich D. Eggers," in Demmon (ed.), *History of Lake
County* (1934), 128, 223; Lake County Deed Records, 10:390; 20:358;
G:602; H:44; I:57, 146, 147, 148; L:115.

[11] Ford, "Heinrich Eggers," in Demmon (ed.), *History of Lake County*
(1934), 223.

The Schrages may be regarded as the "first family" of Whiting. Some time in the 1840's Christof Schrage brought his family from Germany to Chicago. A son, Henry, was destined to play an important role in the development of Whiting. In 1854 the elder Schrage purchased his first land in the area and here the family lived for a time. Although they later returned to Chicago, where Christof was a merchant in his last years, he indicated his continued interest in the Whiting vicinity by the purchase of another tract of land there in 1863.[12]

Henry Schrage joined the Union Army that same year, took part in the fighting around Chattanooga, and was with Sherman on the "March to the Sea." He returned to the Whiting region at the end of the war and found employment as a section hand on one of the railroads at $1.10 a day. In 1868 Schrage was united in marriage with Caroline Wuestenfeldt, whose family was among the first settlers in the area. In the same year he opened the first store on the Whiting site, its few shelves stocked with articles and commodities so necessary to a pioneer community. Mrs. Schrage ran the business, which was located near the Lake Shore and Michigan Southern Station, while her husband continued his work with the section gang. In 1871 the first post office was located in the store with Schrage as postmaster. He was postmaster until 1892 when his son, Henry, Jr., took over the office for a time. The Schrage store was the business, political, and social center of the community until the construction of the refinery was started in 1889.[13]

Henry Schrage was fortunate in the location of his land. The site chosen by the Standard Oil Company for

12 Lake County Deed Records, L:346; X:585; Howat (ed.), *A Standard History of Lake County*, 2:613.
13 Howat (ed.), *op. cit.*, 2:613; Whiting *Call*, September 17, 1909; *Whiting City Almanac and Cook Book*, 21.

its refinery included at least fifty acres of Schrage's property. In 1895 he opened the Bank of Whiting, the first
such institution in the town, reportedly with the money
obtained from the sale of his land to the oil company.[14]
He was a member of the town's first board of trustees
and served in that capacity until 1903. Whiting became
a city in that year and Schrage sat on its council for the
next seven years. He cherished the desire to climax his
career by being mayor of the city in whose interests he
had labored so hard and long. This honor was denied
to him when he suffered defeat in the city elections of
1909.[15] Nevertheless, the old pioneer had the satisfaction
of seeing his son, Walter E. Schrage, serve as mayor of
Whiting from 1914 to 1930. Henry Schrage died in 1932
at the age of eighty-eight.

Most of the early settlers made their living by working as section hands on the railroads, there being little
else to provide them with an income. And yet these
thrifty Germans made the most of what the region had
to offer. The small patches of soil found here and there
on the sand ridges and along the edge of the sloughs
became gardens where watermelons, cabbages, and potatoes grew with varying degrees of success. Nothing
could be grown satisfactorily on the great areas of sand.
A sister of John F. K. Vater came from Germany to
try farming here. According to family reports, when her
potatoes grew no larger than marbles, she tossed hand-
fuls of sand into her brother's face and moved on to
Iowa.[16] A succession of wild berry crops supplemented
the rather monotonous diet of the people. Strawberries

14 Whiting *Call,* September 17, 1909.

15 Walter E. Schrage, Jr., president of the Bank of Whiting, in an
interview on May 12, 1954, told the author of his grandfather's disappointment.

16 Ernst Vater in the Whiting *Times,* August 4, 1939, p. 5.

grew in most of the area and raspberries were plentiful in the vicinity of Berry Lake. The marshes abounded with cranberries, and the pioneers thought nothing of walking the several miles to Tolleston where the finest huckleberries were to be found.

Some of the settlers cut timber and firewood for the Chicago market. Heinrich Eggers was said to have paid for his land and house by selling cedar fence posts in that neighboring city. The timber was lashed into rafts and towed by hand through the shallow water of Lake Michigan to South Chicago. For a time, Jacob Forsythe had a small steamboat on Wolf Lake in connection with his fencing operations and sale of firewood. There was a great demand for fuel in Chicago after the tragic fire of 1871, and Forsythe sold as much as $3,000.00 worth of wood a month.[17] He did not object to the settlers cutting wood off his land for their own use, but he kept a close watch to prevent Chicago timber thieves from stealing trees. The railroads maintained huge tanks of water and sheds filled with wood for use in their locomotives. Although workmen were needed to service the engines with water and fuel, the wood was purchased at places farther east and brought there by rail.

The swamps and marshes teemed with ducks and geese in unbelievable numbers and wild turkeys were numerous on the sand ridges. Several of the pioneers operated hunting lodges for the entertainment of Chicago sportsmen. Charles Kreuter's place on the shore of Lake George was one of the best-known resorts in the region. Frank Reinhart operated a popular sportsmen's retreat near the Lake Shore and Michigan Southern station. Heinrich Eggers entertained hunters and fishermen at

17 Davidson, "A Pioneer Account Book," in Bowers (ed.), *History of Lake County* (1929), 130; *Whiting City Almanac and Cook Book,* 10, 13.

what was considered the most beautiful lodge in the neighborhood, located on Berry Lake where the Standard Oil refinery now stands. While fish could be obtained with ease from Lake Michigan and the inland lakes, apparently there was little commercial fishing at Whiting. The ice business provided seasonal employment for some of the residents. E. A. Shedd and Company was the largest shipper of ice, which it obtained mainly from Wolf Lake.[18]

In 1871 a great fire, similar to the one which almost destroyed Chicago in the same year, swept the Whiting area. The summer had been extremely dry, and there was an abundance of inflammable vegetation. The holocaust, which started in September, burned the homes, barns, livestock, and other possessions cherished by the settlers. The Forsythe family succeeded in burying their library of about a thousand volumes in the sand outside their residence. When it appeared the danger was past, the books were put back on the shelves only to be destroyed a short time later. The Forsythe home burned so quickly that none of its contents were saved. Among the more serious losses was the family piano, probably the only instrument of its kind in the vicinity. The Forsythes fled into one of the swamps where they dug holes in the moist earth as protection against the heat. Soil in the marshes caught fire and burned to a depth of a foot beneath the surface.[19]

Most of the Germans in the area were staunch Republicans after the Civil War. In 1868 Henry Schrage campaigned actively for General Grant in that year's

18 Ford, "Pioneer Days of Robertsdale, Whiting, and Berry Lake," in Demmon (ed.), *History of Lake County* (1934), 225; Goodspeed and Blanchard (eds.), *Counties of Porter and Lake,* 540.
19 *Whiting City Almanac and Cook Book,* 12.

presidential election. The population was so small that a voting precinct was not established until 1870. As a result, the citizens made the long journey of about ten miles to Hessville to cast their ballots. This political chore took at least three days, two of which were spent in making the trip and the third in enjoying the excitement of election holiday. Hessville being a German community, the Whiting contingent welcomed this opportunity to visit with old acquaintances and to make new friends.[20]

Until 1889 the Whiting community was a sleepy hamlet clustering around Henry Schrage's store, its only business establishment. The region had changed but little since the first settler built his log cabin near the railroad tracks. Occasionally, a train stopped to take on water for its engine, and at rare intervals to discharge and receive passengers. There was little commercial activity because Whiting had nothing to ship to distant markets except ice and sand. The citizens went about their daily tasks on the railroad tracks, tending their German gardens, and entertaining groups of sportsmen from Chicago. The children received the rudiments of an education in a tiny schoolhouse in Robertsdale. They were taught for a time by John Quincy Adams Sparks, a lovable derelict who was a plasterer by trade.[21] There were no churches, jails, or other manifestations of civilization. In 1880 the Census Bureau which took notice of the community for the first time, listed a population of 115 souls. A few families were added in 1888 when the Chicago and Calumet Terminal Belt Line Railroad made a connection with the trunk line roads there.[22] As 1888

20 *Whiting City Almanac and Cook Book,* 22.

21 *Ibid.,* 12; Whiting *Times,* August 4, 1939, p. 19.

22 U. S. Bureau of the Census, *Eleventh Census* (1880): *Population* 159; Whiting *Call,* October, 1910.

came to a close, there was little to indicate that a new era was about to begin.

Standard Oil Moves West

The modern oil industry had its origin in Pennsylvania, where its operations were concentrated for some years. The principal products of the refineries before the advent of the automobile era were kerosene for lighting and cooking purposes, lubricating oil for railroads and industry, fuel oil, and greases for wagons and carriages. Gasoline was a nuisance product which many refineries covertly disposed of by dumping into near-by streams at night, thereby causing a fire menace to the surrounding neighborhood. The oil companies tried hard to keep the production of this highly explosive commodity at a minimum.

In 1885 oil was discovered in great quantities in the vicinity of Lima, Ohio. Unfortunately, Lima crude oil, unlike Pennsylvania crude, was "sour." "If you got a drop on you, you smelled like a rotten egg."[23] This was because of its high sulphur content. Kerosene made from Lima crude would not burn in common lamps without smoking and giving off a nauseating odor, and the ordinary refining process of that time would not remove the sulphur. The public refused to buy products made from what it called "pole cat" oil, and the bottom fell out of the price of Lima crude. This presented a serious problem to the Standard Oil Company which had large investments in the Ohio fields. With millions of barrels of crude oil on hand, the company sought to create a market for fuel oil made from Lima crude in Chicago, Milwaukee, and other cities. To overcome the scarcity of tank cars and high freight rates, Standard built an

[23] Paul H. Giddens, *Standard Oil Company (Indiana). Oil Pioneer of the Middle West* (New York, 1955), 2.

eight-inch pipeline from Lima to Chicago. Terminal
facilities and storage tanks were located on Lake Michigan at the foot of 100th Street. The station was called
Fleming Park, now a part of Calumet Park.[24]

In the meantime, Standard Oil officials were trying
desperately to find a method by which Lima crude could
be successfully refined. In 1887 Herman Frasch, a German-born chemist, developed the copper-oxide process for
taking sulphur out of Lima crude oil. The essence of the
Frasch process was "to distill crude oil in the presence
of copper oxide, which reacted with the sulphur [in the
crude oil], formed sulphide of copper, and left the oil
odorless and sweet." The Standard Oil Company bought
the Frasch patents in 1888, and employed the chemist
to perfect the process.[25] In the same year, Dr. William
M. Burton, a young chemist who had just received his
Ph. D. degree from Johns Hopkins University, was
employed by Standard to work with Frasch in the company's laboratories at Cleveland.[26] Encouraged by the
possession of the Frasch process, Standard Oil started
refining Lima crude oil on a large scale.

The choice of the site for the refinery at the southern
end of Lake Michigan was determined largely by the
same considerations that brought other great industries
into the area during the next few years. The nation's
center of population was rapidly moving westward and
industrialists saw the advantage of their plants being
located as close to the midwest markets as possible. Chi-

[24] Giddens, *Standard Oil Company (Indiana)*, 2-4; F. Lawrence Babcock, *The First Fifty, 1889-1939* (Standard Oil Company [Indiana],
1939), 6.

[25] Giddens, *Standard Oil Company (Indiana)*, 5-6.

[26] *Ibid.*, 6-7; Babcock, *op. cit.*, 7; Robert E. Wilson, *Oil Competition
in the Midwest. A Case History* (National Petroleum Association, 1950),
4; Dr. William M. Burton, in *The Stanolind Record*, April, 1927, p. 21.

cago had become the great city of Middle America; more railroads converged there than at any other point in the world. Moreover, Lake Michigan provided cheap water transportation and an abundance of water for industrial purposes. What was of immediate importance, there was not a single important oil refinery in the nation west of Lima, Ohio, at that time.

Standard originally planned to build the refinery at the western end of the Lima pipeline in South Chicago. Although South Chicagoans had welcomed the construction of the pipeline, their enthusiasm for the oil industry waned when they smelled the sickening odor of Lima crude oil. Matters became worse when one of the large storage tanks in Fleming Park collapsed and the foul stench of sulphur lingered in the vicinity for days.[27] Other considerations influenced the company to build the refinery at Whiting. Taxes were lower there than in Chicago where there was a tendency to tax large corporations exorbitantly. Also, South Chicago was a congested district even at this early date, and land for a large refinery could be obtained only at tremendous cost. On the other hand, an abundance of land was to be had at Whiting at prices considered reasonable for industrial sites. The site was convenient to Lake Michigan, and there were three trunk-line railroads in the immediate vicinity. Moreover, the Chicago and Calumet Terminal Belt Line Railroad provided excellent connections with other railroads in the Chicago area.[28]

Theodore M. Towle, Standard's real estate and tax representative, was sent to Whiting to supervise the purchase of the site. Accompanied by Henry Schrage, Towle

[27] Alfred Jones in Gary *Post-Tribune,* May 27, 1937.

[28] In 1890 the Wisconsin Central Railroad, one of Standard Oil's subsidiaries, obtained control of the Chicago and Calumet Terminal Belt Line. See Giddens, *Standard Oil Company (Indiana),* 21.

visited the owners of the land and bought their acreages. The owners did not know who was buying their property. When asked what he was going to do with so much land, Towle said: "I'm going to build a whim-wham for a goose's bridle." About 235 acres were purchased before construction of the refinery was started. No hard bargains were made, but each owner was bound to secrecy both as to the purchaser and the price.[29] In some instances the land was paid for in cash. A study of the deeds shows that the prices paid for the various tracts were largely determined by their location and by the bargaining powers of the owners. The Forsythes, old hands at selling sand, were able to obtain high prices for what they sold. Caroline Forsythe was paid $23,000.00 for one tract of twenty-two acres. On the other hand, Edward A. Shedd received only $10,000.00 for forty-two acres.[30] Most land was purchased in March and April of 1889.

The Standard Oil Company, from the very first, concealed its plans to build a refinery at Whiting. In February, 1889, William P. Cowan, superintendent of the company's Cleveland refinery, who was to be in charge of the construction of the Whiting plant, and other officials arranged with William Curtis, master mechanic at the Cleveland refinery, to make the blueprints for the Whiting project. In accordance with the company's policy of secrecy, Curtis made the drawings in the privacy of his own home. Even after Cowan had arrived at Whiting and construction of the refinery was under way, an atmosphere of mystery as to what was being done pre-

[29] Swartz, "Some Early Days of the Whiting Refinery," in *The Stanolind Record,* August, 1923, pp. 13, 14.

[30] The Forsythes were paid a total of $81,000 and Heinrich Eggers received $7,000 for land sold. See Lake County Deed Records, 44:434; 46:160; 47:132.

vailed. Newspapermen were barred from the plant area, and for a long time the general public and even the laborers did not know the purpose of the project. Incoming shipments of materials and supplies were billed to Cowan, pay checks were signed in his name, and all other matters were similarly handled. Despite such devices, reports appeared in the Chicago newspapers a few days after construction had started that the largest refinery in the world was being built at Whiting.[31]

Construction of the Refinery

Early in May, 1889, the construction of the refinery was started. A month later the Standard Oil trust organized and incorporated a Standard Oil Company in the State of Indiana under whose jurisdiction the plant was to be built and operated. In the meantime, about 1,500 laborers were at work under the direction of experienced construction men from other Standard refineries. The sand ridges were leveled and the intervening sloughs filled in. Loose sand retarded the progress of construction. Horses stumbled and fell while pulling the heavy vehicles and earth-moving machinery. The wagons were equipped with great wide tires and the roads in the plant area were covered with hay and straw to keep the wheels out of the deep ruts in the sand. Workers floundered through water and wet sand, while clouds of mosquitoes made their lives almost unbearable during the summer months. By October, 1889, it was so obvious that an oil refinery was being built that the name of the Standard Oil Company was substituted for that of William P.

31 Swartz, "Some Early Days of the Whiting Refinery," in *The Stanolind Record,* August, 1923, p. 14. Curtis, who became master mechanic at the Whiting Refinery in May, 1889, was prominent in its operations for thirty years. Giddens, *Standard Oil Company (Indiana),* 19.

Cowan, in whose name construction had been carried on from the beginning.[32]

One of the first undertakings was the erection of a water works, the water being obtained through a twenty-inch pipeline that was laid into Lake Michigan. This was superseded a short time later by a tunnel dug under the floor of the Lake to connect with a crib, nearly one-half mile from the water's edge. Water was thereby provided for the refinery and ultimately for the town. Immense sewers, which in time drained the greater part of Berry Lake and many sloughs, were constructed. And yet, while the storage tanks were being constructed, it was necessary to haul sand to build up rings around their foundations to hold back the water. When the tanks were put into service, a boat was used for workers to get from one tank to another to operate valves and read the gauges.[33]

For a time the local people were bewildered by the army of strangers in their midst and shocked by the destruction of homes, gardens, and the leveling of the familiar sand ridges. They came to see that the old way of life was a thing of the past and hastened to find places for themselves in the new order of things. Some found employment at the refinery, while others opened various types of businesses. Heinrich Eggers used the money he had received for his land to erect seventeen rental properties near the plant for newcomers.[34] Property values soared and many citizens divided their farms into lots and disposed of the lots for amounts larger than their farms would have brought before the refinery came. Al-

[32] Giddens, op. cit., 18; Swartz, "Some Early Days of the Whiting Refinery," in The Stanolind Record, September, 1923, p. 9.

[33] Ibid., August, 1923, p. 14.

[34] Ford, "Heinrich D. Eggers," in Demmon (ed.), History of Lake County (1934), 223.

though the company erected several bunk houses for the construction workers, there were not enough accommodations for all. A special train, known as "The Hobo," was put into service by the Lake Shore and Michigan Southern to transport workers each day from Chicago to Whiting. The railroad utilized the locomotive for switching purposes while the coaches sat on a siding until the day's work was done, at which time the workers were returned to their homes in Chicago.

After working hours there was little to occupy the time of the men who lived at the refinery site. The "satchel and trunk men," as the natives called the newcomers, wrote in a homesick vein to their families, describing the community as one of sand burrs, sand fleas, and scrub oaks. Whiting had all the atmosphere of a frontier town. Almost all the buildings on the west side of Front Street, extending from the Pennsylvania Railroad tracks to 119th Street, were saloons. All that was needed to start a saloon, according to reports, were two beer kegs, a bottle of whisky, and a dozen glasses. A public road cut the plant site into two parts of almost equal size, and along this thoroughfare, appropriately called "Oklahoma," a collection of saloons, dance halls, and boarding houses flourished for a time. Here, in the evenings and on paydays, drunken brawls and near riots frequently disturbed the peace. On weekends the trains into Chicago were crowded with young men eager to escape the monotony of Sundays in Whiting.[35]

As the construction of the refinery neared completion in the early summer of 1890, administrative officers and manufacturing personnel began to arrive on the scene. Beaumont Parks, W. S. Rheem, Fred W. Weller, and

35 *The Stanolind Record*, June, 1939, p. 3; Whiting *Call* (souvenir edition), October, 1910.

others came from Oil City, Titusville, Cleveland, and
Buffalo. James A. Moffett, president of the Company,
was placed in charge of operations. William P. Cowan,
vice-president, who had supervised the construction of
the refinery, remained as Moffett's assistant. Dr. William M. Burton, destined to be one of the greatest figures
in the development of the modern oil industry, took
charge of the laboratory and inspection department.
Burton was one of the first trained chemists in the oil
industry. His laboratory was located on the second floor
of the farmhouse formerly owned by Herman C.
Wuestenfeldt, one of the area's pioneers. Research
equipment for experiments was set up in an old cow shed
at the rear of the farmhouse. According to Burton, "this
installation might well be termed the first research department of our company." Recognition of the value of
scientists at this early date gave the Standard Oil Company a tremendous advantage over all other oil companies
and made it an outstanding leader in research. The other
little farmhouses on the plant site were converted into
administrative offices. In the beginning Whiting was the
nerve center of the Standard Oil Company of Indiana,
all the offices of the company being located there with
the exception of the purchasing department which was
in Chicago.[36]

Early in September, 1890, fires were started under the
stills, and on Thanksgiving Day the first shipment of
125 tank cars of kerosene started to market. At this
time the refinery had a charging capacity of about 10,000

[36] Swartz, "Some Early Days of the Whiting Refinery," in *The
Stanolind Record,* August, 1923, p. 14; October, 1923, p. 16; *The Stano-
lind Record,* February, 1922, p. 3; April, 1927, p. 38, Giddens, *Standard
Oil Company (Indiana),* 23-24. Dr. Burton was president of the Standard
Oil Company of Indiana from 1918 to 1927.

barrels of crude oil per day.[37] The great refinery has
never ceased its operations, night or day, in good times
and in periods of depression, since that memorable day
in 1890.

But all was not smooth sailing; Burton was immediately confronted with an exasperating problem. The
Frasch copper oxide process for the removal of sulphur
from the Lima crude oil was not a success at the new
refinery, and its kerosene smelled "to high heaven."
Farmers and housewives, nauseated by its sickening odor,
called it "skunk oil," and refused to use it in their lamps.
The kerosene almost drove customers from the grocery
stores, and what was worse, contaminated butter, vegetables, and other perishable foods. The company had to
dispose of the stuff as second-rate fuel oil. Kerosene
made from Pennsylvania oil was rushed to the dealers
while Burton worked night and day on the problem. The
young chemist found a way to improve the Frasch process
and within a short time the refinery was able to provide
the public with high quality kerosene.[38]

Refined oil, or kerosene, was the most important product made at the refinery prior to 1910. In the 1890's its
annual production of kerosene amounted to about three
million barrels. The production of fuel oil ranked second
in volume in the nineties, with two to four million barrels
going to the market each year. Naphtha, or gasoline,
ranked third in volume, about a million barrels being
manufactured annually. Lubricating oils were fourth in
volume. The railroads bought Fortnite Oil, designed to
burn two weeks at a filling, to light their signal lanterns.

37 Babcock, *The First Fifty,* 9; Giddens, *Standard Oil Company (Indiana),* 25, 28.

38 Conger Reynolds, *Historical Highlights of the Story of Standard
Oil Company (Indiana)* (Mimeographed MS in possession of the
Standard Oil Company of Indiana, Chicago, Illinois), 4.

Candles were made from paraffin wax extracted from crude oil and miners soon discovered that these candles were superior to those made with tallow. The refinery later developed Miner's Sunshine Oil, which burned in a lamp designed and sold by Standard. This lamp soon replaced the candle as the headlight on the miner's cap. The grease works was built a few years after the refinery began operations. Its products, Mica Axle Grease for wagons, Boston Coach Oil for carriages and buggies, Harness Oil, and Hoof Grease, came into general use throughout the nation. The success of the company's products was largely due to the painstaking scientific research conducted by Dr. Burton and his colleagues in the laboratory at Whiting.[39]

When the refinery began operating in 1890, most of the laborers who had been employed on the construction work remained to operate the various departments. As refinery operations expanded more laborers were added, and by 1896 between 2,500 and 3,000 persons were employed. The gates were thronged each morning with anxious men for some weeks after production was started. The foremen took their pick of these, and many who were turned away came back day after day until they obtained the coveted jobs. Standard's policy in the selection of the permanent labor force was to give preference to married men with orderly habits. Yet some rough characters succeeded in getting on the payroll. The company paid as high a wage as industries in the Chicago area and a little more. In 1895 the highest daily wage for skilled labor was $4.50 and for the unskilled worker it was $2.50. The lowest paid adult male employees received $1.50 a day. The average daily pay for women

39 Giddens, *Standard Oil Company (Indiana)*, 33-35; Babcock, *The First Fifty*, 11-13.

and girls was ninety cents and for boys eighty cents. The work day was ten hours in length. The only place where women and girls were employed was in the candle factory. Payday came every two weeks. In the beginning the paymaster and head timekeeper drove over the plant area during the working hours in a light wagon, the top of which was enclosed with a wire screen, to distribute the pay in cash to the workers. When a regular pay house was built the whistle for quitting blew an hour earlier on paydays. This provided a sort of holiday for the workers, and the saloons and stores did a thriving business before darkness closed down on the community.[40] There were no company stores at Whiting and employees traded where they pleased.

Housing and Living Conditions

Standard made an effort to provide adequate housing and living conditions for its supervisory employees. In 1889 a little town site called "The Village" was laid out and construction of houses went on for about two years. The employees moved into these dwellings as fast as they were completed. Most of the houses built by the company were north of what is now 119th Street and in the northeastern part of the community. Sidewalks were laid with boards and water was piped into the houses from the refinery. No other places in town had running water until Whiting was incorporated. Rentals were based on a small per cent of the cost of the homes. All the houses gradually passed into the hands of the tenants with the Company taking the payments out of their pay

---

[40] Giddens, *op. cit.*, 37-38; Swartz, "Some Early Days of the Whiting Refinery," in *The Stanolind Record*, October, 1923, p. 13; Indiana Department of Statistics, *Sixth Biennial Report*, 160.

checks. The "Village" was restricted to the extent that no saloons could be located in that area.[41]

The company's housing did not extend to the rank and file of the workers at the refinery. As a result, many crowded into the south side of the town where slum conditions prevailed for some years. There was no running water, sewers, or sidewalks in this district, conditions which were distasteful to native Americans accustomed to such comforts. On the other hand, this situation did not deter immigrants from the rural areas of central and eastern Europe, who were not familiar with such refinements, from seeking employment at the refinery. Consequently, the foreign born predominated on the south side where alien tongues prevailed over the English in the early years. There were no restrictions in this section which led to the presence of numerous saloons, dance halls, and houses of ill-repute.[42] Housing was woefully inadequate, large families being crowded in small dwellings and in tar-paper shacks. Lack of proper sewerage and pure drinking water permitted epidemics of typhoid fever to sweep the community from time to time.

Native Americans who first came to live and work in Whiting found it a lonely and barren place. Life was particularly drab and lonely for wives and daughters, who had little to break the monotony of each day's existence. There were few trees, no grass, sidewalks, telephones, street lights, parks, or city government. Citizens encountered sand everywhere, in the streets, on what should have been sidewalks, and in the yards of their homes. Sand crept under the doors and through the

[41] Swartz, "Some Early Days of the Whiting Refinery," in *The Stanolind Record*, August, 1923, p. 16; Whiting *Saturday Sun*, August 10, 1907.

[42] Swartz, "Some Early Days of the Whiting Refinery," in *The Stanolind Record*, September, 1923, pp. 9-10.

loose windows of houses and stores. The heat of the summer days was intensified as the sand reflected the sun's rays with great intensity, while in the winter icy blasts from off Lake Michigan kept even the hardy indoors.

Many employees and their families yearned for their former homes in more congenial places. More than one husband returned from the day's work at the refinery to find his wife in tears, her bags packed, and determined to join her parents in Chicago or in the East.[43] There were no theaters or other forms of wholesome entertainment. The sand roads being practically impassable, the trunk-line railroads provided the community with its only contact with the outside world. Even those contacts failed during the railroad strike of 1894, at which time Whiting felt the full impact of its isolation. When the trains stopped running, the flow of food and other necessities into the community was halted for three or four weeks. Numerous stores closed as food, particularly meat, disappeared from their shelves. For a time, the citizens were subjected to a monotonous diet of fish from the neighboring lakes and sloughs.[44]

Such conditions drew the people of the community into closely knit social and religious organizations. The foreign born, who came to form a distinct segment of the area's society, turned to their churches for cultural and social activities. While religious and fraternal organizations were important to the native American population, this segment sought other social outlets. In 1891 a baseball team, the "Whiting Greys" was formed. The Greys more than held their own with teams in the Chicago area for several years. In 1893 the Lakeside

43 *Ibid.*, November, 1923, p. 25.
44 Whiting *News*, July 13, 1894.

Pleasure Club, composed of young married couples and single men and women, afforded its members a chance to dance, play cards, and go bicycling. Though the streets were rough, bicyclists rode on summer nights over a continuous course from Oliver Street through Center Street to Berry Lake, a distance of almost two miles.[45] In 1894 the Fortnightly Club, a literary organization, proved so popular that it was necessary to limit its membership.[46]

The Owls Club, established by young men of the refinery in 1893, was one of the centers of the community's social life. Dr. Burton was one of the leaders of this organization. Club rooms and later a clubhouse provided congenial fellowship for the members. Card games, dances, and bicycling parties were regular features of the club's program. The Owls also sponsored community baseball and basketball teams. One of the club's original members wrote in later years: "In my day it was all that made life bearable, for the young men who came to Whiting to work for the Standard Oil Company found themselves amid surroundings, outside of business hours, that were not conducive to their comfort and their peace of mind."[47] Of the forty-one charter members of the club, many later rose to high positions of responsibility in the company and in the oil industry.[48]

The Fight for Independence

Before the construction of the refinery Whiting had too small a population to justify its incorporation as

---

[45] Giddens, *Standard Oil Company (Indiana)*, 42.

[46] Swartz, "Some Early Days of the Whiting Refinery," in *The Stanolind Record*, November, 1923, pp. 27-28. In 1923 the Fortnightly Club became the Whiting Woman's Club.

[47] Quoted in *The Stanolind Record*, March, 1920, pp. 1-2.

[48] Giddens, *Standard Oil Company (Indiana)*, 42.

a town. The German settlers in the area were law-
abiding citizens and the county sheriff, miles away at
Crown Point, had little reason to visit the community. The need for local government arose with the
construction of the refinery. Maintenance of law and
order was now too great a problem for the sheriff to
handle from his distant office. A municipal government
was also needed to provide the citizens with an adequate
supply of pure water, a sewerage system, streets and
sidewalks, and protection against fire. The problem of
incorporation was not as simple as it seemed at first, the
community achieving the status of a town only after several years of controversy.

Early in 1892 the first effort was made to incorporate
the town. A citizens' committee headed by Dr. W. E.
Putnam and U. G. Swartz proposed to include the territory from the proposed Indiana Harbor Ship Canal
westward to the Indiana-Illinois line and lying north of
Berry Lake, Lake George, and Wolf Lake. This would
give Whiting a frontage of several miles on Lake Michigan for future industrial development.[49] Unfortunately,
the Standard Oil Company and other property owners,
fearing an increase in taxes, were able to block this attempt at incorporation.[50] This lack of vision on the part
of the oil company deprived Whiting of its golden opportunity to become one of the larger cities along the
southern shore of Lake Michigan.

In 1893 a crime was perpetrated that convinced even
the opponents of incorporation that something must be

[49] Swartz, "Some Early Days of the Whiting Refinery," in *The Stanolind Record*, December, 1923, p. 22. Dr. Putnam was said to have been the first physician to settle in Whiting. See Jennie E. Putnam, "Pioneering in Whiting," in Demmon (ed.), *History of Lake County* (1934), 73.

[50] Frank Gavit, History of Whiting, Indiana (Typewritten MS in Whiting Public Library), 2. Gavit, the only attorney in Whiting at that time, was the lawyer for those seeking the incorporation of the town.

done immediately to protect lives and property. On the evening of July 17 seven strangers came to William Timm's Hunter's Resort in near-by Robertsdale. A murderous assault was made upon the resort keeper. When the affair was over, two of the strangers lay dead and a third so seriously wounded that he died a few weeks later. Timm and a friend who came to his assistance were seriously injured. The others in the attacking force escaped. There were no police officers at hand to pursue the assailants or to take charge of the wounded criminal who was secured to a tree with a chain until the next afternoon, when the sheriff arrived to take charge of the situation. The reason for the attack on Timm was never discovered.[51]

The frightened residents of Robertsdale petitioned Hammond to annex their community. Hammond, eager for a frontage on Lake Michigan to assure an adequate water supply and also for future industrial expansion, moved quickly to annex not only Robertsdale but all the area between Atchison Avenue, now the western boundary of Whiting, westward to the Indiana-Illinois State Line before the end of 1893. Whiting, now surrounded by Hammond and East Chicago, thereby lost forever its opportunity for expansion.[52]

Hammond moved next to annex all of Whiting, including the great refinery. Hammond's residents were burdened with heavy taxes and it was thought that the addition of the Whiting area would bring them the relief they so badly needed. In 1894 Hammond's City Council voted to annex all of Whiting except the refinery and the oil company's cottages. In view of Standard's earlier opposition to the incorporation of Whiting, the opinion

[51] Swartz, "Some Early Days of the Whiting Refinery," in *The Stanolind Record,* December, 1923, p. 22.
[52] See above, 163.

prevailed that the oil company would not object to this action. After Whiting was acquired, Hammond's plan called for the annexation of the heavily taxable refinery. Hammond's attempt to place its police on duty at Whiting aroused the latter's citizens to a high pitch of excitement. The Standard Oil Company, convinced it would be far better off in the matter of taxes in an independent Whiting than in debt-ridden Hammond, threw its influence against Hammond's designs and in favor of the incorporation of Whiting. The matter was taken into the courts where the lawyers continued the fight for more than two years.[53]

While the battle against Hammond was being waged in the courts, the Lake County commissioners approved a petition by Whiting's citizens to be allowed to vote on the matter of incorporation. The election was held on June 18, 1895, with Henry Schrage, U. G. Swartz, and C. V. Crane as inspectors. Officials of the refinery urged their employees to vote. William P. Cowan and Jacob Forsythe were interested spectators at the polls. The vote was 685 to 2 in favor of the incorporation of an independent Whiting.[54]

When Hammond withdrew her police from Whiting a few days later, citizens were led to believe the victory had been won. On September 30 an election of town officials was held with the permission of the county commissioners. The oil company's interest in Whiting's gov-

[53] Whiting *Democrat,* June 14, 1894; Swartz, "Some Early Days of the Whiting Refinery," in *The Stanolind Record,* December, 1923, p. 22; Gavit, History of Whiting, Indiana, 2. Indiana law at that time permitted a city to annex adjacent platted territory merely by resolution of its city council. Land owners in the territory to be annexed had the right of appeal to the courts.

[54] Whiting *Democrat,* June 20, 1895; Cannon, Loring and Robb (eds.), *History of the Lake and Calumet Region,* 1:721. U. G. Swartz was editor and publisher of the Whiting *Democrat.*

ernment was indicated by the election of W. S. Rheem, superintendent of the refinery department, to the town board of trustees. Rheem was later chosen president of the town board. Hammond, in the meantime, appealed the order for the election given by the county commissioners. Whiting's independence was thereby delayed until the courts could decide the matter or a compromise could be reached. In the meantime, Whiting's town board went through the formality of holding regular meetings, although no business could be legally transacted.[55]

Whiting's independence was, in part, ultimately achieved through the medium of practical politics. In June, 1896, the Republican convention for the nomination of the candidate for Congress from the Tenth District was held in Hammond. The local city council was greatly interested in the nomination of Edgar D. Crumpacker, of Valparaiso, as against J. Frank Hanly. Crumpacker's brother, Peter Crumpacker, city attorney of Hammond, had been one of the leaders in the effort to annex Whiting. There was also a rumor that Edgar D. Crumpacker had played a part in the annexation proceedings against Whiting. Whiting's delegates to the convention, W. S. Rheem and Dr. W. E. Putnam, were instructed by Whiting Republicans to vote against Crumpacker. At the convention it was discovered that Crumpacker's nomination could be assured if he could win the votes of the Whiting delegates. Consequently, a compromise was arranged by which the Hammond city council would drop its annexation proceedings against Whiting and the Whiting delegates would vote for Crumpacker. Mr. Rheem and Dr. Putnam supported Crum-

55 Whiting *Democrat,* June 27, 1895; Swartz, "Some Early Days of the Whiting Refinery," in *The Stanolind Record,* December, 1923, pp. 25-26; Cannon, Loring and Robb (eds.), *History of the Lake and Calumet Region,* 1 :721.

packer, who was nominated by the narrow margin of one half of a vote. On October 6, 1896, the Hammond city council voted to dismiss its annexation proceedings against Whiting.[56]

Other considerations no doubt played a part in persuading Hammond to drop its designs against Whiting. The Standard Oil Company, financially able to engage the finest legal talent, was obviously prepared to take the case to the highest court in the land. Members of the Hammond city council were weary of the protests made by prominent Whiting leaders who appeared regularly at their sessions. Moreover, the almost unanimous opposition of Whiting's citizens to such a union convinced Hammond it was not wise to insist upon an "unwilling bride."

After so many years of controversy, Whiting rejoiced that its independence was at last a reality. A colorful celebration was held, in the course of which the citizens marched through the town in a torchlight parade. Speeches were made by those who had led the community in its fight for independence and representatives from neighboring communities were present to congratulate the town upon its hard-won victory. The town board immediately granted a franchise for electric lights. Ordinances were passed to install running water, sewers, and sidewalks, and to police the town. Citizens freely admitted that the Standard Oil Company, the largest taxpayer, should have a voice in the affairs of the municipality. The Whiting *Democrat* declared: "Everyone who knows anything about the Standard Oil Company knows that it does what it does well and economically. It follows, therefore, that the town will be well and economically conducted."[57] In 1900 Whiting's population was 3,983.

[56] Swartz, *op. cit.*, 26-27; Cannon, Loring and Robb (eds.), *op. cit.*, 1:721.

[57] Whiting *Democrat*, October 15 and November 12, 1896.

Three years later the community was incorporated as a city. William E. Warwick, a high official of the Oil Company, was elected mayor and served until 1906.[58]

The Burton Cracking Process

The rapid growth of the automobile industry and the general increase in the use of gasoline engines for other purposes ushered in a new era for Whiting. One of the most important problems confronting the petroleum industry in the early years of the century was the rapidly growing demand for gasoline. Between 1903 and 1908 motor car production alone increased 467 per cent. With the failure of crude oil production to keep pace with the demand for gasoline, refiners realized that the normal supply would soon be inadequate and prices would skyrocket. It was obvious that something would have to be done to increase the supply or else the progress of the gasoline-powered automobile would be halted. Standard Oil of Indiana solved the problem with what was called the Burton thermal cracking process, which doubled the amount of gasoline obtained from crude oil. The Burton process, developed in the Whiting laboratory, was said to have been the most significant of all the applications of chemistry and physics to the petroleum industry.[59]

In 1909 Dr. William M. Burton, at that time general manager of manufacturing for Standard of Indiana, instructed Dr. Robert E. Humphreys, chief chemist in charge of the Whiting laboratory, to go to work on the problem of increasing the yield of gasoline from crude oil. While Burton made suggestions from time to time,

[58] *Twelfth Census* (1900): *Population*, pt. 1:139; Howat (ed.), *A Standard History of Lake County*, 1:439-40.

[59] Babcock, *The First Fifty*, 17-18; Wilson, *Oil Competition in the Midwest*, 7. Until this time only about 11 per cent of the crude oil could be turned into gasoline by the prevailing refinery operations.

Humphreys took the initiative, tried various possibilities, and eventually worked out the solution to the problem. Dr. F. M. Rogers and Dr. O. E. Bransky, the other chemists on the Whiting staff, assisted Humphreys on the project.[60]

Humphreys knew that the application of high temperatures would "crack" molecules with a high boiling point into low boiling point fractions, so he experimented with various processes of cracking gas oil by heat. After many futile experiments with heat alone, Humphreys decided to try heat and pressure together on the oil. Heating oil in a still was everyday practice. When this was done, any oil as light as gas oil would distill off when a certain temperature was reached, and there would be no cracking. If the gas oil could be held in a still by the use of pressure until a cracking temperature was reached, Humphreys thought it might provide a good yield of gasoline. But there was very little knowledge of the behavior of oil or steel under extreme heat and pressure. The result might be a terrific explosion and loss of life. And yet Humphreys, a true scientist, was willing to take the risk. A still was built and Humphreys took personal charge of its operation. Afraid of an explosion, regular boilermakers refused to repair the leaks with the still under pressure. Consequently, Humphreys had to climb over the still caulking the leaky spots. The first runs convinced the chemist that the process would work satisfactorily on a large scale. Thus was born the thermal cracking process, destined to be one of the great inventions of modern times.[61]

Until 1911 all the Standard Oil companies were grouped in one organization, the policies of which were

[60] Giddens, *Standard Oil Company (Indiana)*, 141-42.

[61] *Ibid.*, 142-48. See *Stanolind Record*, April, 1927, p. 23, for Robert E. Humphreys' account of his work at the Whiting Refinery.

determined by a board of directors in New York. In
that year the manufacturing committee of this board
refused Burton's request for approximately $1,000,000
to build the first batteries of pressure stills at the Whiting
refinery. According to one of the directors, "Burton
wants to blow the whole state of Indiana into Lake Michigan." Standard of Indiana became an independent company in 1911 when the United States Supreme Court
dissolved the gigantic Standard Oil Trust. The new
board, of which Burton was a member, willingly appropriated $709,000.00 for the construction of pressure
stills when the chemist expressed confidence that he knew
what he was doing.[62]

In January, 1913, twelve Burton stills, each with a
capacity of 8,250 gallons of gas oil every forty-eight
hours, were put into operation at Whiting. Five hundred
pressure stills were in use at Whiting in 1917 and the
number was increased to 893 in 1922.[63] Standard of
Indiana could have enjoyed a great advantage over its
competitors had it kept the Burton process to itself. Instead, the company sold the rights to the process to its
rivals for a royalty of 25 per cent of the net profits from
the savings made by using the Burton stills. This was
a wise move as the tremendous demands for gasoline
during World War I could not have been met without
the general use of the cracking process.[64] The Burton
stills are obsolete today but the principles of the Burton
process are the foundations of modern refining methods.
Thanks to the development of cracking, the industry by
1939 was able to convert 52 per cent of the crude oil

[62] Giddens, op. cit., 149; Wilson, Oil Competition in the Midwest, 7;
Babcock, The First Fifty, 17-20.

[63] Babcock, op. cit., 20.

[64] Ibid.; Wilson, Oil Competition in the Midwest, 7-8.

into gasoline. This was almost five times the yield before the cracking process was put into use.[65]

Shortly after the turn of the century the flow of crude oil through the Lima pipeline began to diminish, an indication that the Ohio field was about exhausted. In 1902 the first of the great mid-continent pools was discovered at Neodesha, Kansas. The oil from this pool was a "sweet crude," a pleasant contrast to the "sour" sulphur-ridden crude from Ohio. In 1904 the Standard Oil Company of Indiana built a refinery at Sugar Creek, Missouri, a suburb of Kansas City, to utilize the Kansas oil. Two years later the Whiting Refinery began to receive its crude oil through a new pipeline from Sugar Creek. This was the end of the Ohio oil, and its sulphur trouble, and of the Frasch process at Whiting.[66] Standard of Indiana acquired a half-interest in the great Sinclair Pipe Line Company in 1921, which extended in a great "Y" from the mid-continent field of Kansas and Oklahoma and from the Salt Creek field of Wyoming and thence to Whiting. In 1930 Standard obtained full ownership of the Sinclair Pipe Line Company, which was renamed the Stanolind Pipe Line Company.[67] Beginning with the mother refinery in 1889, the Standard Oil Company of Indiana was operating twelve refineries in various parts of the nation in 1939, its fiftieth birthday.

Standard's Interest in Whiting

The oil company took an active interest in Whiting's affairs from the very start. This was to be expected as the company was the largest taxpayer and employed

---

[65] Babcock, *The First Fifty*, 22.

[66] *Ibid.*, 24.

[67] Reynolds, *Historical Highlights of the Story of Standard Oil Company (Indiana)*, 12, 13.

the majority of the city's male population. While it would be difficult to determine the extent to which Standard influenced municipal policies, it was significant that William E. Warwick and Beaumont Parks, two of the first three mayors, were officials of the refinery. On the other hand, Walter E. Schrage, a banker with no connection with Standard Oil, was mayor of the city from 1914 to 1930. At no time did the Company support other candidates against Schrage. Refinery employees were encouraged to seek positions on the city council and on the school board.[68]

In 1903 Standard Oil purchased a strip about a mile long and two or three blocks wide in the heart of the refinery area. The little settlement known as "Oklahoma" was included in this acquisition. In order to secure this property the company bought a tract of land on the west edge of Whiting. It then offered to give the property owners in "Oklahoma" an equal amount of land in the new tract, move them free of charge to their new homes, and give them a good price for the old property. Within a short time, "Oklahoma," with its frontier town atmosphere, passed into history.[69]

Within the "Oklahoma" area was an old cemetery, Whiting's first burial ground, owned by Henry Schrage. No interments had been made there for several years. The Company bought the land from Schrage and moved the bodies to a Hammond cemetery at its own expense. Schrage's records showed about seven hundred interments. But when the local undertaker, who had contracted to remove the bodies for $3.00 each, came to do the work, over eleven hundred bodies were found.[70]

[68] This information was obtained in interviews with prominent Whiting citizens.

[69] Giddens, *Standard Oil Company (Indiana)*, 61.

[70] *Ibid.*, 62.

To further the cause of education in the community, the company, in the early years, donated several lots and sold others to the school board at reasonable prices as sites for schools. In 1905 it gave a piece of land to the Public Library Board of Whiting on the condition that within two years from the date of the conveyance a public library should be established.[71]

The Memorial Community House was the most tangible evidence of the Standard Oil Company's interest in the city's welfare. In 1923 the company provided the site and $300,000.00 for the erection of the building, John D. Rockefeller contributed an additional $100,000.00, and John D., Jr., $50,000.00. Standard officials made it clear that the company was making its contribution as a citizen of Whiting, not as an employer, and that the planning, erection, furnishing, and administration would be in the hands of the citizens of Whiting. The gifts of the Rockefellers expressed the interest they still felt in the people of the community where the oldest refinery of the company was located.[72]

The Community House, dedicated as a memorial to the Standard's employees who served in World War I, was a two-story, red brick building patterned after southern Italian architecture. It contained an auditorium, social and reading rooms, a gymnasium and swimming pool, billiard room, and other facilities for cultural and recreational activities. A board of eleven, composed of five employees of Standard at Whiting and six citizens of Whiting, was set up to supervise and administer the Community House.[73]

---

[71] *Ibid.* The library building was erected that same year. Howat (ed.), *A Standard History of Lake County*, 441.

[72] *The Stanolind Record,* December, 1923, p. 15.

[73] *Ibid.,* January, 1924, p. 1.

Population

Whiting, hemmed in by Lake Michigan, East Chicago, and Hammond, had no chance for expansion. In time the refinery area was larger than that of the city. On the other hand, residents of Robertsdale came to have a closer community of interests with Whiting than with Hammond, of which city they were a part. A large number of the refinery's employees found homes in Robertsdale and in time the social, cultural, and economic life of the two communities was merged. Businessmen of the sister communities were united in the Whiting-Robertsdale Chamber of Commerce. The Post Office Department, concerned more with efficiency than with political boundaries, distributed the mail to Robertsdale's citizens through its Whiting office.

The number of employees at the refinery increased from 1,815 in 1910 to 4,080 in 1920.[74] And yet Whiting's population did not increase in proportion, there being 6,587 people in the city in 1910 and 10,145 ten years later. In 1930 Whiting's population was only 10,880, which indicates that the city had reached the saturation point as far as population was concerned.[75] Fortunately, satisfactory transportation by the interurban lines and by the automobiles made it possible for many of the refinery's employees to live in more distant places.

Before World War I, Whiting received its share of immigrants, particularly from the Slavic countries of Europe. A little over 43 per cent of its population in 1910 and more than 36 per cent in 1920 were foreign born. The Slovaks outnumbered any of the other na-

[74] Employment statistics provided by Conger Reynolds, director of public relations for the Standard Oil Company of Indiana, Chicago, Illinois, April 13, 1954.

[75] *Fifteenth Census* (1930) : *Population,* 1 :341.

tionalities in 1920, with the Poles and Hungarians next in order.[76] Slovaks were so numerous in the city that the Catholic bishop asked that a priest be sent to them from Slovakia. Early in 1897 Reverend Father Benedict M. Rajcany arrived to administer to the spiritual and cultural needs of his countrymen. Later in the same year, Father Benedict and his Slovak congregation dedicated a new church to St. John the Baptist. While the church was located in Robertsdale, its history is largely identified with Whiting. In 1910 St. John's congregation reportedly numbered 1,500 members, of which 1,300 were residents of Whiting. By 1924 St. John's had a membership of 3,250, the largest Slovak church in the Calumet Region.[77]

The Negroes and Mexicans, last of the important segments of the Calumet's population to arrive, did not settle in Whiting. The Federal census listed three Negroes in Whiting in 1920 and in 1930 none were reported there. While the Standard Oil Company allegedly had no prejudice against hiring Negroes and Mexicans, apparently few were ever employed at the refinery. Also, the Negroes and Mexicans arrived in the region in large numbers after World War I and by that time Whiting was overcrowded with residents. There was also some evidence that public opinion in Whiting threw up a subtle but effective barrier against the settlement of Negroes in the city.

[76] *Thirteenth Census* (1910): *Population,* pt. 2:572; *Fourteenth Census* (1920): *Population,* pt. 3:304.

[77] Edwin G. Kaiser, *History of St. John's Parish, Whiting, Indiana . . . 1897-1947* (n. p., n.d.), 25, 26, 27; Whiting *Call* (souvenir edition), October, 1910; Cannon, Loring and Robb (eds.), *History of the Lake and Calumet Region,* 1:489-90.

8

EAST CHICAGO, THE TWIN CITY

EAST CHICAGO AND INDIANA HARBOR together form the "Twin City" of the region. While these communities have always been united politically under the name of East Chicago, they were physically separated for many years and a sectional consciousness developed among their citizens that is apparent at the present time. The Indiana Harbor Ship Canal and the great switching yards of the Indiana Harbor Belt Line Railroad divide the city into two almost equal parts. This barrier is so formidable that satisfactory means of transportation between the areas has never been established. As a result, the western half is identified in the minds of the inhabitants as East Chicago, and the eastern side, adjacent to Lake Michigan, as Indiana Harbor. Each community has developed its own business, manufacturing, and residential districts so as to give all the appearance of separate cities. The railroads that pass through the eastern part of the city add to the confusion by listing their stations as Indiana Harbor.[1] Until recent years, the telephone company identified its exchanges as East Chicago and Indiana Harbor respectively. Consequently, unity of thought and action among the citizens of the Twin City has been difficult

---

[1] A few years ago this writer found it necessary to explain to the ticket agent at the Pennsylvania Railroad Station in Fort Wayne that the railroad station listed as Indiana Harbor was in the city of East Chicago.

216

to attain, and on many occasions sectional strife has characterized the various phases of its affairs.

Early Settlement

Because the early settlers avoided this part of the Calumet, it remained in almost a virgin state until the last years of the nineteenth century. Sand ridges with intervening swamps and sloughs covered the area, the part adjacent to Lake Michigan being almost impenetrable. The Grand Calumet River, which crossed the southern edge, made no contribution in the matter of drainage. This stream, almost devoid of a current and clogged with tall grass and reeds, was practically impassable, even by canoes. In 1872 army engineers reported the condition of the surrounding country was such that no commercial advantage could be obtained by dredging the channel of the river.[2] While three trunk-line railroads crossed the area in the early years, not one bothered to establish a station there. This section, on the whole, was more desolate and inaccessible than any other portion of the Calumet Region.

The area was a part of the vast estate of George W. Clark.[3] In 1860 Clark drew a map of his holdings upon which the present Indiana Harbor was identified as Poplar Point. Although this map showed a wooden pier extending into Lake Michigan at Poplar Point, the structure apparently existed only in Clark's mind. He probably planned to build such a pier for the shipment of timber to Chicago. The map also showed an "Indiana Harbor of Wolf River" at the place where that stream, which had its origin in Wolf Lake, emptied into Lake

2 "Examination and Survey of the Mouth of Grand Calumet River, Indiana," 1872, in Report of the Secretary of War, in *Senate Documents,* 42 Congress, 3 session, No. 25, p. 8.

3 See above, 94-95.

Michigan a few miles northwest of Poplar Point. There are some who believe the name Indiana Harbor was borrowed from this old map.[4]

The records indicate that the first settler on the site of East Chicago was a German named Dominick Mutter who purchased 120 acres of land in what is now Indiana Harbor, in 1857.[5] A short time later another German, Louis Ahlendorf, built a house not far from the Mutter homestead.[6] Their nearest neighbors were other German families living along the railroad tracks in what is now Whiting. In 1867 Jacob Forsythe, a brother-in-law of George W. Clark, moved with his family to Poplar Point where he purchased Mutter's property. Forsythe, as noted before, was the administrator of the Clark estate. He erected a sawmill near Lake Michigan and named the place Cassella for his sister, Ella Cass, wife of George W. Cass, president of the Pittsburgh, Fort Wayne and Chicago Railroad.[7] A few cabins were built to house the workers at the sawmill, and the Pittsburgh, Fort Wayne and Chicago constructed a siding for loading timber. In 1871 the little settlement was destroyed by the great fire that swept the region. The Forsythe residence burned and the family moved into the Ahlendorf house.[8] Forsythe did not rebuild the sawmill and once more the quiet of the wilderness prevailed in that vicinity. Cassella persisted as the name for the area until the Inland Steel Company obtained its site there in 1901, when the name was changed to Indiana Harbor.[9]

4 *Whiting City Almanac and Cook Book,* 20.

5 Lake County Deed Records, J:463, 465.

6 The Ahlendorf place was near the site of the Grasselli Chemical Company's plant. See *Calumet Region Historical Guide,* 216.

7 *Whiting City Almanac and Cook Book,* 8.

8 *Ibid.,* 10, 11; Edgar Mills, *A History of East Chicago* (Garman Printing Company, East Chicago, n. d.), 1.

9 According to reports, Indiana Harbor was also known as Brimson

Expansion of the Steel Industry

The expansion of the steel industry in the Chicago area was largely responsible for the origin and development of East Chicago and Gary. This expansion was from the heart of Chicago eastward along the shore of Lake Michigan. Cheap transportation on the Great Lakes was one of the most important factors in the development of the iron and steel industry in the Calumet Region of Illinois and Indiana. The industrialists of the late nineteenth century recognized the value of the excellent facilities afforded by the numerous railroads in the region. They also saw the possibilities of harbors along the Lake for the reception of iron ore, coal, and limestone as well as for the shipment of finished products to market. Moreover, adequate sites were available for industrial purposes at reasonable prices.[10]

Originally, the iron and steel industry in the Chicago area was concentrated along the Chicago River near the heart of the city. Foundries were built there as early as 1839. By the second half of the century the sites near the river were too valuable for industrial purposes. Industrialists then turned their attention to the sparsely settled region known as South Chicago. In 1870 the Federal government started the development of the South Chicago Harbor at the mouth of the Calumet River. Ten years later, the Illinois Steel Company began construction of its South Chicago Works alongside this harbor. In the beginning, the steel officials thought they had a site large enough for all time, but the erection of this great steel mill set off a boom in South Chicago

Switch for a time. See Pearl Ansley, History of Indiana Harbor (Typewritten MS in the Indiana Harbor Public Library, n. d.), 1.

10 John B. Appleton, *The Iron and Steel Industry of the Calumet District. A Study in Economic Geography* (University of Illinois, *Studies in Social Sciences*, Vol. 13, No. 2, June, 1925), 15, 49.

which lasted for several years.[11] Other industries located there, and part of the area was subdivided for residential purposes, with space set aside for parks and schools. As a result, land for industrial purposes became scarce and expensive. Therefore, industrialists and speculators began to seek sites across the state line in Indiana.

Establishment of the City

Early in November, 1881, Jacob and Caroline Forsythe sold 8,000 acres of land for $1,000,000 to William W. Green of Newark, New Jersey. On the same day, Green transferred this huge tract, upon which the greater part of East Chicago now stands, to the East Chicago Improvement Company.[12] This firm, incorporated in New Jersey, was owned by the London Banking House of Melville, Evans and Company.[13] The English financiers, impressed by the boom in South Chicago, saw possibilities of profitable investment in adjacent Indiana. The name, East Chicago Improvement Company, was chosen to identify the location of the property and also to associate it with the South Chicago boom. These considerations no doubt influenced the selection of the name for the city ultimately established there.[14] Since the men behind the East Chicago Improvement Company were bankers, and not industrialists, it is obvious their purpose was speculation in industrial sites.

There is no record of any land sales by the East Chicago Improvement Company. This is not surprising because the area that lay between its holdings and South

[11] Appleton, *The Iron and Steel Industry*, 27-28, 30-31, 56.

[12] Lake County Deed Records, 32:50-53, 54, 55, 56; *Calumet Region Historical Guide*, 216.

[13] Melville, Evans and Company was owned by Ronald Leslie Melville, Henry Evans, and Thomas Fickus. Melville Street in East Chicago was named for Melville, whose title was the Earl of Leven and Melville.

[14] East Chicago *Calumet News*, November 18, 1924.

Chicago was of no concern to industrialists until 1889, when the Standard Oil Company purchased the refinery site at Whiting. In July, 1887, the East Chicago Improvement Company, acting through its attorney, John S. Kennedy, of the New York banking house of J. Kennedy-Tod and Company, transferred its acreage to Joseph Thatcher Torrence and his wife, Libbie, "for and in consideration of the sum of one dollar, lawful money of the United States to it in hand paid and for other good and valuable considerations." This arrangement was common in transactions where the seller retained an interest in the property, generally in the form of stock, and also in instances when the buyer assumed all the debts and other financial obligations incurred by the seller in regard to the property. There is also a possibility that the English syndicate had never fully paid the Forsythes for the land. The Torrences then turned the acreage over to the Calumet Canal and Improvement Company. General Torrence and Marcus M. Towle, the founder of Hammond, organized this firm in 1887, Towle being its first president. The selling price was again "one dollar and other valuable considerations."[15]

General Torrence, an industrial engineer, had experienced some success as a promoter and builder of foundries and steel mills in the Chicago area. In 1885 he established and operated for a time a small iron works in Hammond. The following year he was associated with Marcus M. Towle and James N. Young in the organization of the Chicago and Calumet Terminal Belt Line Railroad. This road, which figured prominently in the development of East Chicago and Whiting, was put into operation in 1888.[16] East Chicago also owes much to

[15] Lake County Deed Records, 42:176, 180.

[16] See H. MacGrath, W. J. Guest, W. James, and H. G. Cutler (eds.), *Encyclopedia of Biography of Illinois* (2 vols. Chicago, 1902), 1:332-34,

the efforts and interest of Robert E. Tod, of the J. Kennedy-Tod Company in New York. Tod, secretary and treasurer of the Calumet Canal and Improvement Company, made his home in East Chicago for a time.[17] According to one report, East Chicago was started with Forsythe's land, Torrence's vision, and Towle's money.[18]

Towle, Torrence, the Forsythes, and the English interests were the principal stockholders in the Calumet Canal and Improvement Company, which was organized in 1887 with a capital of $2,000,000.[19] The English interests operated through J. Kennedy-Tod and Company. In May, 1887, the Standard Steel and Iron Company was formed by Towle, Torrence, the Forsythes, and James N. Young. This firm started operations with about 1,000 acres of land, upon which it later laid out the town of East Chicago.[20] In October, 1887, Caroline Forsythe purchased 637 acres from the Calumet Canal and Improvement Company for $290,000.00. This land was turned over to the Standard Steel and Iron Company.[21] Although the latter company was never anything but a real estate organization, the name indicates that its founders intended, in the beginning at least, to get into the steel business. The officials of these two companies laid out the pattern by which East Chicago ultimately developed. Their plans called for the construction of a ship canal from Lake Michigan south to the

and the Chicago *Sunday Tribune,* November 1, 1896, for accounts of Torrence's career.

17 Hammond *Lake County Times,* July 26, 1919. Robert E. Tod was a nephew of John S. Kennedy. Tod Avenue and Tod Park in East Chicago were named for him. Kennedy Avenue was named for John S. Kennedy.

18 Howat (ed.), *A Standard History of Lake County,* 2:506.

19 *Encyclopedia of Biography of Illinois,* 1:334.

20 East Chicago *Journal,* October 15, 1889.

21 Lake County Deed Records, 47:70.

Grand Calumet River, and the building of a pier into the Lake at Poplar Point. Also, for a belt line railroad to connect the city with other railroads in the Chicago area. When these improvements were accomplished, the promoters believed it would be an easy matter to attract industries to the area.[22]

In the fall of 1887, the Standard Steel and Iron Company laid out the site of East Chicago. The cutting of the thick undergrowth in the swamps, leveling the sand ridges, and filling in the low places between the ridges was an extremely difficult task. By April, 1888, men with forty teams of horses, under the supervision of General Torrence, were busy at work on the roads and streets. The first land to be platted was a subdivision of 110 acres lying between what is now Railroad Avenue and a parallel line drawn just west of the present Indianapolis Boulevard. The northern boundary was what is now the Baltimore and Ohio Terminal Railroad, while the southern limits were just south of what is now 151st Street.[23]

The tracks of the Chicago and Calumet Terminal Belt Line, now the Baltimore and Ohio Terminal Road, were extended from the Indiana-Illinois line eastward into the town site in 1888. Work was started on the ship canal about the same time. In July, 1888, the Standard Steel and Iron Company and the Calumet Canal and Improvement Company offered to convey to the Federal government a strip of land 300 feet wide for the building of a harbor, and another 200 feet in width for the proposed ship canal between the Lake and the Grand Calumet River. The promoters hoped the government would take over the construction of these projects. There is no evi-

22 East Chicago *Journal,* October 15, 1889.
23 *Ibid.; Calumet Region Historical Guide,* 218.

dence that the government ever accepted the land.[24] The Calumet Canal and Improvement Company discontinued its efforts to dig the canal within a short time. In February, 1888, Caroline Forsythe purchased the interests of Marcus M. Towle and James N. Young in the Standard Steel and Iron Company. This transaction gave the Forsythes and General Torrence control of that firm.[25]

In March, 1889, the Lake County Board of Commissioners approved a request for the incorporation of the town. An election was held the following May in which the citizens approved the proposition to incorporate by a vote of 234 to four. The original town site containing 3.75 square miles, was about one third of the city's present size.[26] Several of the avenues were named for prominent stockholders of the land companies or for members of their families. John S. Kennedy, Robert E. Tod, the Forsythes, the wealthy Baring family in England, and Jesse Torrence Magoun, a daughter of General Torrence, were honored in this manner.[27] The real estate

[24] U. S. Army, Chief of Engineers, *Annual Report,* 1910, pt. 2:2156.

[25] East Chicago *Journal,* October 15, 1889.

[26] *East Chicago, Indiana* (a periodical published by the East Chicago Chamber of Commerce), 2:238-39 (August, 1927).

[27] Northcote Avenue, laid out many years later, was named for Amanys N. Northcote, a stockholder of the Lake Michigan Land Company. There is an interesting story about John C. Parrish, a stockholder in the East Chicago Company, for whom Parrish Avenue was named. Pleased by the honor, the Chicagoan ordered the erection of a handsome iron drinking fountain for man and beast at the best location on the avenue. The citizens could not bring themselves to inform Mr. Parrish that there were no water mains as yet in Indiana Harbor. A wooden tank, connected with the fountain by a pipe, was placed in a concealed position. The day of dedication arrived and the proud donor was escorted to the fountain where a short ceremony took place. Mr. Parrish took the first drink followed by the local dignitaries in the crowd. The citizens then hurried him away before the supply of water in the hidden tank was exhausted. See C. A. Westberg, "The Street Nomenclature of the City of East Chicago," in *ibid.,* 1:104, 130 (March, 1926).

companies indicated their desire that the town be associated with Chicago by attaching the east and west streets to the numerical system used in that city. An entire block was presented to the town by the Standard Steel and Iron Company as a site for a town hall and fire department.[28] By 1893 East Chicago's population was large enough for it to be elevated to the status of a city. William H. Penman, whose family established the first permanent home in the community, was its first mayor.[29]

East Chicago's inhabitants were confronted with the same problems experienced by other industrial cities of the region during the first years of their existence. The inevitable sand and the lack of satisfactory communication with the outside world complicated their everyday lives. Mail service was poor, and for some time the postmaster was compelled to use a horse and buggy, which he provided at his own expense, to bring the daily mail from Whiting. Complaints were made that the town, without telegraph facilities and a railroad station, was virtually isolated from the world outside.[30] The editor of the Chesterton *Tribune,* impressed by its frontier character, declared in May, 1890: "East Chicago is a most excellent field for the missionary and evangelist. It is not yet two years old, has 1,500 inhabitants, 13 saloons (and threatened with more), but not a single solitary church."[31] This observation was not completely true. The Methodist congregation of East Chicago erected a building in 1889 and that same year East Chicago's Catholics purchased the site of the present St. Mary's Church from the Standard Steel and Iron Company. The

28 East Chicago *Journal,* October 15, 1889.
29 *East Chicago, Indiana,* 2:238-39 (August, 1927).
30 East Chicago *Journal,* May 25 and June 22, 1889.
31 Chesterton *Tribune,* May 22, 1890.

First Congregational Church was also organized in 1889.[32] Before erection of the Catholic Church, Mass was celebrated in Tod's Opera House. In November, 1888, the first school, with fifteen pupils enrolled, was opened in the town hall. For the first two years, the Standard Steel and Iron Company paid all the expenses of the school. The town's most impressive structure was Tod's Opera House, named for Robert E. Tod. This three-story brick structure was located at the southwest corner of the present Indianapolis Boulevard and Chicago Avenue. According to its admirers, the opera house would have done justice to a city of 20,000 people.[33] In 1890 the town's population numbered 1,255.[34]

Early Industries

The William Graver Tank Works, established early in 1888, was the town's first industry. As early as 1858 its founder, William Graver, manufactured storage tanks for oil companies at Allegheny, Pennsylvania. In 1884 Graver moved his company to Chicago where he demonstrated that lighter and cheaper tanks were more satisfactory than the heavy boilerlike affairs then in use by the oil companies. When the oil field in Ohio was opened the next year, Graver shifted his operations to Lima where he constructed tanks for the Standard Oil Company.[35] The officials of the company apparently informed

[32] Howat (ed.), *A Standard History of Lake County,* 1:430-32. In 1911-12 this Methodist congregation erected its present building at the corner of Chicago and Baring avenues on land donated by the East Chicago Company.

[33] East Chicago *Journal,* May 25, 1889; Magenta D. Kennedy, "Facts Concerning East Chicago," in Demmon (ed.), *History of Lake County* (1934), 93, 94.

[34] U. S. Bureau of the Census, *Compendium of the Eleventh Census* (1890), pt. 1:123.

[35] "Graver Tanks are Monuments to Confidence, Energy, and Skill,"

Graver of their plans to build a refinery at Whiting and also encouraged him to locate his tank works in that vicinity. Graver's East Chicago plant was busy turning out tanks for Standard Oil almost a year before construction of its Whiting refinery was started. In October, 1889, seventy-five men were employed at the tank works.[36] The plant's expansion was so rapid that it was soon one of the city's most substantial industries.

East Chicago experienced an industrial and real estate boom for several years after its founding. The Standard Steel and Iron Company engaged special trains to transport prospective purchasers from Chicago to the town site. Picnics were held on Sundays at the local park where free food, beer, and maps of the community were distributed to the guests. Passenger boats brought people to view the uninhabited lake front, which, according to the boasts of the promoters, was soon to be the "Sheffield" of America.[37] Huge piles of building materials took form as several sawmills cut hardwood lumber from logs shipped from central Indiana.

The C. A. Treat Car Wheel Works was established in 1889. This plant, which employed one hundred men, manufactured two hundred railroad car wheels daily. That same year, Andrew Wickey, who was to be prominent in the city's affairs for many years, erected the Famous Manufacturing Company for the production of hay balers and other farm machinery. In later years Wickey's plant made high-wheel automobile roadsters for physicians and farmers to use on the rough and muddy

in *Southwestern Oil Journal* (Fort Worth, Texas), December 5, 1919, p. 6.

36 Alfred Jones, "John D. Rockefeller First to Industrialize Calumet," in Gary *Post-Tribune*, May 27, 1937; East Chicago *Journal*, October 15, 1889.

37 East Chicago *Journal*, May 25 and August 20, 1889.

roads of that time. Zenas Burns established the Chicago
Horseshoe Factory, which included a foundry, where
one hundred men turned out 270,000 horseshoes daily.
The National Forge and Iron Company employed four
hundred men in the manufacture of merchant bar iron
and railway car axles. In 1892 another important industry, the Grasselli Chemical Company, was attracted
to East Chicago because of its nearness to the Standard
Oil refinery at Whiting. This plant made chemicals used
in the manufacture of petroleum products. While it
employed only twenty-five men in the beginning, Grasselli produced 15,000 tons of chemicals annually.[38]

In 1890 dissension arose between General Torrence
and the English stockholders in the Calumet Canal and
Improvement Company. The latter were apparently dissatisfied with General Torrence because he had concentrated his efforts on the development of the original
site of East Chicago, the greater part of which was
owned by the Standard Steel and Iron Company. The
Englishmen, it appears, were convinced that Torrence
had willfully neglected the vast holdings of their company.
In 1888 Torrence was reported to have said that he
could always sell the land adjacent to Lake Michigan,
which was owned by the Calumet Canal and Improvement
Company, whenever he so desired. The following year
the local newspaper reported that the Calumet Company
"rested from its enterprises while the Standard Steel
and Iron Company engaged in the sale of lots and in
the location of manufacturing plants."[39] The English

[38] *Ibid.*, October 15, 1889; Kennedy, "Facts Concerning East Chicago,"
in Demmon (ed.), *History of Lake County* (1934), 93-94; *Lake County
Directory*, 1909, p. 54; *East Chicago, Indiana*, 4(1929):172.

[39] Lake County Deed Records, 60:165; *Encyclopoedia of Biography of
Illinois*, 1:334; Chicago *Sunday Tribune*, November 1, 1896; East Chicago
Journal, October 15, 1889.

stockholders instructed their agent in New York, J. Kennedy-Tod and Company, to investigate the operations of the land company and if possible eliminate General Torrence from the organization. Accordingly, Robert E. Tod came to East Chicago to study the problem. In the summer of 1892 General Torrence sold his interest in the company to other stockholders and resigned as president of the firm. Robert E. Tod succeeded him as president, a position he held until the merger of the firm with the East Chicago Company in 1901.

Despite the reorganization of the land company, there were no significant industrial developments in the city during the remaining years of the century. The nationwide depression which began in 1893 not only prevented the location of new plants but made it extremely difficult for those already established to survive. The Graver Tank Works and the Grasselli Chemical Company were able to weather the storm only because of the steady demand for their products by the refinery in Whiting. The National Forge and Iron Company, in particular, had trouble keeping its doors open. In 1894 a wage cut resulted in a strike of 250 of its 600 employees. The Company was in the hands of a receiver in 1896 for the third time in eight months. The city's business life was seriously affected when the plant suspended operations for a time.[40] The Company's name was changed several times in the course of its financial troubles, eventually becoming known as the East Chicago Iron and Steel Company.

The city was without a bank until 1899, at which time Andrew Wickey established the East Chicago Bank, a private institution. Within a short time it was purchased by Walter E. Schrage of Whiting, and, in 1910, the

[40] Chesterton *Tribune,* March 2, 1894.

"Schrage Bank" obtained a charter from the state.[41] The "gay nineties" were not so gay for East Chicago; its population in 1900 numbered only 3,411 inhabitants.[42]

As the century neared its close, forces were at work which would soon inaugurate a new era for East Chicago as well as for the other parts of the region. The expansion of industry and the railroads, accompanied by a great increase in the nation's population and the subsequent need for increased farm production, created a demand for steel far beyond the capacity of the existing mills to supply. Obviously, the only solution to the problem lay in the construction of new and more efficient plants. Capital and creative genius were available but appropriate sites for expansion and for new mills were scarce. As a result, the quiet that prevailed along much of the southern shore of Lake Michigan in Indiana was soon destroyed forever.

The Coming of Inland Steel

In 1895 a group of Chicago financiers, which included Owen F. Aldis, Potter Palmer, Jr., and Albert De Wolfe Erskine, organized the Lake Michigan Land Company. This firm began to buy land where Indiana Harbor now stands from the Calumet Canal and Improvement Company. By 1898 its acquisitions amounted to more than 1,300 acres.[43] Another important investor was the industrialist, Henry C. Frick, who bought three hundred acres in the same area from the Calumet Canal and Improvement Company.[44] These were the first large sales made by that company since its organization in 1887.

[41] Howat (ed.), *A Standard History of Lake County,* 2:766.
[42] *Twelfth Census of the United States* (1900): *Population,* pt. 1:447.
[43] Lake County Deed Records, 74:275, 282; 77:276, 310; 83:439; 87:180.
[44] *The Iron Age,* 71:30 (April 16, 1903).

In 1901 the Lake Michigan Land Company made arrangements with Inland Steel to locate a plant in Indiana Harbor. This was probably the most important single event in East Chicago's history. Inland Steel was at that time controlled by its founder, Joseph Block, and his sons, Leopold E. and Philip D. Block. The land company gave fifty acres adjacent to Lake Michigan for a plant site, and also guaranteed that satisfactory belt-line connections would be made with the trunk-line railroads in the Chicago area. In return, the steel company agreed to build within three years an open-hearth plant costing not less than $900,000.00.[45] Inland Steel, from the moment of its arrival, was the largest industry in East Chicago.

The founding of Inland Steel came about in this way. In 1893 Joseph Block was the senior partner and general manager of the Block-Pollack Iron Company in Cincinnati, Ohio. The firm manufactured railroad car axles and also engaged in the iron and steel scrap business. Among its creditors was the Chicago Steel Company which had been forced out of business that year by the depression. This company, which had made harrow teeth and other products used by farmers, was in debt to the Block-Pollack Firm for between $20,000.00 and $30,-000.00 for iron and steel scrap. George H. Jones, one of the owners of the defunct company, purchased its antiquated machinery and moved it to Chicago Heights, Illinois, where a land company had offered financial aid amounting to $20,000.00 and a site for a plant. Money was so scarce that Jones was unable to raise enough funds to unload the machinery from the freight cars. At this juncture, he approached Joseph Block and convinced him

45 Wayde Grinstead, *50 Years of Inland Steel, 1893-1943* (Chicago, 1943), 17.

of the possibilities at Chicago Heights. As a result, the Inland Steel Company was incorporated in October, 1893, with Joseph Block, Philip D. Block, George H. Jones, and Joseph E. Porter as principal stockholders. Porter was the first president of the company. The machinery, which still remained on the railroad cars, was purchased for $8,800.00. Inland Steel also accepted the offer of financial aid and a site by the land company at Chicago Heights.[46]

By 1897 Inland's rolling mill at Chicago Heights was such a prosperous concern that the company was in a position to expand. In November of that year, Philip D. Block purchased the property of the East Chicago Iron and Steel Company at a sheriff's sale for $50,000.00. About three weeks later, Block sold the plant to the Inland Iron and Forge Company, a subsidiary of Inland Steel, for $125,000.00.[47] Leopold E. Block came to East Chicago from Pittsburgh to manage the new member of the Inland family. The plant was put in working order, new machinery was installed, and was soon engaged in the profitable production of forged axles and other railroad equipment. In May, 1899, Inland Steel sold the Inland Iron and Forge for stock in the newly organized Republic Iron and Steel Company. Inland later sold this stock for about a half million dollars. This money was used in the building of the Indiana Harbor plant.[48]

[46] Interview with Leopold E. Block, Chicago, April 29, 1952; Grinstead, *50 Years of Inland Steel,* 5-9, 12, 15.

[47] Grinstead, *op. cit.,* 12, says that this was the East Chicago Iron and Forge Company. However, the deed to the property listed the plant as the East Chicago Iron and Steel Company. For these transactions, see Lake County Deed Records, 83:235-36, 295.

[48] *50 Years at Indiana Harbor* (anniversary edition of the *Inland News,* May, 1951).

When Leopold E. Block visited the site in Indiana Harbor granted Inland Steel by the Lake Michigan Land Company, he found that twenty of the fifty acres were covered by the waters of Lake Michigan. The only person in the area was the watchman in the lonely railroad tower at the intersection of the New York Central and the Elgin, Joliet and Eastern Belt Line Railroad. Block went to New York to make arrangements with the New York Central for transporting from Chicago the workmen who were to build the plant, and he also persuaded Owen F. Aldis to build an excellent hotel, the South Bay, for the accommodation of company officials and engineers during the construction period.[49]

In the late spring of 1901 construction was started. The original plans called for the building of four open-hearth furnaces, a blooming mill, and a standard bar mill. Although blast furnaces were contemplated, Inland for the time being planned to purchase pig iron from other steel companies. R. J. Beatty, general manager of the Midland Iron and Steel Company at Muncie, Indiana, was persuaded by the Blocks to invest money in Inland Steel. Beatty became a director of the company and general manager of the Indiana Harbor plant. Beatty was a "sheet" man, and since he brought men from Muncie who were familiar with sheet-mill operations, the decision was made to add sheet mills.[50] In July, 1902, the first steel ingots to be poured in the East Chicago area were made at the new Inland plant. The blooming mill started operations the following month, and the sheet and bar mills were running by November. According to reports, by 1903 Inland had invested $2,000,000 in

[49] Interview with Leopold E. Block, Chicago, April 29, 1952. Another brother, E. J. Block, joined the Inland organization in 1901.

[50] *The Iron Age,* 67:24 (May 9, 1901); 68:7 (June 20, 1901); Grinstead, *50 Years of Inland Steel,* 20, 25.

its Indiana Harbor Works.[51] The following year about 1,200 men were employed at the plant.[52]

Inland's expansion was more rapid than its founders had anticipated. As Leopold E. Block stated: "We didn't know that we would grow so big."[53] The company soon decided to manufacture its own pig iron for the increasing number of open-hearth furnaces. Within a short time the Laura Iron Ore Mine in the rich Mesaba Range near Hibbing, Minnesota, was purchased. In 1907 the first blast furnace, the "Madeline Number One," named for the daughter of Philip D. Block, was put into operation.[54] By that time the first section of the Indiana Harbor Ship Canal was completed and the ore boats could unload their cargoes at Inland's docks. On August 2, 1907, the Gary *Weekly Tribune* announced: "the first cargo of iron ore ever put off in Indiana will be piled up Sunday [August 4] on the docks of the Inland Steel Company at Indiana Harbor." A second blast furnace, the "Madeline Number Two," was put into use in 1912.[55]

Inland soon outgrew its original site and no land for expansion was available except at excessive prices. In 1907 the Indiana General Assembly passed the "made-land" law, which permitted industries to fill in Lake Michigan out to the limits of the State's jurisdiction. Federal control over the Lake began at the depth of twenty-two feet, at which point the water was considered navigable. As the Lake was filled in, industries could obtain a deed from the State for the land thus made for $25.00 an acre. The companies were required to pay

51 *Iron Age*, 71:30 (April 16, 1903) ; *50 Years at Indiana Harbor*, 4.

52 Employment figures supplied by M. M. McClure, Inland Steel Company, East Chicago, Indiana.

53 Interview with Leopold E. Block, Chicago, April 29, 1952.

54 Grinstead, *50 Years of Inland Steel*, 27.

55 *Ibid.*, 33.

$100.00 a year taxes for each acre acquired. Although the filling-in process provided the mills with an easy means of disposing of worthless slag, the cost of building the land amounted to five or six thousand dollars an acre. Its great value lay in the fact that the industries were provided with contiguous land upon which to expand.[56]

In 1911 Inland organized the Inland Steamship Company. This subsidiary purchased two ore freighters, named the "Joseph Block" and the "N. F. Leopold," and engaged in the transportation of iron ore from the Minnesota mines to Indiana Harbor.[57] As traffic on the upper reaches of the Great Lakes was halted by ice for about four months each year, it was necessary to store enough ore at the plant to feed the blast furnaces through the winter.

Although there was an abundance of ordinary labor to be had, Inland found it difficult to maintain an adequate force of supervisors. Men working and living in well-established industrial communities were reluctant to expose their families to the rough pioneer conditions prevalent in Indiana Harbor in the early years.[58] For this reason the Indiana Homes Company, another subsidiary of the steel company, in 1920 built one hundred duplex houses to accommodate two hundred families in what was called the Sunnyside addition of Indiana Harbor. These six-room apartments were rented to employees at a reasonable rate, and the company provided domestic coke for heating purposes at a price much lower than that offered by private firms.[59] Inland in time was re-

[56] *Laws of Indiana*, 1907, pp. 126-27; interview with Leopold E. Block, Chicago, April 29, 1952.

[57] Grinstead, *50 Years of Inland Steel*, 32.

[58] Interview with Leopold E. Block, Chicago, April 29, 1952.

[59] *The Iron Age*, 105:1037 (April 8, 1920).

garded as the largest independent steel company in the Middle West. Its number of employees increased from 3,900 in 1914 to 7,000 in 1924.[60]

The East Chicago Company

In 1901 the development of the Twin City began in earnest when Albert De Wolfe Erskine organized the East Chicago Company. This firm, in which some of Chicago's first families had a financial interest, was the real builder of the city. Erskine was its president, Honore Palmer, vice-president, and Potter Palmer, Jr., treasurer. The secretary was George W. Lewis, who made his home in the community and was for many years one of its most prominent citizens. The board of directors included Robert E. Tod of New York, Stanley McCormick of the International Harvester Company, S. H. Strawn, and Owen F. Aldis. Among the prominent stockholders were Henry C. Frick, John S. Kennedy, John V. Farwell of the Central Trust Company of New York, and certain English investment companies. The East Chicago Company began operations with a capital of $2,500,000.[61]

The East Chicago Company absorbed the Lake Michigan Land Company in 1901, and within two years acquired all the land owned by the Calumet Canal and Improvement Company and by the Standard Steel and Iron Company. This was regarded as one of the largest and most important real estate transactions ever made in the Chicago area. In 1903 the East Chicago Company was in control of about 5,000 acres in the Twin City. Four thousand lots had been platted by that time, and the remainder was in acreage tracts for sale to indus-

60 Employment figures supplied by M. M. McClure, Inland Steel Company, East Chicago, Indiana.

61 *The Iron Age,* 71:30 (April 16, 1903).

tries.[62] The company owned most of the unoccupied land in the city and the development of the west side, East Chicago, and the east side, Indiana Harbor, proceeded simultaneously.

In 1901 the Company began the construction of the business and residential sections of Indiana Harbor. The platting was accomplished only after the thick growth of bushes and scrub oak were cut, the sand ridges leveled, and the swamps filled in. Several hundred workmen were used in the construction of streets, sewers, and water mains, all of which was done at the Company's expense. Since the Company was in a hurry to sell lots, hard surfacing of the streets was generally done in a haphazard fashion. In some instances, the paving was achieved by pouring a thin covering of asphalt and gravel on a foundation of hay and straw. Some of the streets on the western side of the city were surfaced with bricks laid on the soft sand.[63] The company also constructed business houses and residences for sale or rent to the inhabitants. According to reports, by 1904 nearly six hundred business houses and residences had been erected in Indiana Harbor. The company advertised the city as the "Twentieth Century Wonder." Those who wished to investigate its possibilities could obtain free railroad tickets at the company's Chicago office. Claims were made that "the small investor at Indiana Harbor is making a good thing. The large investor is getting rich." Also, that the community offered workers the opportunity to escape from the demoralizing influence of Chicago.[64]

[62] *Ibid.;* Lake County Deed Records, Vols. 90, 92, 94, and 107.

[63] Interview with Charles M. Reed, East Chicago, October 14, 1953. Reed was an attorney for the East Chicago Company during most of its existence.

[64] *Indiana Harbor. The New Industrial City* (Brochure published by the East Chicago Company, 1904).

Indiana Harbor resembled the mining towns of the Old West in those early years. There was an influx of workers to be sheltered. In 1901 Charles A. Friedrich opened the Harbor Hotel at the corner of Michigan Street and Block Avenue. Although there was not a single bed in the place, sixty-six guests were registered the first night. Many slept in tents or in the open air. Cheap restaurants, boarding houses, and gambling places sprang up almost overnight. In 1910 the Twin City boasted 110 saloons. Single men and married men without their families predominated, the males outnumbering the females by almost two to one in 1910.[65] The babble of foreign tongues was heard on the streets, and the industries found it necessary to print their rules and instructions in several languages.

There was a brighter side to the bustling industrial city. Two recreation areas, Lees Park, on the lake front, and Washington Park, in the south part of Indiana Harbor, were donated to the city by the East Chicago Company. Several hundred young men organized the Indiana Harbor Yacht Club and erected what was considered at that time a handsome club house. The South Bay Hotel, at the intersection of Aldis Avenue and Michigan Street, was the center of Indiana Harbor's social life.[66] Timothy H. Ball, who had predicted years before that large industrial cities would be located on the shore of Lake Michigan, wrote in 1902: "Indiana Harbor is already a town, almost a city of itself." Two years later he wrote: "To one who saw cities try to grow in northern Indiana sixty-seven years ago, and saw them fail, it is amazing how cities now spring up and grow. . . .

---

65 Ball, *Encyclopedia of Genealogy and Biography*, 292-93; Indiana Bureau of Statistics, *Thirteenth Biennial Report*, 1909-10, p. 1150. *Thirteenth Census of the United States* (1910): *Population*, pt. 2:568.

66 *Indiana Harbor. The New Industrial City.*

Money and energy, steam and electricity, are doing much for Lake County in its rapid advance among the counties of the State."[67]

Charles W. Hotchkiss, a civil engineer with years of experience with various railroads, was the promotional genius of East Chicago. Hotchkiss joined the East Chicago Company in 1901 as a vice-president and general manager; he became president of the land company in 1906 and served in that capacity until 1908, at which time he resigned to devote his time to the Indiana Harbor Belt Line Railroad, of which he was also president.[68] Hotchkiss saw the soundness of General Torrence's views that the industrial development of East Chicago depended upon the construction of a ship canal to provide dock facilities for plants, and of a belt-line railroad to connect the industries with other roads in the Chicago area. The engineer persuaded the New York Central to finance the construction of the Indiana Harbor Belt Line Railroad. In 1906 this road, which was built under Hotchkiss' supervision, was opened for traffic.[69]

The East Chicago Company constructed the outer harbor and the Indiana Harbor Ship Canal at its own expense. Work on the outer harbor, which was built at the entrance of the proposed ship canal, was started in 1901. The harbor consisted of a breakwater, known as the north pier, which was built 1,800 feet into Lake Michigan, and a similar wall, 300 feet to the south, ex-

[67] Ball, *Encyclopedia of Genealogy and Biography,* 43-44.

[68] Hammond *Lake County Times,* May 15, 1908. In 1904 Honore Palmer succeeded Albert De Wolfe Erskine as president of the East Chicago Company. Robert E. Tod headed the company after Hotchkiss' resignation. See John W. Leonard, *The Book of Chicagoans. A Biographical Dictionary of the Leading Men of Chicago* (Chicago, 1905), 89, for an account of Hotchkiss' career.

[69] Walter J. Riley in *The Calumet,* June 13, 1913, p. 20; *The Iron Age,* 77:343 (January 25, 1906).

tending 1,200 feet into the Lake. The area between the walls was dredged to a depth of 21 feet. The Federal government assumed the maintenance of the outer harbor when it was completed and also agreed to do the same for the inner harbor, or ship canal, when it should be built. The ship canal, which was to be 200 feet wide and 21 feet deep, was to extend one and one-half miles in a southwesterly direction and thence two miles south to the Grand Calumet River. From the bend of the channel, which was later to be called the "forks," a branch was to extend one and one-half miles to connect with Lake George. There were to be turning basins at convenient intervals to enable the largest lake vessels to navigate it without the aid of tugs.[70]

In October, 1903, in the presence of about three thousand people, Governor Winfield T. Durbin pressed the electric button which started the dredges to work on the canal. All the persuasive powers of Charles W. Hotchkiss were needed to obtain the consent of the railroads for the canal to cross their rights of way, and for the construction of bridges for their tracks across the canal. By 1909 the canal was ready for use for more than a mile inland from the Lake. As the various sections were completed, they were turned over to the Federal government for maintenance. In 1925 the government formally accepted the deed to the canal as well as the full responsibility for keeping it in a navigable condition. Although a drawbridge was built on Chicago Avenue in 1924 to permit the passage of lake steamers from the forks south to the Grand Calumet River, that branch of the canal was never put to profitable use.[71]

70 U. S. Army, Chief of Engineers, *Annual Report,* 1906, pt. 1:603-6; 1910, pt. 1:792; pt. 2:2156.

71 *The Iron Age,* 72:10 (November 5, 1903); Walter Riley, "C. W. Hotchkiss, A Tribute," in Gary *Post-Tribune,* May 9, 1929; U. S. Army,

Courtesy Standard Oil Company of Indiana

BURTON-HUMPHREYS EXPERIMENTAL STILL, BUILT 1910

INLAND STEEL COMPANY, EAST CHICAGO, 1933.
The Indiana Harbor Ship Canal is to the left.

This was because the industries located on this branch had no great need for dock facilities. Consequently, this portion of the canal was permitted to deteriorate until it was of little value to the city.

Other Industries

The building of the ship canal and the construction of the Indiana Harbor Belt Line Railroad inaugurated a new industrial development of the Twin City. Hotchkiss, the Palmers, and other stockholders of the East Chicago Company, aided by the railroads, used their influence to bring industries to the site. Most of those that were established there were the midwestern plants of large nationwide manufacturing corporations.[72] East Chicago is fortunate in that it never has been a one-industry city. The presence of Inland Steel attracted foundries and manufacturers of various steel products. Oil, chemical, and metal-refining industries are also well represented. The Grasselli Chemical Company and the Graver Tank Works, stimulated by the demand for their products by the other industries in the region, expanded their plants. The Republic Iron and Steel Company, which had purchased the Inland Iron and Forge Plant, concentrated on the making of iron and steel bars. Republic was one of the most important industries in the city for many years. Unfortunately, its equipment and processes were permitted to become antiquated, and in the twenties the plant closed its doors.

In 1903 the American Steel Foundries moved its plant from South Chicago to a site on the ship canal. Standard Forgings Company, manufacturer of hammered-iron rail-

Chief of Engineers, *Annual Report*, 1925, pt. 1:1379; East Chicago *Calumet News*, September 9, 1942.

[72] Riley, "C. W. Hotchkiss, A Tribute," in Gary *Post-Tribune*, May 9, 1929.

road car axles, came the next year. In 1909 the Cudahy Packing Company, makers of "Old Dutch Cleanser," erected a plant. Cudahy also repaired refrigerator cars at its East Chicago location. In 1909 the Hubbard Steel Foundries found a place on the ship canal. In 1903 the German American Car Corporation, which had repaired refrigerator cars at the Union Stock Yards in Chicago since 1901, moved to a site near the Graver Tank Works. Here the corporation began to build tank cars in addition to its repair operation. The Graver Company made the tanks and the German American firm made the underframes and trucks upon which the tanks were mounted. In 1910 the plant was moved to its present site where it manufactures tank and freight cars on a large scale. From this time on, the company ceased to depend upon Graver and produced its own tanks. German American not only operated a large fleet of tank and refrigerator cars but also leased a large number to other industries. Because of the anti-German prejudice during World War I, the Company changed its name to the General American Tank Car Corporation.[73]

In 1907 the Harbison-Walker Refractories Company, the first establishment of its kind in the Middle West, began to manufacture silica bricks for use in the open-hearth furnaces and in the coke oven plants of the steel mills. In 1911 the E. B. Lanman Company, whose products were nuts and bolts, moved its plant from Columbus, Ohio, to the city. A year later came the Goldschmidt Detinning Company, later known as the Metal and Thermit Corporation, engaged in the recovery of tin from tin plate scrap. The year 1912 also saw the establishment of the aluminum refinery of the United States Reduction Company and of the International Lead Refining Plant.

[73] *East Chicago, Indiana,* 1:158-59 (June, 1926).

In 1913 the Superheater Company, manufacturers of superheaters for railroad locomotives, found a site in the city.[74]

In 1914 Clayton Mark established the Mark Manufacturing Company, a steel plant, just north of the ship canal from the Inland Steel Works. Shortly afterwards, he constructed the Mark Townsite, more popularly known as Marktown, the first effort on the part of any of East Chicago's industries to provide housing for their employees. One hundred and three white stucco buildings, including stores, residences of the single and duplex type, and dormitories were erected on a tract reclaimed from a swamp near the plant. Recreational facilities, in the form of playgrounds, tennis courts, baseball and football fields, were provided for adults and children. Arrangements were made with the city to locate a school for children up to the fifth grade in the vicinity. The residences were rented to the employees at reasonable rates.[75] In 1920 the American Sheet and Tube Company, which had built a plant on the same side of the canal in 1916, absorbed the Mark Manufacturing Company and also Marktown. Three years later, the Youngstown Sheet and Tube Company, of Youngstown, Ohio, purchased all the property of the American Sheet and Tube. In 1929 this plant, the second largest industry in the Twin City, employed 4,600 workers.[76]

The Edward Valve and Manufacturing Company, one of the most substantial industries in the city, erected its plant in 1914. In the meantime, the Standard Oil Company of Indiana expanded its property to the ship canal, where its tankers took on gasoline and oil for distribution

[74] *Ibid.,* 4:158-59 (December, 1929).
[75] *Ibid.,* 1:129 (March, 1926).
[76] Phyllis Bate, The Development of the Iron and Steel Industry in the Chicago Area (Ph.D. thesis, University of Chicago, 1948), 13.

throughout the Great Lakes Region. The Sinclair Oil
Company's refinery was located in 1917 on the north bank
of the canal. In 1927 the Roxana Petroleum Corporation, a subsidiary of the Shell Oil Company, was established. The refinery part of the Roxana Plant was across
Michigan Street in Hammond. The Empire Oil Company (Cities Service) built its refinery in 1929. In the
latter year, forty-five major industries employing some
25,000 persons were reported in East Chicago.[77]

Problem of Water Transportation

The Indiana Harbor Ship Canal with its outer harbor
was designated a subport by the Federal government and
placed under the jurisdiction of the collector of the port
of Chicago. In time it was regarded as the largest and
busiest harbor in Indiana. Outgoing shipments consisted
mainly of gasoline, oil, and steel, while the incoming cargoes were made up largely of products used in the steel
mills, such as iron ore, coal, and limestone. The amount
of freight handled by the harbor increased from 875,306
tons in 1922 to 5,287,760 tons in 1929. Until 1928 no
shipping facilities were available for industries whose locations were not adjacent to the outer harbor or to the canal.
Nor were boats from foreign countries able to use the
port. In that year the East Chicago Dock Terminal Company constructed docks for public use at the forks of the
canal. Cranes and other equipment for the loading and
unloading of cargoes were installed, and belt-line connections were made with the railroads and the industries
not located on the canal. In May, 1928, a large crowd
celebrated the opening of Indiana Harbor as a world
port when the first ocean-going ship, the "Novodoc,"
arrived from England with a cargo of a special type of

[77] *East Chicago, Indiana,* 4:115 (December, 1929).

pig iron. The claim was made in 1930 that more ships from foreign countries docked at Indiana Harbor than at any other port on lower Lake Michigan.[78]

East Chicago and other cities of the region were enthusiastic advocates of the Great Lakes-to-the-Gulf-of-Mexico Waterway System. Civic leaders saw in this project an opportunity for their steel mills and other industries to compete on more equal terms with the industries of the Pittsburgh area, which enjoyed cheap transportation for their products by way of the Ohio and Mississippi rivers to the rich markets in the lower Mississippi Valley and also in Latin American countries. Such a waterway would bring coal, food, and other vital products from the South at rates much cheaper than the railroads could offer. Local citizens wanted a navigable route by way of the Indiana Harbor Ship Canal and the Grand Calumet River to the Calumet Sag Canal and thence to the Chicago Sanitary and Ship Canal. The last waterway, which was being made navigable in 1926, was planned to connect with the Illinois River at La Salle, Illinois. This canal would permit boats from the Great Lakes Region to reach New Orleans by way of the Mississippi River.[79]

The most formidable obstacle in the path of the Great Lakes-to-the-Gulf Waterway was the reluctance of the Federal government to permit the diversion of sufficient water from the Great Lakes to make it navigable for large ships and also to improve the channel of the Illinois River. The cool, if not hostile, attitude of Governor Ed Jackson and Attorney General Arthur L. Gilliom, of

[78] *Ibid.,* 2(1927):230; *The East Chicagoan* (published by the East Chicago Chamber of Commerce), 1:no. 10 (December, 1930); Hammond *Lake County Times,* May 17, 1928; Gary *Post-Tribune,* May 26, 1928.

[79] Robert I. Randolph in *East Chicago, Indiana,* 1:152 (June, 1926). Randolph was vice-president of the Chicago Association of Commerce.

Indiana, to the project was of concern to the Calumet Region. Local leaders united with Chicagoans to form the Calumet Seaways Association to win the co-operation of the Federal government for the establishment of the waterway. After obtaining Congressional approval in 1927 the project was further blocked by a suit filed in the Federal courts by the State of Wisconsin to enjoin the taking of water from Lake Michigan. Indiana, through its legal department, supported Wisconsin in thus opposing the waterway.[80] The Gary *Post-Tribune* reflected the smoldering resentment against what was regarded as the indifference of other parts of the state to the interests of the Calumet Region: "Indiana was a hundred years old before its people knew that it had a seacoast. It may be another hundred years before the politicians down state realize Indiana in a short time may have one or more of the greatest world harbors. . . . Possibly the time will come when northern Indiana interests will combine to fight the provincial ideas of some of our Hoosier statesmen. . . . Attorney General Gilliom ought to go to night school and study geography."[81] In 1933 the Chicago Sanitary and Ship Canal became a link in the Great Lakes-to-the-Gulf Waterway. The canal was of little benefit to the Calumet's industries because the Grand Calumet River was never improved to permit boats from Indiana Harbor to sail directly to New Orleans.

Walter J. Riley and Carl A. Westberg

Walter J. Riley and Carl A. Westberg played important roles in the development of the Twin City. Westberg was associated with the East Chicago Company

[80] *East Chicago, Indiana,* 2:204 (August, 1927).

[81] Gary *Post-Tribune,* December 16, 1926. Local leaders frequently referred to the Calumet Region as the "State of Lake."

in Indiana Harbor as early as 1905, and two years later became vice-president and treasurer of the Land Company. He also supervised the building of the Indiana Harbor Ship Canal. Riley came from Chicago to Indiana Harbor in 1905 and sold real estate for a time. He later obtained a law degree and in 1911 was appointed city judge of East Chicago by Governor Thomas R. Marshall. Riley and Westberg were lieutenants of Charles W. Hotchkiss as long as that engineer and promoter was active in the operations of the East Chicago Company and in other affairs that involved the development of the city.[82] When the Hotchkiss era ended, Riley and Westberg assumed leadership in banking circles, real estate, and in the bringing of industries to the city.

In 1909 Hotchkiss established the First Calumet Trust and Savings Bank in the southeastern section of the city. He persuaded Riley to become vice-president of the bank, which was housed in a small storeroom. The prospects for a successful financial institution in that part of the city did not appear very bright, and Riley agreed to serve without pay until the bank's earned surplus was equal to its original capital.[83] The success of this institution led Riley in 1914 to organize the First State Trust and Savings Bank. This bank, later known as the United States National Bank, was located at Main and Broadway streets in Indiana Harbor. Despite the drab and forlorn appearance of this neighborhood, Riley had the foresight to see that this part of the city, so near the steel mill, was destined to be a heavily populated area.

82 Cannon, Loring, and Robb (eds.), *The Lake and Calumet Region of Indiana,* 2:3-4, 64; Howat (ed.), *A Standard History of Lake County,* 2:665-66; Riley, "C. W. Hotchkiss, A Tribute," in Gary *Post-Tribune,* May 9, 1929.

83 East Chicago *Calumet News,* November 11, 1927.

In 1918 he extended his operations to the west side where he acquired control of the First National Bank and its sister subsidiary, The First Trust and Savings Bank. These were later combined to form the First National Bank and Trust Company with its location at Chicago Avenue and Indianapolis Boulevard. Riley also established the United States Investment Company to handle the real estate, insurance, and small loan departments of his organization.[84] The Riley banks were the only banks in the Twin City to keep their doors open during the great depression.

Riley's extensive real estate operations were largely responsible for the development of the Calumet community in the southeastern part of the city. He played an important part in the organization of the Calumet-Kennedy Land Company which acquired a large area of land in the Calumet section. Riley, E. T. Davis, and J. Kalman Reppa founded the Philadelphia Land and Improvement Company which was said to have started with a capital of $1,000,000. As early as 1912 this firm began to buy land from the East Chicago Company. The total holdings of the Philadelphia Land and Improvement Company were reported to have been more than six thousand lots.[85] Riley and his associates also engaged in the financing and building of houses.

In 1912 the news that the Baldwin Locomotive Works of Philadelphia had purchased a huge site for a plant in the Calumet section launched a real estate boom of fantastic proportions. For a time crowds of eager buyers stood in line all night before the office of the Calumet-

---

[84] *East Chicago, Indiana,* 4:148-49 (December, 1929). Riley was also president of the O. F. Jordan Company which manufactured snow plows, ditchers, track oilers, and spraying machines for the railroads.

[85] Hammond *Lake County Times,* January 23, 1912; Lake County Deed Records, 175:520, 177:451.

Kennedy Land Company to purchase lots when it opened for business the next morning. In 1913-14 the Baldwin Company fenced its site, built tracks to connect with the railroads, and laid the foundations for a large plant. Due to the uncertain business conditions at that time and to the prospect of strong competition from other companies in the Middle West the plant was never built. The boom collapsed and the hopeful investors, most of whom had made only small payments on their lots, saw the property repossessed by the land company.[86] In 1929 the Empire Oil Company built its refinery on the old Baldwin site.

The Attempt to Annex Hammond and Whiting

The Twin City's population soared from 3,411 in 1900 to 19,098 in 1910. Its total area of only about eleven square miles was surrounded by Gary, Hammond, Whiting, and Lake Michigan. As there were indications that more industries would be located there, civic leaders feared their city would soon be overcrowded. While studying the problem, attorneys discovered Indiana had a law which permitted any town or city, simply by action of its board or council, to annex contiguous territory at any time. To avoid being "kidnaped," at least 51 per cent of the property owners in the contiguous territory must file a remonstrance in the circuit or superior court within thirty days.[87] The burden of the situation thus was put, not on those who did the annexing, but on those who wished to remain independent. As a result, there arose the most complicated matrimonial problem that ever found its way into a divorce court.

[86] Hammond *Lake County Times,* January 20, 1912; interview with Charles M. Reed, East Chicago, October 14, 1953; Howat (ed.), *A Standard History of Lake County,* 1:310-11.

[87] *Laws of Indiana,* 1905, pp. 219-20, 388-90.

The drama began on March 21, 1910, when the city council of East Chicago voted to annex all of Hammond and Whiting. This was done despite the fact that the combined populations of the brides-to-be was 27,512, or about 44 per cent more than that of the eager suitor.[88] Hammond and Whiting were caught unawares by their neighbor's action. Mayor Lawrence Becker of Hammond said "it wasn't a nice thing to do. I don't think we would have done a thing like that to East Chicago." That the Twin City was serious about the matter was indicated by the report that "Hammond was gulped down by a minnow, and the minnow, even after the space of two or three days had not exhibited a solitary symptom of indigestion."[89] The Gary Council, alarmed that East Chicago would later try to absorb its city, in a special meeting held shortly after daybreak on March 28, adopted ordinances annexing the recently enlarged East Chicago, which for the moment included Hammond and Whiting.[90]

This bewildering turn of events, according to one report, "alarmed the postal branch of the Federal government, the railroads, and the interurban companies. Lawyers, educators, and politicians have cudgeled their brains in a common effort to straighten out the muddle but all have failed. No one has been able to say how many towns stand where four stood a month ago. One city is afraid to call anything her own." The officials of the

[88] Wayne A. McDaniel (ed.), *The Municipal Code of the City of East Chicago, Indiana* (East Chicago, 1925), Ordinances 336 and 337, pp. 226, 229; Hammond's population of 20,925 was larger than East Chicago's. Whiting's population at that time was 6,587. See *Thirteenth Census of the United States* (1910): *Population*, pt. 2:531.

[89] Gary *Evening Post*, March 23 and 24, 1910.

[90] *General Ordinances of the City of Gary, Indiana* (n.p., n.d.), 25-26; Gary *Evening Post*, March 28, 1910. Gary's population at that time was 16,803.

various cities finally came to their senses, and parleys were held to untangle the mesh in which they had involved their municipalities. East Chicagoans said they had no desire to seize Gary. The Steel City's officials admitted the only reason they had annexed East Chicago, Hammond, and Whiting was to prevent East Chicago from grabbing their municipality. Hammond said she didn't want to marry anyone.[91] Gary's action had saved Hammond and Whiting from the clutches of East Chicago, and the Twin City was compelled to be content with its inadequate area.

Population and Housing

By 1930 East Chicago had reached its saturation point as far as population was concerned. In 1920 it had 35,967 inhabitants, almost twice as many as in 1910, and in 1930, 54,784, or 5,000 persons per square mile.[92] Since so much of the city's area was occupied by industries and railroads, little space was left for additional residences.

European immigrants seeking employment in the numerous industries flocked into the city in great numbers before World War I. In 1910 the foreign born constituted 53 per cent of the population. Ten years later they numbered more than 40 per cent.[93] Most of the foreign born were from the eastern and southeastern nations of Europe with the Poles, Hungarians, and Aus-

[91] Gary *Evening Post,* March 29 and 30, 1910; Graham H. Taylor, *Satellite Cities. A Study of Industrial Suburbs* (New York, 1915), 178-79.

[92] *Fourteenth Census of the United States* (1920): *Population,* pt. 3:297; *Fifteenth Census* (1930): *Population,* 3:pt. 1:700. East Chicago's population declined during the next ten years, being only 54,637 in 1940. *Sixteenth Census* (1940): *Population,* 1:343.

[93] *Thirteenth Census* (1910): *Population,* pt. 2:568; *Fourteenth Census* (1920): *Population,* pt. 3:297.

trians predominating in that order. The Czechs, Rumanians, Yugo-Slavs, and Greeks were also heavily represented. When the immigration quota laws passed by Congress in 1921 and 1924 practically closed the doors of the nation to the people of eastern and southeastern Europe,[94] the industries turned to the Negroes and to the Mexicans as sources of labor supply. While there were only 28 Negroes in East Chicago in 1910, their number increased to 1,424 in 1920. In 1930 the Negro population was 5,088, or about 9 per cent of the city's inhabitants. [95] There was no satisfactory way of determining the number of Mexicans in East Chicago in the early years. In 1920 and 1930 the Federal Census Bureau listed them as "foreign-born whites" and "other races." Inland Steel's local plant was said to have employed more Mexicans in 1928-29 than did any other steel plant in the nation. The same source placed 9,007 Mexicans in Lake County in 1930, of which 5,343 were residents of East Chicago. If these figures are correct, the Negroes and Mexicans constituted about 18 per cent of the Twin City's population in that year.[96]

With the exception of the Sunnyside and Marktown units, which were largely occupied by supervisory employees, East Chicago's industries made no effort to pro-

[94] *Fourteenth Census* (1920): *Population*, pt. 3:304. The law of 1921 limited the number of immigrants from any European country to 3 per cent of that nationality in the United States in 1910. That of 1924 reduced the quota to 2 per cent, based on the 1890 Census. As the general flood of immigrants from eastern and southeastern Europe came after 1890, only a few could be admitted under the new law.

[95] *Thirteenth Census* (1910): *Population*, pt. 2:568; *Fourteenth Census* (1920): *Population*, pt. 3:297; *Fifteenth Census* (1930): *Population*, 3:pt. 1:700.

[96] Paul S. Taylor, *Mexican Labor in the United States, Chicago, and the Calumet Region* (University of California, *Publications in Economics*, Vol. 7, No. 2, Berkeley, 1932), 26, 61.

vide adequate housing for their workers. The Inland Steel Company lacked the financial resources in the early years to build any sort of accommodations for its employees. Some of the other industries were comparatively small and had started their operations with limited funds. Consequently, housing for common labor in East Chicago was probably the worst in the Calumet Region. A large slum area came into being in the shadows of the mills and factories. Owners of lots rented tenements and shacks for more than such property was worth. Many shacks were built in the rear of lots occupied by larger residences. A large proportion of those living in houses found it necessary to have roomers and boarders to supplement their incomes. Living quarters for the unskilled Negroes and Mexicans were particularly poor. Many, because of their unwillingness or inability to pay the high rents charged for residences, crowded together in cellars and basements. In one place seventy-five men were found living in one dark room in a basement, the ceiling of which was so low that none of them could stand erect. In 1921 forty Negroes were discovered occupying a cellar of a building in Indiana Harbor.[97] In time some of the foreign born and a number of the Negroes and Mexicans were able to establish more comfortable and wholesome homes for their families. Another segment of the population, the business and professional men and the higher-paid employees of the industries, found homes in the Washington Park section of Indiana Harbor and on the quiet residential streets of the far west side. On the whole, high officials of the various industries preferred to live in Chicago.

[97] Interview with Leopold E. Block, Chicago, April 29, 1952; Taylor, *Mexican Labor in the United States, Chicago, and the Calumet Region,* 26; Hammond *Lake County Times,* February 1, 1921.

Hospitals and Schools

Despite its population and numerous industries, the city did not have a hospital for some years. At one time the citizens voted to bond themselves to erect such an institution, the ultimate cost to be paid by taxation. A debate ensued as to the merits of municipal vs. private control of the hospital and the proposed hospital was never built. In 1926 the East Chicago Manufacturer's Association and the Poor Handmaids of Jesus Christ, a Catholic Order, agreed to provide the city with a hospital. The Poor Handmaids, who operated hospitals in other cities, were to contribute $700,000.00 and the Manufacturer's Association $465,000.00 for the erection of a 200-bed institution. The hospital, to be known as St. Catherine's and to be open to all regardless of race, color, or creed, was to be operated and maintained by the Poor Handmaids. Each industry of the city was assessed an amount in proportion to its number of employees. The hospital, construction of which was started in 1927, received its first patients the following year. A number of nuns and other personnel came from St. Joseph's Hospital in Fort Wayne to staff the institution.[98]

As was noted earlier, the city was sharply divided into two sections. Until the construction of the 141st Street viaduct over the Indiana Harbor Belt Line Yards in 1929, West Side citizens had to follow a circuitous route eastward along Chicago Avenue and then north on Euclid Avenue to reach Indiana Harbor. Such an inconvenience discouraged the mingling of the inhabitants of the West Side and the East Side. It also made difficult the satisfactory location of the public schools. For many years the only high school in the city was located in

[98] *East Chicago, Indiana,* 1:269, 335; 2:107, 117; 3:54 (October and December, 1926; April, 1927; April, 1928).

the Harrison Building on the West Side. This arrangement compelled the students who lived in Indiana Harbor
to spend much time and effort to attend high school.
In 1914 the Washington School in Indiana Harbor, which
had been built in 1907 as a grade school, was converted
into a junior-senior high school. Harrison was made a
junior high school containing the seventh, eighth, and
ninth grades.[99] Then it was the turn of the West Siders
to make the long journey to the senior high school at
Washington. Relief was finally provided for the West
Side in 1927 when the newly built Roosevelt School was
made into a senior high school.[1]

Attempt to Rename City

Civic leaders worked hard to promote the unity of
the two sections. Twin City businessmen in 1924 co-
operated in the formation of a joint chamber of commerce. The Kiwanis Club, organized the same year
and in which men from all parts of the city found membership, was hailed as a factor in the interest of unity.[2]
The coming of the automobile and the building of the
141st Street viaduct drew the two sections closer together.

In 1924 a movement was launched by the Kiwanis
Club to change the name of East Chicago. The *Calumet
News* suggested that the school children, the future citizens of the city, be given the opportunity to vote on
the matter. As a result, more than 5,000 pupils in
and above the fifth grade in the public and parochial
schools voted 3,404 against keeping the name East
Chicago and 2,028 against "Indiana Harbor." Others

[99] Howat (ed.), *A Standard History of Lake County,* 1:423.
[1] East Chicago *Calumet News,* April 29, 1927.
[2] *Ibid.,* December 12, 1924.

favored such titles as "Indiana City," "Calumet," "Lake-
port," "Steel City," "Twin City," and "Temulac" (Calumet spelled backwards). A second poll was taken and
59 per cent of the pupils selected "Lake City" as the new
name. Citizens of the West Side showed a strong
tendency to oppose the name Indiana Harbor, their old
rival, as the name for the municipality. The more conservative segment of the city's population, which included
numerous property owners, strongly opposed any change,
insisting that such action would cause many legal complications and would bring only confusion to the city's
neighbors and to those doing business with the various
industries. A large number of irate citizens, who stormed
the chambers of the city council, persuaded that body
to oppose any change. Announcements were also made
that a bill pending before the General Assembly approv-
ing the selection of a new name would be withdrawn.
East Chicago did benefit to a degree from this episode.
The reference of the matter to the school children
brought favorable publicity to the city from many of the
nation's newspapers. Such a referendum was hailed as a
splendid example of the working of the democratic
process.[3]

[3] East Chicago *Calumet News,* February 11, 22, 25, 1927.

9

GARY, THE PIONEER PERIOD

GARY IS THE YOUNGEST of the region's industrial cities.
Its history began with the construction of the huge steel
mills and various subsidiary plants by the United States
Steel Corporation at the southern tip of Lake Michigan
in the Calumet Township of Lake County. Because the
building of the municipality was included in the plans
of the steel company for the area, Gary was truly a "city
by decree." In 1915 it was reported to be the greatest
single calculated achievement of the nation's steel industry. Ten years later it was described as the most interesting and ambitious industrial community ever undertaken in any country.[1] From its very inception Gary was
primarily a steel town and the prosperity of its citizens
was determined by the great mills that were responsible
for its existence. All was well with its inhabitants when
the mills operated at full capacity, but when production
declined or strikes occurred the specter of unemployment and unpaid bills rose to haunt them.

Selection and Purchase of the Site

In 1905 the United States Steel Corporation decided
to construct new steel mills in the Middle West. Officials
were not satisfied with the position held by the corporation's plants in the steel trade. They were barely hold-

[1] Taylor, *Satellite Cities,* 165, 174; Ida M. Tarbell, *The Life of Elbert
H. Gary. A Story of Steel* (New York, 1925), 334.

ing their own in the production of pig iron, making 43.2 per cent of the nation's total in 1901 and 44.2 per cent in 1905. What was more alarming was their decline in production of steel ingots from about 66.2 per cent of total production in 1901 to 60.2 per cent in 1905. The capacity of the corporation's mills in the Chicago area was inadequate to satisfy its customers, which necessitated the shipping of steel at great expense from its eastern plants to the western markets. Space for expansion was not available at its Illinois Steel Company's mills in South Chicago, and the plant at Joliet was not economical because iron ore had to be transshipped from lake boats by rail.[2] A site had to be found large enough for the future expansion of new mills and one that would also provide space for the erection of the corporation's subsidiary manufacturing plants. There must also be adequate room for the housing of workers in the vicinity of the plants.

The steel company's officials laid down certain minimum requirements regarding the choice of a site. Its agents were instructed to seek a moderately priced and compact tract of land adjacent to Lake Michigan. The depth of the water must be sufficient to accommodate the largest lake vessels, and adequate railway facilities must be available. The Gary site not only satisfied these requirements but was also near Chicago, where an abundance of labor could be obtained. Steel officials were familiar with the area because it lay just east of the Buffington Plant of the Universal Portland Cement Company, a subsidiary of the United States Steel Corporation. This cement plant, construction of which was started in 1903, utilized steel slag from the Illinois Steel Company's Mills in South Chicago for the manufacture

2 United States Steel Corporation, *Fourth Annual Report*, 1905, p. 25.

of its product. In 1906 Buffington had an annual capacity of 2,000,000 barrels of cement.[3]

The site selected for the new steel mills and for the city was almost devoid of inhabitants, the population of the township being only 1,408 in 1900.[4] The nearest settlements were the village of Miller and the community around the Aetna Powder Plant to the east, the small village of Clark to the west, and the town of Tolleston about three miles from the lake front to the south. The cottages and clubhouse of the Calumet Gun Club, founded by Chicago sportsmen in 1885 and discussed earlier, occupied a site just east of the present inner harbor of the steel plant. Sand ridges, low dunes, and lakelike sloughs characterized the area, which was covered by a heavy growth of scrub oak, marsh grass, and tangled vines. The sluggish Grand Calumet, more like a bayou than a river, lay half a mile from the lake front across the proposed plant site.

The huge area acquired by the steel company was originally a part of George W. Clark's estate. In 1858 Clark sold a tract of more than four thousand acres to George T. Cline and to Allen Dorsey and his wife, Ann, of Chicago. This tract, which included most of the area upon which the steel mills were built, was bounded on the south by the Grand Calumet. In 1862 Cline and Dorsey sold one eighth of their holdings to Henry Holt, a Baltimore publisher.[5] The Holt purchase of about five hundred acres was in the vicinity of Pine Station.

3 *Ibid., Fifth Annual Report,* 1906, p. 29; Appleton, *The Iron and Steel Industry of the Calumet District,* 29; *The Calumet Region Historical Guide,* 91-92. Employees of the Buffington plant probably lived in East Chicago.

4 U. S. Bureau of the Census, *Thirteenth Census* (1910): *Population,* pt. 2:531.

5 Lake County Deed Records, X:259.

At the time of the packing-house boom in the region in
1890, Philip D. Armour, Gustavus Swift, and Edward
Morris bought about four thousand acres where the city
of Gary now stands. The greater part of this purchase
was made in the names of Albert H. Veeder, attorney
for Swift, and Edward Martyn of Chicago. Among
their most important acquisition was a tract, acreage not
specified in the deed, from Henry Holt and the Dorseys
for $275,000.00.[6] P. Anderson Valentine, of Chicago,
was later associated with Veeder and the packers' tract
was identified on the maps as the Veeder-Valentine Tract.
Gustavus Swift obtained in his own name a section of
640 acres which lay north of the Indian Boundary Line
and east of the southern tip of Lake Michigan.[7] When
the steel company bought its land, it had to bargain
with shrewd businessmen who had held on to their land
against such an eventuality.

In 1905 the purchase of the sites for the mills and
the town began quietly, every effort being made to conceal
the identity of the buyer. The corporation engaged
Armanis F. Knotts, a former mayor of Hammond and
the steel company's attorney for several years, to under-
take the negotiations. In many instances, Knotts acted
as the agent for both the seller and the buyer. Most
transactions were settled in cash, which in one instance,
according to reports, involved the carrying of $1,300,000
through the streets of New York in a handbag.[8] The
deeds were made out to persons in different parts of the

6 Lake County Deed Records, 52:170. See above, 131-35, for an account
of the packing-house boom.

7 Lake County Deed Records, 65:243. The Indian Boundary Line was
also called the Ten Mile Line. It ran eastward from the southern tip
of Lake Michigan and marked the northern boundary of Indiana Territory. See above, 42-43.

8 Robert M. Haig, "The Unearned Increment in Gary," in *Political
Science Quarterly,* 32(1917):82.

country and at the suitable moment transferred to the steel company.[9] According to Knotts, the most difficult transaction was the purchase of 1,500 acres from J. Ogden Armour. This tract, which lay just east of the present Broadway Street, was obtained only after numerous conferences with the packer.[10] The price paid, according to statements made by the steel company's representatives, varied from $500.00 to $2,000.00 an acre, or an average of $800.00. Information from individuals who were concerned in the purchase but not connected with the steel company placed the price at amounts ranging from $350.00 to $1,500.00 an acre, the average being $814.00. The steel company's officials reportedly estimated the cost of the entire nine thousand acres acquired at about $7,200,000.[11] This huge area extended over seven miles along the shore of Lake Michigan and south to the Wabash Railroad tracks.

Policies of the Gary Land Company

The Indiana Steel Company was organized in 1906 as a subsidiary of the United States Steel Corporation to build and operate the steel mills. Eugene J. Buffington, president of the Illinois Steel Company, was chosen to head the new corporation. About the same time the Gary Land Company, a subsidiary of Indiana Steel, was organized to lay out and build the town. Buffington was also president of this company and Armanis F. Knotts

[9] An example of the subterfuge employed was the sale by Veeder and Valentine in January, 1906, of 892 acres to Thomas Murray of New York City for "one dollar and other valuable considerations." In July of the same year, Murray "sold" the tract to the steel company. See Lake County Deed Records, 122:435 and 123:240.

[10] Armanis F. Knotts in the Gary *Post-Tribune,* June 4, 1931, Historical Section, p. 4.

[11] Haig, "The Unearned Increment in Gary," in *Political Science Quarterly,* 32:82.

was its manager. The mills and the town were to be separated by the Grand Calumet River.

A name for the projected town was one of the first concerns of the officials. The name "Corey," in honor of William Ellis Corey, at that time president of the United States Steel Corporation, was considered for a time. At a meeting in the Chicago offices of the Illinois Steel Company, Buffington, Knotts, and William Duff Haynie, a company attorney, named the future town "Gary," for Judge Elbert H. Gary, chairman of the board of directors of the United States Steel Corporation. The Post Office Department was reluctant at first to permit the use of the name, there already being a Gary in Maryland. Fears were expressed that the similarity of "Ind." and "Md." in script would lead to confusion. The postal authorities withdrew their objections when pressure was brought to bear by friendly congressmen.[12] A short time after the town government was formed, its board of trustees asked Judge Gary's permission to place his likeness on the municipal seal. The Judge not only gave his approval but presented the town with a handsome seal prepared by Tiffany of New York.[13]

The steel company, in working out its plans for Gary, was guided by previous experiences with other industrial towns. Steel officials were well acquainted with the sad experiences of the Krupps in Essen, Germany, and the Pullman Company at Pullman, Illinois. These were paternalistic communities in which the companies had owned the houses, stores, schools, and in general had sought

[12] Armanis F. Knotts in the Gary *Post-Tribune*, June 4, 1931, Historical Section, p. 4.

[13] Hammond *Lake County Times*, June 14, 1907; C. Oliver Holmes, "How We Incorporated the Town," in Lake County Old Settler and Historical Association, *Historical Records*, 1924, p. 43.

to regulate the private lives of their employees. Several years after Gary was founded, Eugene J. Buffington stated that "the most successful attempts at industrial social betterment in our country are those farthest removed from the suspicion of domination or control by the employer." "Gary is nothing more than the product of effort along practical lines to secure right living conditions around a steel-manufacturing plant." The steel company was influenced by its success at Ambridge and Vandergrift, Pennsylvania, where the company's subsidiaries provided their employees with streets, proper water and sewerage facilities, and an opportunity to own their own homes. At Gary, with the exception of the Land Company's regulation of the sale of intoxicating liquors, no attempt was made to influence the private lives of the employees.[14]   While Judge Gary hoped that this would be a model town, he was strongly against the use of "fads."[15]

Officials intended for the municipality to be confined to the area purchased by the steel company, which lay between the mill site along the lake front and the Wabash tracks on the south. Strict regulations were prepared to assure that certain standards would be observed in the construction of business houses and residences. The erection of wooden business structures or buildings less than two stories was forbidden on Broadway, the principal commercial street. The officials of the land company wished to discourage speculation in the sale of lots and made every effort to prevent the steel company's employees from being exploited by unscrupulous real estate operators. Their plans called for providing homes

[14] Eugene J. Buffington, "Making Cities for Workmen," in *Harper's Weekly* (New York), May 8, 1909, pp. 15-17; "Vandergrift, A Workman's Paradise," in *Iron Age,* 68:5-7 (November 21, 1901).

[15] Elbert H. Gary in *Iron Age,* 77:1, 417 (April 26, 1906).

for workers, rather than making money by selling lots and houses.[16] Under the contract, an individual could purchase only one lot at a time, and if he did not erect a building of specified quality within eighteen months the company recovered the deed. If the business house or residence was constructed within the allotted time, the owner was free to sell it and purchase another lot.[17]

The land company arranged for private contractors to erect homes for sale or rent to the employees of the steel works. The sale price included the cost of the lot, streets, sidewalks, sewers, and the cost of the house plus 5 per cent interest on the unpaid balance. The total cost could be paid in ten annual installments and the houses were priced so moderately the payments amounted to little more than rent. If the householder was discharged from his job in the mills, or voluntarily quit, or for any other reason wanted to anticipate his payments, he could do so. Or if he wanted to turn his house back to the company, the amount he had paid in would be refunded, minus 9 per cent as rent. In case of death similar terms were open to his heirs.[18]

Intoxicating liquor was to be sold at only four designated places in the area owned by the land company, and these places were to be operated by the company or leased to carefully chosen individuals. Actually, only two bars were ever established in the company's part of the town. The restriction on the sale of liquor was the major departure from the steel company's rules at Ambridge and Vandergrift where prohibition was complete. Officials explained that Gary's nearness to other cities

[16] United States Steel Corporation, *Fifth Annual Report*, 1906, pp. 27-28.

[17] Buffington, "Making Cities for Workmen," in *Harper's Weekly*, May 8, 1909, p. 17.

[18] Taylor, *Satellite Cities*, 188.

in the region and to Chicago would make it impossible for intoxicants to be kept from the workers. By operating a few places under the supervision of the land company it hoped the liquor traffic could be made less harmful and objectionable to the community. If it should get out of hand, the company could always suppress the business in the area north of the Wabash tracks.[19]

Laying Out the Mills and Town

In the fall of 1905 the steel company's engineers began work on the plans for the mills. John Kirk, superintendent of the South Chicago Works of the Illinois Steel Company, and Ralph E. Rowley, a young engineer at the same plant, made preliminary drawings for the great railroad switching and storage yards to be located in the Gary plant site. The plans for the construction of the steel mills were so cloaked in secrecy that Rowley did not know when or where the railroad yards were to be built. Kirk later became superintendent of these yards which were named in his honor. On March 8, 1906, Rowley, who had been chosen chief construction engineer of the proposed mills, made a preliminary survey of the Gary site. Four days later he and his corps of engineers, which included his assistant, Thomas H. Cutler, found living quarters in the cottages of the old Calumet Gun Club on the lake front. The work of laying out the site for the plant and the harbor was started in a snow storm the following day. Grading began a few days later.[20] Armanis F. Knotts, manager of the Gary Land Company, located the places where tents were to be erected for the use of company officials and supervisors,

[19] Buffington, "Making Cities for Workmen," loc. cit.

[20] Ralph E. Rowley, Notes on the City of Gary, Indiana, February 15, 1926 (Typed MS in Office of Bancroft Yarrington, Public Relations Director, United States Steel Corporation, Gary), 1.

and arranged for the digging of wells to provide pure
water for those who were to construct the mills and
to build the town.

The latter part of April, 1906, Arthur P. Melton,
engaged by the Gary Land Company to plan and lay
out the town, joined the group of engineers, many of
whom were old friends, at the gun club.[21] Melton, Rowley, and Cutler, because of the important roles they
played in the development of the mills and of the town,
were popularly known in the early years as the "Three
Industrial Musketeers."[22] Before Melton began his task
of laying out the town, he undertook the construction
of a temporary bridge across the Grand Calumet River
just west of the present Broadway Street Bridge. The
river, which lay across the center of the plant site at that
time, was about one hundred feet wide with a marsh on
its north side about five hundred feet in width.[23] Until
this bridge was built, the only way that part of the plant
site could be reached was by crossing the river at Clark
Road, several miles to the west, and then proceeding
eastward along the Baltimore and Ohio Railroad
tracks.[24] Grading of the plant site north of the river
began when the bridge was completed.

In laying out the town, engineers found it difficult to
mark the line of Broadway Street, which was to be the
principal commercial thoroughfare, because of the series
of sand hills and sloughs over which it passed, the hills
being covered with a thick growth of scrub oak and the
sloughs supporting a dense vegetation of marsh grass

21 Melton was employed as an engineer at the Illinois Steel plant in
South Chicago before coming to Gary. See Howat (ed.), *A Standard
History of Lake County,* 2:852.

22 Cannon, Autobiography, Chap. 47, p. 2.

23 A. P. Melton, "Early Recollections of Gary," in Lester (ed.),
Papers by Various Hands, 1:279.

24 Rowley, Notes on the City of Gary, 3.

and bushes. One slough, in particular, was about a mile long and lay just north of the present Sixth Avenue where the Gary Hotel now stands. This formidable obstacle was about six feet deep and at least seventy-five feet wide. Melton related their troubles at this point: "When our surveying party was measuring Broadway and came to this slough, one of the chainmen made several attempts to throw his tape line across. So he started to wade across but gave that up when he started to sink down in the soft muck bottom. One of the residents of Tolleston was around looking on as was also his dog. The chainman conceived the idea of tieing the tape to the dog's collar, throwing a stick across the slough, sending the dog after the stick and then have the man on the other side call the dog—thus was the first engineering obstacle overcome.[25]

The survey of Fifth Avenue, the city's principal east and west street, was made after the survey of Broadway to the Wabash tracks was completed. When the engineers arrived at what is now Monroe Street, a dense swamp jungle was encountered in the bed of a creek known as Gibson's Run. A day was required to get a line across that morass. In the course of the survey of the land company's first subdivision of about eight hundred acres, the engineering crew was bedeviled by yellow jackets and hornets in the thickets, and by snakes in the swamps. The heat of the sun's rays was at times almost unbearable.[26]

[25] Melton, "Early Recollections of Gary," in Lester (ed.), Papers by Various Hands, 1:279, also article by Melton in Gary Post-Tribune, June 4, 1931, Historical Section, p. 13.

[26] Melton, "Early Recollections of Gary," in loc. cit., 1:280. Gibson's Run had its source near Fifteenth Avenue and Broadway. The stream flowed in a northwesterly direction through what is now Jefferson Park and into the Grand Calumet River west of Buchanan Street.

The city was platted and facilities provided to accommodate a large population. Broadway Street was laid out to be one hundred feet in width and Fifth Avenue, eighty feet. The width of the other streets was greater than generally found in the cities of that time. All conduits such as sewers, water and gas mains, and electric lines were installed in the alleys so that the streets would not be disturbed when repairs were made. In planning the city and installing the public utilities, the land company, unlike the East Chicago Company, was not handicapped by thrifty or short-sighted citizens who might have objected to the expense of such improvements. These matters were accomplished before the future citizens of Gary were given the opportunity to buy the land company's lots.[27]

The direction taken by the city in its expansion and growth soon demonstrated its streets were not laid out properly. This was not the fault of the planners who had fully expected that the city would grow in an east and west direction along Fifth Avenue so that the employees of the steel mills would be able to reach their jobs with a minimum of effort. In fact, it was expected that many would be able to walk to and from the plants.[28] Instead, as illustrated later in this chapter, the expansion of the city was southward. Consequently, thousands of workers were funneled up and down Broadway when the shifts changed in the mills. When the automobile came into general use, Gary was confronted with a traffic problem for which there seemed to be no satisfactory solution.

[27] Gary *Weekly Tribune,* June 21, 1907. The sale of lots began September 3, 1906. See *Iron Age,* 78:599 (September 6, 1906).

[28] Melton, "Early Recollections of Gary," in Lester (ed.), Papers by Various Hands, 1:282; Taylor, *Satellite Cities,* 176-77.

Thomas E. Knotts

Thomas E. Knotts, younger brother of Armanis F. Knotts, was one of the first persons without any connection with the steel company to seek his fortunes in the embryo city. Popularly known as "Tom," this kinsman of the first manager of the Gary Land Company was undoubtedly the most dominant as well as the most controversial figure in the early years of Gary's existence. He was the first and only president of its town board, 1906-9, was elected mayor in 1909, and guided the city's affairs until 1913. Before coming to Gary, Knotts had had an interesting, if not too successful, career. As a very young man he taught school in the vicinity of Medaryville, Indiana, and later attended Valparaiso University. He left the university in 1884 to become superintendent of Indian schools in the Dakota Territory during the first administration of Grover Cleveland. This assignment indicates he was a Democrat at that early date. He left the Indian schools to head the public schools at De Smet in the same territory. In 1891 Knotts moved to Hammond where he entered the real estate and insurance business.[29] One who knew him intimately in later years said he not only had the character of a leader but "had definite and fixed opinions about the things that enlisted his interest. He was definitely on one side or the other of most every question and he apparently preferred to deal with unsettled questions—questions upon which sides could be taken. He did not care for those who were halfheartedly for him, nor did he respect those who mildly opposed him. He loved

---

[29] Knotts was born in Highland County, Ohio, 1861, and in 1866 moved with his parents to Medaryville, Indiana, where he attended public school. See Howat (ed.), *A Standard History of Lake County*, 2:537; Cannon, Loring, and Robb (eds.), *History of the Lake and Calumet Region*, 2:56.

men and women who supported his ideas fully and those
definitely opposed to him commanded his respect. He
preferred to engage in a fight even if he lost the fight."[30]

Knotts demonstrated his ability as a leader and his
liking for controversy during his stay in Hammond. He
joined the Populist party, edited its newspaper, the *Calumet Journal,* and in other ways figured prominently in
the party's affairs in Hammond and Lake County.[31]
Knotts later joined the Hammond Police Department
and rose to the rank of sergeant. In 1905 Governor J.
Frank Hanly, shocked by vice conditions in Hammond,
dismissed the police commissioners and appointed a new
board, which included Knotts. According to reports,
Knotts and his colleagues enforced the laws to the extent
that gamblers and other purveyors of vice transferred
their activities westward across the state line to what
was then West Hammond, now Calumet City.[32] Early
in 1906 Knotts resigned from the police department to
seek a new career in what was to be the city of Gary.

Knotts, being the brother of the manager of the Gary
Land Company, was fully conscious of the opportunities
for position and profit in the new community. Early in
May, 1906, he brought his family, which included his
wife, Ella, and their five children, to the Gary site.[33]
The family came to Tolleston on the Michigan Central
while their household goods were brought from Ham-

30 Ora L. Wildermuth, "Estimate of the Life of Thomas E. Knotts,"
in Biographical Sketches of Gary and Lake County Residents (Scrapbooks in Gary Public Library), Vol. 6 (pages not numbered).

31 Whiting *Democrat,* August 23 and September 13, 1894. See below,
415, 495, for Knotts's part in the Pullman strike in 1894.

32 Chesterton *Tribune,* December 21, 1905. The other commissioners
were Joseph J. Ruff and George P. Pearson. See Howat (ed.), *A
Standard History of Lake County,* 1:339.

33 The children were John, Benjamin, Frank, Eugene, and Hazel.
Frank Knotts was killed in World War I.

mond in wagons. A buggy was borrowed from a local merchant to transport Mrs. Knotts and the younger children to their home in a tent just south of the present location of the South Shore station. There was no road and five hours were required to make the difficult journey of only about two miles. Mrs. Knotts related the story of that ordeal: "We started after the trucks (wagons containing household goods) left, and followed their trail, but it was indistinct in places and we nearly lost it. At every sand dune they had to unload part of the goods and carry them until the trucks got over. After a while we passed them and the trip seemed endless. Finally when I had concluded that we had gotten to the end of nowhere we saw a patch of white in the green foliage and there was the tent." It had three rooms with a board floor and to the rear was a shanty for cooking purposes. Mrs. Knotts was the first, and for a time, the only woman in the vicinity.[34]

There was not a single house in the area, except the cottages of the Calumet Gun Club along the lake front, when the Knotts family arrived. Numerous tents housed the laborers and those in charge of the construction of the mill and town. Many tents were erected on a ridge just south of the present South Shore station to which one of the Knotts children gave the rather impressive name of Euclid Avenue. The only railroad station was located in two boxcars near the New York Central tracks. A post office had not yet been established. Since the only near-by well was in front of the Knotts's tent, the mail, which was brought from Tolleston, Miller, and Pine Station, was left in the care of the Knotts

[34] "Mother of Gary Tells Story of Early Days Here. Mrs. Ella Knotts Relates Her Experiences as a Pioneer," in Lester (ed.), Papers by Various Hands, 2:234.

family. It was placed in a shoe box in front of the tent for the inspection of the inhabitants. There were no stores and the Knotts family obtained supplies from a general store in Tolleston. Fresh meat was a rarity since there were no refrigeration facilities in the community. Within a short time, stores, barber shops, milk depots, and ice cream parlors were established in tents. That the tradesmen catered to the needs rather than to the comforts of the residents was indicated by the report that the local barber shaved thirty-seven men with one towel. There were times when the Knotts's tent leaked and the children slept with their clothes under their pillows. The boys fished and swam in the great slough where the Gary Hotel now stands.[35]

The first building, a small frame affair, was erected in May, 1906, to house the offices of the Gary Land Company. Early in July of the same year the post office was established with Tom Knotts as postmaster. It used part of the building of the land company, the equipment consisting of a dry goods box for a chair and a shoe box to hold stamps and money. The first day's cancellation of postage stamps, which was Knotts's salary as postmaster, was $1.61, and the cancellations for the next three months amounted to $160.85.[36] Knotts was also in the real estate business and on occasions served as a host and guide for those who came to study the possibilities of the place.

Life was not easy for those on the scene in the early days. The sand, disturbed by construction work, was loose and deep, and the thickets and tangled vines sur-

[35] Rowley, Notes on the City of Gary, 2; "Mother of Gary Tells Story of Early Days Here," and Thomas E. Knotts, "Reminiscences," in Lester (ed.), Papers by Various Hands, 2:235, 237; 4:230.

[36] Cannon, Loring, and Robb (eds.), History of the Lake and Calumet Region, 1:752.

From photograph by David Larson, Ogden Dunes

THE DUNES

Courtesy United States Steel Corporation

EXCAVATION FOR OPEN HEARTH FURNACE, GARY WORKS,
UNITED STATES STEEL CORPORATION

CONSTRUCTION AT GARY, 1906

SITE OF MAIN OFFICE OF GARY WORKS

rounding the site discouraged venturing abroad on foot. The mining camp atmosphere of the construction units was such that the women seldom left the immediate vicinity of their tents. Occasionally a few families collected for parties and danced to music furnished by a phonograph. On the Fourth of July, 1906, Tom Knotts raised the United States flag on a pole fashioned by stripping the branches from a pine tree. The celebration included the noise made by two dollar's worth of firecrackers and patriotic music provided by a fiddler and a phonograph. On September 27, 1906, the first child, the daughter of Frank Huff, was born in Gary and was given the appropriate name of "Gary" Huff.[37] At the approach of cold weather in the fall, the Knotts family abandoned their tent for a more comfortable shack. A few ingenious citizens conserved time and energy by erecting tar paper shacks around their tents, and one noble individual quietly built his hut inside his tent. When the work was completed he invited his friends to an "unveiling." A small crowd assembled and at the proper moment a rope was pulled and the tent fluttered down disclosing the new dwelling.[38]

Construction of the Steel Works

Early in June, 1906, William P. Gleason arrived to supervise the construction of the steel mill and to be its superintendent when the work was completed.[39]

[37] "Mother of Gary Tells Story of Early Days Here," and Thomas E. Knotts, "Reminiscences," in Lester (ed.), Papers by Various Hands, 2:237; 4:231-32.

[38] Wildermuth, "Estimate of the Life of Thomas E. Knotts," in Biographical Sketches of Gary and Lake County Residents, Vol. 6.

[39] Gleason, a native of Chicago, spent his boyhood in Joliet, Illinois. He was not a university-trained engineer; instead, he went directly from the public schools to a job at the Joliet Rolling Mills, becoming in time

Gleason, whose character and personality were molded in the school of hard knocks, was to rule the huge mill with an iron hand for twenty-nine years. A rugged individualist of the old order, he was both liked and feared by the personnel of the steel plant and by the citizens of the community. Gleason's most bitter enemies could not deny his interest in Gary's welfare, and all recognized in later years his accomplishments as the "father" of the city's park system.

By July, 1906, several hundred men with teams of horses and mules were busy grading and leveling the plant site.[40] No effort was made by the steel company to provide housing for the construction workers. As a result, a city of tents was erected by the laborers on the company's property along the Grand Calumet River at the plant site. Most of the workers lived through the first winter in these tents, which were made more snug against the cold winds by the banking of sand against their walls. They later abandoned the tents for shacks and huts built of tar paper, boards, tin, or anything else at hand. According to reports, as many as twenty men occupied a single shack.[41] A number of bunkhouses accommodated some of the workers. The most famous of these,

the master mechanic of that plant. Gleason later went to Pueblo, Colorado, where he was employed by the Colorado Fuel and Iron Company. In 1900 he moved to Pittsburgh as an executive of the Crucible Steel Company of America. A short time later he supervised the construction of the Clairton Steel Company's plant at Clairton, Pennsylvania, and thereafter served as assistant general manager of that mill until it was absorbed in 1903 by the United States Steel Corporation. The corporation assigned him to its Carnegie Steel Works where he remained until sent to Gary. See Howat (ed.), *A Standard History of Lake County,* 2:533; Cannon, Loring, and Robb (eds.), *History of the Lake and Calumet Region,* 2:42-43.

40 The Steel Company hired teams from farms as far away as Chesterton, Indiana. See Chesterton *Tribune,* May 17, 1906.

41 Gary *Weekly Tribune,* March 5, 1909.

facetiously named "McFadden's Flats," was located on Broadway just south of the river. This structure contained sixty cots which rented for one dollar a week each. When a guest wished to "wash up," he used the wash pan at the pump outside the back door. McFadden heated the place with an old depot stove, which he purchased in Chicago. Thirty of his lodgers carried this heavy affair through the sand from the railroad station at Miller to the "Flats," a distance of about two miles.[42] Numerous workers lived in boardinghouses conducted by foreign-born families. The cost of a bed and meals, the latter consisting mainly of meat and potatoes, seldom amounted to more than $3.00 a week in these places.[43]

The tremendous task of preparing the mill site continued for a long time after the construction of the plant began. Three railroads, which ran through the plant area, were moved a short distance to the south. Fifty-one miles of new tracks, most of which were elevated to eliminate street crossings, were built for these roads. The elevations were constructed of sand from the dunes east of Miller. The relocation of the Grand Calumet River was an achievement of epic proportions. This stream, which cut the plant site in two, was a thousand feet wide in some places during flood seasons. It was moved more than a thousand feet to the south, where for two miles it was imprisoned in a new and straight bed.[44]

[42] Douglass Wilson, "McFadden's Flats," in Gary *Post-Tribune,* June 4, 1931, Historical Section, p. 8. McFadden was assessor of Calumet Township from 1909 to 1931.

[43] Gary *Weekly Tribune,* March 5, 1909.

[44] *Indiana Steel Company, Gary, Indiana* (Booklet published by Indiana Steel Company, 1912), 23; Rowley, Notes on the City of Gary, Indiana, 3; William P. Gleason, "The Gary Works of the Indiana Steel Company," in Lester (ed.), Papers by Various Hands (scrapbooks in Gary Public Library), 2:315.

The steel plant was originally planned to consist of eight blast furnaces, fifty-six open-hearth furnaces, a rail mill, billet mill, plate mills, merchant bar mills, and a by-products coke oven plant. Such auxiliary units as machine, roll, electric, repair, and blacksmith shops were also built.[45] Construction of a harbor slip to accommodate the largest ore boats, and the Kirk Yards, designed for switching and also for the storage of 15,000 freight cars, was soon a reality. The harbor was formed by the construction of two parallel piers 250 feet apart, 4,950 feet long, and projecting 2,360 feet into Lake Michigan. Between these piers the channel was excavated to a depth of twenty-three feet with a turning basin at its southern end. This harbor was built by the steel company at an estimated cost of $2,450,000. By December, 1908, when the first blast furnace was put into operation, the company's expenditures on the plant, railroads, and the town amounted to $42,797,000. Of the amount appropriated for the Gary projects, $22,500,000 remained to be spent.[46]

Incorporation of the Town

The community had no local government for several months after its inception. The nearest police authorities were in Hammond and East Chicago, and an almost impenetrable stretch of thickets and sloughs separated it from the county sheriff at Crown Point. Preparations for the incorporation of the town were hastened by the large number of construction workers who were arriving

[45] Gleason, "The Gary Works of the Indiana Steel Company," in loc. cit.

[46] "Harbors on the Great Lakes and Elsewhere," in Letter from the Secretary of War, 1910, in U. S. *House Documents,* 61 Congress, 3 session, Vol. 20, No. 1067, p. 24; United States Steel Corporation, *Seventh Annual Report,* 1908, p. 27.

daily and also by a rumor that Tolleston was planning to annex the area. Tom Knotts tramped over the sand hills and through the woods to take a census which showed there were 334 legal residents in the region to be incorporated. He probably took advantage of this opportunity to win the favor of the citizens for any office in the proposed town that he might desire to occupy. Early in June several announcements were posted on trees giving notice that a petition for the incorporation of the area would soon be presented to the county commissioners. The legal requirement that one third of the registered voters approve the petition was met when fourteen citizens signed their names to the document.[47]

On July 14, 1906, shortly after the county commissioners approved the petition, an election on the proposition to incorporate the town was held in the offices of the Gary Land Company. A carriage drawn by large horses labored through the woods all day bringing voters to the polls. Of the thirty-eight votes cast, only one was against incorporation. Tradition has it that the negative vote was cast by one of the duck-hunting citizens who had stopped at a Tolleston saloon to bolster his courage on the way to the election, and that this was his silent protest against the coming of civilization. On July 28 the first town election was held. Millard A. Caldwell, an employee of the steel company, Tom Knotts, and John E. Sears were chosen to represent their respective wards on the town board. C. Oliver Holmes, who was secretary to Armanis F. Knotts and who had moved from Hammond to the site, was elected clerk. Louis A. Bryan, who

---

[47] Thomas E. Knotts, "Reminiscences," in Lester (ed.), Papers by Various Hands, 4:230; Gary *Weekly Tribune*, June 18, 1909; Holmes, "How We Incorporated the Town," in Lake County Old Settler and Historical Association, *Historical Records,* 1924, p. 40.

had large real estate interests south of the Wabash tracks, became treasurer.[48]

The organization of the municipal government proved to be a matter of great significance to the young town. Officials of the steel company were apparently skeptical of Tom Knotts at this early day for they opposed his aspirations to become president of the town board of trustees. According to Louden L. Bomberger, when the time came to choose the president, Millard A. Caldwell, a mill man, voted for Sears; Sears, a representative of the old settlers, voted for Knotts; Knotts, a town man, voted for himself.[49] There is good reason to believe that this marked the beginning of the conflict between Knotts and the steel company's officials which lasted as long as Knotts headed the government of Gary. The new board appointed Louden L. Bomberger of Hammond, who never resided in Gary, attorney; Arthur P. Melton became engineer; and Frank Chambers, town marshal. A short time later, Joseph D. Martin, a member of the Hammond Police Force, was persuaded by Knotts to take charge of Gary's Police Department. Martin was chief of police as long as Knotts was in power. The town began doing business without a dollar of its own. Arrangements were made with a Hammond bank whereby its warrants would be cashed without the necessity of a bond issue. Municipal employees and those doing business with the government received what looked like checks, but on the backs were formal certifications that there were no funds in the treasury and that the bearer would get 6 per cent interest until the treasurer could redeem the warrant.

[48] Gary *Weekly Tribune,* June 18, 1909; Town of Gary, *First Annual Report,* 1908, pp. 9-10; Holmes, "How We Incorporated the Town," *loc. cit.,* 41.

[49] L. L. Bomberger, "Politics Gets Early Start," in Gary *Post-Tribune,* June 4, 1931, Historical Section, p. 4.

The Hammond bank cashed these warrants when the holders so desired.[50]

The area of the new town included the acreage purchased by the steel company, and other land south to the Little Calumet. The first ordinance adopted by the board in the summer of 1906 expanded the boundaries by annexing all the territory westward to East Chicago and Hammond, including Clark and Buffington. This gave Gary an area of twenty-five square miles. The Glen Park area, south of the Little Calumet River, was added in 1909, and Tolleston was annexed the next year. The city extended about seven miles east and west, and its southern limits were about seven and one-half miles south of Lake Michigan at that time.[51]

Knotts and the other trustees were confronted by tremendous responsibilities. The entire municipal government had to be organized and the many problems that inevitably arose had to be solved, not with the view of handling the affairs of a small town, but on a basis broad enough for the city that soon was to rise. Franchises for telephone service, electricity, gas, water, and public transportation had to be framed and granted. Not one of the members of the board had had previous experience in municipal administration. As Knotts expressed it: "We were just three bushwhackers and we had to learn how to manage public affairs as we went along."[52] The administration of the town's affairs was understandingly characterized by controversy. As a result, enmities were engendered among those interested in the community's problems which lasted throughout the remainder of their lives.

[50] Town of Gary, *First Annual Report,* 1908, p. 10; Holmes, "How We Incorporated the Town," in Lake County Old Settler and Historical Association, *Historical Records,* 1924, pp. 41-42.

[51] City of Gary, *Second Annual Report,* 1910, p. 21.

[52] Thomas E. Knotts quoted in Taylor, *Satellite Cities,* 214.

Conflict Between Mill and Town

The steel company's officials were intensely interested in the needs and welfare of the town. Because Knotts and Sears were "town men" who had no connection with the steel company, they kept the influence of the company over municipal policies at a minimum in the early years. Knotts was accused of making it his business to fight the company at every opportunity. He frequently warned its officials to stay on their side of the Grand Calumet River, which separated the mills and the town, and let the people of Gary run their own affairs. Knotts and the steel company's officials, all being men with decided opinions, it would be difficult to arrive at a just conclusion as to the merits of each side. Knotts was frequently accused of being a dictator, a trouble maker, and, in general, of being temperamentally unfit to rule the city. On the other hand, the Gary *Weekly Tribune,* a consistent foe, stated on one occasion: "In T. E. Knotts, the town has a Democrat whose democracy outshines that of Jefferson and Jackson." One of Knotts's friends thought he was aggressive, forceful and even ruthless when he set his eyes upon a civic goal.[53]

The steel company came to the rescue of the young and penniless town in the matter of water, gas, and electricity. In the construction of the great mills the company's officials had the foresight to build a water works system that would not only supply the mills but also the needs of a large city. This involved an outlay of capital far beyond the community's ability to handle. An intake tunnel, three miles long, six feet in diameter, and costing about $750,000.00, was dug eighty feet underground

[53] Thomas H. Cannon, "Tom Knotts As Mayor and Man," in Gary *Evening Post,* March 26, 1921; Gary *Daily Tribune,* May 19, 1911; Gary *Weekly Tribune,* June 8, 1909.

and extended about eight thousand feet into Lake Michigan. The Gary Heat, Light and Water Company, a subsidiary of the steel corporation, was awarded the franchise to provide water, gas, and electricity to the city at rates lower than those generally found in other cities. Gas for all commercial, industrial, and household purposes was manufactured in the coke ovens of the steel plant. It took some time to provide the town with all these utilities, and for more than two years the residents used lanterns to find their way around at night. On May 30, 1908, the first electric lights were turned on, on Broadway.[54]

In 1907 the steel company's officials expressed dissatisfaction with Armanis F. Knotts's administration of the affairs of the Gary Land Company. Little difficulty had been experienced in selling the corner lots on Broadway but the inside lots were selling slowly. Rumors reached the steel people that Knotts was not pushing the sale of the company's lots. Eugene J. Buffington selected Horace S. Norton, secretary to the general superintendent of the Illinois Steel Company's Joliet plant, to investigate the land company's affairs. Norton reported in March, 1907, that Knotts was busy with many private activities and that it was difficult for him to separate his own interests in Gary real estate from those of the Gary Land Company. Since the steel company's officials did not like the course being followed by Tom Knotts as president of the town board it is possible that they felt that the brothers were having things too much their own way in Gary.[55] Armanis F. Knotts soon resigned and Norton succeeded him as manager of the land company.

[54] Town of Gary, *First Annual Report,* 1908, p. 14; Gary *Weekly Tribune,* May 30, 1908.
[55] Quillen, The Industrial City, 121.

Since no statement by Armanis Knotts in regard to this controversy was found, it is impossible to arrive at a definite conclusion as to the various factors that brought about his separation from the land company. The records show Knotts was interested in real estate in that part of Gary which lay outside the company's area, and that he acquired this property at the same time that he was purchasing land for the steel corporation. On November 28, 1905, Knotts purchased 225 lots in the Tolleston area, and on February 17, 1906, forty-three lots in the same district were bought from the auditor of Lake County. There are indications that he was associated with his brother, Tom Knotts, in the real estate business. The latter had also invested in Tolleston property.[56] Tom Knotts said in later years, in regard to his success in the realty business, "It was like picking leaves from a tree."[57] Because the known information about this controversy is scanty, it cannot safely be said that Armanis F. Knotts was primarily interested in the sale of his own lots or that he willfully neglected the affairs of the Land Company. Many early inhabitants were either unwilling or unable to purchase the lots offered for sale by the Land Company; also, almost everyone with capital and ambition speculated in Gary real estate in those early years.

Tom Knotts and his friends apparently resented the steel corporation's course in separating Armanis F. Knotts from the Gary Land Company. It was not unusual for his successor, Captain Norton, to receive a cool reception in the town. Norton's strict enforcement of the company's rules in regard to the sale of lots and the

56 Lake County Deed Records, 103:124; 120:40. See also Vols. 117, 125, 126, 127, 129, and 130 for these transactions.

57 Thomas E. Knotts quoted in Gary *Evening Post,* October 5, 1915. See also Knotts's article in the Chicago *Express,* April 17, 1915.

construction of buildings in its part of the town aroused the enmity of some citizens. Norton was regarded by Knotts's friends as a "mysterious and unwelcome stranger, an arrogant usurper, a man to be shunned." His determination that the steel company should have a voice in the town's affairs soon found him at odds with Tom Knotts who was equally determined that the corporation stay on "its side of the Grand Calumet River" and let the people solve their own problems. The feud which ensued between these strong-willed men was one in which quarter was never asked nor was it ever given by either leader.   A newspaperman who came to Gary in 1910 recalled the talk in Knotts's office of "some strange wretch by the name of Norton, a fellow beyond the pale of polite society." Norton was given the nickname of "Turkey Neck" by Thomas F. Costello, editor of Knotts's newspaper.[58] Norton and his friends were equally as vitriolic in regard to Knotts. The Mayor was frequently denounced as a czar, a dictator, and as the "crazy engineer of Gary." The name of the city, they insisted, should be changed to "Knottsville." Charges were also made that Knotts regarded every friend of the steel company as an enemy.[59] The rough-and-tumble nature of the conflict is indicated by the arrest of the Mayor fourteen times in two years on charges of graft and corruption. Each time he was acquitted.

The main point of conflict between Tom Knotts and his friends on the one side and the steel company on the other was the direction in which Gary should expand. As has been noted, the company's original plan called for the town to expand east and west and to extend only south as far as the Wabash tracks, which was the south-

[58] Erwin C. Rosenau in Gary *Post-Tribune*, August 6, 1947, and Henry Burgess Snyder in *ibid.*, December 13, 1938.

[59] Gary *Daily Tribune*, November 5, 1913.

ern limits of the company's property. By living in that area, the workers would have easy access to the mills. On the other hand, Knotts favored the expansion of the town to the south of the Wabash tracks. In this he was supported by men who owned land in that direction. Aside from their personal interests, there were other considerations that influenced Knotts and his backers in the matter. It would have been difficult for the Gary Land Company to provide housing on its property for all classes of workers in the mills. The standards set up by the land company for housing in its area placed the cost of owning a home at such a level that the common laborers were either unable or unwilling to buy property in that section. Instead, most of them preferred the area south of the Wabash tracks where, for some years at least, there was no building code, no restrictions as to housing, and where liquor and beer could be obtained more conveniently and in unlimited quantities.[60]

The key to expansion was transportation. Knotts and his colleagues pushed the improvement of the streets south of the Wabash tracks. Six weeks after the members

[60] Charles P. Burton, in *The Calumet,* June 16, 1913; Edna Hatfield Edmondson, "Juvenile Delinquency and Adult Crime . . . with special reference to the Immigrant Population," in *Indiana University Studies,* Vol. 8, No. 49, June, 1921, p. 15. By the close of 1907, five hundred dwellings, two lodging houses, one restaurant, and a hotel building of forty rooms, the Hotel Gary, had been constructed by the Gary Land Company. Monthly rentals for the dwellings were as follows: fifty frame houses of four rooms each for from $12.00 to $13.00; ninety frame houses of four, five, and six rooms from $14.00 to $20.00; one hundred frame houses of six rooms, $16.50 to $19.50; and 266 brick, cement, and frame houses of from five to ten rooms with rents ranging from $23.00 to $42.00 a month. These houses were available only to the steel company's employees who had the privilege of purchasing them on easy terms. Because of the lack of specific records, it is impossible to estimate the number of dwellings and buildings erected by individuals on lots purchased from the Land Company. United States Steel Corporation, *Sixth Annual Report,* 1907, p. 31; Taylor, *Satellite Cities,* 184.

of the first town board were inducted into office, Broadway was extended about two miles south of the land company's area to the Little Calumet River. A large part of that section of the street was paved within a short time, and by 1909 an iron bridge was built across the Little Calumet. Eleventh Avenue was improved west of Broadway to Tolleston, and Nineteenth Avenue between Broadway and Madison was widened and paved by 1909. [61] Four miles of Broadway, most of it lying south of the Wabash tracks, was paved by the close of 1910. In the same year the Lake County commissioners were persuaded to extend the street south to Merrillville. In striking contrast to the improvement of Broadway and other streets to the south, Fifth Avenue by 1910 had been paved only about a mile west of Broadway to Tyler Street. From there it was graded, but not paved, for something over a mile to Bridge Street. In 1910 the city council reported that East Fifth Avenue was being "improved" to make a junction with the Miller-Aetna gravel road but nothing was said about the street being paved.[62]

Public transportation facilities were equally as important as street improvements. The area through which the first trolleys were built would be more quickly settled and increase in value more rapidly than would those without such service. The conflict between the steel company's officials and the town board reached a bitter stage over this matter. The steel people organized the Gary and Hammond Traction Company and sought to obtain a franchise from the town trustees. Another firm, the Gary and Interurban Railway Company, headed by Frank Gavit of Whiting, a friend of the Knotts brothers,

[61] Town of Gary, *First Annual Report*, 1908, p. 12.
[62] City of Gary, *Second Annual Report*, 1910, p. 23.

also put in a bid for the right to operate cars on the
town's streets.   Excitement over the matter reached
a high pitch.   On July 6, 1907, the town board met in
Gary's first schoolhouse, which was crowded with citizens
while others peered through the windows, and granted
the franchise to Gavit's company.   Knotts and Sears
favored the Gary and Interurban Company while Caldwell, an employee of the steel company, voted to give
the franchise to his employer's subsidiary.[63]   The steel
company's representative at the meeting, in expressing
his disappointment, said the corporation had striven to
provide Gary with the best public utilities possible and
that it had hoped the streetcar system would be on the
same plane.   He predicted that under the terms of the
franchise, the Gavit Company could not provide satisfactory service.[64]

The terms of the franchise were severe.   Gary and
Interurban was to sell six transportation tickets for
twenty-five cents, and at the end of five years eight fares
for the same amount.   The town was to receive a percentage of the gross profits, and the traction company
was to pave a surface twenty-six feet wide on the streets
over which it ran double tracks.   In addition, the company agreed to build tracks from Fourth Avenue southward on Broadway to the Little Calumet River; on
Eleventh Avenue west to Grant Street, which was the
western limit of the town in that direction; and on Fifth
Avenue to the town's eastern and western boundaries.[65]

Had the steel company's subsidiary obtained the franchise, it is probable that greater emphasis would have

[63] Gary *Weekly Tribune*, July 12, 1907. Frank Gavit was reported
to have had real estate interests south of the Wabash tracks. Quillen,
The Industrial City, 143.

[64] Gary *Weekly Tribune*, July 12, 1907.

[65] City of Gary, *Second Annual Report*, 1910, p. 25.

been placed on providing service for Fifth Avenue. Instead, the Gary and Interurban installed its tracks on Broadway first and was slow to build its line on Fifth Avenue. By the close of 1908 more than two miles of tracks had been laid on Broadway and a mile of track had been built westward on Eleventh Avenue from Broadway to Tolleston. In January, 1910, the line was extended from Tolleston to Hammond. The next year the tracks on Broadway made a connection with the Gary and Southern Railway which proceeded to operate cars from Crown Point over the entire length of Broadway to downtown Gary. On the other hand, the tracks on Fifth Avenue terminated at Fillmore Street, about a mile west of Broadway. In 1911 they were extended to Bridge Street and thence over that thoroughfare to the American Bridge Company's plant.[66] The map of Gary for 1914 showed the area platted and occupied south of the Wabash tracks to be more than four times as large as that platted and occupied in the Gary Land Company's section to the north.

One of the most exasperating problems to confront the steel company involved a five-acre tract owned by Richard Much on the lake front at the foot of Clark Road near Pine Station. Much operated a saloon and restaurant, the latter famous for its fish dinners. In 1908 the Gary police visited the place to find out why the proprietor did not have a license to operate the establishment, only to learn that the town had overlooked the tract when it annexed the surrounding territory. The five acres were immediately made a part of Gary. Clark Road, legally a public thoroughfare, was the only approach to Much's domain. Since his property lay be-

[66] Town of Gary, *First Annual Report*, 1908, p. 31; Cannon, Loring, and Robb (eds.), *History of the Lake and Calumet Region*, 1:679; City of Gary, *Second Annual Report*, 1910, p. 25.

tween the Buffington Cement Plant and the steel company's area to the east, and as Clark Road cut like a dirty gash across the company's otherwise unbroken strip of seven miles along the lake front, steel officials tried in vain to purchase the acreage, offering several times what it was actually worth. Also, that portion of Clark Road to Much's place was crossed by numerous tracks of the Elgin, Joliet and Eastern Belt Line Railroad, a subsidiary of the steel company, a fact which compelled the railroad to maintain crossings at great expense. The steel people brought suit in the state courts to have that part of the road closed. In 1913, after a legal battle of about four years, the Indiana Supreme Court ruled in favor of the roadhouse proprietor. Much celebrated his victory by inviting Tom Knotts and other friends to an elaborate fish dinner, an indication that Knotts encouraged him to defy the steel company.[67]

The First Citizens

Men from every walk of life flocked into the embryo city to seek their fortunes. There were those who came on the orders of the steel company to build the town and to construct and operate the mills. Outstanding among these were Ralph E. Rowley, Thomas H. Cutler, William P. Gleason, Arthur P. Melton, and Captain Horace S. Norton. All remained to become important leaders in the expansion of the steel mills and in the development of Gary.

Until his retirement as manager of the Gary Land Company in 1938, Horace S. Norton, more popularly known as Captain Norton, was one of the most dominant figures in Gary's civic affairs. Norton and William P.

[67] Gary *Weekly Tribune,* October 8, 1908, November 19, 1909; Gary *Evening Post,* March 7, 1913.

Gleason, superintendent of the great steel mill, were the spokesmen for the steel corporation and to Gary's citizens they represented the power and influence of the company in their city. Norton was said to have appeared regularly on Wednesday of each week at the offices of the steel corporation in Chicago, where he received the counsel and ascertained the wishes of Eugene J. Buffington and other high officials in regard to Gary's affairs.[68]

Business and professional men, largely of old American stock, sank their roots in the young community. Most of them were young men whose ambitions more than made up for their lack of capital. Ora L. Wildermuth, Gary's first lawyer, was compelled by lack of clients and office space to find employment on a construction gang and later to serve as the town's first schoolteacher.[69] Another young lawyer, Claude V. Ridgely, arrived with

[68] Quillen, The Industrial City, 488. Citizens who knew Captain Norton intimately said there were three great loyalties in his life: the steel corporation, the Christ Episcopal Church, of which he was a senior warden, and the Republican party. A study of his career indicates that a genuine interest in the welfare of Gary should be added to these. There is little doubt but that Norton was politically minded and that he wanted to be a power in the city's affairs. Also, there is evidence that in more than one instance he found it necessary to compromise with his conscience and support candidates of questionable character and ability in order to retain his influence in the municipality. Despite this weakness, Norton was sincerely interested in the social and spiritual improvement of the people, and many of the steel company's contributions in the form of money and land to churches and social and benevolent agencies, and to the city were brought about by his influence. Norton was born in Lockport, Illinois, in 1865, and was graduated from De Pauw University in 1888. For a time he engaged in the stone business at Bedford, Indiana, and in 1896 was employed by the Illinois Steel Company in Joliet. He obtained his military title from service in the Illinois National Guard. Howat (ed.), A Standard History of Lake County, 2:543; Cannon, Loring, and Robb (eds.), History of the Lake and Calumet Region, 2:20-22.

[69] Ora L. Wildermuth, "The Early Days of Gary," in Cannon, Loring, and Robb (eds.), op. cit., 1:757.

$5.00 in his pockets and also sustained himself for a time by manual labor.[70]   William F. Hodges, mayor of the city in later years, built the first permanent home in the community.[71]   C. Oliver Holmes came from Hammond as the secretary of Armanis F. Knotts.   Dr. Theo B. Templin, only two years out of medical school, started his practice in the town in August, 1906.   In 1907 and 1908 architects and builders such as John A. Brennan, Ingwald Moe, and Marcello Gerometta arrived.   H. Alschuler, operator of Gary's largest department store for many years, and banker Louis Glueck came in 1907. Also, in the same year, Joseph Tittle, native of Bohemia, established the first of a chain of meat stores.   William A. Wirt became superintendent of the Gary schools in 1907, and Louis J. Bailey assumed the direction of the public library the following year.   There were few old people to be seen in the city; everywhere, in the streets, in the mills, in the homes, it appeared that Gary was a city of young people.[72]

Between five and six thousand workmen made up the community's population in the early years of the construction of the mill and of the town.[73]   With the exception of the foremen and skilled workers, these men were chiefly American and immigrant laborers who came without their families.   A considerable number remained in Gary as construction workers, for the work of building went on after the making of steel began.   Some found employment in the mills.   Those who stayed sent for their

70 Interview with Claude V. Ridgely, Gary, April 17, 1953.

71 Other prominent men and the year of their arrival were: William M. Dunn, 1907; Tim W. Englehart, 1907; William J. Fulton, 1907; Harvey J. Curtis, 1907; Ernst L. Schaible, 1908; George H. Manlove, 1908; and Dr. Joseph Toner, 1908.

72 Edmondson, "Juvenile Delinquency and Adult Crime," in *Indiana University Studies*, Vol. 8, No. 49, p. 9.

73 Gary *Weekly Tribune*, December 25, 1908.

families, if they had any, or found wives among the local population. Those who did not marry constituted Gary's boardinghouse population.[74] The early days found adventurers, soldiers of fortune, and other classes of restless humanity crowding into the community. Some were men who had failed elsewhere and were earnestly trying to get a fresh start in life. Others were the sharp kind, who faded away before they became too well known, and many were fugitives from justice.[75] In 1907 Tom Knotts received an average of two dozen letters a day from people inquiring about jobs and possibilities of investments, and from wives seeking errant husbands.[76] Finally, there were the gamblers, saloon keepers, and inmates of houses of prostitution who took advantage of the lack of wholesome recreation to exploit the men from the construction camps.[77]

Police and Fire Departments

In the early days, Gary's Police Department was confronted with all the problems of maintaining law and order that prevailed in the mining towns of the Old West. The crowding of several thousand men into the construction camps along the Grand Calumet River led to fights and riots which often resulted in bloodshed and killings. The presence of "blind pigs," places where liquor was illegally sold, aggravated conditions in the camps.[78]   Chi-

[74] Edmondson, "Juvenile Delinquency and Adult Crime," in *loc. cit.,* 19.

[75] Melton, "Early Recollections of Gary," in Lester (ed.), Papers by Various Hands, 1:282.

[76] Gary *Weekly Tribune,* June 21, 1907.

[77] Quillen, The Industrial City, 155.

[78] Gary *Weekly Tribune,* March 5, 1909. The Gary Land Company originally planned to permit four saloons or bars in its area north of the Wabash tracks. Because two of the sites set aside for this purpose were too remote from the downtown district, only two bars were ever established. The company leased these to private individuals. The best

cago criminals were attracted to the town, where many obtained legitimate jobs to conceal the real reasons for their presence. The absence of electric lights and satisfactory means of transportation were assets to the criminal element. Citizens carried lanterns at night to light their ways across the lonely sand hills, while many carried guns to protect themselves from roving bandits.

The town board, at its first meeting, instructed the clerk to procure a marshal's star, four pairs of handcuffs, and six police clubs. The number of clubs was placed a little higher on the theory that some of the heads might prove unusually hard, hence harder on the clubs. In its first report of 1908 the board explained that in the early days there were "strenuous" men in Gary who, for their own good and the general welfare, had to be restrained. For this purpose a jail consisting of two cells was built at a cost of about $1,000.00.[79] Tom Knotts sought experienced as well as rough and tumble policemen to restrain the strenuous characters in the community.

Drunkenness was the greatest problem for the police. Out of a total of 1,626 arrests made in 1908, 616

known of the two was the Binzenhof at the corner of Fourth and Broadway, where the city hall now stands. It contained a one hundred-foot bar, a restaurant, and on the second floor a large hall which was used for civil gatherings, political meetings, and for plays staged by local talent. It was operated by Ted Binzen, formerly chief of police at Joliet, Illinois. The other bar was located at Sixth and Broadway in the Hotel Gary. It is of interest that these "oases" were located on Broadway, which led to the main gate of the steel mill, and that thousands of workmen passed them each day, a fact resented by the saloon keepers south of the Wabash tracks. Gary *Post-Tribune,* May 25, 1938; Gary *Northern Indianian,* October 25, 1907.

[79] Gary *Weekly Tribune,* October 11, 1907; Holmes, "How We Incorporated the Town," in Lake County Old Settler and Historical Association, *Historical Records,* 1924, p. 42; Town of Gary, *First Annual Report,* 1908, p. 12.

were for public intoxication.[80]   The lack of adequate
lighting and transportation facilities together with
the presence of lonely woods and empty expanses of
sand ridges handicapped the police.   There was the constant danger of drunks freezing to death at night and of
others rolling off the sand hills and drowning in the
sloughs.   The police found it impossible to carry them
individually through the deep sand to the safety of the
jail.   Ingenious methods were devised to solve the problem.   The officers toured the areas several times each
twenty-four hours, handcuffing drunks to small trees
wherever they were found.   It was not unusual for a sod-
den citizen to awake from his sleep to find himself intimately associated with a scrub oak sapling. From time to
time the police made the rounds with a wagon and hauled
them off to jail.   At first an old gray mare and a buck-
board, hired for one dollar a trip, performed this task.[81]
Because of the lack of space in the jail, those arrested for
intoxication and various minor offenses were fined and
released as soon as it was practical.

The task of safeguarding the public's health was also
a responsibility for the police, and in this matter they were
often compelled to resort to unusual methods.   An epidemic of smallpox broke out among some two hundred
Negroes in a construction camp.   The group was immediately quarantined in a "pest" house in the woods.   A
force of physicians from near-by cities was hurried into
the town to vaccinate the entire population.   The process
was a strange one to many of the foreign-born inhabitants who fled in terror when approached by a physician.
Finding the task of explanation too laborious and slow,

[80] Town of Gary, *First Annual Report,* 1908, pp. 36-37.

[81] Douglass Wilson, "Joseph D. Martin, First Police Chief of Gary,"
in Biographical Sketches of Gary and Lake County Residents (scrapbooks in Gary Public Library), Vol. 7.

the police once more demonstrated their ingenuity. Numerous foreigners were hunted down and vaccinated against their will. It was a common sight to see a frightened man running down Broadway pursued by a policeman and doctor—satchel in hand. If captured, the victim was pinned to the pavement, his leg or arm bared, and despite spluttering protestations the job was triumphantly performed. On one occasion a physician was knocked unconscious by muscular workmen.[82] The police also provided temporary shelter for the homeless, "lodgers" in the jail numbering 2,375 during 1908.[83]

For more than two years the Police Department was also the town's fire-fighting force.[84] Late in 1907 Tom Knotts offered the position of chief of the nonexistent fire department to Joseph Feely, a captain in the Chicago Fire Department. Feely, unimpressed by the community, was inclined to refuse the offer until Knotts showed him the water works with five pumps of five-million gallons capacity. This convinced the captain that the steel company was planning a great future for Gary. In December, 1908, Feely organized the fire department, and the Chicago fire officials donated an old fire wagon to the town. Politics did not play a part in the organization of the fire company. Feely wanted men of sound physical condition and about fifty applied for the posts available. The chief's method of selecting his men was simple: "I lined them up and told them to run through the sand over a course which had been measured off. I had Dr. Toner there at the finish. The first men to finish were examined, and if found physically fit, got the jobs." There was no fire alarm system for some time. If a citizen discovered a

---

[82] Horace S. Norton in Fort Wayne *Journal-Gazette*, October 19, 1922; Taylor, *Satellite Cities*, 206.

[83] Town of Gary, *First Annual Report*, 1908, p. 36.

[84] *Ibid.*, 15.

fire, he fired his pistol—almost everyone in Gary in those days owned a gun—and kept firing it until the firemen arrived. Gary's gas-propelled fire truck, purchased in 1909, was said to have been the first of its kind in Indiana.[85]

Early Schools and Libraries

By September, 1906, enough families had settled in the young town to necessitate the establishment of a public school. The Gary schools, soon to be famous, went through a pioneer period as did the other institutions of the city. Tom Knotts engaged Ora L. Wildermuth, who by that time was no doubt weary of his labors on a construction gang, to teach the first school. A few days later a school board composed of C. Oliver Holmes, Thomas H. Cutler, and Edward Jewell, the latter an employee of the Wabash Railroad, was appointed by the town trustees. A small one-room schoolhouse was hastily erected on the east side of Broadway opposite the present South Shore Station. Wildermuth, himself, helped a carpenter construct the rough plank seats for the children. On the first of October the young lawyer-teacher stood on a stump in front of the crude building and rang a bell to summon the children to Gary's first school. The twenty-two pupils responding that day found the bell and a box of writing tablets were the only pieces of educational equipment available.[86] A second teacher, R. R. Quillen, was added a few days later. The number of children in-

[85] H. E. Patterson, "Joseph Feely, Gary's First Fire Chief," in Biographical Sketches of Gary and Lake County Residents (scrapbooks in Gary Public Library), Vol. 4.

[86] Wildermuth, "The Early Days of Gary," in Cannon, Loring, and Robb (eds.), *History of the Lake and Calumet Region*, 1:757; Thomas E. Knotts, "Reminiscences," in Lester (ed.), Papers by Various Hands, 4:231. Wildermuth taught only one year and then devoted his time to the practice of law.

creased so rapidly that another one-room school was
built some distance to the south. By the end of the first
year, four teachers were administering to the needs of 123
pupils. The children south of the Wabash tracks, in
what was soon known as the "Patch," attended a township school at Twenty-second Avenue and Washington
Street the first year.[87]

The visit of William A. Wirt, superintendent of schools
at Bluffton, Indiana, in the fall of 1906, had momentous
consequences for the Gary Public Schools.[88] Tom Knotts
met Wirt during a Sunday morning stroll among the sand
hills where Broadway Street was later built. Knotts discovered that the young man was a schoolteacher, and re-
calling his own experiences as a teacher, thought he would
find out what the stranger knew about education. "We
had not talked long," said Knotts, "when I decided to
quit and listen." Before they parted, Wirt was asked
if he would consider a proposition to head the new school
system if at some time the offer was made to him. Within
a few weeks the school board voted unanimously to employ Wirt as superintendent, beginning July 1, 1907, at a
salary of $2,500.00 a year. Knotts always regarded his
part in bringing Wirt to Gary as one of his greatest
achievements. Although Knotts was a Democrat and
Wirt was a Republican, the former gave the superintendent his loyal support. Knotts, according to reports, never
interfered with Wirt's administration of the schools.
Wirt also had the confidence and support of the steel
company's officials. His success in winning the backing
of these warring factions enabled him to lay a strong
foundation for the work-study-play system of education,

[87] Town of Gary, *First Annual Report*, 1908, p. 49.
[88] The Hammond *Lake County Times*, October 1, 1906, took notice of
Wirt's visit to Gary.

which in time attracted nationwide attention to the Gary schools.[89]

The public schools expanded with the increase of population. In 1907 emergency or portable buildings were erected at Fourteenth and Broadway, and by the end of the second school year there were fifteen teachers and 492 children in the schools. The Gary Land Company came to the aid of the penniless town and erected a brick school of the standard type at the corner of Seventh and Jefferson. This building, known as the Jefferson School, was opened in September, 1908. The school board rented the structure from the Land Company for $7,850.00 a year. This action on the part of the steel company's subsidiary was regarded by the town officials as a philanthropic gesture. In 1912 the school board purchased the building. In September, 1909, the Emerson School, designed to accommodate 1,800 pupils and costing $225,-000.00, was put into use. Until that time the high-school students attended the Jefferson School. Emerson School was the first building planned by Wirt to conform to his work-study-play program of education.[90]

The Gary Public Library, another of the city's institutions which was to attract wide attention, also had its beginning in this period. Ora L. Wildermuth is regarded in some quarters as the founder of the public library. Acting on his suggestion, the women of the neighborhood in the fall of 1906 prepared an oyster supper in the schoolhouse to raise funds for the library. The ladies were

[89] Thomas E. Knotts quoted in Taylor, *Satellite Cities*, 219; *Calumet Region Historical Guide*, 159; Gary *Evening Post*, October 4, 1909; A. H. Bell in the Gary *Post-Tribune*, March 12, 1938. Bell was auditor of the Gary schools during the greater part of the Wirt era. See below, 471-85, for Wirt's career and educational program.

[90] Town of Gary, *First Annual Report*, 1908, pp. 49-50, 53; Gary *Daily Tribune*, September 18, 1912.

agreeably surprised at the number of men from the construction camps who welcomed the opportunity to escape their rough fare for a home-cooked meal. Books purchased from the proceeds of the supper were housed in the tar-paper shack which Wildermuth used for a law office. The following year William A. Wirt suggested that a library board be organized to provide the town with more adequate facilities. Then it was discovered that a state law required five year's residence in a community for a citizen to be eligible to serve as a library trustee. Gary being only about a year old, no one could qualify for the post. The school board somewhat informally appointed a board of four members and delegated to it the organization and management of a public library. The board consisted of Father Thomas Jansen, of Holy Angels Church, Mrs. John E. Sears, wife of the alderman of Gary's Third Ward, Wirt, and Wildermuth. The organization of the new board took place in March, 1908, Father Jansen being elected chairman and Wirt secretary.[91] In June the small collection of books was moved to a storeroom on West Seventh Avenue near Broadway.

The choice of Louis J. Bailey, then on the staff of the Congressional Library in Washington, D.C., as librarian may be compared in importance to the selection of Wirt as superintendent of schools. Bailey, well qualified for the position, possessed an unusually intelligent conception of what a public library should be.[92] Under his supervision the institution not only catered to the reading

[91] Cannon, Loring, and Robb (eds.), *History of the Lake and Calumet Region*, 1:582-85; Wildermuth, "The Early Days of Gary," in *ibid.*, 1:758; Gary *Weekly Tribune*, April 3, 1908.

[92] Bailey was a graduate of the University of Rochester and the New York State Library School at Albany. He was head of the Gary Library until 1922.

public but became a storehouse of source material about the history of the city and the region. Rarely did a current newspaper, directory, municipal report, and other publications so important to students of local history fail to find a place in the library's collection. Bailey's original salary being only $900.00 a year, he and Mrs. Bailey occupied living quarters in the rear of the storeroom-library for some time. In December of 1908 the library was opened to the public with a collection of about 1,500 volumes.[93]

Early in the Norton regime, the Gary Land Company demonstrated its willingness to donate land for civic and benevolent purposes. In 1907 it presented a site for a city hall at Seventh and Massachusetts, and in the same year donated four frame buildings to the Franciscan Sisters for the location of St. Mary's Hospital. The company also created the East Side Park, later known as Buffington Park, and the West Side Park, which in time was called Jefferson Park. The West Side Park was constructed with the view of preserving the original contour of the land. The sand hills and ravines were disturbed only to the extent that they were covered with black dirt in which grass was planted. The Land Company retained ownership of these parks as long as Knotts was mayor. They were presented to the city in 1915.[94]

In 1907 the Gary Commercial Club, Gary's earliest business and civic organization, was founded by Captain

[93] Gary *Post-Tribune,* October 9, 1953; Gary *Weekly Tribune,* September 4, 1908; Cannon, Loring, and Robb (eds.), *History of the Lake and Calumet Region,* 1:584.

[94] Gary *Weekly Tribune,* October 25 and November 15, 1907; William P. Gleason, "Gary's Park System" (Typewritten MS in Superintendent's Office of the Gary Works, United States Steel Corporation), 1; W. H. De Gan, superintendent of the Gary Park System, Report to William P. Gleason, January 26, 1935 (Typewritten MS in Superintendent's Office of the Gary Works, United States Steel Corporation), 2.

Norton. Although the club was intended to be a sort of chamber of commerce, it was more of a social organization in the early years. Captain Norton was the first and only president of the club from its establishment to 1940. The members transformed one of the dining rooms of the Hotel Gary into a clubroom. One of the initial services provided by the organization was the operation of an employment agency. As time passed, the Gary Commercial Club made a distinct contribution in civic affairs as a sounding board or forum for the discussion of community problems and for the expression of protests on graft and corruption in public affairs. Its members were not reluctant to extol the virtues of Gary, and to them may be attributed the term, "Gary, the Magic City of Steel," which was applied to the city for some years.[95]

Production of Steel Begins

On July 23, 1908, the first ore boat, the "Elbert H. Gary," loaded with about 10,000 tons of iron ore from the Lake Superior Region, docked in the harbor at the Gary Works. To celebrate this memorable event, a festive program was arranged and financed by the Gary Commercial Club. Five hundred guests, of whom one hundred were members of the club, wearing badges inscribed "Opening Gary Harbor, July 23, 1908," and singing "Garyland, My Garyland," boarded the ore boat at South Chicago.[96] The "Elbert H. Gary" was escorted

[95] Gary *Weekly Tribune,* September 6 and November 15, 1907; April 24, 1908. The Gary Chamber of Commerce, organized in 1911, merged with the Gary Commercial Club in 1930.

[96] *Ibid.,* July 24 and August 14, 1908. The song was composed by Wilbur D. Nesbit at the request of the Gary Commercial Club. It was sung to the tune of "Maryland, My Maryland." For the words, see Will H. Moore, *"If I Had Known." About Gary in 1909* (Chicago, 1909), 19.

by the United States Navy's gunboat, "Wolverine," the revenue cutter, "Dorothea," and the lighthouse tender, "Sumac." When asked to fire a salute to the steel mill, the commander of the "Wolverine" explained that such action was contrary to regulations but that he could salute the American Flag. A flag was raised at the north end of one of the harbor's piers, and a twenty-one gun salute was fired by the "Wolverine" as the ore boat nosed its way into the slip. This was followed by cheers from several thousand spectators who lined both sides of the harbor. Speeches were made by Indiana's John W. Kern, Democratic candidate for vice-president in that year's election, Congressmen James R. Mann of Illinois and Edgar D. Crumpacker of Indiana, and William P. Gleason. When the first scoopful of ore was deposited in the bins alongside the slip, hundreds of people rushed forward, each seeking a handful of the substance as a souvenir of the momentous occasion. A parade, led by the band from the "Dorothea," made its way down Broadway to the Hotel Gary, where a reception and banquet were held that evening.[97]

On December 21, 1908, Mary Louise Gleason, daughter of the plant's superintendent, lighted the fire in the first blast furnace. When the glare from the furnace was seen at night against the northern sky, some citizens, thinking the mill was burning down, called the Fire Department to put out the fire.[98] The lights from that great mill have never gone completely out. On January 24, 1909, steel rails were rolled from ingots supplied by other plants of the corporation. The first steel was manufactured a week later. Fourteen open-hearth furnaces

[97] *Iron Age,* 82:312 (July-December, 1908); Gary *Weekly Tribune,* August 14, 1908.

[98] Gary *Weekly Tribune,* December 21, 1908; January 1, 1909.

were completed and a like number were near completion by the end of 1908. Three more blast furnaces were put into operation the following year.[99]

Iron Age, the organ of the steel industry, hailed the Gary Works as the greatest steel plant in the world. According to the publication, in Gary was concentrated the most modern methods and appliances for the making of steel from the ore to the finished product. The plant, it asserted, represented in all its units, individually and collectively, the acme of achievement in that branch of the world's industries. *Iron Age* went on to say: "The opportunity of designing a complete steel making plant of such size has never before presented itself to engineers; nor indeed can conditions better suited to successful accomplishment, be easily achieved."[1]

System magazine, in its reference to the plant, declared that "the courage and imagination which have spent forty-two million dollars to clip a few seconds from the birth throes of a steel rail are linked with cool-brained conservatism." Gary was regarded as Pittsburgh's future rival and the article suggested that its name should have been "Economy," Indiana, because economy was its genius and inspiration. The "location, size, arrangement, equipment and every great and lesser detail of the huge plant serve that one master purpose—saving of materials, time, and labor; conserving of energy; elimination of wastes."[2]

By 1909, Gary's pioneer period had come to an end. Although the facilities for manufacturing steel were expanded in the years that followed and the building of the

[99] United States Steel Corporation, *Seventh Annual Report,* 1908, p. 29; *Iron Age,* 84:1571 (July-December, 1909).

[1] *Iron Age,* 83:2 (January-July, 1909). A complete chart and description of the Gary plant were presented in this issue.

[2] *System,* January, 1909, quoted in Gary *Weekly Tribune,* January 8, 1909.

corporation's subsidiaries had not yet started, the fundamental pattern of the city was well established. Much of the frontier atmosphere, so prevalent in the early years, had disappeared when the manufacture of steel began. Eugene J. Buffington, in a review of the steel company's efforts in behalf of the city, saw that a milestone had been reached in its history: "As far as it lies within the power and judgment of the corporation's management there have been provided those basic community conditions which seem best conducive to the highest and best social order of practical life. The material welfare of Gary is an accomplished fact. Its social welfare is held within the desires and aspirations of its future citizens."[3] The steel company, which was responsible for the city's existence, continued to play an important role in its expansion and growth.

[3] Buffington, "Making Cities for Workmen," in *Harper's Weekly,* May 8, 1909, p. 17.

10

GARY, EXPANSION AND MATURITY

THE YEARS FROM 1909 to 1933 were busy and turbulent ones for Gary, the city experiencing all the growing pains of a boom town. The expansion of the steel works and the construction of the corporation's subsidiary plants, which were accelerated by World War I, attracted a steady stream of workers to the city. As a result, Gary's population increased more than sixfold in the years between 1910 and 1930. The rather sudden influx of various races and nationalities was accompanied by problems of housing, education, and general social adjustments. On the political side, the conflict between mill and town disturbed the steel city for some years.

Early Population

There is no way of determining the exact number of people living and working in Gary during the early years of its existence. A large number of the construction workers did not even live in the town. Because of the lack of adequate housing and the rough conditions in the vicinity of the steel mill, many preferred to commute daily by railroad from their homes in Chicago and other nearby places.[1] From time to time the Gary Land Company took a count of the inhabitants and its estimates may be regarded as fairly accurate. The company found that the population increased from 334 in June, 1906, which was

[1] Chicago *Tribune,* October 9, 1908.

before the actual construction of the mills began, to 1,860 on January 1, 1907. A year later, it reported that 10,246 people were living in the town. A census taken in October, 1909, under the direction of the chief of police to determine whether the population was large enough for the town to be made a city, showed there were 11,723 residents within its corporate limits. This seems to have been a conservative estimate as the Federal census of 1910 placed the number of inhabitants at 16,802.[2]

Those concerned with the development of the municipality and its steel industry were not dependent entirely on Chicago and the surrounding area for their labor supply. Workers from a distance were attracted to the area through various media. The steel company advertised the story of Gary in American and European newspapers; editors of various types of publications, on their own initiative, featured articles about its development; real estate brokers depicted in glowing terms the opportunities awaiting those who invested their money in the new steel town; native Americans already on the scene persuaded friends and relatives to seek new careers in the community; and the foreign born passed the word in letters to their people in the old countries. Skilled workmen such as electricians, puddlers, and heaters came from steel mills in Pittsburgh, Youngstown, and other cities to seek employment and advancement in the new plants.[3]

A study of the population in 1910 showed that 26.7 per cent were whites of native American parents, 21.9 per cent were native American whites of foreign or mixed

[2] Gary Land Company, *Annual Report*, 1908, p. 75; Gary *Weekly Tribune*, October 23, 1909; U. S. Bureau of the Census, *Thirteenth Census* (1910): *Population*, pt. 2:531.

[3] Eugene J. Buffington, in the Gary *Post-Tribune*, June 4, 1931; Rose Field, "Growing Up with Gary," in *Success*, October, 1923, p. 14; J. Roy Leevy, The Industrial City (Typewritten MS in Gary Public Library).

parentage, and 49.1 per cent, or almost half of the residents, were foreign-born whites. Hence, the contribution of other countries to Gary's development was particularly impressive, 71 per cent of its people in 1910 being foreign born or having at least one parent who was born outside the United States. There were only 383 Negroes in the city at that time. A startling fact was that Gary's males outnumbered its females 11,521 to 5,281, resulting in the claim that Gary was the best boardinghouse city in the Middle West. The problems of Americanization and education were indicated by the report that 16.9 per cent of the foreign born could neither read nor write. In 1910 the laboring classes obviously comprised the greater part of the city's population.[4]

Housing and Sectionalism

From the very beginning there were two Garys, two differing ways of life, and a degree of sectionalism which affected every phase of the city's affairs. The Gary Land Company's district between the Wabash tracks and the steel mills, known as the North Side, was characterized by regulation, order and planning in building, excellent sanitary conditions, good streets, and strict supervision of the sale of intoxicating liquors. Here, in general, lived the executive and supervisory employees of the steel company, the skilled workmen, and the city's business and professional men, most of whom were native Americans or of the "Old Immigration." South of the Wabash tracks lay the South Side, more popularly known in the early years as the Patch, inhabited largely by people of the "New Immigration."[5] The Patch had all the character-

[4] All the statistics are from the *Thirteenth Census* (1910): *Population*, pt. 2:568. See also Gary *Evening Post*, April 4, 1910.

[5] The term "Old Immigration" is applied to the English, Scotch, Irish, Germans, and Scandinavians who comprised the great bulk of immi-

istics of similar areas around mining camps and fringing other industrial cities. Here were numerous saloons, crowded quarters, poor housing and unsanitary conditions, gambling places, and houses of prostitution. In this district unscrupulous realtors exploited the bewildered foreign born and ignorant American workers. The Patch was compelled in the early years to lay its own sewers and water mains, and its lots were burdened with special assessments to finance those necessities. Since at first there were no building restrictions in this district, every man built as he pleased. Hundreds of boxlike frame cottages and flimsy shacks housed its population.[6]

Gary was a city of strange contrasts in those early years. At its northern extremity, separating its people from the lake front, were the most modern and efficient steel mills in the world. The city's finest residential section was situated a little to the south in sight of the mills where the residents were exposed to the smoke and grime from the open-hearth and blast furnaces. Broadway, the principal business street running north and south through the heart of the city, was paved for about five miles with cement sidewalks running its entire length. On the north side the street was flanked by business houses, hotels, and restaurants of which any city could be proud. And yet just south of the Wabash tracks, and on the same Broadway, was the Patch with its saloons and nondescript buildings of every type and style. To the west of Broadway, in this latter section, lay an immigrant settlement of

grants before 1880. The "New Immigration" was composed largely of Italians, Hungarians, and Slavic people from eastern and southeastern Europe who arrived in America in great numbers in the years after 1880. See Carl Wittke, *We Who Built America* (New York, 1939), 101.

6 Gary *Weekly Tribune,* March 5, 1909; Edmondson, "Juvenile Delinquency and Adult Crime," in *Indiana University Studies,* Vol. 8, No. 49, p. 15.

tar-paper shacks.   Each shack had its accompaniment of
sheds, chicken coops, and stacks of hay or swamp grass
gathered from the near-by open spaces.   Cows, horses,
dogs, pigs, geese, chickens and children mingled in this
Old World community. The Gary Land Company sought
to isolate the Patch by neglecting to improve the adjoining land but this had very little effect on its life and activities.[7]

In the course of the construction of the mills, the steel
company permitted workers to build and occupy huts and
shacks on its property along the Grand Calumet River.
The company charged no rent for this space, and did not
concern itself at all with the conditions that prevailed
among these squatters.   Owners of the shacks, most
of whom worked on the construction gangs, rented
eating and sleeping space to other workers.   According
to reports, frequently from ten to fifteen men occupied
these crude dwellings.   In most instances the wives and
daughters of the proprietors did the cooking for the lodgers.   At least 150 such shacks were reported along the
river at the peak of construction.[8]

Shortly after the first mills were put into operation, the
steel company, desiring to clear the plant site, ordered the
squatters to move off its property. The hegira from the
river's banks began in March, 1909, when about two-
thousand men, women, and children, most of whom were
foreign born, moved southward into the Patch.   Many
owners of the Calumet River shacks purchased lots on the
South Side out of savings accumulated from their boardinghouse operations.   In the absence of building restrictions, numerous one-room shacks, many without windows,

7 Edmondson, "Juvenile Delinquency and Adult Crime," in *loc. cit.,*
8-9, 15, 17-18.

8 Gary *Weekly Tribune,* March 5, 1909.

were erected.   A common practice was the construction of two or three such buildings on the same lot, the owners occupying one and renting the others.   The town board of trustees took notice of such developments only to the extent that such structures were forbidden on Broadway, south of the Wabash Railroad tracks.[9]   Despite the poor housing and unsanitary conditions, the Patch did not experience any serious epidemics of infectious diseases. Climate, sandy soil, and an excellent supply of pure water were important health factors.[10]

The steel company did make an effort to provide proper housing for a portion of its permanent force of workers.   A number of houses, collectively known as Kirkville, were built on the northwest corner of the Gary Land Company's first subdivision. These dwellings were rented mostly to men, many of whom were from Chicago, employed in the Kirk Railroad Yards and by the steel company's belt line railroad, the Elgin, Joliet and Eastern. Another group of houses was erected on Rhode Island and Vermont streets, just north of Sixth Avenue, in the northeast corner of the first subdivision.   These houses, containing four rooms and a bath each and described as "double drygoods boxes," were rented to common laborers in the mills.   This community was called Hunkeyville because of its foreign-born tenants. The term Hunkey was applied indiscriminately by the native-born Americans to all foreigners, regardless of nationality, in the Calumet Region at that time.[11]

The steel company's officials were soon shocked by the

9 *Ibid.*

10 Taylor, *Satellite Cities,* 205.

11 Edmondson, "Juvenile Delinquency and Adult Crime," *loc. cit.,* 14; Taylor, *op. cit.,* 190; William Dale Fisher, Steel City's Culture, An Interpretation of the History of Gary, Indiana (A. B. thesis, Yale University, 1941, in Gary Public Library), 58.

conditions that prevailed in Hunkeyville, and by the abuse of the houses by the foreign-born tenants. Most of these were peasants from the rural areas of their native lands who had no conception of the refinements of the modern American home. Some of the tenants had the impression that something was wrong if the water ever stopped running from the faucets. In one instance the monthly water bill for a single dwelling amounted to $11.50. This was quickly corrected when the tenant, who made about $1.60 a day in the mills, was told that the water used in the home of Mill Superintendent Gleason, the largest in Gary, rarely cost $2.00 a month. The immigrant's penchant for taking in boarders was demonstrated by the report that 1,200 people occupied 50 of the houses in Hunkeyville. The beds were used constantly by members of the day and night shifts in the mills. The company had the foresight to install hardwood floors in these houses so that when kindling wood was scarce they would not be as easy to rip up as the pine boards. Steel officials were also concerned by the reported presence of a criminal element in the community.[12]

On April 1, 1911, the company, despairing of its efforts to teach the tenants better ways of living and not wishing to be responsible for the filth and unsanitary conditions in the houses, ordered the residents of Hunkeyville to move out. Within a short time, they all moved southward into the Patch. The houses were put in order for native and foreign-born workers who knew how to use them properly and who promised not to crowd them with boarders.[13] Thus ended the efforts of the corporation to provide housing for the unskilled workers.

In the meantime, the Gary Land Company had been making a vigorous effort to satisfy the demand for hous-

[12] Taylor, *Satellite Cities*, 192; Gary *Daily Tribune*, April 13, 1911.
[13] Gary *Evening Post*, April 1, 1911; Taylor, *op. cit.*, 192.

ing among its skilled workers. Captain Norton opened additional areas for development and laid out and paved streets in a manner designed to assure the balanced growth of the North Side. More than 1,200 houses were built by the close of 1910, and the following year the company constructed 261 dwellings and apartment houses. The corporation's employees were encouraged to buy these dwellings, and in June, 1910, Norton expressed the hope that there would soon be no company houses.[14]

Steel officials were so concerned with the appearance of the North Side that arrangements were made with the Gary Heat, Light and Water Company, a subsidiary of the corporation, to provide free water for trees and lawns for four months of each year.[15] They also encouraged the occupants of houses to keep their premises attractive by the gift of seeds and prizes which were granted for the best lawns. The company also planted several thousand trees in its area.[16] Despite these efforts, sand from vacant lots and open spaces was often piled by the wind into snowlike drifts on the streets and sidewalks, even on Broadway. Tumbleweeds, their roots loosened by the first frost in the fall, were also a nuisance for the citizens each year. The Gary *Daily Tribune* reported in 1914:

[14] City of Gary, *Second Annual Report,* 1910, p. 19; United States Steel Corporation, *Tenth Annual Report,* 1911, p. 28; Gary *Daily Tribune,* June 8, 1910. The steel corporation's success in dealing with its employees was indicated by the report in 1947 that there had been only one eviction in thirty-one years among the ten thousand tenants of its houses. Erwin C. Rosenau, in Gary *Post-Tribune,* August 7, 1947.

[15] Gary *Daily Tribune,* May 9, 1910. According to reports, the Gary Land Company paid more than $500,000.00 to the Gary Heat, Light and Water Company for this service from 1910 to 1931. Free water service was discontinued in 1931 when Samuel Insull's Midland Utility Company purchased the Gary company. See Gary *Post-Tribune,* June 11, 1931.

[16] Elliott Flower, "Gary, the Magic City," in *Putnam's Magazine,* 5 (January-March, 1909) :652.

"Tumbleweed day is not a fixed holiday in Gary, yet it comes every fall. The fall blizzards pick them up and send them rolling in great waves over the city. By the thousands they were borne down the streets today before the stiff breeze."[17]

The Saloon Controversy

The low state of Gary's morals in the early years, characterized by public intoxication, gambling, and pro-stitution, was blamed by many civic and religious leaders on its abnormal number of saloons. On the North Side, where only two bars were permitted by the Gary Land Company, the liquor traffic was kept under control. In the Patch, where there were no restrictions, Broadway and other streets were lined by solid blocks of saloons, some of which reflected the atmosphere of that community with such names as the "Bucket of Blood" and the "First and Last Chance." In 1910 the city was reported to have 217 saloons, an average of one for every 77 residents.[18] The European immigrant was accustomed to drinking wine without becoming intoxicated, but when confronted by the more potent gin and whisky in an American saloon and with a pay check in his pocket, he had a tendency to drink excessively. In this condition, he was an easy prey for the purveyors of vice who plied their trade in large numbers.

In 1908 a number of civic and religious leaders launched a movement to make Gary a dry city. A state law provided that if a majority of the voters who had voted in the last township election signed a remonstrance peti-tion, the county commissioners were instructed to refuse

[17] Gary *Daily Tribune,* October 26, 1914.

[18] Indiana Bureau of Statistics, *Thirteenth Biennial Report,* 1909-10, p. 1151.

to renew the licenses of saloon keepers for at least two years after their old licenses expired. Since the last general election in Calumet Township was held before the building of Gary began, only 341 votes were cast in that contest. By May, 1908, enough signatures has been collected to invoke the State's local option law. The sponsors of the petition did their work so quietly that the saloon keepers and the wet element were taken unawares and had no opportunity to combat the movement. The county was compelled by the law to deny the applications for the renewal of liquor licenses as they expired. Consequently, the number of legal saloons, those whose licenses had not as yet expired, gradually declined, there being only thirty-eight in operation on January 1, 1909. By April of that year the last of the licenses had expired and the city was legally dry.[19]

The prohibitionists, however, had not considered the attitude and will of Mayor Tom Knotts, who took the side of the saloon keepers and permitted them to operate without licenses. To keep within the law Knotts went through the formality of trying and convicting the saloon keepers for violating the liquor law. Once a month he had every operator of a bar hailed into the city court, of which he was judge by virtue of his office, and imposed a fine of $50.00 and a jail term of thirty days on each. The fines, which went into the city treasury, were approximately the same as the cost of the liquor license, and the jail sentences, termed "immunity baths" by the Gary *Daily Tribune*, were always suspended.[20] As a result, the sa-

[19] Gary *Weekly Tribune,* May 1, 1908, January 8, April 16, 1909. C. Oliver Holmes, a member of the school board and a Methodist layman, was one of the leaders of this movement. See Quillen, The Industrial City, 202.

[20] Cannon, "Tom Knotts As Mayor and Man," in Gary *Evening Post,* March 26, 1921; Gary *Daily Tribune,* May 31, 1911.

loons continued to operate without licenses under the protection of the mayor-judge of the city.

Knotts believed the saloon keepers had been treated unfairly by the dry element. He pointed out that they had much money invested in their property and that some had bought their places on the installment plan. If they were denied the right to continue in business, they would lose their investments. Moreover, the saloon men, along with other property owners, were being taxed by the city for the installation of sewers, sidewalks, and streets. If the bars were closed, the city would suffer a heavy financial loss. He also insisted the closing of the drinking places would cause a scarcity of labor in the mills, that many men would not work where they could not get liquor and beer. Finally, Knotts charged that those behind the remonstrance petition were Republicans who wished to put him in a difficult position because he was a Democrat.[21]

The dry element obtained a writ of mandamus from the superior court to compel the mayor to jail saloon keepers who violated the liquor law. Knotts ignored the court order, and was indicted for conspiracy to violate the local option law. In 1911 the trial was held in Valparaiso where a jury acquitted the mayor.[22] On May 1, 1910, the two-year period, during which liquor licenses could not be obtained, ended for many saloon keepers. On that day the county commissioners granted 138 permits to saloon men in Gary.[23] The effort to restrict the liquor traffic was a failure, the only result being an intensification of the strife between the mayor and his critics.

[21] Gary *Weekly Tribune,* August 6, 1909.
[22] Gary *Daily Tribune,* May 31, 1911; Cannon, "Tom Knotts As Mayor and Man," in Gary *Evening Post,* March 26, 1921.
[23] Gary *Evening Post,* May 2, 1910.

The City Election of 1909

In October, 1909, Gary became a fifth-class city. One may well speculate as to why this change in the political status of the community was delayed until such a late date. Indiana law permitted towns of from two to ten thousand population to become cities of the lowest class, and a census taken by the Gary Land Company in 1908 showed the town's population was more than enough for it to qualify. And yet, no evidence was found to indicate that Tom Knotts and the other members of the town board of trustees concerned themselves about the matter until the fall of 1909.[24]   Apparently the trustees delayed the change in the municipality's status until their term of office neared its end.

The city election of 1909 found Tom Knotts, a Democrat, locked in rough and tumble combat with the local Republican party, in whose affairs the steel company's officials played a prominent part. John A. Brennan, a building contractor, was the Republican candidate for mayor.[25]   The strategy of Knotts's opponents called for the nomination of someone other than Knotts for mayor on the Democratic ticket, then if Knotts ran as an independent the Democratic vote would be so split as to assure the election of Brennan. William C. Crolius, a former mayor of Joliet, Illinois, and a recent arrival in Gary, was selected to capture the Democratic nomination from Knotts. The latter's friends immediately accused Captain Norton and other steel officials of bringing Crolius to Gary for that purpose.[26]   Since Norton and William P.

[24] See above, 305.

[25] See Howat (ed.), *A Standard History of Lake County*, 2:621, for a biography of Brennan.

[26] Gary *Evening Post,* October 14, 1909. Crolius was mayor of Joliet, 1904-6. Several prominent citizens of Gary, who opposed Knotts in those years, told the author that Crolius was put up by the steel people,

Gleason were former residents of Joliet, Crolius' bid for
the Democratic nomination was apparently something
more than a mere coincidence. Crolius was nominated
in a Democratic primary of doubtful legality from which
Knotts and his friends held aloof. Knotts was nominated
by a convention at the Cozy Theater presided over by
Arthur P. Melton and Ora L. Wildermuth. A court
fight followed to determine which candidate, Knotts or
Crolius, could use the Democratic emblem, the crowing
rooster, and the title Democratic party on his ballot in
the election. A superior court in Hammond ruled in
favor of Knotts. According to the *Lake County Times,*
"It really did not matter which candidate had the Democratic emblem as quite a per cent of the voters over there
[Gary] cannot tell a rooster from a humming bird."
Crolius, refusing to run as an independent, urged his supporters to vote for Brennan.[27] He soon departed from
Gary.

Knotts founded the Gary *Evening Post* during this
campaign. His only instructions to those in charge of the
paper were: "Make it hot. Give 'em hell."[28] Knotts's
platform, expressed in a speech before his friends at the
Binzenhof bar, was equally as brief: "If you will elect me
to the office of mayor I will go and do exactly as I have
done in the past."[29] The Democrats charged that the
Republican ticket was a "steel company ticket," that

and that it was a mistake for Captain Norton to try to run both political
parties.

[27] Cannon, "Tom Knotts As Mayor and Man," in Gary *Evening Post,*
March 26, 1921; Gary *Weekly Tribune,* October 22, 29, 1909; Hammond
Lake County Times, November 5, 1909; Gary *Daily Tribune,* November
1, 1909.

[28] Cannon, "Tom Knotts as Mayor and Man," in Gary *Evening
Post,* March 26, 1921. Cannon and Frank Patrick, Chicago newspapermen, were employed by Knotts to run the *Evening Post.*

[29] Gary *Weekly Tribune,* October 8, 1909.

Brennan was Captain Norton's "Stooge," and that if he was elected, the steel company would control Gary. The company, it was said, would transform Gary into a "company town" and would own and operate the schools, stores, and houses as the Pullman Company had done in its town in South Chicago.[30] The Republicans also injected the steel corporation into the campaign. William F. Hodges said the campaign narrowed down to two issues: "Knotts and the steel company," that if Knotts, whom he alleged was hostile to the corporation, was elected, other industries would not locate in Gary.[31] Knotts was also criticized for permitting the saloon keepers to operate their business without licenses. On the other hand, John A. Brennan insisted he was not against the saloons but that they should be regulated so that if "you go in on pay night you won't be in danger of getting your brains knocked out."[32]

Both parties sought the vote of the foreign born. An act passed by the Indiana General Assembly in 1881 permitted aliens to vote who had formally declared their intention of becoming American citizens and who had been residents of the state for six months, of the township for sixty days, and of the precinct for thirty days immediately preceding an election.[33] Consequently, hundreds of the foreign born were hustled to the Federal building in Hammond for their first papers. When that office was overtaxed with applications, the prospective voters were taken to Valparaiso.[34]

---

[30] Gary *Evening Post,* October 16, 26, 30, 1909.

[31] Gary *Daily Tribune,* October 20, 1909.

[32] *Ibid.,* October 14, 1909.

[33] *Constitution of Indiana,* Art. II, Sec. 2; *Laws of Indiana,* 1881, p. 482.

[34] Gary *Daily Tribune,* November 1, 1909.

As the bitter campaign neared its end, Governor Thomas R. Marshall ordered a company of the state militia to be ready in case things got out of hand in Gary. The Governor also ordered the sheriff of Lake County to send enough deputies to the steel city to keep order on election day. The Democrats accused the sheriff, who was a Republican, of sending only Republican deputies. On the night before the election the entire Gary police force was arrested on a warrant sworn out by a Negro charging Knotts and the police with defamation of his character. The town board hastily provided bail for the policemen as they were about to be taken to jail in Hammond. Police Chief Martin appointed a large number of deputy marshals to supplement his police force, and finding his supply of clubs exhausted, armed them with clubs sawed from curtain poles. On election day many clashes occurred between the deputy sheriffs and the city's police. Despite this turmoil, few arrests were made and the militia was not called in.[35]

Knotts emerged the victor by the narrow margin of 71 votes, the total being 1,790 for him and 1,719 for Brennan. The voters in the Patch and in Hunkeyville reportedly gave Knotts his greatest support. The general results of the election indicated that Knotts's victory was a personal one since the newly elected city council was composed of four Republicans and three Democrats. The Gary *Evening Post* hailed Knotts's election as a victory for the people against the steel company.[36]

[35] See Gary *Weekly Tribune,* November 5, 1909; Gary *Post-Tribune,* June 4, 1931, Historical Section, p. 7; and Cannon, "Tom Knotts As Mayor and Man," in Gary *Evening Post,* March 26, 1921, for the best accounts of this campaign and election.

[36] Gary *Weekly Tribune,* November 5, 1909; Gary *Evening Post,* November 5, 1909.

Political Strife, 1909-1913

While controversy during the next four years centered around the picturesque and strong-willed Knotts, it should be kept in mind that he had to work with a Republican-controlled city council. The council, while it contained several well-qualified members such as Ralph E. Rowley, was subject generally to the will of men not so solicitous for the welfare of the city. For a time six of the nine councilmen were saloon keepers, some of them most disreputable.[37] Nor could the mayor always depend on the support of the Democratic members. One of them, Maurice N. Castleman, popularly known as "Battleaxe" for his favorite brand of chewing tobacco, was the stormy petrel of the council. According to reports, his hand was against every official he could not control. Knotts could and did insist upon the complete loyalty of the officials responsible to him. One luckless cabinet member, who sided with the administration's critics in a traction dispute, felt the full force of the mayor's wrath. Knotts's letter of dismissal to him was brief and to the point: "Sir: This is to notify you that you are dismissed from the position of Commissioner of Public Works of the city of Gary for lying. To take effect forthwith."[38]

As the mayor of a fifth-class city, Knotts presided over the city court. According to one report, his court was neither decorous nor technical but his extraordinary sense of justice and his excellent judgment of human nature enabled him to dispense justice as well as a seasoned jurist could have done. The mayor-judge did not hesitate to

[37] Taylor, *Satellite Cities,* 214. The newly elected city clerk was a Democrat while the treasurer was a Republican. The number of councilmen was increased from seven to nine when Gary became a fourth-class city in October, 1910.

[38] Cannon, Autobiography, Chap. 51, p. 2; Gary *Evening Post,* May 18, 1911.

take the field in the interest of law and order. One Saturday night in July, 1910, the city's police force was crippled by the resignations of six of its members. On Sunday Knotts, dressed in plain clothes and without a star, helped arrest and haul to jail the largest number of drunks and other disturbers of the peace in many a Sunday. He also acted as the desk sergeant in booking the prisoners. Monday morning the culprits were startled to recognize the judge as the "fat cop" who had arrested them.[39] When Gary became a city of the fourth class in October, 1910, Ora L. Wildermuth was appointed city judge by the mayor with the approval of Governor Marshall.

Knotts was intensely proud of Gary. Governor Marshall won his enmity by vetoing a bill to locate a superior court in Gary for which Knotts had labored hard and long. About this same time the Governor heaped fuel on the flames by saying he was not sure but that Indiana would be better off if Gary slid into Lake Michigan. Although both were Democrats, Knotts never forgave Marshall for that remark.[40]

Knotts was arrested fourteen times in two years with never a charge being proved against him. The accusations ranged from election frauds, embezzlement, and perjury, to general misconduct and malfeasance in office. Apparently the purpose of the various indictments was to drive him from office. In the early stages of the Dean affair, discussion of which will follow, the Gary *Daily Tribune* said the case was the beginning of a campaign for civil purification in the city and that the time for a

[39] Wildermuth, "Estimate of the Life of Tom Knotts," in Biographical Sketches of Gary and Lake County Residents (scrapbooks in Gary Public Library), Vol. 6; Gary *Daily Tribune*, August 1, 1910.

[40] Wildermuth, *op. cit.;* Indiana *Senate Journal*, 1909, pp. 172, 205, 241, 242, 243, 263, 270, 1415-17 (veto).

"cleanup in Gary's municipal affairs" had been too long delayed. On the other hand, some of the mayor's opponents were apparently influenced by their personal dislike of him, or by desire for political power. There is no way to determine the extent to which certain officials of the steel corporation were behind the movements against the mayor. Knotts frequently charged that the steel officials were behind the attacks against him and in this he was consistently supported by the Gary *Evening Post*.[41] It should be noted that the actions of the officials as individuals did not necessarily reflect the wishes of the steel corporation.

The Thomas B. Dean case, which attracted nation-wide attention, was the most sensational of the attacks against the mayor. Dean, a newcomer to the city, who claimed to represent Chicago and Louisville capitalists, sought a franchise for a central heating plant in the community. In August, 1911, the city council granted Dean the franchise, which Mayor Knotts approved.[42] A few days later Dean had the mayor arrested for allegedly accepting a five thousand dollar bribe for signing the franchise. The money, in marked bills, was found in a pigeonhole of the mayor's desk. Knotts insisted it had been "planted" there. Dean next produced a Dictograph record of a purported conversation between himself and several members of the city council in the course of which, it was claimed, the councilmen accepted a bribe to approve the franchise. Dean said the Dictograph had

[41] Taylor, *Satellite Cities,* 195; Cannon, "Tom Knotts As Mayor and Man," in Gary *Evening Post,* March 26, 1921; Gary *Daily Tribune,* September 8, 1911. Several prominent citizens of Gary who were political foes of Knotts told this author that the steel officials were leaders of the movements against Knotts.

[42] The city council granted the franchise by a vote of eight to one. See Gary *Evening Post,* August 26, 1911.

been hung under the bed in the room of the Hotel Gary where the payment of the bribe took place.[43] Knotts recalled that Dean acted peculiarly from the start of the negotiations for the heating franchise, that he willingly agreed to conditions in the contract that his alleged company could not possibly fulfill with any prospect of profit. Among those arrested in the case along with Knotts were a former city commissioner of public works, the city engineer, and four councilmen, only one of the latter being a Democrat.[44]

In the course of the trials that followed, Knotts and the other defendants accused Dean of being a tool of the United States Steel Corporation, that the whole affair was an effort to seize the reins of the city government and to run it in the interest of the steel company which they said had provided the money involved in the case.[45] The Democratic councilman was convicted but never served his sentence since he died while awaiting an appeal of the case. The jury disagreed in the case of the city engineer. Mayor Knotts's trial at Valparaiso, which lasted a week, was attended by large crowds from Gary. The case against him and the remaining defendants collapsed when the Dictograph operator signed an affidavit that the records of the alleged conversations between Dean and the councilmen were actually dictated by Dean.[46] The city clerk, who had testified against the

---

[43] Gary *Evening Post* and Gary *Daily Tribune,* September 8, 1911. The Dictograph episode recalls the placing of a microphone, which was attached to a tape recorder, in the office of an assistant prosecutor of Lake County in 1950 by the Gary Crime Commission. See "The Microphone Speaks" (MS in Gary Public Library).

[44] Gary *Evening Post,* September 8, 1911.

[45] *Ibid.,* November 15, 16, 1911.

[46] *Ibid.,* February 17, July 2, 1912; Taylor, *Satellite Cities,* 214; Cannon, "Tom Knotts As Mayor and Man," in Gary *Evening Post,* September 26, 1921.

mayor and the councilmen, disappeared and later sent
back a statement that his testimony was perjured, that
he had been bribed by two Gary bankers and several local
Republican politicians to take the stand for the prosecu-
tion. The clerk, who returned to the city a few months
later, claimed he had been paid by Knotts's friends to
leave the state and repudiate his testimony against the
mayor. He was convicted of compounding a felony and
sentenced to prison.[47] The case against Knotts was not
reopened.

The City Election of 1913

Knotts was confronted by a formidable combination
of forces when he sought re-election in 1913. He had
alienated many of his own party; a large number of
independent citizens, who did not believe all the charges
leveled against the mayor were, nevertheless, weary of
the seemingly endless strife that centered around him;
and, lastly, many foreign-born voters who had been such
a source of strength to him in 1909, had been alienated
by what they regarded as the high-handed methods of
his police force.[48] The Republicans and the steel com-

[47] Gary *Evening Post,* April 22, 1912; Gary *Daily Tribune,* November
5 and 20, 1912. The disposition made of the $5,000.00 "bribe" money,
which remained for a time in the care of the sheriff, was an interesting
aftermath to the case. Dean refused to claim it; Knotts said that the
money did not belong to him and suggested that it be turned over
to the city's school fund. The Michigan Avenue Trust Company of
Chicago, represented locally by William F. Hodges, was awarded the
money by the circuit court. An echo of the case was heard as late
as 1921 when the failure of the trust company brought the disclosure
that the money had originally been deposited to the account of Thomas
B. Dean in that bank. There was no record as to who deposited the
money in his name. Gary *Evening Post,* April 12, 1912, July 24, 1921;
Gary *Daily Tribune,* December 13, 1912.
[48] Cannon, "Tom Knotts As Mayor and Man," in Gary *Evening
Post,* March 26, 1921; Taylor *Satellite Cities,* 216-17.

pany's officials, who had fought the mayor for years,
drew these various elements together into what was
called the Citizens party. A convention, headed by William F. Hodges and Captain Norton, nominated Roswell
O. Johnson, a popular real estate man, for mayor. Two
Democrats were placed on the aldermanic slate, one of
whom was at the time a member of the city council.
Among the bolting Democrats at this convention were
Maurice N. Castleman and Frank Zawadski, the latter
a leader of the Polish element in the city.[49]

Knotts was nominated to head the Democratic ticket
which included Ora L. Wildermuth as candidate for city
judge. The mayor was portrayed by the Democrats as
"The Man Who Made Good." They said that Johnson
was a tool of the steel company, whom Captain Norton
had chosen because he could be easily controlled.
Knotts recalled that "the men who nominated Johnson
were the same men who tried to send me to the penitentiary."[50] In Roswell O. Johnson the Citizens party
had a candidate who was able to make an appeal to voters
in every walk of life. Possessed of an attractive and
colorful personality, Johnson mingled intimately with the
foreign born of the South Side to win their confidence
and votes. A member of the Gary Commercial Club and
popular with businessmen along Broadway, he appealed
to conservatives and independents by promising to bring
peace to the city and by the insistence that what Gary
needed was a businesslike administration of its civic
affairs. The Citizens party candidate was widely heralded
by the Gary *Daily Tribune* as the Hoosier schoolmaster,
justice of the wild west, and the conqueror of the Indians.[51]   These themes apparently had more influence

49 Gary *Evening Post,* July 14, 1913.
50 *Ibid.,* October 6, 1913.
51 Johnson, forty-one years old, was born in Adams County where

with the voters than did the old charges that Knotts was a tyrant, a troublemaker, and in general unfit to head the city's government.

As the voters went to the polls on election day, Governor Samuel M. Ralston kept in touch with the mayor and the county sheriff regarding their ability to maintain law and order. Thanks to the co-operation of the chief of police and the sheriff, which was in striking contrast to 1909, the militia was not needed. The entire Citizens' ticket was elected, Johnson defeating Knotts by 1,516 votes. The South Side, which had been Knotts's stronghold in the past, gave Johnson an overwhelming majority of its votes. On the other hand, the English-speaking precincts on the North Side, which previously had the tendency to side with Knotts's opponents, voted heavily for him.[52] The only protest made by the Gary *Evening Post,* which had supported Knotts, was its charge that the foreman in the steel mills had forced workers, on threat of dismissal from their jobs, to vote for the Citizens' candidate. The *Post* also alleged that a score of automobiles were used by Johnson's friends to bring workers from within the mills to the polls and that the mill officials denied this privilege to the Democrats.[53]

The Gary *Daily Tribune* hailed Knotts's defeat as a victory for the steel company, that would permit the

he taught school for a time. He received an LL.B. Degree from the Indiana Law School at Indianapolis. In 1900 President McKinley appointed him collector of customs in the Arizona Territory, in which office he served three years. This was followed by a three-year term as a police judge in Arizona. He moved to Kendallville in 1907, and two years later came to Gary. Gary *Daily Tribune,* June 7, October 1, 13, 1913.

[52] Gary *Evening Post,* November 5, 1913. Johnson's total vote was 4,984 and Knotts's, 3,468.

[53] Charges were also made that William P. Gleason, superintendent of the Steel Works, brought pressure on plant officials to see that the workers voted for Johnson. *Ibid.*

corporation to carry forward its plans for the city it had founded.[54]

Mill officials immediately assumed positions of leadership in the Johnson administration. William P. Gleason was appointed president of the Park Board and began the development of a planned park system. Ralph E. Rowley, elected president of the City Council, was soon known as the "watch dog" of the treasury. Rowley was the unquestioned leader of the city's legislative branch for many years. Pontius Heintz, chief inspector for the Gary Land Company since 1908 and generally regarded as Captain Norton's bodyguard, became chief of police. Some citizens thought of Norton as the controlling power behind Mayor Johnson and a few termed him the real mayor of Gary. While the steel officials played an important part in the city's affairs for several years, the extent to which their influence was decisive in local elections is debatable.[55]

Tom Knotts devoted his last years to his insurance and real estate business. He found it difficult to resist the lure of public office and in 1916 was nominated for sheriff of Lake County. His defeat in that year's elections was not unexpected, Lake County being normally Republican in those years. Knotts died on March 26, 1921, and the entire city mourned his passing. The body lay in state at the city hall and two thousand people attended the funeral services in the Orpheum Theater. Before leaving for Rochester, Minnesota, to undergo an operation, Knotts had told his friend, Ora L. Wildermuth, that in case of his death he wanted Clarence Darrow, the famous Chicago lawyer, to deliver an address at his funeral. Darrow came from Denver, Colorado, where he was

---

[54] Gary *Daily Tribune*, November 5, 1913.
[55] Quillen, The Industrial City, 269; Taylor, *Satellite Cities*, 217-18.

engaged at that time in legal business, to carry out the request and was introduced by Wildermuth.[56]

Industrial Expansion

After the actual production of steel began in 1909, there was no letup in the expansion and construction of the steel corporation's plants. By 1910 the Works of the Indiana Steel Company as originally planned were almost completed. At that time there were 4,204 employees on its payroll.[57] In 1909 the corporation authorized the construction of plants for two of its subsidiaries, the American Bridge Company and the American Sheet and Tin Plate Company, both of which made large use of steel.[58] These were built west of the great steel mill which in time was flanked on both sides by subsidiaries dependent upon it for the steel from which their products were made.

Construction of the American Bridge Company's plant was started late in 1909 in what was later known as the Ambridge section of the city. This plant, which produced structural steel for bridges and various types of buildings, was put into operation the following year. In 1910 the Gary Land Company began the erection of 250 houses in Ambridge to be rented or sold to the Bridge Company's employees. About 1,500 workers were reported employed at this plant in 1915. In 1910 work was started on the American Sheet and Tin Plate Works. Its manufacture of steel sheets and plates began the next year. This plant was reported in 1915 to be employing about two thousand men. Arrangements were

[56] Gary *Evening Post,* March 28 and 30, 1921.

[57] Employment figures supplied by John H. Vohr, superintendent of the Gary Works, October 20, 1954.

[58] United States Steel Corporation, *Eighth Annual Report,* 1909, pp. 29-30.

made in 1910 for the Gary Land Company to build 110 houses for the Sheet and Tin Plate's supervisors and skilled workers.[59]

Only two plants not owned or controlled by the steel company were established in the early years. The Gary Screw and Bolt Company's plant, whose products were indicated by its name, began production in 1912.[60] In 1917 the Union Drawn Steel Company, manufacturer of steel wire, bars, and rods, began operations. These plants came to the city largely because of the presence of the steel mills.

The fact that Gary was practically a "one industry" city for many years raises the question as to whether the United States Steel Corporation discouraged the coming of other industries. Charges were made from time to time that Captain Norton used the Gary Commercial Club to do just that, because the steel company wanted to control the labor market and also wanted to keep labor unions out of the city. Allegations were made that the corporation did not want other industries to challenge its power in municipal affairs. There is some evidence that the steel company's officials, while not active in their opposition to other industries, did not go out of their way to bring them to the city. However, the Gary situation was not attractive for the location of other major plants. The steel company owned practically every foot of the city's frontage on Lake Michigan as well as the only harbor. An industry needing a position on the Lake could get it only with the permission of the corporation. Also, Gary was not within the limits of the Chicago shipping district in the early years, which would have been a serious handicap to independent industries. This

[59] Gary *Evening Post,* August 23, 1910; Howat (ed.), *A Standard History of Lake County,* 2:622, 864; 1:319.

[60] Gary *Evening Post,* May 16, 1912.

was no problem for the steel company which had its own belt-line railroad. If the corporation did maintain a subtle barrier around Gary, it was removed in 1928 when the Gary Land Company subdivided the area west of Ambridge and advertised the sale of industrial sites. The merger of the Gary Commercial Club and the Gary Chamber of Commerce in 1930 was interpreted as being indicative of the corporation's recognition that the city needed diversified industries.[61]

In 1914 the steel industry, the bellwether of American industry, was the first to feel the effects of the recession experienced by the nation at that time. Gary was confronted with the problem of unemployment for the first time in its history.[62] The recession was brief, the city soon feeling the impact of World War I with its great demand for steel. By July, 1915, the steel mills were operating at 100 per cent capacity for the first time in two years. The city was bursting its seams in 1916 with a reported 20,000 men on the payrolls of its various plants. By 1917 the plants were in desperate need of workers. Immigration from Europe having been curtailed by the war, the industries turned to the South for laborers. Hundreds of Negroes flocked to the city and within a short time this new segment of its population began to figure prominently in the local news. By the latter part of 1916 about three thousand Negroes were reported in the city.[63]

As steel production leveled off after the war, the specter of unemployment again arose to haunt the city.

[61] Gary *Republican,* May 6, 1916; Hammond *Lake County Times,* July 21, 1928; Gary *Post-Tribune,* March 8, May 8, 1930.

[62] Many steel workers lived in East Chicago and South Chicago. To assure jobs for local men, the steel company issued an order that employees in the Gary mills must live in Gary. Gary *Daily Tribune,* September 25, 1914.

[63] *Ibid.,* July 9, 1915, September 8, 1916.

Steel officials reported that five hundred to one thousand men were being turned away from the gates of the mills each day, and warned those seeking work not to come to Gary.[64] Nevertheless, two developments infused new life into the region's industrial cities during the twenties. Construction of the National Tube Company's plant, another subsidiary of the steel corporation, was started in 1922 with an initial appropriation of $20,000,000. In 1928 this plant, which was put in operation in 1924, employed 3,100 workers.[65] The second development was the action of the Federal Trade Commission in 1924 abolishing the "Pittsburgh Plus" price-fixing system, a step which was hailed as the inauguration of a new era for the area's steel cities.[66]

The Pittsburgh Plus system meant that all steel prices were quoted f.o.b. Pittsburgh regardless of the place of production. Hence the steel mills of the Calumet Region added $7.60 a ton to the price of their products sold in the Chicago area because that was the freight rate from Pittsburgh. This gave Pittsburgh an advantage over the Calumet Region's producers, for while Pittsburgh could compete with them in the West and, in fact, all over the United States, at no loss in price, outside producers received less money per ton the closer they sold to Pittsburgh. The United States Steel Corporation maintained the Pittsburgh Plus to protect its heavy investments in the many out-of-date plants in the Pittsburgh area, to better control its eastern competitors, and to make a higher profit on steel produced in the Calumet area.[67] The abolition of this pricing system con-

64 Hammond *Lake County Times,* February 7, 1921.

65 Employment figures supplied by John H. Vohr, superintendent of the Gary Works, October 20, 1954.

66 Gary *Post-Tribune,* September 18, 1924.

67 F. B. Garver, "Pittsburgh Plus," in *American Economic Review,* 14 (1924) :192-93.

tributed to plant expansion in Gary and the high rate of production in the local mills from 1924 to 1929.[68] The Gary plants, being the most modern and efficient in the corporation's empire, were kept at a high capacity of production even during seasonal slack periods.[69]

The Corporation's Contributions to Gary

Judge Gary took a direct and paternalistic interest in the affairs and well-being of the city. He inspected its parks and public buildings on his frequent visits to the region and did not hesitate to lecture public officials when he considered them derelict in their duties. The Judge and Mrs. Gary were proud, if not vain, of the city that bore their name. According to Captain Norton, when they drove down Broadway and saw a building such as the Gary State Bank, Mrs. Gary would turn to the Judge and say, "Look there is a bank named after us."[70] Apparently, the steel company's contributions to the civic, social, and spiritual welfare of the city were largely due to Judge Gary's interest and influence. It was estimated in 1927, at the time of his death, that he, personally, and the corporation had donated at least $5,000,000 in cash and land to worthwhile projects in the city. Gary citizens, in turn, took pride in their patron saint. The Judge's opinions and public announcements together with news about him made the front pages and often the headlines of the local newspapers. The news of his death threw the city into mourning. Business houses and schools were closed for two hours on the day of his funeral, and hun-

68 Quillen, The Industrial City, 385.

69 In June, 1927, the private harbor of the Buffington Cement Plant was dedicated, Vice-President Charles G. Dawes being the principal speaker. This harbor was said to be the deepest on the Great Lakes. See Gary Post-Tribune, June 12, 1927.

70 Horace S. Norton, quoted in Quillen, The Industrial City, 488.

dreds of citizens attended a memorial service at the City
Methodist Church. The city of Gary, it was said, was a
monument to the dead steel executive.[71]

Hardly a church, hospital, welfare or civic organization in the city failed to receive a contribution from the
steel company. In 1910 Judge Gary donated $200,000.00
for the construction of a Y. M. C. A. building and the
Gary Land Company gave a full block on Fifth Avenue
for a site. The various subsidiaries of the corporation
in the city contributed $40,000.00 to furnish the build-
ing.[72] The Y. M. C. A., a four-story stone structure, was
opened to the public early in 1912. William P. Gleason,
Captain Norton, and John Kirk, all officials of the steel
company, were on its board of trustees. The corporation
reportedly paid the cost of the maintenance and upkeep
of the Y. M. C. A. for many years and the organization's
officials and employees received their salaries from the
Gary Land Company. In 1910 Andrew Carnegie gave
$65,000.00 to the city for the erection of a public library,
and the Gary Land Company donated the block on Fifth
Avenue opposite the Y. M. C. A. as its site.[73] In 1922
Judge Gary contributed an undisclosed sum for the
erection of a Y. W. C. A. building.[74]

The steel company made many of its contributions to
the city through its subsidiary, the Gary Land Company.
In 1911 the Land Company donated the playgrounds
of the Emerson and Froebel schools to the school board.[75]
It will be recalled that in 1907 the Land Company pre-

[71] Gary *Post-Tribune,* October 1, 1925, August 16, 1927.

[72] Gary *Daily Tribune,* May 14, 1910; Gary *Evening Post,* July 12,
1911.

[73] Gary *Daily Tribune,* September 12, 1910.

[74] Gary *Evening Post and Daily Tribune,* May 15, 1922.

[75] Report of W. H. De Gan, superintendent of the Gary Park System, to William P. Gleason, January 26, 1935 (typewritten MS in
office of Gary Works, United States Steel Corporation), 1.

sented four frame buildings on Carolina Street between 6th and 7th avenues to the Franciscan Sisters for a hospital. This institution, the "Old St. Mary's," was a crude affair, its buildings being connected by hallways to protect the Sisters and the patients from the weather. In 1912 the company gave a huge site on West Sixth Avenue between Tyler and Polk streets for a modern hospital. A year later the Poor Handmaids of Jesus Christ assumed the administration of the new institution which was given the name of St. Mary's Mercy Hospital. The Gary Commercial Club, under the leadership of Captain Norton, raised $50,000.00 to help equip the hospital.[76] A Federal Building, which included the Post Office, was erected in 1916 on the southeast corner of Fifth Avenue and Adams Street on a site donated by the Land Company. In 1923 a large area at Eleventh Avenue and Madison Street was presented to the city and to the state for the construction of an armory to house the 113th Engineers. In 1925 a gift of seven lots at Seventh Avenue and Massachusetts Street provided the site for the Central School Gymnasium, later known as the Memorial Auditorium.[77]

In 1918 the Gary International Institute was established to help the foreign born adjust themselves to the American way of life. The Institute, organized with funds provided by the National War Council, was later affiliated with the Y. W. C. A. When the funds of the War Council were exhausted, the steel company assumed a large part of the Institute's financial burden.[78] The

[76] *St. Mary's Mercy Hospital* (booklet published by the hospital, n.d., in Gary Public Library), 2, 3; Howat (ed.), *A Standard History of Lake County,* 1:406.

[77] Cannon. Loring, and Robb (eds.), *History of the Lake and Calumet Region,* 1:752-54; Gary *Post-Tribune,* October 31, 1925.

[78] The International Institute of Gary, Indiana, 1918-1948 (Typewritten MS in files of the Institute), 1.

Gary-Alerding Settlement House, an adjunct of St. Anthony's Roman Catholic Church and named for Judge Gary and Bishop Herman J. Alerding of the Fort Wayne Diocese, was erected in 1924 with funds contributed by the steel executive. This institution was concerned principally with the needs of the foreign born and the underprivileged, particularly women and children. In 1927 it was providing educational and recreational facilities for about five thousand children.[79]

Apparently, the largest contribution of Judge Gary and the steel company was made to the First Methodist Episcopal Church, now the City Methodist Church. The Judge, an active Methodist layman, indicated his interest in Gary Methodism as early as 1909 when the Gary Land Company donated five lots at the southwest corner of Seventh Avenue and Adams Street as the site of the church's first building, which was dedicated in 1912. In 1916 Dr. William Grant Seaman, formerly president of the University of South Dakota and earlier a professor of philosophy at De Pauw University, became pastor of the church. Dr. Seaman believed the traditional church building could not carry on the comprehensive program needed in the heart of the city's business district; that what was needed was a combination church and community house. His plan called for a church that would present the most beautiful in architecture and music, and one that would be open seven days a week. To this structure would be attached a community house to provide facilities for Christian education, healthful recreation, and clean wholesome entertainment for people of all ages. A third feature would be a wing containing space for stores and offices, the rent from which would supplement the budget of the Church.[80]

79 Cannon, Loring, and Robb (eds.), *A History of the Lake and Calumet Region,* 1:487-89.

80 Howat (ed.), *A Standard History of Lake County,* 1:409; Gary

Dr. Seaman went to New York where he made an appeal to the finance committee of the United States Steel Corporation for assistance. Judge Gary overruled the objections of the younger J. Pierpont Morgan who wished to delay a decision on the matter. Subsequently, the Gary Land Company donated six lots at the corner of Sixth Avenue and Washington Street as a site for the institution. The corporation also agreed to match dollar for dollar the amount the Methodists were willing to spend on construction. According to Dr. Seaman, the steel company ultimately contributed $388,625.20 toward the total cost of the edifice which amounted to about $800,000.00.[81] The structure, a splendid example of Gothic architecture, was built of Indiana limestone. More popularly known as the "City Church" it was dedicated October 10, 1926.[82]

The Park System

The park system was established largely through the generosity of the steel company and by the individual efforts of Captain Norton and William P. Gleason. It will be recalled that the Gary Land Company created Buffington Park on the East Side and Jefferson Park on the West Side, in the very early years of the city's existence. In 1915 these parks, along with Tyler Park, were presented to the city.[83]

The most perplexing and exasperating problem to confront the citizens was that of creating a park that would

Evening Post, October 7, 1916; Cannon, Loring, and Robb (eds.), A History of the Lake and Calumet Region, 1:455-58.

[81] Sketch of Seaman in Biographical Sketches of Gary and Lake County Residents (Scrapbooks in Gary Public Library), Vol. 9.

[82] Gary Post-Tribune, October 2, 11, 1926. The community hall and theater, later known as Seaman Hall, seated one thousand persons.

[83] Report of W. H. De Gan to William P. Gleason, January 26, 1935, p. 1.

give them access to the beach and the cooling waters of
Lake Michigan. The steel company had by necessity
located its plants on the lake front and needed every
foot of the lake frontage which it owned in Gary for
future expansion. As East Chicago was situated on the
lake west of the city, the only space available for a park
was in the vicinity of Miller to the east. But Miller, a
town of 638 people in 1910, was not in Gary. Hobart
Township, in which it was located, was unwilling to
finance a park for the use of Gary's citizens, nor did the
township look with favor upon the annexation of that
part of its area by the steel city. The problem was
further complicated by the tendency of property owners
along the beach and those who claimed property rights
there to demand what were considered exorbitant prices
for their sandy acres. In 1913, according to reports, real
estate operators were asking $1,200.00 an acre for land
that was not worth one third of that amount.[84]

As the summer's heat descended upon the city each
year, its citizens contemplated the lake front with a sense
of frustration. The whistle of the ore-laden boats of
the steel company reminded them that Lake Michigan,
to which they were denied access, was at their very doorstep. Only the workers in the mills could see the great
body of water, a privilege not available for their swelter-
ing families. Gary inhabitants who came to Miller by
public transportation were compelled to trudge more
than a mile through the deep sand and over the dunes
to reach the beach. Only a few could be accommodated
by the lone carriage which in 1913 operated between the
town and the Grand Calumet River. From the river they
had to complete the journey to the beach on foot. The
first automobile reached the lake front at Miller in 1914

[84] Gary *Daily Tribune,* July 5, 1913.

the calum

Whiting

Indiana Harbor

EAST CHICAGO

Lake

GARY

East G

HAMMOND

Little Calumet River

Munster

Highland

Hobart

Griffith

Crown Point

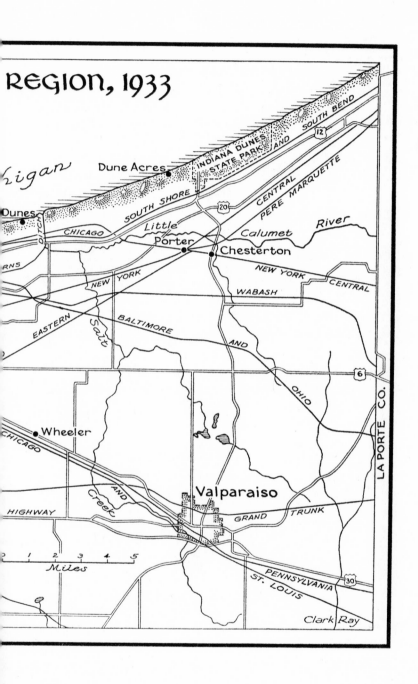

REGION, 1933

higan

Dune Acres

INDIANA DUNES
STATE PARK AND

SOUTH BEND

12

CENTRAL

PERE MARQUETTE

Dunes

DITCH

CHICAGO

SOUTH SHORE

20

Little

Calumet

River

Porter

Chesterton

RNS

NEW YORK

NEW YORK

CENTRAL

WABASH

EASTERN

Salt

BALTIMORE

AND

OHIO

6

LA PORTE CO.

Wheeler

CHICAGO

Valparaiso

AND

Creek

GRAND

TRUNK

HIGHWAY

R   1   2   3   4   5
Miles

PENNSYLVANIA
ST. LOUIS

30

Clark Ray

but managed to do so only after the miniature dunes, which had drifted across Lake Street, were covered with straw. Despite these obstacles, Gary's more determined citizens managed to visit the beach by the hundreds, particularly on Sundays. Drusilla Carr, one of the pioneer settlers at Miller, and her sons operated the only bathhouse at the beach.[85]

In 1913 the Gary Park Board sought to lease a portion of the beach area but was rebuffed by the local property owners. A ray of hope for the solution to the problem appeared in 1915 when the Indiana General Assembly passed a law to permit the formation of a park district comprised of municipalities along Lake Michigan for the purpose of maintaining a park and a boulevard system on the lake front. The Gary-Miller Joint Park Board, with William P. Gleason as chairman, was formed, a step which opened the way for Gary and Miller to co-operate in the establishment of a lake front park. Once more, property owners, who now feared they would receive only a small price for their land if it was condemned for park purposes, arrayed themselves solidly against the creation of any kind of park.[86]

Advocates of the park decided that Gary's dream of a recreation spot on the lake could never be realized as long as the desired area lay outside the city. Consequently, in December, 1918, Gary annexed that portion of Hobart Township which lay near the lake, including the town of Miller. The Park Board condemned 179

[85] *Ibid.*, June 25, 1913, August 19, 1914; Hammond *Lake County Times,* July 31, 1919.

[86] Gary *Evening Post,* May 10, 1913; Gary *Daily Tribune,* February 27, 1915, August 26, 1916. From time to time aspirants for public offices sought to make the steel company the "whipping boy" in the beach park problem by blaming it for shutting the people away from the Lake. See Gary *Republican,* May 6, 1916.

acres lying north of the lagoon, which was a remnant of
the old bed of the Grand Calumet River, in June, 1919,
for the proposed park. These proceedings were abandoned when numerous property owners filed remon-
strances against the action of the Park Board. The steel
corporation finally cut the Gordian knot by purchasing
120 acres along the lake front in Miller, and on September 3, 1919, donated the area to the city. This gift,
which included a frontage of three quarters of a mile
along the Lake, was reported to be worth $500,000.00.
The Park Board proceeded immediately to prepare the
spot for public use. The greater part of the area was
covered with a dense growth of thickets and underbrush.
These were removed and the larger oaks and pines were
trimmed. Thousand of cubic yards of sand were removed
from the ridges and dunes to permit the construction of
a temporary road of cinders so that the people could
reach the beach.[87]

Annexation of Miller and the acquisition of the park
brought about the construction of streets between those
areas and Gary proper. These, in turn, hastened the development of the northeastern part of the city and its
subsequent expansion in that direction.[88]

Gary's citizens were soon able to reach Miller and the
park by automobile and various means of public transportation.

In the meantime comfortable facilities were provided
for the public at the park. In 1922 the bathing pavilion,
containing two thousand lockers and lighted by flood-
lights on the outside, was opened. The following year a

[87] Gary *Daily Tribune,* December 23, 1918; Report of W. H. De Gan
to William P. Gleason, January 26, 1935, p. 2; Gleason, Gary's Park
System, 2. By 1929 subsequent purchases by the Park Board increased
the area of the park to 135 acres.

[88] Report of W. H. De Gan to William P. Gleason, January 26,
1935, p. 4.

combined restaurant and recreation building was started. This structure provided space for dancing and contained a banquet hall designed to seat six hundred persons.[89] The city's "breathing spot" was known as the Lake Front Park until 1930, at which time its name was changed to Marquette Park, in memory of Father Jacques Marquette.[90]

The creation of Gateway Park and the building of twin municipal and county buildings adjacent to that park were the crowning achievements of the city's formative period. For many years the appearance of the municipality's front yard between Fifth Avenue, its principal railroad stations, and the gates of the steel mill had been of concern to civic leaders. This area with its dilapidated buildings and vacant lots gave visitors and those who passed through on the trains a poor impression of the city. Others who traveled the principal east and west highway through the municipality saw only its worst side. The improvement of the district was assured when the steel company, which owned most of the vacant land there, donated its holdings to the city. The municipal building, dedicated in December, 1928, was erected on the east side of Broadway at Fourth Avenue. Its twin structure, the county building which houses the Gary offices of the various county officials, occupies a site across the street on the west side of Broadway and was opened in September, 1929.[91] Gateway Park lays to the north on both sides of Broadway.

[89] Gleason, Gary's Park System, 7, 8.

[90] Gary *Post-Tribune,* April 24, 1930. Father Marquette skirted the southern and eastern sides of Lake Michigan in a canoe in 1675. Being seriously ill at the time it is possible that he rested on the beach in the Gary area. See above, 24-25n.

[91] Report of W. H. De Gan to William P. Gleason, January 26, 1935, pp. 2, 3.

Miscellaneous Developments

The Gary State Bank, now the Gary National Bank, destined to become the city's strongest financial institution, was organized in 1908 under the direction of George Campbell, a son-in-law of Judge Gary. Henry G. Hay, son of the assistant treasurer of the United States Steel Corporation, was the first president of this institution. In 1923 Hay was succeeded by Lawrence W. McNamee, former auditor of the Gary Works of the Indiana Steel Company and of the Gary Land Company, and president of the Gary Heat, Light, and Water Company. William P. Gleason was on the bank's board of directors. The Gary State Bank, while not owned by the steel corporation, was its local depository and assisted the various plants in their payroll operations. In 1928 the bank moved into a new ten-story bank and office building, the largest in Gary, constructed on its first and only site on the southwest corner of Fifth and Broadway. In the same year the institution moved away from the direct control of the steel company's officials. Although the bank had flourished under their direction, its affairs had reached the stage at which the directors felt it should be guided by a practical banker. William W. Gasser, vice-president of the Union National Bank in Marquette, Michigan, was chosen vice-president and manager of the institution.[92] Gasser, who became president of the bank a few months later, was soon a power in the city's financial circles.

[92] Interview with William W. Gasser, chairman of the board of directors, Gary National Bank, December 15, 1954. The Gary State Bank was the second bank to be established in Gary, the first being the First National Bank, founded in November, 1906. The Gary State Bank became the Gary National Bank in 1943. See Howat (ed.), *A Standard History of Lake County,* 1:333; 2:638; Cannon, Loring, and Robb (eds.), *A History of the Lake and Calumet Region,* 1:652.

The city grew so rapidly after World War I that housing could not catch up with the population. Consequently, the 1920's were years of building activity not only of residences but of apartment houses. More than 1,800 apartment houses were erected in the short period of eight years, and in 1926 alone a reported $22,000,000 was spent on nonindustrial construction.[93] In that year the Gary Hotel and Masonic Temple were erected, and work was started on the million-dollar Knights of Columbus Temple and Hotel. Burns Ditch, also completed in 1926, rescued the city from periodic floods by diverting the waters of the Little Calumet and Deep rivers into Lake Michigan east of Ogden Dunes. This project led to the development of the Little Calumet Valley on the South Side. It also drew the Glen Park community, which lay south of Ridge Road, into a more intimate association with other parts of the city.

Population After World War I

Gary's population increased in proportion to its industrial expansion. By 1920 the municipality, which became a second-class city in 1915, had 55,378 inhabitants. Ten years later there were 100,426 residents in the city. Gary continued to be a "man's town," there being 31,810 males and 25,568 females in the community in 1920. Ten years later almost 55 per cent of the inhabitants were males. World War I and the Federal immigration quota laws of the early 1920's adversely affected the movement of the people from Europe to the United States. As a result, the steel city's foreign-born population decreased from almost 50 per cent of its total number of inhabitants in 1910 to a little more than 29 per cent in 1920, and to 19 per cent in 1930. Gary be-

[93] Cannon, Loring, and Robb (eds.), *op. cit.,* 1:749.

came the center of the region's Negro population in those
years, more than 9 per cent of its population being Negro
in 1920. In 1930 there were 17,922 Negroes in the city,
which was about 17 per cent of all its residents. The
Mexicans, the last important segment of population to
arrive, numbered 3,486 in 1930.[94] The advent of the
Negroes and Mexicans had some effect on the distribution
of population. Many of the foreign-born families moved
from the Central District, formerly known as the Patch,
to the North Side while others found homes in the Glen
Park neighborhood south of the Little Calumet River.
The Negroes and Mexicans, the greater part of whom
were in the lower-income bracket, moved into the tenements, basements, and substandard houses formerly occupied by the foreign born.

The steel city was a mixing bowl of races and nationalities. In 1930 there were 15 nationality groups numbering five hundred or more within its limits, the most numerous being the Mexicans, Poles, Czecho-Slovaks, Yugo-
slavs, Greeks, Italians, and Russians, in the order
named.[96] The sound of European tongues blending with
the soft-spoken Spanish of the Mexicans and with the slow
drawl of the Southern Negroes gave Gary a flavor
approached only by East Chicago of the region's cities.
The South Side was a section of foreign churches, restaurants with strange names on their windows specializing

[94] See the *Fourteenth Census* (1920): *Population,* pt. 3:286, 297, 307,
and the *Fifteenth Census* (1930): *Population,* 3:pt. 1:63, 700, 715, 721, for
verification of statistics given. In 1915 the second-class cities in Indiana,
those with populations between 35,000 and 250,000, were Fort Wayne,
South Bend, Terre Haute, and Gary. Indianapolis was, and still is,
the only first-class city in the state.

[95] Stillman K. Taylor, The International Institute of Gary (Typewritten MS in the files of the Institute), 9.

[96] *Fifteenth Census* (1930): *Population,* 3:pt. 1:721.

in foreign foods, and numerous eating places serving the fish, barbecued pork, and hamburgers so favored by the Negroes.   Coffee houses were patronized by swarthy Greeks and Turks who passed their leisure hours with card games brought from their native lands.   This was the Old World and the gulf between it and the North Side was much wider than the Wabash tracks which separated the two.

11

POPULATION

THE CALUMET REGION became a mixing bowl, rather than a melting pot, of races and nationalities. Melting pot suggests a oneness of features and characteristics produced by a simultaneous amalgamation of different elements. That did not occur in the Calumet area. Instead, the movement of the population groups into the region during the first fifty years was such that each had the opportunity to make its presence felt. Those of the "New Immigration" who followed came in such great numbers as to accentuate the varied character of the population for years to come. The late arrival of the Negroes and Mexicans made it even more diversified. The presence of so many nationalities and races produced a variety of flavors almost unique to the Calumet Region.

Native-born American Settlers

The early settlers in the region were largely of native American stock. Cheap land, along with unsatisfactory conditions in the older states, stimulated the great movement of people into the West.[1] When Indiana became a state in 1816, the bulk of its population was concentrated in the southern part. By 1825 settlers were crowding into the northern half as far as the Wabash River and by

[1] The land law of 1820 permitted the purchase from the Federal government of a minimum of 80 acres for $1.25 per acre. In 1832 the minimum tract that could be purchased was reduced to 40 acres.

344

1830 pioneers regarded the valley of that stream as "finished."[2] The land hungry people moved next into the northeastern part of the state, and when the best land in that area was occupied, others moved westward into the northwestern corner near Lake Michigan. Since the Calumet Region was the last to be settled, it may truly be regarded as Indiana's last frontier.

While the settlement of Porter County began in 1833 and that of Lake County in 1834, the first detailed study of the area's population was not made until 1850. In that year the Federal census listed 5,234 residents in Porter County and 3,991 in Lake. Valparaiso, with 522 inhabitants, was the only incorporated town in the region. Of the 1,102 men fifteen years old and over in Lake County, 917 were farmers, most of whom lived south of the Little Calumet River. The sand dunes and swamps adjacent to Lake Michigan were almost devoid of inhabitants. North Township, where the cities of East Chicago, Whiting, Hammond, and a part of Gary now stand, had only 97 residents, 28 of whom were associated with the six inns in the area. According to the census report, no marriages were performed and no children attended school that year in North Township. The townships along the Lake in Porter County, because of their more extensive farming areas, had more residents, there being 360 in Westchester and 263 in Portage.[3]

Indiana provided more settlers for Lake County than did any other state. In 1850 more than 28.74 per cent of its population were native Hoosiers. Ohio, which was

[2] Turner, *The United States, 1830-1850*, 260.

[3] U. S. Bureau of the Census, *Seventh Census* (1850), 756, 768, 772; Census of North Township, Lake County, 1850 (microfilm copy, in Genealogy Division, Indiana State Library); Lang, "The Inhabitants of Center Township, Lake County," in *Indiana Magazine of History*, 44 (1948) :287.

well settled by 1830, was the source of 12.78 per cent of
Lake's residents.[4] Since population movements, like rivers,
tend to follow the line of least resistance, it is not surprising that such a large proportion of the region's inhabitants came from the Middle Atlantic and New England
states in the early years.   Thousands of Easterners came
into the Old Northwest by way of the Erie Canal and the
Great Lakes.   The Yankee exodus was also stimulated
by the completion of the first railroads from the East to
Chicago in 1852.

The Yankees and the "Yorkers," New Yorkers, provided much of the leadership for the region in the early
years, their influence being greater than their numbers
would indicate.   Solon Robinson, regarded by some as
the "father" of Lake County, and his brother, Milo, were
from Connecticut.   The Robinson brothers operated the
first store in the county, and Solon was instrumental in
the location of the county seat at Crown Point.   John
Wheeler and Zerah F. Summers, the "fathers" of Lake
County journalism, were also from Connecticut.[5]

From Massachusetts came John Wood, Lake County's
earliest industrialist, who established the first grist- and
sawmill in the county; Henry Wells, first sheriff of Lake
County; and Hervey Ball, surveyor and father of the
region's historian, Timothy H. Ball.   Also from the
Bay State came Harriet Warner Holton, who taught the
first school in Lake County; Lewis Warriner, the region's
earliest representative in the Indiana General Assembly;
and George H. Hammond, one of the founders of the
packing house at Hammond and for whom that city was
named.   Marcus M. Towle, associate in the packing
house and founder of Hammond, was from New Hamp-

4 Lang, *op. cit.*, 44:281.

5 Kellar (ed.), *Solon Robinson*, 1:3-41; Howat (ed.), *A Standard History of Lake County*, 1:246-47.

shire. A Vermonter, Ebenezer Saxton, was one of the founders of Merrillville. The "Yorkers" were also conspicuously present: Thomas A. E. Campbell helped start the town of Valparaiso; Henry D. Palmer paused at a spring in Lake County to repair his wagon and remained to be its first physician; and Obadiah Taylor, reported to be the only Revolutionary War veteran buried in Lake County, came with his sons, Horace and Adonijah, to establish one of its most prominent families.[6]

The Old Immigration

The foreign born who came to the region in the early years were a part of what has come to be called the "Old Immigration," composed in the main of people from England, Ireland, Germany, and the Scandinavian countries. This migration was at its peak in the period between 1820 and about 1880.

The Germans, the greatest in number and influence for more than fifty years, arrived in the region almost as early as did the native-born Americans. Most of them migrated from their homeland for economic reasons although some came because of political considerations. Overpopulation, overproduction, and overcrowding in the farming districts and the ruin of small hand industries in competition with the new factory system were factors that uprooted them from their native land. Conditions were so bad in some areas that the local governments encouraged the emigration of the surplus population.[7] The failure of revolutions in Germany in 1830 and 1848 compelled many intellectual liberals to flee to America. Those

6 Howat, *op. cit.*, 1:53, 89-90, 150, 292; Ball, *Encyclopedia of Genealogy and Biography,* 669; Bowers (ed.), *History of Lake County* (1929), 115-16, 124, 139-42; Demmon (ed.), *History of Lake County* (1934), 216.

7 Albert B. Faust, *The German Element in the United States* (2 vols. Boston, 1909), 1:583-84.

348 THE CALUMET REGION

who came after the second revolution were known as the "Forty-Eighters," and of these, Carl Schurz is well known to Americans. Although few in number compared to the rank and file who came for economic reasons, the "Forty-Eighters" provided intellectual and political leadership for the German-Americans.[8] A few years later, the wars to unify Germany, culminating in the Franco-Prussian War, 1870-71, and the subsequent development of Germany as a great military power, caused many Germans to flee to America to escape military service.[9]

Chicago, at an early date, was one of the largest German centers in the Middle West. Many Germans who had intended to make Chicago their permanent home, backtracked eastward into the Calumet Region on hearing of the opportunities offered there. This was true of Henry Reese, Heinrich D. Eggers, John F. K. Vater, and Henry Schrage who founded the Whiting settlement. Ernst W. Hohman, Joseph Hess, and Jacob Rimbach came to the Hammond area from Chicago. Apparently most of the Germans who worked on the railroads in the region originally lived in Chicago. Whiting, Tolleston, Miller, Hessville, and Schererville were founded by Germans; the greatest concentration of this nationality was in Hammond.[10] Germans began to settle in St. John's Township in 1837; by 1850 more than half of the population of that township was German. Also, in 1838 German Lutherans began the settlement of what was later Hanover Township including the villages of Brunswick, Klassville, and Hanover Center.[11]

[8] Wittke, *We Who Built America*, 189.

[9] John R. Commons, *Races and Immigrants in America* (New York, 1907), 68.

[10] See above, 141-44, 156-60, 181-88.

[11] John N. Beckman, "Reminiscences of Brunswick and Hanover Townships," in Demmon (ed.), *History of Lake County* (1934), 106-8; Howat (ed.), *A Standard History of Lake County*, 1:162-65.

In 1850 the Germans comprised 14 per cent of Lake County's population, whereas in Indiana as a whole they make up only 3 per cent of the inhabitants. Their proportion in regard to other nationalities in Lake County was the largest in 1880 when they constituted more than 18 per cent of the total population. In 1910 the Federal census reported that almost 30 per cent of Hammond's residents were either born in Germany and Austria or their parents were born in those countries.[12] Although earlier census reports did not analyze Hammond's population, the city's percentage of Germans was no doubt greater in 1890. Porter County, being farther removed from Chicago, did not experience as early or as large a settlement of Germans as did Lake County. They made up about 9 per cent of that county's population in 1870, and of the 18,052 inhabitants there in 1890, only 1,770 were born in Germany.[13] Nor did Porter County have the German communities that Lake had. Most of the Germans were concentrated in the town of Valparaiso, and in Portage and Westchester townships.

The great majority of the Germans who settled in the region were enterprising peasants and artisans. They were better supplied with funds when they came than were the Slavs and Hungarians in later years. A study of the German settlers in Hanover and St. John's townships showed that most of them were men of considerable means, that they bought the best land, erected comfortable houses, and built substantial barns. The Germans enjoyed an excellent reputation for industry, thrift, and a wholesome respect for the law. The Whiting commun-

[12] Lang, "The Inhabitants of Center Township," in *Indiana Magazine of History*, 44:283; *Tenth Census* (1880): *Population*, 506; *Thirteenth Census* (1910): *Population*, pt. 2:568.

[13] *Ninth Census* (1870): *Population*, 353; *Eleventh Census* (1890): *Population*, pt. 1:125, 621.

ity did not have a jail until the refinery came nor did the sheriff bother to visit the place except on rare occasions. A. Murray Turner, sheriff of Lake County from 1888 to 1892, recalled that he did not serve a legal paper on any citizen of Hanover Township during his term of office, nor was any property in that township on the delinquent list during that time.[14]

The Germans loved their beer and their beer gardens. Good beer, good food, and good music went together, and Sundays were especially popular for picnics and other outings. Beer gardens frequently came into conflict with Sunday closing laws, and the more conservative of the non-German Protestants frowned upon what they considered to be the desecration of the Sabbath by the fun-loving Germans. And yet it was generally admitted that German beer gardens were orderly places to which children often accompanied their parents, that a drunken customer would be immediately ejected by the proprietor or guests. In Hammond, Drackert's and Kendel's groves were popular recreation spots, and Towle's Opera House was liberally patronized by German citizens. Conrad's Grove in Tolleston was the scene of picnics, where on occasions a German orchestra from Chicago provided music for young and old at the open-air dancing pavilion.[15]

Numerous organizations and societies satisfied the convivial and gregarious instincts of the Germans. Among those in Hammond in 1909 were the Turnverein, a gymnastic society which emphasized both mental and phy-

[14] Gettler, "Town of Dyer," and Beckman, "Reminiscenses of Brunswick and Hanover Township," in Demmon (ed.), *History of Lake County* (1934), 79-80, 107-8; Howat (ed.), *A Standard History of Lake County,* 1:162-67.

[15] Hammond *Times,* June 17, 1951; Reminiscences of Mrs. J. J. Roberts, in Gary *Post-Tribune,* July 6, 1951, p. 14.

sical development; the Kriegerbund, an organization of veterans of the Germany army; and the Plattdeutsche Grot Gelde, a fraternal and benevolent society. In 1914 there were nine German cultural and singing societies in Hammond, and the local chapter of the German-American National Union had 1,200 members enrolled the same year.[16] While the great influx of Slavs and Hungarians in later years tended to overshadow the Germans, the visitor to Hammond, Valparaiso, and to the rural parts of the region could not but notice their presence and their contributions.

Around 1850 the Swedes began to settle in the region, and in time constituted an important segment of the population in certain localities. The primary cause of their migration to America was economic, and most of those who came in the early years were peasants and agricultural laborers. Tillable land was scarce in Sweden and a series of crop failures, culminating in the "Great Famine" from 1867 to 1869, caused much suffering. Swedes were easily infected with "America Fever" when they read the alluring accounts of opportunities to be had in the New World, which emigrant agents and the steamship lines kept before them. Tales of Swedish-Americans who returned to the homeland, often at the expense of the steamship lines, also made a great impression. The prospect of cheap and fertile farms in America was too much for numerous Swedes to resist.[17]

Unlike the Germans, the Swedes preferred Porter County to Lake County, probably because more fertile land was available there. In 1870 the former had 561

---

[16] *Lake County Directory,* 1909, p. 99; Hammond *Lake County Times,* May 14, 1914.

[17] Florence E. Janson, *The Background of Swedish Immigration, 1840-1930* (University of Chicago Press, 1931), 7, 14, 222; Wittke, *We Who Built America,* 263-64.

Swedish and Norwegian residents while there were only 224 in Lake County. Porter County Swedes numbered 974 in 1890 and Lake's total was 641. The second wave of Swedish immigration occurred after 1890, being caused largely by industrial crises and labor troubles in the homeland. Most of those who came in the later period were laborers and skilled workers who sought employment in the industrial cities of Lake County. Their number was never large in comparison with the Slavic immigrants, there being only 147 in Gary, and 473 in East Chicago in 1910.[18]

The most reliable evidence as to when the Swedes arrived in the area and where they settled in the largest numbers may be found in the history of their churches. In the early 1850's the first concentration of Swedes was apparently in the Baillytown community just north of the old Bailly homestead in Westchester Township, Porter County. They found employment in this vicinity cutting timber for the railroads and for the local market. When there was no more such work, the Swedes remained as farmers or in other capacities. In 1857 a Swedish Lutheran Church, probably the first in the region, was established at Baillytown. In 1879 Chesterton Swedes organized the Evangelical Bethlehem Church with the assistance of their countrymen at Baillytown. The Swedish population of Chesterton apparently increased after 1880 when C. O. Hillstrom moved his organ factory from Chicago to Chesterton. Hillstrom employed Swedish workmen in the manufacture of organs and piano stools. As early as 1862 the Swedes were numerous enough in Hobart to

18 *Ninth Census* (1870): *Population,* 353. Although the census of 1870 grouped the Swedes and Norwegians together, apparently few Norwegians settled in Porter County. *Eleventh Census* (1890): *Population,* pt. 1:622; *Thirteenth Census* (1910): *Population,* pt. 2:568; Janson, *The Background of Swedish Immigration,* 11.

establish the Swedish Lutheran Augustana Church. The
Swedes were as numerous as the Germans in Miller, and
in 1874 the Bethel Evangelical Lutheran Church was
organized in that community. Portage Township, in Porter County, was rather heavily settled by Swedish farmers. The Swedes were noted for their adaptability to
American conditions and for their willingness to work
and save their money. They came to this country to
stay, and a study showed that no other immigrant group
was so quickly Americanized.[19]

The Irish migration, which reached its peak in the
1840's, was stimulated by a terrible famine which lasted
for several years. As was the case with the Germans,
they found their way into the region from Chicago. The
majority of those who came in the early years settled in
Porter County. In 1870 there were 527 residing in that
county and only 269 in Lake.[20] The Irish did not leave
their imprint on the region as did the Swedes and Germans, there being no distinctly Irish communities.

Of the Old Immigration, the Dutch were the smallest
in numbers and yet were the most concentrated of any of
the national groups. Dutch migration to the United
States began to reach real proportions around 1850. Holland was overcrowded, taxes were high, and unemployment was the rule instead of the exception. A large number of the Dutch who came to the Chicago area were
attracted to the rich, black soil adjacent to the Little
Calumet River. By 1850 settlements had been made at
Roseland and South Holland in Illinois. From there the
Dutch moved eastward into Indiana where they found
fertile land on both sides of what is now Ridge Road.

[19] Cannon, Loring, and Robb (eds.), *A History of the Lake and
Calumet Region*, 1:503, 509, 510; Wittke, *We Who Built America*, 272.
[20] *Ninth Census* (1870): *Population*, 353.

Here in 1855 they established the village of Munster. The founders of this community were Dingernon Jabaay, Antonie Bonevman, and Eldert Munster. The entire group came directly from Holland. A little later, Cornelius Klootwyk and Peter Kooy joined the little community.

Within fifteen years there was a continuous Dutch settlement stretching more than five miles along the Little Calumet in Indiana and Illinois. Here was truly a bit of old Holland; the spotless Dutch homes, the quaint dress of their occupants, the huge beds of flowers, and the truck gardens which produced luxuriant yields of vegetables for the Chicago market. The Hollanders at Munster worshiped at the Dutch Reformed Church just across the state line in Illinois. While the Dutch sought American citizenship soon after their arrival, they nevertheless clung to their national dress, including the wooden shoes.[21]

The New Immigration

In 1890 the Bureau of the Census officially declared the frontier at an end, which meant that the era of free and cheap lands in the United States was a thing of the past. As a result, northern Europeans were less attracted to the United States than they had been in the earlier years. Also, in the case of the Germans, their country's rise as an industrial power and the development of her empire kept them fully occupied. The steamship companies, industrialists, and others interested in the immigrant trade and in an abundant supply of cheap labor, then turned their attention to the Mediterranean area and to eastern Europe. Immigration from the Balkans, Italy, central Europe, and Russia was characterized as the "New Immigration." The advertising campaign which had

[21] Wittke, *We Who Built America*, 305; Howat (ed.), *A Standard History of Lake County,* 1:175; Wilhelmine S. Kaske, "Early Days in Munster," in Demmon (ed.), *History of Lake County* (1934), 87-89.

been so successful in luring immigrants in the earlier years was now turned upon the Italians, Slavs, Hungarians, and upon the Jews in the interior of Europe. In the years between 1897 and 1914 a total of 13,041,124 Europeans, of which 10,057,576 were classified as "New Immigrants," entered the United States. This flood reached its crest in 1907 when 1,199,566 European immigrants, both "Old" and "New," came to this country.[22]

The principal cause of this great immigration was economic, although some came for political reasons, and others, as in the case of some of the Jews, to escape religious persecution. The new immigrant came to this country not merely to make a living, but to make a better living than was possible at home. He was essentially a seller of labor, seeking a more favorable market for his product. A large proportion of the immigration from southern and eastern Europe may be traced directly to the inability of the peasantry to gain an adequate livelihood in agricultural pursuits, either as laborers or as proprietors. Desire to escape military service was a cause of emigration from some countries, but on the whole it was relatively unimportant.[23] These people had endured their hard lot for centuries because there was no place for them to go. When the call came from America for their labor, the peasants and workers of eastern and southern Europe were all too ready to respond.

On the whole, the new immigrants sought employment in the cities. At first glance this seems something of a paradox since most of them were peasants from the agricultural areas of the old countries. They turned to the industries and to the mines because that was where money

22 Edith Abbott, *Immigration: Select Documents and Case Records* (University of Chicago Press, 1924), 233; *Emigration Conditions in Europe* (41 vols. U. S. Immigration Commission, *Reports*, 1907-10), 4:11.
23 *Emigration Conditions in Europe*, 4:53-54.

could immediately be made. Many wished to accumulate funds in order to bring their families or relatives to America, while others looked forward to the day when they could return to the homeland and become land-owners. Also, most of them were too poor to pay the high prices then asked for land in the United States.[24]

Immigrants were not required by law to possess a certain amount of money when they entered this country, but immigration officials asked each to volunteer such information. From 1905 to 1909, according to their own statements, the average amount possessed by the Poles was $14.60, by the Bulgarians, Serbians, and Montene-grins, $18.05, and by the Hungarians, $19.37. These figures may not be correct as the peasants, traditionally suspicious of public officials, may not have told the whole truth. The rate of illiteracy among the new immigrants was high. In the period 1899-1909, the percentage of illiteracy among the various nationalities was as follows: South Italians, 54.2; Bulgarians, Serbians, and Montene-grins, 41.8; Poles, 35.4; Roumanians, 34.7; North Italians, 11.8; Hungarians, 11.4; Germans, 5.1; Czechs from Bohemia and Moravia, 1.7; Scotch, .7; and Scandinavians, .4.[25]

Seventy-three per cent of those belonging to the "New Immigration," who entered the country in the years from 1899 to 1909, were males. A large number could not afford to bring their wives and children but hoped to send for them later, while many were "birds of passage." The latter came, not to stay and become American citizens, but to save money and return as speedily as possible to the homeland. The birds of passage were not concerned about American standards of living and were content to

24 Emil Lengyel, *Americans from Hungary* (New York, 1948), 127.
25 *Emigration Conditions in Europe*, 4:30, 37.

reside in the worst quarters of industrial cities. Nor did they take any interest in the economic and political problems which were of concern to workmen with a more permanent stake in Americn society. In 1920 Emerson Hough reported an interview with a Turk in Gary: "Then you don't intend to be a citizen of America? He shook his head. I got farm in Toorkey. In six-seven mont' I go back to Toorkey. I got money, plenty now. I asked the man if he liked America. He did not understand and gave it some thought. She good place for mon (money). He said at last." A large number who did return found their native lands not as attractive as they expected. Others discovered that landowners and speculators took advantage of their kind and increased the price of land they so desired to buy with money saved in America. In disillusionment, many returned to this country.[26]

Native Americans and those of the old immigration had a tendency to regard the new immigrants with distaste and suspicion. They differed in language, customs, political ideas, and personal standards of living. The new immigrant was represented as being of the offscourings and unwanted people of Europe, in contrast to the old immigrant who was presumed to represent a highly selected, adventurous, resourceful type. While the older immigrants were still considering themselves heroes, the newer ones were being viewed as a problem.[27] Peter Finley Dunne's "Mr. Dooley" lampooned the attitude of the earlier arrivals toward the new immigrants: "As a pilgrim father that missed th' first boats, I must raise me

[26] Ibid., 4:23; Wittke, We Who Built America, 405-6; Emerson Hough, "Round Our Town," in Saturday Evening Post, February 14, 1920, pp. 18-19; Lengyel, Americans from Hungary, 130.

[27] Marcus Lee Hansen, The Immigrant in American History (Harvard University Press, 1940), 26-27.

Claryon voice again' th' invasion iv this fair land be th' paupers an' arnychists iv effete Europe. Ye bet I must —because I'm here first—.''[28]   People were inclined to forget that many of the colonists had been indentured servants who had to pay their passage to the New World by working from four to seven years, and that many of the English and "old stock" immigrants had been paupers and persons who had been imprisoned for debt and petty crimes. Also, that in the not too far distant past Americans had spoken with fear of the "wild Irishmen," and the "ignorant" Germans. Actually, the new immigrants represented desirable stock, the great majority being males in the prime of life. The home countries bore the expense of rearing them up to the productive period of their lives, and America, without that heavy expense, reaped the profits of the old country's investment.[29] Also, it may well be doubted that American industry could have expanded and reached its degree of efficiency without the cheap and abundant labor from eastern and southern Europe.

It is not possible to obtain the exact number of each nationality to enter the United States before World War I as the political boundaries of European nations did not correspond with the national groups. The Czechs were classified as Austrians and the Slovaks as Hungarians because they were politically a part of those countries. Actually the Czechs belonged as much to the old immigration as they did to the new immigration, there being about 20,000 in this country by 1850. Those who came to the Calumet Region were a part of the new immigration, the majority settling in Gary and East Chicago. The Czechs came largely from Bohemia and Moravia, and the rea-

[28] Quoted in Wittke, *We Who Built America*, 408.
[29] Commons, *Races and Immigrants in America*, 121.

sons for their migration were economic and political. The spirit of nationalism was usually strong among them and they bitterly resented their domination by Austria. Czech immigrants were probably the most advanced of all the Slavic groups to come to the United States. As has been noted, the degree of illiteracy among them was much lower than most Europeans, even the Germans. Also, of those coming to this country between 1899 and 1909, 24.6 per cent were skilled workers. Most of the Czechs brought their families and came to the United States as permanent residents. They mingled well with the Germans and most of them were proficient in the use of the German language. In the beginning the Czechs held their social functions in halls owned by Germans, and they also had a tendency to marry Germans.[30]

The home of the Slovaks is the southern slopes of the Carpathian Mountains which were under the domination of Hungary before World War. I. Large numbers came to America because of the persistent efforts of Hungarians to "Magyarize" them, that is to force the Hungarian language and culture upon them. The Slovaks were also denied representation in the Hungarian Parliament. A large number migrated to escape service in the Hungarian Army. Those who came to America for those reasons came to stay. On the other hand, many who came for economic reasons were often birds of passage, the majority being males. According to reports, the Slovaks were here to get money, and to get as much of it as they could and as quickly as possible, so that they could improve their status here, and bring their families

[30] Francis J. Brown and Joseph S. Roucek (eds.), *One America. The History, Contributions, and Present Problems of our Racial and National Minorities* (New York, 1952), 160; *Emigration Conditions in Europe*, 4:28; Thomas Capek, *The Czechs (Bohemians) in America . . .* (Boston, 1920), 56, 96.

over, or return to the homeland with a tidy sum in savings. To achieve these ends, they would endure harder
work, longer hours, and poorer living conditions than
would the native American workmen. The Slovaks came
as common laborers, only 3.5 per cent of those entering
the United States from 1899 to 1909 being skilled workmen. They were largely Roman Catholics although a
few were Lutherans. The Slovaks settled largely in
Gary, East Chicago, Whiting, and the Robertsdale section of Hammond. Although they were close to the
Czechs in language and blood, and were united politically
with them after World War I, the two groups did not
mingle intimately in America. The Czechs were inclined
to be clannish and often ignored other national groups in
their vicinity, while the Slovaks were not particular and
were more willing to mix socially with others.[31]

Racially, the majority of the Hungarians were Magyars rather than Slavs. They belonged to the Finno-
Ugrian branch of the human family and their only
relatives in Europe were the Finns and possibly the
Esthonians. There are some who think the Magyars
came from the interior of Asia while others believe their
original abode was on the European side of the Ural
Mountains. A native of Hungary is not necessarily,
racially speaking, a Magyar, which has been confusing to
those concerned with Hungary. According to reports,
only 54 per cent of Hungary's population was Magyar
before World War I. The principal reasons for the
Hungarian migration to America was economic. Hungary
was an agricultural country and there was insufficient land
to support the population. What was worse, most of
the tillable area was controlled by feudal landlords. The

[31] Kenneth D. Miller, *The Czecho-Slovaks in America* (New York, 1922), 60, 74; *Emigration Conditions in Europe*, 4:28; Capek, *The Czechs (Bohemians) in America*, ix.

movement to America was primarily a peasant migration,
93.2 per cent of all who came from 1899 to 1909 being
unskilled workmen. East Chicago received the largest
number of Hungarians, 2,154 residing there in 1920. On
the same date, Gary had 895, Hammond 450, and Whiting 406. The great majority of Hungarians were Roman
Catholics although there was a sprinkling of Protestants
among them.[32]

The Poles settled in the region in larger numbers
than did the Hungarians or any of the Slavic groups.
Poland was divided between Germany, Russia, and Austria-Hungary before World War I, and it was not possible to determine the exact number of its people who
came to the region before 1914. It is certain they
came to East Chicago in the early 1890's since St.
Stanislaus' Church was founded in 1896 to serve the
Poles in the twin city. In 1920 East Chicago, with 4,074
Polish residents, had the largest number of any of the
area's cities. On the same date, there were 2,703 living
in Gary, 1,826 in Hammond, and 726 in Whiting. The
principal reason for the Polish migration was economic.
Poland was overcrowded and there was not enough land
to support her population. Wages were low, taxes high,
and industries few in number. A large number left German Poland because of the linguistic and religious persecution resulting from Bismarck's "Kultur-kampf" policy.
Most of the Poles who came were peasants, only 5.1
per cent being skilled workmen. Most of them who migrated to America came to stay. About 93 per cent were
Roman Catholics.[33]

[32] David A. Souders, *The Magyars in America* (New York, 1922),
13; Lengyel, *Americans from Hungary*, 14, 120; Brown and Roucek,
One America, 223; *Emigration Conditions in Europe*, 4:28, 361-62;
Fourteenth Census (1920): *Population*, pt. 3:304, 307.

[33] Howat (ed.), *A Standard History of Lake County*, 1:431; *Four-*

Serbs, Montenegrins, Slovenes, and Croats, united politically in Yugoslavia after World War I, made up an important segment of the region's foreign-born population. Since immigrants representing these groups came largely from the old Austria-Hungarian Empire before World War I, it was not possible to arrive at the exact number of each. Gary and East Chicago had large Serbian and Croatian populations at an early date. The largest Eastern Orthodox Church (St. Sava's) in Gary is Serbian. The majority of the Serbs were of the Eastern Orthodox faith while the Croatians and Slovenes were mostly Roman Catholics. They migrated to America mainly for economic reasons but partly because of their domination by Austria-Hungary. In 1920 Gary had 1,558 Yugoslav residents, East Chicago 987, and Whiting 380.[34]

The Roumanians and Greeks made their presence felt in the area. Most of the Roumanians came from Transylvania and the Banat in the Austria-Hungarian Empire. Apparently only a few came from Roumania proper. Poverty at home, political oppression, and weariness from too many wars stimulated their migration. The Roumanian immigrants were divided into three Christian bodies: the Greek Orthodox Church, the Roman Catholics of Eastern Rites (Uniates), and the Protestant groups with a large predominance of Baptists. The Roumanians preferred East Chicago to Gary, there being 841 in the Twin City and 435 in Gary in 1920. Greece was a backward agricultural country with little manufacturing. Low

teenth Census (1920): Population, pt. 3:304, 307; Paul Fox, The Poles in America (New York, 1922), 59; Emigration Conditions in Europe, 4:28; Wittke, We Who Built America, 425.

34 Martin E. Carlson, A Study of the Eastern Orthodox Churches in Gary, Indiana (M.A. thesis, University of Chicago, 1942, in Gary Public Library); Fourteenth Census (1920): Population, pt. 3:304, 307.

wages, high prices, and a low standard of living set many Greeks in motion to the United States. The majority were men and boys. Most of the Greeks belonged to the Greek Orthodox Church. In 1920 Gary's Greek population numbered 1,392 and East Chicago's 488.[35]

Before World War I, immigration officials were content to classify all immigrants from Russia as "Russian." Apparently, the majority who came here were Jews and Russian peasants along with a small number of Finns, Esthonians, Latvians, and Lithuanians. Most of the Jews in the new immigration from Russia came because there they were crowded into certain areas where they suffered religious persecution and economic discrimination. Since the Jews were not listed as such in the census reports, it is impossible to determine the exact number that came to the United States. Russian peasants left the old country because of political oppression under the Czarist regime, oppression at the hands of feudal landlords, and because of a desire for complete religious freedom. Most of the Russian peasants were males and highly illiterate. As a result, they found work in the heavy industries as the lowest ranks of common laborers. In 1920 East Chicago had 837 Russian residents, Gary 1,435, and Hammond 765. Most of the Russian peasants were Greek Orthodox in their religious faith. In 1920 there were 323 Lithuanians living in Gary, most of them being males who had migrated to escape military service in the Russian army. Many wrote friends and relatives to send marriageable Lithuanian girls, and they did not insist on having known the prospective brides before leaving the old country.[36] The Lithuanians were mostly Roman Catholics.

[35] Brown and Roucek, *One America*, 225, 227; *Fourteenth Census* (1920): *Population*, pt. 3:304, 307; Wittke, *We Who Built America*, 447.
[36] Wittke, *op. cit.*, 331-32; Jerome Davis, *The Russians and Rutheni-*

A large majority of the Italians who came into the region were from southern Italy. That part of the country was overcrowded, and the land was poor and owned in the main by landlords who took little interest in the peasant's welfare. The industry that did exist was in a state of stagnation. Most of the Italian immigrants were men, among whom the rate of illiteracy was high. They were said to have been the first birds of passage to enter this country, a large proportion of the early arrivals eventually returning to their native land. The Roman Catholic Church was probably the greatest influence in their lives. In 1920 there were 982 Italians residing in Gary and 381 in East Chicago.[37]

Other nationalities came in small numbers, the most important being the Albanians, Bulgarians, and Turks. The Turkish immigrants were mostly bachelors and many returned to Turkey after World War I. The majority who came to the Calumet Region settled in Whiting where they obtained employment in the Standard Oil Company's refinery. Because of their unusual resistance to heat they were especially proficient in the cleaning of the distilling units. In 1952 it was reported that of the original migration of 1912 and 1913, only about six to eight hundred remained in the United States, the majority being in Whiting.[38]

It would be a difficult task to identify specifically all the nationalities in the region, since the immigrant, after his arrival, had a tendency to be more specific in classifying himself than were the immigration officials. In 1912 the

ans in America (New York, 1922), 13, 14; Fourteenth Census (1920): Population, pt. 3:304, 307; interview with Lithuanian-Americans at the Gary International Institute, April 21, 1952.

37 Wittke, We Who Built America, 437-38, 441; Fourteenth Census (1920): Population, pt. 3:304, 307.

38 Brown and Roucek, One America, 292.

Gary police arrest sheets listed thirty-three nationalities in the city. In 1916 an officer of the Lake County juvenile court reported forty-seven national and racial groups in the county. A survey of the East Chicago public schools in 1925 listed thirty-six races and nationalities among the children enrolled. At that time only 20.8 per cent of the children in East Chicago's school were reported to have native-born parents. Also, the children of native-born white parents numbered only about 10 per cent of the enrollment in the parochial schools of the city.[39]

Since the cities of East Chicago, Whiting, and Gary were founded and their industrial development began during the period of the new immigration, it was logical for these cities to be largely populated by that group of immigrants. They were on the ground as early as the native-born Americans and whatever those cities represent today is due to these immigrants as well as to those of American stock.

Problems of the New Immigrants

The foreign born were confronted by conditions and problems in their new home entirely different from those they had known in the old countries. From a simple and orderly existence, principally in the rural areas of Europe, they were suddenly faced by all the complexities of urban life and by strange conditions in the industries. Their inability to speak and read English not only added to their bewilderment but also erected a barrier between them and the Americans. Immigrants were often victimized by unscrupulous merchants, by shady employment

[39] Gary *Evening Post,* July 24, 1912; Edmondson, "Juvenile Delinquency and Adult Crime," in *Indiana University Studies,* Vol. 8, No. 49, p. 8; East Chicago *Calumet News,* June 25, 1925.

agencies, and in some instances by their straw bosses in
the mills.   Such exploitation aroused suspicion and distrust of Americans in general.   As a result, the foreign
born sought the company of their fellow countrymen and
entire neighborhoods were populated by the same nationalities.   They found security among their own kind
who understood their language and ideas, who sympath-
ized with their feelings of loneliness and confusion, who
enjoyed the same kind of food, adhered to the same customs, and celebrated the same holidays.   Those of each
nationality were brought even closer together in their
churches under the guidance of priests and ministers who
administered to their spiritual needs in their own languages.   Colonies occupied by a single nationality sprang
up south of the Wabash tracks in Gary, in the Indiana
Harbor and south-side sections of East Chicago, on the
east side and in the Robertsdale part of Hammond, and
in Whiting.   In this manner, the foreign born isolated
themselves from the native American segment of the
population for some years.

Originally, the areas inhabited by the new immigrants
possessed all the atmosphere and color of the Old World.
Foreign languages were heard on every side, in the stores,
on the streets, in the social halls, and in the churches.
The industries published their rules and directives in several foreign languages.   Foreign-language newspapers
were read more avidly than were American publications.
In defense of this practice, priests and other leaders
pointed out that the large majority of their people could
not read English and the only way they could teach them
American ways and customs was through such mediums.

The immigrants clung to the traditions of their native
countries, thereby deriving a feeling of security.   Their
amusements were largely national in character.   They

were very fond of dancing and feasting, and it was a poor sort of an occasion which was not celebrated by one or the other or both. In some instances christenings were followed by dances and feasts at which gifts of money were made to the baby to be placed in a bank until it was of age. Weddings were generally followed by banquets and dances at which each man made a gift of money for the privilege of dancing with the bride. The money, which was often pinned on her dress, was generally used to buy furniture and equipment for her new home. The success of these affairs was sometimes judged by the number of empty beer kegs on the outside of the social hall the next morning.

In 1916 one who lived and worked among Gary's foreign born depicted the Old World atmosphere and color on the South Side:[40]

A bridal party dressed in the bright colors dear to the immigrant heart gaily escort the white-veiled bride and the proud faced groom through the streets; a solemn funeral procession slowly marches behind the hearse on the way to the photographer who will take a picture of the dead covered over with flowers and surrounded by living friends and relatives; or finally as many groups join together in native folk costume, each group with its band playing its own national airs, in one big political parade, shouting over and over again "Knotts, Knotts, Knotts," the name of the candidate for mayor, the only English word many of them know.

The city is full of strange inconsistencies. . . . Two squares west of Broadway and only a few squares south of the city's beautiful residential district is a typical immigrant settlement of tar paper shacks promiscuously set down in the sand at various angles, forming a little village community: each shack has its number, 56, 57, etc. . . . In the evening the women come in along the paths from the prairies, wearing their shawls and

[40] Edmondson, "Juvenile Delinquency and Adult Crime," *loc. cit.,* 8-9.

kerchiefs over their heads and their short, full skirts, and bending under bundles of sticks tied on their backs. As they gather in groups laughing and chatting a few minutes before separating for their various shacks, the red of the setting sun behind them throws this picture of peasant life into a bold relief that quite blots out another picture only two squares away, a picture of the hustle and bustle of an American business day drawing to a close.

A street car loaded with workmen from one of the most perfectly appointed and equipped modern steel plants in the country turns off Broadway and clangs past, disturbing the line of march of a flock of geese which two little Italian girls, Santina and Carmella, are driving home to their father's shack—geese whose feathers are to go into great fluffy mattresses between which the children will sleep snug and warm against the winter winds filtering through the cracks and crevices of their poor little shack.

Since most of the immigrants came to the region emptyhanded, and as the industries did not provide housing for common laborers, appalling conditions prevailed among some. The homes of many were tar-paper shacks of from one to three rooms with outside toilets, communal pumps, and no screens. Dogs, pigs, goats, chickens, and, in some instances, cows shared the dwellings with their human occupants. In 1910 the Gary Board of Health found a man and his wife, their five children, seven boarders, and seven cows all living in a one-room shack with no partitions. In 1913 sanitary conditions in most of the shacks were reported to be bad, with filth and dirt everywhere. In the winter it was almost impossible for an outsider to breathe the air in the close rooms, which often had no windows or other means of ventilation. Under such conditions, typhoid fever and tuberculosis took a heavy toll.[41] Apparently, many of the foreign born, guided by the standards of living they had known

41 Gary *Evening Post,* July 8, 1910; Edna C. Hatfield, "Problem of Housing Foreign Population Is Presented," in *ibid.,* March 5, 1913. Miss Hatfield was an officer of the Lake County Juvenile Court.

in the old countries, could not understand at first that a decent home, neat furniture, and good clothes were for them. They knew these things existed, also that they did not cost much, but they felt such refinements were only for those of another class.

The desire for money to send to their families in the old countries, to pay the passage of relatives to America, and to own property was uppermost in the minds of most of the foreign born. To achieve these ends, they were willing to work and live under conditions that repelled native American workmen. Groups of single men, as many as twenty in number, erected large one-room shacks. In some instances there were no beds in these rude dwellings, the occupants sleeping on the floor. The wardrobe of each man generally included two blankets, a suit of cheap clothes, and a pair of shiny patent leather shoes for Sunday and holiday wear. A group usually hired a man and his wife to cook for them. Each man provided his own food, generally meat and potatoes. The cost of board and lodging was around $2.50 a week.[42]

Married couples usually bought their homes on credit, and to meet the payments the common practice was to keep boarders. Under one system, the wife in the family received three or four dollars a month from each man in return for doing his laundry, his cooking, and furnishing him a place to sleep. Each man bought his own food under this plan. Overcrowding and lack of privacy in the boardinghouses frequently resulted in a lowering of moral standards. Actual cases of polyandry were reported in Gary and East Chicago; the boarders who lived with a couple in some instances had relations with the wife with the knowledge and consent of the husband. Also, many of the boarding foreigners lived in such a way that relations

42 Gary *Daily Tribune,* March 5, 1909.

with the woman of the household were taken as a matter of course along with board and lodgings. Despite what appeared to be extremely low charges for board and lodging, many thrifty and hard-working families accumulated considerable sums from such operations. In 1909 a man on Gary's South Side was reported to have boarded fifty-five men and grossed $7,000.00 in that year. The only helpers he had were his wife and two daughters.[43]

The handling and use of money was one of the most perplexing problems encountered by the new immigrants. In the rural regions of the old countries wealth was generally measured in land and material things produced, and many peasants had never handled money before coming here. In America they worked for money, obtained the necessities of life with money, and their savings were in the form of money which could easily be stolen. On the whole, they avoided the American banks, looking with awe and suspicion at their magnificent proportions and equipment. Moreover, the American banker did not seek what were thought to be the small accounts of the foreign born nor did his clerks understand their language. So the immigrants took their money to members of their own group, saloonkeepers or merchants who had safes. These were known as immigrant bankers. The immigrant bank was convenient, it being located in the neighborhood and was open at night, on Sundays, and on holidays. The immigrant banker provided other services to his customers. He wrote letters for the illiterate, cashed pay checks, forwarded money to relatives in the old countries, and acted as an interpreter and legal adviser. The immigrant banker was compensated for his services by the trade of the foreign born at his grocery store or

43 Edmondson, "Juvenile Delinquency and Adult Crime," *loc. cit.*, 20; Taylor, *Satellite Cities,* 204; Gary *Evening Post,* April 4, 1910.

saloon. He also deposited his client's money in the
regular banks, often keeping the interest for himself.
The immigrant banker was usually a power in local politics, and his place of business was a social club where his
customers enjoyed the companionship of their fellow
countrymen.[44]

Some of the foreign born converted their savings into
postal money orders which they carried around on their
persons or secreted in their homes. This form of protection was not entirely satisfactory as money orders were
frequently lost or stolen and the signatures could be
forged. The establishment of postal savings banks in
1910 provided the security so eagerly desired by the
immigrants, who in the main had great confidence in the
United States Government. They were also impressed by
the payment of interest on deposits in the postal savings
banks. Consequently, large sums of money that had
been out of circulation found their way to the post office.
In 1911 the Gary postmaster reported that 90 per cent
of the depositors were foreign born. In 1915 the average amount deposited by native Americans in the postal
savings bank in Gary was reported to be $115.00, while
that of the immigrants was $194.00. Also, that of the
fifty-four depositors having the maximum of $500.00,
fifty were foreign born.[45] The immigrants also used the
post office service to send money to relatives and friends
in the old countries. In 1911 the Gary postmaster estimated that at least $5,000,000 was sent through the post
office the year before; also, that large amounts had no
doubt been sent in registered letters and parcels.[46]

The confidence of the immigrants in the post office was
not entirely complete, as was demonstrated by their sus-

[44] Abbott, *Immigration: Select Documents and Case Records,* 498-99.
[45] Gary *Evening Post,* June 3, 1911, August 12, 1915.
[46] Gary *Daily Tribune,* May 2, 1911.

picion of what lay behind the offer to deliver the mail to their homes free of charge. When free mail delivery was started in Gary in 1909, the mail carriers who took a census of the routes encountered a wall of opposition in the immigrant districts. Several hundred of the foreign born refused to give their names or to have their houses numbered. The stock reply was "no got it house number. Got a box at the post office so we don't want it the free delivery." Many were afraid they were being asked to sign papers whereby their lots and houses would be mortgaged. Others could not understand why some strange fellow should be entrusted with their mail when they, themselves, could go to the post office, as they had always done, and get their letters and packages. They were also suspicious of the offer to bring their mail to their homes without extra cost.[47]

The immigrants encountered the language barrier on every side when they came into contact with various phases of American life. This was particularly the case for those who became involved in legal matters. Unscrupulous lawyers took advantage of their ignorance of the English language and of legal procedures to exploit and even swindle them. While it was the policy of the circuit and superior courts to employ interpreters, the city courts, local magistrates, and the police did not provide this service. As a result, professional interpreters hung around the lower courts and the police stations where they sold their services to the foreign born, their fee being added to the amount of the fine in case the defendants were found guilty.[48] Because of their work in the mills and the necessity of dealing with Americans on the outside, the men were the first to learn to speak English.

[47] Gary *Daily Tribune*, June 11, 1909.
[48] Gary *Weekly Tribune*, August 27, 1908.

Unfortunately, the first English they came to use was acquired from their association with the foremen and their fellow workmen in the mills and was usually on the rough and profane side. Americans, particularly the ladies, found it difficult to reconcile the immigrants' politeness and quaint Old World bows with the profanity that poured from their lips. They came to understand that the foreign born were not being disrespectful but were merely demonstrating their knowledge of English, however crude it may have been.[49]

The churches were the last stronghold of the Old World languages. In the earlier years the Germans, Swedes, and others of the old immigration preferred their church services to be conducted in their native tongues. It was also necessary that those of the new immigration, most of whom were Roman Catholics, have priests who knew their language to hear confessions, preach sermons, and administer to their spiritual needs in general. In some instances priests were summoned from the old countries because those born and educated in America were not always proficient in the use of this or that language. Most priests were farsighted men who, realizing their congregations were here to stay, encouraged the process of Americanization and the use of the English language. Their policy called for a lessening of the use of the mother tongue and an increasing use of English as their parishioners demonstrated the ability to understand it. The priests often encountered obstacles as a considerable number of the older people insisted that their native language be used in the sermons and sincerely believed their religion suffered when handed down in another tongue. In 1921 this feeling reached such intensity

---

[49] Edmondson, "Juvenile Delinquency and Adult Crime," *loc. cit.*, 21.

among some members of the largest Slovak Church in
the region that an attempt was made upon the life of its
first priest because of his emphasis on the use of the English language and on the Americanization of his people.
Others were critical of the churchman because of his
enthusiasm for the American game of baseball. In 1927
some of the more conservative parishioners sought to
effect a change of pastors largely because of what they
considered the too streamlined Americanism of the priest.
The churchman stood his ground and the crisis passed
without any ill effects on the congregation.[50]

The Problem of Americanization

The process of Americanization was not easy for the
older of the foreign born and many did not concern themselves seriously about it. This was particularly true of
numerous wives and mothers who had little desire to
learn English nor did they see any need to do so. Others
refrained because they feared the ridicule of their children who had learned to speak English fluently in the
public schools and from their assocation with American
children. Many parents insisted on giving their children
a working foundation in the mother tongue, making it a
practice to converse at home in their native language to
the exclusion of English. It was noticeable among the
children of immigrants, that while the first born spoke
the parent's mother tongue passably well, the younger
children spoke it poorly or not at all. This was because
when the first child came, both parents in all probability
knew no other language except their own native tongue.
Meanwhile, as the other children were born, the parents
had acquired a speaking knowledge of English. In consequence, the later-born children, no longer needing the

[50] Kaiser, *History of St. John's Parish,* 40.

"other language" in their intercourse with their parents or older relatives, never learned it. There were also prejudices to overcome, especially the prejudice that a large number of immigrant men had against the education of the women. In 1919 the director of the public night school in Gary told of an incident that occurred in one of the schools which many of the foreign-born women were accustomed to attend. The husband of one of them happened to come one evening, and discovering his wife was there using the facilities of the gymnasium and swimming pool, ordered her to "go home," but he himself went into the men's gymnasium.[51]

None of the region's cities had a centralized and co-ordinated program of Americanization and education for their foreign-born population. Instead, civic, industrial, religious, and patriotic organizations approached the problem independently and from different viewpoints. The foremost agencies in this work were the public schools whose efforts in behalf of adults were made through the medium of night classes. These placed particular emphasis on the teaching of English, simple mathematics, manual training, and citizenship. As early as 1909 William A. Wirt, superintendent of Gary Public Schools, started night classes in English at the public library. Later a comprehensive program was launched in the Gary school buildings, 1,900 men and women being enrolled in 1917 and 1918. Wirt refused to use the term "Americanization" in connection with any part of his program. It was his opinion that the aggressive attitude which characterized most such efforts did more harm than good, that the foreign born resented an approach which, in their minds, aimed to crush out every spark of love

[51] Estelle M. Sternberger, "Gary and the Foreigner's Opportunity," in *The Survey,* 42 (April-September, 1919) :482.

and attachment they had toward the land of their birth. In 1912 Hammond started a night school with 942 adults enrolled. East Chicago's night school had five hundred in attendance in 1915.[52]

The Gary Y.M.C.A. conducted classes for adults and also made extensive use of films and slides in its Americanization program. The steel company in Gary provided classes in the various technical subjects pertaining to the manufacture of steel and also in English, the classes being held inside the plant. Men engaged in certain forms of night work were given the opportunity to leave their tasks to attend weekly classes in English. Despite the efforts of the various agencies, only a small proportion of the foreign born were ever reached. Illiterate when they arrived in America, many could not appreciate the benefits that came from educational opportunities. Another obstacle was the fatigue of workmen after a strenuous twelve hours or so in the mills. These men did not have the inclination to go to the public school classes or to return to the educational quarters of the steel plant, which was quite a distance from their homes.[53]

Children of immigrants and the younger of the foreign born were more easily educated and taught American ways and customs. The public schools made their greatest contribution to the children, for their Americanization began in the first grade. Also, the emphasis on vocational training kept many in school after they had passed the age of compulsory attendance. And yet it was wrong for Americans to insist that all immigrants divest themselves of their culture and heritage immediately and take over a standardized American pattern for their lives. There

[52] Gary *Weekly Tribune,* January 1, 1909; Howat (ed.), *A Standard History of Lake County,* 1:354, 424.

[53] Sternberger, "Gary and the Foreigner's Opportunity," *loc. cit.,* 42:480-82.

was much in their culture, customs, and general background that should have been retained in America. Instead, the young people in their eagerness to be like the native Americans were inclined to be ashamed of their parents and their Old World ways. Children were frequently heard to refer to their parents as foreigners, and to place emphasis on the fact that they themselves were born in the region. A large number whose names appeared difficult to Americans found it necessary or desirable to change them to the American version. This was also true of some of the older people because the foremen and clerks in the mills arbitrarily insisted upon names more easily pronounced or recorded. The Roumanian name Parschina Rotarin became Pearl Rotar, the Croatian family name Millocivich was changed to Miller, the Polish Christian name Kalada was Clara, Wladislaw was Walter, Aniello became Nellie, and Michaelo was known as Mike. A young man whose name was Majerski had great difficulty in proving his right to an inheritance in his native country because a clerk in the steel mill was too hurried to get his name correct and the man himself too indifferent to insist that Majerski and not Morris was his name.[54]

The International Institute of Gary, established in 1919, was the only agency that devoted its efforts entirely to the needs of the foreign born. As mentioned earlier, for a short time the War Council, created by the Federal government during World War I, provided funds for its support. When this aid was no longer available, the United States Steel Corporation assumed the greater part of the financial burden. While the Institute was interested in making good Americans out of the foreign

[54] Edmondson, "Juvenile Delinquency and Adult Crime," loc. cit., 23-24.

born, it also encouraged them to preserve the richer and
finer things in their culture and customs. In the 1920's
the agency was primarily concerned with the wives and
mothers whom the industries and the public schools had
been unable to reach. The Institute provided assistance
in the matter of naturalization and also served as a clearing house of information for the often-confused aliens.
Its personnel operated on the theory that if friendship
and understanding were offered the foreign born by Americans speaking their language, the problems of adjustment would be eased. English classes were held at the
Institute and also in the homes of women with small
children who could not leave their homes. In the summers they were taken for outings in the dune country and
at Miller Beach. Films about America were shown and
lectures explaining American organizations, institutions,
and ways of life were given in the winter. Many nationality groups used the rooms of the Institute as club rooms
and as a social center. Because of its efforts, large numbers of immigrants were fitted more easily into the American pattern of life.[55]

The Immigrants and the Homeland

The immigrants followed closely the fortunes of their
native lands. In 1911 and 1912 at least one hundred
Turks left Gary for their homeland to fight against
Italy in the Turko-Italian War. The Balkan Wars of
1912 and 1913 aroused great excitement among the
Slavic groups whose native lands were involved in that
conflict. On October 7, 1912, three thousand Greeks,
Serbians, Bulgarians, and Montenegrins paraded through

[55] Interview with Elizabeth Wilson, director of the Gary International Institute, April 14, 1951; Taylor, The International Institute
of Gary, 3.

Gary's streets to demonstrate their sympathy for the mother countries in their war against the Turks. The King of Montenegro sent a battle flag to the reservists of his army in the region calling upon them to return for military service. Macedonians in Gary received a telegram from the Bulgarian government urging them to return at once. Three hundred Montenegrins announced their intention to fight in the war, and a meeting was held in Gary's Binzenhof Hall to raise money to pay their expenses to the homeland. Fifty Serbians were reported to have sold their property in Gary preparatory to returning to their native land. So many workmen went back to their homelands that steel officials feared a shortage of labor would occur.[56] Since the Turks were the enemies of the Balkan nations in the First Balkan War, and since they were all aligned against Bulgaria in the Second Balkan War, little friendship existed between the region's Turks and Bulgarians on the one side and the Serbians, Greeks, Roumanians, and Montenegrins on the other.

World War I, which found the Slavic peoples of Europe, with the exception of the Bulgarians who were allies of the Central Powers, arrayed against Germany and Austria-Hungary, had profound repercussions in the region. On July 28, 1914, when Austria-Hungary precipitated the great conflict by declaring war on Serbia, fifteen hundred Serbian men and women paraded through Gary's streets singing the war hymn of their native land on their way to a meeting at Turner Hall. At this gathering they sent a telegram to King Peter offering their support. Indignation among the Serbians and Montenegrins reached a fever heat as they gathered on the street corners, in the saloons, and at private residences

[56] Gary *Daily Tribune,* March 9, October 7, 12, 14, 16, 1912; Hammond *Lake County Times,* October 6, 1912.

to discuss the news about the war. Those in Gary appealed to all Americans for sympathy and aid for their mother countries. On the other hand, two hundred Hungarians met in East Chicago to pledge fealty to their native land. Although deprecating the war, they announced their intention to do all in their power to help Hungary in the conflict. Resolutions were also adopted lamenting what they regarded as the unfriendly attitude of the American press toward Hungary and her allies.[57]

In June, 1915, 125 Gary Serbians, together with a large number of their countrymen in East Chicago, left for Europe to fight in the war. In April, 1917, shortly after the United States entered the war, 250 of the region's Serbians, preferring to fight under the flag of the native land, departed for Europe. It would be difficult to determine the exact number of the region's foreign born who returned to the old countries during the Balkan Wars and World War I. A local historian put the number at "several thousand."[58] No evidence was found that any of the Germans returned to Europe to participate in the war although most of them did side with the fatherland before the United States entered the struggle. As has been noted, the Germans of Hammond in 1914 appealed to Americans to accord the German cause in the war unbiased consideration. They also deprecated the ease with which Germany's enemies were able to obtain food and materials of war in the United States.[59]

The murder of the Reverend Edmund E. A. Kayser, pro-German pastor of the German Evangelical Church in Gary in August, 1915, aroused great excitement in

[57] Gary *Daily Tribune,* July 28, 1914; Hammond *Lake County Times,* August 1, 6, 1914.

[58] Gary *Daily Tribune,* June 25, 1915, April 23, 1917; Cannon, Autobiography of Tom Cannon, Chap. 25, p. 6.

[59] See above, 159-60.

the region. Mr. Kayser, born and educated in Germany, was the pastor of a church in Chesterton before coming to Gary. He founded the Gary church, made frequent visits to Germany, and persuaded a number of Germans to migrate to the steel city. Kayser, probably the region's most aggressive advocate of the German cause in World War I, frequently engaged in bitter controversy with other citizens and with the newspapers about the European conflict. Shortly after the war began, the pastor published a half-page article in the Gary *Daily Tribune* in which he blamed England, whom he termed that "pious old hypocrite and the professional land-grabber of the World," for causing the war. Kayser also protested against what he regarded as the thinly veiled hatred of Germany on the part of Americans and the press. He went on to say: "I do not think Germany is going to be defeated. As long as the heavens are blue, the German Empire will not perish." Later, Kayser wrote a lengthy public letter to the newspaper in which he defended Germany's course in the war.[60]

The pastor's murder occurred at night and his body, riddled with bullets, was found near the sidewalk outside his house. The interior of the residence was in shambles which indicated that a ghastly and terrific struggle had started there. His last known visitor was a Gary attorney, who testified that he and Kayser were engaged in forming organizations among the Germans in Gary and Hammond to disseminate literature opposing further shipments of munitions of war from the United States to the nations at war with Germany. Some people believed the pastor was killed because of his pro-German views, while others thought that enemies in his congregation were responsible for his death. An investigation revealed

[60] Gary *Daily Tribune,* August 19, 1914; August 25, 1915.

that Kayser opposed the proposal of the Saxon Society of the church to build a large hall for dances and other social affairs, that he had received threatening letters, several of which were written in German. In one letter, he was warned that his life would be taken "before the snow falls."[61] The real reason for the pastor's murder and the identity of its perpetrators are still a mystery.

Some of the foreign born returned to their native lands after the war, although the exact number is not known. In 1919 a rather large number of Serbians and Slovaks, who had made an unusual amount of money in the mills during the war, returned to Europe during the steel strike. Many of the nationalities, whose countries were enlarged by the various treaties at the end of the war, were tempted to go back. A check of Gary's churches and of the foreign exchange departments of the city's banks indicated that numerous single men returned to Europe. According to one report, more Serbians, Greeks, and Roumanians went back than did other nationalities. Any mass movement from the region was discouraged by letters from the old countries telling of hard times, threats of war, and of compulsory military service.[62]

The Foreign Born and American Citizenship

Those of the new immigration were slow to seek American citizenship. In 1910 only 3,444 or 20 per cent of the 17,157 foreign-born white males of voting age in Gary, East Chicago, Hammond, and Whiting were naturalized. Ten years later only 24 per cent were American

61 Gary *Evening Post,* August 27, 1915; Gary *Daily Tribune,* August 26, 1915.

62 Taylor, *Mexican Labor in the United States, Chicago, and the Calumet Region,* 17; Mary Sternberger, "Are Our Foreign-Born Emigrating, An Analysis of the Experience of an Industrial City," in *The Survey,* 43 (October, 1919-March, 1920) : 539-40.

citizens. In 1930 only 45 per cent were naturalized. The depression years put a premium on a person being an American citizen, the industries bringing pressure on their workers to seek naturalization. As a result, by 1940 the number of citizens among the foreign born reached 68 per cent.[63]

Of interest is the fact that immigrant women showed a stronger tendency to seek citizenship than did the men. In 1920 more than 31 per cent of Gary's foreign-born women were citizens in contrast to 24 per cent of the men. At the same time, 42 per cent of the foreign-born women of adult age in Hammond were naturalized while only 34 per cent of the immigrant men were citizens.[64] The lower citizenship rate among the men was probably because single men, more inclined to return to the old countries, were less interested in being American citizens. It was not surprising that the aliens showed such little interest in citizenship except during World War I, when numerous Germans were moved by public opinion to become citizens. The Federal government did not put pressure on them and the American people were indifferent to the matter except in wartime. Some of the more thrifty aliens objected to the five-dollar fee charged for filing the first and second naturalization papers, becoming more reluctant after 1929 when the charge was increased to ten dollars.[65] The naturalization process took time and was inconvenient for some, the prospective citizens having to go to Hammond or Valparaiso to file their papers and take the oath of allegiance.

[63] *Thirteenth Census* (1910): *Population,* pt. 2:568, 572; *Fourteenth Census* (1920): *Population,* pt. 3:297, 299; *Fifteenth Census* (1930): *Population,* 3: pt. 1:715, 717; *Sixteenth Census* (1940): *Population,* 2:pt. 2:784-85, 807.

[64] *Fourteenth Census* (1920): *Population,* pt. 3:297.

[65] Taylor, The International Institute of Gary, 6.

On the other hand, there were factors and considerations which stimulated many to seek citizenship. As has been noted, Indiana law permitted aliens who had been in the state six months and who had filed their first papers to vote. In 1913 predictions were made that at least three thousand would take out their first papers before the municipal elections in November. Unfortunately, the zeal for citizenship on the part of a large number did not extend beyond the initial papers. In 1919 reports spread of a great wave of patriotism sweeping through the foreign sections of Lake County, that hundreds who had lived in the country from five to twenty years had suddenly become possessed of a throbbing impulse to become American citizens. The rush for the first papers was such that the clerk of the Federal court ran out of application blanks. This surge of interest was caused by the new Federal income tax law which allowed no exemptions for aliens who had not filed their intentions to become American citizens.[66] Again, it is doubtful that more than a few went beyond the filing of the first papers.

Immigration Restrictions

The era of comparatively unrestricted immigration came to an end shortly after World War I. For years, organized labor had insisted that a check be placed on European immigration. Three presidents, Grover Cleveland, William Howard Taft, and Woodrow Wilson, vetoed laws setting up a literacy test for immigrants. Their reasons for blocking such legislation were substantially the same, that a literacy test merely showed whether the immigrant could read and write and not

[66] Hammond *Lake County Times,* October 13, 1913; March 17, 1919; Gary *Daily Tribune,* March 15, 1919.

whether he would be a desirable or undesirable addition to the American stock. The requirement of a literacy test became a law in 1917 when passed over Wilson's veto during the excitement and hysteria engendered by the war. The law required all over sixteen who were physically capable of reading to pass a test showing their ability to read English or some other language. This legislation was suspended a year later to admit much needed labor from Canada, Mexico, and the West Indies.[67]

The literacy test law, which had been designed to restrict immigration from eastern and southern Europe, apparently did not meet the expectations of those who feared that the United States would be flooded with immigrants from the devastated areas of Europe. The American Legion and the American Federation of Labor asked for more effective barriers against immigration. For the first time important numbers of American businessmen, fearing that immigrants might propagate the ideas of the Russian Revolution, took a stand for the restriction of immigration. In 1921 Congress passed an emergency law limiting annual European immigration to 3 per cent of the number of foreign born in the country in 1910. The quota basis was changed in 1924 to 2 per cent, the percentage to be computed on the census of 1890 instead of 1910. Obviously, this change was intended to favor immigration from the British Isles, northern and western Europe, and strike with special discriminatory force against the Italians, Hungarians, and Slavs from eastern and southern Europe. The same act provided that after July, 1927, the total number of immigrants who might be admitted in any one year was to be arbitrarily fixed at 150,000; the number to be ad-

[67] Sidney Kansas, *U. S. Immigration. Exclusion and Deportation and Citizenship of the United States of America* (New York, 1940), 6, 10-11.

mitted from any one country was to be apportioned in accordance with the contribution of that stock to the national population in 1920. Under this law, 127,266 immigrants from northern and western Europe and only 23,235 from eastern and southern Europe were to be admitted each year. Great Britain and Northern Ireland were allowed 65,721, while Poland was allotted 6,524, Czechoslovakia 2,874, and Yugoslavia only 845. The total number to be admitted was slightly increased in 1929.[68] As northern and western Europeans had little inclination to migrate, American industries turned to other quarters for their supply of laborers.

The Negroes Arrive

It may seem strange that Negroes who had complained since the Civil War of intolerable persecution in the South never made any great efforts to leave until offered economic advantages in the North. Unpleasant as conditions were in the South, the Negroes found it easier to live there than in the North. Trade unions regarded them as interlopers and strikebreakers, and industries preferred white immigrant labor as long as it was available. Few Negroes lived in the Calumet Region before World War I. Gary had 383 in 1910, which was more than there were in all the other cities of the area. Most of these were employed in the construction of the mills and in the building of the city of Gary. Porter County, because of its rural character, did not attract Negroes; the 1910 Census listed eight, while in 1920 only two were living in the county and none in Valparaiso. As late as 1930, Porter County had only 17 Negro residents.[69]

68 William S. Bernard (ed.), *American Immigration Policy* (New York, 1950), 18-19, 24-28; Wittke, *We Who Built America,* 516-17.
69 Carter G. Woodson, *The Negro in Our History* (Washington, D. C., 1931), 510; *Thirteenth Census* (1910): *Population,* pt. 2:561, 568;

The first wave of Negro migration occurred just before and during World War I. While discrimination on the part of the whites in the South was in part the reason for their exodus, it was not the dominant one. The most important factor was the opportunity for employment caused by the expansion of the industries in wartime, by the great number of enlistments in the armed services, and by the curtailment of European immigration by the war.[70] After years of discontent because of Jim Crowism and the denial of civil rights and adequate educational privileges in the South, the Negroes were ready and willing to migrate when the call came from the North.

The Negroes were not merely invited, they were sent for. Employment agencies and industries sent agents into the South to lure the Negroes with prospects of high wages, steady jobs, no race discrimination, better housing and schools, and, in some instances, free transportation and money for food along the way. The Chicago *Defender,* a Negro newspaper which circulated in the South, pictured in glowing terms the opportunities awaiting Negroes in the Chicago area. The *Defender* also maintained an employment agency for those seeking jobs. Letters from Negroes already on the scene influenced relatives and friends to follow their example. A Negro woman in East Chicago wrote of the marvels of the region to a friend in the South: "I have children in school every day with white children."[71] The prospect of good jobs and social equality were too attractive for many Southern Negroes to resist.

Fourteenth Census (1920): *Population,* pt. 3:294, 302; *Fifteenth Census* (1930): *Population,* 3: pt. 1:707.

[70] Edwin R. A. Seligman and Alvin Johnson (eds.), *Encyclopaedia of the Social Sciences* (15 vols. New York, 1930-34), 11:342.

[71] Edward Franklin Frazier, *The Negro Family in the United States* (Chicago, 1939), 293, 297.

Gary became the center of the region's Negro population. In September, 1916, at least three thousand were
reported in the steel city. By that time the news of
Negroes and their activities occupied prominent space in
the local newspapers. In 1917 the Gary *Daily Tribune,*
when referring to the construction of the Negro Baptist
Church at 21st and Washington, said the Negroes "are
to be a constantly growing factor in our industrial development and in our growth as a municipality." In
1920 Gary's Negro residents numbered 5,299, which was
9.6 per cent of her population. The steel company was the
heaviest employer of Negro labor, the number increasing
from 189 in 1915, which was 1.4 per cent of the total
number of employees, to 1,325 in 1919, or 8.83 per cent
of the plant's workers.[72] In 1920 East Chicago had 1,424
Negroes within its borders, which was 4 per cent of its
total population. In the same year, Hammond's Negro
population was only 137, an indication that they found
better opportunities in the heavy industries which were
largely concentrated in Gary and East Chicago. The
Negroes never gained a foothold in Whiting, there being
only three residing there in 1920.[73]

The number of Negro women to migrate to the region
was almost as large as that of the men. In 1930 Gary's
Negro population was composed of 9,393 males and
8,529 females, while the ratio in East Chicago was 2,724
males to 2,364 females. Of Gary's Negro population in
1920, 92.9 per cent were born in other states. In 1930

[72] Gary *Evening Post,* September 8, 1916; Gary *Daily Tribune,* September 18, 1917; *Fourteenth Census* (1920): *Population,* pt. 3:307; John
Foster Potts, A History of the Growth of the Negro Population of Gary,
Indiana (M.A. thesis, Cornell University, 1937, in Gary Public Library),
7. Potts obtained his employment figures from W. S. McNabb, superintendent of Industrial Relations at the Gary Works of the United
States Steel Corporation.

[73] *Fourteenth Census* (1920): *Population,* pt. 3:297, 299.

86 per cent of those in Gary who were not born in Indiana gave the southern states as their birthplace, about three fourths of them being from Alabama, Mississippi, Tennessee, Georgia, and Arkansas.[74]

The second wave of Negro migration came in the years immediately after World War I. The first phase of this movement occurred during the steel strike in 1919, when large numbers were brought in by the industries to take the places of workers then on strike. Negroes were extremely resistant to the overtures of unions at that early date, it being alleged that they were eager and willing to replace the workers then on strike. The number of Negroes employed at the Gary Works of the United States Steel Corporation increased during the labor crisis from 1,295 in 1918 to 2,060 in 1920.[75]

A momentary slackening in the Negro migration occurred during the business recession of 1920 and 1921, at which time the steel mills operated at between 40 and 50 per cent capacity. A large number of Negroes were thrown out of work. Their distress in East Chicago was such that public appeals were made for food and clothing and the police department opened a bread line in the city hall. Some Negroes were reported seeking funds to return to their old homes in the South.[76]

Increased industrial activity and the shutting off of European immigration by the Federal government brought another flood of Negroes to the region. By 1930 Gary's Negro population had increased to 17,922, which

[74] *Fifteenth Census* (1930): *Population,* 3: pt. 1:715; U. S. Department of Commerce, Bureau of the Census, *Negroes in the United States, 1920-1932* (Washington, D. C., 1935), 34-36.

[75] Potts, A History of the Growth of the Negro Population of Gary, 7, 31; William Z. Foster, *The Great Steel Strike and Its Lessons* (New York, 1920), 205.

[76] Hammond *Lake County Times,* February 1 and 7, 1921.

was 17.8 per cent of her total residents. In the same year East Chicago had 5,088 Negroes, which was about 10 per cent of her population. The Gary Works of the Steel Corporation was employing 3,181 Negroes in 1923, the largest number in any year before the depression. At that time almost 21 per cent of the plant's employees were Negroes. Also, in 1923 a Negro teacher in the Gary schools, who could see a railroad station from her building, saw as many as a hundred Negroes getting off the trains in one day. As was true in the earlier years, the Negroes showed a decided preference for Gary and East Chicago, there being only 623 in Hammond and none in Whiting in 1930.[77]

Segregation of the Negroes

The Negroes encountered racial barriers in the region almost as severe as those they had known in the South. If the Northern whites showed more respect for the legal and political rights of the Negroes than did the Southern whites, they were less inclined to tolerate intimate personal relations. The Northern whites professed an affection for the Negroes in a general or abstract way and yet gave evidence of being hostile toward them individually. As a result, the residential segregation imposed upon them was as rigid as that experienced in the South. Almost without exception, the Negroes were restricted to the more undesirable sections of each city. Gary Negroes largely supplanted the foreign born in what became known as the central district, formerly called the Patch. A subtle barrier was erected against them on the North Side and in Glen Park south of the Little Calumet River. The cleavage between the Negroes and the whites of East Chicago was just as sharp. They were crowded

77 *Fifteenth Census* (1930): *Population,* 3:pt. 1:715, 716, 717; Potts, *op. cit.,* 7, 8.

into that part of Indiana Harbor close to the steel mills, while the majority of the whites resided farther south, in Calumet, and on the West Side. The left arm of the Indiana Harbor Ship Canal was a boundary that the Negroes were unable to cross in their search for homes. Hammond's small Negro population was not solidified socially or economically. A small colony existed just north of the downtown business district, while the majority lived near the Standard Steel Car Company's plant in what was known as the Maywood district. Residential segregation was not difficult for the whites to impose upon the Negroes in any of the cities because only a few possessed the means to purchase their own homes.

Gary, no doubt because of its large Negro population, had more trouble with the problem of segregation than did the other cities. In 1913 Negroes were refused admission to the Art and to the Orpheum theaters. While such a ban prevailed for only a short time, efforts were made for some years by the theaters to seat the races separately. In 1916 the mayor, fearing a clash between Negroes and whites, forbade the showing of the motion picture "Birth of a Nation" in the city. He later changed his mind and the picture was shown without causing any trouble. The races did not mingle in the public parks and swimming pools. Riverside, later Gleason Park, was divided into two parts, one for Negroes and one for whites, equal recreational facilities being provided in each. A policeman was kept on duty there to keep the races separated. Negroes were denied access to Lakeside, now Marquette Park, the city's only recreational area on Lake Michigan. In 1926 Negro businessmen leased the Richard Much property on the Lake near Pine Station to give their people an opportunity to enjoy the beach.[78]

[78] Gary *Evening Post,* July 15, 1913, December 1, 1916; Taylor,

A degree of segregation also prevailed in the Gary Public Schools for some years. In 1908 the board of education rented a Negro church on Washington Street between 16th and 18th avenues for use as a school. A Negro teacher was employed to teach the twenty-five pupils enrolled at that time. Only the elementary grades were segregated at that early date, there being two Negroes in the high school. William A. Wirt, superintendent of the city's schools, was reported as saying: "We believe that it is only in justice to the Negro children that they be segregated. There is naturally a feeling between the Negroes and the whites in the lower grades and we believe the Negroes will be better cared for in their own schools. Besides they will take a pride in their work and will accomplish better results."[79] A portable building was erected when the Negroes objected to the use of the church structure as a school. A compromise was effected a few years later at the Froebel School whereby Negroes were admitted but were taught in separate classes by Negro teachers. When the great influx of Negroes from the South occurred, the school board for some years adhered to the policy of having the majority of the Negro pupils taught by instructors of their own race.[80]

In 1927 the most serious clash between the races occurred at the Emerson School. Although six Negro students were already enrolled at Emerson, nearly 1,200

Mexican Labor in the United States, Chicago, and the Calumet Region, 17; Potts, A History of the Growth of the Negro Population of Gary, 54; Hammond *Lake County Times,* May 13, 1926.

79 William A. Wirt, quoted in Gary *Weekly Tribune,* December 18, 1908.

80 Gary *Weekly Tribune,* January 8, 1909; Gary *Evening Post,* September 29, 1916. Four Negro teachers were reported in the Gary school system in 1918-19, sixteen in 1919-20, fifty-three in 1925-26, and eighty-four in 1931-32. Potts, A History of the Growth of the Negro Population of Gary, 12.

white students walked out in protest against the transfer of eighteen Negro pupils from the overcrowded Negro school on Virginia Street. The striking students chanted the slogan: "We won't go back until Emerson's white." Superintendent Wirt believed some of the parents were behind the walkout. He went on to say: "Segregation is impossible now . . . there can be no segregation of white and colored students in Emerson School this year, next year, and perhaps never." The Superintendent pointed out there had never been any trouble at the Froebel School, where eight hundred Negro students were enrolled. In some quarters, the Ku Klux Klan, which was active in the region at that time, was blamed for the strike. The walkout ended on September 30, four days after the trouble started, with a victory for the striking students who were given "excused absences" for the time they were away from classes. An agreement was also made that three Negro students, who were seniors and who had been in attendance at Emerson for three years, were to remain and graduate with their class. Three more seniors were transferred to Froebel and the other Negro students were to be cared for in a temporary school to be erected at 25th and Georgia, pending the construction of an "all Negro" school to cost six hundred thousand dollars.[81] This action led to the establishment in 1928 of the Roosevelt School, one of the largest Negro schools in the Middle West.

East Chicago, with a smaller Negro population, was more liberal in its handling of the race problem. Only

[81] Gary *Post-Tribune*, September 26, 27, 29, 1927; *The Congregationalist* (Whiting), October 27, 1927; Gary *Post-Tribune*, September 30, 1927. The magazine, *School and Society* (26 [July-December, 1927]: 453), reported the cost of the building as $1,000,000. The Negroes became a power in local politics, three being members of the Gary City Council from 1925 to 1929.

white students attended the schools on the West Side, there being no Negroes living in that part of the city. Segregation was not practiced in the Indiana Harbor section. In 1925 the Superintendent of East Chicago's schools made it clear that the city's schools were open to pupils of all races. In 1932 the Gary police forbade the playing of a baseball game in Marquette Park between teams sponsored by the American Legion posts of Gary and East Chicago because there were two Negroes on the East Chicago nine. The reason given for this action was that a rule of the Gary Park Board excluded Negroes from Marquette Park. The game was transferred to Washington Park in East Chicago.[82]

The concentration of Negroes in Hammond's Maywood district aroused the resentment of the Slavic and Hungarian residents, who considered the area their own. In 1929 tension approached the breaking point, a race riot being averted only by the quick action of the police who quelled a mob of about six hundred whites, armed with clubs, rocks, and other weapons, which was about to attack the Negro settlement. Hammond's Negro population was too small to be an issue in regard to segregation in the public schools.[83]

The Mexicans

The Mexicans were the last of the long succession of nationalities to arrive in the region. Most of them were unskilled workers of the peon class, with a high percentage of illiteracy.[84] While the Federal immigration quota laws did not apply to them, large numbers entered the United States illegally across the long and poorly guarded

82 East Chicago *Calumet News,* January 9, 1925; July 22, 1932.

83 Hammond *Lake County Times,* August 26, 1929.

84 Manuel Gamio, *Mexican Immigration to the United States. A Study of Human Migration and Adjustment* (Chicago, 1930), 71.

border. The Mexican's tendency to regard himself as a temporary resident of this country attracted the favorable attention of industrialists. According to Eugene G. Grace, president of the Bethlehem Steel Company, "the Mexicans assuredly fill the prescription of willingness to work hard, and return to their homeland when the need for them has passed."[85] What was also important, as workers they were found to be superior to many of the Europeans and Americans. Mexicans, it was said, were usually honest, trustworthy, steady, clean, and safe workmen who stood heat well. They were inclined to be less husky than other national groups, but this was not a handicap as the mechanization of the steel mills progressed.[86]

Mexicans were attracted to the region by the prospect of employment during World War I. The railroads, using them as track workers, were the first to bring them into the area in large numbers. As early as 1916, little colonies of Mexican laborers were to be found in the vicinity of the railroad yards. In 1923 more than 57 per cent of the employees of the Indiana Harbor Belt Line Railroad were Mexicans. By 1928 the number had soared to more than 64 per cent.[87] The Baltimore and Ohio Terminal Railroad and the Pennsylvania line were also large users of Mexican labor.

Employment of Mexicans in large numbers by the steel mills began in 1919 during the steel strike. The steel companies sent agents as far as Laredo and El Paso, Texas, to recruit workers, who were brought to the region in car and train-load lots. In 1920 about three thousand

[85] Eugene G. Grace, quoted in the Hammond *Lake County Times,* May 12, 1923.

[86] Taylor, *Mexican Labor in the United States, Chicago and the Calumet Region,* 17.

[87] *Ibid.,* 30.

were reported in East Chicago. The number of Mexicans employed by the Inland Steel Company increased from 90 in 1918 to 945 in 1919, which was more than 18 per cent of the workers in that plant. East Chicago became the center of the region's Mexican population, with Inland Steel in 1928 and 1929 being the greatest single employer of Mexican labor in the United States. In 1925, of Inland's 7,305 employees, 2,526 were Mexicans. In 1930 East Chicago had 5,343 Mexican inhabitants. The Gary mills also dipped into this reservoir of labor, nearly two thousand Mexicans being reported at work in 1923 at its various plants. In 1930 Gary's Mexican population was 3,486. The Mexicans were concentrated in the heavy steel industries, only 86 being reported in Hammond.[88]

A large number of Mexican workers were originally housed in bunkhouses and fed in cafeterias inside the various plants. Some of these bunkhouses were erected in 1919 during the steel strike. As the Mexicans became accustomed to the community, they generally preferred to live outside the plants where they were closer to friends and amusements. In 1928 Inland Steel was the only plant operating bunkhouses. The Mexicans found they could live more cheaply outside the plants. According to reports, board and room cost $1.50 a day in Inland's bunkhouses in 1928 while the Mexicans could live for as low as 90 cents a day on the outside. The Mexicans made a favorable impression on officials while living inside the plants. A foreman reported there were no vermin in their bunkhouses although vermin were found in those occupied by the whites. Also, the Mexicans, who wanted clean sheets twice a week, were the first to protest when the laundry was late and when there was no hot water.[89]

[88] Taylor, op. cit., 26, 36, 41, 182; Gary Daily Tribune, November 5, 1920; Fifteenth Census (1930): Population, 3:pt. 1:720; Gary Post-Tribune, May 24, 1923.

[89] Gary Post-Tribune, May 24, 1923; Taylor, op. cit., 183, 188.

The housing for Mexicans in Indiana Harbor was said to have been the poorest in the region. A large number lived in dark basements and in little shacks in the rear of larger houses which would have been condemned in many cities. Because of their common poverty, the Mexicans established their quarters on the same streets and often shared the same houses with the Negroes.[90] Also, as was the case with the Negroes, efforts were made by the whites to isolate and segregate the Mexicans. Two theaters in Indiana Harbor made a practice of seating the Mexicans separately. The Mexican consul in Chicago came to Indiana Harbor in 1924 to investigate the conditions among his countrymen. In 1928 an appeal for fair play by Mexico's ambassador had the effect of partially removing some of the social barriers against the Mexicans.[91]

The high proportion of young single men put a premium on the few Mexican women in the region which frequently led to fights over wives. Mexican men, believing that American-born girls wanted too much liberty, preferred brides from Mexico. Also, a large number of the first generation Mexicans regarded themselves as temporary expatriates and preferred to remain single as long as they were in the United States.[92]

Mexicans were the most reluctant of all the immigrant nationalities to become citizens of the United States. No matter what their feelings were about their homeland before they left, the Mexicans demonstrated an intense love of country after they came to the United States. A large number were convinced that naturalization would not improve their position here, that they would still be treated as Mexicans and foreigners. Also, their experiences with

[90] Hammond *Lake County Times,* April 15, 1924.
[91] Taylor, *op. cit.,* 234.
[92] Gamio, *Mexican Immigration to the United States,* 129.

social segregation and discrimination at the hands of native-born Americans caused citizenship to be less attractice to them. Mexican flags were displayed in most of their homes. In 1926 about 2,500 Mexicans participated in a colorful pageant and parade in Indiana Harbor in celebration of the anniversary of the winning of Mexico's Independence.[93] Some of the first generation of Mexicans were confused and disillusioned by conditions in American industries. Others watched in dismay the Americanization of their wives and children.

Such was the region's mixing bowl of races and nationalities. It was little short of remarkable that peasants, peons, and Negroes, accustomed as they were to rural simplicity, could adjust themselves so well to the complexities of urban and industrial life. Also, that European nationalities with a background of suspicion and conflict with each other in the Old World could live together in peace. The fact that whites and blacks could share a small and congested region without the troubles that occurred in other places was a tribute to the restraint and good nature of both races. Each race and nationality made its own contribution to the cultural and economic life of the region. Together they provided a color and flavor to each of the industrial cities. In 1929 an observer caught the color of Gary:[94]

Stand half an hour any day at the foreign money order window of the post office and watch the American dollars go flitting off to become rubles, marks, pesos, lire, kronen and all manner of

[93] In the year ending June 30, 1932, a total of 136,111 persons were naturalized in the United States, but of these only 248 were Mexicans. See Emory S. Bogardus, *The Mexican in the United States* (University of Southern California, School of Research Studies, No. 5, Los Angeles, 1934), 77-78; East Chicago *Calumet News,* September 17, 1926.

[94] Arthur Shumway, "Gary, Shrine of the Steel God," in *The American Parade* (Mishawaka), January, 1929.

foreign coins. Go to the south side and listen in vain for English speech in the coffee houses, the national centers and clubs. In the churches few sermons are in English. Up and down Broadway they go, all of them, to and from the Works. Carl Sandburg, poet of sweat and steel, in a verse about Gary, said of these men on Broadway: "They looked to me like men who had been somewhere."

"Hunkietown" is on the south side. It is where the distinctive flavor is to be found in Gary; it is where aliens and newly made Americans congregate in the national cluster. Here are the Serbs, here the Croats, there the Mexicans, there the Poles, and here, there and everywhere are the Negros, living much as they lived in the "bottoms" and "darktowns" of the South, save a few who lead in wealth and learning.

There is the living, breathing, sweating, drinking, cursing, laughing, singing Gary. This is the old world. Streets are narrow, houses of every type of shack, bungalow, and tenement; stores have exotic names and advertisements; cafes have distinct national airs, featuring tomales, ravioli, or whatever the favorite dish may be; national club houses display strange and interesting posters in their mysterious windows; coffee houses, those rendezvous of the Balkans, shelter gossiping, cardplaying men who read papers with L's and P's crazily inverted; churches even bearing Byzantine domes, hawkers shouting their wares in all versions of the bewildering jumble of tongues; children skip and run half-naked in the streets; mothers sing to dark babies strange, alien lullabies, remembered from European hearthsides—all this is Gary's real charm.

The same racial and national pattern existed in the Indiana Harbor section of East Chicago and was present on a somewhat lesser scale in Whiting and Hammond.

12

THE NEWSPAPER PRESS

THE FIRST NEWSPAPERS in the region were published in the county seat towns of Valparaiso and Crown Point. County seats were generally the oldest and largest communities in newly settled areas. Moreover, lawyers and county officials preferred to live in these towns because the political activities of the county were concentrated around the courthouse. Printing legal forms and documents for the county departments and for lawyers assured a publisher a more dependable income than he could expect from subscriptions, advertisements, and required public notices. Not all publishers had printer's ink in their veins nor did all establish newspapers with the intention of remaining in the profession permanently. The possession of a newspaper was an asset to those with political ambitions, and some were founded for the sole purpose of improving the owner's chances for election to public office. Also, it was a common practice to appoint editors to political sinecures such as postmasterships and as census takers. These factors caused the frequent transfer of some papers and the early death of others.

Early newspapers were usually printed on single sheets folded once, thus providing four pages, each carrying from four to six columns of type. The number of pages and columns increased or decreased as the paper prospered or declined. Advertisements usually occupied two or three columns on the front and back pages while articles of national and international interest, which the editor frequently borrowed from other newspapers, took up space on all pages. Local news, usually brief paragraphs about the comings and goings of local residents, occupied a column or two on the inside sections. The early newspapers were generally weekly affairs. Subscription rates, which varied from $1.00 to $2.00 a year, were sometimes higher if not paid in advance. It was not unusual for hard-pressed publishers to welcome payments in meat, fruit, and other foodstuffs. On one occasion the editor of the Crown Point *Register* was pleased when a customer settled long-standing arrears and also ordered a year's subscription in advance, the payment being made with potatoes.[1]

In 1836 or 1837 Solon Robinson published the first newspaper in the region at Lake Court House, later called Crown Point. Robinson owned a small press on which he printed handbills, legal notices, songs, and poems expressing his political and temperance views. Occasionally he published a newspaper variously known as the *Great Western* or *Western Ranger*. Robinson was particularly active in behalf of William Henry Harrison, the Whig candidate for the presidency in 1840, his campaign songs and poems being distributed to many newspapers in the state. He took his printing equipment to the Log Cabin Convention in honor of Harrison at the Tippecanoe Battleground, where he turned out songs and other literature for distribution to the crowd.[2]

The Valparaiso Press

Robinson sold the press and type in 1842 to James S. Castle of Valparaiso. Castle had brought a printing

---

[1] Crown Point *Register,* July 29, 1859, cited in "Old Time News" in Crown Point *Lake County Star,* October 14, 1901.

[2] Kellar (ed.), *Solon Robinson,* 1:19, 136-37.

press with him when he emigrated from Utica, New York, in 1835, and shortly after his arrival he began publication of the Michigan City *Gazette,* La Porte County's first newspaper. After a year or so the paper passed into other hands and Castle moved to Valparaiso where in 1842 he started the *Porter County Republican* with Robinson's press. This newspaper, a weekly, was independent in politics while under Castle's direction. At the end of two years, he sold the paper to William M. Harrison, who changed its name to the *Western Ranger* and made it a Democratic sheet. In 1847 William C. Talcott, a Free Soil Democrat, bought a half interest in the paper. Valparaiso's *Western Ranger* enjoyed unique distinction with abolitionist articles by Talcott and Democratic editorials by Harrison appearing on the same page. Talcott bought Harrison's interest in 1849, and the paper became the *Practical Observer.*[3]

In addition to the weekly edition, Talcott began publishing a triweekly edition in January, 1853, and a daily the following September. At that time the publisher claimed the *Practical Observer* was: "1. The largest paper in the State of Indiana; 2. That it was the largest paper in the world published in so small a town; 3. That it was the only semiweekly published either in so small a town, so sparse a county, or at so low a price." It continued to be an abolitionist paper until 1854, when Talcott joined the newly organized Republican party. In 1857 Robert A. Cameron purchased the *Practical Observer* and changed its name to the *Valparaiso Republican.* As such the paper was the official spokesman of the Republi-

3 Goodspeed and Blanchard (eds.), *Counties of Porter and Lake,* 67; Daniels, *La Porte County,* 244-45; Valparaiso *Vidette and Republic,* December 17, 1868. The major Valparaiso newspapers published since 1875 are in the county clerk's office at Valparaiso. A number of scattered issues before that date may also be found there.

can party in Porter County. In 1858 it passed into the hands of Thomas McConnell, William C. Talcott, and Henry W. Talcott. Cameron recovered control of the paper the following year and changed its name to *Valparaiso Republic;* he also discontinued the daily edition.[4]

With the coming of the Civil War, Cameron turned the paper over to Edward R. Beebee and joined the Union Army; as corresponding editor he sent home long spicy letters about his experiences in the war. Beebee was unable to finance the paper and in 1863 it reverted to Cameron and his wife Jane. She tried to carry it on with the help of Aaron Gurney as editor, but gave it up at the end of the year. During the next two years Valparaiso had no paper. Following Cameron's return from the war he revived the *Republic* in January, 1866. After a few months he sold it to G. A. Pierce who in turn sold it to Aaron Gurney, who had founded the *Porter County Vidette* the previous January. These papers were merged and issued as the *Vidette and Republic.* Pierce immediately founded a new paper the *Republican,* which was merged with the *Vidette and Republic* in July, 1868, under the joint ownership of Gurney and Pierce. In June, 1874, the ownership of the paper was transferred to William C. Talcott and his son, C. R. Talcott. In the meantime, the name had been changed to *Porter County Vidette.*[5]

Democratic papers had a difficult time in Porter County. The *Porter Democrat* was founded by a Mr. Berry

[4] Goodspeed and Blanchard (eds.), *Counties of Porter and Lake,* 68-69; Valparaiso *Vidette-Messenger,* August 16, 1936 (Centennial edition), Sec. 1, p. 10.

[5] Goodspeed and Blanchard (eds.), *Counties of Porter and Lake,* 69-70; Valparaiso *Vidette-Messenger,* August 16, 1936 (Centennial edition), Sec. 1, p. 10; Valparaiso *Republic,* January 4, 1866; *Vidette and Republic,* November 27, 1866; *Porter County Vidette,* June 10, 1869, and June 4, 1874.

in 1856, but after changing hands several times in the next four years it expired shortly after the election of 1860.[6]   C. C. Morricle established the *Valparaiso Democrat* in 1864 but it was discontinued after a few weeks for lack of patronage.[7]   Finally, in 1871 the German-born Englebert Zimmerman founded the *Messenger,* the first successful Democratic paper in the Calumet Region. He had formerly published newspapers in Columbia City, and was located at Upper Sandusky, Ohio, when Democratic leaders in Valparaiso persuaded him to move his equipment there.   Zimmerman was an unusually able journalist and under his guidance the *Messenger* became vigorous and prosperous. He supplemented his income by doing printing for the Northern Indiana Normal School, later Valparaiso University.   In 1881 Henry Baker Brown, principal of the Normal School, bought a half interest in the *Messenger* but held it only for a short time.   Englebert Zimmerman died in 1906, and his son Arthur F. was city editor and manager of the *Messenger* until his death in 1914.   The following year Hinman F. Strother of Pittsfield, Illinois, purchased the paper from the Zimmerman estate.   In 1924 Strother sold a half interest to Lynn M. Whipple of Niles, Michigan, who gained complete control of the organ the following year.[8]

In 1881 the Valparaiso *Herald* was started by P. O'Sullivan.   It was well edited and popular because of its full coverage of local news, but unable to survive on subscriptions alone, it stopped publication in two or three

6 Goodspeed and Blanchard (eds.), *Counties of Porter and Lake,* 70.   This was probably J. A. Berry, who later founded the *Lake County Jeffersonian.*

7 Valparaiso *Vidette and Republic,* December 17, 1868.

8 Goodspeed and Blanchard (eds.), *Counties of Porter and Lake,* 71; Valparaiso *Vidette-Messenger,* August 16, 1936 (Centennial edition), Sec. 1, p. 10.

years.[9] James A. McConahy founded the Valparaiso
Star in 1889, ran it as a daily for two years and then as a
weekly until 1898, when it was merged with the *Porter
County Vidette*. The paper was published as the *Star-
Vidette* until 1903, when John M. Mavity of Cambridge,
Illinois, bought it and dropped the *Star* from its name.
In 1927 the *Vidette* and the *Messenger* were merged and
issued as the *Vidette-Messenger*. In 1929 Lynn Whipple
bought the interests of the Mavitys, who retired from the
local newspaper field.[10]

The Chesterton Tribune

Chesterton was the only other town in the Porter
County part of the Calumet area to have a prosperous
newspaper. The Chesterton *Tribune,* published by W.
W. Mikels, was started on October 28, 1882.[11] During
the latter part of 1883 the paper passed into the hands of
a group of Chesterton businessmen headed by John T.
Taylor. In June, 1884, Arthur J. Bowser and Samuel
D. Watson purchased the *Tribune*. Bowser gained complete control of the paper in September, 1884, following
which he published and edited it for almost forty years. A
native of Valparaiso, Bowser had attended the Northern
Indiana Normal School and was one of the editors of the
Porter County Vidette before coming to Chesterton. An
able newspaperman, he made the Chesterton *Tribune* one
of the most widely read weeklies in the region. Bowser

9 Cutler, *History of Porter County,* 1:92-93.

10 *Ibid.*; Valparaiso *Vidette-Messenger,* August 16, 1936 (Centennial
edition), Sec. 1, p. 10.

11 There was a statement in the Chesterton *Tribune,* April 8, 1904,
that the paper was started in 1881 as an organ of the Greenback
party. No further evidence has been found that such was the case.
The first issue of the *Tribune,* October 28, 1882, was numbered Volume
I, Number 1. The complete files of the paper are in the office in
Chesterton.

kept a sharp eye on local and regional events which were faithfully reported to the *Tribune's* readers. The local news was fully covered in the columns, "Chesterton Chips" and "Porter Pointers," the latter containing news of Porter, Chesterton's sister community.

Although Chesterton and Porter were less than a mile apart, Bowser in July, 1894, demonstrated his faith in the latter's industrial potential by establishing the Porter *Tribune,* which he also edited. But Porter's subsequent development did not justify his hopes, and in April, 1896, Bowser combined his two papers into the *Westchester Tribune,* published at Chesterton. Through this step he hoped to provide better services for Chesterton, Porter, Baillytown, and Waverly, all in Westchester Township.[12] The name of the paper again became the Chesterton *Tribune* in November, 1897. In April, 1923, Bowser sold the paper to John G. Graessle, who had been his foreman for almost thirty years.[13] After Graessle's death in 1928 his widow sold the Chesterton *Tribune* to Warren R. Canright, a graduate of Lawrence College, at Appleton, Wisconsin, who had operated a printing company in North Chicago, Illinois, for three years after World War I. Canright was with the Chicago *Tribune* for five years before coming to Chesterton.[14]

[12] Chesterton *Tribune,* April 16, November 14, 1896; Valparaiso *Vidette-Messenger,* July 17, 1935; Porter *Tribune,* July 6, 1894.

[13] Arthur G. Bowser had too much printer's ink in his veins to remain out of the newspaper field. Early in 1934 he began to edit a column known as "Siftings—Gleaned from Hither and Yon and Now and Then—And Way Back When" for the Valparaiso *Vidette-Messenger.* This interesting column, which he continued until shortly before his death in July, 1935, was devoted largely to local history as recalled by himself and by contributors. See *Vidette-Messenger,* July 17, 1935.

[14] Chesterton *Tribune,* December 6, 1928.

Crown Point Newspapers

The Lake County portion of the region was without
a newspaper for fifteen years after Solon Robinson discontinued his little sheet in 1842. Lake's population apparently did not justify a journalistic endeavor in those
years, there being only 3,991 persons in the entire county
in 1850. Crown Point, a village of thirty-five dwellings
and three stores in 1849, was not incorporated as a town
until 1868.[15] The *Western Ranger,* later the *Practical
Observer,* of Valparaiso devoted space to news of Crown
Point and had a large circulation in that vicinity for several years. The success of the *Observer* in Lake County
convinced Janna S. Holton, John Wheeler, and Zerah F.
Summers, all related by marriage, that a local Republican
newspaper was needed at Crown Point. They invested
$300.00 in the purchase of a press and type and estab-
lished the *Lake County Herald* at the county seat in 1857.
Rodney Dunning, a Valparaiso newspaperman, was persuaded by a guarantee of subscriptions equivalent to
$300.00 a year to edit the paper. Dunning proved to be
a poor choice to guide the paper; at least its failure after
a few months was blamed on what was regarded as his
"shiftless unconcern." Wheeler and Summers purchased
Holton's interest in the *Herald's* equipment and founded
the Crown Point *Register* in August, 1857.[16]

The publishers of the Crown Point *Register* may well
be regarded as the fathers of Lake County journalism.
Wheeler was born in Connecticut and came to Crown
Point in 1847. The next few years he worked as a farm-

15 U. S. Bureau of the Census, *Seventh Census* (1850), 768; *The
Indiana Gazetteer,* 1849, p. 202.

16 Howat (ed.), *A Standard History of Lake County,* 1:246; Goodspeed and Blanchard (eds.), *Counties of Porter and Lake,* 440. The
first issue of the *Register* appeared August 4, 1857. Valparaiso *Republican,* August 11, 1857; Crown Point *Lake County Star,* January 4, 1901.

er in the summers and as a teacher in the winters. Wheeler learned surveying from his father in the Kankakee swamps and in 1853 was elected surveyor of Lake County. Summers, also a surveyor, had worked on the Cleveland and Toledo Railroad and came to Crown Point in 1854. He was Wheeler's assistant as county surveyor.[17]

The Crown Point *Register,* being the spokesman of the Republican party in Lake County, enjoyed a large circulation from the very beginning. Wheeler and Summers soon discovered, as did many publishers in the early period, that a successful journal needed subscribers who would pay cash in advance for the paper. At the end of the first year of the *Register's* existence they announced that $800.00 had been "trusted out" and that henceforth the credit system was to be abandoned.[18] John Wheeler's newspaper career ended in April, 1861, when he joined th Union Army. Summers, who was elected clerk of Lake County in 1859, evidently found the task of publishing a newspaper too arduous, and the *Register* was sold to B. D. Harper and A. E. Beattie in 1862.[19]

Meanwhile the Democrats had challenged the Republicans by establishing the *Lake County Jeffersonian* at Crown Point in January, 1860. The paper was owned by J. A. Berry and its first editor was B. D. Harper. The latter was soon succeeded by Joseph P. Smith. Smith's connection with the paper immediately brought favors from the Buchanan administration, and he became the local postmaster and was also made census taker for

[17] Ball, *Encyclopedia of Genealogy and Biography of Lake County,* 577-79; Howat (ed.), *op. cit.,* 1 :246.

[18] Crown Point *Register,* July 29, 1858, cited in "Old Time News," Crown Point *Lake County Star,* June 7, 1901. Most of the issues of the *Register* and the *Star* since 1881 are on microfilm in the Gary Public Library.

[19] Goodspeed and Blanchard (eds.), *Counties of Porter and Lake,* 441. John Wheeler was killed at the battle of Gettysburg, July 2, 1863.

Lake County in 1860. The strength demonstrated by the Republicans in the elections of 1860 was proof that a Democratic paper could not be published successfully at Crown Point, at least at that time. In April, 1861, the *Jeffersonian's* plant was sold to two tramp printers, Charles Alvord and one Desmond, who immediately sold it to a third party whose identity has never been discovered. Alvord and Desmond hurriedly left Crown Point owing the original proprietors of the paper $600.00 of the purchase price. The presses and type mysteriously disappeared one night from the old Chapman Hotel on the west side of the public square, where the paper had been printed; "not a track was left for a trail to show which way it had gone."[20]

The arrival of the first railroad in 1865 immediately increased the population of Crown Point and that part of the country through which it passed. The boom that followed was characterized by increased activity in the local newspaper field. Harper and Beattie published the Crown Point *Register* from 1862 to 1866, when Samuel E. Ball purchased Harper's interest. The following year Ball sold out to Frank S. Bedell, a veteran newspaperman formerly with the Dubuque (Iowa) *Daily Times* and the Detroit *Free Press*. Bedell became the *Register's* sole owner in 1869 but sold an interest in the paper to C. W. Ainsworth in 1875. H. M. Ingrim started the Crown Point *Herald* in 1872 to support Horace Greeley for the Presidency in that year's election. In October, 1872, Timothy Cleveland purchased the *Herald* but sold it to James J. Miller and John F. Rowins in November, 1873. Although the plant was immediately destroyed by fire, new equipment was installed and the Crown Point *Herald*

[20] Crown Point *Jeffersonian,* February 9, 1860 ff. and *Register,* April 4, 1861, cited in "Old Time News," *Lake County Star,* September 26, 1902 and November 17 and 24, 1911.

was continued. Miller bought Rowins' interest in January, 1875, and in December of that year sold the paper to Bedell and Ainsworth, who merged it with the Crown Point *Register.* The following year John J. Wheeler purchased Ainsworth's interest in the paper. In 1880 Wheeler disposed of his share of the *Register* to John Millikan.[21]

Millikan was one of the most experienced as well as one of the ablest of the editors at Crown Point in this period. He had been connected with the South Bend *Free Press* from 1837 to 1845, when he moved to La Porte and purchased the La Porte *Whig,* which became the La Porte *Union* in 1852. Millikan went to Plymouth, Indiana, in 1871 and bought the Plymouth *Republican.* He came to Crown Point in 1877 and established the Crown Point *Cosmos,* an unusually interesting paper. Much of the material in the *Cosmos* reportedly came from La Porte. Millikan discontinued the paper after three years to do active work on the Crown Point *Register.* In 1882 Millikan bought Bedell's interest in the *Register* and became its sole owner. The paper prospered under his guidance and was a strong influence in behalf of the Republican party in Lake County. In 1891 Millikan sold the Crown Point *Register* to Allison A. Bibler and retired from newspaper work. Bibler, who had worked on the Chesterton *Tribune* before coming to Crown Point, published the paper for seven years and then sold it to Charles J. Davidson. He recovered control of the Crown Point *Register* in 1914 and ran the paper until his death in 1941.[22]

[21] Crown Point *Register,* October 14, 1902; Goodspeed and Blanchard (eds.), *Counties of Porter and Lake,* 441-42; Cannon, Loring, and Robb (eds.), *History of the Lake and Calumet Region,* 1:372-74.

[22] Howat (ed.), *A Standard History of Lake County,* 1:248; Good-

The position of the Wheeler family as the first family of Crown Point journalism was largely due to John J. Wheeler, the able son of John Wheeler, one of the founders of the Crown Point *Register*. John J. Wheeler married Belle Holton, a granddaughter of Solon Robinson. His first journalistic effort was the publication of the *Young Hoosier* for about five months in 1875 at Crown Point. In October, 1880, Wheeler bought the Crown Point *Herald,* a Democratic paper founded in 1878, from John Griswold and began the publication of the *Lake County Star,* a Republican organ. From its very beginning, the *Star* was probably the strongest weekly in Lake County. In 1904 it was said to have the best equipment and the largest circulation of any paper in northwestern Indiana. John J. Wheeler died in 1917. The *Lake County Star* came under the control of his son, Fred Young Wheeler, who had been schooled in newspaper business by his father since he was seventeen years old.[23]

The Crown Point *Freie Presse* was one of the best edited and most influential of the German-language newspapers in the Calumet Region. It began in 1874 and was originally owned by John Lehmann, John H. Meyers, and John J. Wheeler. Lehmann, who was born in Switzerland, became sole owner of the paper after a short time and converted it into a Democratic organ. The *Freie Presse* had a large circulation among the Germans of the county, many of whom could not read English. In 1900 Henry Barck was editor of the paper.[24] No evi-

speed and Blanchard (eds.), *op. cit.,* 442; Ball, *Northwestern Indiana,* 534-35; Gary *Post-Tribune,* March 7, 1941.

23 Goodspeed and Blanchard (eds.), *op. cit.,* 442; Cannon, Loring, and Robb (eds.), *op. cit.,* 1:373; Ball, *Encyclopedia of Genealogy and Biography of Lake County,* 577-79.

24 Goodspeed and Blanchard (eds.), *Counties of Porter and Lake,* 443; Ball, *Northwestern Indiana,* 534.

dence was found to indicate when the *Freie Presse* was discontinued. Its demise was probably due to the little need for German-language newspapers among the descendants of German immigrants.

Hobart Newspapers

Hobart, one of the smaller communities in the area, was more than adequately served by newspapers in the early years. The Hobart *Journal,* founded by Paul J. Kelly in 1877, was the town's earliest newspaper. The *Journal* was absorbed by the Hammond *Western Indiana Tribune,* later the Hammond *Tribune,* when that paper was established in 1880. As the Hobart *Tribune,* a Republican paper, it was printed in Hammond and was issued as late as 1889. In 1882 Porter B. Towle, a brother of Marcus M. Towle, the founder of Hammond, started the Hobart *Transcript.* Towle published the *Transcript,* which was also printed in Hammond, for only a short time. The Hobart *Gazette* was founded in 1889 by George Narpass and George Bender. Andrew J. Smith purchased the paper in 1890 and two years later sold a half interest to Nevin B. White. Smith being a Democrat and White a Republican, the Hobart *Gazette* was published as an independent paper. The Hobart *News,* a Republican journal, was started in 1907 by A. A. Keelor. In 1912 the *News* came into the possession of A. L. Pattee.[25]

Newspapers in Hammond

Newspapers started slowly in Hammond. Most of the original settlers in that area were Germans. Their

[25] East Chicago *Journal,* October 15, 1889; Goodspeed and Blanchard (eds.), *op. cit.,* 443; Cannon, Loring, and Robb (eds.), *op. cit.,* 1:373-75; Hobart *Gazette,* Souvenir Supplement, May, 1898, p. 6.

numbers increased when the George H. Hammond Packing Company, established in 1869, showed a preference for German butchers and sausage-makers. Since a large number came directly from the old country and could not read English, German-language newspapers from Chicago and Milwaukee had a large circulation in the community. English-language papers did not do well there until the second generation of Germans matured and until native-born workers from near-by states found employment in the city's other industries. Crown Point and Hobart papers circulated in Hammond among people who had originated in those communities.[26] Hammond remained an unincorporated town until 1883, and the lack of political activity there until that time made the community a less attractive place for newspapers.

Porter B. Towle founded the *Western Indiana Tribune,* a Republican newspaper, at Hammond in December, 1880. In July, 1881, the paper was sold to Alfred A. Winslow, under whom it became the Hammond *Tribune.* The *Tribune* ran as a weekly until 1883 when Winslow started the first daily in Lake County. Winslow may rightfully be called the father of the English-language press in Hammond. The success of the Hammond *Tribune* was due largely to its support of Marcus M. Towle, mayor of Hammond from 1884 to 1888. The paper's mission was largely political and, according to one report, it "went strong during campaign years and slumped terribly between fights." Winslow sold the *Tribune* in 1893 to W. J. Maxwell when he entered the consular service of the United States.[27]

26 Hammond *Times* (centennial edition), June 17, 1951, p. 2C.
27 Hammond *Lake County Times,* July 21, 1906; Goodspeed and Blanchard (eds.), *Counties of Porter and Lake,* 443; Hammond *Times,* June 17, 1951, p. 2C; Chesterton *Tribune,* August 11, 1893. Winslow held posts in Belgium, Guatemala, Chile, New Zealand, South Africa,

The Hammond *Tribune* changed hands frequently after Winslow left the city. Thomas J. Hyman of Chicago bought the paper in 1894 and sold it to James G. and Henry Davidson of Whiting, who in turn disposed of it to Allison A. Bibler, the publisher of the Crown Point *Register*. Winslow returned to Hammond newspaper circles for a short time when he purchased the *Tribune* from Bibler in July, 1904. But in September, 1905, Winslow sold the paper back to Bibler, who immediately disposed of it to a syndicate headed by Ralph B. Bradford.[28]

James B. Woods, postmaster and also city clerk, founded the Hammond *Independent* in 1888 to support Thomas Hammond for mayor against the incumbent, Marcus M. Towle, in the election of that year. Hammond's victory apparently convinced Woods that the *Independent* had achieved its objective and the paper was discontinued. In 1890 Mr. and Mrs. Silas E. Swaim started the *Lake County News,* a Democratic paper, in Hammond. Swaim ranks with Winslow as one of the brightest figures in Hammond's journalistic history. The Democratic party's ability to compete on fairly equal terms with the Republicans in the city was largely due to Swaim's paper. In 1891 Swaim bought the Hammond *Standard,* which had been started as the Hammond *Echo* by Marcus M. Towle and Charles A. Cleveland in 1889 or 1890. This was a Republican paper which was published and edited by Cleveland and Elmer E. Ragon. Swaim merged the *Standard* with the *Lake County News* under the name of the Hammond *Daily News.* The

and Canada. Cannon, Loring, and Robb (eds.), *op. cit.,* 2:70, incorrectly gives 1896 as the date of the sale of the Hammond *Times* by Winslow to Maxwell.

28 Hammond *Lake County Times,* July 21, 1906; Chesterton *Tribune,* September 28, 1905.

reputation and influence of the *News* were enhanced when Percy A. Parry became its editor, but the paper suffered an almost crippling blow when Parry went to the *Lake County Times* in 1906.[29] The *News* was unable to compete successfully with its more wealthy rival, the *Lake County Times,* and was discontinued sometime in the early twenties.

In 1891 Armanis F. Knotts founded the *Calumet Journal,* a Populist newspaper, at Hammond.[30] This paper, edited by his brother, Thomas E. Knotts, was particularly active in the support of labor during the Pullman and railroad strikes in 1894. Thomas E. Knotts encouraged the strikers and their sympathizers to defy a Federal court injunction which ordered them to refrain from interfering with trains as they passed through Hammond to and from Chicago. He was arrested for contempt of court and taken to Indianapolis, where he was released on his own recognizance. Knotts was never brought to trial.[31] The *Calumet Journal* was discontinued shortly after the strike when Thomas E. Knotts joined the Hammond police force and Armanis F. Knotts became occupied with business and legal affairs.

Porter B. Towle, who had founded the *Western Indiana Tribune* in 1880, continued active in Hammond's newspaper circles. In 1891 he founded the Hammond *Leader,* a daily, and published it until 1899. In 1900 Towle was listed as the publisher of the Hammond *Daily Republican,* which was apparently the *Leader* under a new

[29] Howat (ed.), *A Standard History of Lake County,* 1:249-50, 2:827-28; Chesterton *Tribune,* January 22 and May 22, 1891; Hammond *Times,* June 17, 1951, p. 2C.

[30] Geros (ed.), *Hammond City Directory, 1891-1892,* 23; Armanis F. Knotts was mayor of Hammond from 1902 to 1904.

[31] Chicago *Tribune,* July 2, 1894; Cannon, "Tom Knotts As Mayor and Man," in Gary *Evening Post,* March 26, 1921.

name. This paper was still in existence in 1902, but how much longer is not known.[32]

In 1888 the *Deutsche Volks-Zeitung*, a German-language weekly newspaper, was started in Hammond. Wilhelm Schnett was listed as its publisher in 1900. The paper must have died during the next few years for it was not listed in the Hammond City Directory of 1911. The *Nord-Indiana Post*, also a German-language sheet, was started on August 29, 1914, which was the opening day of the Indiana State Convention of the German-American National Union in Hammond.[33]

The purchase of the Hammond *Tribune* in 1906 by Sidmon McHie, a wealthy Chicago grain and stock-broker, marked the beginning of a new era in the newspaper history of the region. Until that time most of the publishers in the area had been men of limited means and their papers, on the whole, led a hand-to-mouth existence. McHie possessed the business genius, energy, and capital to publish a newspaper on a scale never before attempted in the Calumet area. He had already demonstrated his confidence that Hammond was destined to be an important industrial city by building the Hammond Building, at Hohman and Fayette streets, and the Hammond grain elevator, and by making heavy investments in local real estate. The capitalist reasoned that a good newspaper was needed to advertise the city.[34]

32 Geros (ed.), *Hammond City Directory, 1891-1892*, 23; Chesterton *Tribune*, March 18, 1899; Ball, *Northwestern Indiana*, 534. The Hammond *Times* of June 17, 1951, published items from the Hammond *Daily Republican* issued the day after Knotts was inaugurated mayor of Hammond. He was elected in May, 1902, and probably took office shortly thereafter.

33 Oscar L. Bockstahler, "The German Press in Indiana," in *Indiana Magazine of History*, 48(1952):166; Ball, *Northwestern Indiana*, 534; Hammond *Lake County Times*, August 29, 1914.

34 Hammond *Times*, June 17, 1951, p. 2C.

McHie changed the name of the Hammond *Tribune* to the *Lake County Times,* a step which indicated that he did not intend to limit its circulation to Hammond alone. The first issue of the *Times,* a Republican paper, was published June 18, 1906. The proprietor brought his brothers into the publishing organization, William A. McHie as president and Richard A. McHie as secretary. Matthew P. Ludwig and Ralph B. Bradford, who had been connected with the old Hammond *Tribune,* were retained. Sidmon McHie persuaded Hugh E. Keough, a Chicago newspaperman, to edit the paper for a time. Percy A. Parry, as has already been noted, succeeded Keough as editor. Parry guided the paper for about thirty years. The Hammond *Tribune* had a daily circulation of only 137 when McHie bought it, while that of the *Lake County Times* immediately jumped to five thousand and within a short time a high-pressure campaign increased it to ten thousand, though most of its circulation was free.[35]

The McHies invaded Gary in June, 1906, a few weeks before that community was incorporated. An edition of the *Lake County Times,* called the Gary *Evening Times,* was compiled and edited in a tar-paper shack among Gary's sand hills by C. Oliver Holmes. Holmes, the first town clerk of Gary and a member of its first school board, had formerly lived in Hammond. The Gary *Evening Times* was printed in the *Lake County Times'* plant in Hammond. The publishers of the locally owned newspapers, particularly the *Northern Indianian,* a Democratic paper, resented this invasion of what they considered to be their private domain. The feud between

[35] *Ibid.* The complete files of the *Lake County Times* and of the *Times* are on microfilm at the Hammond Public Library. Keough was later famed for his column, "The Wake of the News," in the Chicago *Tribune.*

the McHies and the *Indianian* and its successor, the *Evening Post,* lasted while Thomas E. Knotts was president of the town board and mayor of Gary from 1906 to 1913. On more than one occasion, the *Evening Post* accused the McHies of being hostile to Knotts and to Gary in general. Such able newspapermen as Roy G. Parry, Alfred Jones, Elmer Ragon, and Leslie J. Parry edited the Gary *Evening Times.* This Gary edition of the *Lake County Times* was discontinued in August, 1933.[36]

The territory of the *Lake County Times* also included East Chicago, Whiting, and Calumet City, the latter just across the Illinois State Line from Hammond. For many years the McHies published the Calumet City *Times* and the Whiting *Times;* the edition devoted to the "Twin City," East Chicago and Indiana Harbor, bore the name *East Chicago—The Times—Indiana Harbor* on the front page. Each of these seemed to the uninitiated to be locally owned newspapers, but actually there was little difference in the various editions except for the name of the paper and some variation in local news. This arrangement apparently proved too expensive during the depression, and on August 28, 1933, the *Lake County Times* became the Hammond *Times.* As such, special editions were issued to the neighboring cities although there was little difference in any of them.

The competition provided by the *Lake County Times* discouraged the publication of daily papers in the near-by cities with the exception of Gary. Hammond's population was 64,560 and that of East Chicago was 54,784 in 1930.[37] It is doubtful whether any other city in the nation of East Chicago's size was without a locally

[36] Howat (ed.), *A Standard History of Lake County,* 1:252-53, 384; Gary *Evening Post,* September 29, 1911; Hammond *Times,* August 28, 1933.

[37] *Fifteenth Census* (1930) : *Population,* 3:pt. 1:700-1..

published daily at that time. The situation in regard to the newspapers, along with the fact that Hammond, East Chicago, Whiting, and Calumet City were all served by the same traction system, favored the retail merchants of Hammond and harmed those in the other cities. Since it cost a resident of East Chicago no more to go to Hammond than to the local business section, people were drawn to Hammond to shop by its merchants' advertisements in the *Lake County Times*. As a result, Hammond became a city of large department stores while small retail outlets predominated in East Chicago.

Whiting Journalism

Whiting was a fertile field for weekly newspapers in its early years. Although Whiting's population was small compared with neighboring cities, the community was from its inception the most prosperous and stable in the region. The Standard Oil Company's refinery, around which the city was built, provided steady employment for its workers in periods of depression as well as in boom times. The reading public of Whiting was unusually numerous for a city of its size because the refinery employed a larger proportion of skilled workers than did most industries.

Whiting's earliest newspaper was founded about a year after the construction of the refinery began. In November, 1890, David A. Holman, pastor of the Plymouth Congregational Church, started *The Congregationalist* for circulation among the members of his flock. The publication was so well received that Holman expanded its scope and in January, 1891, changed its name to the Whiting *News*. As such, it was the purveyor of local news and gossip. When ministerial duties called him elsewhere, Holman sold the paper to James G. Davidson, a young real estate dealer who intended to use it to advertise his business. The new publisher made a big splurge and printed ten thousand copies each week to circulate in a Whiting that then boasted less than three thousand people. The magnitude of these operations was such a drain on the young realtor's pocketbook that he sold the *News* to his brother, Henry S. Davidson, in June, 1891.[38]

The Whiting *Standard* was started in 1892 with Edwin S. Gilbert as publisher and Edward A. Gowe as editor, but after a short time it was sold to Henry S. Davidson, who merged it with the Whiting *News*, a Republican paper. Whiting was isolated for a time in 1894 by the Pullman and railroad strikes. The trains stopped running and with them the flow of food and other necessities into the community. Publisher Davidson's ingenuity was put to a test during this crisis. His supply of newsprint being exhausted, one issue of the Whiting *News* was printed on the back of ordinary wallpaper. Henry S. Davidson's interest in the *News* waned, and in 1895 he sold it back to his brother James G. From 1895 to 1900 the paper led an erratic existence, and it was said that if the editor had any other duty to perform on print day the paper simply did not appear. James G. Davidson had a talent for writing, and his pungent articles published under the name of "Pocahontas" were a popular feature of the *News*. In 1900 he sold the paper to Edwin S. Gilbert, a former East Chicago newspaperman who, as has been noted, had already showed an interest in Whiting's press. Then in 1904 Edwin H. Farr leased the paper, but a disagreement between him and Gilbert over its political policies led Farr to establish the Whiting *Call*, beginning

[38] Howat (ed.), *op. cit.*, 1:250; Whiting *Call* (souvenir edition), October, 1910. Most of the Whiting newspapers since 1892 are on file at the Whiting public library.

June, 1906. Gilbert soon discontinued the Whiting *News*.[39]

In 1894 U. G. Swartz, an employee of the Standard Oil Company, purchased modern equipment and founded the Whiting *Democrat*. Swartz, an able man, was prominent in Whiting's affairs for many years. His appointment as postmaster of Whiting and a subsequent promotion at the refinery made it necessary for him to dispose of the paper. On January 1, 1897, it was sold to William E. Ingham, an East Chicago journalist. Ingham named the paper the Whiting *Sun* and made it Republican in politics. Cecil Ingham became editor of the paper when his brother died in June, 1898. Four years later Brooks B. Bowman bought the *Sun* and published it until 1904, when he sold it to Frank S. Vance. Vance, whose wife was an excellent printer, published the paper with success and profit. Under his direction the *Sun* was known as the "Official Paper of the City." The *Sun* passed into the hands of William A. Hickey, a "Jeffersonian Democrat," in September, 1908, and he published it until the presidential election of that year. Toward the end of 1908 Edwin H. Farr bought the *Sun* and merged it with the Whiting *Call*. Farr published the paper as the Whiting *Call-Sun* for a few months in 1909 and then reverted to the original title, the Whiting *Call*.[40]

Farr had edited the *Farmer's Advocate* in Moline, New York, and had had many years of newspaper experience before coming to Whiting. He was among the ablest of Whiting's editors and under his direction the

39 Howat (ed.), *op. cit.*, 1:250-51; Whiting *News*, July 13, 1894; Whiting *Call* (souvenir edition), October, 1910; Whiting *Times* (historical edition) August 4, 1939, p. 44.

40 Whiting *Sun*, January 1, 1897; Whiting *Call*, August 6, 1909; (souvenir edition), October, 1910; Howat (ed.), *op. cit.*, 1:251; Whiting *Times* (historical edition), August 4, 1939, p. 14.

Call was a very interesting and widely-read weekly. The paper was strictly Republican except in 1912, when the editor supported the Progressive or "Bull Moose" ticket. In 1917 James J. Griffith, who had been foreman of the *Twin City Sentinel* in East Chicago from 1912 to 1915, became part owner of the Whiting *Call*. Griffith's journalistic career was interrupted by service in the army during World War I. In 1920 the owners of the Ben Franklin Press, a successful job printing firm, took over the Whiting *Call*. The paper was converted into a daily in 1926 with James J. Griffith as editor, and its name was changed to the Whiting *Daily Times*. It took only a year to convince the publishers that Whiting was not the place for a daily paper and the *Times* reverted to its weekly status. Late in 1926 Griffith became the sole owner of the Ben Franklin Press. The newspaper was published for a time as the *Ben Franklin News* and then under its former name of the Whiting *Times*.[41]

The East Chicago Press

There were fewer newspapers in East Chicago than in any other of the larger cities of the region. Its first, the East Chicago *Journal,* owned and published by Joseph Hirsch, appeared on March 30, 1889, about a month before the young community was incorporated as a town. The paper was apparently printed in Hammond. Hirsch published the *Journal* until October, 1889, when he sold it to the Calumet Printing and Publishing Company of Hammond, the reputed owner of the Hammond *Tribune* and the Hobart *Tribune*.[42] No record was found that the *Journal* was published after Hirsch disposed of it.

41 Whiting *Times* (historical edition), August 4, 1939, p. 46.

42 East Chicago *Journal,* October 15, 1889. The issues of the *Journal* are in the East Chicago Public Library.

In 1891 Edwin S. Gilbert founded the East Chicago *Globe,* the first newspaper to be printed in the town itself. Gilbert published the paper until August, 1899, when it was purchased by Allison P. Brown. Brown, one of the city's ablest journalists, edited the *Globe* for about thirty-five years; during all that time the paper remained a weekly and in politics was generally Republican. As was noted earlier, Edwin S. Gilbert purchased the Whiting *News* in 1900. From that year until about 1904, he published at his Whiting plant an edition known as the Indiana Harbor *News.* Gilbert's newspaper work brought about his appointment as the first postmaster of Indiana Harbor in 1902.[43]

The development of the Indiana Harbor section of East Chicago dates from 1901, when the Inland Steel Company began to build its plant along the shore of Lake Michigan. The *Lake County Directory, 1909,* reported the existence of the *Harbor Sentinel,* established in 1902 and edited by William W. Moberly. This was probably the first paper published and printed in that part of East Chicago. Evidence is lacking to indicate how long Moberly conducted the *Harbor Sentinel.* By 1913 the *Twin City Sentinel,* published by Harry M. Dill, was being circulated in East Chicago, probably as the successor of Moberly's paper. Dill also had the agency for the circulation locally of Chicago newspapers. Subsequently, Dill sold the newspaper agency and also the *Twin City Sentinel* to Joseph J. Freeman and his wife, Marion H. Freeman.[44]

[43] Ball, *Encyclopedia of Genealogy and Biography of Lake County,* 542-43; Kennedy, "Facts Concerning East Chicago," in Demmon (ed.), *History of Lake County* (1934), 95.

[44] *Lake County Directory,* 1909, p. 412. Marion H. Freeman, Wheaton, Illinois, to the author, July 15, 1955. Mrs. Freeman placed the date of their purchase of the *Twin City Sentinel* as about 1910, but evidence

Mrs. Freeman had the most distinguished career of any of the newspaper women in the region. Joseph J. Freeman, said to have been an excellent reporter, was more interested in the advertising and business sides of newspaper work. Mrs. Freeman's association with the Calumet Region began in 1906 when she joined the staff of the newly established *Lake County Times,* now the Hammond *Times,* as an associate editor in the editorial department. In 1907 her husband took charge of the East Chicago and Indiana Harbor edition of the *Lake County Times.* Next year the Freemans moved from Chicago to East Chicago. The equipment of the *Twin City Sentinel* was meager and antiquated when the Freemans bought it. Gradually over a period of years, they purchased the most modern linotype machines, presses, and eventually a stereotyping outfit.[45] Their plant came to be one of the best printing establishments in Lake County.

Because East Chicago lacked a locally published daily paper, prominent citizens began to urge the Freemans to issue a daily edition of the *Sentinel.* They were opposed to such a step, pointing out that a large segment of the city's population was foreign born who could not or would not read an English language newspaper.[46] As the muni-

indicates that it occurred during or shortly after 1913. Mrs. Freeman was 86 years old at the time she wrote the above letter. Joseph J. Freeman died in 1945.

[45] Mrs. Freeman began her newspaper career as a reporter for the City Press Association, now the City News Bureau, in Chicago during the World's Columbian Exposition, 1893. She was also employed by the Chicago *Inter-Ocean* and by the Chicago *Tribune* before coming to Hammond. Joseph J. Freeman's first newspaper work was with the Topeka (Kansas) *Capital.* Marion H. Freeman to the author, July 15, 1955; E. Palma Beaudette, *East Chicago-Indiana Harbor. Twin Cities of Indiana. Political . . . Historical . . . Industrial Sketch* (Chicago, 1913), 49; Hammond *Times,* June 17, 1951.

[46] As noted above, East Chicago's foreign born constituted 53 per cent of its population in 1910 and 40 per cent in 1920. See page 251.

cipal elections of 1921 approached, increased pressure was brought to bear on the Freemans to make the *Sentinel* a daily. Since the *Lake County Times* in Hammond had indicated at an early date its intention to support the Independent party, Republican leaders felt desperately the need of a daily paper. They turned to the Freemans for such a paper, promising unlimited moral and financial support if they would convert their paper to a daily. Sincere in their belief that the Republicans had the best candidate for mayor and encouraged by such efforts of support, the Freemans began to issue the *Sentinel* as a daily a few months before the election.[47]

The ensuing campaign was probably the most bitter in the city's history. Friendships were broken because of the invectives and insults hurled at each other by the candidates for mayor. The *Lake County Times* and the *Twin City Sentinel* "pulled all the stops" in their support of their respective candidates. On election day Governor Warren T. McCray had the Gary unit of the state militia ready to move into the city in case local authorities were unable to maintain law and order.[48] The Independent party was victorious in the election. In the course of the excitement that occurred when the results were known, a number of the more exuberant supporters of the winning ticket decided to celebrate their victory by wrecking the Sentinel's plant. Mrs. Freeman described what followed:[49]

[47] Marion H. Freeman to the author, July 15, 1955.

[48] Hammond *Lake County Times,* November 8, 1921.

[49] Marion H. Freeman to the author, July 15, 1955. The Gary *Evening Post and Daily Tribune,* November 9, 1921, reported that the presses were started and pieces of scrap iron were tossed into the machinery. This was taken as evidence that at least one of the vandals knew how to start the presses. Also see Hammond *Lake County Times,* November 9, 1921, for an account of the destruction of the plant.

On election night, fearing that the rowdy element roistering about might throw a rock through one of our front windows or otherwise damage our property in our absence if the shop was closed down at the usual hour, my husband and I decided to remain within until things quieted down, regardless of which side won, never dreaming however of what was really in store. Before midnight it was evident that Callahan was the victor but the shouting was in full swing until long past that hour and we stayed on until 3 a.m. A taxi stopped across the street and believing it to be the one we had ordered, Joe locked the door and we started across. But just as we reached it, it pulled out, the driver muttering: "No more fares tonight." We stood there expecting our own taxi momentarily. While we waited, another car, not however the taxi, drove up and stopped in front of the shop. A number of men piled out of it at once, but immediately piled in again, one of them remarking loudly as he glanced our way: "This isn't the place, it's a block down." Joe thought he recognized the car but in the dim light that filtered through the window it was impossible to recognize the faces of the passengers. As it drove off our taxi appeared from the opposite direction, stopped to pick us up, and we were driven to our home.

In view of what happened shortly afterwards we later became convinced that the car we had been watching contained the men responsible for the wrecking of our plant. Our belief was confirmed later. We learned that the same car returned very shortly after we took our departure, and its occupants went into action. Albert, the porter, an old derelict who slept on the premises had been a witness to everything. He related that shortly after 3 o'clock hearing a racket he rose from his bed which was at the back of the shop and ran out to see what was doing. He encountered six or eight well-dressed men wearing masks who after threatening him with revolvers into silence went to work on the machinery. They smashed and hacked at everything in sight, not only the presses and linotype machines but the furniture, telegraph instruments, typewriters and even an umbrella had been attacked with sledge hammers and other damage-dealing implements . . . It was not long before Joe learned the identity of those who participated in the raid; and I knew from him at the time who they were. But at this late date I have forgotten most of them and of those I do recall hazily I have forgotten the first names, or their initials.

The damage done to the plant was estimated at $25,-000.00. Editorially, the leading newspapers in the area denounced those involved in the vandalism. The *Gary Evening Post & Daily Tribune* called it "as dastardly a deed as has been committed in Lake County in many years." Hammond's *Lake County Times,* which supported the victors in the recent campaign, demanded that "the guilty be brought to bay so that the courts may have an opportunity to deal with those responsible for such a shameful deed." "The perpetrators [should] be punished no matter who they are." According to Mrs. Freeman, the wreckers were not ordinary goons or hoodlums, but well-to-do men of reasonably good standing in the community.[50]

Such was the end of the *Twin City Sentinel* and of the efforts of the Freemans to publish a newspaper in East Chicago. Not one of the Republican leaders who had joined in the hue and cry for a daily newspaper and who had lavishly pledged both capital and influence to make it a success came forward to redeem his promises. After a brief and futile effort to revive the paper, the Freemans saw it pass into bankruptcy. Mrs. Freeman was employed about a year by the Gary *Post-Tribune* during the course of an effort by that paper to publish an East Chicago edition. The project was curtailed because of the lack of local advertising. Later she worked on the staff of the Chicago *Daily Journal* from 1925 to 1931 and conducted a column on the woman's page of the Chicago *Daily News* from 1931 to 1934.[51]

[50] Gary *Evening Post and Daily Tribune,* November 9 and 10, 1921; Hammond *Lake County Times,* November 11, 1921; Marion H. Freeman to the author, July 15, 1955.

[51] Marion H. Freeman to the author, July 15, 1955. Joseph Freeman did free lance writing for a short time after the destruction of the plant but soon retired because of ill health. Mrs. Freeman covered

George Huish, who had been associated with the *Twin City Sentinel,* purchased the remains of the Freeman plant from the receiver and founded the *Calumet News* in 1923.[52] A capable and aggressive newspaperman, Huish soon had the newspaper on a paying basis. In November, 1923, the *News* was converted from a weekly to a bi-weekly, issued on Tuesdays and Thursdays. Alfred G. Parry, one of the ablest journalists in the region, was installed as editor. In 1926 John De Jong became city editor. While Huish was a Republican, the *News* was more often independent than partisan in local political affairs. The paper weathered the depression years, although it was forced to revert to a weekly in January, 1933. The *Calumet News* and the East Chicago *Globe* were the only newspapers in East Chicago at that time.

Gary Newspapers

The *Calumet Advance,* founded by Louis A. Bryan in 1896, was the earliest newspaper on the site of Gary. In that year Bryan, a Chicago lawyer and real estate dealer, acquired a large acreage between the Wabash tracks and the Little Calumet River and laid out the town of Calumet. He started the weekly *Calumet Advance* to publicize the community and to promote the sale of lots. The *Advance* was issued until 1907.[53]

The region where Gary now stands was virtually a

the Loeb-Leopold trial in 1925 for the Chicago *Daily Journal.* Her last newspaper assignment was in 1947 when, at 77 years of age, she began a two-year period on the Richland (Washington) *Villager.*

[52] Statement of George Huish to the author, East Chicago, June 12, 1955. The issues of the *Calumet News* are in the newspaper office in East Chicago; those from 1926 to the present are on file at the East Chicago Public Library.

[53] Horace S. Norton, "Reminiscences," in Biographical Sketches of Gary and Lake County Residents (scrapbooks in Gary Public Library), Vol. 7; Howat (ed.), *A Standard History of Lake County,* 2:475-79.

wilderness of sand ridges, sloughs, and scrub oak until 1906, when the United States Steel Corporation began the construction of its great mills along the shore of Lake Michigan there. In July, 1906, the town of Gary was incorporated. On May 10 the Chesterton *Tribune* announced the publication of the *Northern Indianian,* a Democratic weekly, in the embryo steel city. The paper was published by J. O. Benthal and edited by Thomas F. Costello, Chicago newspapermen. Its early issues were printed in Indiana Harbor. A few months later the offices and equipment of the *Indianian* were located in the Knotts Building at Seventh and Broadway. The paper was a staunch supporter of Armanis F. Knotts, the first manager of the Gary Land Company, and also of his brother, Thomas E. Knotts, president of the town board and later mayor of the city. The Knotts brothers, backed by the *Northern Indianian,* frequently challenged the power of the Steel Company in the management of Gary's affairs. While Armanis F. Knotts denied that he had any connection with the paper, he and his brother encouraged and favored it in various ways.[54]

The *Northern Indianian's* failure within three years of its establishment was apparently caused by a combination of circumstances. The Steel Company, which supplied the young community with electricity, gas, and water, also sought the franchise to build and operate the street railway system, but the town board, largely through the influence of Thomas E. Knotts, granted the concession to the privately owned Gary and Interurban Traction Company. When the *Northern Indianian* went out of business, the claim was made that its demise was due to the failure of the Gary and Interurban Railway Company to keep its

[54] Chesterton *Tribune,* May 10, 1906. Most of the issues of the *Northern Indianian* are on microfilm in the Gary Public Library.

promise to pay for the presses and other equipment of the paper, but no proof was ever offered that such was the case. Other factors apparently affected the fortunes of the *Indianian*. For instance, Costello's aggressive and vitriolic editorials were resented by the steel company's officials and also by the conservative segment of Gary's citizens. The editor's favorite target was Horace S. Norton, the steel company's most prominent official at that time, whom he persistently called "Turkey Neck." Norton was the founder and president of the Gary Commercial Club, an association of merchants and professional men, which functioned as a sort of chamber of commerce. A study showed that the leading merchants favored the Gary *Daily Tribune* for advertising while the *Northern Indian* depended upon the uncertain support of small scale realtors. This situation may have been due to Norton's influence. Costello's associate Benthal was thought to be a Socialist and such a rumor may have been a liability to the paper. The *Northern Indian* closed its doors in March, 1909. Costello left a bewildered foreman in charge of the offices and equipment and returned to Chicago. The paper's creditors petitioned the circuit court to determine its ownership. There were rumors that Thomas E. Knotts would assume control of the establishment when the matter was settled in the courts.[55] When that time came, Knotts and his brother, Armanis F., did buy the equipment and began the publication of the Gary *Evening Post*.

The founding of the Gary *Weekly Tribune* in June, 1907, by Homer J. Carr and George R. Scott was a notable event in Gary's journalistic history. Carr was editor and Scott was in charge of its business office. Both were

---

55 Gary *Weekly Tribune,* March 12, August 16, 1909; Erwin C. Rosenau in Gary *Post-Tribune,* August 6, 1947; Cannon, Autobiography of Tom Cannon, Chap. 50, p. 3.

veteran newspapermen who had worked together in Chicago for some years. Carr was marine correspondent for the Chicago *Tribune* when he came to Gary. Because Carr had long been connected with the Chicago *Tribune,* he and Scott apparently chose the name of the Gary *Weekly Tribune* for the new journal. The office of the paper was first located in a rude shack on what was then Euclid Avenue, just west of Broadway. Later it was moved across Broadway to where the Union Railway Station now stands. For some months the local news and advertisements were collected by Mark Goodnow and Fred Carr and mailed to Chicago, where the editor and business manager had the type set and the papers printed. They were then sent back to Gary for distribution on Saturday mornings. This procedure was followed until the spring of 1908, when Carr and Scott built a plant at 670 Broadway and installed modern equipment. By 1912 the paper had outgrown its quarters and moved to its second home at Fifth and Washington.[56] On Labor Day, September 7, 1908, the *Tribune* became a daily, the first to be printed in Gary, though the weekly edition was continued for several years. Carl O. Dennewitz, another prominent figure in the city's newspaper circles, joined the staff of the *Weekly Tribune* as a cub reporter. He later became managing editor of the Gary *Daily Tribune* and remained in that position until he joined the army in 1917.[57]

[56] Howat (ed.), *A Standard History of Lake County,* 2:850-51; Cannon, Loring, and Robb (eds.), *History of the Lake and Calumet Region,* 1:375-77; Gary *Daily Tribune,* June 21, 1912. The complete files of the weekly and daily *Tribune* are on microfilm in the Gary Public Library.

[57] Dennewitz was a foreign correspondent after World War I for the New York *Tribune* (now the *Herald-Tribune*), and the New York *Times.* He was an editorial and advertising executive of the Crowell Publishing Company at the time of his death in 1934. See Gary *Post-Tribune,* November 3, 1934.

Carr and Scott were Republicans and, except for the election of 1912 when they supported the "Bull Moose" ticket, their papers were the partisan spokesmen for the Republican party in national and local politics. The *Tribune* papers were also the spokesmen of the United States Steel Corporation in civic affairs, Carr being an intimate friend of William P. Gleason, superintendent of the Steel Works. Nevertheless, a few Democrats were connected with the *Tribune* papers. Arthur P. Melton, city engineer in the Democratic administration of Mayor Thomas E. Knotts, was reported in 1909 to be one of their stockholders, and Dennewitz was the Democratic candidate for city clerk in the election of 1913.[58]

The great real estate boom, which provided profitable advertising coupled with the unsettled state of political affairs during Gary's early years, attracted other newspapers to the city. The Gary *Daily News,* edited by Carl J. Cooper and Alfred Jones, was started in November, 1907. This paper, printed in Chicago, was reportedly owned by the Daily News Publishing Company of that city. The *News* ended its short career on a sour note. A subscription drive was launched in December, 1908, with a piano as the grand prize. Several of the town's most prominent young ladies entered the contest, and numerous people were persuaded to pay for subscriptions six years in advance, but the paper failed in March, 1909. The subscribers lost their money and the winner of the contest never saw the piano.[59] Next came the *Lake County Democrat* in August, 1909, to oppose Thomas E. Knotts for mayor in the city elections of that year. Alfred Jones was one of its editors, and John F. Dorman was one of

[58] Gary *Weekly Tribune,* November 10, 1909; Gary *Evening Post,* June 13, 1913.

[59] Cannon, Autobiography, Chap. 50, p. 5; Gary *Weekly Tribune,* March 26, 1909.

its founders. The success of Knotts in the election caused
the demise of the paper early in 1910.[60]

In October, 1909, Gary became a city of the fifth class.
Thomas E. Knotts, president of the town board since
1906, was eager to be the city's first mayor. A strong
and controversial figure, he was opposed not only by the
Republicans but also by an insurgent faction in the Democratic party. Since the *Northern Indianian* had closed
its doors in March, 1909, none of the papers in Gary
were friendly to him. Both the Gary *Daily Tribune*
and the Gary *Evening Times,* the latter an edition of the
Lake County Times of Hammond, supported John A.
Brennan, the Republican candidate. The *Lake County
Democrat,* as has been noted, was founded to prevent
Knotts from getting the Democratic nomination. Therefore, in August, 1909, Knotts and his brother Armanis
bought the equipment of the defunct *Northern Indianian*
at a mortgage sale and established the Gary *Evening
Post.*[61] The new paper, a daily, occupied the old quarters
of the *Northern Indianian* in the basement and a portion
of the second floor of the Knotts Building at Seventh and
Broadway.

Thomas H. Cannon and Frank Patrick, veteran Chicago newspapermen, were engaged to run the *Post.*
Patrick was the publisher and business manager while
Cannon wrote the editorials and worked as a reporter.
A. Howard Bell, later auditor of the Gary Public Schools,
was installed as circulation manager. Thomas E. Knotts's
instructions to the staff of the *Post* in regard to the forth-
coming campaign were brief and to the point: "Make it
hot. Give 'em hell."[62] The first issue of the *Post* ap-

[60] Gary *Weekly Tribune,* August 6, 1909; Cannon, Autobiography,
Chap. 50, p. 5.

[61] Gary *Weekly Tribune,* August 6, 1909.

[62] Cannon, "Tom Knotts As Mayor and Man," in Gary *Evening*

peared on October 2, 1909, about a month before the election. After Knotts had been elected mayor, his interest in the *Post* waned immediately, and Cannon and Patrick were left with a white elephant. They organized a stock company with a proposed capital of $15,000.00 but could find few purchasers in the lull that followed the election. In later years Cannon recalled their troubles: "We were living at the Victoria Hotel. The proprietor could have testified to the insolvency of the paper. Nevertheless, we kept the *Post* alive until January, 1910, when two young men from Ohio dropped into town. They were J. Ralph Snyder and his brother H. B. [Henry Burgess] Snyder." The brothers were the sons of Henry Richard Snyder, a prominent Ohio newspaperman, and both were well launched on newspaper careers of their own, the former as manager of the Marion *Mirror* and the latter as publisher of the Urbana *Citizen*.[63]

There was good reason for the Snyders to be impressed with the opportunities in the young steel city. Its population had risen to almost 17,000 in 1910. Already there were 4,204 employees in the works of the Steel Corporation and the construction of that large plant continued. The erection of the American Bridge Company's plant had been started in 1909 and that of the American Sheet and Tube Company began in 1910. Both were important subsidiaries of the United States Steel Corporation. The Gary Screw and Bolt Company's plant, an independent, was also begun in 1910. These industries rapidly increased Gary's population in the next few years, and there were indications that other companies intended to seek sites in the city.[64]

Post, March 26, 1921. The complete files of the *Post* are on microfilm in the Gary Public Library.

[63] Cannon, Autobiography, Chap. 50, p. 3; interview with Henry Burgess Snyder, June 14, 1955.

[64] *Thirteenth Census* (1910) : *Population,* pt. 2:568, Employment statis-

In March, 1910, the Snyder brothers purchased controlling interest in the *Post* with capital obtained from the sale of the Urbana *Citizen*. Thomas E. Knotts retained a small interest in the paper until about 1916, when the Snyders bought his share. The brothers gained full ownership by buying the few shares of stock held by others, mainly saloonkeepers.[65] The new officers of the Gary *Evening Post* were Thomas E. Knotts, president, Henry Burgess Snyder, editor, and J. Ralph Snyder, business manager. The Snyders announced that the *Post* would be a Democratic paper and its editorial policy would be along the lines of true democracy. Thomas H. Cannon remained on the staff as an editor and reporter. Henry Richard Snyder joined his sons in 1912 and was associate editor of the Gary *Evening Post* and later of the Gary *Post-Tribune* until his death in 1925. A third son, Herbert R. Snyder, came to Gary in 1913 to become advertising manager of the paper. The equipment of the *Post* was antiquated and in poor condition when the Snyders purchased it, but they moved to a new site on west Fifth Avenue between Washington and Adams and installed modern equipment. For the first time since its birth the *Evening Post* began to look like a real newspaper. In 1913 it moved to a new home on the north side of Fifth Avenue between Broadway and Washington, where it remained until its merger with the Gary *Daily Tribune* in 1921.[66]

tics provided by John H. Vohr, superintendent of the Gary Steel Works, United States Steel Corporation, October 21, 1954. Gary's population was 55,378 in 1920 and 100,426 in 1930. *Fifteenth Census* (1930) : *Population,* 3 :pt. 1 :715.

[65] Interview with Henry Burgess Snyder, June 14, 1955. According to Snyder, their original investment in the Gary *Evening Post* was about $8,000.00.

[66] Gary *Evening Post,* March 10, 1910; Cannon, Autobiography, Chap. 50, p. 3.

From 1910 to 1921 the Gary *Evening Post* and the Gary *Daily Tribune* were the city's leading newspapers and also antagonists in the political arena. The Snyders backed Thomas E. Knotts in his futile bid for another term as mayor of Gary in 1913. The day following the election the *Post* announced that henceforth it would be a free lance in public matters, yet for some years the Snyders showed a tendency to support the Democratic party. In 1915 Henry Burgess Snyder was appointed postmaster of Gary by President Wilson and held that position until late in 1920. The *Post* urged the United States to join the League of Nations after World War I and was a consistent advocate of closer co-operation between the United States and other nations of the world. It also agreed with the Democrats that the tariff should be kept at a low level, while it went down the line in support of the Democratic tickets, both national and local, in the elections of 1920.[67]

The Snyders again announced in January, 1921, that in the future their paper would be independent in politics. They denied that the decision to retire as spokesmen for a particular party was due to any political disappointments. The Gary *Evening Post,* they said, had been Democratic because it believed in the principles of Woodrow Wilson. It would support the Democratic party in the future whenever that party stood for the interests of men, women, and children everywhere. But the political situation was different in the state, county, and city, particularly in the last two. These, the announcement continued, were business institutions that should be conducted on business principles, and that in the city and county there was no inherent reason why anyone should vote either the Republican or Democratic ticket. In conclusion the opinion

[67] Gary *Evening Post,* November 5, 1913, November 3, 1920.

was expressed that "without a party we believe we can stand for the best interests of this community in a way that the public will understand and appreciate." The Snyders went on to praise the administration of Mayor William F. Hodges of Gary, a Republican, but declared that Lake County, also with a Republican administration, was not so fortunate.[68] The Snyders probably realized the futility of supporting the Democratic party in the city and county, which were consistently Republican before the depression which began in 1929. Thomas E. Knotts, whose victory in 1909 was largely a personal one, was the only Democratic mayor of Gary until 1935.[69] In view of this political situation, one can understand the reasoning on the part of the Snyders that they could be a greater influence for good in local affairs if they were independent rather than on the "outside" as Democrats. Whether their course strengthened the Republicans and weakened the Democrats in Gary and in the county is an open question.

The depression that followed World War I, combined with an increase in the cost of newspaper publication, brought financial difficulties to the *Daily Tribune* and the *Evening Post*. Their incomes were further diminished because merchants could not afford to advertise in both papers. As a result, the two papers were hardly more than breaking even.[70] Under existing conditions, it was doubtful that Gary was large enough to support two daily newspapers. Of the two, the *Evening Post* presented the more sprightly appearance and was also in better financial condition.

[68] *Ibid.,* January 3, 1921.

[69] The Republicans elected the city treasurer and a majority of the city council in the elections of 1909. Gary *Weekly Tribune,* November 5, 1909.

[70] Cannon, Autobiography, Chap. 50, p. 4.

Early in May, 1921, Homer J. Carr sold the controlling interest in the Gary *Daily Tribune* to Carl O. Dennewitz and Charles Emley. A short time later, on May
21, they sold it to Edward C. Toner, publisher of the
Anderson *Herald* at Anderson, Indiana.[71]   Robert B.
Phillips, also of the Anderson *Herald,* who had had five
years of newspaper experience in Gary, became editor
while Emley remained on the staff as business manager.
The paper was to be independent in politics. Toner was
soon beset with the same financial problems that had
troubled the previous owners of the *Tribune.* On July 9,
1921, he sold the paper to the Snyders and returned to
Anderson.[72]

The Snyders combined the *Post* and the *Tribune* into
the Gary *Evening Post and Daily Tribune.* The new
paper, which was housed in the old Gary *Daily Tribune*
Building at Fifth and Washington, was put into circulation on July 11, 1921. Its officials were Henry Burgess
Snyder, editor; Henry Richard Snyder, associate editor;
J. Ralph Snyder, business manager; and Herbert R. Snyder, in charge of commercial printing. George R. Scott,
one of the founders of the Gary *Daily Tribune* who had
retained a financial interest in the paper, was secretary of
the new organization. The Snyders began the publication
of the Gary *Sunday Post* in the same month only to discover within a short time that Gary was not yet ready for
a Sunday paper.[73]   On August 26, 1922, the name of the

71 Dennewitz's and Emley's reasons for disposing of the *Tribune*
so quickly are not entirely clear. Henry Burgess Snyder, in an interview with the author at Gary, February 16, 1956, said it was possible
that Dennewitz and Emley had miscalculated their financial strength
or that they had acted as the intermediaries for Toner in the purchase
of the paper.

72 Gary *Evening Post,* May 21 and July 9, 1921.

73 The first Sunday issue, containing 34 pages, appeared July 24.
The Gary *Post-Tribune* began the publication of a Sunday edition in
the fall of 1955.

combined papers was simplified to the Gary *Post-Tribune*. Although officially labeled as independent in politics, the paper consistently supported Republican candidates for local, state, and national offices in the 1920's.

The Gary *Post-Tribune* prospered as business conditions improved and as merchants saw the advantage of advertising in only one paper. The circulation of the *Evening Post* had averaged 6,241 copies in 1920, while that of the *Post-Tribune* was 20,026 in 1930.[74] A new building erected at Fourth Place and Broadway for a reported $500,000.00 was dedicated and put into use in 1927. The position of the Snyders as the "first family" of Gary's journalism was further strengthened in 1930 when Henry Burgess Snyder married Mary Rennels, literary editor of the New York *Telegram*, who had served in a similar capacity on the Cleveland *Times* and also the Cleveland *Press*. Mrs. Snyder wrote articles occasionally for the *Post-Tribune* and was on the staff of the Chicago *Daily News* during the Century of Progress Exposition in Chicago, 1933-34.[75]

The Gary *Colored American*, labeled as "Indiana's Greatest Colored Newspaper," was founded by Arthur B. Whitlock in 1927.[76] Whitlock, a graduate of Tuskegee University, was a member of Gary's city council from 1921 to 1929. In the beginning the paper, a weekly, was published by David Eugene Taylor and edited by Chaun-

[74] Circulation figures provided by Henry Burgess Snyder, June 14, 1955.

[75] Gary *Post-Tribune*, January 15, 1930; interview with Henry Burgess Snyder, June 14, 1955. Mary Rennels Snyder edited the book section of the *Post-Tribune* which was started late in 1954.

[76] The Gary *Sun*, established in 1922 or 1923, was apparently the first Negro newspaper in the region. This paper, edited by Zenobia Bagby, and owned by her husband, was purchased by Arthur B. Whitlock in 1931. Interview with Arthur B. Whitlock, Gary, April 16, 1959.

cey Townsend.[77] Whitlock acted as both publisher and editor in later years. Republican in sentiment, the *American* was the voice of the city's Negro citizens in public affairs.

Any history of the region's newspapers would be incomplete without the story of Thomas H. Cannon, one of its very able newspapermen. Cannon started his newspaper career in 1874 and for more than fifteen years worked as a reporter and editor on papers in Colorado, Kansas, and Missouri. In 1890 he became political editor of the Chicago *Times* and was later employed by the Chicago *American* and by the Chicago *Daily Tribune*. Cannon covered numerous assignments for Chicago papers in the Calumet Region of Indiana and was thoroughly familiar with the area before coming to Gary. At the time Thomas E. Knotts engaged him and Frank Patrick to run the newly established Gary *Evening Post* in 1909, Cannon was chief editorial writer for the Chicago *Daily Journal*. The Snyders persuaded him to remain on the staff of the *Post* when they purchased it the following year. Cannon worked on the *Post* and on the *Post-Tribune* until shortly before his death in 1936. The great steel strike of 1919 was his last bit of heavy newspaper reporting. Feeling the weight of the years, Cannon devoted most of his time after that to editorial duties and to his daily columns. To quote his own words: "The end of the trail had been reached. The swivel chair was calling."[78]

Cannon's fame and wide acquaintance among the readers of the *Evening Post* and of the *Post-Tribune* were due largely to his columns, "Flue Dust" and "Lud Wrang-

[77] Gary *Colored American*, November 10, 1927. This was the first issue of the paper.

[78] Cannon, Autobiography, Chap. 50, p. 9; Cannon, Loring, and Robb (eds.), *History of the Lake and Calumet Region*, 2:33-37.

ler," which were daily features of those papers for many years. The title "Flue Dust" was no doubt inspired by the smoke and dust which poured constantly from the flues and stacks of the great steel mills and which, when the atmosphere was heavy and the wind came from off the lake, moved like a fog over the city. Cannon started the "Flue Dust" column in 1913 and conducted it until shortly before his death. The column consisted at first of verse and prose written by Cannon in which he interspersed satirical and humorous comments about current events, both local and national. Beginning in 1915 contributions were received from his readers and from members of the newspaper staff. The first contributor was Margaret K. Hanlan, society editor of the paper, who as "Pandora" sent in exceptionally fine poems and sprightly skits. As time went on, poems, jokes, and timely bits of wisdom came from the pens of contributors under such names as "The Grey Courier," "Merely Gene," "Uncle Spud," "Shoe-Shine Socrates," "Rhoda Dendron," "Oh Hek," and numerous others. Contributions came not only from Gary's citizens but from people in nearby states. For some years Cannon published the best of the "Flue Dust" material annually in a booklet called "The Log Book." Cannon also created "Lud Wrangler," whose letters and musings were daily features of the editorial page.[79] He also ventured into the historical field, serving as editor-in-chief of the *History of the Lake and Calumet Region of Indiana,* a two-volume combination of history and biography, published in 1927.

By 1933 the region's newspaper pattern was well established. Because of its nearness to Chicago there had never been a morning daily in the area nor were there

[79] Cannon, Autobiography, Chap. 55, pp. 1-2; Gary *Post-Tribune,* August 28, 1936.

prospects of one.   Instead, the citizens read the metro-
politan papers in the mornings for items of national and
international interest and in the evenings turned to the
locally published dailies for local and regional news.   The
Vidette-Messenger dominated the Valparaiso scene, the
Gary *Post-Tribune* held sway in the steel city, and the
Hammond *Times* circulated heavily in Hammond, Whiting, and East Chicago.   The weeklies, East Chicago's
Globe and *Calumet News,* Whiting's *Times,* Crown
Point's *Register* and *Lake County Star,* Hobart's *Gazette,* and Chesterton's *Tribune* brought news and notices
of a more intimate nature to their readers.   The fact
that all these newspapers survived the depression indicated that they were permanent fixtures in their respective
communities.

13

EDUCATION

IN THE CALUMET REGION as elsewhere in Indiana the earliest settlers had little time for education. They had to establish themselves before education was possible on any significant scale. There were forests to clear, the tough prairie sod to convert into tillable land, and houses to build while they were trying to make a living from the soil. Because of the absence of adequate roads, travel during the winter months and in periods of rain was at times impossible. The sparseness of the population also handicapped the progress of education. As noted above, in 1850 Valparaiso, with 522 inhabitants, was the only incorporated town in the region. In the same year Center Township, where Crown Point was located, had only 966 inhabitants and North Township, where the cities of East Chicago, Hammond, and Whiting now stand, had 97 residents, none of whom were attending school.[1] Also, because of the lack of opportunities in fields of endeavor other than farming in the West during the early years, young people were discouraged from seeking anything more than the rudiments of an education.

Some of the residents of the Calumet area no doubt shared in the general prejudice against a system of public

---

[1] U. S. Bureau of the Census, *Seventh Census of the United States,* 1850, pp. 768, 772; microfilm of Census for North Township, Lake County, 1850, in Indiana State Library. Statistics for the entire county showed sixteen common schools with a total enrollment of 375. *Seventh Census* (1850), 784.

443

schools whose doors were open to all without tuition charges. Many people were unwilling to pay taxes to educate the children of others, and the churches were skeptical of schools in which children of all denominations and even those with "no faith" were thrown together. Although the Constitution of 1816 had made provision for state-supported public schools, the General Assembly was reluctant to provide funds for that purpose.

Early Schools

Despite the slow progress of education in the early years, the school situation was perhaps better in the Calumet area than it was generally throughout the state. In 1850 about 30 per cent of its inhabitants were from New England, New York, and Pennsylvania where they had had the opportunity to attend district schools, academies, and even colleges.[2] In contrast, a large proportion of those who settled in southern and central Indiana came from the South which until that time had been largely dependent on private schools, usually few and far between. Probably the greatest weakness of the pioneer schools was the lack of competent teachers; those who were capable had a tendency to avoid the teaching profession because of the meager pay and to choose instead to become lawyers, doctors, ministers, businessmen, or farmers.[3] The Calumet area was fortunate in this respect for many of the early schools there were taught by wives, widows, and ministers who had received a fairly good education in the East and were not dependent solely upon their pay as teachers for a livelihod .

[2] Lang, "Inhabitants of Center Township, Lake County," in *Indiana Magazine of History*, 44:282-84.

[3] Buley, *The Old Northwest*, 2:329-31, 370-71; Barnhart and Carmony, *Indiana*, 1:258-61, 267.

Information about the earliest schools in the Porter
County area is scanty. The first school was said to have
been held during the winter of 1833 and 1834 in the
home of Jesse Morgan just north of the present Chesterton. What appeared to be the first important educational
venture in the county was the erection in 1851 of a building costing $2,000 in Valparaiso to house a county semin-
ary. Ashley M. Pierce was the first principal and 120
students were enrolled during its initial session. The
adoption of the public school law in 1852 resulted in the
sale of the seminary's property, the proceeds being placed
in the Common School Fund. In 1853 the Valparaiso
school trustees purchased the building and established the
Union School of Valparaiso, which was organized into
what was called "three grades" corresponding to the
present elementary, junior high, and senior high schools.
Although considered a public school, the tuition rate for
each student in the first grade was $1.50, for the second
grade $2.00, and for those in the third grade $2.50 for
each session. In 1857 this school was terminated when
its building was destroyed by fire.[4]

Harriet Warner Holton taught the first school in Lake
County in 1835-36 at Lake Court House, now Crown
Point. Mrs. Holton, a widow, was educated in Massachusetts and taught school in Vermont before coming to
Indiana. In 1840 Hervey Ball and his wife Jane, parents
of Timothy H. Ball, started an academy and boarding
school on the west side of Cedar Lake. Mrs. Ball was
also educated in Massachusetts while her husband was a
graduate of Middlebury College in Vermont. A large
log building which housed the school also served as a
social and religious center for that part of the county.

[4] Cutler, *History of Porter County,* 1:71, 75-77; Goodspeed and
Blanchard (eds.), *Counties of Porter and Lake,* 53-54.

Along with the three R's, more advanced subjects such as botany, Latin, natural philosophy, drawing, and painting were taught. Mrs. Ball was also a skilled mapmaker, an art her son Timothy found profitable in later years. The academy was said to have had the largest library in the region at that time, its students having access to eastern periodicals as well as to some of the classics. Two literary societies were the pride of the school. One, the Cedar Lake Lyceum, which excluded girls from its membership, met weekly. The other, known as the Cedar Lake Belles Lettres Society, was composed of both sexes. The Balls operated the academy for sixteen years, in the course of which six students, including Timothy H. Ball, were sent forth to colleges and seminaries.[5]

In 1847 William Townley, pastor and one of the founders of the First Presbyterian Church in Crown Point, established a school in the county seat for the training of teachers. Townley, who was educated in New Jersey, was said to have had a master of arts degree. On August 11, 1847, the following announcement was published in Valparaiso's *Western Ranger:*

A high school is being started at Crown Point for the instruction of young gentlemen and ladies embracing also a department for young children. Particular attention will be given to the work of qualifying those, who may contemplate it, for the business of teaching in our public schools. Diligent attention will be given to the health and morals of the pupils. No charge will be made for rent and fuel. Board, it is believed, may be obtained in the village for $1.25 to $1.50 a week.[6]

5 Ball, *Northwestern Indiana,* 369, 387; Howat (ed.), *A Standard History of Lake County,* 1:203-7. The Census of 1850 reported a county library of 250 volumes in Lake County and one of 450 volumes in Porter County. The library in Lake County was probably the one located in Ball's academy. See *Seventh Census* (1850), p. 798.

6 The laws at that time regarding the licensing of teachers were extremely lax. An act of 1837 provided for the appointment by the

The school was divided into the three grades common at that time. The first grade included orthography, reading, writing, and arithmetic, with tuition at $2.50 a quarter; the second grade included geography, English, grammar, natural philosophy, and chemistry, with tuition at $3.00 a quarter; algebra, geometry, surveying, and Latin were taught in the third grade, the tuition being $3.50 a quarter. Classes met five days a week for a period of twelve weeks.[7]

In 1848 Townley called his school the Crown Point Literary Institute. Young ladies, he announced, would receive instruction in ornamental needle work if desired. Also, a few more young ladies could be accommodated with board at his home.[8] The institute continued under Townley's direction until 1855 when it was purchased by a group of prominent Crown Point citizens who changed its name to the Associate Academy of Crown Point. Townley remained as principal. The school was closed in 1856 when Townley severed his connection with the Presbyterian Church and departed for the West. Its building was later sold to Crown Point merchants and converted into a storeroom. Townley's school was said to have provided women teachers for most of the region's schools in this period. His failure to attract young men to the teaching profession was, no doubt, due to the low pay received by teachers in those years. In 1852 Townley said that of the five hundred students to graduate

circuit court of three examiners in each county to examine prospective teachers and grant licenses. In many instances the examiners were poorly qualified to pass upon the capabilities of applicants for licenses. *Revised Statutes of Indiana*, 1837, p. 527; Fassett A. Cotton, *Education in Indiana, 1793-1934* (Bluffton, Ind., 1934), 31, 35.

[7] John H. Thomas, "The Academies of Indiana," in *Indiana Magazine of History*, 10(1914) :339.

[8] Valparaiso *Western Ranger*, April 5, 1848.

from his school since it was started only five young men had gone out as teachers.[9]

Mary Elizabeth Parsons, a graduate of Mount Holyoke Seminary in Massachusetts, opened the Parsons' Seminary for young ladies in 1856 at Crown Point. Miss Parsons, who had taught at Oxford, Ohio, and at Greensburg, Indiana, wished to found a second Mount Holyoke for the young ladies of the West. The curriculum, which was on a high scholastic level, was designed to provide a cultural education and also to prepare those who were interested in careers as teachers. Miss Parsons died in 1860 and the brief career of the seminary came to an end. She made a lasting impression on the Crown Point community, it being said that she "left behind delightful memories among her students of loving womanhood, scholarly devotion, and inspiring life."[10]

William W. Cheshire was a prominent figure in the educational circles of the region during the third quarter of the century. Born in North Carolina, he was said to have traveled on foot to Indiana in 1854. Cheshire attended Franklin College and in 1858 was graduated from the normal department of Miami University at Oxford, Ohio. In 1861 he opened a school at Crown Point. A short time later, he was made supervisor of the public schools comprising the lower grades at Crown Point. In 1864 he was appointed examiner of the Lake County schools and teachers, serving in that capacity for

9 Thomas, "The Academies of Indiana," in *Indiana Magazine of History,* 10(1914):339; Howat (ed.), *A Standard History of Lake County,* 1:209; Ball, *Northwestern Indiana,* 387-88.

10 Richard G. Boone, *A History of Education in Indiana* (New York, 1892, reprinted by offset process by Indiana Historical Bureau, 1941), 229; Ball, *Lake County, Indiana, 1834-1872,* 244. Martha and Kate Knight started the Knight school for girls in 1865 at Crown Point. Available records do not show how long it continued. Howat (ed.), *A Standard History of Lake County,* 1:209.

three years. After a term as clerk of Lake County, Cheshire in 1878 became county superintendent of schools.[11] In the meantime, he had joined three other men in erecting in 1873 a building, popularly known as Cheshire Hall, at Crown Point. This structure contained a large room equipped for the presentation of concerts, plays, and public lectures. It was also used for political rallies, teachers' institutes, and other public gatherings. Cheshire Hall was for several years the cultural, social, and political center for that part of the region.[12]

Timothy H. Ball

Timothy H. Ball, Baptist minister, teacher, and historian, played an important role in the area's cultural and educational life. Ball was born in Massachusetts in 1826, his boyhood was spent in the Bay State and at his father's old home at Columbus, Georgia. In 1837 he moved with his parents to old City West, one of the "dream cities" on the shore of Lake Michigan in Porter County, and later in the same year to Cedar Lake. Ball attended his parents' academy at Cedar Lake and was graduated from Franklin College in 1850. After teaching a few years he studied for the ministry, then in 1863 took up his residence at Crown Point where he remained until his death in 1913.[13]

11 Howat (ed.), *op. cit.,* 1:211-12; Crown Point *Register,* August 22, 1861, in "Old Time News," in Crown Point *Lake County Star,* January 23, 1903. In 1881 Cheshire left Lake County to accept an appointment as an examiner of pensions for the Federal government at Washington.

12 Belle Holton Wheeler, in Ball (ed.), *Lake County, Indiana, 1884,* 148-49. The records of the Crown Point Lecture Club, of which Mrs. J. W. Youche was secretary in 1884, reveal an impressive list of lecturers, readers, entertainers, and political leaders who graced the Cheshire Hall stage. Most prominent among these was Susan B. Anthony and the Hutchinson family. *Ibid.*

13 Ball, *Encyclopedia of Genealogy and Biography,* 671-72.

In 1865 Ball established the Crown Point Institute, which included primary, preparatory, and collegiate departments. Although he was a Baptist, the school was neither owned nor operated by the Baptist Church. Ball was listed in the school's announcements as "proprietor and trustee." A substantial building was erected and equipped at a cost of $5,300, a large sum for that time. The school, which employed several instructors, was open to both girls and boys. Tuition for each term of ten weeks was $3.00 for the primary course, $4.00 for the intermediate, preparatory $5.00, and $6.00 for the collegiate course. The regular school year had four terms. Board, with laundry and lights extra, was $30.00 a term, and "self boarders," those who furnished their own food, could obtain a room for $2.50 per term. Students taking music were charged $8.00 a term for the use of a melodeon and $10.00 for a piano. The institute published *The Pierian,* later known as *The Castalian. The Pierian,* an eight-page monthly, was said to have been the first literary and educational publication in Lake County. Printed in Chicago, it was issued from November, 1867, to March, 1870. Ball did not neglect the recreational side. The students took daily exercises, made frequent excursions to Cedar Lake, and were treated to sleigh rides in the winters. At one time the school had sixty boarding students.[14]

The development of tax-supported and free public schools after the Civil War weakened the Crown Point Institute. In 1871 the property was sold for $3,600 to the town of Crown Point for use as a public school.[15] Ball founded the Lake County Gymnasium and Normal School in 1873, his last venture in the field of school

14 Ball, *Lake County, Indiana, 1834-1872,* 128-31.
15 *Ibid.,* 129.

administration. The normal school, which stressed the training of teachers, was the only one of its type ever to operate in the Lake County portion of the region. A business course was added shortly after the school opened. Classes were never large and the one term a year was seldom more than thirteen weeks in length. Ball was the only member of the faculty. His lectures were designed merely to acquaint prospective teachers with the general nature of the liberal arts and sciences, and also the best methods of teaching each. The school was closed in 1879 when other interests began to occupy Ball's attention.[16]

According to Ball's own statement, the "three departments" of his life were teaching, writing and preaching.[17] There seems to be but little doubt that he excelled in all three activities. His fame rests largely on his work as the pioneer historian of the Calumet Region and upon his efforts to interest the people of the area in their past. Ball, who was eleven years old when he arrived in the area in 1837, resided about seventy years in Lake County. He witnessed or had first-hand knowledge of important happenings from the time of the log cabins and slow plodding oxen to the coming of the railroads and the beginning of the region's great industrial era around the turn of the present century. Most of Ball's observations and writings may be accepted as original source material. He made mistakes, many of them, but the same can be said of others who wrote about their times. Ball watched closely the founding and development of Hammond, Whiting, East Chicago, and the smaller communities in the region. He seldom failed to record his observations and opinions and in more than one instance his pro-

---

16 Howat (ed.), *A Standard History of Lake County*, 1:213-14.
17 See Ball, *Encyclopedia of Genealogy and Biography*, 671-73.

phecies as to what the future held for those places came true. Ball had a keen sense of historical values and was reasonably successful in persuading his contemporaries to write their memoirs and reminiscences. It is not surprising that those concerned with the history of the region have consistently "deferred to and referred to" the writings of this unusual man.

Ball, according to his own statement, wrote and published thirteen books and six pamphlets on historical, genealogical, and religious subjects. He published his own works, most of which were written and printed at Crown Point, and did not hesitate to admit that some of his efforts were profitable. Ball also derived a considerable income from the making and publishing of maps, an art he learned from his mother. Teaching, preaching, and writing were not great sources of wealth in the last century as evidenced by his statement that seldom more than $2,000 ever passed through his hands in the course of a year. In 1873 Ball's first and probably his best work, *Lake County, Indiana, 1834-1872,* was published in Chicago. This was followed in 1880 by *The Lake of the Red Cedars: or Will It Live?* written under the pen name of "Y. N. L." Published at Crown Point, this volume was a narrative of the first thirty years of Baptist activity around Cedar Lake and in Lake County.

In 1875 Ball was instrumental in the organization of the Old Settler's Association of Lake County, the purpose of which was to stimulate interest in the county's history among the descendants of the original settlers. Ball was chosen historian or historical secretary of this organization and in that capacity was its guiding force until 1910. In 1903 its name was changed to the Old Settler and Historical Association of Lake County and as such is still in existence. Ball published the annual reports which recorded the activities of the association, from 1884 to 1910.[18]   Following the celebration of the county's semicentennial, Ball published *Lake County, Indiana, 1884,* containing memoirs and reminiscences of some of the county's pioneers.

In 1890 *The Sunday Schools of Lake, 1840-1890,* was issued by Ball at Crown Point.   Ten years later, *Northwestern Indiana from 1800-1900* appeared.   In this work Ball presented a brief history of La Porte, Porter, and Lake counties.   His last historical effort, *An Encyclopedia of Genealogy and Biography of Lake County, Indiana, with a Compendium of History, 1834-1904,* was published in 1904 at Chicago.   This volume, while valuable to students of the region's history, was apparently Ball's most commercialized work.   The historian found time between his heavier writings to publish two periodicals, *The Prairie Voice* and *Our Banner,* the latter an organ of the Indiana Sunday School Union.   He also wrote articles for such religious journals as *The Southwest Baptist, The Tennessee Baptist,* and *The Witness.* Ball did not actively crusade against the use of liquor, tobacco, or for woman suffrage as did some minister-writers of his period.   Apparently his primary interest was to record the events of his time.

Early Interest in Higher Education

Since 1859 Valparaiso has been a center of higher education in the region.   In that year the Valparaiso Male and Female College was established by the Northwestern Indiana Conference of the Methodist Church.   Apparently, the opening of what is now Northwestern Univer-

[18] "Old Settler and Historical Association of Lake County," in Demmon (ed.), *History of Lake County* (1934), 296-97.

sity by the Methodists in 1855 influenced those in Valparaiso to start a similar institution there. Also, the arrival of the first railroad, accompanied by a rapid increase in the population of Valparaiso and the county, no doubt made the time seem propitious for such an educational enterprise.[19] In the course of a meeting at the courthouse, citizens of the town and county donated $6,000 for the purchase of a site and for the erection of a building. Fifteen acres were acquired on a summit overlooking the town from the southeast. This site was fondly known through the years that followed as "The Hill" and "College Hill." A wooden building was erected immediately but was replaced by a substantial brick structure the next year. The school was designed to accommodate from three to five hundred students from the lowest grades through the college level.

The doors of the college were opened in September, 1859, with a faculty of six and 75 students in attendance, the number of students increasing to 104 by the middle of November. The enrollment increased to 327 the following year. A normal department for the training of teachers was added at that time. The college greatly stimulated the cultural life of the town and county. Commencement exercises, which continued for an entire week,

[19] Valparaiso's population increased from 522 in 1850 to 1,698 in 1860, and that of Porter County from 5,234 to 10,313 in the same period. In 1870 Valparaiso had 2,765 inhabitants. The information presented below concerning the Valparaiso Male and Female College and its successor the Northern Indiana Normal School, which in time became Valparaiso University, is taken chiefly from the two manuscript histories of the University written by Katherine E. Bowden and W. C. Dickmeyer, typed copies of which are in the Valparaiso University Library; from John Strietelmeier, *Valparaiso's First Century,* published by the University in 1959, and from George W. Stimpson, *The Story of Valparaiso University* (Chicago, 1921); from an article by W. H. T. Dau, in Cannon, Loring, and Robb (eds.), *History of the Lake and Calumet Region,* 541-48; and from the catalogues issued by the schools.

were attended by residents of the county and by friends from more distant places. On these occasions the town was said to have been "thronged with visitors from abroad, and bright with its continued festivities." The graduates were publicly quizzed by their various instructors during the final exercises. Following that examination, textbooks were passed out to the college's visitors who, in turn, tried to stump the seniors with questions from the texts. Such attempts, it was said, were seldom successful.[20]

The Civil War, which brought a general lack of interest in education, dealt a crippling blow to the Valparaiso Male and Female College. Attendance declined and the school soon found its treasury depleted. Moreover, its location almost a mile from the center of the town had been a handicap from the very beginning. The road to the college was often impassable in wet weather and during the winter months. Most of the students traveled a winding path through the woods from their homes, a trying ordeal in time of rains and extreme cold. Nor was there adequate housing for boarding students on the campus. Finally, the college had serious competition from the Valparaiso Collegiate Institute. This school, founded by the Presbyterians in 1859, occupied a handsome building in the very center of town. Accordingly, parents found it more convenient and practical to send their sons and daughters there. After the war, the Methodists and other friends of the Male and Female College contributed $25,000 to keep it in operation. Their efforts were futile, as indicated in 1869 when only about one hundred students enrolled. The trustees, after suspending the operation of the college for one year,

[20] See Bill Scifres, "Valparaiso University, Dies Twice, Prospers Three Times in History," in Fort Wayne *Journal-Gazette*, April 19, 1953.

closed its doors in 1871. As a final act, they announced that no matter what happened, the college property would never be sold for any other purpose than education.

The nation's rapid commercial and industrial development after the Civil War placed a premium on education. Opportunities were opened to young Americans which had not existed before the war when the country's economy was largely agricultural. Teachers were needed for the expanding public-school program. Industries and the railroads needed engineers, accountants, chemists, and other trained personnel, while the increase in the nation's population created a great demand for physicians, dentists, lawyers, and other professional people.

This situation, coupled with the lax requirements for the licensing of those in the various professions, tempted enterprising educators to establish privately owned colleges and normals. Those that came into being in Indiana were apparently patterned after the National Normal School at Lebanon, Ohio. While none of these institutions were exactly alike, the general plan was the same among them all. The private or independent normal schools filled a gap in the educational system caused by the incomplete work of the secondary schools and the general need for prepared teachers. Their most important work was the training of teachers for the common schools. The more prosperous of the private colleges and normals acquired substantial buildings, fairly adequate equipment, and in time adopted a solid academic curriculum. They also added other departments such as medicine, dentistry, law, engineering, and pharmacy. A few became permanent institutions and are in existence today. At least fifteen such institutions were established in Indiana from 1873 to 1892.[21]

21 Boone, *A History of Education in Indiana,* 434-37.

Valparaiso University

One of the most successful of these privately owned institutions was the Northern Indiana Normal School, later Valparaiso University, founded by Henry Baker Brown in 1873 on the campus of the defunct Valparaiso Male and Female College. Brown, who was only twenty-six years old at the time he came to Valparaiso, had graduated in 1871 from the National Normal School at Lebanon, Ohio. He was an instructor at the North-western Normal School in Republic, Ohio, when he heard of the vacant buildings of the Valparaiso Male and Female College from one of its former students. Brown came to Valparaiso early in the summer of 1873, in-spected the property on College Hill, and had a confer-ence with the trustees who were eager to revive the school in some form. He decided to open a normal school when the trustees offered to repair the buildings and permit him to use them rent free. Brown, according to one source, undertook the project as a money-making propo-sition. In 1875 he made an interesting arrangement with the city of Valparaiso by which he was enabled to buy the college property, the price being $12,000. The city then bought the property from Brown for $12,000 and gave him the privilege of redeeming it within ten years, which he did. In 1877 Porter County donated $10,000 at the rate of $1,000 a year for the support of the school. This was the only financial assistance the institution ever re-ceived from an outside source until the Lutherans took it over in 1925.

After deciding to open the school, Brown spent the remainder of the summer of 1873 soliciting students in the city and county, attending teachers' institutes, and in general publicizing his new school. He also recruited students from among his friends in Ohio. There being no facilities for the housing of students on the campus, several prominent families in the city agreed to provide rooms and board so that no one would be turned away. In September, 1873, Brown's institution, which he called the Northern Indiana Normal School, opened its doors to students of both sexes from the primary grade through the college level. Thirty-five students were present the first day and by the end of the term sixty-one were enrolled. There were four members on the faculty in addition to Brown, all of whom came from Ohio.[22] The curriculum consisted of four courses of study: preparatory, music, teacher training, and scientific. Tuition was $7.00 a term and board and room could be had for $3.00 a week.[23] The institution's name was changed at the beginning of the second term to the Northern Indiana Normal School and Business Institute. Board and room were reduced to $2.25 a week at this time; the catalogue for 1874 stated that young people could obtain an education there for less money than at any other school in the United States.

The school's enrollment increased by leaps and bounds as students from Indiana and from neighboring states flocked to this only institution of higher learning in northwestern Indiana. The catalogue for 1876-77 announced that 1,320 were enrolled, which led to the claim that the institution was the largest normal school in the United States. At that time five departments were listed: preparatory, teachers, business, engineering, and collegiate. Board and room were $2.00 a week. In 1878 telegraphy, to satisfy the demands of the railroads for telegraph operators, and phonography were added to the

22 Statement of Henry Baker Brown, in Valparaiso *Vidette-Messenger* (Centennial edition), August 16, 1936, Sec. 2, p. 18; Goodspeed and Blanchard (eds.), *Counties of Porter and Lake,* 138.
23 Valparaiso *Porter County Vidette,* June 26, 1873.

curriculum. A law school, whose students received a bachelor of law degree at the completion of the two-year course, was started in 1879. Ninety dollars paid the tuition, board, and room for thirty-three weeks in the law school. In 1878 Henry Baker Brown expressed his philosophy of education by which the school was guided as long as he was in control.[24]

We have learned by observation that there are thousands of people with strong minds passing through life without any education whatever for the following reasons: 1. They are unable to meet the enormous expenses common to our schools, and should they be able to do this they are unwilling to expend their money for that which is not practical, 2. The time required to secure even an ordinary education is too long in most of our institutions of learning, 3. Students are compelled to study many branches that are not practical, and, perhaps, distasteful to them, and thus their progress is retarded. Our curriculum embraces only those studies that are practical.

The school's motto, "Donde la Teoria se und la Practica" —"Where Theory Squares with Practice" was in harmony with this philosophy.

By 1880 the school had grown too large for Brown to administer alone. There were almost a thousand students on the campus that year and it was apparent that the number would increase. Consequently, he persuaded Oliver Perry Kinsey, an old friend who was on the faculty of the normal school at Lebanon, Ohio, to join him as part owner and co-administrator of the mushrooming institution. Before coming to Valparaiso, Kinsey and his wife Sarah spent several months in the East where they visited the leading normal schools and later made a tour of Europe. Kinsey was listed in the school's catalogue, 1880-81, as an instructor of history, literature,

[24] Valparaiso Normal and Business Institute, *Catalogue*, 1878-79, p. 3.

and commercial arithmetic, and Sarah J. Kinsey as a
teacher of geography. Mrs. Kinsey, later dean of women,
remained on the faculty as long as her husband was associated with the institution. Henry Baker Brown continued as principal of the school and Kinsey bore the
title of associate principal. In the years that followed,
Valparaiso's citizens frequently referred to the institution
as the "Brown and Kinsey School."

The success of the school, an educational wonder in
the years before World War I, was largely due to the
following policies: 1. The low cost of tuition, board,
lodgings, and other essentials which made an education
possible for thousands of young men and women who
otherwise could not have afforded to go to college. 2. The
concentration on undergraduate work with emphasis on a
practical education. The school tried to fit young people
for useful work in life and to do this as quickly as possible. 3. The absence of entrance requirements. New
classes were started each term and students could enter
and leave as they pleased. They were advanced and
graduated as they demonstrated their ability. The state
schools and church colleges were critical of the Brown
and Kinsey program and Brown was compelled to attend
sessions of the General Assembly to block legislation
hostile to the institution. 4. Emphasis on hard work—
classes began at 6:30 A. M. in the morning and continued until 8 or 9 o'clock in the evening. The catalogue
warned prospective students they must devote their spare
time to study and to nothing else. As such a large proportion of the students were older than the average
college students today, this was not considered unreasonable. 5. The ban on athletics, dancing, fraternities,
sororities, and other activities which might have diverted
the attention of some students from their studies. Brown

and Kinsey ruled the student body with an iron hand. Student spies, or informers, were frequently utilized to keep the administration informed of what went on among the student body. The catalogue of 1880-81 announced that the names of students expelled from the school would in the future be listed in the catalogues. This threat, however, was never put into practice. Brown and Kinsey did not turn out great scholars or savants, nor did they attempt to educate men and women for profound and epoch-making investigations in any field of scientific research, but they did try to give their students an adequate preparation for the duties and responsibilities of life.

Kinsey demonstrated a genius for economy and resourcefulness. He took charge of the boarding and rooming facilities, which the school then owned, and which were expanded as the number of students increased. Because of his skill, living costs were kept so low that the school was widely known as "The Poor Man's Harvard." Meat, flour, and other staples were purchased in carload lots from the wholesalers and on occasions directly from the packers and processors. Kinsey visited the Water Street Market in Chicago on Saturday afternoons where he bought large quantities of fresh fruit and vegetables from distributors who preferred not to carry such perishables over the weekend. The nutritious value of these foods was not diminished by the time they were served to the students. He also purchased the entire crops of cabbage and potatoes raised by various farmers in the vicinity as well as the yield of their apple and peach orchards. The school also set aside several acres for the raising of vegetables by student labor.[25] In

[25] Interview with Katherine E. Bowden, Valparaiso University, May 19, 1953; Stimpson, *Story of Valparaiso University,* 58, 86.

the spring of 1889, a student paid $1.75 a week for board and room.[26] Kinsey's achievements attracted nation-wide attention. In 1908 *McClure's Magazine* reported that board and room could be had for twenty-three cents a day, breakfast being four cents, dinner ten cents, and supper five cents. Also, that butter was served regularly as long as its price was not more than twenty cents a pound.[27] In 1913 *The Hotel Monthly,* organ for the nation's hotels, found Valparaiso's students were bountifully fed with wholesome foods three times a day for twenty cents.[28] Brown and Kinsey also persuaded the railroads to give reduced rates to their students.

Valparaiso was an oasis of culture in the Calumet Region around the turn of the century. As early as 1878, the city's first historian said the normal school had "introduced a new element in Valparaiso society. The opera house and the Academy of Music, during the past season, have opened a continuous round of entertainments such as is scarcely known in cities many times the size of ours." Lectures, plays, vocal and instrumental concerts were brought to The Hill to enrich the lives of the students and of the community's citizens. While Brown and Kinsey regulated the lives of the students in a strict manner, their generosity and sense of justice inspired a deep affection among them for the school. Chicago alumni, in large numbers, made annual pilgrimages to Valparaiso where they were received in a fatherly manner by the educators.

The school's facilities were gradually expanded in the last years of the century. In 1880 a reading course for

26 Valparaiso *Messenger,* April 18, 1889.

27 George Kennan, "The Cost of Living," in *McClure's Magazine,* 30(1907-8) :647.

28 John Willy, "Catering Extraordinary," in *The Hotel Monthly* (Chicago), November, 1913, p. 77.

pre-medical students, which included anatomy, physiology, and materia medica, was added to the curriculum. A school of pharmacy was established in 1893. By 1890 more than forty debating societies, numerous literary and dramatic clubs, a normal congress, and a moot court provided students with practical experience in their chosen fields. In 1891 the institution's name was changed from the Northern Indiana Normal School and Business Institute to the Northern Indiana Normal School and Business College. The catalogue of that year placed the enrollment at 2,000 students, listed 33 instructors, and estimated the library at 10,000 volumes. Salaries of teachers, which ranged from $1,000 to $1,800 a year, were divulged as evidence that only the best were employed. The college was advertised as the largest normal school in the nation.

It would be difficult to determine just how many students were on the campus at any one time. The student body was in a constant state of change, especially during the spring and summer months when many students withdrew to earn money for further tuition and other expenses. It is doubtful if more than two thirds of the number listed as being enrolled were on the campus at any one time. Brown and Kinsey sought more students as new buildings were added. Advertisements were placed in the newspapers and catalogues, and other material was sent through the mails to teachers, public schools, and libraries over the nation. On June 22, 1893, the Chesterton *Tribune* reported the college was mailing its quarterly output of 500,000 circulars at the rate of 25,000 a day. The school's enrollment was reported in 1901 to be nearly 4,000 students.

The name of the institution was changed in 1900 to Valparaiso College. In 1901 a medical school was es-

tablished, this being the most ambitious step taken by the
school since its birth. This was followed shortly by the
addition of a school of dentistry. The medical school was
located in Chicago where Brown and Kinsey purchased
the building and equipment of the Chicago College of
Medicine and Surgery. Instructors were recruited from
among the physicians on the staff of Cook County Hospital. Students had the opportunity for further study in
Cook County and Frances E. Willard hospitals which
were nearby. Students had the choice of taking their
pre-medical work on the Valparaiso campus or they could
spend the entire four years in Chicago. Only high school
graduates were admitted to the medical school. The
college of dentistry was located in a five-story building on
Harrison and Wood streets, also in Chicago. In 1908
the dental school, known as the Chicago College of
Dental Surgery, was reported to have 85 chairs and that
an income of $30,000 a year was derived from the stu-
dents' practice on the public.[29]

In 1907 the Brown and Kinsey school became Valparaiso University. As such, the institution enjoyed its
most prosperous years before the nation entered World
War I. Its enrollment reached 5,625 in 1912-13, which
led to the claim that the school was the largest "university
and training school" in the United States. Since Brown
and Kinsey enrolled students from the kindergarten
through the university level, it is probable that Valparaiso
was the largest school of its kind in the nation. According to Kinsey, the enrollment in 1914-15 was the largest
in its history.[30] Six thousand students registered in that
year and there were 218 instructors on the faculty. Only
the universities of Chicago, Wisconsin, and Illinois re-

[29] Kennan, "The Cost of Living," in *McClure's Magazine,* 30:649;
Valparaiso University, *Catalogue,* 1912-13, p. 83.
[30] Valparaiso *Vidette-Messenger,* August 16, 1936, Sec. 2, p. 18.

ported more students than did the Brown and Kinsey school at that time.[31] It should be remembered though that all the students on Valparaiso's rolls were never on the campus at one time. Nevertheless, the school had a fine reputation and its prestige, as yet, was undiminished. Logan Esarey paid tribute to the university at that time: "This, in some respects is the most remarkable educational institution in the state. Until recently, when it little needed it, it has had no financial assistance from any source. From an enrollment of 200 it has grown to over 5,000. It teaches everything and its only entrance requirements are health and energy. It has reached the great middle class in a way that no other institution of the state has. It has fulfilled the ideal of the independent normal."[32]

Valparaiso's decline during and after World War I was brought about by factors and influences beyond its control. The development of free public schools weakened its preparatory department which had been supported by tuition fees. Also, the rapid expansion of the state universities and teachers' colleges, financed by appropriations from public funds, provided facilities such as libraries, laboratories, and living quarters for students at a cost far below Valparaiso's ability to equal. Moreover, the more strict and higher standards set up for teachers, lawyers, physicians, and other professions made obsolete the Brown and Kinsey philosophy of education. There was no longer a place in the educational world for a university where students could attend without entrance requirements, where they could enter and leave whenever they pleased, and where the requirements for graduation

[31] In 1914-15 Chicago reported an enrollment of 7,701, Wisconsin, 7,596, and Illinois, 6,004. *Chicago Daily News Almanac and Year Book,* 1915, p. 240.

[32] Esarey, *History of Indiana,* 2:1004.

were restricted only to demonstration of the student's
ability. Whether the academic ideas of Brown and
Kinsey were inferior to those that came to be regarded
as orthodox after World War I is beside the point, the
fact remains that they were unable to survive in the new
era. While these were the fundamental reasons for the
University's collapse, others hastened its near demise.

Henry Baker Brown suffered a stroke of paralysis in
the fall of 1912 from which he never recovered, although
he lingered until 1917. Kinsey became acting president
of the University and Brown's son, Henry Kinsey Brown,
came from California, where he was engaged in the
brokerage business, to assist in the management of the
school. World War I dealt a financial blow to the institution. Hundreds of students left to enter the armed
services while others, whose expenses were being paid by
relatives and friends in foreign countries involved in the
war, were forced to withdraw. Despite this setback,
Kinsey carried the school through the war. In the meantime, serious differences of opinion as to finances and
university policies developed between Kinsey on one side
and Mrs. Henry Baker Brown and her son on the other.
Although Kinsey and Henry Baker Brown had been
regarded as wealthy men during the best years of the
school, most of their funds had gone to finance its expansion. Mrs. Brown, now that her husband was dead,
reportedly regarded the University as an accumulation
of wealth to be handed down to her children. Originally,
Henry Baker Brown and Kinsey planned to bequeath the
University to a self-perpetuating board of trustees, but
this was not carried out. Early in 1919, Mrs. Brown
decided to make her son president of the University.
This situation proved to be intolerable to Kinsey, who
was then more than seventy years old. In May, 1919,

the firm of Brown and Kinsey, proprietors of the school, was formally dissolved, Kinsey going into retirement. Henry Kinsey Brown assumed control, the university becoming the property of the Brown family as it had been in the beginning. Oliver Perry Kinsey's departure from the institution ended an important era in the region's cultural history.

Apparently, Henry Kinsey Brown was neither an educator nor an executive with sufficient experience to manage the university. Moreover, he was said to have been reluctant to form a connection with the school and did so only at his mother's insistence. Brown's ideas as to what a university should be were also entirely different from those held by his father. The younger Brown wanted Valparaiso to function like the state universities and the heavily endowed institutions. To this end, an intercollegiate athletic program was launched, fraternities and sororities were permitted, and dances and other activities were encouraged. Early in 1917, when the younger Brown's association with the university began, reference was made for the first time to a program of athletics. The catalogue of that year carried the announcement that an athletic field, baseball diamond, and tennis courts were being constructed, also a gymnasium designed to seat fifteen hundred people. Each student was assessed a fee to help finance these improvements.

Henry Kinsey Brown's appointment of Daniel Russell Hodgdon as president in 1920 proved to be an unfortunate setback for the struggling institution. Public confidence in the university and the morale of the faculty and student body were lowered during the new president's brief tenure. Hodgdon, who listed the M.S., Sc.D., and LL.D. degrees after his name, was said to have formerly headed the "Newark College of Technology" at Newark,

New Jersey. The new executive began his administration
of the school with a flourish. Because of the similarity of
its name with one of the principal cities of Chile, he
announced that the school should attract students from
the Latin American countries. Accordingly, a Spanish
language edition of the university's catalogue for 1920-21
was published and distributed among our sister republics
to the South. Despite this ambitious program, the flow
of students from "south of the border" did not material-
ize. An effort was made to revive the medical school
which had closed its doors during the war. Hodgdon
announced the university had "affiliated" with the Hahnemann Medical College in Chicago. If such an arrangement was made, it appears that Hahnemann merely
agreed to accept students who had completed the pre-
medical course at Valparaiso.[33]

Within a short time, at least three fourths of the University's faculty, alienated by Hodgdon's dictatorial attitude and by his general lack of tact, were convinced he
was neither an educator nor an executive.[34] Suspicions
were aroused as to the origin of the president's numerous
degrees, some coming to believe these academic honors
were but products of the so-called diploma mills, so prevalent at that time.[35] Faculty unrest soon spread to the
student body. The climax was reached in April, 1921,
when a mass meeting of students, which included a hundred veterans of World War I, condemned Hodgdon
for what they regarded as his effort to make "the poor
man's Harvard a regular Harvard," and also for the
introduction of policies which did not conform to the

[33] The history of Hahnemann Medical College, in *The History of
Medicine and Surgery . . . of Chicago* (Chicago, 1922), does not
mention any formal connection with Valparaiso University.

[34] Chicago *Herald-Examiner*, April 27, 1921.

[35] Interview with Katherine E. Bowden, May 19, 1953.

traditions of the university. The president, in turn, accused the students involved of being Bolshevists, saying the school was a hotbed of Communism. Hodgdon resigned late in April, 1921, when the Federal government refused to sign a contract for five hundred disabled veterans to attend the university for vocational training as long as he was associated with the school. The contract, so desperately needed by the tottering institution, was reported to have been signed one hour after the president's resignation.[36]

The influx of veterans brought only temporary relief to Valparaiso. Between 1921 and 1925 three presidents in succession followed Hodgdon.[37] Since Henry Kinsey Brown, who acted as bursar of the university when Hodgdon was president, was not listed in subsequent catalogues, he apparently had no active part in the administration of the school. These were lean years for the university as the number of students steadily declined. As early as 1920, Oliver Perry Kinsey's methods of feeding and housing students, which had made the school famous, were apparently abandoned. Students were informed in the catalogue for 1921-22 that food could be had in the university's cafeteria and at restaurants and private boarding houses in the city. In the meantime instructors often went unpaid, forcing some to leave the institution; the grounds went untended and buildings deteriorated for lack of funds to keep them in repair. "A great school had been built and gone to seed."[38]

36 Chicago *Herald-Examiner,* April 25 and 27, 1921.

37 The presidents were John E. Roessler, a former dean, 1921-22; Milo M. Bowman, 1922-23; and Horace M. Evans, 1923-25.

38 Dickmeyer, History of Valparaiso University, 8. The enrollment in 1924-25, the year before the Lutherans assumed control of the school, was 614 students. Information obtained from Paul E. Thune, Associate Registrar, November 17, 1955.

In 1923 the Ku Klux Klan, which was unusually strong in Indiana at that time, made an effort to get control of the university for the teaching of "Americanism." The Klan and the university's trustees even reached an agreement as to the purchase price, reported to have been $350,000. Fortunately, as the national headquarters of the Klan took a dim view of the matter, the deal was never consummated. And yet for some years erroneous reports persisted that Valparaiso had once been a Klan school.[39]

In 1919 and again in 1925 the trustees offered the university's property to the state for use as a teacher's college, there being no institution of that type in northern Indiana. The offer was rejected both times.[40] The school, which had educated and enriched the lives of hundreds of the region's young men and women, appeared doomed when relief came from an unexpected quarter.

In the summer of 1925 a group of laymen of the Lutheran Church of the Synod of Missouri had its attention drawn to the university. An inspection of the property convinced the group that the school could be reorganized to serve the needs of its church body. Accordingly, the Lutheran University Association was organized with executive offices at Fort Wayne. Membership was restricted to members of the Synodical Conference of the Evangelical Lutheran Church of America, of which the Synod of Missouri was the largest and most influential part. The Association, incorporated under the laws of

[39] Interview with Katherine E. Bowden, May 19, 1953; Gary *Post-Tribune,* August 16, 1923; Strietelmeier, *Valparaiso's First Century,* 74.

[40] Indianapolis *Star,* January 10, 1919, p. 11; Indianapolis *News,* March 16, 1925; Cannon, Loring, and Robb (eds.), *History of the Lake and Calumet Region,* 1:547-48; Fort Wayne *Journal-Gazette,* April 19, 1953. In 1925 a bill was introduced in the General Assembly to make Valparaiso University a branch of the State Normal School; it passed both houses but the Governor refused to sign it.

Indiana, became the holding company of the university's property. A drive was launched among the members of the church to obtain the purchase price of $176,500, and also for funds to renovate the buildings and to operate the school. While the Lutheran Church gave no direct financial support to the university, there was a close connection between the two.[41]

In September, 1925, the university opened its doors under Lutheran control. The new owners proceeded slowly and conservatively to put the school on a sound foundation. The 1926-27 catalogue listed the following departments: preparatory, arts and sciences, teacher training, law, engineering, music, pharmacy, commerce, pre-medical, and pre-dental. Approximately six hundred students and forty-five instructors were reported at the school in that year. Although the preparatory, pre-medical and pre-dental departments were dropped during the great depression, the university survived that crisis better than did many church schools. In 1932-33 Valparaiso had 560 students on its rolls.[42] By that time the school which had almost died was once more an important influence in the cultural life of the region.

William A. Wirt and the Platoon School

Gary was the scene of one of the most original and thoroughly constructive attempts at educational reorganization in the history of American education, and one that profoundly influenced school organization and instruction throughout the nation. This was the work-study-play school, more popularly known as the platoon

[41] See Streitelmeier, op. cit., 77-108, for a complete account of the acquisition of the school by the Lutheran University Association.

[42] Chicago Daily News Almanac and Year-Book, 1927, p. 426; 1932, p. 290.

school, which was developed in the steel city by William A. Wirt, superintendent of public schools.[43]   Wirt, generally recognized as the "Father of the Platoon System," was a disciple and student of John Dewey and his work-study-play idea represented the Dewey educational philosophy in a new and original manner.   Dewey believed the schools should be a miniature of society itself and that the child should be taught how to live amid the complexities and problems of modern industrial society not by studying about them but by actually living them in his daily school contacts.   The child should learn by doing.[44]   Dewey and Wirt believed the "subject-matter" schools, whose objective was to impart a specific amount of knowledge from certain printed material, were obsolete in the new industrial and urban age upon which the nation had embarked.   The time had come for the public schools to prepare young people for the "business of living."

In 1900 Wirt established the first platoon school in America at Bluffton, Indiana, where he was superintendent of schools.[45]   Consequently, his ideas were not untried when he came to Gary in 1907.   Wirt's platoon system

[43] William A. Wirt was born January 21, 1874, on a farm near Markle, Indiana, attended the public schools at Markle and Bluffton, and was graduated from De Pauw University in 1898. Prior to this time he had served as principal and superintendent of the Redkey schools, and while taking graduate work at De Pauw he taught in the Greencastle schools. In 1899 he became superintendent of schools at Bluffton where he remained until accepting the position at Gary in 1907. During this interval he had also taken graduate work at the University of Chicago and made a study of educational systems in England, France, Belgium, and Germany. *Dictionary of American Biography, Supplement Two* (New York, 1958), 727-28; Gary *Post-Tribune,* January 21, 1936, March 11, 1938.

[44] John Dewey and Evelyn Dewey, *Schools of Tomorrow* (New York, 1915), 290-316.

[45] Bluffton reverted to the conventional type of school organization after Wirt's departure.

was distinguished by two features, both intimately connected with each other: (1) the enrichment and diversi-
fication of the curriculum; (2) on the administrative side,
provision for the full use of the school plant at all times
by the maintenance of two student bodies or platoons,
sometimes known as the duplicate school. The curriculum
was designed to adjust the students to the social, economic, and political problems which in the new industrial
age could no longer be satisfactorily solved by the parents in the homes. Wirt believed that the "whole child"
should be educated—the schools had the responsibility
of educating him physically, artistically, manually, scien-
tifically as well as intellectually. That by putting in the
child's way all the opportunities for varied development,
the child would be able to select those activties for which
he was best suited, and thus develop his capacities to their
highest power. This could be done only in a school which
provided, besides the ordinary classrooms, playgrounds
and gardens, gymnasiums and swimming pools, special
drawing and music studios, science laboratories, printing
and machine shops, and an auditorium. The school, with
the possible exception of the first two or three grades,
should be departmentalized with special teachers for each
subject. Home-room registration would counteract extreme departmentalization.[46]

Wirt's work-study-play school was divided into two
student bodies, later known as platoons, and identified in
Gary as Alpha and Beta schools. The schedule called for
one platoon to spend a period of the day in home-rooms
studying the fundamental subjects while the other was
engaged with activity subjects in special rooms or in
recreation. At the end of the period, the platoons alter-

[46] Randolph S. Bourne, *The Gary Schools* (New York, 1916), 14-15.
The term "platoon" did not originate with Wirt but came into general
use about 1912 at Kalamazoo, Michigan.

nated from the special rooms and recreational activities to the home-rooms, and vice versa. This form of organization made possible a richer curriculum at a cost no greater than that provided by the traditional school, and made it possible to provide for twice as many children as the classrooms alone would accommodate.

Wirt could not have chosen a better site than the infant Gary to put his educational ideas into practical operation. Here the field was open for the development of an educational system adapted to local conditions. There were no antiquated buildings, there was no teaching staff with uniform, fixed habits. The very mobility and rawness of a large part of the population from this point of view was an advantage, for the patrons of the schools, the majority of whom had recently arrived from Europe, were without the educational traditions that might readily have resisted departures from common usage. In short, no place could have been chosen where, in most respects, there were fewer obstacles and where conditions were more favorable to innovations. There seemed, for the moment, however, some rather formidable problems. The town, incorporated in 1906, started with an empty treasury. State laws provided that school revenues for any given year were to be obtained on an assessment made almost two years before, and yet in Gary school facilities had to be provided for a population that doubled each year for several years. Actually, this situation favored Wirt and his platoon plan, for the schools would have been swamped had they been organized along traditional lines. Mayor Thomas E. Knotts and the school board saw the wisdom of Wirt's ideas and gave him their whole-hearted support.[47] As a result,

[47] The Hammond *Lake County Times,* a consistent foe of Mayor Thomas E. Knotts, said on September 4, 1914, that "in a great measure William Wirt attained his success because of the free hand Tom

Gary's children were not only provided with adequate school facilities but with a richer curriculum than prevailed in other cities at that time.

Wirt was one of the first to see that urbanization of the nation's population placed additional responsibilities upon the public schools. He pointed out that in the earlier years children on the farms grew up in a more wholesome atmosphere than was possible for young people in the cities. They had a more intimate acquaintance with nature and had the great out-of-doors for a playground. Rural children were also kept busy with farm and household duties. Consequently, it was not necessary for the little red schoolhouse to teach much more than the three R's. The activities of the rural home which had educational value for children such as the raising of food and the making of clothes had, in the cities, been taken out of the home and shut away from the children. The open spaces of the farm had shrunk to a "yard," too small for real play. As a result, city children sought recreation in the unwholesome atmosphere of alleys, street corners, and cheap theaters. The schools should return to children the opportunities for wholesome work and play of which the city had deprived them.[48]

Gary's work-study-play school was designed to create a child's world within the adult world of the city. To achieve this end, the school day was lengthened to eight hours. Teachers taught six hours but physical education instructors were on duty throughout the school day. Wirt thought the long summer vacation was a waste of time. Accordingly, a summer school, attendance at which was

Knotts gave him. Of course, Mr. Wirt is entitled to the chief glory. But it must be said in behalf of Mr. Knotts that were his cooperation lacking that Gary schools would not be as famous as they are."

[48] William A. Wirt, *The Great Lockout in America's Citizenship Plants* (Gary, 1937), front and back covers.

voluntary, was established. Enrollments in the summer
schools in the early years were approximately one third
that of the regular year. On Saturdays three hours of
classes were held for those who wished to strengthen
themselves in courses in which they were weak and for
those who wished to progress more rapidly. In 1927
and 1928 attendance in the Saturday school was more
than one third that of the regular school.[49]

All the classrooms, shops, laboratories, studios, and
athletic facilities were thrown open to adults in the
evenings. Wirt intended for the schools to be club houses
for adults. In 1922 enrollments in Gary's evening schools
were 10,320 while those in the regular day schools, including kindergarten, were 10,991. More men over
twenty-one years old were reported attending evening
schools in 1916 than there were boys of all ages in the
regular schools.[50] In 1931 the number of hours in which
the Gary schools were in use was double the average of
the public schools in the nation and yet the cost to the
taxpayers was no more than that of the traditional
school.[51]

There were no "high schools" in Gary. Instead, the
larger centers, known as "complete" schools, contained
all the classes from kindergarten through the common
school and high school. From an economic point of view,
it was cheaper to have large, completely equipped centers
than to duplicate the equipment in a number of small
centers. From an educational point of view, the complete
schools enabled students to bridge the chasm between
the elementary grades and the high schools. By ceasing

[49] Roscoe D. Case, *The Platoon School in America* (Stanford, Calif.,
1931), 42.

[50] Wirt, *op. cit.*, 51; Bourne, *The Gary Schools*, 82.

[51] Case, *op. cit.*, 42; A. H. Bell, *The Work-Study-Play Program* (Columbus, Ohio, 1932). Bell was auditor of the Gary Public Schools.

to make the high school a separate institution to be "entered" or "graduated from," pupils found no place to stop when they completed the first eight grades. Also, the association of pupils of all ages in the same building had a tendency to break down what was termed "the snobbery of age." Wirt also pointed out that many students did not go to high school because they were timid. Moreover, some parents believed that children in high school must dress unusually well, buy expensive books, belong to societies, and live on a social plane which they could not afford. Finally, Wirt learned from experience that more students went to high school when it and the elementary schools were in the same building.[52]

One of the most controversial features of Wirt's system was that a student did not have exclusive use of a desk as was the case in the traditional school. The educator explained that sole possession of a desk by each pupil was expensive and a waste of valuable space. It was no more practical for a school to provide each child with a desk than it was for the city to allot a separate seat in a park for each of its citizens. The elimination of private desks doubled the capacity of a building. It also made the desks available for use by adults in the evening school. Instead of private desks, each pupil was provided with a steel wall locker for his wraps, books, and other equipment. The lockers, which were cheaper than desks and cloak rooms, occupied space along the wall in the halls that could be used for no other purpose.[53] Wirt was successful in overcoming local prejudice against the multiple desk idea but numerous other cities that adopted the platoon system retained the individual desks of the traditional school.

[52] William A. Wirt, in Town of Gary, *First Annual Report,* 1908, p. 67.

[53] *Ibid.,* 61-62.

The auditorium was the assembly hall and theater of Gary's student community. Its use and purposes were different from the auditoriums of the traditional schools where the school day was opened generally with patriotic or religious exercises and then remained vacant for the remainder of the day. In Gary the auditorium hours came at different periods of the day and the program differed for different classes. It was intended as an occasion when happenings of peculiar interest in any part of the school could be brought to the attention of the rest of the student body. Each child was in the auditorium for an hour each day where programs were staged by the pupils, teachers, or by outside visitors. The program generally included choral singing, instrumental or phonograph music. Lantern slides and motion pictures were also shown. Folk dancing, student plays, and debates on school issues were often on the program. Pupils of widely different ages were sent together to the auditorium hour so that the younger might have their curiosity stimulated about the work of classes they had not yet reached. Here again, was another effort to break down the "snobbery of age." The auditoriums were also available in the evenings to adults for concerts, political meetings, and other gatherings of interest to the community.[54]

Almost from the beginning of the Gary school system some form of constructive work was a feature of the regular school course. In time, this program was devoted to the industrial arts and to domestic science. This program was not designed to be a system of vocational training nor was its purpose the training of the child for any particular trade. Instead, its objective was the presentation of a liberal set of industrial experiences calculated to

[54] Bourne, *The Gary Schools,* 49-52; Dewey and Dewey, *Schools of Tomorrow,* 196-97.

broaden, enrich, and stimulate the school life of the pupils. On the more practical side, it was possible that such training might help the child make an intelligent choice of an occupation, the training for which could be obtained after he had completed his public school years. Wirt's critics frequently charged that this phase of the Gary plan was fathered and supported by the United States Steel Corporation as a device to train a supply of labor for the mills. In regard to this allegation, a competent observer said: "whatever else may be said of the Gary plan, it must be evident to any serious observer that the mind of man could hardly devise a plan less calculated to accomplish this particular object than the system of training represented in the school shops."[55] While Wirt got along well with the officials of the steel corporation, available evidence failed to indicate that they ever sought to influence his educational program.

This constructive program was connected with the maintenance and repair of the school buildings. The large, well equipped school plants in Gary required a large force of mechanics and other artisans to keep them in repair. The usual way of doing this would have been to hire outside labor at considerable expense to do the necessary work during the school year and in the vacation periods. Since Gary's schools had no long summer vacations, a permanent force of trained personnel was needed throughout the year. Regular union artisans, such as plumbers, electricians, sheet-metal workers, carpenters, foundry-men, printers, etc., were selected with care, not only for their knowledge of their trade, but for personal qualities of intelligence, teaching ability, and sympathy

[55] Charles R. Richards, *The Gary Public Schools, Industrial Work* (New York, 1918), 5, 119-20, 122. Richards made this study for the General Educational Board in New York City.

for young people. Shopmen were not listed as instructors in the school records but as workers in the department of maintenance and repair. The pupils worked with these men in much the same way as old-time apprentices, though, of course, for only a fraction of their time. Shops of these artisans became the regular industrial shops of the school. Economy was a feature of this plan for the teacher-workmen would be doing the work whether the pupils assisted or not. For example, the printing shop did all the printing work for the schools and, in addition, the pupils obtained practical knowledge of that useful and interesting trade.

Domestic science was not taught as a separate "subject" in Wirt's system of schools. Girls were given practical experience in the school's lunchrooms under the direction of an instructor and a cook assistant. The domestic science room was a real kitchen, dining room, and pantry for the preparation of daily lunches for students and teachers. All expenses and supplies were charged to the lunch department and the salary of the assistant was paid out of its profits. The sewing room was operated on a similar plan, the instructor having practical dressmakers, milliners, and laundresses as assistants. Their salaries and all materials were paid from the savings made by doing the necessary laundry and needlework for the schools. All the other shops were self-supporting in the sense that the ordinary appropriations for painting, electrical work, plumbing, printing, etc. (which would have had to be paid anyway) generally paid the salaries of the teacher-workmen and the cost of materials. The ideal was to make all the shops and the domestic science work self-sustaining community-service affairs.[56]

56 Bourne, *The Gary Schools,* 40-49.

Such were the original and unique educational ideas that William A. Wirt put into operation in Gary in the early years, and yet it should be understood that the plan was not entirely the same in the smaller elementary schools as in the larger centers. Nor did Wirt hesitate to make changes in the program and, also, to adjust it to the city's rapid growth. In 1918, the educator said he had tried approximately fifty different programs for the work-study-play schools.[57] Nevertheless, his educational goal remained unchanged as indicated by his statement in 1937 that the objectives of the Gary schools had not changed in thirty years.[58]

In September, 1908, Wirt established the first platoon system in Gary at the Jefferson School. This structure was erected by the Gary Land Company at a cost of $90,000 and was leased to the town's school board, whose treasury was empty at that early date. A traditional school building, Jefferson was completed just before Wirt came to Gary. The steel company officials were startled when Wirt asked that the structure be remodeled to house a platoon school. He called their attention to the intelligence they were putting into the construction of the steel mills and reminded them that the mills would not be permited to lie idle half the time. Yet, Jefferson School, if conducted along traditional lines would be utilized to only one half of its capacity and the classrooms would be vacant about one half of the day. The building was altered to conform with Wirt's ideas, its original capacity of 360 pupils being more than doubled. The Jefferson School is the oldest platoon school in the United States.[59]

[57] William A. Wirt quoted in *ibid.*, xvii-xviii.

[58] Wirt, *The Great Lockout*, 5.

[59] Burton J. Hendrick, "Children of the Steel Kings," in *McClure's Magazine*, 41:no. 5 (September, 1913):61-69; Case, *The Platoon School*, 21.

Wirt had almost complete freedom in planning the large educational centers in the city. He engaged William B. Ittner, regarded as one of the nation's foremost school architects, to take charge of the construction of the Emerson School, which opened in 1909. Ittner also supervised the building of Froebel, 1912, Horace Mann, 1926, Roosevelt, 1928, and Lew Wallace in 1931.[60] These buildings, which accommodated pupils from the kindergarten through high school, were not alike in appearance and design. Each was a stately structure with a distinct beauty and charm of its own. In all instances, Wirt obtained sites large enough to conform to the play feature of the platoon school, insisting that each child should have playground space of at least forty-nine square feet.[61] In 1929 Emerson School, the nation's second oldest platoon school, had 2,584 pupils enrolled. In the same year Froebel, the third oldest platoon school in the country, was the largest institution of its kind in the United States, its enrollment being 3,173.[62]

From the very beginning, Wirt's Gary plan attracted the attention of educators, school boards, and teachers throughout the nation and in some foreign countries. Such large numbers of visitors came to inspect the schools of the steel city that the school board found it necessary to set up an organization to accommodate them. In 1911, a pamphlet, containing an explanation of the Gary plan, its curriculum, school costs, teachers' loads and salaries, was distributed to those who came to study the city's schools. In the same year an information bureau was established in the Gary Commercial Club where visitors

[60] Ittner was employed as commissioner of school buildings in St. Louis before coming to Gary. See Gary *Post-Tribune,* January 27, 1936.

[61] Town of Gary, *First Anual Report,* 52.

[62] *Indiana School Directory,* 1929-30 (State Department of Public Instruction, Indianapolis, 1930), 129, 130.

could register and obtain programs and descriptive literature. Also in 1911 inspection and study of the schools
by outsiders were restricted to four designated periods
of the year. Visiting educators and teachers were asked
to stay an entire week and not just one day. The suggestion was also made that a visitor stay with one class
throughout the day. By 1919 so many requests for information were coming in that the school board assigned
a specialist to give her entire time to the collection and
distribution of information. School administrators from
other cities were provided with school-building programs
portraying both the traditional and platoon systems of
organization.[63]

Apparently no attempt was made by other cities to
duplicate in its entirety the plan which Wirt developed
in Gary.[64] This did not mean that the general idea of
the plan failed of acceptance by other officials. It was
accepted. Numerous educators studied Wirt's system,
and then set up plans, patterned after his ideas but modi-
fied, as he insisted should be done, to fit local conditions
and needs. Despite what others did to change the original

[63] See *Notes to Visitors* (Gary, 1911) and *Regulation of Visitors*
(Gary, 1911), pamphlets in the Gary Public Library; Case, *The
Platoon School,* 22.

[64] In 1914 Wirt was engaged by the board of education in New
York City to make a study of its schools with the object of reorganizing
them according to the platoon system. Wirt devoted one week of each
month to the New York assignment until January, 1919, his salary being
$10,000 a year. Mayor John P. Mitchel and some of the newspapers
supported Wirt's program. According to reports, by the end of 1916
the platoon system was in operation in 120 of the city's schools. Tammany
Hall opposed Wirt's system and was critical of what it considered to
be the unusually high salary paid to the Gary man. In 1918 John
F. Hylan made the platoon system one of the major issues in his
campaign for mayor, his slogan being "a seat for every child." Hylan's
election terminated Wirt's assignment and New York City eventually
abandoned the platoon system. Gary *Evening Post,* September 2, 1914;
New York *Times,* March 3, 1938.

structure, the plan which represented Wirt's philosophy remained very much the same as when first organized. By 1929 the platoon system was being used by 1,068 schools in 202 cities in 41 states.[65]

There seems to be little doubt but that the work-study-play system of schools contributed more toward the education of Gary's children and adults than the traditional schools could have done. This was also true of the region's other cities, all of which adopted various features of the Gary plan. Gary's population increased at such a fantastic rate that there would not have been enough time or money to provide adequate facilities had the schools been organized along traditional lines. Nor would there have been an adequate program for adults. One of Gary's most serious problems was the Americanization and education of its foreign-born residents who at one time composed more than 50 per cent of its population. Moreover, a large proportion of the common laborers in the steel mills were native Americans who had never been overly concerned with education for themselves or their children. While apparently the evening adult schools were of little cultural value to the foreign born, they did provide an opportunity for large numbers to

[65] Case, *The Platoon School,* 26, 34, 42. Detroit, with 121 schools, in 1929 was the outstanding platoon school city in the United States. Other cities in order of usage were Pittsburgh, Birmingham, Dallas, Newark, Portland, Akron, and Seattle. In 1925 the National Association for the Study of the Platoon or Work-Study-Play School Organization was formed in co-operation with the United States Office of Education. This organization served as a clearing house for the ideas, theories, and methods of educators applying the platoon-school philosophy. In 1927 it began the publication of a magazine, *The Platoon School.* In 1930 this organization was converted into the "Platoon School Department" of the National Education Association. John G. Rossman, at the time assistant superintendent of the Gary schools and later superintendent of the East Chicago schools, was the first secretary of this association. *Ibid.,* 268-73.

learn American ways and the English version of the three R's. Although there were certainly imperfections in Wirt's work-study-play plan, the system was a success in Gary where school facilities were so few and an education was needed by so many.

Higher Education in Lake County

Some of Lake County's young people attended Valparaiso University in the neighboring county, but by the close of World War I local educators felt the need for an institution of higher learning in their county. The Extension Division of Indiana University sought to fill this need by offering regular college courses on the freshman and sophomore level, as well as those of junior and senior rating which did not require extensive laboratory and library facilities. Students were permitted to take sixty semester hours in extension classes which was one half of the regular college requirement for a degree.

The first of these extension classes was given at Gary's Jefferson School in 1920; the following year courses were offered at Hammond, and in 1922 at East Chicago and Valparaiso. That year there were 206 students enrolled in classes at Gary.[66] Teachers were obtained from the University faculty at Bloomington and from universities in Chicago. Tuition fees, which were reasonable, were applied toward the cost of instruction. The University subsidized the program as the amount paid by the students seldom took care of all the expenses.

Despite these efforts by Indiana University, local educators and the newspapers, moved in part by local pride, demanded that a state university or state normal school

[66] Statistics provided by Helen Duncan of the Division of Adult Education and Public Services, Indiana University, Bloomington, Indiana, from the files of that division, November 14, 1954.

be located in Lake County. They emphasized the need of an institution for the training of teachers, pointing out that, with the exception of Marion County, the number of teachers in Lake County was larger than in any other county in the state.[67] When it became apparent it was not practical to locate a state university in the area, Superintendent Wirt and Horace S. Norton, of Gary, and A. Murray Turner, of Hammond, announced in 1922 their intention to seek legislation which would enable counties of from 150,000 to 350,000 population to establish junior colleges. Local residents would pay no tuition in these institutions. Wirt, who suggested that Lake County's school be called Calumet College, went so far as to select a site for the proposed institution at Fifth Avenue and Cline Street in Gary.[68] While this location was convenient to Hammond and East Chicago, a huge area in its vicinity was uninhabited at that time and public transportation facilities were poor. The General Assembly refused to act on the proposal.

In the meantime, Indiana University expanded its program in the region by establishing the Gary Extension Center in 1925, with Albert Fertsch, director of adult education in the Gary Public Schools, in charge. The offices of the Center were first located in the Memorial Auditorium but were later moved to the Horace Mann School, where most of the classes were held. Although classes were organized wherever there was a demand, most of the University's work was given in Gary. During the 1931-32 school year, sixty-seven classes were offered in the steel city, nine in Hammond, and three in East Chicago.[69]

[67] Gary *Evening Post,* February 9, 1921; Gary *Evening Post and Daily Tribune,* May 20, 1922.

[68] Gary *Evening Post and Daily Tribune,* December 16, 1922.

[69] Information provided by Helen Duncan, November 14, 1954.

William A. Wirt for many years had toyed with the idea of extending one of Gary's "complete" schools through the first two years of college.[70] The success of Indiana University's classes in Gary led him to believe a municipal junior college would do equally well. Accordingly, Gary College was founded in 1932. Albert Fertsch was appointed director of the new institution which was housed in the Horace Mann School. The Gary School Board subsidized the college only to the extent that it continued to pay Fertsch's salary as director of adult education in the city's schools and, also, the salaries of office employees of the college.[71] Born in a time of great depression, with no funds, and inadequate library and laboratory facilities, the new college had a rough time. The student body did not exceed one hundred fifty the first year and most of them were unable to pay the required tuition. Salaries of instructors, most of whom were from the University of Chicago, were only partially paid for several years. Despite these handicaps, Gary College survived the depression years, in the course of which numerous young people, who could not have financed their education in distant institutions, were given the opportunity to continue their studies beyond the high school years.[72]

[70] Bourne, *The Gary Schools,* 18-19.

[71] Interview with Ruth Wall Nelson, November 11, 1955. Mrs. Nelson was associated with Gary College as a student and as secretary to its director from 1933 to 1948, at which time the college was taken over by Indiana University.

[72] Interview with Ruth Wall Nelson, November 11, 1955. The back salaries were paid in full by 1936. In time a working arrangement was made with the University of Illinois for the acceptance of credits earned by Gary College students. Indiana University also took a favorable view toward the college. In 1948 the College was absorbed by Indiana University which immediately established its Gary Center in the annex of the City Methodist Church at Sixth Avenue and Washington Street. Albert Fertsch was retained as director of the new center.

Indiana University had discontinued its Gary center upon the establishment of the junior college, but agreed to offer such advanced courses as might be needed in the steel city. This action led educators and civic leaders in Hammond, Whiting, and East Chicago to seek an expansion of the University's program in their area. Accordingly, the Hammond-Whiting-East Chicago Center was established during the summer of 1932 with offices in East Chicago's Roosevelt High School. Instead of placing a local educator in charge as had been done in Gary, Hugh W. Norman, head of the Bureau of Visual Education in the Extension Division and a member of the University faculty, became the Center's executive secretary. The selection of Norman assured a more intimate tie with the University than had been enjoyed by the Gary Center.[73] The University's program for the region was announced in the new Center's first catalogue:

The center is organized to give a fuller program of University Extension Service to the northern part of the state, not only to students who are beginning their college work but also to advanced students. Courses of graduate level will be organized when the demand justifies. In addition, the University provides various services for community groups such as parent-teacher associations, clubs, civic organizations, and industries. The Center office is a clearing-house for such services as correspondence study, reading courses, lectures, package libraries, visual aids for school and community, and general information. The Executive Secretary, a member of the University faculty, will give advisory service to individuals or groups concerning ways through which the University may serve Indiana citizens.

[73] Hammond *Lake County Times,* April 14, June 14, 1932. Norman guided the Hammond-Whiting-East Chicago Center, the name of which was changed in 1936 to Calumet Center, until 1946 when he moved to the Bloomington campus as associate dean of the Division of Adult Education and Public Services, the successor of the Extension Division. In 1955 Norman became dean of this part of the University.

This statement was an indication that opportunities for
a higher education as well as for other cultural services,
which had heretofore been lacking, were to be presented
to the area's residents.

During the first semester of 1932-33, the new center
had 253 students enrolled in 32 classes. Classes were
held in the late afternoons and evenings at Roosevelt and
Washington high schools in East Chicago, and at Hammond High School. A few courses were also given in
La Porte and Michigan City. While the majority of
the center's students were from the major industrial
cities, others from Munster, Highland, Griffith, and
from the Illinois communities of Lansing and Calumet
City, attended the classes in Hammond and East Chicago.
Norman also supervised the organization of advanced
and graduate courses in Gary, most of which were taught
by instructors from the University's Bloomington faculty.
The center opened its doors with a faculty of twelve
instructors, four of whom took up their residence in
the region. The others were part-time teachers from the
Bloomington campus and from universities in Chicago.[74]
In 1933 a summer school became a permanent feature
of the center's program in the area. The first semester
of 1933-34 found 427 students enrolled in 41 classes
taught by sixteen instructors, five of whom made their
homes in the area.

The Hammond-Whiting-East Chicago Center enabled
hundreds of high school graduates in the depression ridden years to obtain at least half of the regular four-year
college course at home. Moreover, many parents who

[74] The resident instructors, all of whom had recently graduated
from Indiana University, were William L. Bright, chemistry; Irvin
S. Goldman, English; Harold E. Burns, mathematics; and Powell A.
Moore, history. In 1946 Burns succeeded Norman as director of the
Calumet Center.

could afford to send their children away to college, but
who thought they were not sufficiently matured to leave
home, sent them to the local center. As the nation
recovered from the depression, numerous young people
attended evening classes while working in the region's
industries to finance the remainder of their education on
the Bloomington campus or at other colleges and universities. The center also enriched the lives of adults
who had no need for college credits but were eager to
continue the education they had received in high school
or college. By the end of 1933, the University's center
was a vital part of the cultural life of the region.[75]

[75] In 1939-40 the University erected a building in East Chicago to
house the Calumet Center. While classes were held in this building
during the day and evenings, courses were continued in the evenings
at East Chicago's Roosevelt High School and at Hammond High School.
The Calumet Center's largest enrollment before World War II was
1,733 during the first semester of 1940-41. Enrollment reached 1,847 in
1947-48, the largest in its history.

14

LABOR AND LABOR TROUBLES

THE GREAT MAJORITY of the region's inhabitants, after the turn of the present century, were industrial workers. Those in Gary, Hammond, and East Chicago nearly all worked in steel mills or were engaged in the fabrication and manufacture of products made from steel. In Whiting, the Standard Oil Company's refinery absorbed most of the working population. The employees of these industries were for the most part unskilled workers, not craftsmen in the traditional sense of the term. White collar workers were in the minority and the region never had a leisure class. Thus, the average family was concerned with such items as hourly wages, the length of the workday, and the conditions under which its wage earners labored in the industrial plants.

Labor in the Region's Earliest Industries

The first industries to be established in the region had no serious labor troubles in their early years. This was largely due to their size, nature, and to their distance from Chicago, the nearest center of the organized labor movement. The George H. Hammond meat-packing plant in Hammond and the Standard Oil Company's Whiting refinery were the only industries large enough to be of interest to labor unions. The Hammond packing house had little trouble with its employees although wages and working conditions were no better than those that caused riots and bloodshed at the large packing plants in Chicago. Many workers at the Hammond plant were Germans who were inclined to be conservative in their thinking and acting. Hammond's other industries, those in East Chicago, and the plants in more isolated places as Valparaiso and the Porter-Chesterton area were too small and, in some instances, too poor to invite much attention from organized labor. Moreover, the personal and friendly relationships that frequently prevailed between employers and employees in small plants discouraged union activity.

The Standard Oil Company in Whiting, which early gained a reputation as a considerate employer, enjoyed through the years a greater measure of employee loyalty than did the other large corporations in the area. Work at the refinery was regular, the plant being little affected by industrial disturbances and by national business recessions. Standard Oil insisted on the seven-day week with common labor and mechanics working ten hours and stillmen twelve hours daily. As to wages, the company paid about 5 per cent more than did other industries in the region. In 1895 the highest daily wage was $4.50 for skilled labor and $2.50 for unskilled workmen. The lowest paid adult males received 15 cents an hour or an average of $1.50 a day. The average daily wage for women and girls was 90 cents and that for boys was 80 cents.[1] The oil company provided free medical treatment for all employees injured at work through no negligence of their own. Seriously injured employees were sent to a Chicago hospital and cared for until fully recovered. There was no limit to the length of time a worker might

[1] Indiana Department of Statistics, *Sixth Biennial Report*, 1895-96, p. 160.

receive medical care and full wages were paid while he was off the job.[2]

Standard Oil was one of the first American industries to provide pensions for its employees. The plan, started January 1, 1903, to which the employees paid nothing, provided that any worker with twenty-five years of continuous and satisfactory service who had reached the age of 65 might be retired on 25 per cent of his average pay for the preceding ten years. An employee between the ages of 60 and 64 with twenty years of continuous service might retire at his own request on a pension averaging 50 per cent of his average earnings for the ten preceding years; upon reaching the age of 65, the rate was reduced to 25 per cent. The system was liberalized in 1910 by reducing the time of service from 25 to 20 years, while during the first year of retirement an annuity of 50 per cent of the average pay for the preceding decade was to be paid, then 25 per cent thereafter.[3]

Bricklayers, carpenters, boilermakers, stationary engineers, firemen, and nearly all the workers in the mechanical department belonged to unions but, in general, Standard Oil did not recognize unions, did not bargain collectively, and avoided, if possible, any formal contract with labor organizations. When strikes did occur, the company did not hesitate to use court injunctions and strikebreakers. The most serious strike at the Whiting refinery began in July, 1906, when several hundred workers struck for higher wages. Within a few weeks almost every department of the plant was closed because of the walkout or for lack of materials. The strikers besieged the plant when strikebreakers were brought in, but the

2 Giddens, *Standard Oil Company (Indiana)*, 41.

3 *Ibid.*, 62-63; John R. Commons, *et al., History of Labour in the United States* (4 vols. New York, 1918-35), 3:388.

company immediately secured an injunction which forbade picketing and interference with nonunion workers. An agreement was made between company officials and a committee of the strikers in which the former agreed to reinstate leaders discharged for causing the strike and to discuss wage demands. The strike ended in November with a 5 to 10 per cent increase in wages for all employees.[4]

In June and July, 1894, workers and other citizens of the region took an active part in the Pullman strike, one of the most violent episodes of that time. This strike in South Chicago, which was caused by a wage reduction, began early in May. It was followed, in the latter part of June, by a sympathetic strike by the railroad unions. Trains carrying Pullman cars were stopped on all sides of Chicago and by July freight, passenger, and mail services into and out of the city were seriously affected. The unions blocked railroad tracks in Hammond, Whiting and East Chicago. For a time trains destined for Chicago remained on sidings at Crown Point, Tolleston, and Miller. Eventually, the regon's cities and towns were faced with a shortage of food and other necessities. Grocers in Crown Point brought supplies from Chicago in horse-drawn wagons as had been customary before the railroads were built. Whiting felt the effects of the blockade more than did the other communities since the roads between it and Chicago were so deep with sand as to be almost impassable for heavy vehicles. Hammond and East Chicago fared better as they were connected with Chicago by an electric trolley line.[5]

4 Giddens, *op. cit.,* 41-42, 63-65.
5 Howat (ed.), *A Standard History of Lake County,* 1:273; Ball, *Encyclopedia of Genealogy and Biography of Lake County,* 41. For a general account of the Pullman strike, see Almont Lindsey, *The Pullman Strike* . . . (University of Chicago Press, 1942).

Numerous citizens of Hammond, East Chicago, and Whiting helped the strikers maintain the blockade. Most of the merchants, some of the ministers, and a majority of the inhabitants were reported to be in sympathy with the strikers. This was largely because many of the region's residents were employed in various capacities by the railroads. A Federal court issued a blanket injunction enjoining all persons from interfering with the transportation of the mails and the flow of interstate commerce. The strikers and sympathetic citizens retaliated with violence. Freight and passenger cars parked in the Hammond yards were overturned and burned. Nonunion trainmen were assaulted and beaten. A railroad bridge was burned in East Chicago. Thomas E. Knotts, later the first mayor of Gary, figured prominently in these troubles. Knotts, editor of a Populist organ, the *Calumet Journal,* urged the strikers to defy the Federal injunction. He was arrested by a United States marshal on the charge that he climbed into the cab of a locomotive and "intimidated" the engineer and fireman. Knotts was taken to Indianapolis and arraigned for contempt of court before a Federal judge but was released immediately on his own recognizance and was never brought to trial.[6]

On July 8 the peak of violence was reached when several United States soldiers, accompanying a work train, fired on strikers and citizens engaged in destroying a Pullman car in the Hammond yards; when the smoke cleared away it was found that an innocent bystander had been killed and three others wounded. Two com-

[6] Chicago *Daily Tribune,* July 2, 7, 9, 1894; Whiting *Democrat,* July 12, 1894. The Chicago *Tribune* accused Knotts of being an agent of Eugene V. Debs, the Socialist leader who called the railroad strike. Debs was sentenced on the same charge to six months imprisonment in a Federal prison. See Cannon, "Tom Knotts As Mayor and Man," in Gary *Evening Post,* March 26, 1921.

panies of Federal troops were rushed from Fort Sheridan, Illinois, to Hammond to rescue the soldiers and restore order. Additional troops were sent to Whiting and both cities were placed under martial law. This ban was lifted on July 11 when four companies of the Indiana state militia replaced the Federal troops. The militia threw a strong guard around the railroad yards in Hammond. A Gatling gun was set on the platform of the Erie station where passengers came under the scrutiny of sentries posted there. On July 17 a freight train was wrecked in East Chicago when strike sympathizers rioted against the militia. The governor immediately dispatched four more companies of state troops into the region, thereby bringing an end to the violence so far as the Calumet Region was concerned.[7]

Organized Labor and the Steel Industry

The effort of the unions to organize the workers in the nation's leading industry, steel, is one of the classic stories of American industry. Not only did the steel companies resist unionization but the very nature of the industry stood as a barrier against such a program. The variety of labor in the steel mills, ranging from skilled, semi-skilled, to unskilled, bewildered labor leaders accustomed to the craft union idea. Moreover, the tremendous amount of capital needed to produce steel efficiently and at low cost led to the formation of gigantic corporations. Such combinations possessed the wealth and able leadership to exclude the unions from their plants for many years. On the other hand, organized labor operated with insufficient funds and was too often handicapped by

[7] Hammond *Lake County News,* July 5, 12, 19, 1894; Chicago *Daily Tribune,* July 9, 10, 1894; Whiting *Democrat,* July 12, 19, 1894; Ball, *Encyclopedia of Genealogy and Biography,* 41.

inferior and, at times, by radical leadership. Moreover, management was centralized and labor decentralized throughout the early years. In fairness to all, however, it should be remembered the majority of the American public, a large segment of labor, and many industralists were then honestly skeptical of the need for and the wisdom of labor unions.

One of the earliest important developments in the unionization of the iron and steel industry occurred in 1856 when a group of Pittsburgh iron puddlers founded the Sons of Vulcan. In 1876 other unions such as the Associated Brotherhood of Iron and Steel Heaters and the Iron and Steel Roll Hand's Union united with the Sons of Vulcan to form the Amalgamated Association of Iron, Steel, and Tin Workers. Amalgamated's membership was restricted to skilled workers which proved to be a hindrance to the effort to organize all classes of labor in the steel industry. The skilled workers were generally unwilling to sacrifice their high wages in prolonged strikes to organize the unskilled. Moreover, some mill owners, fearful of any efforts to organize all their workers, made contracts with Amalgamated because of its stand in regard to the unskilled workers. Amalgamated also closed its doors to Negroes, a course which encouraged their use as strikebreakers. The union blocked or, at best, half-heartedly supported efforts in later years to organize all classes of steel workers. Amalgamated enjoyed a fair degree of success until 1892 when it was weakened by its defeat in the Homestead strike against the Carnegie interests.[8]

[8] Lewis L. Lorwin and Jean A. Flexner, *The American Federation of Labor* (Brookings Institution, Washington, D. C., 1933), 33, 180; Sterling Spero and Abram L. Harris, *The Black Worker. The Negro and the Labor Movement* (New York, 1931), 249-50.

United States Steel Corporation and Organized Labor

In 1901 the organization of the United States Steel Corporation inaugurated a new era in the steel industry. It also started a new chapter in the tug of war between management and organized labor. The company was the prime target of unions from its very beginning. Since it was the nation's largest producer of steel, labor leaders reasoned if it could be compelled to deal with the unions the smaller companies would also fall in line. On the other hand, officials of the steel corporation believed if they stood firm for the open shop in their mills, the industry in general would present a united front against organized labor. In June, 1901, the corporation's executive committee sent the following directive to the presidents of its various subsidiary companies: "We are unalterably opposed to any extension of union labor and advise subsidiary companies to take a firm position . . ."[9]

In the summer of 1901 Amalgamated, which had contracts with several of the Carnegie mills recently absorbed by United States Steel, called a strike against the corporation on the assumption that the first stages of the formation of the company afforded the best opportunity to organize its nonunion mills. J. Pierpont Morgan, the principal founder of United States Steel, affirmed that he was not an enemy of organized labor and expressed a willingness to negotiate with the union. And yet, it was soon apparent that the steel officials were by no means eager for peace at any price. Morgan, Charles M. Schwab, and Judge Elbert H. Gary agreed to the wage scale demanded on condition that Amalgamated refrain from organizing their nonunion mills. The union rejected this proposal. In the end, Amalgamated was

[9] *Investigation of the United States Steel Corporation* (*House Reports,* 62 Congress, 2 session, No. 1127, August 2, 1912), 128.

compelled to accept an agreement covering fewer mills than any of the previous proposed settlements included. Loss of the strike seriously weakened the union.[10]   In July, 1909, Amalgamated again went on strike.   The walkout, which did not involve the newly opened Gary mills, was a complete failure and marked the elimination of unions from the corporation's mills.[11]

The American Federation of Labor hammered away at United States Steel from time to time.   In 1909 it referred to the corporation as the greatest enemy of organized labor.[12]   Two years later the A. F. of L., which had consistently urged the restriction of foreign immigration on the grounds that immigrants threatened the standard of living of American workers, held the corporation responsible for the flood of foreigners to this country.   In referring to the steel company's original stand against the unions, the Federation made the following statement:[13]

Following that declaration, the evidence clearly shows how American labor felt. Justly or unjustly, they considered themselves persona non grata and the works of the United States Steel Corporation. The process of filling the places of the union laborers is interesting and important to observe. American laborers loyal to the unions could not be had. Something had to be done to get laborers. Southern Europe was appealed to. Hordes of laborers from Southern Europe poured into the United States. They were almost entirely from the agricultural classes, knew absolutely nothing about iron and steel manufacturing, but were sufficient

[10] Lorwin and Flexner, *The American Federation of Labor,* 63-65.

[11] Charles A. Gulick, *Labor Policy of the United States Steel Corporation* (Columbia University, *Studies in History, Economics, and Public Law,* Vol. 116, No. 1, 1924), 103.

[12] *Ibid.,* 185. The American Federation of Labor had been organized in 1886 to promote independent trade unionism based upon craft autonomy. *Dictionary of American History,* edited by James Truslow Adams (5 vols. and index. New York, 1940), 1:60.

[13] *Investigation of the United States Steel Corporation,* 129.

to fight the unions. They were absolutely unskilled, but they could work, especially as common laborers. . . . The result is that about 80% of the unskilled laborers in the iron and steel business are foreigners of these classes. With the benefit of a skilled American foreman, such a crew can work out results in unskilled labor production. The profits of this system of labor employment go to the Steel Corporation, while the displaced American laborer shifted as best he could.

Labor Policies of United States Steel Corporation

In the early years, the corporation's labor policies were characterized as paternalistic and autocratic—paternalistic primarily in its welfare program and autocratic in its handling of grievances and its methods of fixing wages and hours of labor. There was concrete evidence of paternalism in Gary where the corporation was unusually generous in its grants of land and money to churches, hospitals, social agencies, and also to the city. William P. Gleason, superintendent of the corporation's Gary works, as head of the city's park board, was largely responsible for the development of Gary's park and recreation areas. The steel company made it possible for hundreds of its employees to own their own homes. It even furnished water for their lawns and gardens free of charge. In 1910 the corporation inaugurated a pension plan to which the workers contributed nothing. A hospital to provide treatment for employees injured in the mills was established on the grounds of the Gary Works, and visiting nurses were employed to protect the health of worker's families. Critics of the steel company alleged the welfare program and its generosity to the communities where its plants were located were designed to make the workmen feel that labor unions were unnecessary.[14]

14 Gulick, *Labor Policy of the United States Steel Corporation*, 185;

As far as the corporation's autocratic tendencies were concerned, there was little to indicate that it possessed them to a greater extent that did other large combinations of that time. As the largest producer of steel in the nation, it did enjoy an advantage in the determination of wages and hours of labor. The smaller companies obviously could not pay higher wages for a shorter working day and, at the same time, compete with the corporation whose mills were, in general, the most efficient in the industry. United States Steel made it clear to its employees that union activity would not be permitted in its mills. Accordingly, as early as 1911 men were discharged from the Gary Works for union membership. William P. Gleason was widely regarded as an autocrat who ruled with an iron hand, and it was believed that the men below him had little security in their jobs. In fairness to Gleason, however, his strongest critics agreed those were rough and tumble times in the mills and that a strong hand was necessary to secure production. The charge was often made that Gary was a "one industry" city because the steel company wanted to control the labor market and, also, to prevent unions from being established at its doorstep.[15] It is likely that steel officials saw an advantage in the corporation being the heart and core of the city's life.

Judge Gary saw no need for unions. Instead, he insisted employees could secure adjustments of their grievances by personal appeals—over the heads, if need be, of foremen to plant superintendents and even to the corporation's New York office. Gary often said his office door was open to any employee with a grievance. That

United States Steel Corporation, *Ninth Annual Report,* 1910, p. 6; Quillen, The Industrial City, 316.

[15] Quillen, *op. cit.,* 317; Gary *Republican,* May 6, 1916; Hammond *Lake County Times,* July 21, 1928.

the "high command" was sincere in this attitude seems unquestionable, but the fact remained that individual workers seldom dared to make such complaints. Moreover, an employee could seldom afford the expense and time to make the journey from Gary to New York to inform Judge Gary of his troubles. The foremen were all too often the voice of authority, particularly to the foreign-born workers. Nepotism, favoritism, and bribery were known to prevail in the mills. Stories still circulate in Gary of foremen who had the employees under them paint their houses, mow their lawns, and perform other tasks at no cost to themselves. Hence, it was not surprising that numerous workers were easily persuaded to join the unions when the opportunity came in the troubled months after World War I.

The major complaint of the steelworkers was directed at the shift system with its long working days and weeks. The fundamental process in the steel industry, the conversion of iron ore into steel in the blast and open-hearth furnaces, is a continuous operation. Once a furnace is put into blast, it is not put out except for a complete cessation of work. If a blast furnace is allowed to cool, it must be completely rebuilt at tremendous cost. In case of strikes, a furnace is "banked," a process that requires several days. An equal amount of time is necessary to put it back into operation. The simplest method of maintaining a continuous labor force was to operate with two shifts of men, each working a twelve-hour turn seven days a week. In 1914, 41 per cent of the employees in the blast furnaces were working seven shifts of twelve hours each, a total of eighty-four hours a week.[16] Such an arrangement carried with it the "long turn"

[16] U. S. Department of Labor, Bureau of Labor Statistics, *Bulletin 305. Wages and Hours of Labor in the Iron and Steel Industry, 1907-1920* (Washington, D. C., 1922), 17.

when a shift made the change from the day to the night turn.   On Sunday mornings the incoming workers tended the furnaces until Monday morning, a full 24-hour "day."   This put them on the night shift for that week and the others changed to the day; a week later their positions were reversed.   Critics referred to such an arrangement as the "eight-day week."[17]

The seven-day week was confined almost exclusively to the blast furnaces and, more specifically, to such essential workmen as the "blowers" who had the highest earnings of workers in the blast furnaces.   The steel companies did not insist upon a seven-day week in other departments except for a few workers who made repairs or did other work that was essential.   In 1912 only about 15 per cent of all the steelworkers were on the seven-day week.   The others worked a twelve-hour day for six days each week and alternated from day to night shifts.   Nevertheless, the work week in the steel mills was longer than that in other industries, the 53.5 hour week being the average in all American manufacturing establishments in 1914.[18]   The American Federation of Labor, whose objective was the eight-hour day, made vigorous efforts to focus public attention on the steel industry.   That America's leading industry should lag far behind in such vital measures was also intolerable to humanitarians.   Carl Sandburg, poet of smoke and steel, in 1915 looked with critical eyes on those who condoned the labor policies of the steel companies:

[17] John A. Fitch, "Old Age at Forty," in *The American Magazine,* 71:656 (March, 1911).

[18] *Labor Conditions in the Iron and Steel Industry* (4 vols. *Senate Documents,* 62 Congress, 1 session, No. 110); 3:160; Commons, *et al., History of Labour in the United States,* 3:109.

The Mayor of Gary

I asked the Mayor of Gary about the 12-hour day
      and the 7-day week.
And the Mayor of Gary answered more workmen steal
      time on the job in Gary than any other place in
      the United States.
"Go into the plants and you will see men sitting
      around doing nothing—machinery does every-
      thing," said the Mayor of Gary when I asked
      him about the 12-hour day and the 7-day week.
And he wore cool cream pants, the Mayor of Gary,
      and white shoes, and a barber had fixed him up
      with a shampoo and a shave and he was easy
      and imperturbable though the government weather
      bureau thermometer said 96 and children were
      soaking their heads at bubbling fountains on the
      street corners.
And I said good-by to the Mayor of Gary and went
      out from the city hall and turned the corner into
      Broadway.
And I saw workmen wearing leather shoes scruffed
      with fire and cinders, and pitted with little holes
      from running molten steel,
And some had bunches of specialized muscles around
      their shoulder blades hard as pig iron, muscles
      of their fore-arms were sheet steel and they looked
      to me like men who had been somewhere.[19]

Gary, Indiana, 1915.

On the other hand, a large proportion of the steelworkers
were either indifferent or were actively opposed to the
shorter working day. This was particularly true of the
foreign born who had been accustomed to long hours of
labor in the old countries. Moreover, numerous workers
feared an eight-hour day would mean smaller pay checks.

[19] Carl Sandburg, *Smoke and Steel* (Copyright, 1920, by Harcourt,
Brace and Company, Inc.; renewed by Carl Sandburg. Reprinted by
permission of the publishers), 25.

The Background of the Steel Strike of 1919

World War I provided the stimulation for the steel strike which occurred in 1919. When the nation entered the war the need for a united front against the enemy and for maximum production resulted in important concessions to organized labor. The War Labor Board, while forbidding strikes and lockouts, recognized the right of labor to organize and bargain collectively through its chosen representatives. Employers were forbidden to discharge workers for joining the unions. The board also insisted upon the basic eight-hour day in all cases in which existing laws required it. Despite these guarantees, the demands of the workers were never fully granted by the steel industry which subtly warded off the efforts of the Labor Board.[20] The war presented labor with the opportunity to organize the steel industry which it had never possessed and might never have again when peace came. According to William Z. Foster, one of the leaders in the organization movement, and, in later years, prominent in the Communist party in the United States, "as the war wore on . . . the situation changed rapidly in favor of the unions. The demand for soldiers and munitions had made labor scarce; the Federal administration was friendly; . . . the steel industry was the master-clock of the whole war program and had to be kept in operation at all costs. . . . It was an opportunity to organize the industry such as might never again occur."[21]

The American Federation of Labor at its annual convention in 1918 appointed a national committee to organize the iron and steel industry, of which William Z. Foster became secretary. Organization of industries in the Calumet Region was started in September of the

[20] Lorwin and Flexner, *The American Federation of Labor,* 165, 171.
[21] Foster, *The Great Steel Strike,* 17.

same year.   Because of the War Labor Board, which prevented the steel companies from discharging employees for joining the unions, considerable success was achieved by the labor groups before the war ended.   On October 1, 1918, the United States Steel Corporation, followed by many of the independents, inaugurated the basic eight-hour day.   This was done, it was said, to weaken the union's efforts to organize the industry.[22]   Actually, the basic eight-hour day had nothing at all to do with the length of the work day but was a method of wage payment that gave "time and a half" for all work over eight hours.   This was equivalent to a 16 2/3 per cent increase in pay for the thousands who continued to work, as they had always done, the twelve-hour day.

The Gary *Daily Tribune* on September 23, 1918, for the first time took notice of the presence of labor organizers in the steel city.   The *Tribune* accused the organizers of undermining the morale of the workers, thereby lessening production at a time when the companies were endeavoring to provide the nation with steel to win the war.   Of the two daily papers in Gary, the *Tribune* was the most partisan in the support of the steel corporation during the crisis that followed, while the Gary *Evening Post* pursued a more moderate and objective course in its presentation of the news.   Despite the efforts of the *Post* to deal fairly with both sides, William Z. Foster said it was also hostile to organized labor:

The new unions immediately boycotted the *Tribune*. Result: The *Gary Post,* somewhat friendly inclined, doubled its circulation at once. The *Post* then became more friendly; whereupon, it is alleged, a leading banker called the editor to his office and told him that if he did not take a stand against the unions his credit would be stopped, which would have meant suspension within a week. That very day the *Post* joined the *Tribune's* campaign of

22 Lorwin and Flexner, *The American Federation of Labor,* 180-81.

abuse. Apparently, the *Post's* youthful editor had learned a new wrinkle in journalism.[23]

The *Post's* editorials and columns during the strike failed to substantiate Foster's allegations. On the contrary, the *Post* on October 2, 1919, several days after the beginning of the strike, editorially criticized Judge Gary for his refusal to negotiate with the union leaders.

The United States Steel Corporation repeatedly sought to convince the public that the movement to organize the steelworkers was the work of radicals and foreigners, that it was the beginning of a concerted effort by "Reds" to destroy the American industrial system. The presence of such a heavy foreign-born element in the region, a large proportion of which were persuaded to join the unions, assured a degree of success to such a campaign. Numerous native American citizens, already disturbed by war hysteria and social unrest, often regarded those who joined the unions as alien revolutionaries. Moreover, the Red scare was more readily invoked because William Z. Foster had been associated with the I. W. W. (International Workers of the World), and was generally regarded as being a radical. Doubtless there were radicals of various stripes in the region's cities who cooperated with agitators from the outside to foment discontent and violence. Apparently, these troublemakers were not so much interested in the cause of organized labor as they were eager to bring about a rift between employer and employee.[24]

[23] Foster, *op. cit.*, 169.

[24] Commons, *et al., History of Labour in the United States,* 3:297; Rowland H. Harvey, *Samuel Gompers, Champion of the Toiling Masses* (Stanford University, 1935), 275. Gen. Leonard Wood, commander of the Fifth Army whose troops were sent to Gary during the strike, said the steelworkers were loyal Americans. The Red element, according to Wood, used the strike situation to foment violence and discontent. See Wood's statement in Gary *Daily Tribune,* October 16, 1919.

Tension increased as the organizing of the steel mills progressed. Gary's newspapers and Hammond's *Lake County Times* repeatedly warned the public of probable trouble. In January, 1919, several hundred businessmen gathered in Gary's Broadway Theater to pledge themselves to put a stop to the "infamous Bolshevik and Red propaganda which was intended to stir up trouble in local steel plants." Serious trouble was probably averted when the mayors of Gary, Hammond, and East Chicago forbade parades and public meetings which radicals had scheduled for Sunday, May 4, 1919, to commemorate the anniversary of the Haymarket riots which occurred in 1886 in Chicago. Despite this precaution, near-riots broke out in Gary and East Chicago. The police, aided by irate citizens, dispersed informal street gatherings which were being addressed by speakers in various foreign languages. Red badges and red neckties were reportedly stripped from the orators.[25] The *Lake County Times,* of May 5, in referring to these episodes, declared: "the way to stop Bolshevism in Lake County is to stop the haranguing of the excitable foreign-born by speakers in Russian, Croatian or any foreign language. The police cannot understand them. They would not dare say in English what they rant in a foreign tongue. The minute any man talks to a crowd in a foreign tongue, clap him in jail. Arrest him for provoke [*sic*], for he is inciting a riot." The region was sitting on a powder keg.

In 1919 a wave of strikes swept over the nation. The dissolution of the War Labor Board and other government agencies for dealing with industrial relations almost immediately after the Armistice was generally accepted by labor and management alike as the end of the uneasy industrial truce which had prevailed during the war. The

25 Gary *Evening Post,* January 6, May 5, 1919.

situation grew tense when business stagnation gave way to the hectic post-Armistice boom. Those favoring strikes urged that the industrial boom and the labor shortage promised success, while further delay might jeopardize, the cause of labor. Labor's unrest was stimulated by an increase in the cost of living. In addition, workers in the steel mills felt they had not secured their full share of the war prosperity. The typical work day in the steel industry had remained at twelve hours, and the cost of living had so nearly kept pace with the wage increases that standards of living had not noticeably improved. What followed was characteristic of newly organized labor. The rank and file of the members of the new unions, many of whom associated unions with the idea of a strike, demanded immediate action. They had organized to obtain better pay, shorter hours, and improved working conditions. When employers did not accede to their demands immediately, they felt their only recourse was to strike even though the time might not be right.[26]

The Eve of the Steel Strike

During the summer of 1919 the movement for a strike against the steel industry gained momentum. Samuel Gompers, president of the American Federation of Labor, wrote Judge Gary in June of that year requesting a conference between representatives of the unions and officials of the United States Steel Corporation. Judge Gary did not answer the letter. On July 20 the national committee of the A. F. of L. for organizing the steel industry drew up a list of demands, the most important of which called for the abolition of the twenty-four hour,

---

[26] Lorwin and Flexner, *The American Federation of Labor,* 181; Quillen, The Industrial City, 316; *Wages and Hours of Labor in the Iron and Steel Industry,* 15; Harvey, *Samuel Gompers,* 275.

shift, an eight-hour day, one day's rest in seven, wage increases to guarantee an American standard of living, the right of collective bargaining, the checkoff system for collecting dues, and the abolition of "company unions." A short time later the statement was made before a Senate committee that what labor most desired was a recognition from the steel corporation of the principle of collective bargaining. The questions of hours, wages, and other demands could be adjusted later.[27]

On August 27, 1919, Judge Gary answered a letter from the strike committee asking for a conference:

We do not think you are authorized to represent the sentiment of a majority of the employees of the United States Steel Corporation and its subsidiaries. We express no opinion concerning any other members of the iron and steel industry.

As heretofore publicly stated and repeated, our corporation and subsidiaries, although they do not combat labor unions as such, decline to discuss business with them. The corporation and subsidiaries are opposed to the "closed shop." They stand for the "open shop" which permits one to engage in any line of employment whether one does or does not belong to a labor union. This best promotes the welfare of both employees and employers.

In view of the well-known attitude as above expressed, the officers of the corporation respectfully decline to discuss with you, as representatives of a labor union, any matters relating to employees. In doing so no personal discourtesy is intended.

In all decisions and acts of the corporation and subsidiaries pertaining to employees and employment their interests are of the highest importance. In wage rates, living and working conditions, conservation for life and health, care and comfort in times of sickness or old age, and providing facilities for the general welfare and happiness of employees and their families, the corporation and subsidiaries have endeavored to occupy a leading and advanced position amongst employers.

27 Arundel Cotter, *United States Steel, A Corporation with a Soul* (New York, 1921), 253, 254. Harvey, *Samuel Gompers*, 284-86. Cotter, who was sympathetic with the corporation, appeared to be sure of his facts.

It will be the object of the corporation and subsidiaries to give such consideration to employees as to show them their loyal and efficient service in the past is appreciated, and that they may expect in the future fair treatment.[28]

Judge Gary's refusal to deal with the unions hastened the day of the strike. He was denounced by speakers as "Kaiser Gary" at the Labor Day celebration in the steel city, his picture being displayed hanging upside down.[29] On September 9, the presidents of the unions, despite Gompers' warning that the strike would be a failure, scheduled the walkout for September 22. On September 10, President Wilson asked the committee to delay the strike until after the opening of the National Industrial Conference early in October. Gompers and various other labor officials supported the President's request but the national strike committee proceeded with plans for the strike.[30]

The Steel Strike in Gary

Regarded by organized labor as the Gibraltar of the United States Steel Corporation, the Gary units were singled out as the most important objectives of the unions. As a labor organizer expressed it: "As Gary goes, so goes the strike. This is the stronghold of the trust. It built the town and runs it. If we win in Gary, the trust is licked."[31] Gary was the storm center within the Chicago district throughout the strike. Not only did the unions

[28] See Cotter, *United States Steel,* 254; Harvey, *Samuel Gompers,* 286; and Gary *Daily Tribune,* August 27, 1919, for this letter. Also see *Investigation of Strike in Steel Industries, Hearings before the Committee on Education and Labor* (U. S. Senate, 66 Congress, 1 session, Washington, D. C., 1919), 6, for details of this episode.

[29] Gary *Daily Tribune,* September 2, 1919.

[30] Lorwin and Flexner, *The American Federation of Labor,* 181-83; Harvey, *Samuel Gompers,* 276.

[31] Quoted in the Chicago *Sunday Tribune,* September 21, 1919.

concentrate their forces there, but radical leaders of
almost every type came to stir up unrest and confusion.

As the strike date approached, the city and the mills
girded themselves for the crisis. Practically all building
construction was stopped and merchants cancelled a large
part of their orders for winter goods.[32]   Mindful of
the recent riots and bloodshed in Hammond during the
Standard Steel Car strike, civic leaders took steps to
prevent such troubles in their city. The Loyal American
League was formed with Samuel Reck, a prominent
realtor, as president. Actually, this organization was a
revival of the American Protective League founded
during the recent war to combat German and Austrian
propaganda. The League was composed of business
and professional men and war veterans. Most of its
members were native Americans. The organization ran
full-page notices in the Gary *Daily Tribune* during the
first three weeks in September indicating law and order
were to be maintained in the city. The League recognized the right of men to strike, but it also insisted any
man desiring to work must not be prevented from doing
so. It also called upon the foreign born to prove themselves worthy of American citizenship.[33]   Shortly after
the strike began, about six hundred business and professional men, alarmed by the blunt warning of the steel
company's officials that unless the mills were kept running
they would be shut down for at least nine months, pledged
themselves to do everything possible to keep the mills in
operation despite the strike.[34]

[32] Chicago *Sunday Tribune,* September 21, 1919.

[33] Gary *Evening Post,* October 8, 1919; Gary *Daily Tribune,* September 16 and 18, 1919. The Memorial Post of the American Legion
protested the use of the name "Loyal American League," pointing out
that union men were confusing the two organizations. It also announced that if Legionnaires belonged to the League they did so as
individuals. See Gary *Daily Tribune,* October 7, 1919.

[34] Chicago *Daily Tribune,* September 27, 1919.

Five days before the start of the strike there were indications that enough workers would live in the mills to keep them in operation when the walkout occurred. Cots for sleeping purposes and carloads of food were brought into the plants. While steel officials denied that fire arms and ammunition were stored in the mills, rumors persisted that rifles were at hand for the defense of the company's property. Maps were published in the newspapers showing how easily the corporation's plants could be defended. It was pointed out that the mills were separated from the city to the south by the Grand Calumet River which would serve as an effective moat against mob violence. Since the corporation controlled the lake front, strikebreakers and supplies could be brought in boats directly to the mills. Probably no other industrial establishment occupied a position so impregnably arranged as to withstand a prolonged industrial siege.[35]

It is difficult to determine the exact number of workers who struck when the walkout was called on September 22. Union officials claimed 97 per cent were idle while the steel corporation insisted 80 per cent of its employees continued on the job. A Chicago newspaper man, who visited the plants on the day the strike began, reported about 27 per cent of the employees of the various plants were not at work. A study of the local newspapers during the first few days of the strike indicate that the claims of unions and management alike were exaggerated. Uncertainty as to the number of men who would join the strike necessitated the "banking" of the furnaces, thereby causing a general disruption of operations. Nevertheless, the mills were kept running sufficiently to provide the city with an adequate supply of gas, electricity, and

[35] Hammond *Lake County Times,* September 17, 1919; Chicago *Daily Tribune,* September 27, 1919.

water.   Native white Americans and Negroes were reported to have paid little attention to the strike order.[36]

The lull in production which occurred when the strike began was brief.   Strikebreakers soon replaced those who had struck.   Agents of the corporation reportedly made a house-to-house canvass for workers in Crown Point and other nearby towns.   Negroes were used as strikebreakers, large numbers being imported from Chicago and the Southern states.   Some Negroes were reported living in the mills at the beginning of the strike.   The corporation's agents were said to have marched Negroes "ostentatiously" through the streets to their jobs in the plants.   On September 29, Mayor William F. Hodges announced that the police would protect any who wished to return to work.   The following day a newspaper reporter found the Gary Steel Works operating at half capacity with about four thousand men on the job.   On October 2, an unbroken line of automobiles was seen moving for more than a half hour into the plant at the change of the afternoon shift.   Also, forty men, each with a lunch bucket, were observed on a streetcar headed for the mills.[37]

A feeling of unrest and uncertainty developed among the strikers when it became evident that the mills were operating without them. The foreign born, in particular, were confused by this unexpected turn of events.   Union leaders worked night and day urging them to stand firm and not to return to work.   Radicals, outside the unions,

[36] Gary *Daily Tribune,* September 21 and 22, 1919. In 1920 the various plants of the United States Steel Corporation in Gary employed a total of 17,760 workers.

[37] Hammond *Lake County Times,* September 25, 1919; Chicago *Daily Tribune,* September 24 and 30, 1919; Gulick, *Labor Policy of the United States Steel Corporation,* 119; Gary *Daily Tribune,* September 2 9, 1919; Gary *Evening Post,* October 2, 1919.

added to the confusion by haranguing crowds on the streets in various languages. A large proportion of the foreign born were unfamiliar with strike methods and procedures. Some were reported to be disappointed that the unions refused to pay them for joining the strike, claiming they had been led to believe they would be paid as much money to stay away from work as the plants gave them to work.[38] One was said to have worked three days in the mills and eleven days as a picket on strike. He went back to the mill and wanted pay for the whole fourteen days and was angry when he was unable to get it.[39] The stage was set for trouble as strikers watched other workers take their jobs in the plants.

On Saturday afternoon, October 4, the peace and quiet which had prevailed since the strike began was suddenly ended. A large crowd of strikers returning from a mass meeting in the East Side Park attacked a streetcar loaded with workers, many of whom were Negroes, on its way up Broadway to the mills. Within a few minutes a serious riot raged along Gary's main street between Tenth and Seventeenth avenues. Policemen, businessmen, and members of the Loyal American League battled the crowd for more than an hour. Firemen assisted in the restoration of order by turning their hose on groups of strikers. While there were no fatalities, dozens of injured crowded the hospitals when the affair ended. Thirty of the riot's leaders were arrested and hurried to the safety of the Crown Point jail. A year later William Z. Foster insisted the outbreak was a trivial affair, a matter for the police. He also charged that the local newspapers were influenced by the steel company's officials to magnify the incident so as to justify the summoning of the state

[38] Chicago *Daily Tribune,* September 30, 1919.

[39] Hough, "Round Our Town," in *Saturday Evening Post,* February 14, 1920, p. 14.

militia to break the strike. Following the riot, Mayor Hodges immediately issued orders forbidding parades and open air meetings for the duration of the strike. Despite this precaution, the city was kept in turmoil by sporadic outbursts of violence throughout Saturday night and Sunday. When it was apparent that the situation was beyond local control, the mayor requested the governor to send the state militia to Gary. Toward Sunday midnight, October 5, four companies of state troops arrived in the city.[40]

But the worst trouble was still yet to come. The presence of the militia, coupled with an announcement by the corporation that all its mills were to be put into operation on Monday inflamed the ardor of the radicals and increased the excitement of the strikers, already at a high pitch. On October 6 the peak of the crisis was reached. It became apparent that war veterans who were among the strikers had no respect for the militia. The former soldiers taunted the state troops with shouts of "Who won the war?" and "Run the tin soldiers home." The Gary *Daily Tribune* reflected the seriousness of the situation:[41]

Thousands of men lined the sidewalks and hooted at the militia as they marched by. Still there was little serious trouble, only seven men being arrested. In the afternoon groups of returned soldiers began to appear on the streets, mingling with the strikers and hooting at the militia. The word was sent out to mobilize

[40] Gary *Daily Tribune*, October 4, 1919; Chicago *Sunday Tribune*, October 5, 1919; Gary *Evening Post*, October 6, 1919; Foster, *The Great Steel Strike*, 170.

[41] Gary *Daily Tribune*, October 7, 1919. The Gary *Evening Post*, more conservatively inclined, in its issue of the same date, estimated the number in the parade at two thousand, of whom between two and three hundred were ex-soldiers in uniform. Several citizens who witnessed the parade told the author it was a "frightening sight" and anything could have happened.

for a parade (parades being forbidden since October 4). It was
led by five hundred men in uniform. Thousands fell in behind
the ex-soldiers, waving their hats and shouting themselves hoarse.
Somebody struck up a soldier's song. As the parade neared the
center of the town, the officials became greatly disturbed. The
militia was assembled in front of the city hall and called to
attention. And they remained that way while the shouting, jeering
column moved past. The troops were ordered to follow and break
up the parade. Then Mayor Hodges appeared, "Hell no," he
shouted. "It would be suicide. Let it go. I've just requested
federal troops and they are on their way. We can control the
situation tonight.

The parade made its way over Seventh Avenue to the
East Side Park where it was addressed by several ex-
service men, all of whom insisted they wished to prevent,
not make, trouble. The speakers declared they wanted
to show the authorities they could keep the peace in
Gary without the help of the militia.[42]

Governor James P. Goodrich, in relaying Mayor
Hodges' request for Federal troops to Gen. Leonard
Wood at Fort Sheridan, said that the militia could not
cope with the situation in Gary.[43] The Gary *Evening
Post* editorially supported the Mayor's action in calling
for Federal troops:[44]

Fortunately, the strikers were actuated by no spirit of disorder.
They had no desire to start anything. They simply failed to realize
that the orders of the mayor had to be obeyed if Gary is to
remain a community in which lives are safe.

But mobs seldom do act from intention of wrong doing in
the beginning. They start innocently enough. But the trouble is
their intentions change. The parade was a very orderly affair
except for the spirit of mob law which it engendered. But by
evening ex-soldiers were playing horse with the militia. And

[42] Gary *Evening Post*, October 7, 1919.

[43] Gen. Leonard Wood, quoted in Hough, "Round Our Town," in
Saturday Evening Post, February 14, 1920, p. 14.

[44] Gary *Evening Post*, October 7, 1919.

horse play in a time of such seriousness might lead in the end
to an overt act that would have had a terrible result.

Mayor Hodges could only call in any element of law on which
he could lay his hands after such an outbreak. He had been defied.
He had been told that not he but the crowd would decide what
could be done in Gary. No mayor worthy of the name could sit
quietly under such a challenge. The strikers forced his hand and
he did not hesitate when it came to a showdown.

Now there will be no further disorder. There will be no more
horse play. The laws will be enforced and the mayor's orders
will be obeyed. Let this be a lesson to Gary that will not soon be
lost.

A few hours after the defiance of the militia by the
paraders, more than a thousand well-equipped United
States Army troops arrived. They were men of the
4th Division, under the command of Col. William S.
Mapes, who had seen combat in France during the recent
war. Five hundred of them were quartered in the corporation's new tin mills, while others were billeted temporarily in the rooms of the Gary Commercial Club, the
Y. M. C. A., the University Club, the Elks Club, and in
the local armory. Colonel Mapes established his headquarters in the city hall and Gary was placed under
martial law.[45] When things quieted down, the troops
were encamped at Aetna, a few miles from the business
section of the city.

The strike, for all practical purposes, ended when the
Federal troops came to Gary. Soldiers patrolled the
streets, providing protection for those who wished to
work in the mills. Parades and public gatherings were
forbidden and strict limitations were placed on picketing.
Within a few days after the troops arrived, so many men
had returned to work that one would not have known a
strike was in progress. On October 14 the corporation

45 Gary *Evening Post* and Gary *Daily Tribune*, October 7, 1919.

announced that its steel works was operating at 50 per cent capacity; its subsidiary, the American Sheet and Tin Plate's tin mill was operating at 65 per cent and its sheet mill at 85 per cent of their normal capacity. By November 26 all the mills were operating at 90 per cent capacity, which was considered normal production in steel circles.[46]

When peace was restored in the city, Colonel Mapes turned his attention toward the elimination of the Reds, I. W. W.'s, and other radicals who had caused trouble during the strike. Since Gary was under martial law, search warrants were not needed to search the houses and quarters occupied by those thought to be troublemakers. In some instances, the military was overly zealous and invaded the homes of people who had no connection with radicals. And yet, quantities of Communist literature, badges, and flags were seized. Several Russians, admitted Communists, were turned over to the immigration authorities for deportation. Colonel Mapes had prisoners erect a barbed wire stockade and a guardhouse across the street from the city hall where the Memorial Auditorium now stands. Others were put to work sweeping the downtown streets. Such harassment was believed to have led many radicals to leave the city. Only about a score of prisoners were ever placed in the "Hotel de Mapes," as the stockade was facetiously called. Mapes later said the stockade was built mainly as a bluff to the radicals. When searching for troublemakers, the soldiers found alcohol stills, quantities of bootleg whisky, houses of prostitution, and instances of white slavery. Colonel Mapes sought to disassociate the workers who had joined the strike from the rabble rousers in the minds of the

[46] Gary *Evening Post,* October 14, 1919; Gary *Daily Tribune,* November 26, 1919. William Z. Foster said the steel mills in the Chicago district were operating at 85 per cent capacity by November 15, 1919. Foster, *The Great Steel Strike,* 172.

public. He made it clear that the radicals were outside the unions entirely. However, it was unfair to credit all the peaceable and law-abiding strikers as "Americans," and all the lawless and violent elements as "foreigners."[47]

The citizens of Gary, not involved in the strike, extended a warm welcome to the soldiers. Dances, motion picture shows, and athletic events provided entertainment and amusement for them. As the community and the mills returned to normal, the troops were kept occupied for a time with manuevers in the sand dunes east of Gary. A battalion of five hundred men was assigned to guard powder stored at the defunct Aetna powder plant. But, as the army stayed on, difficulties with restless and inactive soldiers arose. Several sold their revolvers to civilians, alcoholic beverages seized from bootleggers disappeared from storage, and, late in December, a poolroom brawl between soldiers and civilians occurred. The citizens were obviously weary of the military and of martial law. On December 29 Mayor Hodges informed Gen. Leonard Wood that the crisis had passed and requested the end of martial law. The order to withdraw the troops was given at midnight, December 31. On January 8, 1920, the strike officially ended when the last pickets were withdrawn from the gates of the mills. Four days later, the troops returned to Fort Sheridan. It was a tribute to the good sense and restraint of all parties in the strike that not a single shot was fired by the troops during their three-month rule of Gary.[48]

[47] Gen. Leonard Wood quoted in Gary *Daily Tribune,* October 11, 1919, and in Gary *Evening Post,* October 17, 1919; Foster, *The Great Steel Strike,* 170; Gary *Evening Post,* March 25, 1920; Gary *Daily Tribune,* November 26, 1919; Graham R. Taylor, "At Gary, Some Impressions and Interviews," in *The Survey,* 43:65-66 (November 8, 1919).

[48] Gary *Daily Tribune,* December 29, 1919, January 2 and 8, 1920; Gary *Evening Post,* January 12, 1920.

The Steel Strike in East Chicago

The steel manufacturing plants in East Chicago felt the impact of the strike. Walkouts occurred at the Inland Steel Company's mills and at the Mark Manufacturing Company's plant on September 22, the same day the strike began in Gary.[49] Inland Steel, according to reports, did not expect a strike. The company was said to have been more friendly to organized labor than the other steel interests. Inland had the eight-hour day, not basic but actual for both working and wage purposes, the workers being divided into three shifts. Moreover, the company had recognized the principle of collective bargaining and had permitted its employees to join unions. Inland's workers were said to have had no grievances and to have made no demands prior to the strike.[50] Perhaps the Inland strike was called in the interest of union solidarity in an effort to strengthen organized labor's cause in the other plants of the community.[51]

Inland continued operations when the strike occurred. Living facilities were provided in the plant for the supervisory employees, strikebreakers, and for the loyal workers who chose to remain inside the gates for the duration of the strike. When it was apparent the strike had not curtailed Inland's operations, every effort was made by the unions to prevent workers from entering its gates. Mayor Leo P. McCormick, who took pride in the three

[49] The Mark Manufacturing Company was purchased in 1920 by the American Sheet and Tube Company. In 1923 the Youngstown Sheet and Tube Company absorbed the American Sheet and Tube.

[50] Chicago *Sunday Tribune,* September 28, 1919.

[51] Strikes also occurred at the American Steel Foundries, Standard Forging Company's plant, and the Hubbard Steel Foundries, all of which made large use of steel. The Republic Iron and Steel Company and the Interstate Iron and Steel plant, which had contracts with the Amalgamated Iron, Steel and Tin Union, were not affected by the strike. See Hammond *Lake County Times,* September 22, 1919.

union cards he carried, apparently made no special effort to provide police protection for those who wanted to work. On October 4 a riot of major proportions occurred near the Inland plant when a strikebreaker shot a union picket. A shouting and threatening crowd of about two thousand men and women, which gathered at Inland's main gate, refused to disperse when ordered to do so by local authorities. Realizing the situation was out of hand, the mayor called upon the governor to send in the militia, five hundred state troops arriving the next day. Their commanding officer announced protection would be given to any workers desiring to enter the plant. The soldiers "dried up" the Indiana Harbor section of the city by closing about two dozen "soft drink" parlors which had sold liquor to the strikers. The only trouble the militia had in East Chicago occurred on October 10 when it dispersed a parade of about five hundred foreign women near the Inland plant.[52]

The strike in East Chicago was broken within a few days. By October 10 the noise and smoke coming from the various mills indicated that they were operating at better than 50 per cent capacity. A few days later, Inland Steel was reported working at 65 per cent capacity and 80 per cent of the employees of the Mark Manufacturing Company's plant were said to be back at their jobs. On November 3 the state troops were withdrawn from the city. A major factor in the failure of the strike in East Chicago's steel mills was the use of strikebreakers, mainly Negroes and Mexicans. Some Negroes came in from Chicago and others from the Southern states. Inland Steel showed a preference for Mexicans, the number employed increasing from 90 in 1918 to 945 in 1919,

[52] Chicago *Daily Tribune*, September 26, 1919; Gary *Evening Post*, October 8, 11, 1919; Hammond *Lake County Times*, October 6, 1919.

which was more than 18 per cent of the workers in the plant on the latter date. The Mexicans were housed in bunkhouses and fed in cafeterias in the Inland plant during the strike.[53]

Why the Steel Strike Failed

Why did the steel strike fail? In general, it may be said the major cause was the determined attitude of the United States Steel Corporation to prevent the unionization of its mills at any cost. Lack of funds and lack of unity on the part of the two dozen unions involved were important contributory causes. Gompers believed the strike was poorly timed, and the American Federation of Labor was reluctant to go all out in its support of the young steel unions. Moreover, Gomper's distrust of William Z. Foster and the latter's radical background were handicaps from the very beginning.[54] The indifference and even hostility of the native-born white workers and Negroes to organized labor was another factor. According to Foster, "the foreign workers were simple, sincere, earnest-minded folk, naturally disposed to co-operative effort. While the individualistic, sophisticated American workers all too often attended the ball games and filled the pool rooms, the foreigners packed the union meeting

[53] Gary *Evening Post,* October 15, 1919; Taylor, *Mexican Labor in the United States, Chicago, and the Calumet Region,* 41, 182; Gary *Post-Tribune,* May 24, 1923.

[54] Gompers, in his autobiography, said that when Foster insisted that the strike be called on September 22 despite President Wilson's request that it be postponed until after the start of the National Economic Conference on October 6, "I began to doubt his sincerity and to believe, as I am now convinced, that his whole conciliatory policy toward the American Federation of Labor and the trade union movement was for no other reason than to gain some foothold by which he could undermine and destroy the bona fide labor movement of America and to try to reconstruct it upon the Soviet revolutionary basis." *Seventy Years of Life and Labor,* 2:516-19.

halls. Their worst fault was a woeful unacquaintance with trade-union methods." When well educated in these matters, the foreigner was loyal to the unions. The presence of Federal troops made a profound impression upon the foreign born who had a great respect for military authority. Consequently, they returned to work in large numbers when the soldiers arrived.[55]

The Negroes gave the strike less co-operation than any other element, skilled or unskilled, foreign or native. Their willingness to act as strikebreakers was largely due to the efforts of organized labor in the past to bar them from industry and, too, its reluctance to take those who were employed into the unions. Negro leaders argued that a strike was the one chance for members of their race to prove their competence as industrial workers and to win the good will of employers. Moreover, it was a way of showing organized labor that the Negroes could not be excluded from its ranks forever.[56] While it was true that the steel companies were inclined to replace Negro strikebreakers with white workers, including those who had been on strike, when the walkout was over, the Negro's position in the mills was strengthened.

The unions met their Waterloo at Gary and East Chicago. The failure of the strikes in those cities was said to have doomed, for the time being, the movement to organize the entire steel industry.[57]

Hammond's Standard Steel Car Strike

In March, 1919, one of the most violent strikes in the region's history began at the Standard Steel Car Com-

---

[55] Foster, *The Great Steel Strike,* 171, 205.

[56] *Ibid.,* 205, 207; Spero and Harris, *The Black Worker,* 128.

[57] William Z. Foster said the failure of the strikes in Gary and East Chicago affected adversely the whole Chicago district, thereby weakening

pany's plant in Hammond. This plant, which manufactured railroad cars, was the city's largest industry, employing about three thousand workers at the time of the walkout. Most of the employees at the Standard Steel Car establishment, which was located in an isolated part of southeast Hammond, were foreign born, a large number of whom lived in the immediate vicinity. The American Federation of Labor's various craft unions had been reasonably successful in organizing the foreign-born element, but the native Americans showed a preference for a company-sponsored union. This split among the workers was partly responsible for the violence that occurred during the strike. A demand for an increase in wages was the primary cause for the walkout.[58]

On March 25, 1919, about six hundred men left the plant when the company refused to confer with representatives of the American Federation of Labor's unions. The strikers returned to work when Federal mediators were sent to the plant at the request of Samuel Gompers, president of the Federation. The strike was resumed on July 17 when the company refused to recognize the closed shop. Ten days later the company obtained a temporary injunction from the Federal court forbidding strikers and all persons associated with them to interfere with the operations of the plant in any manner. The *Lake County Times,* which was inclined to be critical of organized labor, disapproved of the court's action. The strike, it reported, had been a very tame affair, the acts of violence alleged by the company consisting of the turning of men around by the pickets as they attempted to enter the

the morale of union members everywhere. Thus undermined, the strike gradually disintegrated. *The Great Steel Strike,* 172.

[58] See Hammond *Lake County Times.* especially issues of March 24-25, July 18 and 28, August 7, 13-14, 21, 28, September 5 and 9, 1919, for reports on the progress of the strike.

plant. On August 7, the Federal court extended the injunction until its October meeting. Subsequently, a large number of employees, mostly native Americans who belonged to the company union, returned to their jobs at the plant.

The situation grew worse as time passed. Local grocers ceased giving credit to strikers, leaving many families short of food. On August 13 crowds were reported loitering in the streets leading to the plant and women were said to be throwing salt and pepper in the eyes of persons seeking to enter the car works. A riot of major proportions occurred the next day when the police and deputy sheriffs tried to protect the men who had returned to work at the plant. About four thousand men and women, stimulated by radical agitators, erected barricades in the streets. Shots were fired and, for a time, the plant was in a state of siege. When it became obvious the local authorities could not control the situation, the mayor requested Governor Goodrich for the militia. On August 20, eleven companies of state troops, totaling 850 men, arrived. Order was restored, the plant resuming operations the next day. The soldiers were withdrawn in about a week when it appeared there would be no more trouble. And yet, only 300 of the original 1,500 on strike had returned to work while the soldiers were on duty.

On August 28, the company inserted a full page statement in the *Lake County Times* that no new orders for railroad cars had been received since the Armistice, while previous orders for 12,000 had been canceled. The strikers were offered employment at the same rates and on the same conditions as prevailed before the walkout, but the company refused to recognize the closed shop. The strikers rejected the offer.

Trouble broke out again on September 5, when the police battled crowds who sought to attack those employed in the plant. On September 8, about two hundred men marched in a body through the streets to their jobs in the plant. This touched off what was probably the worst riot in the region's history. The next day about one thousand men—women were conspicuously absent—armed with bricks, rocks, and, as it was later alleged, with revolvers, gathered at the corner of Calumet Avenue and Highland Street. A parade was formed and the strikers, led by a man in a soldier's uniform and carrying an American flag, moved eastward on Highland Street toward the plant. A pitched battle occurred in the vicinity of what is now the Lyndora Hotel when the paraders ran into police and company guards. Within a few minutes the streets were littered with dead and wounded strikers. In all, four were killed and about sixty wounded. Although the charge was later made that the strikers fired first, it was significant that the police and the plant's guards emerged from the melee comparatively unscathed. A few hours after this clash, a hundred deputy sheriffs and a large number of the city's business and professional men were added to the forces protecting the plant. Local authorities announced the situation was well in hand and that the state militia would not be needed.

A few days later the steelworkers' national strike committee cited the Hammond incident as one of many reasons for not postponing the steel strike, as requested by President Wilson. The committee accused the steel companies of high-handed methods, giving the Hammond tragedy as an example. On the other hand, the strikers were obviously headed for the car works and had they reached its gates a worse situation might have ensued. Disheartened by their failure to close the plant and by

the exhaustion of their savings, the strikers began to return to work. The more stubborn capitulated when the
company warned that all residents of its tenement houses
who were not employees were to be evicted. On October
29, the strike, which had lasted fifteen weeks, officially
ended. The only concession made by the company was a
7 per cent increase in wages.[59]

The Steel Industry and Labor in the 1920's

The failure of the steel strike coupled with the open
shop campaign launched by industrialists caused organized labor to lose ground in the decade that followed.
Judge Gary played a leading role in the open shop movement. For instance, in 1921 he left no doubt in the
minds of the corporation's stockholders as to his position
regarding unions.

As stated and repeated publicly, we do not combat, though
we do not contract or deal with labor unions as such. Personally,
I believe they may have been justified in the long past, for I think
the workmen were not always treated justly, that because of their
lack of experience or otherwise they were unable to protect themselves and, therefore, needed the assistance of outsiders in order to
secure their rights.

But whatever may have been the conditions of employment
in the long past, and whatever may have been the results of
unionism, concerning which there is at least much uncertainty,
there is at present in the opinion of the large majority of both
employers and employees no necessity for labor unions, and that
no benefit or advantage through them will occur to anyone except
the union labor leaders. The "open shop" as heretofore publicly
defined is what we believe in and stand for.[60]

[59] Harvey, *Samuel Gompers*, 285; Hammond *Lake County Times,*
October 23 and 29. 1919.

[60] Elbert H. Gary, *Principles and Policies of the United States Steel
Corporation,* address by Judge Gary at the annual meeting of the
stockholders, April 18, 1921, pp. 10-11. Pamphlet in Gary Public Library.

The United States Steel Corporation did not waiver from Judge Gary's opinions in regard to organized labor. Since it produced more steel than all the other companies combined, the latter followed its example concerning unions. Consequently, the 1920's and early 1930's were reasonably devoid of union activity in the steel mills.

And yet, some good came out of the postwar strike. On its last day (January 8, 1920), the Gary *Evening Post* said "the strike has accomplished much good. It has given a great deal of publicity to an industry which does not seek publicity." The strike focused the attention of the public upon the steel industry with its long work day and long work week, the pressure of public opinion being largely responsible for the gains made by the steelworkers in the next few years. On February 1, 1920, the United States Steel Corporation gave a 10 per cent increase in wages to common laborers for a ten-hour day. This was followed on September 1, 1922, by a 20 per cent increase. A third advance of 10 per cent a year later brought the average wage for common labor to about 60c an hour. Early in March, 1921, the corporation abolished the seven-day week for most of its employees. By 1924 only 5 per cent of its men were working 84 hours a week.[61]

The corporation found it more difficult to grant the eight-hour day. In July, 1923, Judge Gary announced that while the eight-hour day would add about 15 per cent to the cost of steel, the corporation would put it into effect as soon as sufficient labor was available. Hammond's *Lake County Times* predicted that the migration of Negroes and Mexicans into the region would end the

[61] United States Steel Corporation, *Annual Report*, 1920, p. 29; 1922, p. 24; 1923, p. 29; Gary *Evening Post*. March 8, 1921; United States Department of Labor, Bureau of Labor Statistics, *Bulletin 513, Wages and Hours of Labor in the Iron and Steel Industry, 1929* (Washington, D. C., 1930), 7.

labor shortage. Also, that the eight-hour day would add from 25,000 to 35,000 people to Lake County's population within a year. In August, 1923, the corporation inaugurated the eight-hour day for all employees "connected with continuous processes." Wages were increased 25 per cent to compensate for the hours of work thus lost. All other employees remained on the ten-hour day with, as has been noted, a 10 per cent increase in wages. By February, 1924, the change over to the shorter work day was completed.[62] Other steel companies soon adopted the same policies in regard to wages and hours of labor. The industry's willingness to make these concessions and to improve working conditions in general no doubt lessened the interest of its employees in the union movement.

Standard Oil and Labor After World War I

The Standard Oil Company of Indiana was able to avoid the labor troubles which shook the very foundations of the steel industry. The Standard moved quickly to establish improved employer-employee relationships in its plants when the war ended. In 1919 the Industrial Relations Plan, which could well have served as a model for other industries, was put into operation. The purpose of this plan was to provide effective means of contact between management and employees and to give the latter a voice in matters pertaining to their employment such as wages and working conditions. A department of industrial relations was created under the supervision of a director, and an assistant director was appointed at each refinery. Within the department, divisions relating to employment, safety and accident, health and welfare,

---

[62] Hammond *Lake County Times,* July 7, 1923; Gulick, *Labor Policy of the United States Steel Corporation,* 49, 53; United States Steel Corporation, *Annual Report,* 1923, p. 29; 1924, p. 29.

workmen's compensation, statistics, and publication were organized. Managers, superintendents, and employees were free to communicate in person or by letter with the director of industrial relations at any time. A joint general committee was established at each refinery. These committees were composed of representatives elected by the employees and an equal number appointed by the management. The joint committees had jurisdiction over wages, hours, employment, working conditions, safety and accident, recreation, and any other matters which might be brought before them by representatives of either management or employees. If a committee made a recommendation to the management which was not accepted, an appeal could be made to the president of the company and ultimately to the Secretary of Labor in Washington by whose decision both employees and management were to abide. This program lessened the interest of employees in the unions and also the danger of strikes.[63]

In 1920 the Whiting Joint General Committee initiated a move for a six-day week for those who did shift work. Until 1915 these employees had worked twelve hours a day seven days a week. At that time, the company adopted the eight-hour day with no loss of pay but the seven-day week was continued. On May 1, 1920, a schedule was inaugurated by which shift workers received thirty-two consecutive hours off each week. On April 3, 1920, the company adopted a vacation plan by which all employees in continuous service of the company for twenty years or more were to be entitled to an annual vacation of two weeks with pay.[64]

[63] Giddens, *Standard Oil Company (Indiana)*, 337-43. The company began the publication at this time of the *Stanolind Record,* a monthly devoted to company affairs and to the activities of its employees and families.

[64] *Ibid.,* 348-49.

To encourage thrift among its employees and also to stimulate greater interest on their part in the company's affairs, an employee stock purchase plan was set up in March, 1921. This gave employees an opportunity to become partners in the business. Any employee who had been with the company for more than a year was eligible to purchase an amount of stock not in excess of 20 per cent of his annual pay. Regular deductions were made from the employee's pay and deposited by the company to his credit in a special fund. The company also paid into the fund to his credit a sum equal to 50 per cent of his deposit. At the end of five years 15,325 or about 70 per cent of the company's eligible employees had purchased 384,638 shares of stock costing $11,800,000 and which was then worth $34,350,000.[65] In view of these efforts by the Standard Oil Company of Indiana to be a considerate employer, it was not surprising that the Whiting refinery enjoyed a long period of industrial peace.

Such was the story of labor during the first half century of the region's industrial history. While labor gained much in the way of higher wages, shorter hours, and better working conditions, it failed to achieve its major objective, the unionization of the area's industries. This was finally accomplished during the turbulent years of Franklin D. Roosevelt's New Deal program before World War II.

[65] Giddens, *Standard Oil Company (Indiana)*, 351-54.

15

POLITICS, PROHIBITION AND DEPRESSION

THE POLITICAL PATTERN in the region before the Civil War was, in general, similar to that of Indiana and the Old Northwest. Indiana supported Andrew Jackson in his three races for the Presidency. But the nomination of William Henry Harrison, the Northwest's first candidate for the Presidency, to run against Martin Van Buren in 1836 caused political sentiment to turn in favor of the Whigs. Harrison, first governor of the Indiana Territory and the hero of Tippecanoe, was highly popular throughout the state. Porter County gave its vote to him in 1836, its first election, and again in 1840, but Lake County, which cast its initial vote in the latter election, was carried by Martin Van Buren, a Democrat. After Harrison's death in 1841, the Whig party grew weaker in Indiana. In the national election of 1844 the Democrats won in Lake County and in the state as a whole, but lost in Porter County by six votes. In the presidential elections of 1848 and 1852 both Lake and Porter counties as well as the state were carried by the Democrats.[1]

County Politics, 1848-1933

Antislavery sentiment in the region was strong as early as 1848 since a large proportion of its inhabitants came

[1] For election returns, see the *Tribune Almanac for the Years 1838*

533

from the eastern states and from Germany, and were, for the most part hostile to slavery. In September, 1848, the Free Soil party was established in Lake County by Bartlett Woods, Judge William Clark, Wellington Clark, and other prominent citizens. Enthusiastic meetings were held in Crown Point and other places in the county during the ensuing presidential campaign.[2] More than one fourth of the votes cast in Lake County in that year's election went to Martin Van Buren, the Free Soil candidate for the Presidency.[3]

Lake and Porter counties were strongholds of the Republican party from the time it was founded in 1854. Citizens in the central and southern parts of the state, on the other hand, were slower to join the new party. Indiana went Democratic in the presidential election of 1856, whereas Lake and Porter counties were carried by the Republicans. Although Abraham Lincoln won the state by a small margin in 1860, more than two thirds of the votes in Lake and Porter counties were cast for him.[4]

While Indiana wavered between the two major political parties after the Civil War, Lake and Porter continued to be banner Republican counties.[5] In the years from 1854 to 1930, Porter was consistently Republican and Lake's only defection occurred in 1892 when the

to 1868, Inclusive; Comprehending the Politician's Register and the Whig Almanac (2 vols. New York, 1868), 1:27, 47, 56.

[2] Bartlett Woods, "The First Free Soil Meeting in Lake County," in Ball (ed.), Lake County, Indiana, 1884, 468-69. Woods, born in England, was one of the founders of the Republican party in Lake County.

[3] Tribune Almanac, 1:56.

[4] Lincoln's total vote in Lake and Porter counties was 2,754 and Stephen A. Douglas' was 1,344. The state polled 139,033 for Lincoln and 115,509 for Douglas. See ibid., 2:62.

[5] Indiana, a "doubtful" state, went Democratic in the presidential elections of 1876, 1884, and 1892.

Democrats carried it by a small margin in that year's presidential election. While tradition and memory of the Civil War kept many citizens loyal to the Republican party, another important factor was the prosperity of the farmers.[6] Both counties were heavy producers of poultry, eggs, and dairy products, all of which found an excellent market in near-by Chicago. As noted above, in 1870 Lake led the counties of the state in the production of butter, hay, and oats, and in 1880 was first in the amount of cheese produced on farms. As a result, agrarian discontent which adversely affected the fortunes of the Republican party in various areas during those years, was noticeably absent in Lake and Porter counties.[7]

Despite the development of the region's industrial cities in the early years of the century, the Democratic party was unable to challenge the power of the Republicans in county political circles. Republican strength and Democratic weakness were demonstrated in Lake County in 1926 when 32,475 Republicans and only 957 Democrats voted in their respective primaries.[8] In the 1920's, it was generally recognized that nomination for office in the Republican primary in Lake County was tantamount to election. The Gary *Post-Tribune* reviewed the situation:[9]

[6] William G. Carleton, "Why Was the Democratic Party in Indiana a Radical Party, 1865-1890?" in *Indiana Magazine of History,* 42(1916): 224.

[7] *Compendium of the Ninth Census* (1870), 730-31; *Compendium of the Tenth Census* (1880), 856-57. In 1892 the Populist party obtained only 174 out of a total of 10,558 votes in Lake and Porter counties. See *The Tribune Almanac for 1893* (New York, 1893), 273.

[8] Hammond *Lake County Times,* May 6, 1926. By 1900, 52 per cent of Lake County's population was classified as urban. This percentage increased rapidly, reaching 90 per cent by 1920 and 92 per cent by 1930. *Fourteenth Census* (1920): *Population,* pt. 1:156; *Fifteenth Census* (1930): *Population,* 3:pt. 1:705.

[9] Gary *Post-Tribune,* November 6, 1930.

Year after year Democratic candidates have been put up for office, and when we say "put up" that is what we mean, merely as sacrifices to the party and year after year the county has seen the party dwindle away until only a handful of stalwarts stood as a reminder of the two party system in the county. Just as in the South the election has been in the primary so it has developed in Lake County.

But troublous times were ahead for the Republicans. As the twenties came to a close, a political storm, of which neither party was conscious, was building up just beyond the horizon.

In 1930 the nationwide depression, which paralyzed the economic life of the area's industrial cities, together with the prohibition scandals involving prominent Republican officials, swept the party from power in Lake County. Every Democratic candidate for a state, county, and township office was elected. However, the Democrats, obviously expecting defeat, failed to nominate candidates for judges of the five superior courts. The Gary *Post-Tribune* analyzed the reasons for the Republican collapse:[10]

For years upon years it [the Republican party] has been telling the public it is the party of prosperity. Keep us in power and we will keep economic conditions good. . . .

The party was lucky for many years and people grew into the belief that there was some actual connection between prosperity and the Republican party. And then came the depression. By no possible means could it be saddled on the backs of Democrats. If it was made by a political party then that political party was the Republican party. Quickly sensing the changed situation, Republican leaders began telling the truth about prosperity and depression. The Republican party did not cause this depression, they said, the depressions are not caused by political parties but by fundamental economic conditions. . . . That is to say Republican leaders built up a Frankenstein monster to devour them.

10 Gary *Post-Tribune,* November 6, 1930.

Then there was the local issue, the issue of waste and corruption. Through a long succession of reports of the state board of accounts, actions of grand juries and trials of officials a picture of the Republican party in Lake County, culpable and lacking responsibility, was built up in the minds of the voters. . . .

In the 1932 elections the Democrats again made a clean sweep of all offices in Lake County. Yet, despite the fact that the Republican party became the minority party in Lake County, it continued to be the dominant power in Porter County, where the population was largely rural.

Urban Politics, a General View

In the early years, the towns of the Calumet Region were not as consistent in their political loyalties as were the strictly rural areas. Local issues and local problems frequently determined the outcome of urban elections. There were also instances when the reputations and personalities of candidates influenced voters to cross party lines. Moreover, city elections were, with few exceptions, held in odd years and were not directly influenced by congressional and presidential campaigns.

Whiting demonstrated the power of candidates possessing local prestige and administrative ability. Its first three mayors from 1903 to 1914 were Democrats, two of whom were officials of the Standard Oil Company's local refinery. William E. Warwick, superintendent of the refinery, became mayor in 1903 and was re-elected for the then two-year term the next year. In 1909 Beaumont Parks, assistant superintendent of the refinery and later a director and vice-president of the Standard Oil Company of Indiana, was elected for a four-year term. The political trend was reversed in 1913 when Walter E. Schrage, a Republican, defeated Parks. Schrage, Whiting's leading banker and the son of Henry Schrage, one of the community's pioneers, was mayor of the city until 1930 when he was succeeded by Thomas S. Boyle, a Democrat.

East Chicago and Gary were Republican strongholds. The Democrats carried East Chicago in only two elections and even then they deemed it wise to conceal their identity from the voters. For instance, Frank Callahan, a Democrat, was elected mayor on the Citizens' ticket in 1913 and again in 1921 as the candidate of the Independent party. In the 1920's Republican nomination in the primaries was equivalent to election. Raleigh P. Hale, Republican candidate for mayor in 1925, and others of his party were unopposed by the Democrats. Republican strength was further indicated by Hale's re-election in 1929 while under indictment by a Federal grand jury for conspiracy to violate the prohibition laws.[11]

Thomas E. Knotts was the only Democratic mayor of Gary from 1910 to 1933. Knotts was president of the town board from 1906 to 1909 and mayor from 1910 to 1914. And yet while Knotts was mayor the city treasurer and a majority of the municipal council were Republicans.[12] In the mayoralty election of 1917 the Republicans were split between William F. Hodges, the regular Republican candidate, and Roswell O. Johnson, the incumbent, who ran as an independent. Harvey J. Curtis, the Democratic candidate, was unable to poll the

[11] Mayors of East Chicago were: William Penman, 1893-99, William F. Hale, 1899-1905, Edward De Briae, 1906-10, Alexander G. Schlieker, 1910-14, Frank Callahan, 1914-18, Leo P. McCormick, 1918-22, Frank Callahan, 1922-26, Raleigh P. Hale, 1926-30. Hale who resigned in January, 1930, was succeeded by Thomas W. O'Connor, city comptroller.

[12] Gary's other mayors were Roswell O. Johnson, 1914-18, William F. Hodges, 1918-22, Roswell O. Johnson, 1922-25 (resigned March, 1925, and was succeeded by William J. Fulton, city comptroller), Floyd E. Williams, 1926-29 (resigned in December, 1929, and was succeeded by Henry J. Hay, city comptroller), Roswell O. Johnson, 1930-34.

largest plurality of the votes. The Gary *Evening Post* wryly remarked that the result of the election "indicated above everything else that it is very difficult to elect a Democrat in Gary."[13] The prohibition scandals which characterized the second administration of Roswell O. Johnson, 1922-25, and the subsequent imprisonment of the mayor and other city officials failed to lessen the power of the Republicans in the steel city.

Political power in Hammond was rather evenly divided between the major political parties. Here, as in Whiting, the popularity and personal qualifications of the candidates frequently determined the outcome of elections. Marcus M. Towle, founder of the city and one of the owners of the George H. Hammond packing company, was its Republican mayor from 1884 to 1888 when he was defeated by the Democratic candidate, Thomas Hammond, brother of George H. Hammond and one of the city's leading financiers. Hammond resigned in 1893 to go to Congress. Fred Mott, son-in-law of Ernst and Caroline Hohman, was the Republican mayor from 1894 to 1898. Patrick Reilley, a Democrat, headed the city's administration from 1898 to 1902. Armanis F. Knotts, the Republican brother of Thomas E. Knotts and one of the ablest lawyers in the region, guided Hammond's affairs in the troubled times that followed the burning of the great packing house. Knotts was succeeded by Lawrence Becker, German-born Democrat and popular with the city's large German population, who served from 1904 to 1911, when he resigned to become the judge of one of the superior courts. Another Democrat, John D. Smalley, succeeded Becker and was elected for a full term in 1913. Hammond was consistently Republican in the years after World War I.[14]

13 Gary *Evening Post,* November 7, 1917.
14 Hammond's other mayors were Patrick Reilley, Democrat, 1893-94

The influence of the industries on the political affairs of the region was a source of controversy and speculation among the citizens. Plant officials, particularly in Gary and Whiting, kept a close watch on the local political scene. They recognized the value of schools, libraries, social agencies such as the Y. M. C. A. and the Y. W. C. A., and adequate recreational facilities for their employees. Company officials also threw their influence against gambling, prostitution, and excessive use of intoxicating liquors. Because they were fully aware of their workers' tendency to resent any efforts of the industries to regulate their lives outside the gates of the plants, they made no efforts in that direction. Instead the industries sought a voice in civic affairs largely by indirection, encouraging their employees to seek positions on the city councils, and school, library, and park boards.

Officials of the United States Steel Corporation in Gary engaged in open warfare against Mayor Thomas E. Knotts. Knotts in return made every effort to restrict the power of the corporation to its plant area north of the Grand Calumet River. His defeat by Roswell O. Johnson in the election of 1913 was attributed to the influence of the corporation's officials. Johnson was friendly to the steel company and its officials exercised a great deal of influence in his administration. Ralph E. Rowley, elected president of the city council in 1913, was regarded for many years as the "watch dog" of the treasury. William P. Gleason was appointed president of the park board in 1914 and held the position for more than thirty years. Horace S. Norton, head of the Gary Land Company, a subsidiary of the steel corporation, was said to be the real mayor of Gary during Johnson's first

and 1898-1902; Daniel Brown, Republican, 1918-26; Adrian Tinkham, Republican, 1926-30; Charles O. Schonert, Republican, 1930-34.

term.[15] Critics of the administration said that Gary had government by "proxy," its real rulers being the "Trustees under God," a term applied to the corporation's officials.[16]

Despite Johnson's friendly attitude toward the steel corporation, the officials were disturbed by the mayor's indifference to the prevalence of gambling and prostitution and by the general laxity of his administration. They opposed his re-election in 1917, and threw their support to William F. Hodges who had resigned as city attorney some months before in protest against the widespread vice in the city.[17] Hodges, who won the election, followed an independent course as mayor. While he was friendly to the corporation, there was little to indicate that it exercised any undue influence in his administration. In the years that followed the steel company kept in the background in regard to political affairs. Newspapers gave no indication that it sought to influence the selection of candidates for public office or the will of the voters. Norton, Gleason, and Rowley, however, continued to play important parts in public affairs.

Whiting, like Gary, was a one-industry city, the majority of its citizens being employed at the local refinery of the Standard Oil Company of Indiana. When Whiting was incorporated as a town in 1895, its citizens expected that the oil company, its largest taxpayer, should have a voice in the town's affairs. The Whiting *Democrat* said: "Everyone who knows anything about the Standard Oil Company knows that it does what it does well and economically. It follows, therefore, that the town will

[15] Quillen, The Industrial City, 269.

[16] Gary *Republican,* May 6, December 16, 1916.

[17] Gary *Evening Post,* December 7, 1916; Hammond *Lake County Times,* October 31, 1917. Johnson ran as an Independent in this election.

be governed well and economically."[18] As was noted earlier, Whiting's first two mayors were officials of the refinery. The oil company also encouraged its employees to participate in civic affairs. Apparently the only instance in which the company openly sought to influence the voters in a presidential election was in 1908, when about two hundred employees were given yearly subscriptions to *Harper's Weekly* which contained articles advocating the election of William Howard Taft.[19]

The numerous industries in Hammond and East Chicago apparently had little influence in local political affairs. While Marcus M. Towle and Thomas Hammond were at one time connected with the George H. Hammond packing company, Hammond's largest industry, their participation in civic affairs occurred after they had severed their relations with that company. Not one of the industries in East Chicago was large enough in the early years to be a power in city political circles. The Inland Steel Company, East Chicago's largest plant, began operations in 1901 on a small scale and with little money, and the Youngstown Sheet and Tube Company, the city's second largest industry, arrived on the scene at the late date of 1923. Although the officials of East Chicago's industries banded together in the Manufacturer's Association, that organization appeared to have little interest in local politics.

National and Racial Elements in Politics

In 1910 the foreign born constituted more than half of East Chicago's population, almost one half of Gary's, and more than 43 per cent of Whiting's. About 17 per cent of Gary's foreign born in 1910 were unable to read

18 Whiting *Democrat*, November 12, 1896.
19 Hammond *Lake County Times*, September 14, 1908.

or write.[20] The overwhelming majority of these immigrants came from European countries where democracy was unknown. Another national segment comprised the Mexicans, who came to the region after World War I and were largely of the peon class with little experience in the political life of their own country. As a result, these national groups had little conception of the duties and responsibilities of American citizens.

Most of the immigrants, desperately poor when they came to the region, were primarily interested in making money and establishing homes. Absorbed with these personal problems, the foreign born were all too ready to accept the leadership of native Americans in political affairs. They were also inclined to vote as directed by their mill foremen, saloonkeepers, and neighborhood merchants. Such a segment of the voting population was easily regimented by the professional politicians.

Political leaders recognized the voting potential of the foreign born at an early date. Since Indiana law gave the right to vote to aliens who had resided in the United States one year and in the state six months and who had filed their intentions to become American citizens, both the Republican and Democratic parties had naturalization committees whose duty it was to encourage aliens to file their first papers. On a single day in 1908 the Republican committee in Gary conducted sixty-five persons to Hammond where they filed their intentions to become American citizens with the Federal court. The *Lake County Times* predicted in 1913 that three thousand would file their intentions before the municipal elections of that year.[21] During the political campaigns both par-

---

[20] *Thirteenth Census* (1910) : *Population*, pt. 2:568, 572.

[21] Gary *Daily Tribune,* October 24, 1908; Hammond *Lake County Times,* October 13, 1913.

ties printed literature in several foreign languages and employed speakers who could address the voters in their various tongues.

And yet the foreign born were content to vote for candidates who were native Americans, as indicated by the fact that in the years before 1933 all the candidates for mayor in the area's industrial cities, with the exception of Hammond's Lawrence Becker, who came from Germany, were born in the United States. Only on rare occasions were Slavs and Hungarians able to win seats on the various municipal councils. Moreover, the Mexicans showed even less interest in political affairs. No evidence was found that they ever held, or even sought, public offices.

The Negroes, the largest racial group in the region, demonstrated more interest in political affairs than did the immigrant population. Three Negroes sat on Gary's city council from 1925 to 1929. Since most of them came directly from the Southern states where they had been largely excluded from political activity by the Democrats, they showed a decided preference for the Republican party. Moreover, that party had a great appeal for the Negroes because Abraham Lincoln, a Republican, had freed the slaves, a fact which campaign orators did not let them forget. In 1917 the Gary *Evening Post* tried in vain to convince the Negroes that the great Emancipator had nothing to do with the city's mayoralty election.[22] The Negroes continued to be a source of strength for the Republican party during the next fifteen years. Despite the hardships imposed upon them by the depression which began in 1929, they cast a heavy vote for Herbert Hoover against Franklin D. Roosevelt in 1932. However, by the end of 1933 Roosevelt's concern for

[22] Gary *Evening Post*, November 6, 1917.

the Negroes as expressed in his New Deal program of relief, recovery, and reform caused those in the Calumet Region to desert the Republican party almost en masse.[23]

The Prohibition Era

The prohibition era was probably the most lurid and fantastic phase of the region's history. The Eighteenth Amendment met open defiance from a large proportion of the citizens and was never really enforced in the larger cities. The presence of such a large foreign-born population, accustomed to the use of alcoholic beverages in one form or another, the region's close proximity to Chicago where the organization of the illicit liquor traffic reached its greatest perfection, and the area's easy access to Canada by way of the Great Lakes and by automobile made the success of the "noble experiment" impossible. In 1926 the public's attitude was indicated when a poll showed that seven out of eight persons interviewed were against the dry law.[24] The demand for liquor led to the corruption of public officials and the tarnishing of many reputations. Federal authorities made a heroic effort to enforce the Volstead Act while local officials in general pursued a passive course and in some instances encouraged violations of the law. The prohibition era was characterized by a general lowering of the moral tone of the region's life.

In 1917, when it was evident that Indiana would soon have prohibition by state law, predictions were made that the region's saloonkeepers would continue to sell liquor under one guise or another. Indiana's dry law went into effect at midnight, April 2, 1918, and the next day a

[23] Potts, A History of the Growth of the Negro Population of Gary, 39, 40.

[24] Hammond Lake County Times, April 1, 1926.

large number of saloonkeepers were reported to have
gone into the "soft drink" business.[25] The area's first
important liquor violation occurred on April 20, when a
wagon loaded with forty gallons of whisky was seized in
East Chicago while en route from Chicago to a justice of
the peace in Gary. Until the national prohibition law
went into effect on July 1, 1919, hundreds of the region's
citizens quenched their thirst daily in West Hammond
(now Calumet City), Burnham, and other Illinois communities.[26]

With the nation legally dry, the underworld and numerous heretofore law-abiding citizens turned quickly to
making beer, wine, alcohol, and whisky for sale directly
to the public and for distribution to the operators of
soft-drink parlors and other types of "blind tigers." In
1922 an immigrant woman, reportedly poor two years
before, purchased $11,000 in traveler's checks at a Ham-
mond bank with profits obtained from the operation of
a "kitchen still," and returned to the old country with
her new wealth. The story still circulates in East Chicago
of a prominent local undertaker who used his ambulances
and hearses to transport liquor into the city. A popular
restaurant along the lake front in Hammond had a little
house in the rear where whisky was sold to the diners.
A Federal grand jury found that more arrests were made,
more whisky was seized, and more stills were captured
in Gary in 1922 than in any other city in the state. In
1924 bootleggers raided the warehouse of the former

25 *Ibid.*, April 3, 1918. The typical "soft drink" parlor dispensed
soft drinks at the front while in the rear of the building, generally behind
a curtain or partition, alcoholic beverages were sold. In 1921 more than
two hundred such places were reported in Gary alone. Gary *Evening
Post*, May 23, 1921.

26 Gary *Daily Tribune*, April 20, 1918; Hammond *Lake County Times*,
July 1, 1919.

Hammond Distilling Company where whisky was stored under Federal supervision. The raiders compelled the guards to help load two trucks with sixty barrels of whisky worth $30,000 and assured their safe getaway by forcing the guards to drink themselves into a state of helpless intoxication.[27]

Elaborate equipment was necessary to satisfy the demand for liquor. In 1921 a still capable of producing 275 gallons of whisky a day was found in the sand dunes two miles east of Miller. In 1929 a complete brewery was discovered in Hammond only five doors away from the home of a policeman. Gary civic leaders in 1926 hailed the establishment of a new industry, the Indiana Lined Pipe and Drum Company, in their city. This plant, which was supposed to manufacture chemical-proof steel-lined pipes and drums, was located in the buildings of the former O. K. Giant Battery Company on Eleventh Street at the E. J. & E. belt-line tracks. Two months later, eleven members of the concern, all of whom had been welcomed to Gary as officials of a promising industry, occupied cells in the city jail. Their plant, instead of manufacturing pipes and drums, housed a distillery capable of producing 2,500 gallons of alcohol a day. The distillery, staffed by skilled chemists and expert distillers, was thought to be the central distilling headquarters for a midwestern ring of bootleggers. The real owners of the distillery were never discovered.[28]

27 Hammond *Lake County Times,* June 6, August 24, 1922; January 29, 1924; Gary *Post-Tribune,* January 20, 1923. The Hammond Distilling Company, one of Hammond's most prosperous industries, was sold to the Nowak Milling Company shortly after the Eighteenth Amendment went into effect.

28 Gary *Evening Post,* May 23, 1921; Hammond *Lake County Times,* September 5, 1929; Gary *Post-Tribune,* October 9 and 13, 1926. The raid on the plant was made by the Gary police.

It was obvious that operations of such magnitude were not possible without the knowledge of public officials. In 1921 the chief of police and a police captain in East Chicago were sentenced to serve two years in a Federal prison for alleged conspiracy to violate the prohibition laws. Federal officers testified at the trial that the East Chicago police would not co-operate with them in the enforcement of the liquor laws and that the defendants notified bootleggers when Federal officers planned a raid. Early in 1925 East Chicago's city judge resigned and the mayor announced he would not be a candidate for re-election in that year's contest. Both reportedly gave as reasons their inability to enforce the liquor laws.[29]

In August, 1922, Federal agents descended on Gary and arrested 127 bootleggers and operators of soft-drink parlors. They announced that evidence had been found that would involve public officials from the highest to the lowest in a conspiracy to violate the prohibition laws. Gary was said to be the wettest city in Indiana. In January, 1923, what was described as a United States "dry bomb" exploded in the city. Sixty-two persons were indicted and arrested by Federal authorities for conspiracy to violate the national prohibition laws. Among those involved besides the bootleggers were Mayor Roswell O. Johnson; Lewis E. Barnes, president of the city's board of public works; William M. Dunn, city judge; Clyde Hunter, a police sergeant; William H. Olds, sheriff of Lake County; Dwight M. Kinder, county prosecutor; three policemen; a justice of the peace; a city constable; and three prominent lawyers. A few days before their arrest evidence had been presented to a Federal grand jury in Indianapolis alleging that the defendants conspired to elect public officials hostile to the prohibition

29 East Chicago *Calumet News,* January 23 and 27, 1925.

laws; that they had assigned various districts in Gary to certain bootleggers, whose competitors were driven out; and that in some instances bootleggers had been given prison sentences which were never served.[30]

In March, 1923, all but seven of those indicted were convicted in a Federal district court at Indianapolis.[31] Mayor Johnson received the heaviest sentence, a fine of $2,000 and eighteen months in the Atlanta penitentiary. Sheriff Olds demanded a new trial and later the case against him was dropped for lack of evidence. Judge Dunn refused to appeal his case and left immediately for Atlanta to serve his sentence of a year and a day. Johnson, Barnes, Kinder, and Hunter carried their cases to the United States Supreme Court which affirmed the decision of the district court. The defendants left for Atlanta the latter part of April, 1925, to serve their terms in the Federal prison.[32]

Gary's citizens viewed the conviction of their officials with mixed emotions. The following quotation from the Indianapolis *News* indicated the unfavorable reputation that Gary was enjoying in the newspapers throughout the country: "The trial has shown one thing very clearly, and that is that there was not the slightest idea in Gary that the liquor laws were meant to be obeyed. . . . Gary ought now to realize that it is really a part of the United

[30] Gary *Post-Tribune,* August 31, 1922, January 15, 18, and 22, 1923.

[31] *Ibid.,* March 31, 1923. On the eve of the trial, Gaspari Monti, reportedly head of the Italian underworld in Gary and one of the government's principal witnesses against the defendants, was killed in broad daylight outside the Italian Club in Gary. His assassin, who used a sawed-off shotgun, escaped in an automobile. The United States district attorney immediately announced that other witnesses would be given adequate protection. The perpetrators of the crime were never apprehended. See *ibid.,* March 13, 1923. For further details of the Gary scandal, see the *Literary Digest,* April 21, 1923, pp. 15-16.

[32] Gary *Post-Tribune,* May 5 and 9, 1923; April 20 and 28, 1925.

States."[33] The Gary *Post-Tribune,* distressed by the unfavorable publicity the city was receiving in the national
press, insisted the mayor and other officers who had been
convicted and were awaiting appeal, resign their offices,
that it was unfair to advertise a past that Gary wanted
the world to forget.[34] When Johnson showed a reluctance to step aside, the newspaper launched a movement
to replace the mayor and council form of government
with the city manager plan, but in June, 1923, the voters
rejected this change by a large majority. When the Supreme Court upheld the conviction, Johnson resigned.
At this time William P. Gleason, superintendent of the
Gary steel mills and president of the city's park board,
apparently voiced the feeling of that body: "We lose
no whit of our respect for the law and the enforcement
of the law when we express our sympathy for Mayor
Johnson. I would suggest that we express our sympathy
by rising to our feet."[35]

Johnson was released from prison in November, 1925,
after serving one third of his original sentence. In
March, 1929, a pardon by President Coolidge restored
to him the privileges of a United States citizen and a
short time later a superior court judge in East Chicago
ruled that he was legally eligible to hold public office. In
1929 Johnson won the Republican nomination for mayor
of Gary and was elected by a substantial majority the
following November. Concerning Johnson's past troubles
the Gary *Post-Tribune* remarked: "This newspaper has

[33] Quoted in *Literary Digest.* April 21, 1923, p. 16. This issue of
the *Digest* also contained excerpts critical of Gary from newspapers in
Chicago, Peoria, Fort Wayne and other cities.

[34] Gary *Post-Tribune,* April 2 and 5, 1923. Johnson continued to
serve as mayor until his resignation on March 28, 1925, two years after
his conviction and a few days before he entered the penitentiary.

[35] Quoted in *ibid.,* March 28, 1925.

never felt that Mr. Johnson was guilty of violating the law so much as he was guilty of laxness in enforcing it."[36]

East Chicago's officials also continued to have trouble with the Federal authorities. In August, 1929, prohibition agents swooped down upon the city arresting 125 men and women for conspiracy to violate the dry laws. Among those seized were Mayor Raleigh P. Hale, recently nominated for re-election by the Republican party; James W. Regan, chief of police; the reported leader of the Negro underworld in the city; two men said to be representatives of Chicago's Capone gang; and numerous bootleggers. On the first day of the arrests, agents captured four stills with a daily capacity of 200 gallons of alcohol each, 7,000 gallons of mash, and 575 gallons of alcohol. The United States district attorney in charge of the raids reported that all manner of vice, gambling, prostitution, and liquor violations were rampant in the city. "No city in the state," he declared, "has been run as openly as East Chicago. It would be impossible to imagine vice resorts run more openly and liquor sold more openly than has been done here." Federal agents had operated in the city since the previous January. Several obtained employment in local industries and circulated freely as "mill workers" in the community. The agents used the central post office as their headquarters in order to keep the investigation a secret from the local authorities.[37]

In October, Mayor Hale, Chief Regan, the head of the city's safety board, a member of the board of public works, a police captain, the resident manager of the East Chicago Dock Terminal, and about two hundred others

[36] *Ibid.*, November 6, 1929.

[37] *Ibid.*. August 14 and 15, 1929; Hammond *Lake County Times,* August 13, 14, and 31, 1929.

were indicted for conspiring to violate the prohibition
laws. The manager of the dock terminal was charged
with permitting lake vessels loaded with liquor from
Canada to enter the local harbor and to unload their
cargoes at his company's wharf.[38]   In the course of the
grand jury hearings, Federal officers charged that there
was a tie between the Capone gang and East Chicago
racketeers.[39]   Despite these disclosures, Hale was re-
elected mayor of the city by a large majority a few days
later.

In January, 1930, Hale, Regan, two policemen, and
eleven others were found guilty by a Federal district
court. A few days later the Mayor resigned his office,
reportedly to avoid impeachment by the city council.
Regan also resigned as chief of police. Early in March,
Hale and Regan were given similar sentences, a fine of
$2,000 and two years in the Federal prison at Fort
Leavenworth. In May, 1931, the circuit court of appeals
reversed the decision of the district court and ordered a
retrial of the case against the two former officials.[40] The
government's case collapsed when Hale died at his home
in East Chicago on December 1, 1931.[41] The case against
Regan was later dropped, reportedly for lack of evidence.

National prohibition was one of the victims of the
depression. Sentiment against the dry laws in industrial
areas like the Calumet Region increased as the nation
found itself in the throes of an economic collapse. The

38 Gary *Post-Tribune,* October 4 and 11, 1929; East Chicago *Calumet
News,* October 11, 1929. The case against the manager of the dock
terminal was later dismissed on a plea of misnomer.

39 It may or may not be significant that Regan was on the Cicero,
Illinois, police force when appointed by Mayor Hale in 1926. Cicero
was generally regarded as the headquarters of the Capone gang.

40 Gary *Post-Tribune,* January 18, March 4, 1930, May 18, 1931;
Hammond *Lake County Times,* March 4, 1930.

41 Gary *Post-Tribune,* December 1, 1931.

election in 1932 of Franklin D. Roosevelt, who had promised an end to prohibition, was hailed by most of the region's citizens. Predictions were made that the return of legal liquors would help break the back of the depression by bringing new business to local industries. In February, 1933, Congress submitted the Twenty-first Amendment, which repealed the Eighteenth, to the states and it was declared adopted by December of the same year. Prohibition for all practical purposes ended in the Calumet Region in March, 1933, when Indiana repealed its dry law. Local authorities immediately turned over the enforcement of the national prohibition law to the Federal government. The prosecutor of Lake County dismissed more than 150 liquor cases then pending in the state courts. When the Federal government legalized the sale of beer and wine late in March, 1933, nearly every store and restaurant in the region was reported ready to file applications for permits to sell those beverages. Lake County, it was said, would soon be one vast beer garden—a prediction which almost came true.[42]

The Ku Klux Klan

In the 1920's the Invisible Empire, Knights of the Ku Klux Klan, was a power in the region's political affairs. The Klan was essentially a product of the hatreds and hysteria engendered among some Americans by World War I. It was at one and the same time anti-Catholic, anti-foreign, anti-Jewish, anti-Negro, and to a degree anti-organized labor. The Negro, according to the Klan, had been spoiled by high wages earned during the recent war and by stories of racial equality that colored veterans had brought back from Europe. He needed

[42] *Ibid.*, March 2, 1933; Hammond *Lake County Times*, March 18, 1933.

to be "put in his place." The Jews were denounced as un-American radicals and as unscrupulous profiteers. Immigrants, particularly those whom the Klan chose to regard as not of "Nordic" blood, were regarded as radicals dangerous to American institutions. Catholics were baited as half-hearted Americans who placed their religion above their patriotism and owed allegiance to a foreign potentate, the Pope.[43] Klansmen marched in white hoods and shrouds through village and city streets, burned "fiery crosses" in conspicuous places, and posed as advocates of what they chose to call "one hundred per cent Americanism." The order preferred to take the law into its own hands and those who incurred its wrath were on occasions beaten, tarred and feathered, or even killed.

The Klan was unusually strong in Indiana. D. C. Stephenson was said to have initiated over half a million members in Indiana and Ohio. Indiana membership was estimated at 178,000.[44] The Indiana Klan supported and sought to control the Republican party. Stephenson was said to have captured the Republican state machine, forced two United States senators to adopt a friendly attitude toward the Klan, and elected his candidate for governor, Ed Jackson, in 1924. It was generally believed that the majority of the Republicans elected to office in Indiana in 1924 had no dealings with Stephenson. His support, according to reports, was thrown into their laps and "they did not pitch it out."[45]

43 John M. Mecklin, *The Ku Klux Klan. A Study of the American Mind* (New York. 1924), 17; Stanley Frost, *The Challenge of the Klan* (Indianapolis, 1924) 64-65, 69.

44 Mecklin, *The Ku Klux Klan,* 32; Barnhart and Carmony, *Indiana,* 2:394.

45 Barnhart and Carmony, *Indiana,* 2:395; Dixon Merritt, "Klan and Anti-Klan in Indiana," in *The Outlook,* 144:466 (December 1, 1926).

The Grand Dragon frequently boasted that he was the law in Indiana.

The Calumet Region with its large foreign-born, Catholic, and Jewish population, and its increasing number of Negroes was a fertile area for the operations of the Klan. The Klan's stand against organized labor attracted many citizens who had been unduly aroused against the foreign born because of their support of the unions during the 1919 steel strike.[46] Also, the so-called "Red" scare which turned the finger of suspicion against the foreign born during that strike provided a favorable atmosphere for Klan activity. As early as 1921, the order was said to have a membership of 500 in Gary and 2,500 in Lake County.[47] The Klan turned to the Protestant churches for members. Twelve robed and masked Klansmen walked into a Hammond church in September, 1922, where a revival meeting was being held and handed the minister an envelope containing $200.00. The order reportedly held meetings in several East Chicago churches in 1923. In the same year, Klansmen offered $2,000 to the pastor of one of Hammond's largest Methodist churches for religious education in the public schools; the pastor refused the money, but a few minutes later the offer was accepted by the minister of another church. The Hammond Council of Religious Education refused to accept this donation.[48]

The Klan sought to obtain public support and attract new members by holding spectacular demonstrations. In

[46] The American Federation of Labor, at its Cincinnati convention in 1922, urged its members not to join the Klan. See Mecklin, *The Ku Klux Klan*, 97, and Frost, *The Challenge of the Klan*, 65, for the Klan's attitude toward organized labor.

[47] Gary *Post-Tribune*, September 24, 1921.

[48] Hammond *Lake County Times*, September 25, 1922; February 22, 1923; East Chicago *Calumet News*, September 20 and November 15, 1923.

September, 1922, it inserted in the *Lake County Times* a full-page invitation to the public to attend a lecture by a Klansman from Atlanta, Georgia, at Harrison Park in Hammond. A large crowd estimated from five to twelve thousand was present at the meeting. Early in April, 1923, a reported five thousand fully attired Klansmen paraded through the streets of Hammond while several of their number on motorcycles directed traffic. The following June several thousand held an initiation in Hammond's Maywood Park from which the public was excluded. Such assumption of authority by the Klan led to a ruling by the Hammond Park Board that permission for use of its parks by such organizations as the Klan would have to be obtained from the board. In May, 1923, at Valparaiso, the order staged its greatest demonstration, attended by a reported ten thousand members from the "Domain of Lake Michigan," said to include sections of Indiana, Ohio, Michigan, Illinois, and Wisconsin. Special trains brought crowds from Chicago and other places. The "Grand Goblin" of the Domain presided over an all-day picnic and in the evening headed a parade of more than 2,000, of whom 350 were said to be women.[49]

As in the rest of the state, the Klan operated largely within the Republican party, the peak of its political power being reached in the middle twenties. The order's greatest success in Lake County was achieved in 1924 when most of its candidates for state and county offices were nominated in the Republican primaries. The *Lake County Times* hailed this new power in local politics:[50]

[49] Hammond *Lake County Times,* September 30, 1922; Gary *Post-Tribune,* April 3, May 21, June 14, 1923.

[50] Hammond *Lake County Times,* May 9, 1924. Governor Warren T. McCray of Indiana was sentenced in 1924 to ten years in the Federal prison and fined $10,000 for using the mails to defraud. Barnhart and Carmony, *Indiana,* 2:392-93.

The Republican party has reason for thanking the Klan for coming to its rescue. The Lake County booze and graft scandal which ended in the conviction of Mayor Johnson, the prosecutor and 53 others including Lew Barnes, the political boss of the county, combined with the disgrace of Governor McCray might have meant its doom had not Cleveland [Clyde Cleveland], Hammond's Republican city chairman, built up an organization of such strength and enthusiasm that it not only kept the rank and file within the party lines but drew thousands from the Democratic camp. But to get this support, it was necessary to promise good government, an end to booze, graft and open gambling in the county.

The Gary *Post-Tribune,* while acknowledging the quality of the Klan's nominees, sounded a more sober note: "The other policies of the Klan in regard to religion and race are the ones to fear and deplore. It is the deeper issue that is being created which interests us. Where is the religious and racial feeling that is being fostered going to lead us?"[51] The Democrats sought to make the Klan a major campaign issue. They insisted that the Republican party was a tool of the order. The slogan of the Democratic party in the local election of 1924 was "Liberty and Americanism against the Klan."[52]

The Klan apparently achieved success in the city elections in 1925 in Gary and Hammond. Two of the three candidates for the Republican nomination for mayor in Gary, Floyd E. Williams and C. Oliver Holmes, were said to be Klansmen although both denied membership

[51] Gary *Post-Tribune,* May 8, 1924. *Tolerance,* an anti-Klan publication, in June, 1923, listed the mayor of Hammond, Hammond's chief of police, the Hammond city judge, a Hammond publisher, and a prominent East Chicago attorney as members of the Klan. *Ibid.,* June 23, 1923.

[52] East Chicago *Calumet News,* October 7 and 21, 1924. Frank Callahan, Democratic mayor of East Chicago, in June, 1923, dismissed a member of the city's board of safety for alleged membership in the Klan. In May, 1923, the East Chicago city council forbade Klan parades in the city. Hammond *Lake County Times,* May 1, June 14, 1923.

in the order. Holmes admitted the receipt of a telegram from Klan leaders urging him to withdraw in favor of Williams because the latter was the Klan's candidate. Holmes refused, but Williams won the nomination anyway. Five of the Republicans nominated for councilmen-at-large were reportedly backed by the Klan.[53] The extremely light vote cast for Williams, the victor in the November election, was, no doubt, due to the fact that Catholic, Negro, and foreign-born Republicans lacked enthusiasm for his candidacy.[54] While Adrian Tinkham, elected mayor of Hammond, was not linked with the Klan, he appointed Clyde Cleveland, reputed political head of the order in Lake County, as city attorney.[55]

The prestige of the Klan in the region waned as suddenly as it had waxed. Its demise as a power in local politics coincided with its decline in the state. The scandals involving D. C. Stephenson and Governor Ed Jackson exposed the corruption and graft in the order that had posed as the exponent of morality, religion, and "true Americanism." Its masks and shrouds, parades and public demonstrations, which were so impressive in its heyday now appeared foolish and ridiculous to fair-minded citizens. The Klan's failure to nominate a single candidate in the local primaries in 1926 was evident that it had lost its appeal for the voters.[56]

The Depression

The depression, foreshadowed by the stock market crash in October, 1929, brought unemployment, relief

[53] Gary *Post-Tribune*, April 25, 27, 28, May 2 and 6, 1925.

[54] The vote for Williams in the primary was 9,349, for William G. Fulton 7,988, and for C. Oliver Holmes 1,126. Williams received only 7,660 votes in the November election. Gary *Post-Tribune*, May 7 and November 4, 1925.

[55] Hammond *Lake County Times*, November 25, 1925.

[56] East Chicago *Calumet News*, October 26, 1926.

lines, and widespread suffering to the region. As in other heavily industrialized communities, unemployment was the source of many troubles. The steel industry, which employed at least 40,000 persons, was the life blood of the region, and as the mills curtailed production, hardships increased in proportion. In the spring of 1929 the Gary mills were operating at 100 per cent capacity, a unique situation for peacetime history. Production in United States Steel's plants throughout the country was down to about 47 per cent in the last quarter of 1930 and to about 24 per cent in December, 1931.[57] In 1932 none of the region's steel mills operated at more than 15 per cent capacity, the lowest at any time during the crisis. In April, 1932, the Buffington cement plant in Gary, a subsidiary of the United States Steel Corporation, closed down completely, throwing about one thousand men out of work, most of whom lived in Indiana Harbor. A number of smaller industries, connected one way or another with the steel industry, closed their doors. The railway-equipment industry, which ranked next to steel and oil in importance, was reported in 1932 to be completely prostrate.[58]

By the end of 1932 United States Steel found it necessary to cut wages 25 per cent.[59] The Standard Oil Company of Indiana, Whiting's only major industry, saved that community from the worst effects of the depression. When gasoline and oil sales declined, the company kept its employees at work by launching a plant rehabilitation

[57] Gary *Post-Tribune*, March 29, 1929; United States Steel Corporation, *Annual Report*, 1930, p. 3; 1931, p. 3.

[58] Walter J. Riley, *The Story of Unemployment Relief Work in Lake County, Indiana, December 31, 1932* (n. p., n. d), 2. Riley was the chairman of the Lake County Relief Committee. Hammond *Lake County Times*, April 13, 1932.

[59] United States Steel Corporation, *Thirty-first Annual Report*, 1932, p. 9.

and construction program at a reported cost of ten million dollars. Whiting, it was said in 1932, "laughs at the depression." Ninety-eight per cent of its taxes were paid, its banks were open, its teachers and city employees were being paid regularly.[60]

Early in the summer of 1930, the area received the full impact of the crisis when its banks began to fail. By the end of 1932, thirty-three banks in Lake County had closed their doors. Many of these institutions were legally solvent, their funds being tied up in such frozen assets as mortgages and long-term loans. As property values declined, many of the loans proved worthless, at least for the time being. The failure of the first banks affected the public's confidence in all such institutions, and large withdrawals were made and money taken out of circulation. The Gary *Post-Tribune* commented: "In the old sock, back of chimney corners, in hidden safety boxes, perhaps in the lining of forgotten trunks, repose the bits of engraved paper representing this vast wealth. . . . [These] are the old-fashioned people who feel safer holding a lien against Uncle Sam that bears no interest than when they have their savings in some other investment." The bank closures impounded millions of dollars belonging to the public schools, cities, counties, and townships. Private depositors had an estimated $27,000,000 tied up in the defunct banks.[61]

Every bank in Hammond closed its doors, and from January to December, 1932, that city of more than 64,000 people had no banks. The Chamber of Commerce established a currency exchange in the lobby of one of the closed institutions for the accommodation of industries

[60] Gary *Post-Tribune*, June 29, 1932; Standard Oil Company of Indiana, *Annual Report*, 1931.

[61] Gary *Post-Tribune*, November 4, 1930; Hammond *Lake County Times*, September 9, 1932.

and business houses.   Individuals did their banking business in the other cities of the region.   In East Chicago
the Riley banks, the Union National and the First National, were the only ones to survive.   The city's industries
came to their rescue in March, 1931, an announcement
being made at that time that officers of the various companies were to occupy seats on the bank's board of directors.[62] The Gary State Bank was the only one in the
steel city to stay open.   This institution weathered the
storm alone, receiving no assistance from the steel corporation or from any other source.[63] The Standard Oil
Company of Indiana intervened to save Whiting's banks.
In 1932 Walter E. Schrage of the Bank of Whiting told
what happened:[64]

We used to have five banks here. On Dec. 12 (last) two of
them began having difficulties. The big blow-up in Hammond
was the cause. Officials of the Standard Oil Company realized
that the banks, the First National and the First Trust and Savings, would close if something wasn't done quickly. A conference
was held and a new institution—the State Bank of Whiting, was
organized. It arranged to and subsequently did assume the depository liability of the two struggling institutions. E. G. Seubert,
president of the Standard Oil Company of Indiana, was selected
to head the new bank.

Knowing that the Sandard Oil Company and the Schrage
family were behind the new bank, the confidence of the
people was restored.   The new bank opened its doors the
latter part of December, 1931, with four officials of the

62 Hammond *Lake County Times,* March 7, 1931. The Standard Oil
Company of Indiana subscribed $50,000 to aid in the reorganization of
the Riley banks. Giddens, *Standard Oil Company (Indiana),* 470.

63 Interview with W. W. Gasser, president of the Gary National
Bank, December 9, 1954.

64 Walter E. Schrage quoted in Gary *Post-Tribune,* January 29, 1932;
Giddens, *Standard Oil Company (Indiana),* 470.

oil company on its board of directors. All of Hobart's banks were closed by October, 1931.

Public confidence in the banks was also shaken when several officials were found to be involved in irregularities and others suffered mental relapses brought on by the shock of the crisis. In August, 1930, the suicide of the president of the American State Bank in Gary started a run of withdrawals which immediately spread to other institutions. When the American State Bank in East Chicago closed its doors, its director disappeared, to be found a week later in Peoria, Illinois, reportedly a victim of amnesia. In September, 1931, the president of the defunct Northern Trust and Savings Bank of Hammond was found guilty of making illegal loans and overdrafts and sentenced to prison for from two to fourteen years. A high official of the Indiana State Bank in Indiana Harbor was indicted for embezzlement in April, 1932. Business and social circles in Hammond were shocked when the president of the First Trust and Savings Bank, the city's largest bank, and his son, the institution's vice-president, were convicted of making loans without the approval of the board of directors. The father was given a suspended sentence because of his age, and the son died shortly after he entered the Michigan City prison.[65]

Gary, East Chicago, and Hammond, with their reserve funds tied up in closed banks and with tax collections below normal, had difficulty meeting payrolls and other expenses. As a result, a new type of "currency" came into being. The three cities and Lake County issued tax anticipation warrants, more popularly known as "scrip," and hoped this paper would circulate as money. Much of this scrip was sold to local industries who later used it to

65 Gary *Post-Tribune,* August 19 and September 27, 1930; Hammond *Lake County Times,* September 28, 1931; February 10 and June 23, 1932; East Chicago *Calumet News,* April 22, 1932.

pay taxes. Brokers, speculators, and others who had money to invest purchased the paper at a discount as high as 10 per cent. When no market existed for scrip, the city employees and schoolteachers were paid with the paper. It was soon discovered that the scrip dollar did not have the purchasing power of the cash dollar. Merchants and professional men charged more for their goods and services because they had to wait one or two years until the taxes were collected to turn the scrip in for cash. There were times when there was no market at all for scrip. In August, 1932, Hammond paid its municipal employees with checks dated ninety days ahead. Such checks were known as "shin plasters."[66]

Lake County, the industrial cities, and the townships with large urban populations found themselves totally unprepared to handle the heavy relief burden. Because the farmers were more self-sufficient than the industrial workers, Porter County and the rural townships had little trouble with matters of relief. By the end of 1930, North Township, in which Whiting, East Chicago, and Hammond were located, had 16,935 families on its relief rolls. It also led the townships of the state in money spent on relief. In 1930, Calumet Township, which included Gary, ranked third in the state, with 6,979 families on relief. In December, 1932, about half of East Chicago's population was receiving aid, and by February, 1933, over 25,000 people in Calumet Township were on the relief rolls, 90 per cent of whom were in Gary. The high was reached in March, 1933, when more than 30 per cent of the population of North and Calumet townships were dependent on relief.[67]

66 Gary *Post-Tribune*, August 3, 1932.

67 *Ibid.*, September 8, 1931; February 25, 1933; Hammond *Lake County Times*, December 3, 1932.

Emergency relief commissions were organized in Hammond, Gary, and East Chicago to obtain aid for the jobless. In October, 1930, a Hammond bank provided a large building for the housing and feeding of the unemployed and a local industry donated money for food and equipment. Three hundred men applied to the Salvation Army for the fifteen jobs offered by a Hammond department store to deliver handbills, the pay to be three dollars worth of groceries for a day's work. In November, 1930, employees of the Gary retail store of a large Chicago mail order house agreed to donate a day's pay a month for four months which the company matched dollar for dollar, to be used to buy food and fuel for the unemployed. The following year Gary's municipal employees contributed one day's pay each month, an example that the city's relief commission asked all employed persons to follow. Tag days were scheduled to raise funds. In January, 1932, the East Chicago Teacher's Association voted to donate $1,900 to the local community chest.[68] The public schools donated the proceeds from athletic contests and music concerts for relief purposes. The cities also sought to provide jobs on public work projects, the pay for which was made in clothing, groceries, and other necessities. Soup kitchens were also established. Meritorious as these efforts were, they did not begin to solve the relief problem.

Social agencies such as the Red Cross, Community Chest, and the Salvation Army, together with the larger industries were able to provide more solid contributions. Estimates placed the total expenditures of the social agencies in Gary, East Chicago, Hammond and Whiting at $478,000 in 1931 and $641,000 in 1932. The Federal

[68] Hammond *Lake County Times,* October 8 and 31, 1930; Gary *Post-Tribune,* November 10, 1930; October 10 and 24, 1931; East Chicago *Calumet News,* January 5 and 12, 1932.

government channeled large quantities of flour and cotton goods to the indigents through these agencies.[69] Several industries matched the contributions of their employees to the Community Chest, and Inland Steel in East Chicago established a relief agency for its unemployed. In 1932 the United State Steel Corporation came to the rescue of Gary and the county by paying its taxes amounting to $1,017,918 several months in advance. Land for more than 5,000 industrial gardens and over 20,000 private gardens, where the unemployed raised vegetables for their own use, was provided by the industries and the various social agencies. These gardens were said to have occupied the time and labor of more than 35,000 people. The sandy soil in the greater part of North and Calumet townships being unfit for cultivation, most of these vegetable plots were in the valley of the Little Calumet River. Seeds, fertilizer, trucks, tractors, and plows as well as technical information were provided free of charge. On one occasion the state prison farm at Michigan City donated almost a million cabbage and tomato plants to the Calumet unemployed.[70]

The larger part of the relief burden in the region fell upon Lake County. Under the law, the county appropriated funds for the poor which were administered by the township trustees. Its original appropriation for poor relief for 1930 was $195,650, and by August of that year the disbursements for such purposes amounted

69 Riley, *The Story of Unemployment Relief in Lake County,* 4, 6, 8.

70 *Ibid.,* 11-14; Gary *Post-Tribune,* November 4, 1930; November 4, 1932. The various plants of the United States Steel Corporation in Gary provided 2,034 garden plots for their employees. Youngstown Sheet and Tube Company in East Chicago allotted 617 garden plots to its unemployed. The *Post-Tribune,* May 19, 1932, reported that 650 acres in the Little Calumet River Valley were devoted to private and industrial gardens.

to $325,826 in Calumet Township alone. By November
of 1930, the county was reported "broke" with no money
for payrolls or for the maintenance of its roads. An
effort to float a bond issue in 1931 failed for lack of
buyers. Unable to borrow money, the county began to
issue tax anticipation warrants in October, 1931, which
totaled $1,200,000 by the close of 1932, of which $800,-
000 were still outstanding. At that time, the county
relief fund was reported to have overdrafts from Calumet and North townships amounting to $1,221,412. In
October, 1932, an effort to borrow $1,000,000 from the
Reconstruction Finance Corporation failed when Governor Harry Leslie refused to approve the loan. The Governor insisted that if Lake County would eliminate graft
and politics from its relief program, it could care for its
needy.[71]

The administration of poor relief in Lake County
was characterized by inefficiency, waste, and petty politics. The township trustees were too often influenced by
political considerations in the employment of investigators, the majority of whom were reported to have had no
social service experience. The trustees designated the
grocers, coal dealers, physicians, and dentists to whom
the indigents must take their relief orders. Some grocers
allegedly "short-ordered" and overcharged on food for
the poor. Two prominent physicians, one of whom was
a brother-in-law of the North Township trustee, were indicted by a grand jury on charges of filing false claims for
medical service to the unemployed. Investigation dis-
closed that another physician had sought to collect a fee
for medical aid to a man whose address was found to be

[71] Gary *Post-Tribune*, November 7, 1930; October 26, 1932; Hammond
Lake County Times, October 12, 1931; Riley, *The Story of Unemployment
Relief in Lake County*, 5.

in Lake Michigan off Indiana Harbor. Another case involved a dentist who filed a claim for a set of false teeth
for a woman who later denied she wore dentures.[72]   Evidence that politics handicapped the relief program in Lake
County was indicated by the statement of Governor Leslie
that "Republicans were rotten up there and the Democrats were rottener. I hope somebody converts them."[73]

In January, 1933, Governor Paul V. McNutt came to
the rescue of the bankrupt county.   McNutt approved a
$750,000 loan to the county from the Reconstruction
Finance Corporation with these reservations: that the
money would not be used to pay old relief bills, and that
it be administered by a committee to be appointed by the
Governor.[74]   The loan was made for the purpose of providing employment on worthwhile public work projects.
Trained investigators were engaged by the committee to
choose the men for work on these projects.   The committee also established commissaries where food and
clothing were packaged for distribution to the poor.   The
unemployed to whom food orders were issued were permitted to take them to grocers of their own choosing.
The purchasing power of these orders, redeemable immediately in cash, was reported to be 15 per cent greater
than those issued by the township trustees.[75]   By the time

[72] Gary *Post-Tribune,* December 29, 1932; March 16, 1933; Hammond
Lake County Times, November 16, 1932.

[73] Governor Harry Leslie quoted in Gary *Post-Tribune,* December 29,
1932.   Walter J. Riley, on resigning as chairman of the relief commission
in Lake County, reported great waste of tax money in the administration
of relief to the unemployed. *Ibid.,* January 14, 1933.

[74] The Governor's committee included Peter Hein, Crown Point
banker; Judge Maurice E. Crites of East Chicago; John L. Rohde of
Hammond; Ora L. Wildermuth of Gary; and P. D. Sullivan of Whiting.
Virgil Sheppard was director of the program. *Ibid.,* February 4 and
March 16, 1933.

[75] Hammond *Lake County Times,* April 3, 1933.

the fund was exhausted, the Federal government had assumed much of the distress-ridden area's relief burden.

The voluntary repatriation of a large part of the Mexican population was one of the most unique and constructive methods devised to cope with the relief problem. Suffering among the Mexicans, most of whom had worked in the mills as common laborers and were poor when the depression began, was unusually severe, particularly in the winter months. Early in the depression several hundred returned to the homeland at their own expense. Others were provided with work by the industries to obtain sufficient funds to go back home, while some were aided by local citizens and by the township trustees. But, as the economic crisis worsened and public and private funds diminished, a large number still remained in the area, particularly in East Chicago and Gary.

The American Legion in East Chicago suggested the plan by which the mass repatriation was accomplished. Legion officials pointed out to the East Chicago Relief Commission that it would cost less to send the Mexicans back home than to keep them on the relief rolls, that the amount expended to provide relief for an individual or a family for a week would pay the railroad fare to the border. Also, the cities would be spared the expense of educating Mexican children. Moreover, when conditions improved, the Mexican would not be on the scene to compete for jobs with American citizens. Finally, the success of the plan would be assured by the willingness of the Mexicans, most of whom had retained their Mexican citizenship, to return to their native land.

This unusual population movement began early in 1932. Several American railroads agreed to handle the exodus and to provide a special rate of $15.00 for adults and $7.50 for children. There was no charge for children

under five years of age. The passengers were permitted
to take only their personal possessions under this arrangement. Beyond the border, the Mexican government
offered to provide transportation for the repatriates to
their ultimate destinations without further cost. Several
local industries advanced the money for the movement to
the trustees of North and Calumet townships, accepting
in return tax anticipation warrants.[76]

In May, 1932, the first train, composed of three passenger and two baggage cars, and carrying 150 persons,
left East Chicago. About a month later another train
loaded with 350 Mexicans departed for the border.[77]
A supervisor, designated by the township trustee, accompanied each train. Efforts were made to assure the comfort and to protect the health of the passengers. The
trustees provided a package of food for each person,
and coffee and milk were served on the train twice a day
during the journey.[78] By the end of 1932 about 1,800
Mexicans were reported to have left East Chicago, and
almost 1,500 were said to have been sent back to their
homeland from Gary.[79]

Conditions began to improve throughout the region in
1933. The various New Deal agencies, such as the
Federal Emergency Relief Administration, the Civil
Works Administration, and the Civilian Conservation
Corps, lightened the burden of the county and townships
by taking large numbers off the local relief rolls. About
2,500 families were reportedly removed from the relief
list between March and July, 1933. Also, local industries

[76] Riley, *The Story of Unemployment Relief in Lake County,* 10-11;
Gary *Post-Tribune,* January 14, 1932.

[77] Hammond *Lake County Times,* May 9 and June 9, 1932.

[78] Interview with Paul E. Kelly, East Chicago, November 14, 1952.
Kelly accompanied several of the trains as a supervisor.

[79] Riley, *op. cit.,* 10.

began to feel the effects of the general betterment of economic conditions throughout the nation. Approximately 35,000 persons were reported at work in the region's steel mills in June, 1933, as compared to 20,000 the previous March. The huge Buffington cement plant resumed operations on a moderate scale in June. Plants of the United States Steel Corporation increased production on an average of about 30 per cent, and wage increases totaling 25 per cent were given to its employees.[80] By the close of the year, the most tragic period in the region's history was about over.

[80] Hammond *Lake County Times,* June 9 and July 15, 1933; United States Steel Corporation, *Thirty-second Annual Report,* 1933, pp. 9-10.

16

TALES OF THE INDIANA DUNES

THE INDIANA DUNES which extend along the shore of Lake Michigan between Gary and Michigan City were the last part of the Calumet Region to feel the touch of civilization. Until recent years this stretch of lonely sand hills and marshes, only a short distance from Chicago and bordered by the industrial cities of northwestern Indiana, was a fragment of untamed wilderness. Jens Jensen, Chicago landscape artist and popularly known as the "Apostle of the Dunes," described the area in 1923 :[1]

Just a little beyond our eastern gateway lies the Dune Country, the vast garden of Mid-America. Within easy reach of millions, it has remained practically unknown. . . . The Dune Country possesses all the charm, mystery and beauty that primitive America has to offer anywhere. Countless ages are written in its sand-hills, and its to-morrow is in the making. . . .

It is a native arboretum of vast instruction to those who seek knowledge in the out-of-doors of plant and animal life. It is a shrine for solace and quietness in contrast to the turbulent life of the great city. . . .

There is an ocean-like grandeur in the broad stretches of beaches; the waves chasing one another in madness, pitch high; the west wind roars and the sand blizzard rules; seagulls fill the air like giant snowflakes. Then the Dune Country is in its making, and a grand drama is enacted on those Indiana shores.

The dunes remained in their virgin state because they were worthless for agricultural purposes and because in-

[1] Jens Jensen, quoted in the Introduction to Brennan's, *The Wonders of the Dunes.*

dustries found more suitable sites elsewhere in the region. As late as the early 1920's the beach could be reached by automobile only at Miller, Waverly Beach, and at Michigan City. Along the lake front there were no harbors or other facilities for the accommodation of freight and passenger boats. Most of the dune country remained for many years a wild and mysterious land, while settlement and industrialization encircled it.

The Carr Family at Miller Beach

The Miller settlement, in what is now the eastern part of Gary, began shortly after the Lake Shore and Michigan Southern Railroad penetrated the edge of the dune country in 1851. This community, originally located about a mile from the lake, was composed largely of Swedes and Germans who came to work as section hands on the railroad. Its importance increased in 1874 when the Baltimore and Ohio Railroad was constructed a short distance to the south. The village soon became an important center for the shipping of fish, ice, and sand.[2] Its only connection with the outside, with the exception of the railroads, was a township road which led to Hobart a few miles to the south.

About 1862 Robert Carr settled on the lake front at the foot of the present Lake Street, soon to be known as Carr's Beach. This was a lonely area at that time, the only other residents being a boat builder from Michigan City, a trapper from South Chicago, and a Negro by the name of Davy Crockett who had come to the dunes as a fugitive slave before the Civil War. Carr fished for sturgeon and white fish most of which he sold in

[2] Miller had a post office as early as 1865. William O. Enos was the first postmaster. Index of Indiana Post Offices, in Indiana Division, Indiana State Library.

Chicago. Some were traded to farmers who lived south of the dune belt for flour, pork, and butter. Robert Carr's wife, Drusilla, who had come to the beach to live with her brother in 1872 and married Robert Carr two years later, said that she was the only woman on the lake front at that time, and the region was so wild that "the wolves stood back in the hills and cried like a woman and when we went along the beach we could see an eagle on every hill."[3]

The area where the Carrs lived became involved in one of the most unusual legal entanglements in the region's history. Although they were squatters, the Carrs occupied the site without molestation for more than forty years. Since it had no agricultural or commercial value during that long period, its legal owners, in most instances, did not bother to pay the taxes. But when Gary was founded in 1906 the value of the heretofore worthless land rose to fantastic levels. The United States Steel Corporation, which owned the entire lake front in Gary, took steps to add Carr's Beach and the surrounding area to its holdings. The corporation, through its subsidiary, the Gary Land Company, paid up the taxes on most of the property, thereby obtaining liens against it. The Carrs, on the other hand, claimed title to the area by right of "adverse possession," more popularly known as "squatter's rights."[4] The legal battle over this sandy wasteland, which amounted to more than two hundred acres, began in 1908 and lasted for more than thirty years. Since the disputed area contained several different tracts, each was the subject of a separate law suit. Although the

[3] "Mrs. Drusilla Carr Tells of Early Days at Miller Beach," in Lester (ed.), Papers by Various Hands, 1:228-32.

[4] Both Indiana and Federal laws recognized the claims of squatters to land which they had occupied "peacefully and without interruption" for twenty years or more.

Carrs resisted stubbornly, parcel after parcel was awarded by the courts to the corporation. By 1939 it was in possession of most of the area.[5] The Carrs, retaining their residence, remained as fishermen along that part of the beach.

Octave Chanute at Miller and Dune Park

In 1896 the dune country was the scene of significant developments in the history of aviation, for here Octave Chanute, one of the pioneers of human flight, performed his experiments with gliders.

Chanute, born in France in 1832, had already achieved a position among America's most eminent civil engineers when he became interested in aeronautics. In 1853 he worked as a surveyor on the construction of the Joliet and Bloomington portion of the Chicago and Alton Railroad, and in the years that followed held other assignments with railroads in the Middle West. Chanute designed and supervised the building of Chicago's Union Stockyards in 1867 and was chief engineer for the Erie Railroad from 1873 to 1883. Perhaps his greatest engineering achievement was the design and construction of the railroad bridge across the Missouri River at Kansas City, which was completed in 1869. In 1889 he established his home in Chicago.[6]

When he was almost sixty years of age Chanute became interested in Otto Lilienthal's experiments with

[5] Gary *Post-Tribune,* March 22, 1927; February 25, 1939; Brennan, *The Wonders of the Dunes,* 138-40. A portion of the disputed area was sold by the steel corporation to the city of Gary.

[6] *The Aeronautical Annual* (Boston, 1896), 56-59. Since this unsigned biography accompanies an article, "Sailing Flight," by Chanute, the information apparently came from him. See also Marvin W. McFarland (ed.), *The Papers of Wilbur and Orville Wright: Including the Chanute-Wright Letters and Other Papers of Octave Chanute, 1899-1948* (2 vols. New York, 1953), 1:15-16n.

gliders. Lilienthal, a German, is regarded as the most important of the "modern fathers" of aviation. Chanute collected and sifted every bit of information he could find about aeronautical work done in Europe, even from the earliest times. The result was a volume, *Progress in Flying Machines,* published in 1894, which became one of the bibles of aeronautics. This work was said to have been the first reasoned analysis of aviation experiments to be published; it was symbolic of one of Chanute's chief functions in the history of flight, for he was the great collector and disseminator of accurate information about aviation as well as a pioneer in his own right.[7]

Having published his book, Chanute decided to experiment with gliders of his own design. His immediate objective was not to perfect a machine that would fly farther than any other had flown nor to excel in any of the spectacular aspects of aviation. Instead, Chanute believed that of all the problems involved in aeronautics the most important was equilibrium, for until automatic stability at all angles of flight and conditions of wind was achieved, and safety therefore secured, it would be premature to place a motor in a flying machine. Chanute was certain that lack of balance was the chief weakness of the Lilienthal machines and that the German's success was due largely to his superb physical and mental co-ordination. Lilienthal's death as a result of a glider accident in 1896 strengthened Chanute's opinion that the problem of equilibrium must be solved before man could fly with safety.[8]

[7] Charles Gibbs-Smith, *A History of Flying* (New York, 1954), 207.

[8] Octave Chanute, Opening Address, International Conference on Aerial Navigation, Paris (undated typewritten manuscript in the Collected Papers of Octave Chanute, in John G. Crerar Library, Chicago). In this paper Chanute speaks of Lilienthal in the present tense. Since the latter died in August 1896, the address must have been given before that date.

While Lilienthal experimented with both monoplane and biplane gliders, the operational principles of the two were fundamentally the same. The pilot stood in the middle of the apparatus, thrusting his arms through the padded openings in the frame, so that the weight in flight rested on his elbows. Thus he sailed through the air with a portion of his body and legs hanging below the machine. He maintained balance while in flight by moving his body and swinging his legs back and forth as the occasion demanded. Lilienthal made his flights from hills, one of which was artificially constructed, and from low mountains.[9] In 1896, aware of the need of a better method of control, he installed a movable rudder on a biplane glider, the apparatus being operated by a rope fastened to a band around the pilot's head. The plan called for the machine to climb when the head was moved forward and to descend when it moved backward. While testing this device, Lilienthal apparently became confused by the unfamiliar controls and was killed when the glider plunged fifty feet to the ground.[10]

In contrast to Lilienthal, Chanute's objective was to discover better means of control than that of shifting the weight of the pilot and also to obtain some measure of automatic stability. He sought to achieve these ends with the use of adjustable surfaces and parts which could be controlled with a minimum of effort on the part of the pilot. Because of the success of his efforts, Chanute must be given credit for the development of the first reasonably stable flying machine.[11]

[9] Lewin B. Barringer, *Flight Without Power: The Art of Gliding and Soaring* (New York, 1940), 2.

[10] Cecil L. Brown, *The Conquest of the Air: An Historical Survey* (London, 1927), 65-66; Edwin Way Teale, *The Book of Gliders* (New York, 1930), 31.

[11] *Scientific American Supplement,* 70 (July-December, 1910) :No. 1826 :427.

Chanute selected Miller Beach for his experiments because the high sand dunes were reasonably devoid of vegetation and because of the frequent north and northwest winds, which were the best for glider flights in that area. Moreover, the soft sand assured maximum safety for the operators of the machines. Chanute also hoped, but mistakenly, that at Miller he would escape the attention of the newspapers and curiosity seekers. His party, which arrived at Miller on June 22, 1896, consisted of Augustus M. Herring, a pupil of Lilienthal who had been associated with Samuel P. Langley at the Smithsonian Institution; Paul Butusov, a young Russian aeronautical enthusiast; William Avery, a carpenter; and James Ricketts, a young Chicago physician.[12] A camp was established northeast of what is now the Lake Street bridge over the Grand Calumet River.

The engineer's desire to keep his experiments a secret from the public was blasted immediately. According to Chanute, "As soon as we left the train at Miller with our suspicious baggage, we soon had more visitors than was altogether pleasant in preliminary experiments."[13] Within a short time several Chicago, New York, and Boston newspapers had reporters on the scene. A representative of the *Westchester Tribune,* Chesterton, Indiana, who arrived at the camp site while the tents were being erected, described Chanute as a little man with gray hair and a "French style" beard. On being told that the Chesterton visitor was a newspaper man, Chanute said:

[12] "Octave Chanute's Diary, 1896," in McFarland (ed.), *Papers of Wilbur and Orville Wright,* 1:641n. Chanute, conscious of the possibility of injuries to his glider pilots, insisted on having a physician in his party. Ricketts also served as the camp cook. See the *Scientific American,* 105:275 (July-December, 1911). In this article, Ricketts was referred to as "Howard" and not "James."

[13] Octave Chanute, "Recent Experiments in Gliding Flight," in *The Aeronautical Annual* (1897), 33.

I did not come here seeking notoriety. We have a machine that is an improvement on the one made in Berlin (Lilienthal's) which we are going to test but do not expect these tests to be successful. We want nothing said of our work or that we are here, because we do not want to be classed with the army of aerial cranks that have been and are exciting the country. We want nothing said in the newspapers and we want no visitors.[14]

Nevertheless, some of the dunes' people did regard Chanute as a crank, and fantastic stories were told in later years about the "Crazy Old Man of the Sand Dunes." His first wings, the natives insisted, were thatched with chicken feathers. A famous naturalist, while spending the summers of his boyhood in the sand hills, was impressed by the stories of the "lonely old man" and of his efforts to fly.[15]

The site was ideal for Chanute's experiments, for the dunes in that area were about seventy feet high. Adjacent to the camp was a long dune which bordered the river for some distance. A few hundred feet to the north was another dune which ran east and west, and beyond it to the north was a wide, level beach extending to the edge of Lake Michigan.[16] Since Chanute was too old to pilot the machines himself, he left the testing to Herring and occasionally to other members of the party. The operators, who were suspended from the wing of the Lilienthal glider and from beneath the lower wing of Chanute's multiple-winged machine, would make running starts of several steps and launch themselves into the wind from the top of the dune. About a hundred glides, the longest being 116 feet, were made with the Lilienthal machine. Chanute found the German's glider

14 Chesterton *Westchester Tribune*, June 27, 1896.

15 Teale, *Dune Boy*, 118-19.

16 Chanute, "Recent Experiments in Gliding Flight," in *The Aeronautical Annual* (1897), 32; Brennan, *The Wonders of the Dunes*, 141.

dangerous and hard to handle, however, and tests with it were discontinued.[17]

The Chanute glider, the wings of which were arranged so as to swerve fore and aft to adjust the center of lift, was a fantastic machine with five tiers of wings on each side of the center structure. It had two small wings like rudders in the rear. Although its longest flight was only eighty-two feet, this "Venetian blind" affair was flown at least three hundred times without the slightest injury to the pilots.[18]   Chanute, who was concerned with principles of construction that would achieve balance for the operators, was satisfied with its performance.   The members of the party, all of whom were no doubt familiar with Lilienthal's book, *Bird Flight as the Basis of Aviation,* also spent hours watching the hawks, eagles, and gulls of the area, comparing notes on what they saw.[19] In 1897 Chanute stated that more was learned from the experiments at Miller than he had gathered during many years of study of the principles involved and from experiments with models.[20]

The experiments were terminated on July 4 and the machines taken back to Chicago.   Chanute, Herring, and Butusov spent the next few weeks supervising the construction of new gliders which incorporated the principles learned during the tests.   Chanute returned to the Indiana dunes on August 20, 1896, but not to Miller where the public had interfered with his work.   Instead, the

17 Chanute, "Recent Experiments in Gliding Flight," in *The Aeronautical Annual* (1897), 36.

18 *Ibid.*

19 Teale, *The Book of Gliders,* 24, 36. Lilienthal's study of bird flight was published in Berlin in 1889 as *Der Vogelflug als Grudlage der Fliegekunst.* In 1911 an English translation of the second edition was published under the title, *Bird Flight as a Basis of Aviation.*

20 Chanute, "Recent Experiments in Gliding Flight," in *The Aeronautical Annual* (1897), 37.

party came on a sailing vessel, the "Scorpion," to Dune
Park, several miles east of Miller, where a site was
selected in an unsettled area about two miles from the
station of Dune Park, now Wilson, on the Lake Shore
and Michigan Southern Railroad. The only road through
the woods, swamps, and dunes was so indistinct that
visitors frequently lost their way when they sought to
reach the camp. But Chanute's hopes for privacy were
again shattered when a storm wrecked the camp and much
of the equipment on the night of their arrival. Replace-
ments were sent by railroad to the Dune Park station,
thereby attracting the attention of the public and the
newspapers.[21]   The *Westchester Tribune* gleefully remarked that Chanute had discovered he could not get
away from newspapermen.[22]

Chanute tested three types of machines at Dune Park:
his original multiple-winged affair; a glider with three
wings; and a monoplane invented by Butusov. The
three-winged affair was designed by Chanute with the
exception of an automatic device which operated the rudder perfected by Herring for the purpose of securing
stability.[23]   All the machines were constructed at Chanute's expense. As Butusov's glider was too heavy for
the operator to take off from a flying start, a slanting
"trestle" was erected. Its runways were greased with
tallow and two men pulled the machine into the wind.
The glider never flew more than seventy-five feet and
was soon abandoned as unsatisfactory.[24]   The greatest

21 Chanute, "Recent Experiments in Gliding Flight," in *The Aeronautical Annual* (1897), 40-41.

22 *Westchester Tribune,* August 26, 1896.

23 Octave Chanute, "The Evolution of the 'Two-Surface' Flying
Machine," in *Aeronautics* (New York), 3:28-29 (October, 1908).

24 Chanute, "Recent Experiments in Gliding Flight," *loc. cit.,* 42.

distance achieved by the multiple-winged type was 188
feet in 7.8 seconds with Avery as the operator.[25]

The first trials of the three-winged machine showed
that the lower surface was too close to the ground. It
was removed and the glider became a biplane.[26] Unusual
success was had with this machine, numerous flights of
from 199 to 359 feet being made without any injury to
the pilots. The flight of 359 feet was made by Herring
at a maximum height of 62 feet in 14 seconds, or something more than seventeen miles an hour.[27] Glides were
made in winds of as much as thirty miles an hour velocity,
something which Lilienthal was reported to have said
would surely bring disaster to any pilot.[28] Such confidence was acquired in the biplane that all in the party
were permitted to fly it. Chanute believed that any young
man could become expert in the use of the machine within
a week.[29] However, he did not consider his biplane
sufficiently stable or airworthy to justify the attempt to
fit it with an engine and make motor-driven flights.[30] At

[25] "Octave Chanute's Diary, 1896." in McFarland (ed.), *Papers of Wilbur and Orville Wright,* 1:648.

[26] Chanute, "The Evolution of the 'Two-Surface' Flying Machine," in *Aeronautics,* 3:28.

[27] "Octave Chanute's Diary, 1896," in McFarland (ed.), *Papers of Wilbur and Orville Wright,* 1:649. Teale, *The Book of Gliders,* 37, reports that the gliders at Dune Park achieved a maximum speed of fifty-two miles an hour, and Barringer, *Flight Without Power,* 3, states that Herring reported a flight of 927 feet in 48 seconds. No verification of such unusual performances was found in Chanute's writings.

[28] Chelsea Fraser, *The Story of Aircraft* (New York, 1933), 291.

[29] Octave Chanute, "Some American Experiments," in *The Aeronautical Journal* (London), January, 1898, p. 9. According to Chanute, accidents were so rare at Dune Park that Dr. Ricketts could only exhibit his talents as a cook. See Chanute, "Recent Experiments in Gliding Flight," in *The Aeronautical Annual* (1897), 41.

[30] Brown, *The Conquest of the Air,* 72. Chanute's opinion that the biplane was not as yet sufficiently stable to perform motor-driven flights

the termination of the tests, Chanute estimated the costs of the experiments at Miller and Dune Park at $14,000, all of which he paid personally.[31]

The biplane glider, as developed by Chanute, was his greatest achievement in the field of aeronautics. This machine, which later became famous as the "Chanute type," was the model upon which the first successfully powered airplanes were built. While Chanute did not invent the biplane, he was the first to apply the principles of the modern truss bridge to glider construction.[32]   In describing the wings of the machine Chanute said: ". . . being a builder of bridges, I trussed these surfaces together in order to obtain strength and stiffness. The surfaces were connected by a girder composed of vertical posts and diagonal ties (wires), specifically known as a 'Pratt truss.' "[33]   The wings, which were straight and slightly cambered to diminish the pressure of wind gusts, were referred to by Chanute in another instance as "aerocurves."[34]   The vertical and horizonal rudder, an invention of Herring's, was held in place by a spring which

was justified in October, 1898, when Herring failed in his efforts to perform such flights. Herring's experiments, which were witnessed by Chanute, took place at St. Joseph, Michigan. See McFarland (ed.), Papers of Wilbur and Orville Wright, 1:651n.

[31] Octave Chanute, "Development and Future of Flying Machines," in The City Club Bulletin, 2 (Chicago, 1898):No. 15:192, in The Collected Papers of Octave Chanute, in John G. Crerar Library, Chicago. Herring conducted experiments, partly at Chanute's expense, with a biplane glider at Dune Park in September, 1897. These experiments were erroneously referred to as "Chanute glides of 1897." See McFarland (ed.), Papers of Wilbur and Orville Wright, 1:651n.

[32] Wilbur Wright, "Some Aeronautical Experiments," an address delivered before the Western Society of Engineers, Chicago, September 18, 1901, in McFarland (ed.), Papers of Wilbur and Orville Wright, 1:102.

[33] Chanute, "The Evolution of the 'Two-Surface' Flying Machine," in Aeronautics, 3:29.

[34] Chanute, "Some American Experiments," in The Aeronautical Journal, January, 1898, p. 10.

permitted it to move upward or downward with reference to its normal position, thus modifying the action of the wind gusts upon it and thereby achieving more satisfactory longitudinal stability.[35]   Otherwise, the pilot, who was suspended beneath the lower wing, controlled the glider by throwing his legs to the left or to the right as the occasion demanded, but with much less effort than in the Lilienthal machines.   The glider was light but very strong. Weighing only 23 pounds, it carried a maximum weight of 178 pounds.[36]   This was the machine upon which the Wright brothers based the design of their gliders and later of the first motor-driven airplane.[37]

Chanute stands out most prominently as the man who directly encouraged the Wright brothers and provided

[35] Wright, "Some Aeronautical Experiments," in McFarland (ed.), *Papers of Wilbur and Orville Wright,* 1:103. For several years a controversy was waged between Chanute and Herring in regard to the "Chanute type" of glider, Herring and his friends insisting that Chanute was not giving Herring sufficient credit for his part in the development of the machine. Although Chanute in his diary refers to the biplane as the "Herring machine," he also speaks of it in the same document as the glider Herring "called his own." On several occasions Chanute gave Herring full credit for the "automatic regulator" which operated the rudder. At one point of the controversy Chanute declared that he "did not claim to have made any invention at all, but simply designs to study automatic stability." For details of this affair, see "Octave Chanute's Diary, 1896," in McFarland (ed.), *Papers of Wilbur and Orville Wright,* 1:648-52; Chanute to James Means, September 29, 1897, and Chanute to Matthias S. Arnot, March 24, 1901, in *ibid.,* 1:650n-52n; Chanute, "Recent Experiments in Gliding Flight," in *The Aeronautical Annual* (1897), 39; Chanute, "Some American Experiments," in *The Aeronautical Journal,* January, 1898, p. 10; Chanute "The Evolution of the 'Two-Surface' Flying Machine," in *Aeronautics,* 3:28-29.

[36] Barringer, *Flight with Power,* 3; *Scientific American Supplement,* 70:no. 1826:427.

[37] The most important improvement made by the Wright brothers on the Chanute glider was the elimination of its vertical and horizontal rudder in the rear and the placing of a "horizontal rudder" in front of the machine. This innovation proved useful in securing fore and aft balance. See Brown, *Conquest of the Air,* 94-95.

them with a practical example of biplane construction. In May, 1900, Wilbur Wright, who was acquainted with Chanute's writings and accomplishments, wrote him the first of numerous letters exchanged by the two during the next ten years. The Chanute-Wright correspondence is said to be

unquestionably among the most important, not to say fascinating, chapters in all of aeronautical literature and certainly of aeronautical history. It is seldom that mankind's epochal achievements on the history-making and history-changing scale of practical aerial flight have ever been recorded, discussed, and elucidated with such clarity, candor, and simple charm as are found in the Wright-Chanute letters. . . . These precious documents are instinct with the scientific intelligence and philosophic spirit out of which flight was born.[38]

Wilbur Wright, in his first letter to Chanute, revealed his ideas and ambitions in regard to flying, and also sought advice as to the best locations for winter experiments with gliders. A short time later he asked Chanute where spruce could be obtained and what type of varnish was the best for use in the constructing of gliders. In May, 1901, Wright invited Chanute to visit him and his brother, Orville, at their camp at Kitty Hawk, North Carolina.[39] Chanute accepted, returning in 1902 and 1903 to witness their experiments. The Chanute-Wright letters are filled with highly technical discussion and information about aeronautics. Throughout the correspondence one sees Chanute's encouragement of the brothers in their efforts to solve the problem of heavier-than-air flying machines.

38 Marvin W. McFarland and Arthur G. Renstrom, "The Papers of Wilbur and Orville Wright," in The Library of Congress, Quarterly Journal of Current Acquisitions, 7:no. 4:22-34 (August, 1950).

39 Wilbur Wright to Octave Chanute, May 13 and August 10, 1900, May 12, 1901, in McFarland (ed.), Papers of Wilbur and Orville Wright, 1:15-19, 22, 54.

In January, 1911, about a month after Chanute's death, Wilbur Wright paid tribute to his friend and also reminded the world that important aeronautical achievements had been made in the Indiana dunes.

Mr. Chanute was one of six very remarkable men who in the last decade of the 19th century raised studies relating to flying to a point never before attained. Lilienthal, Chanute, Langley, Maxim, Ader, and Hargrave formed by far the strongest group of workers in the field that the world has seen. Lilienthal and Chanute were peculiarly missionaries of the cause, and by their writings gave their experimental work an influence on the progress of the art not equalled by the others. Mr. Chanute's book, *Progress in Flying Machines,* was one of the greatest contributions ever made to the advancement of the art. His Dune Park experiments, in combination with the clear manner in which they were presented to the public, constituted another very important contribution, and finally his encouragement of workers in all countries vastly influenced the trend of events accompanying the birth of the art. From all of these causes I think I was fully justified in saying that if he had not lived the history of human flight would have been quite different from what it has been.[40]

Today, a small plaque northeast of the Lake Street bridge over the Grand Calumet River in Miller marks the site of Chanute's initial efforts to conquer the skies over the Indiana dunes.

[40] Wilbur Wright to Charles L. Strobel, January 27, 1911, in *ibid.,* 2:1017-18. See also Wilbur Wright, "The Death of Octave Chanute," in *Aeronautics,* 8:4 (January, 1911). Samuel P. Langley (1834-1906), for some years head of the Smithsonian Institution, experimented with steam-powered and gasoline-driven airplanes; Sir Hiram Stevens Maxim (1840-1916), American-born English citizen and inventor of the Maxim machine gun, also conducted experiments with steam-driven flying machine; Clément Ader (1841-1925), French engineer, worked with gliders and attempted to perfect a steam-powered airplane; Lawrence Hargrave (1850-1915) invented box kites which provided the foundation for the development of the power airplane in Europe. See Gibbs-Smith, *A History of Flying,* 193, 198, 199, 209.

Scientists, Artists, and Writers in the Dunes

The dune country was "discovered" by scientists, artists, and writers at an early date, and they in turn acquainted the public with its beauties and unusual features. In 1897, William S. Blatchley, Indiana state geologist, directed the attention of students and nature lovers to the dunes with his informative report, "The Geology of Lake and Porter Counties," which appeared in the *Geological Report* for 1897. Scientists at the University of Chicago, only about thirty miles away, made studies of the dune country before the close of the last century. Henry Chandler Cowles, eminent botanist on the University's faculty, attracted botanists to the area with a scholarly study, "The Ecological Relations of the Vegetation of the Sand Dunes of Lake Michigan," published in the *Botanical Gazette* in 1899. Years later the newspapers gave wide publicity to Cowles's statement that European botanists regarded the Indiana dunes as one of the wonders of America.[41] Cowles made an intensive study of plant life in the beautiful tamarack swamp north of Mineral Springs which now bears his name. Frank Leverett, also of the University of Chicago, started a procession of geologists into the dune country with an article, "The Pleistocene Features and Deposits of the Chicago Area," which appeared in the Chicago Academy of Science *Bulletin* in May, 1897. In the years that followed, botany and geology teachers and students from various colleges and universities made expeditions to the dunes. In 1917 George Pinneo, botanist and for some years physical director of the Gary Y.M.C.A., published a fine study, *The Flora of the Dunes,* in behalf of the movement for a dunes national park. Pinneo spent

41 Brennan, *The Wonders of the Dunes,* 210.

much of his time while in Gary studying the botany of the area, particularly in the vicinity of Liverpool.

Through the years artists haunted the dune country in search of refreshment for their souls and subjects for their brushes. In 1906 or 1907 Earl H. Reed, artist and author, abandoned his business as a Chicago grain broker to depict the dune country in etchings and books with rare insight and charm. Reed was probably the most prolific of duneland's artists and writers. He was the friend and confidant of numerous human derelicts who fled from the busy world of strife and turmoil to the peace and quiet of the sand hills. These fugitives from society lived as squatters in little shacks of driftwood scattered here and there among the depressions and dunes along the shore of the lake. They eked out a bare existence by fishing, and by shooting and trapping small game. In the pages of Reed's books we meet "Old Sipes" who wore a patch over one eye because "as long as there was nothin' going' out, he didn't want nothin' comin' in"; "Happy Cal," who was so named because he wasn't happy at all; "Catfish John" and his horse, Napoleon; "Holy Zeke," to whom Catfish John was always willing to give a fish "when'e's hungry, even if 'e does think I'm goin' to hell"; J. Ledyard Symington, whose cabin door bore the notice that he was at home on Tuesdays and Thursdays and that visitors should leave their cards if he was absent; and other picturesque characters. Reed illustrated his books with etchings which beautifully portrayed the color and flavor of the dune country. In 1912, *Voices of the Dunes,* an anthology of duneland poetry, appeared. This was followed by *The Dune Country,* 1916; *Sketches in Duneland,* 1918; and *Tales of a Vanishing River,* which portrayed the atmosphere and characters in the Kankakee River country, in 1920. *The*

Silver Arrow, a volume of legendary Indian romances, was published in 1926.[42]

Among the artists who frequented this region, Frank V. Dudley probably more than any other possessed the genius to portray the real beauty and majesty of the dunes. His pictures, which won him high acclaim as early as 1907, were exhibited biennially at the Chicago Art Institute from 1918 to 1956.[43] Today, they adorn the walls of universities, public schools, and libraries throughout the Middle West. When the dunes are gone, Dudley's paintings will serve to depict for later generations the beauty that once existed along the Indiana shore of Lake Michigan.

George Brennan, Chicago writer and historian, spent several years in the dunes while preparing his work, *The Wonders of the Dunes,* completed in 1923. In 1922 John O. Bowers, Gary attorney and historian, published *The Old Bailly Homestead,* an account of the life of Joseph Bailly, fur trader and first white settler in the dune region. Bowers drew heavily on the papers and business records of Bailly which he obtained in 1919 shortly after the death of Frances Howe, the pioneer's granddaughter. Bowers also told the story of the ill-fated "cities," "City West," "Manchester," and "Indiana City," which promoters laid out in the dune country in the first half of the last century, in *Dream Cities of the Calumet,* published in 1929. The naturalist, Edwin Way Teale, described the golden summers of his boyhood at Lone Oak, the farm of his grandparents, on the edge of the dune country near Furnessville, in *Dune Boy,* which appeared in 1943.

42 For an account of Reed's life, see John Drury, "Artist-Author Discovered the Dunes," in Gary *Post-Tribune,* April 22, 1956.

43 "Famous Artist Finds Subjects at Dunes State Park," in *Outdoor Indiana* (published by the Indiana Department of Conservation), 14no. 6: 14-16 (September, 1947).

The Carbarn Bandits

Around the turn of the century the dune country was a favorite refuge for local and Chicago criminals. Since it was easily accessible to horsemen, thieves had little trouble concealing stolen animals there. Drifting sand, which quickly covered their tracks, made it difficult for the authorities to ferret them out. In 1891 the Chesterton *Tribune* reported that numerous places had been found in the sand hills where stolen horses had been fed and kept.[44] The sand ridges and swamps in the vicinity of the railroad tracks near the lake front in what is now the western part of Gary afforded cover for fugitives from justice. Dugouts of a permanent nature were built in the sides of the ridges and served as comfortable hideouts for those on the wrong side of the law.

The capture of the carbarn bandits is the most dramatic crime story of the dunes. In August, 1903, the bandits, Peter Neidermeier, Gustave Marx, Emil Roeski, and Harley Van Dine, robbed a street railway barn in Chicago of about $2,500.00, in the course of which two employees were killed.[45] The following November, Marx was captured in Chicago after fatally wounding a policeman. He disclosed the names of the others involved in the carbarn robbery and killings. On hearing of their betrayal, Neidermeier, Roeski, and Van Dine fled by railroad to East Chicago and thence on foot to a dugout just west of Clark Station. The following morning, Thanksgiving Day, the bandits were recognized by a local schoolteacher while they were purchasing food in a store at Clark Station.[46] South Chicago police were notified and the man hunt began.

[44] Chesterton *Tribune*, November 6, 1891.

[45] Chicago *Daily News*, August 29, 1903.

[46] Neidermeier was familiar with the area. In 1901 he and a companion stopped a Baltimore and Ohio passenger train near Clark

Eight Chicago detectives were sent to Indiana Harbor by railroad and from there traveled in a wagon to the dugout, which they found deserted. After spending the night with a local farmer, the officers followed the trail of the bandits from Clark Station through the snow to another dugout south of the Baltimore and Ohio tracks about a mile to the east. Although surrounded in their hideaway, the bandits fought their way out and reached the safety of the near-by woods. In the course of this battle, two officers were shot and Neidermeier and Roeski were wounded. Roeski, unable to keep up with the other fugitives, made his way to Aetna where he was captured later in the day while waiting for a train at the Wabash Station.

In the meantime, Neidermeier and Van Dine reached East Tolleston where they found a Pennsylvania sand train on a siding. Only the fireman was in the engine's cab, the engineer and conductor being at lunch a short distance away. The fireman was quickly overpowered by the bandits and forced to disconnect the engine from the train. At this stage, Neidermeier shot and killed a brakeman who attempted to prevent the theft of the engine. The bandits then directed the fireman to drive the engine toward Liverpool. The East Tolleston telegraph operator notified the Liverpool Station of what had happened and a switch was closed across the path of the oncoming locomotive. On seeing this avenue of escape blocked, the criminals ordered the fireman to stop the engine and then put it in reverse. They abandoned it about a half mile west of Liverpool and fled on foot toward the Little Calumet River to the north. A short time later the fugitives were surrounded and captured in a corn field by

Station and attempted to rob its express car. They hid out in one of the dugouts in that vicinity for several days. See Chicago *Sunday Tribune,* November 29, 1903.

local farmers armed with shotguns and rifles. The bandits were turned over to the Chicago police and taken back to Chicago for trial.[47]

Motion Pictures in the Dunes

The dune country was a favorite location for the making of motion pictures when Chicago was one of the centers of that industry. Lake Michigan and its beaches provided a fairly authentic setting for pictures requiring an ocean background while the dunes and the magnificent open stretches of sand were ideal for Arab and desert scenes. The area's proximity to Chicago suited the purposes of the early producers who generally operated with small budgets. Moreover, in this isolated region, interference by the public in the making of pictures could be kept to a minimum.

In June, 1910, a Chicago company made a picture about the "carbarn bandits" at Dune Park.[48] The Essanay Company chose the region near Miller in 1912 for the setting of the "Conquest of Mexico" by Hernando Cortes.[49] The famous conquistador landed on the beach at the foot of Lake Street with 160 "Spaniards" dressed in early sixteenth-century costumes. Here a terrific battle was fought with the "Aztecs" led by their emperor, Montezuma. The "Aztecs" were decisively beaten while sev-

[47] Neidermeier and Marx were sentenced to death while Roeski and Van Dine were sent to prison for life. For complete accounts of this episode, see the Chicago *Daily Tribune,* November 29, 1903; the Chicago *Daily News,* November 29, 1903; and the Chesterton *Tribune,* December 4, 1903.

[48] Gary *Evening Post,* June 13, 1910.

[49] The Essanay Company, one of the pioneers of the motion picture industry, was organized in Chicago by George K. Spoor in 1907 and continued in business until 1916. George K. Spoor, "The Essanay Days," in *Theatre Arts,* July, 1951, p. 7; Chicago *Sunday Tribune,* December 21, 1947.

eral hundred residents of the dunes watched from the crest of the near-by hills. Ten Pullman cars on a siding at Miller housed the actors for a week while the picture was being made. A large number of the "extras" were students from the Art Institute in Chicago who enjoyed a vacation in the dunes while being paid a dollar a day and expenses.[50]

In 1914, Francis X. Bushman was Essanay's star in "The Plum," a Mexican drama, filmed in the dunes near Miller.[51] Stark realism was added to the experiences of an actor who played the character part in "Lost in the Desert," a picture made by a Chicago company near Dune Park in 1919. The company, with numerous men and women representing British soldiers, Bedouin warriors, and Moslem maidens, with camels and horses spent three days enacting battles, kidnappings, and attacks on desert caravans. In the final scene the leading man played the part of a British officer who escaped from the Bedouin bandits and wandered aimlessly about the desert until rescued by the cavalry. The actor was made up with long flowing hair and untrimmed beard. His clothing was in tatters and a leopard skin covered his shoulders. The part also called for him to carry a heavy club. The scene finished, the exhausted actor fell asleep in the shade of a tree. The company packed its equipment and returned to Miller leaving him truly "lost in the desert." He was not missed until the group reached the railroad station and the guide refused to lead a search party into the dunes during the night.[52]

In the meantime, the deserted actor awakened from his sleep when the cool of the evening descended upon him.

[50] Gary *Daily Tribune,* May 31, 1912.

[51] *Ibid.,* September 2, 1914.

[52] Alfred E. Jones, "An Amateur Wild Man" (undated newspaper clipping in scrapbook in Gary Public Library).

Unable to find his way out of the wilderness, he spent the night there tormented by mosquitoes and suffering from lack of water. The next morning a trapper from the village of Crisman, making his way through the marshes, was startled to see a ragged, unkempt, half-naked man with long hair and a beard. The strange figure was stumbling through the sand, carrying a club. At times it paused, tried to shout, then moaned inarticulately, and went on his way. The frightened trapper hurried back to Crisman to tell what he had seen. A sheriff's posse tracked down and rescued the lost man about sunset.[53]

Horse Racing at Mineral Springs

In the early part of the century Mineral Springs, on the edge of the dune belt near Porter, was a favorite summer resort and recreation spot for Chicagoans and other residents of the region. One of the features of the area was the excellent spring water which could be tapped only a few feet below the surface of the ground. The resort was also more easily accessible by railroad than were the dunes bordering Lake Michigan. Armanis F. Knotts, a former mayor of Hammond who acquired a summer cottage there in 1907, was one of the promoters of the resort. For a time in 1909, Knotts bottled water from the local springs for sale in Gary.[54]

In 1912, Knotts and a group of the region's businessmen organized the "Racing Foundation Corporation of America," locally known as the Mineral Springs Jockey Club. About $80,000.00 was invested in the project.[55] The first meeting was held in October at the close of the

53 *Ibid.*

54 Chesterton *Tribune,* August 12, 1909. John E. Sears, a member of Gary's town board, distributed the water locally.

55 Gary *Daily Tribune,* October 9, 1912; Chicago *Daily Tribune,* October 16, 1912.

Chicago racing season. Better than average horses from the Chicago tracks were stationed there and special trains were run on the Lake Shore and Michigan Southern Railroad from Chicago to the track. A crowd of about 3,500 fans attended the races on opening day. According to reports, it was not a typical race track crowd with wildly whooping touts and hangers on. Instead, jewels and automobiles were conspicuous by their presence. Six races were scheduled for each day of the two-and-a-half-week season with a daily distribution of $3,000.00 in purses to horsemen.[56] The Chicago newspapers gave the track as much space on their sports pages as they did those in New York and other racing centers.

Since gambling on horse races was illegal in Indiana, the owners of the track insisted none would be permitted there. And yet the racing editor of a Chicago newspaper, who inspected the track before opening day, found evidence to the contrary. The gamblers were advised, he said, to "go light" at the start. The editor continued: "There is a large tent just north of the grandstand. To just what use this may be put to is not clear. It would make an excellent place for 'friends' to meet, but far be it from us to be accessory even by the remote suggestion to a compound fracture of the laws of the commonwealth of Indiana."[57] On opening day the mysterious tent was on another site where it was being used as a temporary stable for horses, a move apparently inspired by the presence of the county sheriff and state officials. And yet bookmakers handled bets for the crowd from the very start. On the second day of the meeting regular "bookies" of a Chicago syndicate were reported stationed

56 Chicago *Daily Tribune,* October 16 and 17, 1912; Gary *Daily Tribune,* October 17, 1912.

57 Chicago *Daily Tribune,* October 16, 1912.

wherever they could hang their hats in the enclosure under the grandstand.[58]

When it became obvious that open gambling prevailed, Governor Thomas R. Marshall ordered the Porter County sheriff to close the track. The sheriff refused, insisting he had seen no gambling there.[59] The Governor then resorted to more strenuous measures. At noon on October 22 a company of the state militia from South Bend, followed shortly thereafter by another from Rensselaer, arrived at the track. By the time the first race train arrived from Chicago, the soldiers were in possession of the racing property. Sentries at the gates admitted only track officials and newspapermen inside the grounds. Despite the presence of the state troops, the management insisted on running the races as scheduled. The horses were ridden by their jockeys onto the course only to be stopped by soldiers with fixed bayonets who were lined across the track in front of the judge's stand. Racing at Mineral Springs ended for that year when the Superior Court in Valparaiso refused to enjoin the militia from interfering with the operation of the track. When informed of the court's action, Governor Marshall declared: "That's fine. I'll show them they can't dump all those Chicago gamblers in Indiana."[60] The soldiers left the track in about two weeks.

Successful races were held at Mineral Springs in June and July of 1913, and while track officials insisted there was no betting, a newspaper reporter said that bookmakers were openly plying their trade.[61] When racing was renewed on August 21 of the same year, Governor

[58] *Ibid.,* October 18, 1912.

[59] Gary *Daily Tribune,* October 19, 1912.

[60] Quoted in *ibid.,* October 22, 1912; Chicago *Daily Tribune,* October 22, 1912.

[61] Gary *Evening Post,* July 7, 1913.

Samuel M. Ralston sent two companies of the state militia to close the track. Thus ended horse racing at Mineral Springs.[62] The following year, Armanis F. Knotts purchased 120 acres on the bluffs of the Little Calumet River near the race course which he divided into lots for sale as sites for summer cottages.[63] Mineral Springs continued to be one of the popular resorts in the region.

The Dunes State Park

Just before the first World War the public became concerned about preserving the dune country in its natural state. By then the demand for sand for elevation and filling-in purposes had brought about the destruction of some of the finest dunes. Large areas of sand hills in the vicinity of Miller and Dune Park had been removed, leaving only desertlike plains. Hoosier Slide, a magnificent dune almost two hundred feet high on the western edge of Michigan City, was sacrificed to commercialism. The dune country was further threatened as industrial development pushed steadily along the lake shore, leaving in its wake the cities of Whiting, East Chicago, and Gary with their refineries, furnaces, and bellowing smoke. Industrialists seeking new sites for plants or for room to expand those already established acquired large tracts in the dune area.[64] Private interests purchased hundreds of acres for speculative purposes. Lovers of the dunes realized that unless something was done the great sand hills and beautiful marshes would soon be gone forever.

[62] Gary *Evening Post,* August 28, 1913.

[63] *Ibid.,* April 6, 1914.

[64] By 1919 the Inland Steel Company had acquired 265 acres of the dune area and by 1927 its purchases totaled about 741 acres, most of which lay just east of Miller in Porter County. See Porter County Deed Records, 80:568-73; 83:438-40; 85:367-68; 91:245-46.

The Prairie Club of Chicago, whose members discovered the dunes in the course of their organized walks or hikes in the city's vicinity, first called public attention to the threatened destruction of the area.[65] In 1913, the club, under its president, Jens Jensen, leased a large tract of land on the lake front just east of Mt. Tom near Tremont. Here, in what was then one of the wildest and most picturesque parts of the dunes, it erected the "Beach House" for the use of its members.[66] With the building of the clubhouse, members of the organization largely restricted their hiking activities to exploration of the thousands of acres in the dune region.

The movement to "save the dunes" was given impetus in the spring of 1916 by rumors that sand companies intended to move several of the finest dunes to Chicago for filling-in purposes. One report had it that Fort Creek at Waverly Beach was to be dredged so that lake vessels could come up the stream and receive sand by way of a small railway from Mt. Tom, the highest of the dunes.[67] In July the National Dunes Park Association was organized during a large meeting of dune enthusiasts at Waverly Beach. Three special trains from Chicago brought the number of those present to about five thousand. The purpose of the organization was to raise funds to purchase land which would be turned over to the Federal government as a national park.[68]

[65] The Prairie Club was organized in 1908 as "Saturday Afternoon Walks" by the Playground Association of Chicago. It was incorporated in 1911 as the Prairie Club.

[66] John O. Bowers, History of Dune Park (MS in Gary Public Library, 1927), 2. Jens Jensen, landscape artist, was superintendent of the Chicago park system.

[67] Ibid.; Brennan, The Wonder of the Dunes, 188.

[68] The officers of the National Dunes Park Association were Armanis F. Knotts, president, and Thomas H. Cannon, secretary. The directors were Jens Jensen, Henry C. Cowles, John O. Bowers, George M. Pinneo,

In October, 1916, Stephen T. Mather, Assistant Secretary of the Interior and Director of National Parks, conducted a hearing in Chicago regarding the proposed park. Among those who spoke in favor of the preservation of the dunes were Henry Chandler Cowles, botanist at the University of Chicago; Lorado Taft, the famous sculptor; T. C. Chamberlain, geologist at the University of Chicago; Julius Rosenwald, head of Sears, Roebuck and Company; George Ade; Otis Caldwell, president of the Chicago Historical Society; John W. O'Leary, president of the Chicago Association of Commerce; and Earl H. Reed, artist and writer.[69] Impressed by this imposing array of persons, Mather made a personal inspection of the dunes. His report to the Interior Department in 1917 favored the creation of a national park in the dune country.

Unfortunately, there was opposition to the park project in Porter County. The Valparaiso Chamber of Commerce, the county press, and numerous citizens were critical of the movement to locate a national park in their area. While they were not opposed to the conversion of a part of the dune region into a park, they were fearful that the entire lake front would be closed to industry. Citizens also pointed out that the county would lose the taxes on any section turned into a park. Charges were made that the United States Steel Corporation was behind the park movement in order to prevent its compet-

and Mrs. Frank Sheehan. Mrs. Sheehan, of Gary, came to be known as the "Lady of the Dunes" because of her efforts in behalf of a dunes park. See Minutes of the National Dunes Park Association (MS in Gary Public Library), 1. The Association was incorporated under the laws of Indiana in 1917.

[69] Organizations represented at this meeting were the Prairie Club, the Indiana Academy of Science, Chicago Association of Commerce, and the Illinois Audubon Society. For a complete account, see Mather, *Report on the Proposed Sand Dunes National Park.*

itors from locating plants in Porter County.[70] Such
opposition no doubt contributed to the delay in the plan
to preserve the dunes.

In 1917 a magnificent historical pageant entitled "The
Dunes Under Four Flags" was prepared under the aus-
pices of the Prairie Club to promote interest in the proposed park. The spectacle was scheduled for Memorial
Day and the following Sunday in the Jens Jensen Blow-
out, a short distance west of Fort Creek at Waverly
Beach.[71] The Memorial Day performance was rained out,
but on the following Sunday an estimated crowd of twenty-five thousand people gathered to witness the pageant.
The vast amphitheater was packed. The pageant closed
with a grand review of the hundreds of participants followed by the singing of the national anthem by the huge
audience.[72] Probably in no other manner could it have
been possible to impress so many people with the beauties
of the dunes and with the urgent need for their preservation.

The coming of World War I, together with the opposition of Porter County residents, brought to a standstill
further efforts to convert the dunes area into a national
park. Indiana and Illinois organizations then turned
their attention toward the creation of a state park. New
threats appeared which convinced advocates of a park

[70] Bowers, History of Dune Park, 3; Gary *Daily Tribune,* June 28,
1920.

[71] The pageant was produced by the Dunes Pageant Association, in-
corporated in Chicago in 1917. Among the incorporators were Jane
Addams, Lorado Taft, Earl H. Reed, Henry C. Cowles, and Mrs. Frank
Sheehan. The Chicago Art Institute, Illinois Federation of Women's
Clubs, Chicago Historical Society, Illinois Audubon Society, and the
National Dunes Park Association of Indiana co-operated in the staging
of the pageant.

[72] Brennan, *The Wonders of the Dunes,* 170-72. Copies of the pageant
program are on file in the Gary Public Library.

that time was rapidly running out for preservation of the area. The Dunes Highway, now Highway 12, which skirted the dune country between Gary and Michigan City, was completed in 1923. While this road made the region more accessible, it also increased the danger that commercial interests would exploit the area. By 1923 hundreds of acres had been acquired by real estate companies for residential development. Moreover, the long agitation for a park caused the price of the land to rise to almost a prohibitive level. Fortunately, Porter County's opposition to the park plan was lessened by the willingness of park advocates to have only a portion of the lake front set aside for the enjoyment of the public. In 1923 a bill was rushed through the Indiana General Assembly to place a tax of two mills on each $100.00 of taxable property in the state over a period of seven years to purchase a tract of land three miles in length along the lake front. The right of condemnation of land for park purposes and the right to accept donations of land and money were included in the bill.[73]

Since no funds were available until the taxes were collected and since land prices were advancing as rapidly as the tax money was accumulating, industrialists and public-spirited citizens came to the rescue of the project. In 1925 Judge Elbert H. Gary, acting for the United States Steel Corporation, contributed $250,000.00, a check for $135,000.00 being sent immediately to Governor Ed Jackson to start the purchase of the area. Julius Rosenwald donated $50,000.00 and Samuel Insull, Jr., provided funds for the purchase of a strip of land five-hundred feet wide and three fifths of a mile long between the Dunes Highway and the park at Waverly Beach.

[73] Cannon, Loring, and Robb (eds.), *History of the Lake and Calumet Region,* 1:619; *Laws of Indiana,* 1923, pp. 266-68.

By May, 1927, the entire park area had been purchased at a cost of about $1,000,000. The park, soon opened to the public, contained approximately three and one half square miles or 2,210 acres.[74]

Diana of the Dunes

In 1916 the attention of the public was called to a strange figure who occupied an abandoned shack in the sand hills between Dune Park and Mineral Springs. Fishermen told of seeing a woman now and then along the beach and among the dunes. For a time no one knew who she was and her reluctance to be interviewed stimulated local curiosity. The woman hermit captured the imagination of newspaper reporters who proceeded to weave an atmosphere of mystery and romance around her. The press referred to the recluse as the "Nymph of the Dunes," "Psyche," and finally as "Diana of the Dunes." She was pictured as a winsome maiden who hovered about the flowers and ferns by day, bathing daily in the nude in the lake, and disappearing as if by magic at the approach of a man. Tales were told that she had fled from civilization because of disappointment in love. Rumors also spread that Diana was a graduate of the University of Chicago, where she had been an honor student.

Diana of the Dunes was Alice Mable Gray, daughter of a Chicago physician. She entered the University of Chicago in 1897 when sixteen years of age. University records showed she received her junior college certificate with honors in 1899, was elected to Phi Beta Kappa in 1901, and was graduated with an A.B. degree in 1903.

[74] Cannon, Loring, and Robb (eds.), *op. cit.*, 1:619-20; George S. Cottman, *Indiana Dunes State Park. A History and Description* (Indiana Department of Conservation, 1930), 40; Gary *Post-Tribune*, September 2, 1925; January 11, 1926.

She received honorable mention for excellence in astronomy, mathematics, Greek, and Latin. Miss Gray enrolled in the graduate school for ten quarters at various times between 1903 and 1912. There was a statement on her record cards at the University that transcripts of her credits had been sent in August, 1906, to the University of Goettingen in Germany and also to the United States Naval Observatory in Washington, D.C. If she attended the German university or formed a connection with the observatory, her stay was brief as she enrolled in the graduate school of the University of Chicago in the autumn quarter of 1908.[75]

Diana was typical of the many intellectuals who fled the restraints of civilization to the peace and quiet of the wilderness. She was well acquainted with the dune country, having made frequent pilgrimages there during her student days in Chicago. In 1916 she explained her presence in the dunes:[76]

I wanted to live my own life—a free life. The life of a salary earner in the cities is slavery, a constant fight for the means of living. Here it is so different. My salary when I worked was nothing extraordinary, and yet here I have lived all winter and summer on the last pay envelope that I received in Chicago. I buy only bread and salt.

When I came here in October, 1915, I had nothing but a jelly glass, a knife, a spoon, a blanket and two guns. For four nights before discovering this abandoned hut, I slept under the stars. Then I began housekeeping, and all the furniture I have is made

75 Evidence is lacking as to her work after she graduated from the University of Chicago. Recently, an official of the University recalled that she worked for "somebody" there. It was variously reported that she was secretary to the president, worked as editorial secretary of the *Astrophysical Journal* (published by the University), and that she was employed by a Chicago publishing house, but no evidence has been found to verify any of these reports.

76 Quoted in Chicago *Examiner,* July 23, 1916.

of driftwood. Everything is driftwood here, including myself, and I have named the place "Driftwood."

It was a poem of Byron's called "Solitude" that gave me my first longings to get away from the conventional world, and I never gave up the idea, although a long time passed before I could fulfill it.

The line in Byron's poem that so impressed her was "In solitude when we are least alone." A fisherman's wife, who won the confidence of the recluse, described her in a sympathetic manner:[77]

She wears her hair bobbed. She has no mirror and knows when her hair is too long by the length of the shadow it casts on the ground. When she thinks it needs bobbing she cuts it by the shadow. Her winter dress consists of a short coarse skirt, big boots, ragged waist, and a little cap. In the summer she wears just an old light dress and the ragged waist. She never wears shoes or stockings. She cooks outside her hut. She has a few boxes which she keeps scrupulously clean and uses for chairs and tables. She has a sort of fire place, and her only utensils are an old coffee pot and a cup she found on the railroad tracks.

She must have quite a bit of money. At different times she has presented to the store a $5 and $10 dollar bill and several checks. She makes money by picking wild berries and selling wild animals. She says that when she was at the University of Chicago she grew discontented with the way things were run. She was always crazy about the Lake and people would not let her go down in the night and swim. It is hard to make her talk at all. Generally she will not listen and chases people away with a revolver if they ever come near. She will not take any assistance of any kind and shuns discourse of any kind at all. She is still crazy about the water and walks only on the lake shore in the sand.

Those who ventured to peer through the small windows of Diana's cabin saw a cot well-stocked with blankets, a small wood stove, a box or two, and great piles of books and magazines, the whole suggesting a mix-

[77] Mrs. Matilda Burton quoted in Gary *Evening Post*, July 24, 1916.

ture of culture and abandon.[78]   Occasionally she walked
to Porter or Baillytown for supplies.   Diana lived about
four years at Driftwood, apparently unconcerned by the
World War or by the steel strikes which convulsed the
region's industrial cities only a short distance away.

In 1920 Diana married Paul Wilson, a beachcomber,
fisherman, and maker of rustic outdoor furniture.   Wilson, a giant of a man whose physical feats were legendary
along the beach, claimed to have been a pugilist before
coming to the dunes.[79]   The couple moved to a shack,
which they called the "Wren's Nest," in the western part
of what is now Ogden Dunes.   Here Diana reportedly
compiled in manuscript form her observations and experiences in the dunes and also recorded stories about the
area as told by fishermen and trappers.[80]   As Ogden
Dunes was only about three miles from Miller, the Wilsons soon felt the press of civilization.   Paul, in particular, resented the Chicago sightseers who were brought by
boat from Miller to view Diana and the Wren's Nest
from the safety of the lake.[81]

The year 1922 was crowded with troubles for the
Wilsons.   In May a University of Chicago student found
the body of an unidentified man on a desolate section of
the beach and for the moment the police suspected Paul
of being the murderer.   He was absolved a short time
later when evidence was found that the dead man had
been killed elsewhere and his body dumped on the beach.

[78] J. William Lester, "Orchids and Tumbleweeds," in Gary *Post-
Tribune,* January 12, 1929.

[79] According to reports, Wilson's real name was Izenblater. Prior
to his marriage, he was said to have spent six months at the state penal
farm for stealing chickens. Gary *Evening Post,* July 6, 1920; Gary
Evening Post and Daily Tribune, June 14, 1922.

[80] Lester, "Orchids and Tumbleweeds," in Gary *Post-Tribune,* January 21 and 23, 1929.

[81] Gary *Evening Post and Daily Tribune,* June 17, 1922.

In June Diana suffered a skull fracture and Paul was shot in the course of a fight with a deputy sheriff who had accused them of looting summer cottages and robbing fish nets. The Wilsons were not prosecuted as the police found the deputy sheriff was intoxicated at the time of the trouble.[82] Reports were heard in November that Diana and Paul were going to Texas in their motor-driven boat.

They returned to the dunes a few months later and Diana died there early in 1925. Paul remained in Ogden Dunes for only a short time afterward. He removed Diana's books and manuscripts and sold the shack to a neighbor who set fire to it, thereby obliterating all but the memories of duneland's tragic recluse.[83]

Dune Acres and Ogden Dunes

Construction of the Dunes Highway between Gary and Michigan City in the early 1920's led to the development of a portion of the dune country for residential purposes. While the South Shore electric line provided transportation for the public to the southern edge of the area, the sand hills and the Lake Michigan beaches were not accessible for practical use. Moreover, the industries and private investors, who owned large tracts in the area, were not interested in disposing of small plots for use as summer or permanent homes. Now that the highway permitted automobiles to penetrate the region, promoters saw the possibility of the creation of residential sections similar to Evanston, Winnetka, and other communities along the north shore of Lake Michigan.[84]

[82] *Ibid.*, June 14, 17, 19, 1922.

[83] Gary *Post-Tribune*, February 10, 11, October 9, 1925. According to reports, Wilson later worked in a Gary garage, married an Indian woman, and lived in the dunes near Michigan City. *Ibid.*, April 28, 1926; March 14 and 17, 1927.

[84] *Ibid.*, December 9, 1922.

Late in 1922 William A. Wirt, superintendent of the Gary Public Schools, obtained a ninety-nine year lease of approximately 582 acres from Henry A. Leman of Chicago. This section, popularly known as the "Leman tract" and containing several of the highest dunes along the Indiana shore of the Lake, lay just west of the proposed Indiana Dunes State Park and north of Baillytown and Mineral Springs.[85] Early in 1923 Wirt assigned the lease to Dune Acres Incorporated, a realty company organized to lay out and administer the town site. Arthur P. Melton, former planning engineer of the city of Gary, was put in charge of the project.[86]

About the same time, Samuel H. Reck, a Gary realtor, organized a syndicate which purchased 513 acres of the sand hills from the Francis A. Ogden estate.[87] This area, which was named Ogden Dunes, was located on the lake front a few miles west of Dune Acres. In 1925, despite its sparse population, the community was incorporated as a town, its residents voting 24 to 0 in favor of such a step. This was done to assure a right-of-way from the Dunes Highway across the New York Central tracks which skirted the southern edge of the area. The promoters of the two communities had ambitious plans for their

85 William A. Wirt, who was to pay an annual rent of $17,460.00 as long as the original lease was in effect, was to have the privilege of purchasing land in the area in plots of not less than 25 acres for $600.00 per acre. See Porter County Miscellaneous Records, 9:53-59.

86 The incorporators of the Dune Acres Company were William A. Wirt, Arthur P. Melton, C. R. Kuss, and Claude V. Ridgely, all prominent in Gary's business and legal circles. For details about the company, see ibid., 9:185. In 1926 they purchased 175 acres of the leased area for $105,000.00. Porter County Deed Records, 89:414.

87 Gary Post-Tribune, February 22, 1923. This syndicate, known as Ogden Dunes Incorporated, was formed by Samuel H. Reck, Joseph A. Boo, and Colin S. Mackenzie. The latter, a civil engineer, platted and laid out the Ogden Dunes site. See Porter County Miscellaneous Records, P:464.

development.   Each was to have a hotel, golf course, club house, and a small harbor for the accommodation of pleasure craft.[88]   Stores and other commercial establishments were forbidden, a rule strictly enforced in the years that followed.   In 1927 a ski jump with a 240-foot drop, said to have been the highest slide in the nation, was erected in Ogden Dunes by local sportsmen.   Annual tournaments, in which skiers from various European countries as well as the United States participated, were held for several years.   In January, 1932, about 8,000 people watched several members of Norway's Olympic team carry off first honors.[89]

And yet the development of duneland towns as year-round residential communities did not come up to the expectations of their promoters.   In 1930 Ogden Dunes had fifty permanent residents while Dune Acres listed only twelve inhabitants.[90]   As a result, with the exception of the club house in Dune Acres, the hotels, golf courses, and harbors were never built.   Poor roads and inadequate snow-moving equipment no doubt deterred people from spending winters in the dunes.   Moreover, Gary and the other cities of the region still had excellent sites for the better type of residences.   Finally, the depression which began in 1929 retarded the growth of the lake shore communities.

At the end of 1933 the dune country was largely a vacation land.   Although a few permanent homes, sum-

[88] Gary *Post-Tribune,* December 9, 1922; February 22, 1923; August 17, 1925.

[89] *Ibid.,* January 25, 1932; *South Shore Lines* (published by the Chicago, South Shore, and South Bend Railroad), January, 1928, p. 6.

[90] In 1940 the population of Ogden Dunes was 144 and that of Dune Acres was only 46.   In 1950 there were 429 permanent residents in Ogden Dunes and 86 in Dune Acres. *Seventeenth Census* (1950): *Population,* 1 :sec 14-17.   A census taken by the Ogden Dunes Woman's Club in July, 1956, listed 788 permanent residents in the community.

mer houses, and the shacks of squatters were to be seen here and there, most of the area remained in its virgin state. But as the Calumet Region shook off the effects of the depression and as World War II expanded its industries and overcrowded its cities, the great sand hills and extensive marshes, which had been thousands of years in the making, once again were faced with destruction.[91]

[91] In 1930 the Midwest Steel Company, a subsidiary of the National Steel Company, purchased a large area of land near Ogden Dunes and east of Burns Ditch. Officials of the company informed the Gary *Post-Tribune* that a steel mill costing $30,000,000 was to be built on the site and that a town, to be known as Port Williams (for John Williams, president of the National Steel Company), was to be built to accommodate its employees. It is probable that the depression prevented the building of the mill. National Steel still owns this tract. Gary *Post-Tribune*, February 3, June 6, 1930. In 1957 the Bethlehem Steel Company completed the purchase of a reported 3,500 acres in the vicinity of Burns Ditch and adjacent to the holdings of National Steel. When its acquisitions were announced, Bethlehem made public its plans to build a steel plant on the site.

BIBLIOGRAPHY
[Limited to sources cited]

Manuscripts

Ansley, Pearl, History of Indiana Harbor (Typewritten MS in the Indiana Harbor branch of the East Chicago Public Library, no date).

Bailly, Joseph, Miscellaneous Papers of Joseph Bailly, in possession of Mrs. John O. Bowers, Gary.

Bate, Phyllis, The Development of the Iron and Steel Industry in the Chicago Area (Ph.D. thesis, University of Chicago, 1948).

Biographical Sketches of Gary and Lake County Residents (Scrapbooks of newspaper clippings in Gary Public Library). Sketches cited include those of Joseph Feely, Thomas E. Knotts, Joseph D. Martin, Horace S. Norton.

Bowden, Katherine E., A Short History of Valparaiso University (Typewritten MS in Valparaiso University Library).

Bowers, John O., History of Dune Park (MS in Gary Public Library, 1927).

Cannon, Thomas H., The Autobiography of Tom Cannon (Typewritten MS in Gary Public Library).

Carlson, Martin E., A Study of the Eastern Orthodox Churches in Gary, Indiana (M. A. thesis, University of Chicago, 1942, in Gary Public Library).

Chanute, Octave, Opening Address, International Conference on Aerial Navigation, Paris (undated typewritten MS in Collected Papers of Octave Chanute, in John G. Crerar Library, Chicago).

De Gan, W. H., Report as Superintendent of Gary Park System to William P. Gleason, January 26, 1935, in Office of Gary Works, United States Steel Corporation.

Dickmeyer, W. C., History of Valparaiso University (Typewritten MS in Valparaiso University Library).

Fisher, William D., Steel City's Culture. An Interpretation of the History of Gary, Indiana (A. B. thesis, Yale University, 1941, in Gary Public Library).

Gavit, Frank, History of Whiting, Indiana (Typewritten MS in Whiting Public Library).

609

Gleason, William P., Gary's Park System (Typewritten MS in Superintendent's Office, Gary Works, United States Steel Corporation).

Hammond, Thomas, Brief History of the City of Hammond (MS found in the cornerstone of the Hammond Central High School, built in 1893, and now in the cornerstone of the Hammond Technical High School).

Hohman, Caroline, Diary, April 26, 1850 to June, 1870 (typewritten copy in possession of Warren A. Reeder, Hammond).

Index of Indiana Post Offices, in Indiana Division, Indiana State Library.

The International Institute of Gary, Indiana, 1918-1948 (Typewritten MS in the files of the Institute).

Jones, Alfred E., "An Amateur Wild Man," in Scrapbook of newspaper clippings, Gary Public Library.

Lake County Deed Records, in Recorder's Office, Courthouse, Crown Point.

Lake County Miscellaneous Records, in Recorder's Office, Courthouse, Crown Point.

Leevy, J. Roy, The Industrial City (Typewritten MS in Gary Public Library).

Lester, J. W., Papers by Various Hands (4 vols. Scrapbooks in Gary Public Library). Reminiscences cited include those of Darius Blake, John O. Bowers, Drusilla Carr, Isaac Crisman, William Earle, Henrietta Gibson, William P. Gleason, Ruby M. Graham, Silas E. Green, Ella Knotts, and Thomas E. Knotts.

National Dunes Park Association, Minutes, 1916 (MS in Gary Public Library).

Porter County Deed Records, in Recorder's Office, Courthouse, Valparaiso.

Porter County Miscellaneous Records, in Recorder's Office, Courthouse, Valparaiso.

Potts, John Foster, A History of the Growth of the Negro Population of Gary, Indiana (M. A. thesis, Cornell University, 1937, in Gary Public Library).

Quillen, J. J., The Industrial City (Ph. D. thesis, Yale University, 1942, microfilm in Gary Public Library).

Reynolds, Conger, Historical Highlights of the Story of Standard Oil Company (Indiana) (Mimeographed MS in office of Standard Oil Company of Indiana, Chicago, Ill.).

Rowley, Ralph E., Notes on the City of Gary, Indiana, February 15, 1926 (Typewritten MS in Public Relations Office, Gary Works, United States Steel Corporation).

Skinner, Hubert M., Complete History of Porter County, prepared for Valparaiso *Messenger,* 1878 (Typewritten MS in Indiana State Library; printed in *Messenger,* February 26, 1878 ff.).

Taylor, Stillman K., The International Institute of Gary (Typewritten MS in files of the Institute).

United States Weather Bureau, Ogden Dunes Co-operative Station, "Local Climatological Summary for the Ten-Year Period, 1949-1958," compiled by Robert Allen Ward (mimeographed report).

Books, Articles, Periodicals, Printed Records and Reports

Abbott, Edith, *Immigration: Select Documents and Case Records* (University of Chicago Press, 1924).

Alvord, Clarence W., "The Conquest of St. Joseph, Michigan, by the Spaniards in 1781," in *Missouri Historical Review*, 2 (Columbia, 1908): 195-210.

———, *The Mississippi Valley in British Politics* . . . (2 vols. Cleveland, 1917).

Andreas, Alfred T., *History of Chicago from the Earliest Period to the Present Time* (3 vols. Chicago, 1884-87).

Appleton, John B., *The Iron and Steel Industry of the Calumet District. A Study in Economic Geography* (University of Illinois, *Studies in Social Sciences*, Vol. 13, No. 2, June, 1925).

Babcock, F. Lawrence, *The First Fifty, 1889-1939* (Standard Oil Company [Indiana], 1939).

Bailey, E. Stillman, *The Sand Dunes of Indiana* . . . (Chicago, 1917).

Baird, Elizabeth Thérèse, "Reminiscences of Early Days on Mackinac Island," in *Wisconsin Historical Collections*, 14 (Madison, 1898) :17-64.

Ball, Timothy H., "The Cady Marsh," in *Proceedings* of the Indiana Academy of Science, 1897, p. 240.

———, *Encyclopedia of Genealogy and Biography of Lake County, Indiana* (Chicago, 1904).

———, *Lake County, Indiana, from 1834 to 1872* (Chicago, 1873).

———, *Northwestern Indiana from 1800 to 1900* . . . (Crown Point, Ind., 1900).

——— (ed.), *Lake County, Indiana, 1884* . . . (Crown Point, Ind., 1884).

Barnhart, John D., *Henry Hamilton and George Rogers Clark in the American Revolution* (Crawfordsville, Ind., 1951).

Barnhart, John D., and Carmony, Donald F., *Indiana. From Frontier to Industrial Commonwealth* (4 vols. New York, 1954).

Barringer, Lewin B., *Flight Without Power: The Art of Gliding and Soaring* (New York, 1940).

Beaudette, E. Palma, *East Chicago-Indiana Harbor. Twin Cities of Indiana. Political* . . . *Historical* . . . *Industrial Sketch* (Chicago, 1913).

Bell, A. H., *The Work—Study—Play Program* (Columbus, Ohio, 1932).

Bernard, William S. (ed.), *American Immigration Policy. A Reappraisal* (New York, 1950).

Bieber, C. L., "Tolleston and Post-Tolleston Beaches and Bars in Lake County, Indiana," in *Proceedings* of the Indiana Academy of Science, 1951, pp. 176-79.

Blackburn, Glen A., "Interurban Railroads of Indiana," in *Indiana Magazine of History,* 20(1924) :400-64.

Blatchley, Willis S., "The Geology of Lake and Porter Counties, Indiana," in Indiana *Geological Report,* 1897, pp. 26-104.

Bockstahler, Oscar L., "The German Press in Indiana," in *Indiana Magazine of History,* 48(1952):161-68.

Bogardus, Emory S., *The Mexican in the United States* (University of Southern California, School of Research Studies, No. 5, Los Angeles, 1934).

Boone, Richard G., *A History of Education in Indiana* (New York, 1892, reprinted by offset process by Indiana Historical Bureau, 1941).

Bourne, Randolph S., *The Gary Schools* (New York, 1916).

Bowers, John O., *Dream Cities of the Calumet* (Gary, 1929).

————, *The Old Bailly Homestead* (Gary, 1922).

————, Taylor, Arthur G., and Woods, Sam B. (eds.), *History of Lake County (Publication* of the Lake County Historical Association, Vol. 10, Gary, 1929). Proceedings of meetings including papers presented. Those cited include papers by Hiram Barton, Darus P. Blake, Henry S. Davidson, Alys Hess, Armanis F. Knotts, Hattie Palmer, Arthur Patterson, Arthur G. Taylor.

Brennan, George A., "De Linctot, Guardian of the Frontier," in *Journal* of the Illinois State Historical Society, 10 (Springfield, 1917-18): 323-66.

————, *The Wonders of the Dunes* (Indianapolis, 1923).

Bretz, J. Harlen, *Geology of the Chicago Region, Part II—The Pleistocene* (Illinois State Geological Survey, *Bulletin No. 65,* Part 2, Urbana, Ill., 1955).

————, "The Stages of Lake Chicago: Their Causes and Correlations," in *American Journal of Science,* 249 (New Haven, Conn., 1951) :401-6.

"Brickmaking in Porter," by Herman F. Wagner as told to Warren R. Canright, in Chesterton *Tribune,* November 25 and December 2, 1954.

Brown, Cecil L., *The Conquest of the Air: An Historical Survey* (London, 1927).

Brown, Francis J., and Roucek, Joseph S. (eds.), *One America. The History, Contributions, and Present Problems of our Racial and National Minorities* (New York, 1952).

Brown, Sister Mary Borromeo, *The History of the Sisters of Providence of Saint Mary-of-the-Woods, Vol. I* (New York, 1949).

Buffington, Eugene J., "Making Cities for Workmen," in *Harper's Weekly* (New York), May 8, 1909.

Buley, R. Carlyle, *The Old Northwest. Pioneer Period, 1815-1840* (Indiana Historical Society, 1950).

The Calumet (published by Gary Commercial Club), June 13, August 1, 1913.

The Calumet Region Historical Guide . . . , compiled by the Writers' Program of the Work Projects Administration ([East Chicago], 1939).

Cannon, Thomas H., "Tom Knotts as Mayor and Man," in Gary *Evening Post,* March 26, 1921.

——————, Loring, H. H., and Robb, Charles J. (eds.), *History of the Lake and Calumet Region of Indiana* (2 vols. Indianapolis, 1927).

Capek, Thomas, *The Czechs (Bohemians) in America* . . . (Boston, 1920).

Carleton, William G., "Why was the Democratic Party in Indiana a Radical Party, 1865-1890," in *Indiana Magazine of History,* 42(1946): 207-28.

Carmony, Donald F., *see* Barnhart, John D.

Case, Roscoe D., *The Platoon School in America* (Stanford, Calif., 1931).

Chanute, Octave, "Development and Future of Flying Machines," in *The City Club Bulletin,* 2 (Chicago, 1898). No. 15, in The Collected Papers of Chanute, in John G. Crerar Library, Chicago.

——————, "The Evolution of the 'Two-Surface' Flying Machine," in *Aeronautics,* 3 (New York, 1908) :28-29.

——————, "Recent Experiments in Gliding Flight," in *The Aeronautical Annual* (Boston, 1897), 30-53.

——————, "Some American Experiments," in *The Aeronautical Journal* (London), January, 1898.

Chicago-Tolleston Land and Improvement Company, Circular and Map (n.p., n.d.). Pamphlet in Gary Public Library.

Chicago Daily News Almanac and Year-Book, 1915, 1927, 1932.

Clemen, Rudolf A., *The American Livestock and Meat Industry* (New York, 1923).

——————, *George H. Hammond, 1838-1886, Pioneer in Refrigerator Transportation* (New York, 1946).

Colton, J. H., *Indiana, Delineated, Geographical, Historical* (New York, 1838).

Commons, John R., *Races and Immigrants in America* (New York, 1907).

——————, *et al., History of Labour in the United States* (4 vols. New York, 1918-35).

The Congregationalist (Whiting), October 27, 1927.

Cotter, Sister Anita, "Mother Mary Cecilia Bailly," in *In God's Acre. Biographical Sketches, Series I* (Sisters of Providence, Saint Mary-of-the-Woods, 1940).

Cotter, Arundel, *United States Steel, A Corporation with a Soul* (New York, 1921).

Cottman, George S., *Indiana Dunes State Park. A History and Description* (Indiana Department of Conservation, 1930).

Cotton, Fassett A ., *Education in Indiana, 1793-1934* (Bluffton, 1934).

Cowles, Henry C., "The Ecological Relations of the Vegetation of the Sand Dunes of Lake Michigan," in *Botanical Gazette,* 27 (Chicago, 1899) :107-8.

Cox, Isaac J. (ed.), *The Journeys of Réné Robert Cavelier, Sieur de la Salle* . . . (2 vols. New York, 1922).

Cox, Sandford C., *Recollections of the Early Settlement of the Wabash Valley* (Lafayette, Ind., 1860).

Cressey, George B., *Indiana Dunes and Shore Lines of the Lake Michigan Basin* (The Geographical Society of Chicago, *Bulletin No. 8,* 1928).

Cutler, Harry G., *History of Porter County, Indiana* . . . (2 vols. Chicago, 1912).

Daniels, E. D., *A Twentieth Century History and Biographical Record of La Porte County Indiana* . . . (Chicago, 1904).

De Bow, J. D., *Statistical View of the United States* . . . *Being a Compendium of the Seventh Census* . . . (Washington, D. C., 1854).

Demmon, Alice M., Little, Jesse, McNay, Phillip M., and Taylor, Arthur G. (eds.), *History of Lake County* (*Publication* of the Lake County Historical Association, Vol. 11, Gary, 1934). Report of observance of centennial of permanent settlement of Lake County including speeches made and papers read at various meetings. Articles by John E. Beckman, Frank Borman, William Earle, Clara E. Ford, Alma K. Gettler, Myrtelle Huehn, Wilhelmine S. Kaske, Magenta D. Kennedy, Arthur Patterson, Jennie E. Putnam, and August Rump have been cited.

De Peyster, Arent S., to H. Watson Powell, January 8 and March 17, 1781, in *Michigan Pioneer and Historical Collections,* 19 (Lansing, 1892) :591.

Dewey, John and Evelyn, *Schools of Tomorrow* (New York, 1915).

Dictionary of American Biography, Supplement II, edited by Robert L. Schuyler (New York, 1958).

Dinwiddie, Edwin W., "The Fauna of Lake County," in Timothy H. Ball (ed.), *Lake County, Indiana, 1884,* 150-57.

————, "The Flora of Lake County," in Ball (ed.), *Lake County, Indiana, 1884,* 158-71.

Dunn, Jacob P., "Indiana Geographical Nomenclature," in *Indiana Magazine of History,* 8 (1912) :109.

————, *Indiana, A Redemption from Slavery* (Boston and New York, 1905).

————, *The Word Hoosier* (Indiana Historical Society Publications, Vol. 4, No. 2, Indianapolis, 1907).

East Chicago, Indiana (published by East Chicago Chamber of Commerce), 1925-29.

The East Chicagoan (published by East Chicago Chamber of Commerce), December, 1930.

Edmondson, Edna N., "Juvenile Delinquency and Adult Crime. Certain Associations of Juvenile Delinquency and Adult Crime in Gary, Ind., with special reference to the Immigrant Population," in *Indiana University Studies,* Vol. 8, No. 49 (June, 1921).

Emigration Conditions in Europe (41 vols. U. S. Immigration Commission, *Reports,* 1907-10, Vol. 4 [U. S. *Senate Documents,* 61 Congress, 3 session, Vol. 12, No. 748]).

Esarey, Logan, *A History of Indiana from Its Exploration to 1850* (3d ed., 2 vols. Fort Wayne, 1924).

Faust, Albert B., *The German Element in the United States . . .* (2 vols. Boston, 1909).

Field, Rose, "Growing Up With Gary," in *Success* (New York), October, 1923.

50 Years at Indiana Harbor (Anniversary edition of *Inland News,* May, 1951).

Fitch, John A., "Old Age at Forty," in *The American Magazine,* 71 (New York, 1910-11) :655-64.

Flower, Elliott, "Gary, the Magic City," in *Putnam's Magazine,* 5 (New York, January-March, 1909) :643-53.

Folwell, William W., *A History of Minnesota* (4 vols. St. Paul, Minn., 1921-30).

Foster, William Z., *The Great Steel Strike and Its Lessons* (New York, 1920).

Fox, Paul, *The Poles in America* (New York, 1922).

Fraser, Chelsea C., *The Story of Aircraft* (New York, 1933).

Frazier, Edward F., *The Negro Family in the United States* (Chicago, 1939).

Friends of Our Native Landscape (Chicago), Spring, 1956.

Frost, Stanley, *The Challenge of the Klan* (Indianapolis, 1924).

Fryxell, Fritiof M., *The Physiography of the Region of Chicago* (Chicago, 1927).

Fuess, Claude M., *Daniel Webster* (2 vols. New York, 1930).

Gamio, Manuel, *Mexican Immigration to the United States. A Study of Human Migration and Adjustment* (Chicago, 1930).

Gannett, Henry, "Indiana Geographical Nomenclature," in *Indiana Magazine of History,* 8(1912) :71.

Garner, F. B., "Pittsburgh Plus," in *American Economic Review,* 14 (New York, 1924) :192-93.

Gary, City of, *Second Annual Report, December 31, 1910* (Gary, 1911).

Gary, Town of, *First Annual Report of the Board of Trustees, December 31, 1908* (Gary, 1909).

"Gary,—Pittsburg's Future Rival," in *American Review of Reviews,* 39 (New York, 1908-9) :236-37.

Gary Land Company, *Annual Report,* 1908 (Gary, 1908).

Gary Public Schools, *Notes to Visitors,* published by Board of Education (Gary, 1911) and *Regulation of Visitors,* published by Board of Education (Gary, 1911).

Gates, Paul W., *The Illinois Central Railroad and Its Colonization Work* (*Harvard Economic Studies,* Vol. 42, 1934).

Geros, Frank E., *Hammond City Directory, 1891-1892* (Hammond, 1891).

Gibbs-Smith, Charles H., *A History of Flying* (New York, 1954).

Giddens, Paul H., *Standard Oil Company (Indiana). Oil Pioneer of the Middle West* (New York, 1955).

Gompers, Samuel, *Seventy Years of Life and Labor. An Autobiography* (2 vols. New York, 1925).

Goodspeed, Weston A., and Blanchard, Charles (eds.), *Counties of Porter and Lake, Indiana* (Chicago, 1882).

"Graver Tanks Are Monuments to Confidence, Energy, and Skill," in *Southwestern Oil Journal* (Fort Worth, Texas), December 5, 1919.

Grinstead, Wayde, *50 Years of Inland Steel, 1893-1943* (Chicago, 1943).

Gulick, Charles A., *Labor Policy of the United States Steel Corporation* (Columbia University *Studies in History, Economics, and Public Law,* Vol. 116, No. 1, 1924).

Haig, Robert M., "The Unearned Increment in Gary," in *Political Science Quarterly,* 32 (New York, 1917) :80-94.

Hale, Albert, *see* Oglesbee, Rollo B.

Hansen, Marcus Lee, *The Immigrant in American History* (Harvard University Press, 1940).

Hargrave, Frank F., *A Pioneer Indiana Railroad. The Origin and Development of the Monon* (Indianapolis, 1932).

Harlow, Alvin F., *The Road of the Century. The Story of the New York Central* (New York, 1947).

Harvey, Rowland H., *Samuel Gompers, Champion of the Toiling Masses* (Stanford University, 1935).

Hatfield, Edna C., "Problem of Housing Foreign Population Is Presented," in Gary *Evening Post,* March 5, 1913.

Hendrick, Burton J., "Children of the Steel Kings," in *McClure's Magazine,"* 41, no. 5 (New York, 1913) :61-69.

Hibbard, Benjamin H., *A History of the Public Land Policies* (New York, 1924).

The History of Medicine and Surgery . . . of Chicago (Chicago, 1922).

History of St. Joseph County, Indiana (Charles C. Chapman and Co., Chicago, 1880).

Hodge, Frederick W. (ed.), *Handbook of American Indians North of Mexico* (2 vols. Smithsonian Institution, Bureau of American Ethnology, *Bulletin 30,* Washington, D. C., 1907, 1910).

Hoffman, Charles F., *A Winter in the West* (2 vols. New York, 1835).

Holmes, C. Oliver, "How We Incorporated the Town," in *Historical Records* of the Lake County Old Settler and Historical Association, 1924, pp. 40-44.

Hough, Emerson, "Round Our Town," in *Saturday Evening Post* (Philadelphia), February 14, 1920.

Howat, William F. (ed.), *A Standard History of Lake County, Indiana and the Calumet Region* (2 vols. Chicago, 1915).

Howe, Frances R., *The Story of a French Homestead in the Old Northwest* (Columbus, Ohio, 1907).

Hungerford, Edward, *The Story of the Baltimore and Ohio Railroad, 1827-1927* (2 vols. New York, 1928).

Hurlbut, Henry H., *Chicago Antiquities* . . . (Chicago, 1881).

Indiana. *Laws of Indiana,* 1834-35 (local); 1836-37 (local), 1842-43 (local), 1895, 1905, 1907, 1911, 1917, 1923, 1927.

————, Supreme Court Reports, 147 Ind. 466-76 (State *v.* Forsythe).

Indiana Bureau of Statistics, *Thirteenth Biennial Report,* 1909-10.

Indiana Department of Statistics, *Fifth Annual Report,* 1883; *Sixth Biennial Report,* 1895-96.

Indiana *Documentary Journal,* 1851-52, 1854.

The Indiana Gazetteer, or Topographical Dictionary of the State of Indiana (3d ed., Indianapolis, 1849).

Indiana Harbor. The New Industrial City (Brochure published by the East Chicago Company, 1904).

Indiana History Bulletin, 30 (Indianapolis, 1953) :169.

Indiana Magazine of History (Vols. 1- , Indianapolis and Bloomington, 1905-   ). Vols. 8, 10, 18, 20, 42, 44, 48.

Indiana State Gazetteer and Business Directory, 1882-83, compiled by R. L. Polk & Co. (Indianapolis, 1882).

The Indiana State Gazetteer and Shippers' Guide for 1866-1867 (Lafayette, Ind., 1866).

Indiana Steel Company, Gary, Indiana (Indiana Steel Company, 1912).

Inland News (published by Inland Steel Company, East Chicago), Anniversary edition, May, 1951.

Investigation of Strike in Steel Industries, Hearings before the Committee on Education and Labor (U. S. Senate, 66 Congress, 1 session [Washington, D. C., 1919]).

Investigation of the United States Steel Corporation (*House Reports,* 62 Congress, 2 session, No. 1127, August 2, 1912).

The Iron Age (Vol. 1- , New York, 1859-   ). Vols. 67-68, 71, 78, 82-84.

Janson, Florence E., *The Background of Swedish Immigration, 1840-1930* (University of Chicago Press, 1931).

Johnson, Howard, *A Home in the Woods. Oliver Johnson's Reminiscences of Early Marion County* (*Indiana Historical Society Publications,* Vol. 16, No. 2, Indianapolis, 1951).

Johnson, Ida Amanda, *The Michigan Fur Trade* (Lansing, 1919).

Jones, Alfred, "John D. Rockefeller First to Industrialize Calumet," in Gary *Post-Tribune,* May 27, 1937.

Kaiser, Rev. Edwin G., *History of St. John's Parish, Whiting, Indiana . . . 1897-1947* (n. p., n. d.).

Kansas, Sidney, *U. S. Immigration. Exclusion and Deportation and Citizenship of the United States of America* (New York, 1940).

Kellar, Herbert A. (ed.), *Solon Robinson. Pioneer and Agriculturist* (2 vols. *Indiana Historical Collections,* Vols. 21 and 22, Indianapolis, 1936, 1937).

Kellogg, Louise Phelps, *The British Régime in Wisconsin and the Northwest* (State Historical Society of Wisconsin, 1935).

—————, *The French Régime in Wisconsin and the Northwest* (State Historical Society of Wisconsin, 1925).

Kennan, George, "The Cost of Living," in *McClure's Magazine,* 30 (New York, 1907-8) :639-50

Kenton, Edna (ed.), *The Jesuit Relations and Allied Documents* (New York, 1925).

Kettleborough, Charles (ed.), *Constitution Making in Indiana . . . Volume I, 1780-1851* (*Indiana Historical Collections,* Vol. 1, Indianapolis, 1916).

Kinnaird, Lawrence, "The Spanish Expedition against Fort St. Joseph in 1781, A New Interpretation," in *Mississippi Valley Historical Review,* 19 (1932-33) :173-91.

Labor Conditions in the Iron and Steel Industry (4 vols. *Senate Documents,* 62 Congress, 1 session, No. 110).

The Lake County Directory . . . , 1909 (Gary, 1909).

Lang, Elfrieda (ed.), "The Inhabitants of Center Township, Lake County, Indiana, According to the Federal Census of 1850," in *Indiana Magazine of History,* 44 (1948) :281-304.

Larzelere, Claude S., "The Boundaries of Michigan," in *Michigan Pioneer and Historical Collections,* 30 (Lansing, 1906) :1-27.

Latrobe, Charles J., *The Rambler in North America, MDCCCXXXII-MDCCCXXXIII* (2 vols. New York, 1835).

Leech, Harper, and Carroll, John C., *Armour and His Times* (New York, 1938).

Lengyel, Emil, *Americans from Hungary* (New York, 1948).

Leonard, John W., *The Book of Chicagoans. A Biographical Dictionary of the Leading Men of Chicago* (Chicago, 1905).

Lester, J. W. (ed.), "Pioneer Stories of the Calumet," in *Indiana Magazine of History,* 18(1922) :166-76, 347-58.

Leverett, Frank, *The Pleistocene Features and Deposits of the Chicago Area* (Chicago Academy of Sciences, Geological and Natural History Survey, *Bulletin No. II,* May, 1897).

Lindsey, Almont, *The Pullman Strike . . .* (University of Chicago Press, 1942).

Literary Digest (125 vols. New York, 1890-1938), April 21, 1923.

Little, Jesse, *see* Demmon, Alice M.

Loring, H. H., *see* Cannon, Thomas H.

Lorwin, Lewis L., and Flexner, Jean A., *The American Federation of Labor . . .* (Brookings Institution, Washington, D. C., 1933).

Luther, James H., "History of Northern Lake County," in Timothy H. Ball (ed.), *Lake County, Indiana, 1884,* 112-21.

McCoy, Daniel, "Old Fort St. Joseph," in *Michigan Pioneer and Historical Collections,* 35(Lansing, 1907) :545-52.

McDaniel, Wayne A. (ed.), *The Municipal Code of the City of East Chicago, Indiana* (East Chicago, 1925).

McFarland, Marvin W. (ed.), *The Papers of Wilbur and Orville Wright: Including the Chanute-Wright Letters and Other Papers of Octave Chanute, 1899-1948* (2 vols. New York, 1953).

MacGill, Caroline E., *History of Transportation in the United States before 1860* (Washington, D. C., 1917).

MacGrath, H., Guest, W. J., James, W., and Cutler, H. G. (eds.), *Encyclopedia of Biography of Illinois* (2 vols. Chicago, 1892).

McNay, Philip M., *see* Demmon, Alice M.

Martineau, Harriet, *Society in America* (2 vols. New York and London, 1837).

Mather, Stephen T., *Report on the Proposed Sand Dunes National Park, Indiana* (Department of the Interior, Washington, D. C., 1917).

Mecklin, John M., *The Ku Klux Klan. A Study of the American Mind* (New York, 1924).

Melton, Arthur P., article in Gary *Daily Tribune,* February 26, 1915.

Menke, Louis G., "The Story of Chesterton," in *Chesterton Retail Merchants' Directory* (Chesterton, 1949), 27-47.

Merritt, Dixon, "Klan and Anti-Klan in Indiana," in *The Outlook* (New York), December 1, 1926, pp. 465-69.

Meyer, Alfred H., "The Kankakee Marsh of Northern Indiana and Illinois," in Michigan Academy of Science, Arts and Letters, *Papers,* 21(1935) :359-96.

————, "Toponomy in Sequent Occupance Geography, Calumet Region, Indiana-Illinois," in *Proceedings* of the Indiana Academy of Science, 1944, pp. 142-59.

Michigan Central Railroad, *Annual Reports,* 1851-55.

Michigan Southern and Northern Indiana Rail-Road Companies, *Reports,* 1850, 1853, 1855.

Miller, Kenneth D., *The Czecho-Slovaks in America* (New York, 1922).

Mills, Edgar, *A History of East Chicago* (Garman Printing Company, East Chicago, n. d.).

Moore, Will H., *"If I Had Known." About Gary in 1909* (Chicago, 1909).

Morgan, Mary, and Schiemann, Olga Mae, "Coffee Creek Post Office," in *Indiana History Bulletin,* 30(1953):48-50.

Munro, William Bennett, *Crusaders of New France . ..* (Yale University Press, 1921).

Nute, Grace Lee, *Caesars of the Wilderness, Médard Chouart, Sieur des Groseilliers, and Pierre Esprit Radisson, 1618-1710* (New York, 1943).

Oglesbee, Rollo B., and Hale, Albert, *History of Michigan City* (La Porte, Ind., 1908).

Packard, Jasper, *History of La Porte County, Indiana* (La Porte, Ind., 1876).

Paré, George, "The St. Joseph Mission," in *Mississippi Valley Historical Review,* 17(1930-31):24-54.

———, and Quaife, Milo M. (eds.), "The St. Joseph Baptismal Register," in *Mississippi Valley Historical Review,* 13(1926-27):201-39.

Parkman, Francis, *The Conspiracy of Pontiac and the Indian War after the Conquest of Canada* (Frontenac edition, 2 vols. Boston, 1905).

———, *La Salle and the Discovery of the Great West* (Frontenac edition, Boston, 1905).

Peattie, Donald C., *Flora of the Indiana Dunes . . .* (Chicago, 1930).

Peckham, Howard, *Pontiac and the Indian Uprising* (Princeton University Press, 1947).

Pence, George, and Armstrong, Nellie C., *Indiana Boundaries, Territory, State, and County* (Indiana Historical Collections, Vol. 19, Indianapolis, 1933).

Pierce, Bessie L., *A. History of Chicago. Volume I* (Chicago, 1937).

Putnam's Magazine (New York), Vols. 5, 11.

Quaife, Milo M., *Chicago and the Old Northwest, 1673-1835* (Chicago, 1913).

———, *Chicago Highways, Old and New, from Indian Trail to Motor Road* (Chicago, 1923).

———, *Lake Michigan* (Indianapolis, 1944).

———, *see also* Paré, George.

Reck, Franklin M., *Sand In Their Shoes. The Story of American Steel Foundries* (Chicago, 1952).

Richards, Charles R., *The Gary Public Schools, Industrial Work* (New York, 1915).

Riley, Walter J., *The Story of Unemployment Relief Work in Lake County, Indiana, Dec. 31, 1932* (n. p., n. d.).

Robb, Charles J., *see* Cannon, Thomas H.

Roberts, Mrs. J. J., reminiscences in Gary *Post-Tribune,* July 6, 1951, p. 14.

Robertson, Nellie A., and Riker, Dorothy (eds.), *The John Tipton Papers* (3 vols. *Indiana Historical Collections,* Vols. 24-26, Indianapolis, 1942).

Roll, Charles, *Indiana, One Hundred and Fifty Years of American Development* (5 vols. Chicago, 1931).

Royce, Charles C. (comp.), *Indian Land Cessions in the United States* (2 vols. U. S. Bureau of American Ethnology, *Eighteenth Annual Report,* 1896-97).

Russell, Nelson Vance, *The British Régime in Michigan and the Old Northwest, 1760-1796* (Northfield, Minn., 1939).

St. Mary's Mercy Hospital [Gary] (booklet published by the hospital, n.d., in Gary Public Library).

Sandburg, Carl, *Smoke and Steel* (Harcourt, Brace and Company, New York, 1921).

Schantz, Orpheus M., "Indiana's Unrivaled Sand-Dunes," in *The National Geographic Magazine,* 35 (Washington, D. C. 1919) :430-41.

School and Society (vols 1- , New York, 1915-   ). Vol. 26 (July December, 1927).

Schoolcraft, Henry R., *Narrative Journal of Travels from Detroit Northwest through the Great Chain of American Lakes to the Sources of the Mississippi River in the Year 1820* (Albany, N. Y., 1821).

Scientific American (New Series, vol. 1- , New York, 1859-   ). Vol. 105 (July-December, 1911).

Scientific American Supplement (88 vols. New York, 1876-1919). Vol. 70, No. 1826.

Scifres, Bill, "Valparaiso University, Dies Twice, Prospers Three Times in History," in Fort Wayne *Journal-Gazette,* April 19, 1953.

Seligman, Edwin R. A., and Johnson, Alvin (eds.), *Encyclopaedia of the Social Sciences* (15 vols. New York, 1930-34).

Sheehan, Mrs. Frank J., *The Northern Boundary of Indiana* (*Indiana Historical Society Publications,* Vol. 8, No. 6, Indianapolis, 1928).

Shirreff, Patrick, *A Tour through North America* (New York, 1837).

Shockley, Ernest V., "County Seats and County Seat Wars in Indiana," in *Indiana Magazine of History,* 10 :no. 1 (March, 1914) :1-46.

Shumway, Arthur, "Gary, Shrine of the Steel God," in *American Parade* (American Wheelabrator & Equipment Corporation, Mishawaka), 3 :28 (January, 1929).

Skinner, Hubert M., *History of Valparaiso from the Earliest Times to the Present* (Valparaiso, 1876).

Smith, Dwight L., "A Continuation of the Journal of an Emigrating Party of Potawatomi Indians, 1838," in *Indiana Magazine of History,* 44 (1948) :393-408.

Smith, Edgar (ed.), *Directory of Hammond, Indiana,* 1911 (Gary [1911]).

Souders, David A., *The Magyars in America* (New York, 1922).

South Shore Lines (published by Chicago, South Shore, and South Bend Railroad), January, 1928.

Spero, Sterling, and Harris, Abram L., *The Black Worker. The Negro and the Labor Movement* (New York, 1931).

Spoor, George K., "The Essanay Days," in *Theatre Arts,* July, 1951.

Standard Oil Company (Indiana), *Annual Report,* 1931.

The Stanolind Record (published by the Standard Oil Company, vols. 1- , Chicago, 1919-). Issues of February, 1922, July, 1923, April, 1927.

Sternberger, Mary, "Are Our Foreign-Born Emigrating. An Analysis of the Experience of An Industrial City," in *The Survey,* 43(New York, October, 1919-March, 1920):539-40.

————, "Gary and the Foreigner's Opportunity," in *The Survey,* 42 (April-September, 1919):480-82.

Stimpson, George W., *The Story of Valparaiso University* (Chicago, 1921).

Strietelmeier, John, *Valparaiso's First Century* (Valparaiso University, 1959).

Swartz, U. G., "Some Early Days of the Whiting Refinery," in *The Stanolind Record,* July, 1923, p. 6.

Swift, Louis F., *The Yankee of the Yards. The Biography of Gustavus F. Swift* (Chicago and New York, 1927).

Tarbell, Ida M., *The Life of Elbert H. Gary. A Story of Steel* (New York, 1925).

Taylor, Arthur G., *see* Bowers, John O., and Demmon, Alice M.

Taylor, Graham R., "At Gary, Some Impressions and Interviews," in *The Survey,* 43(New York, 1919-20):65-66.

————, *Satellite Cities. A Study of Industrial Suburbs* (New York, 1915).

Taylor, Paul S., *Mexican Labor in the United States, Chicago, and the Calumet Region* (University of California, *Publications in Economics,* Vol. 7, No. 2, Berkeley, 1932).

Teale, Edwin Way, *The Book of Gliders* (New York, 1930).

————, *Dune Boy, The Early Years of a Naturalist* (New York, 1943).

Thomas, John H., "The Academies of Indiana," in *Indiana Magazine of History,* 10(1914):323-58.

Thwaites, Reuben Gold, *Father Marquette* (New York, 1902).

———— (ed.), *The Jesuit Relations and Allied Documents . . .* (73 vols. Cleveland, 1896-1901).

The Tolleston Club of Chicago (Published by the Tolleston Club, 1902). Pamphlet in Gary Public Library.

The Tribune Almanac for the Years 1838 to *1868, Inclusive; Compre-hending the Politician's Register and the Whig Almanac* . . . (2 vols. New York, 1868).

The Tribune Almanac for 1893 (New York, 1893).

Tucker, Sara Jones (comp.), *Indian Villages of the Illinois Country* (Illinois State Museum, *Scientific Papers,* Vol. 2, Part 1, Atlas, Spring-field, 1942).

Turner, Frederick Jackson, *The United States, 1830-1850, The Nation and Its Sections* (New York, 1935).

United States Army, Chief of Engineers, *Annual Report,* 1906, 1910, 1925.

United States Bureau of the Census, Seventh through Sixteenth Census, 1850-1950.

————, Compendiums of the Ninth Census and Tenth Census (1870, 1880).

————, *Negroes in the United States, 1920-1932* (Washington, D. C., 1935).

United States Congress, *Annals of Congress,* 14 Congress, 1 session.

————, *House Documents:*

58 Congress, 2 session, No. 172 (Examination of Calumet River)

61 Congress, 3 session, Vol. 20, No. 1067 (Harbors)

64 Congress, 1 session, No. 470 (Examination of Calumet River)

————, *House Reports:*

62 Congress, 2 Session, No. 1127 (Investigation of United States Steel Corporation)

————, *Senate Documents:*

42 Congress, 3 session, No. 25 (Grand Calumet River)

61 Congress, 3 session, No. 748 (Emigration Conditions in Europe)

62 Congress, 1 session, No. 110 (Labor Conditions in Iron and Steel Industry)

United States Department of Labor, Bureau of Labor Statistics, *Bulletin 305. Wages and Hours of Labor in the Iron and Steel Industry, 1907 to 1920* (Washington, D. C., 1922).

————, *Bulletin 513. Wages and Hours of Labor in the Iron and Steel Industry, 1929* (Washington, D. C., 1930).

United States Steel Corporation, *Annual Report,* 1905 to 1933.

United States Supreme Court, *Reports,* Vol. 15.

Van Tyne, Claude H. (ed.), *The Letters of Daniel Webster* (New York, 1902).

Visher, Stephen S., *Climate of Indiana* (Bloomington, Ind., 1944).

Westberg, C. A., "The Street Nomenclature of the City of East Chicago," in *East Chicago, Indiana,* 1(March, 1926):104, 130.

Whiting City Almanac and Cook Book (Whiting Savings and Loan Association, 1911).

Willy, John, "Catering Extraordinary," in *The Hotel Monthly* (Chicago), November, 1913, p. 77.

Wilson, Robert E., *Oil Competition in the Midwest. A Case History* (National Petroleum Association, Washington, D. C., 1950).

Wirt, William A., *The Great Lockout in America's Citizenship Plants* (Gary, 1937).

Wittke, Carl, *We Who Built America. The Saga of the Immigrant* (New York, 1939).

Woods, Sam B., *see* Bowers, John O.

Woodson, Carter G., *The Negro in Our History* (Washington, D. C., 1931).

Wright, Wilbur, "The Death of Octave Chanute," in *Aeronautics*, 8 (New York, 1911) :4.

Newspapers

Scattered issues of Chicago newspapers containing accounts of happenings in the Calumet Region:

Chicago *Examiner,* July 23, 1916.

Chicago *Express,* April 17, 1915.

Chicago *Daily News,* August 29, November 29, 1903.

Chicago *Daily Tribune,* June 20, 1890; June 13, 1893; July 2, 9, 10, 18, 1894; November 1, 1897; August 24, October 24, 1901; October 9, 16, 17, 1912; September 23, 1918; September 24, 26, 27, 30, 1919.

Chicago *Herald,* July 18, 1892.

Chicago *Herald-Examiner,* April 25 and 27, 1921.

Chicago *Inter-Ocean,* June 11, 1891.

Chicago *Sunday Tribune,* March 22, November 1, 1896; January 17, 1897; November 29, 1903; October 23, 1912; September 21, 28, 1919; December 21, 1947.

Chicago *Times,* August 1, 1892.

Indiana Newspapers

Chesterton *Tribune,* 1882-1896, 1897-1933.

Chesterton *Westchester-Tribune,* April 1896-November 1897.

Crown Point *Register,* 1913-1929.

Crown Point *Lake County Star,* 1882-1933.

East Chicago *Calumet News,* 1923-1933.

East Chicago *Journal,* March 30 to October 15, 1889.

Fort Wayne *Journal-Gazette,* April 19, 1953.

Gary *Daily Tribune,* 1908-1921.

Gary *Evening Post,* 1909-1921.

Gary *Evening Post and Daily Tribune,* 1921-1922.

Gary *Northern Indianian,* 1906-1909.
Gary *Post-Tribune,* 1921-1933.
Gary *Republican,* 1916-1917.
Gary *Sunday Tribune,* 1921.
Gary *Weekly Tribune,* 1907-1912.
Hammond *Lake County News,* July, 1894.
Hammond *Lake County Times,* 1906-1933.
Hammond *Times,* August 28, 1933, July 2, 1939, June 17, 1951 (historical edition).
Hobart *Gazette,* May 19, 1891, souvenir edition, May, 1898.
Indianapolis *News,* March 16, 1925.
Indianapolis *Star,* January 10, 1919.
Porter *Tribune,* 1894-1896.
Valparaiso *Daily Vidette,* 1903-1927.
Valparaiso *Messenger,* 1871-1927.
Valparaiso *Porter County Vidette,* 1866, 1869-1898.
Valparaiso *Republic,* 1866.
Valparaiso *Republican,* 1857-1859, 1866-1868.
Valparaiso *Star-Vidette,* 1898-1903.
Valparaiso *Vidette and Republic,* 1868-1869.
Valparaiso *Vidette-Messenger,* 1927-1936.
Valparaiso *Western Ranger,* 1847-1848.
Whiting *Call,* 1909-1916.
Whiting *Democrat,* 1894-1897.
Whiting *News,* 1894.
Whiting *Sun,* 1897-1908.
Whiting *Times,* August 4, 1939 (historical edition).

INDEX

INDEX

Aetna community, incorporated, 124; annexed to Gary, 125; powder plant, 96, 122-25, 259.

Agricultural implements and machinery, manufacture of, 118, 175, 227-28.

Agriculture, areas best suited to, 14-15; conditions affecting, 80-81, 89, 90-92; products, 80, 91, 535. *See also* Fruits and berries.

Ahlendorf, August, 144.

Ahlendorf, Louis, 218.

Ahlendorf, Theodore, 144.

Ainsworth, C. W., 409, 410.

Albanians, 364. *See also* Foreign born; Immigration, new.

Aldis, Owen F., 230, 233, 236.

Alschuler, H., 290.

Alvord, Charles, 409.

American Brass Works, 128.

American Bridge Company, 327.

American citizenship, attitude of foreign born toward, 317, 382-84, 397-98n, 543.

American Federation of Labor, attempt to organize steel industry, 499-528 *passim.;* members urged not to join Klan, 555n.

American Fur Company, 44, 45.

American Maize Products Company, 113.

American Revolution, 30-34.

American Sheet and Tin Plate Company, 327-28.

American Sheet and Tube Company, 243.

American Steel Foundries, 166, 241.

Animals, wild, 21, 23, 103.

Antislavery movement, 402, 533-34.

Armour, J. Ogden, meat packer, 104, 173-74n, 261.

Armour, Philip D., meat packer, 131-35, 260.

Avery, William, 577.

Bailey, Louis J., librarian, 290, 298-99.

Bailly, Agatha, *see* Agatha Biddle.

Bailly, Alexis, 45-46.

Bailly, Eleanor Cecilia, 43, 49-51.

Bailly, Esther, *see* Esther Whistler.

Bailly, Francis, 45.

Bailly, Hortense, *see* Hortense Wicker.

Bailly, Joseph, 61, 75n; biographical sketch, 43-45n; home and trading post on Little Calumet, 39, 40, 43-49n; marriages, 45, 46; inn, 47-48; education of children, 49-50; plats town, 51-52; business interests other than fur trading, 51-52n; burial ground, 52n; story of, published, 588.

Bailly, Joseph, son, 45.

Bailly, Marie Le Fevre (Mrs. Joseph), 43, 46-47, 52.

Bailly, Michel, 45.

Bailly, Philip, 45.

Bailly, Robert, 43, 49, 52n.

Bailly, Rose, *see* Rose Bailly Howe.

Bailly, Sophia, 45.

Pittsburgh, Fort Wayne, and Chicago Railroad, construction, 83, 89, 181; towns and stations on, 89-90, 98, 218.

"Pittsburgh Plus" price-fixing system, 330-31.

Plumer, George W., partner in Hammond Packing Company, 147, 150, 154.

Pokagon, Simon, 36n.

Poles, 361. See also Foreign born; Immigration, new.

Politics, nomination of Congressional candidates (1896), 206-7; vote in presidential elections (1836-1930), 533-35; in local elections, 535-39. See also Democratic party; Elections and Election campaigns; Republican party.

Pontiac, Ottawa chief, 28-29n.

Pontiac's conspiracy, 26, 27-28.

Poor relief, handling of, during depression, 563-70.

Poplar Point, 217.

Population, see under Lake and Porter counties and under names of towns and cities.

Populist party, newspaper, 270, 415, 495; votes received, 535n.

Porter (Porter Co.), clay deposits, 15, 120; development of, 125-31; industries, 126, 127, 128-31; newspaper, 128; railroad station, 87.

Porter, David Dixon, county named for, 63.

Porter, Joseph E., 232.

Porter County, formation, 63; origin of name, 63; seal, 64n; settlement of, 60-63, 65, 347; county-seat sites, 64; courts, 168; early schools, 445; population: (1840 to 1850), 79, 345; (1850

to 1860), 454n; (1870 to 1890), 349; Negroes, 386; source of population (United States), 62; (foreign), 349, 351-53; vote cast in presidential elections, 533-35.

Porteret, Pierre, 23.

Portersville (Porter Co.), platted, 64; offered for county seat, 64; name changed to Valparaiso, 64-65.

Post offices, Calumet, 62; Chesterton, 62-63; Coffee Creek, 62; Gary, 271-72; Hammond, 154; Hessville, 144; Indiana Harbor, 423; Jerusalem, 135; Lake Court House, 68, 69; Whiting, 184.

Potawatomi Indians, in Calumet Region, 23, 26-27, 36-37n, 48, 69; loyalty to French, 27-28, 30; aid English, 30, 32, 34; land cessions, 35-36; reserves in Lake County, 70-71n.

Pothier, Toussaint, 44n.

Prehistoric animals, 7.

Prize fighting, at Roby, 109-12.

Proclamation of 1763, p. 29.

Prohibition, local option law, 312-14; defiance and enforcement of Volstead Act, 545-53. See also Liquor.

Public lands, survey of, 60; sale of, 61, 70, 183, 344n; effect of railroads on value of, 83, 94, 141-42, 181; speculation in, 94-97, 122, 181. See also Swamp lands.

Quebec Act, 29-30.

Quillen, R. R., 295.

Ragon, Elmer E., 414, 418.

Railroad cars, manufacture of, 175-76; development of refrigerated car, 146-47.

DATE DUE